HANDBOOK ON THE EUROPEAN UNION AND BREXIT

Handbook on the European Union and Brexit

Edited by

John Erik Fossum

Professor, ARENA Centre for European Studies, University of Oslo, Norway

Christopher Lord

Professor, ARENA Centre for European Studies, University of Oslo, Norway

Edward Elgar
PUBLISHING

Cheltenham, UK • Northampton, MA, USA

Published by
Edward Elgar Publishing Limited
The Lypiatts
15 Lansdown Road
Cheltenham
Glos GL50 2JA
UK

Edward Elgar Publishing, Inc.
William Pratt House
9 Dewey Court
Northampton
Massachusetts 01060
USA

A catalogue record for this book
is available from the British Library

Library of Congress Control Number: 2022948502

This book is available electronically in the **Elgar**online
Political Science and Public Policy subject collection
http://dx.doi.org/10.4337/9781839100697

Printed on elemental chlorine free (ECF)
recycled paper containing 30% Post-Consumer Waste

ISBN 978 1 83910 068 0 (cased)
ISBN 978 1 83910 069 7 (eBook)

Printed and bound in the USA

Contents

Figures

Tables

Contributors

Richard Bellamy, Professor of Political Science, Department of Political Science, University College London, UK.

Monika Brusenbauch Meislová, Associate Professor, Department of International Relations and European Studies, Masaryk University, Czechia; Visiting Professor, Aston University, UK.

Birgit Bujard, Senior Research Fellow, Centre for Turkey and European Union Studies (CETEUS), University of Cologne, Germany.

Ian Cooper, Research Fellow, Brexit Institute, Dublin City University, Ireland.

James Dennison, Migration Policy Centre, European University Institute, Italy and School of Politics, Philosophy, Language and Communication Studies, University of East Anglia, UK.

Helen Drake, Professor and Director, Institute for Diplomacy and International Governance, Loughborough University London, UK.

Federico Fabbrini, Full Professor of EU Law and Founding Director, Brexit Institute, Dublin City University, Ireland.

John Erik Fossum, Professor, ARENA Centre for European Studies, University of Oslo, Norway.

Christian Frommelt, Director and Head of Research Politics, Liechtenstein Institute, Liechtenstein.

Roy H. Ginsberg, Professor of Political Science Emeritus, Skidmore College, USA.

Andrew Glencross, Professor, European School of Political and Social Sciences, Catholic University of Lille, France.

Sieglinde Gstöhl, Director of Studies, EU International Relations and Diplomacy Studies Department, College of Europe in Bruges, Belgium.

Michael Kaeding, Professor for European Integration and European Union Politics, Institute of Political Science, University of Duisburg-Essen, Germany.

Hussein Kassim, Professor of Politics, School of Politics, Philosophy, Language and Communication Studies, University of East Anglia, UK.

Michael Keating, Emeritus Professor, School of Social Science, University of Aberdeen, UK.

Brigid Laffan, Emeritus Professor, Robert Schuman Centre for Advanced Studies, European University Institute, Italy.

Sandra Lavenex, Professor of European and International Politics, University of Geneva, Switzerland.

Christopher Lord, Professor, ARENA Centre for European Studies, University of Oslo, Norway.

Nanette Neuwahl, Associated Professor, Faculté de Droit, Université de Montréal and invited researcher, Centre de Recherche en Droit Prospectif (CRDP), Canada.

Kalypso Nicolaïdis, Chair in International Affairs, School of Transnational Governance, EUI.

Craig Parsons, University of Oregon, USA and ARENA Centre for European Studies, University of Oslo, Norway.

Jean-Claude Piris, Consultant EU Law and International Public Law, Member of the EU3D Advisory Board and Former Director General of the Legal Service of the EU Council, France.

Uwe Puetter, Professor of European Integration and European Politics, Europa-Universität Flensburg, Germany.

Rafał Riedel, Professor, University of Opole, Poland and Guest Professor, University of Sankt Gallen, Switzerland.

Justus Schönlau, European Committee of the Regions, Belgium.

Julie Smith, Professor of European Politics, Department of Politics and International Studies (POLIS), Cambridge University, UK.

Russell Solomon, School of Global, Urban and Social Studies, RMIT University, Australia.

Amy Verdun, Professor of Political Science and founding Director of the European Studies Program, University of Victoria, British Columbia, Canada. She is also guest professor at Leiden University, the Netherlands.

Alexandre Veuthey, Global Studies Institute, University of Geneva, Switzerland.

Albert Weale, Emeritus Professor of Political Theory and Public Policy, School of Public Policy, University College London, UK.

Wolfgang Wessels, Jean Monnet Chair *ad personam* for Political Science and Director, Centre for Turkey and European Union Studies (CETEUS), University of Cologne, Germany.

Shaohua Yan, Research Associate Professor, Center for China–Europe Relations, Fudan University, China.

Biao Zhang, Associate Professor in International Relations, China University of Political Science and Law, China.

Preface and acknowledgements

The UK's decision to leave the European Union (EU) is a momentous change whose effects are not confined to the relations between the UK and the EU (and its member and affiliated states) but has ripple effects across the entire globe.

From 2016 to 2019 Brexit dominated British politics. The EU, on the other hand, largely 'parked' or compartmentalized Brexit so that it interfered as little as possible with many other things on the Union's political agenda. Yet, all the time, Brexit remained as important to the Union as to the UK. Since the beginning of 2020 even Brexit has often appeared largely submerged first by the COVID pandemic and then by the war in Ukraine. However, Brexit contains many unresolved problems. For neither the UK nor the EU is Brexit likely to go away.

The contents of this *Handbook* aim to capture what is both important and enduring in Brexit. Rather than provide a template for each contributor to respond to a set of prefixed questions designed by us as editors, we asked the contributors to focus on those aspects they considered most salient from their specialized and particular vantage-points. That ensures a book which combines a clear focus on Brexit with a wide range of contextually sensitive contributions written by highly specialized contributors in each aspect of Brexit.

Every book is a collective effort, and this is no less so. We would like to thank all our contributors who have done so much to make the *Handbook* such an insightful survey of the many aspects of Brexit. We are also grateful to ARENA and the excellent research support we have received from the ARENA staff and assistants, including Janna van Diepen, Anne Gaspers, Mathias Weseth Opdal, Birte Einen, Silva Malin Hoffmann, Ingrid Christensen, and Andrijana Zivic. We also thank everyone at Edward Elgar involved in the editing and production of the *Handbook*.

Part of the research that has gone into this *Handbook* (notably Chapters 1, 10 and 21) has received support from the EU's Horizon 2020 programme (Societal Challenges 6: 'Europe in a Changing World – Inclusive, Innovative and Reflective Societies') under Grant Agreement No. 822419).

John Erik Fossum and Christopher Lord
Oslo and Brussels, 2022

1. Introduction to the European Union and Brexit[1]

John Erik Fossum and Christopher Lord

Much of the already vast literature on Brexit focuses on the UK, and on a rather unitary conception of it. But Brexit is also hugely important for the European Union; for single countries within and beyond Europe; and, indeed, for the international system. Even within the UK, Brexit means different things to different social groups; to different generations; to the different tribes (Nicolaïdis 2019) of leave and remain created by the 2016 referendum, and to the different territories and peoples of England, Scotland, Wales and Northern Ireland. Brexit even means different things to those who wanted it, especially to those who wanted it.

Nor is that necessarily a criticism or even much of a surprise. It is perhaps of the nature of pluralist democratic politics in complex societies that winning coalitions – such as those which won the 2016 referendum and the 2019 election which most recently endorsed a specific approach to Brexit – are heterogeneous agglomerations of those who want the same thing for different and even contradictory reasons.

Some things in the Brexit story are, in any case, clear enough. In January 2013 David Cameron committed the Conservative Party to an in-out referendum on the UK's continued membership of the European Union. The Conservatives unexpectedly won an overall majority in the 2015 election (albeit with only 36.9 per cent of the vote). On 23 June 2016 voters were asked to vote on the following question: Should the United Kingdom remain a member of the European Union or leave the European Union? On a turnout of 72.2 per cent the UK public voted 51.9 per cent to leave and 48.1 to remain. On 27 March 2017 the UK used Article 50 of the Treaty on European Union to notify its intention to leave.

After some extensions of a procedure that was meant to be completed within two years the UK left the Union on 31 January 2020 after 47 years of membership that had often been troubled and turbulent but which had also done much to shape the contemporary Union. However, the Union insisted that the withdrawal agreement (WA) should only cover the bare essentials of the UK's exit: citizens' rights, financial liabilities and the Northern Ireland border. Anything further in the UK's future relationship would need to be negotiated later, once the UK was a non-member. On 31 December 2020, the UK agreed a Trade and Cooperation (TCA) with the EU. This consists of a free trade area in goods and a wider association agreement that creates a framework for multiple further forms of cooperation, as well as a shared governance structure with a partnership council and a mechanism for resolving disputes. The TCA – or other relationships – could turn out to be sparse or ambitious depending on the EU and future British Governments.

Throughout, Brexit has been handled by Conservative Governments, just as, incidentally, it was a Conservative Government that took the UK into the EU (1973) and a Conservative Government that first applied to join (1961). But the three Conservative Governments since 2015 have been quite different from one another. The briefly re-elected Cameron Government (2015–16) hoped to remain in the EU but exorcise divisions on Europe from the Conservative Party. The May Government (2016–19) sought doggedly to implement an instruction from the voters to leave the EU. But it had no clear majority for any one approach to Brexit, especially in the 2017–19 Parliament. Its own proposals were voted down by majorities of 230, 149 and 58. Yet indicative votes failed to get a parliamentary majority for any other solution. In contrast, the Johnson Government (2019) was elected with a clear majority to 'get Brexit done'. Even more so than the May Government, the Johnson Government claimed that Brexit is not a simple matter of subtracting the UK from the EU. Rather, it is also a means of transforming the UK's economy, society and international relations.

May was much derided for proclaiming that 'Brexit means Brexit' when determining the meaning of Brexit was precisely the problem. The referendum had only decided that the UK should leave the EU. It had not decided how the UK should leave. The referendum decided a great deal and very little. It constrained the form of any Brexit whilst leaving unanswered many questions needed to specify Brexit. Throughout, a hard Brexit was contrasted to a softer Brexit. Since a soft Brexit was defined as remaining in some form of single market or customs union with the EU, a hard Brexit assumed that the UK should go no further than a free trade area with the EU. The point needs labouring – since it is so often forgotten – that a free trade area is quite different to a single market. The first only involves the removal of 'at-border' restrictions to trade such as tariffs. Only a single market attempts to remove the multiple 'behind border' restrictions that form the main obstacles to trade in modern service economies: different regulations, uncompetitive public procurement, aids and tax breaks to favoured producers or providers and so on. Tackling those 'behind border' restrictions means that a single market is a large undertaking in shared law-making. Hence, what really made different versions of Brexit hard and soft was not just that they involved quite different trading relationships. They also had contrasting implications for how law would be made and power exercised after Brexit.

If, though, they were largely agreed in wanting to avoid shared law-making with the EU, hard Brexiters differed in how and how far they wanted to use Brexit to transform the UK internally and externally. Here we need to be careful. To suggest that domestic and international transformation was the preserve of hard Brexiters is to assume what many remainers most bitterly contest; namely, that domestic and international change was not possible as long as the UK remained within the EU. Conceivably many changes that are now used to justify a hard Brexit – a fairer society and more global forms of cooperation and competition – could have been even more feasible as a member, let alone as part of a soft Brexit. But that does not alter the point that different ideas of Brexit have contrasting implications for what kind of a state, political system, legal order, international actor, economy and society the UK is likely to be outside the EU. So, choosing one version of Brexit over another – let alone choosing leaving over remaining – is a huge exercise in political power. Even if taken by democratic majorities, decisions about the nature of Brexit involve fundamental choices that many would rather have been decided otherwise. Later, we will briefly discuss how far the British political system has the means of resolving disagreements inherent to Brexit.

A further unknown was that much in Brexit depended on the EU and not just the UK. Even if exiting the EU involves less than breaking or seceding from a state, the UK is, none the less, exiting a distinctive political and legal order to which its own constitution, law and economy had adapted over 47 years. Even the procedure for UK withdrawal was defined and constrained by EU Treaties (Hillion 2015). Just one condition the EU required for a withdrawal agreement has shaped alternative versions of Brexit: namely, that Brexit should not disrupt the peace process in Northern Ireland or create a physical border between Northern Ireland and the Republic of Ireland. Their contrasting solutions to that problem was one reason why the Brexits agreed by the May and Johnson Governments were so different. The EU has also constrained Brexit more generally. To an extent that is not always well understood in the UK, the EU is also constrained in the kind of relationships it can offer non-members. We will come back to that.

A final unknown is that the full meaning of Brexit will remain unclear until the UK settles the question of exit to what: until it fully decides what other relationships, if any, will replace its membership of the EU. Of course that could include relationships with the EU itself. But alternative relationships will also depend on many other states and international bodies with goals, beliefs and constraints of their own. Obvious examples are suggestions that the UK should seek ambitious trade agreements with the US or China or join multilateral frameworks such as the US-Mexico-Canada trade agreement (USMCA) or Trans Pacific Partnership (TPP). In so far as any one version of Brexit depends on such relationships for its own domestic or international ambitions, Brexit is not fully owned or controlled by the UK.

RIPPLE OR RUPTURE?

As the foregoing suggests, only a multi-perspectival approach can identify the many different meanings, implications, problems and solutions to Brexit within and beyond the UK. This *Handbook* responds to that challenge. Its first part begins with an overview of the literature with regard to the causes of Brexit, proceeds with chapters on voters, parties and the territorial parts of the UK, and ends with one chapter on the role of economic ideas in the Brexit story and one chapter on the political economy of Brexit. Its second part turns to the role in Brexit of different EU institutions, the European Council, the European Commission, the European Parliament, EU agencies and the Committee of the Regions (COR). The third part considers implications of Brexit for different countries within the EU, including Ireland as the most directly affected EU member as well as some of the most powerful member states (France, Germany and Poland), and ends with a chapter on regions as clusters of member states. The fourth part considers some countries that have long demonstrated the problems and possibilities of being a European democracy without being a member of the EU (Liechtenstein, Norway and Switzerland). The fifth part focuses on some non-European countries that have also been identified as models for how the UK might relate to the EU from the outside (Canada and Australia), and some of the world's most powerful states, the US and China. A sixth and final part focuses on some of the many issues of legitimacy brought up by the Brexit process.

The remainder of this introduction frames the rest of the *Handbook* by briefly discussing the origins of Brexit in UK politics; by suggesting a framework for distinguishing the likely implications of different forms of Brexit; and by identifying options and constraints in the EU's own responses to Brexit. The chapter concludes with brief chapter summaries of all the book's contributions.

A core question that is important from all perspectives is how far Brexit is likely to be a rupture for the UK, for the EU, or even the international system. Just before the referendum, Andrew Moravcsik (Financial Times 8 April 2016) argued that 'regardless' of its

> result, Britain would under no circumstances … leave Europe … Europe is real because globalisation means every day more British people rely on the EU to secure and stabilise trade, investment, travel, litigation, national security and political values. So the same politicians who lead a majority of Britons down the path to leave Europe would lead them back up again.

On that understanding, closely interconnected economies and societies need to cooperate; and there are functional and political limits to how far any one state can determine the terms of that cooperation. The UK and EU might continue to cooperate in ways that limit the impact of Brexit, now or in the future. First, the UK could, one day, simply rejoin. It could variously be a non-member state, an ex-member state and a future 'second-time lucky' member state. Second, the UK could participate in some EU policies as a non-member state. Xavier Bettel, Prime Minister of Luxembourg, has joked that, for many years, the UK has been a member seeking opt-outs. Now it will be a non-member seeking opt-ins. Moving from internal differentiated integration (where a member state does not participate in all Union policies) to external differentiated integration (where a non-member seeks at least some policies) could conceivably leave the UK in much the same place in terms of policy participation. Third, the UK and EU could cooperate *sotto voce* through a complex mix of bilateral understandings and unilateral approximations. Its supporters seem keenly aware of what, for them, would be the dangers of disguised, partial or minimal forms of Brexit. Johnson dismissed May's Brexit as remaining in the EU's orbit. Other versions of Brexit, including perhaps his own, contain elements that seem to burn bridges or to signal a determination not to drift quietly back to forms of cooperation that might amount to membership without membership.

Whilst, though, it is too soon to tell whether Brexit will be a ripple or a rupture, we can begin to discuss the questions that make the one or the other more probable. Why did Brexit happen? How far is there a coherent core to Brexit that rules some things in and some things out? Can we identify what must be involved in transitioning from being a state that was once organized for being a member of the EU to one that is now organized for leaving it? And, interacting with all of that, how far are different versions of Brexit likely to be constrained or enabled by different relationships that the EU, or others internationally, can offer the UK?

ORIGINS OF BREXIT

Accounts vary in how far they attribute Brexit to contingent happenings; to deeper problems in British politics, economy and society; to flaws and contradictions in the UK's membership of the EU; or to a wider crisis in democratic politics. To Dominic Cummings (2017), director of the leave campaign, much in Brexit was 'non-linear' or part of a 'branching history' in which events and individual calculations tilted an otherwise fine balance between factors making for a continuation or termination of British membership of the EU. Cummings continues as follows:

> There are strong psychological pressures that lead people to create *post facto* stories that seem to add up to 'I always said X and X happened' … The big event must have had an equally big cause … If about 600,000 people – just over 1 per cent of registered voters – had decided differently, IN would have won. This is a small enough margin that it could easily have happened if quite a few specific events and decisions had turned out differently. If just one person had behaved differently the dominant story now would be 'the economy was *always* going to trump a revolt against the elites … For example, if Michael Gove had stayed out of the campaign then *Vote Leave* would almost certainly have either collapsed (which it nearly did anyway) or been forced into fighting the campaign on a losing message like 'Go Global' … Without Boris, Farage would have been a much more prominent face on TV during the crucial final weeks, probably *the* most prominent face … It is extremely plausible that this would have lost us over 600,000 vital middle class votes. (Cummings 2017)

A second account focuses on the politics of the Conservative Party. Until the 1980s the Conservatives claimed to be 'the party of Europe' (see campaign guide for the European elections in 1984). In his *Official History of Britain and the European Community*, Stephen Wall (2019: 289) presents the single market as 'Thatcherism on a European Scale'. Whether intentionally or not, the EU's single market programme – and, therefore, UK membership of the Union – constrained how radically any Labour Government could reverse the market solutions chosen by the Conservative Party for the UK's economy and society after 1979. Yet, from the 1990s the Conservatives increasingly split on questions of European integration. By the time they returned to government in 2010, the rise of the United Kingdom Independence Party (UKIP) faced the Conservatives with the added problem of an anti-European and anti-immigration party to their right. Interviews for the Brexit archive recorded by the UK in a changing Europe programme argue that, had Cameron done nothing, his successor would probably have had to commit to leaving the Union as the price of winning the leadership of the Conservative Party. For its defenders, a referendum was the best chance of pre-empting that possibility; and, therefore, of keeping the UK inside the Union. Yet, it remains unclear how far there was a public demand for a referendum beyond the needs of the Conservative Party to ensure its internal cohesion and to compete with other parties. The EU had rarely been popular with the public. But it had rarely been salient either. EU questions usually ranked low in surveys of issues most important to the public. The 2016 referendum was not required to resolve deep divisions amongst the public on the UK's membership of the Union. It created those divisions.

A third account attributes Brexit to inequalities and injustices in British society. As Cummings (2017) also puts it: 'we voted to leave because so many British people had been left behind economically and culturally for so long and they were furious about it'. One question that raises is how far the referendum – or even Brexit more generally – had really been about the European Union. Was the EU, and the UK's membership of it, just collateral damage in a protest against decades of neglect that originated in domestic politics and policy? Was the EU really an obstacle to regenerating 'left behind' parts of the UK? Membership of the EU had not obstructed the far larger task of regenerating East Germany between 1990 and 2020. Maybe, though, the EU's commitment to free movement was partly at fault in helping British Governments to operate a growth model that was likely to lead to inequality. As soon as earnings rose for the 'left behind', they could be brought back down again by using free movement to recruit from elsewhere in the Union. Famously the number of EU citizens resident in the UK rose to at least 4 million. Meanwhile the real earnings of the lowest income groups fell by about 25 per cent after the financial crisis with little recovery before the 2016 referendum. Once again, it is unclear whether these were problems that could not have been resolved by domestic policies on minimum wages or retraining. But what mattered was the perception, not the reality, of the link between EU membership, free movement and declining earnings.

A fourth account sees Brexit as an unravelling of the particular form of membership that the UK developed after the Treaty on European Union (1992). The UK had opted out of Monetary Union and large parts of Justice and Home Affairs (JHA) whilst keeping the Common Foreign and Security Policy (CFSP) largely intergovernmental. So extraordinary was its ability to construct what often seemed its own private form of membership that – even after opting out of JHA – the UK was able to opt back into 130 JHA measures. Yet, on one matter, the UK was firmly on the side of uniformity. It sought neither exception nor differentiation from the single market; and insisted none should be given to others. The UK's Permanent Representative to the EU, Sir Ivan Rogers (2017), described the UK as having a largely 'single market only' membership.

Yet that configuration was unstable. In one way, the UK was anything but a monetary union 'out'. London developed as the financial centre for the euro without being in the euro (Jones 2015). It dominated euro currency and bond trading. It headquartered most non-EU banks with access to the Union's single financial market. Hence, British Governments worried about institutional incongruence between the European Union and its monetary union. For sure the UK participated in making single market rules that governed its paradoxical role as banker of the Eurozone (EZ). However, with its widening to 19 members, the EZ approximated on its own to a qualified majority of 55 per cent of member states representing 65 per cent of the Union population. The EZ could potentially dominate single market decisions on which rules regulating the UK's financial sector depended. The difficulty became acute with the financial crisis. For EZ countries, the survival of the euro depended on their being able to insist on conditions for safe banking in the Union's own currency. Yet measures needed to make the EZ safe could be deeply harmful to the UK. Financial sectors are creations of rules: as Rogers (2017) has also put it 'a successful financial sector cannot be a rule-taker'. The EZ needed to control the rules of any single financial market in its own currency. London needed to control the rules of any single financial market on which its own financial sector depended.

Even if such *arcania* are far from voter concerns, they contributed to difficulties in the UK's membership that occasioned the referendum. Incongruence between the UK's participation in the single market and its absence from the single currency is an important explanation for why there was a referendum even if it was unimportant to voter behaviour in the referendum.

Such were the domestic constraints posed by Eurosceptics in his own party and by UKIP that Cameron felt obliged in 2011 to veto a Fiscal Compact aimed at alleviating the euro crisis. However, the other members persisted with the Fiscal Compact by international treaty. But, what if Conservative Governments were constrained by their own party to block every major change where the UK still had a veto; and what if other members responded by merely acting outside the EU Treaties? Wouldn't that mean the slow death of British membership, at once self-excluded from new initiatives and at risk of being outvoted in the single market matters at the core of its existing membership. Cameron concluded that he needed a referendum to settle the UK's future in the EU if he was to regain sufficient control from his own party to bargain successfully at the European level.

According to a fifth account, things did not just go wrong in the last years of British membership. EU membership had always been hard to reconcile with British conceptions of identity, sovereignty and democratic self-rule. Both the UK and European integration changed fundamentally between 1950 and 2016.

But the British Governments of the 1950s that declined participation in the early stages of European integration would have recognized the argument of the leave campaign in 2016 that the UK could not be a part of a body in which it did not have full control of its own laws (Lord 1996, 2020). Not only might the UK be obliged to adopt laws that had not been approved and could not be changed by the Westminster Parliament. Membership also involved a commitment to cumulative integration. For sure, the 1975 referendum to leave or remain demonstrated how UK membership could be reframed as autonomy-gained or sovereignty-pooled rather than sovereignty-lost (Saunders 2018). Then and later cooperating with others through the European Communities was often defended as a way of enlarging the UK's ability to make choices and reducing its need to follow the choices of others. What was the use of the UK having the final say if, on its own, it had little say?[2]

Still, the sovereignty of the UK Parliament and the primacy of EU laws always had potential to become a tale of two colliding absolutisms (Bogdanor 2019). The tying of assumptions about justified political authority so closely and so absolutely to the sovereignty of the UK's Parliament (Milward 2002: 79) and low identification with the Union at best made UK membership transactional. At worst, they meant that the Union was more likely to be understood as an alien and imposed political order, rather than a form of joint decision-making in which the UK itself participated.

The UK itself then supported the development of the Union in ways that made sovereignty conflicts more likely. As seen, a single market is a massive undertaking in shared law-making. It was largely through the single market that the EU and its law became so important to how the UK and its public were governed. It was precisely its claims to legal supremacy that made the EU uniquely suited to constructing a multi-state internal market. The priority of EU law and the monopoly final interpretation of EU law by its Court facilitated certainty and coherence in the rules needed to create a single market. Yet, by creating a large body of law that the UK could not easily change alone, the single market made it plausible to argue that the UK could only regain full control of its own laws by exiting the Union. That suggests something quite different to a widely held view that it was the post-Maastricht European Union – and its creation of a single currency of which the UK was not a part – that undermined UK membership. Rather, it was the pooling of sovereignty to which British Governments had earlier bound themselves by so enthusiastically promoting a single market.

A sixth interpretation sees Brexit as part of a wider crisis in government and representative democracy; or of what Schonfeld and Winter-Levy (2019) call a 'wider populist upsurge across the western world'. The Brexit referendum and the election of Trump are often bracketed as twin events of 2016. Voters for both had similar sociological profiles: older, less skilled, less likely to have a university education, more likely to have suffered years of stagnant earnings, more threatened by immigration (Sobolewska and Ford 2020). Those similarities suggest something of a new cleavage in advanced democracies that has fed off a drastic loss of trust in political authority and a mobilization of 'the people' against elites. For populists, representatives are turned into unrepresentative and unaccountable elites by the very process of representation. By forming a European Freedom and Direct Democracy Group in the European Parliament, UKIP alluded to a critique of representative democracy that was increasingly a part of its case for Brexit. Still, support for Brexit only overlapped with populist ideas. The two were by no means identical. It is to the complexity of the Brexit coalition that we now turn.

THE CORE OF BREXIT?

The accounts of its origins set out in the last section are oddly limited in how much they tell us about Brexit. That is because Brexit has been heavily endogenous. It has changed and evolved through the very process of deciding Brexit. As seen, it was the referendum itself that divided the British public into tribes of leavers and remainers. Above all, what has ultimately decided the nature of Brexit has not just been the factors making for it; but, rather, the distinctive ways those factors were then combined into winning coalitions by the leave campaign and then the

Johnson Government. Leave could have made more of economic arguments, more of global Britain and less of arguments about sovereignty and control. However, once it mobilized votes by emphasizing sovereignty and control, the leave campaign changed what counted as delivering Brexit.

Holding together a winning coalition then created a form of Brexit that few would have predicted in 2016. Looked at from the outside, the UK has made a hard Brexit. With the exception of Northern Ireland, the UK has insisted on a complete exit from the EU's political and legal order and, therefore, from any single market or customs union. Yet looked at from the inside, Brexit has been soft to the point of attempting a new social compromise. Brexit has been a move to the right externally that has emphasized sovereignty, national identity and global markets. Yet Brexit has been a move to the left internally on questions of distribution and state responsibility for the UK's own economy and society. This section briefly retraces how Brexit had to reinvent itself to win and then survive.

Leave is often accused of being an inconsistent coalition. Many of its donors, policy entrepreneurs or advocates saw Brexit as an opportunity to turn the UK into a radically deregulated and globalized economy. Twelve days after the Brexit referendum the former chair of the leave campaign told the House of Lords that Brexit was an 'opportunity to finish the job that Margaret Thatcher started' (House of Lords Debates 5 July 2016). Yet, as seen, for many of its voters, Brexit was a protest of left-behind communities or threatened identities against Europeanization, let alone globalization. There would have been no majority for Brexit without the support of those 'left behind' by the marketization, Europeanization and globalization of British economy and society. Their demand was not for a Brexit that would complete the Thatcher revolution but for a revolution that would roll it back. So, some of its supporters understand Brexit as an opportunity to create a kind of Singapore-on-Thames: a radically deregulated and maximally open economy with a minimal state. Others understand it as an opportunity to create a more communitarian economy and society or at least a new social compromise. For some, a hard Brexit means a hard break from the EU as a form of economic governance and regulation. For others, a hard Brexit means being hard on immigration. Still others argued for a 'Lexit'; or, in other words, a left-wing form of Brexit aimed at more redistribution, social justice and public support for developing the means of economic production than would be possible under EU rules (Bickerton and Tuck 2017). Given the closeness of the vote to leave the Union, each of the foregoing ideologies of Brexit has some claim to being essential to it. However, those versions of Brexit differ hugely in the beliefs about economy and society they use to justify withdrawal from the EU.

Yet, whatever their other contradictions, most who voted for Brexit agreed with some part of the idea that the UK had insufficient 'control' of its laws, money and borders. In a huge survey (Ashcroft 2016) of 12,639 voters on referendum day itself, the idea of 'regaining control' dominated any other reason for voting to leave the EU; 49 per cent of those who voted leave said their main reason for doing so was 'the principle that decisions about the UK should be taken by the UK'; and an overlapping group of 33 per cent said their main reason was that the UK should 'regain control of immigration and its own borders'. When a subsequent YouGov poll asked respondents to pick 'two or three of the most important issues when deciding on Britain's future relationship with the EU', 54 per cent of all leave voters chose 'ensuring Britain has control over its own laws' as an answer. In contrast, that response was chosen by only 17 per cent of remain voters. Hobolt et al. (2020), accordingly, classify the Brexit vote as a 'sovereignty referendum'.

However, we cannot understand the leave vote without understanding that component of it that saw itself as doing something more than return powers transferred to the European Union. They also saw themselves as taking back their share of control within the UK's own system of government. Communities neglected for decades by a political system that normally encourages political competition for just 10 per cent of the vote in 10 per cent of constituencies made themselves pivotal to the referendum outcome. They remained pivotal in the 2019 election as the UK realigned along a leave/remain cleavage. The result has been the lumping together of the contrasting economic and social ideologies of Brexit discussed earlier. Before discussing prospects of satisfying those different elements, we must first discuss what Brexit means to the EU and, therefore, to the relationships the EU can offer the UK.

BREXIT AND THE EUROPEAN UNION

It is not enough to trace evolutions of Brexit within British politics. As said, the shape of Brexit will also depend on the EU. For the first time the EU has lost a member. That raises at least the following questions. Is Brexit part of a process of disintegration? Is it a sign that something has gone very wrong with the Union; that it is losing popular support or failing to meet the needs of its member states? Does Brexit create new perils for the EU? Or has the EU lost a member that constrained its further development? Could it even be the Union, and not the UK, that gets to have its cake and eat it? Could the UK end up having to align with EU policies and rules without the Union having to incur the 'decision-costs' of accommodating an awkward partner (George 1998)? Or could the EU and UK both benefit from replacing a dysfunctional relationship with mutually advantageous forms of policy competition? Whatever happens, Catherine De Vries (2017) is surely right that Brexit has created a 'counterfactual': a clearer means of evaluating membership against an example of non-membership.

A key question is how far the choices of both the EU and the UK will now depend on the choices of the other; and will any interdependence then be symmetric or asymmetric? Will one side dominate if only by virtue of being able to get by however the other decides? Some clues might be found in how the EU has managed Brexit so far. Apart from the Union being unsentimental – often seeming to treat Brexit as largely an administrative question of identifying what needs to be done technically to withdraw a member from the Union – member states have been disciplined in holding to a multilateral approach to negotiation and foregoing temptations to get a better deal for themselves by bargaining bilaterally with the UK. That is crucial, since, of course, the EU's position as the larger player depends on its being a block negotiator.

Another key question is how far Brexit is likely to create novel ways of organizing relations between the EU and European democracies that are not members of the Union. Michel Barnier was fond of a chart that arranged the EU's relations with non-members on a staircase. Just one step down from membership were the European Economic Area (EEA) countries: Norway, Iceland and Liechtenstein. Two steps down was Switzerland. Furthest away were those without any relationship with the EU beyond shared membership of other international bodies such as the World Trade Organization. Yet Barnier's staircase assumed what many Brexiters disputed: namely, that existing arrangements exhausted all possible ways of organizing relations with non-members or that it made sense to compare the UK with any existing example of a European state that is not a member of the EU. In their view, the UK is unique in its size as the world's fifth largest single state economy; in its membership of the United

Nations Security Council; in its status as a nuclear power; and in its privileged access to US intelligence. Even the fact that it has been a member of the European Union might count in its favour. The UK will be able to choose where to do things differently whilst benefiting from many other ways in which it starts off aligned with the EU (Legatum Institute 2016).

There are different versions of the argument that the UK will find its own *Sonderweg* as a non-member state. One assumes that, even if the UK would be better off with a relationship with the EU than without one, it could get by without any relationship at all. A second assumes the UK needs a relationship with the EU but no more than vice versa. A third is cautious of any relationship that is not strictly on the UK's terms. Leaving was the idea of leaving. No agreement should involve any constraint on the UK; and, anyway, Europeanization was the past. Globalization should be the UK's future. Not only will the UK be a different kind of non-member state. Brexit is also happening at a distinct historical juncture in which transformations in economy and society are opening up new possibilities, and, with them, new ways of cooperating between states and democracies. Two of those arguments assume that the UK could sit comfortably at the bottom of Barnier's staircase without much relationship with the Union beyond the wider rules and relationships of the international system. All three suggest scope for the UK to coax the Union into better and more balanced relationships with non-member European democracies.

However those arguments turn out, there will, of course, be one way in which the UK will be one of a kind: it will be the one non-member state that is also an ex-member state. The European Free Trade Association (EFTA) and EEA countries have, as it were, developed 'coming together' forms of non-membership: forms of non-membership that involve more cooperation and inclusion. Any relationship the UK forms with the European Union will likely be a 'falling apart' form of non-membership: an arrangement that will involve less integration than before to the policies, institutions and laws of the Union. Both sides are also likely to be wary of any form of non-membership that repeats the difficulties of UK membership.

Still the Union itself may have an interest in viable forms of ex-membership. Ease of exit is a defining feature of any political order (Hirschman 1970); and even a rather paradoxical factor in their legitimacy. In the case of the EU, the more its undertakings constrain it to insist on the supremacy of its law, the more its legitimacy with its member states may depend on their ultimate right to 'regain control' of their laws by leaving the Union (Garben 2019). Yet, ease of exit depends on the availability of alternatives.

Still, when the Union says that it is constrained in the relationships it can offer non-members it is not just being stubborn or unimaginative, nor is it necessarily trying to dominate anyone or drive a hard bargain. The Union cannot offer non-members the benefits and rights of membership without the costs and obligations. Only by excluding free-riders can the Union work as a club for managing externalities and solving collective action problems between its members; and only by insisting that degrees of inclusion are linked to rights and values can it operate internally as a community of rights and values. The most the EU can offer a non-member is participation in the preparation or implementation of decisions. Only members can have decision-rights and, therefore, votes or vetoes, if the benefits of membership are to be restricted to those prepared to contribute to the costs of membership. In that sense the EU is a 'vulnerable hegemon' (Fossum et al. 2021), constrained to insist on the hegemonic exclusion of outsiders from full decision-rights by its own vulnerability to what would follow from according those rights for free. It is here that we begin to understand the vast difference between membership and non-membership. It is possible to imagine a non-member participating or approximating unilaterally to so many Union policies that its citizens' lives are affected in much the same way as they would be if their country was a full member. But, still, there would be a fundamental difference in being outside the Union's political and legal order: in being outside the EU's supremacy and direct effect and correlative political decision-rights.

FROM MEMBER STATE TO BREXIT STATE

We have sketched what winning coalitions within the UK might demand from Brexit, as well as the relationships the EU and others may be able to supply. Only by considering the demand and supply sides of Brexit in combination can we now identify what might make it a ripple or a rupture.

As Christopher Bickerton (2012) has argued, states that are members of the Union are particular kinds of state: namely, states that are organized for participation in the policies, institutions and rule-making of the EU. Within each member state that has profound implications for relations between governments and parliaments, for public administration, and for its own internal legal order, which has to adapt to the priority of EU law. To be a member state is also to be a different kind of democracy that makes some of its decisions with other democracies whilst accepting some limits on what can be determined by democratic choice, competition and compromise within its own democracy. Membership creates new ways of cooperating to manage externalities and solve collective action problems. But it also constrains what economic and social models are possible within member states (see Fossum's chapter in this volume). To be a member is also to be a certain kind of international actor. The EU constrains what its members can do and agree internationally. Finally, free movement constrains how member states can manage their boundaries and decide who can live and work on their territory.

If membership transforms so much, we might expect withdrawing from the Union to be a rupture. But not so fast. Non-members can also be significantly organized for relations with the EU. The EEA countries – and to a lesser extent Switzerland – are examples. A leaving state might, conversely, choose to magnify, rather than smooth, differences between its future goals and its past membership. Either way, structural factors, imperfectly understood, may mean that a withdrawing state ends up diverging less or more than it intends. Whilst, though, the range of possibilities is wide we can anticipate some choices the UK will have to make in any transition from member state to what we might call the 'Brexit state': from being a state organized for membership of the Union to being a state organized for leaving the Union. The 'Brexit state' will presumably need to do at least the following:

1. Deliver on the outcome of the referendum. As well as leaving the EU Treaties, the Brexit state may need to develop concepts and practices of sovereignty and statehood that credibly deliver on a mandate to regain control of the UK's own laws, borders and money.
2. The Brexit state will need to review everything in the UK's own political and legal order that presupposes membership of the EU. That will require much more than merely subtracting the UK from the Union's Treaties, supremacy, direct effect and decision-rules. As Vernon Bogdanor (2019) observes, the starting point for Brexit is the UK's Europeanized constitution. The UK's political and legal order has itself been fundamentally changed by membership of the EU. Rights, law, territoriality and government – or, in other words,

many of the fundamentals of political order – all evolved between 1973 and 2016 in ways that assumed membership of the European Union. The Brexit state will need to review those parts of the UK's political and legal order that depend on EU membership either discarding them or giving them some other foundation.

Attempting to do that by simply reasserting UK parliamentary sovereignty as the basic norm and organizing principle of the British political and legal order may only risk multiple, acute, overlapping sovereignty conflicts within the UK itself (Bickerton 2019). First, between parliamentary and constitutional sovereignty as forms of rights protections. Second, as we will see, between the sovereignty of the UK Parliament and the sovereignty of the parliaments and peoples of the UK. Third, between different forms of sovereignty – parliamentary and popular – favoured by different varieties of Brexit. Is Brexit better understood as a rediscovery of parliamentary sovereignty or an innovation in popular sovereignty? A critique of unrepresentative elites plainly contributed to the no vote. But that complaint was directed at British parliamentary and political elites, and not just the European Union. More than return powers transferred to the European Union, some leave voters saw themselves as taking back their share of control within the UK's own system of government.

3. As Michael Keating discusses in this volume, the Brexit state will need to choose between exiting as one demos or many. Northern Ireland and Scotland voted to remain. For some, the idea that a majority of the whole of the UK should trump majorities in its parts in determining the nature of Brexit has already begged the very question of whether the UK should decide fundamental questions as a democratic people or a democracy of more than one democratic people. For some of that view, the referendum has not been a legitimating moment. It has been used to impose Brexit on parts of the UK that should have had a larger role in discussing and deciding it. Even others who accept the final say belongs with a majority of the UK as a whole might feel that more should have been done to hear, accommodate and respect majorities of the parts in deciding the nature of any Brexit. Another acute difficulty is that the same constraints on the sovereignty of the British state that convinced many Brexiters of the need to leave the European Union were understood by many in Northern Ireland and Scotland as necessary protections if they were to be guaranteed roles in governing themselves within their parts of the UK. In Brendan O'Leary's view (2018: 234), Brexit 'brutally re-advertised' 'the inability of the English to establish entrenched constitutional arrangements with others'. Northern Ireland and Scotland remain unresolved questions of Brexit.
4. The Brexit state will need to choose between the contrasting ideologies of Brexit discussed earlier. As seen, contrasting ideas that Brexit should lead to radical marketization or to social protection and reconstruction can both claim to be essential to the winning coalition in the referendum. There may be some scope to apply contrasting solutions to different regions, social groups or sectors. But perhaps the key question is whether Brexit will generate a sufficient economic surplus to pay its political debts. For many of its supporters Brexit releases the UK from the ponderous European Union just at the moment that new technologies – such as Artificial Intelligence – offer huge new possibilities to fast movers. But the gamble is huge. Hopes that technological transformation will make it as easy to trade with any other part of the world will need to compensate for any downside to UK trade within the European region. So a lot rides on the assumption that the world is changing from one in which countries are much more likely to trade with their neighbours,

especially those with similar GNPs and, therefore, similar patterns of supply and demand. The UK trades more with Ireland (with a population of 5 million) than with India (with a population of 1 billion). Such trade data may even understate economic interdependence within the European area. It is one thing to trade huge quantities of *finished* goods and services. Interdependence is quite different where supply chains and processes of producing key goods and services are themselves integrated across borders. Processes of production are often physically distributed across European states. Another difficulty is that the UK is really two economies. As Mark Blythe (2021: 23) points out, the rest of the UK detracts from GDP (it is 'value added' negative and therefore partially dependent on 'central transfers) outside London and the South East. Brexit may, therefore, rest on an implicit assumption that London can pay for Brexit. Yet, perhaps the largest economic unknown is what Brexit will mean for London with its special dependence on finance, services and free movement of labour and capital. Finally, Brexit does not just free the UK from the EU. It also frees the EU from the UK. As long as it was a member, the UK only needed to persuade a few other member states to hold the EU to a largely neoliberal interpretation of the single market. What if the EU now pivots to a more social market economy? Could that affect decisions on standards and equivalence in ways that make it harder for the UK to sell into the single market?

5. The Brexit state will need to choose between the different relationships that can be negotiated with the EU or others. Large though the difference is between membership and non-membership, there are, as seen, many varieties of non-membership (Eriksen and Fossum 2015; Gstöhl 2015) that vary in how far they approximate or deviate from what it is to be member state. At one end of a range, non-members can aim at dynamic or 'real-time' convergence through regular and institutionalized participation in the shaping of Union policies and laws, rather than merely approximating unilaterally and case-by-case. At the other end of the range of options, non-members can have little relationship with the EU beyond common membership of third bodies such as the World Trade Organization.[3] Hence, in discussing whether Brexit is likely to be a ripple or rupture we need to be careful to distinguish two factors: first, the large difference between membership and any form of non-membership; second, the fact that Brexit will nonetheless be defined by the difference between the highly distinctive form of membership the UK is giving up and the specific form of non-membership(s) it ultimately develops.

Choices between alternative forms of non-membership will also greatly affect the kind of international actor the Brexit state is likely to be. In vetoing the UK's membership of the European Communities in 1963, De Gaulle spoke of a British preference for the Open Sea over European commitments. Yet, even the UK's ability to ignore Europe has historically depended on Europe: on an absence of European problems that the UK itself wants a hand in solving. As remainers have often taunted, the UK inescapably shares a continent with the European Union; and, as some leavers have replied, they aim only to leave the European Union, not Europe. All that raises a problem to which we will return: does taking back control confer control or does control in the modern world depend on the pooling of sovereignty rather than its hoarding?

It is not hard to see how withdrawing from the European Union may require the Brexit state to confront deep and difficult questions about its sovereignty, autonomy, constitution, law, territoriality, rights protections, political order, economy, society and international relations. Hence, deciding the form of Brexit will unavoidably be a huge exercise of political power over fundamental questions of politics. Whilst, though, disagreements on such matters are only to be expected, that need not be a problem if there is agreement on procedures by which the Brexit state can resolve its disagreements. Where Brexit ends up on a continuum from Singapore-on-Thames to Lexit, how far the UK exits as one or several territorial units, and how far it repools some sovereignty through a Brexit of varying softness or other international cooperations are all questions that can be decided by elections and referendums over time.

At least two difficulties need to be anticipated. One is that prospects of agreement on the exact nature of Brexit have already been weakened by the referendum itself. Maybe it was never fully tested – not even in the 2019 election which was decided by a mere plurality – whether one way of leaving the European Union was a Condorcet winner; that is to say, a choice that would have been preferred to all other possible choices had those also been put to the public (Weale 2017: 178). Hence, the referendum sowed division. Leavers saw a clear mandate to leave. Remainers saw an unspecified mandate and some other choices that might have defeated a hard Brexit. Choices should perhaps have been more thoroughly deliberated in relation to one another before being narrowed to just those most likely to produce a majority that could beat all other possible majorities (Miller 1996). A second difficulty is with the nature of the UK's electoral system. Here it needs to be stressed that it is the electoral system that will be crucial to deciding the fundamentals of the Brexit state and resolving disagreements over time. Even future referendums would need to be authorized by prior elections (Lord 2021). Whilst, however, much of the British public has a certain affection for the UK's electoral system, the latter is famously adversarial and prone to rather arbitrary outcomes. That may limit its ability to resolve disagreements left over from Brexit.

TAKING BACK CONTROL

We can doubt how far voters – or even democratic peoples – normally get to choose and control the systems under which they live (Dunn 2000). Yet, remaining or leaving the European Union has been a fundamental choice over the laws, institutions and economic and social systems under which British citizens live their lives. The same might be said of choices between different versions of Brexit, different ways of relating to the EU from the outside and different ways of substituting for relationships with the Union.

But it is less clear that Brexit is a convincing answer to its own question of what it is for individual citizens or whole democratic peoples to control their own laws. Future historians may amuse themselves by debating how many crises the European Union faced between 2008 and 2022. Financial Crisis. Migration crisis. Geopolitical crisis. A Pandemic. A Membership crisis, including Brexit. Pluri-crisis has been the context of Brexit. That raises the question not just of how people should govern themselves in their individual democracies. But of how they should govern themselves in an interconnected world. Indeed, the first question is unanswerable without the second. As Philip Pettit (2010) has argued, highly interconnected democracies can only control their own laws by deciding how they should be internationally ordered for non-domination within and between themselves.

For sure, international organizations and international treaties have proliferated globally (Zürn 2018). Neither Europe nor the European Union have a monopoly on the means of coordination needed to solve collective action problems under conditions of interdependence. Yet Europe has become by far the most 'internationally governed' region in the world.

International cooperations within Europe have also overwhelmingly tended to concentrate on the European Union: even where cooperations have started outside the Union, they have tended to gravitate towards it. Tiresome though the cliché may be, it really is hard to play cricket when others want to play football. Whether they are members or non-members of the Union there are limits to how far any single European democracy can choose the frameworks by which all European democracies manage their interdependence.

It may also be structurally difficult to arrange relations between European democracies that are and are not members of the Union so that all those democracies and their citizens can fully control all of their own laws as equals. Thus, it is not just choices between joining, remaining or leaving the European Union that have profound implications for what it is to be a self-governing democratic people in contemporary Europe. So do choices between the different ways of *not* being a member of the Union. A European democracy outside the European Union is unlikely to free itself from any need to consider how its internal political order and system of democratic rule are affected by its relationship with the EU. Exiting just raises that question in new ways.

Yet individual European democracies can have some shared control (Lindseth 2010) over the constraints by which they are themselves constrained. That, though, implies a pooling of sovereignty. Democracies have collective action problems they cannot solve individually, so they reciprocally commit to using their sovereignty together and in ways that change how each uses its own sovereignty (Keohane and Hoffman 1991; Keohane 2002). But, if the pooling of sovereignty is a requirement of control, and not its abdication, it is unclear that the Brexit state has taken back control.

PLAN OF THE BOOK

Part I: The UK and Brexit

The first part focuses specifically on the UK. It starts with a chapter by James Dennison which provides an overview and brief assessment of those causes of Brexit that the literature has brought forth thus far. Dennison finds that possible explanations highlight historical and identitarian factors with emphasis on the UK's awkward relationship with the EU. Further, there are socio-political explanations that highlight such issues as marginalization, changes in the party system and the rise of populism; these are found across advanced democracies, although Brexit represented a unique opportunity for their articulation. Finally are explanations that see the referendum as a proxy for other issues than the UK's EU relationship. Dennison concludes by highlighting several important underexplored themes. Julie Smith's chapter focuses on the Brexit referendum. The chapter starts by providing a historical background that includes the UK's 1975 referendum, which failed to lay the question of membership to rest. The next section discusses the implications of the UK's not holding a referendum on the Lisbon Treaty as a possible 'safety-valve'. The remainder of the chapter documents the process leading up to the referendum, the government's preparations (including Cameron's effort to renegotiate some of the UK's terms of EU membership), and the different sides' handling of the referendum, where the leave side played their cards better than the remain side. The chapter by Andrew Glencross and Monika Brusenbauch Meislová complements Smith's chapter by focusing on how UK political parties defined themselves in relation to Brexit. They move beyond a binary for or against and focus on how internal tensions especially within the Labour and Conservative Parties drove the Brexit process, and document the important changes to the landscape of UK politics that this process has unleashed. The authors show how territorial politics and the question of the future of the UK is bound up with party politics. The territorial dimension is the focus of Michael Keating's chapter. His point of departure is that there is no single agreed-upon interpretation of the UK as a polity but rather two, one that sees the UK as a homogeneous nation-state, the other that sees the UK as a plurinational union. Brexit brought these two interpretations to a head, given that 'taking back control' drew its sustenance from the former unitary account, which draws on a classical Bodinian notion of sovereignty. The second account is steeped in a post-sovereign account wherein devolution and the UK's plurinational character are compatible with the EU's transformation of sovereignty. Keating discusses the territorial implications of the Brexit decision, with regard to the process of devolution, the Irish conundrum and the future of the UK as a union. Brexit was not only a contestation over different conceptions of the UK as a polity; it was equally a contestation over the UK's role in the world, and as Ben Rosamond has noted, 'the referendum result was delivered through an alliance between hyperglobalist neoliberals and nativist economic nationalists' (Rosamond 2019: 414). In his chapter Craig Parsons examines the role of economic ideas in the Brexit story, given the importance attached to the role of ideology in driving the Brexit process. Parsons re-examines Thatcher's neoliberal position and notes that contrary to what is frequently stated that 'Thatcherites consistently rejected the notion that robust European institutions were desirable, *even for liberalisation*' (italic in original), Parsons proceeds to examine how this early and consistent antipathy to EU institutions, a rather peculiar version of neoliberalism, came about and concludes by noting that the EU's insistence on the indivisibility of the single market represented another version of neoliberalism. The Brexit process thus pitted two different versions of neoliberalism against each other. In her chapter on the political economy of Brexit, Amy Verdun notes that TCA even if far from solidified gives us some sense of how future EU-UK relations will be structured. Through Brexit, the UK has sought to de-link itself from the EU institutions, and especially the EU's attempt to deepen European integration. That certainly applies to the area of economic and monetary union. On financial matters, and in terms of the single market, there has been a greater interest both on the part of the UK government and certainly on the part of the business community and among voters, to be more closely aligned with the EU. These relations are, however, likely to be affected by the rather unstable situation surrounding the Northern Ireland Protocol. Brexit itself may have implications for the UK's constitutional make-up. With regard to the EU it is interesting that it managed to stay united during the negotiations. For the period post-Brexit, the EU must ensure that the EU-UK relationship is not considered so favourable as to entice other states to leave the EU. The relationship the EU has with the UK is not so comfortable that Eurosceptics may more easily point to the UK situation as one that is desirable. She concludes by noting that 'for the foreseeable future, both sides have some incentive in demonstrating that the relationship with the EU and the UK will remain somewhat rocky'.

Part II: Brexit and the European Union Institutions

Contributions to the next two parts turn to Brexit within the EU context; The second part of the *Handbook* deals with EU institutions. The third with EU member states. The second part starts with an overview of the legal aspects of the EU-UK negotiations. It then shifts the focus to a selection of EU institutions (the European Council, the European Commission, the European Parliament, EU agencies and the EU's regional dimension).

The part on the institutions starts with a chapter by Jean-Claude Piris, former Director General of the Legal Service of the EU Council. His experience places him in a unique position to outline key legal issues and challenges associated with Brexit. He starts the chapter by outlining the UK's distinct legal position in the EU with regard to rights and obligations. He then proceeds to chronicle the process of negotiations with regard to the negotiation procedures and the different stages, the UK's initial stance of keeping single market benefits, the Withdrawal Agreement, the UK's Internal Market Bill (2020), the Protocol on Northern Ireland, and the Trade and Cooperation Agreement (TCA). He underlines that the UK's main aim was national independence and sovereignty, not economic benefits. Thus, 'the aim of the TCA was not, as it is usual for a FTA, to reduce obstacles to trade, but to try and reduce the obstacles to trade created by the exit of the UK from the EU'. In this context the TCA is a framework for further negotiations not a final settlement. The next chapter by Birgit Bujard and Wolfgang Wessels focuses on the European Council, the EU's august body composed of the heads of states and government. Article 15(1) TEU states that the European Council's main purpose is to set out the EU's general political directions and priorities thereof. The authors underline the central role of the European Council in outlining the UK's role and status in the EU whilst a member, and it is the EU body that was in charge of setting out the details of the Brexit process and in terms of hammering out the EU-UK relationship. The authors use process-tracing to detail the European Council's involvement in the Brexit process and conclude by spelling out what they see as the EU's 'exit doctrine'. The next chapter by Christopher Lord is on the world's first and most significant supranational legislature, the European Parliament. Lord notes that the European Parliament (EP) has an important treaty-based role to play in international agreements (Article 218 TFEU). The EP's approval was needed for the Withdrawal Agreement (WA) and for the TCA. Lord argues that the EP can function as 'an informal agenda setter and an informal source of amendments even where it has neither of those powers formally'. The EP played an important role in sustaining EU coherence during the negotiations of both the WA and TCA. In his chapter Hussein Kassim uses extensive interviews with key practitioners to explore the role of the European Commission in the negotiation of the Withdrawal and Trade Cooperation agreements. The findings confirm the crucial importance of the expertise of the Commission as the one body that could identify the possible consequences of Brexit across the range of the Union's policies and powers. However much less known is how far the Commission developed its role in continuous communication with the member states. That was helped by trust in Barnier. It was also an important reason why the EU maintained its powerful position as a bloc negotiator throughout, without fragmentation, as many had feared, into a series of competing bilateral discussions with the UK. In the next chapter, Michael Kaeding focuses on EU agencies and Brexit. An important aspect of EU integration is 'agencification', or the formation of EU decentralized agencies. Kaeding notes that the EU at present has 34 such agencies spread across 22 EU member states. An interesting and explicitly Brexit-relevant fact is that EU agencies are open for participation from third countries. Kaeding notes that the UK during its EU membership was an important contributor to the EU's agencies. Post-Brexit the UK's role has changed to third country and what is notable is that the TCA only covers seven EU agencies. The political declaration initially envisaged cooperation also in foreign policy, external security and defence, but the UK walked away from this. The final chapter of this part is the chapter by Justus Schönlau, which considers

Brexit from the vantage-point of the European Committee of the Regions. The point of departure is that European integration has fostered the development of a dense network of vertical and horizontal relationships among national subunits within the EU, making the EU a highly complex and composite multilevel entity. Schönlau in his chapter discusses the implications of Brexit from the vantage-point of the Committee of the Regions which is a political assembly composed of locally and regionally elected representatives from the EU's member states. The chapter underlines that Brexit will likely have repercussions for the relations between levels of governance within individual member states and within the broader context of EU multilevel governance (Keating's chapter pointed to the possible effects for the subnational level within the UK). Further, the EU will feel the loss of a net contributor to its cohesion policy. Finally, Schönlau notes that the territorial effects of Brexit are likely to be asymmetrically distributed across regions.

Part III: Member States and Brexit

The third part of the book covers chapters on central member states, that is, Ireland, Germany, France and Poland. Brigid Laffan notes that '(f)or the Irish state, Brexit was an existential matter involving high politics and geopolitics'. History and geography ensured that Ireland was the EU member state that would be the most affected by Brexit, perhaps even more so than the UK itself. Laffan in her chapter discusses what Ireland as a small state could do under such circumstances. She notes that '(a)rguably there was far more analysis of Brexit in Ireland than there was across the entire UK administrative system prior to the referendum'. This is hardly surprising given the implications Brexit could have not only for the Northern Ireland peace process but for the entire island. Laffan shows how Ireland mobilized state capacity and sought to ensure domestic elite cohesion and support from the EU and the US as two external protectors. The EU's support and coherent stance meant that Ireland could relate to the UK from a position of strength rather than weakness. Nevertheless, the Northern Ireland issue has not been laid to rest.

In his chapter on Brexit and Germany, Uwe Puetter notes that despite diverging on their long-term objectives for the EU integration process, the two countries have collaborated on a wide range of important EU projects, notably the single market. Puetter labels the period 1990s to 2010s as a transition from engagement to disengagement. With regard to Brexit, Puetter points to 'the striking absence of Germany as an independent voice in the Brexit negotiations. There is almost no evidence of the country seeking to secure particular relative advantages for its export-oriented economy.' In a similar vein, there is no evidence that Germany sought to control the Brexit process. Germany's main aim was EU unity; hence, it was comfortable with attributing a central negotiating role to the European Commission. Puetter examines the prospects for UK-German bilateralism post-Brexit and finds that these are quite limited. In her chapter on France and Brexit, Helen Drake notes that France was among those bent on imposing hard terms on the UK. Drake notes that both the UK and France have been labelled as 'awkward' member states, the UK for its penchant for semi-detached membership and France for its insistence on retaining sovereignty. She notes, however, that France has continued to support the pooling and sharing of sovereignty that is taking place within the ambit of the EU. Through Brexit, France as well as Germany faced a choice between pursuing a bilateral France-UK relationship or EU unity. As Germany opted for the latter. Brexit thus drove a wedge into the well-entrenched Franco-British Bilateral Relationship (FBBR) which had existed for almost 50 years. Drake notes that France is experiencing an ongoing political crisis of lack of trust that may dwarf the role of Brexit. In his chapter on Poland, Rafał Riedel starts by noting how Brexit increases asymmetrical power relations within the EU in favour of Germany. Riedel examines whether Brexit served to give impetus to or stymie the Polish PiS party government's sovereignty pursuit. Nevertheless, there is an important difference between the Euroscepticism that is found in the UK and Poland's view of the EU. Poland is generally speaking very positive towards the European Union, but Poles are against specific policies, and in particular supranational monetary integration. Brexit may, if the UK is perceived to be a success outside the EU, tilt the balance towards a more sovereigntist stance against Brussels. The last two chapters in this part focus on two aspects of the regional dimension within the EU. Ian Cooper and Federico Fabbrini focus on regions as clusters of member states, or what they term bottom-up regional groups (BURGs) of cooperation within the EU. This phenomenon has received very little attention in the scholarly literature on European integration. The authors identify 13 such groups and note that every EU member state is involved in at least one of these (pre-Brexit examples are the bilateral UK-Ireland relationship, the New Hanseatic League, the Three Seas Initiative and the Baltic Assembly). The chapter clarifies the different forms of cooperation involved in the various BURGs, and discusses the implications of this form of EU differentiation for relations post-Brexit. The authors find that BURGs may represent a means for re-including the UK, along various BURG-inspired arrangements.

Part IV: Brexit and Affiliated Non-Members in Europe

The fourth part considers implications of Brexit for closely affiliated non-member countries in Europe. It starts with a chapter by Sieglinde Gstöhl that examines what pattern(s) of affiliations the EU has developed with its neighbouring countries. This overview of affiliations includes the EEA model (which includes the three EEA-EFTA states Iceland, Liechtenstein and Norway and the EU's 27 member states); the Swiss model; the Turkish model; the small states Andorra, Monaco and Marino; the Ukrainian model; sectoral communities; and the British model, including the special case of Northern Ireland. These affiliations vary considerably in substance and depth but there is an overall pattern: the broader and deeper the substance of the arrangement, the stronger the governance arrangements, and the more these countries are included in the EU's decision-making processes. This is labelled a form of decision-shaping, not decision-making because third countries do not participate in the EU's main law-making bodies. In this context, the substance of the UK's TCA is quite narrow, and is 'more inspired by FTAs [free trade agreements] with countries further afar than those with EU neighbours'. The next chapter by Sandra Lavenex and Alexandre Veuthey discusses the Swiss model, which was a frequently referred to model in the Brexit debate. The authors start by tracing the trajectory of this model of bilateral agreements, which they label as a side-street because the Swiss in a popular referendum in 1992 rejected EEA accession. This arrangement the authors note has run into problems in particular with regard to freedom of movement. The failure to reach an agreement for five current and all future agreements means that the model has over time moved from a 'side-street' to a 'dead-end'. Thereafter the authors discuss Brexit and Swiss-EU relations, the role of the Swiss model in the Brexit debates and Brexit's impact on Swiss-EU relations. They note that Brexit has reinforced EU pressure on the Swiss model. They conclude that '(b)eyond the specific case of Switzerland and Brexit, the developments in this chapter highlight a new approach in the EU's relations with third countries, in which the homogeneity of the single market and the balance of benefits and obligations predominate over economic or other functional interests in promoting integration below the threshold of membership'. In the next chapter John Erik Fossum discusses the Norwegian model, which also figured in the Brexit debate. Fossum's point of departure is that there are at least three different readings of the Norway model: two steeped in law; the third steeped in distinct socio-economic and political conditions associated with the Nordic model. The Nordic region has historically speaking been a carrier of a distinct socio-economic structure embedded in and upheld by political parties and state institutions (including tripartite cooperation and concertation). Thus, the Norway model is not only a legal mode of affiliation; it is also steeped in distinct socio-economic conditions with stronger social democratic anchorage than the UK's neoliberalized socio-economic structure. Fossum argues that despite the fact that Norway is not an EU member it has been heavily Europeanized; hence there are few grounds for seeing Norway as a particularly strong carrier of the Nordic model. Nevertheless, 'in order to establish how distinctive the Norway Model is as a mode of EU affiliation, it may be more important to clarify how extensively the Nordic region has been Europeanized than to look at the distinctive traits of Norway's legal affiliation with the EU'. In the next chapter, Christian Frommelt focuses on Liechtenstein's relations with the EU in the context of Brexit. Liechtenstein is a very small state, which raises questions of autonomy, recognition and how to manage the extreme asymmetry that marks the relationship with the EU. In this context, as Frommelt notes, EEA membership, in contrast to how it is discussed in Norway, was for Liechtenstein seen as a step to independence and recognition. Liechtenstein has then also obtained a range of exceptions unique to it. Some of these were discussed in the context of Brexit. Frommelt explains that Liechtenstein's path to the EEA was contested. Concerns were raised pertaining to administrative capacity, immigration, democratic deficit and financial pressures. Liechtenstein, as the other EEA states, has a host of additional arrangements with the EU. At the same time, Liechtenstein has a very close relationship with Switzerland which places it in a precarious position when as now Swiss-EU relations are at a low. In the context of Brexit, Frommelt discusses how Liechtenstein should relate to the UK. Liechtenstein was part of the agreement between the EEA-EFTA states and the UK. For technical reasons to do with free movement, Liechtenstein also needed to be a part of the bilateral agreement between the UK and Switzerland. The instance of Brexit meant that those states that are closely affiliated with the EU faced a new dynamic when the UK left the EU: how to manage the new triangular dynamics EU-UK-EEA-EFTA? The development of EU-UK relations obviously matters a lot here.

Part V: Brexit Beyond Europe

The fifth part of the book focuses on the implications of Brexit beyond Europe, including some of the most powerful players in the international system (the US and China), and Canada and Australia, the former as a possible template for the UK's post-Brexit EU affiliation; the latter as an intrinsic element of the 'global Britain' notion. In her chapter on Canada, Nanette Neuwahl focuses on whether or the extent to which the EU-UK Trade and Commerce Act is a Canada-style agreement; in other words, resemblant of the Comprehensive Economic and Trade Agreement with Canada (CETA), or whether an agreement between a regional organization such as the EU and a former member state such as the UK may in fact be in a category of its own. Neuwahl assesses the TCA in terms of its substantive remit, institutional features (including dispute settlement) and dynamics of alignment and compares the TCA with the

CETA on these counts. She finds that 'in many fields the TCA resembles a new generation deep trade agreement like CETA', and its forging benefited from the EU's experience with developing the latter. In the next chapter Roy H. Ginsberg discusses the impact of Brexit on EU-US political relations and NATO. Ginsberg notes that 'Brexit is not an advantageous development in EU-US and transatlantic relations, at least in the short-term. It complicates and divides the European pillar of the western security alliance.' In the chapter Ginsberg chronicles the Brexit process thus far with reference to the first 3–4 years as 'the parting' and projects the future EU-UK and EU-US relations as 'together apart'. He concludes by offering two future scenarios for a multipolar world wherein China will play a more prominent role. The first is an EU-UK association agreement that would strengthen the European pillar of NATO, the other is a trilateral cooperation scenario that focuses on EU-UK-US consultation and cooperation (under the heading of an EU-US FTA) bent on countering Chinese influence. In the next chapter, Russell Solomon focuses on what Australia might offer the EU and the UK in the post-Brexit period. Some of the Brexiteers saw UK-Australia relations as an intrinsic part of the Brexit slogan of 'global Britain'. Such a view might be consonant with Solomon's observation to the effect that '(h)istorically, Australia's relations with the EU have been the converse of those with the UK where antagonism and only episodic engagement with the EU was in contrast to a deep ongoing and often close one with the UK'. In this context, Australia felt betrayed when the UK joined the EU in the early 1970s because Australia conceived of the EU as an obstacle to the liberalization of trade, mainly due to the EU's common agricultural policy. Solomon notes that Australia has developed a global trade outlook with a natural gravitational pull towards markets closer to home, such as China. Nevertheless, Australia recognizes the need to branch out, and the EU figures significantly, as evidenced by the negotiations over an Australia-EU FTA. It is notable that Brexit might serve to institutionalize rather than undermine EU-Australia relations. In the final chapter of this part, Biao Zhang and Shaohua Yan examine how China views Brexit. The authors draw on a wide range of Chinese sources to analyse how Chinese scholars and policy-makers assess Brexit's impact on the UK; how the Chinese assess Brexit's effects on China-UK relations; what impacts Brexit will have on China-EU relations; and more indirect effects pertaining to Brexit's implications for what the authors term 'great power relations'. The authors provide a comprehensive and very nuanced overview. The main points are with regard to the first, that the general view in China appears to be that Brexit will harm the UK. On the second, Chinese assessments are more positive in terms of how Brexit will affect China-UK relations, even if these assessments are also somewhat mixed. On the third, Chinese assessments with regard to Brexit's effects on China-EU relations in general are negative. On the final dimension, Chinese assessments are that Brexit will render the UK vulnerable to US influence; it will likely move the UK closer to Japan; and (prior to the Russian invasion of Ukraine) may improve EU-Russia relations.

Part VI: Brexit and Questions of Legitimacy

The sixth and final part contains two chapters that deal with aspects of Brexit and questions of legitimacy. In his chapter, Albert Weale starts by noting that the Brexit decision brings up a number of important questions pertaining to political legitimacy. These range from the role of referendums in settling core constitutional questions, including in terms of holding a referendum, the conduct of the referendum, and 'the authority of the result and its implications for the conduct of government and the obligations of citizens'. Weale provides a careful assessment of these points and notes that whereas there were problems on all counts, that does not amount to stating that Brexit was illegitimate. At the same time, he notes on the question of citizens' obligations that '(t)here is no inconsistency in supposing that the referendum was a genuine act of authorization, on the basis of which the government could pursue a policy of leaving the EU and continuing to campaign for a reversal of that decision'. Weale also addresses legitimacy in the context of inter-state relations, in terms of the UK's external conduct. The critical issue is the UK's willingness to abide by the agreements it has entered into, especially with regard to the Northern Ireland Protocol. Finally, Weale also discusses the issue of legitimacy in relation to the future integrity of the UK state, especially given the distribution of support and the issue of Scottish separation. In the next chapter, Richard Bellamy discusses Brexit in the light of political constitutionalism and referendums. Bellamy notes that Brexit brought up two views of political constitutionalism and its relationship to referendums. One is that referendums are deviations from representative democracy and serve to disfigure democracy, given that 'they deny the pluralism and tolerance of true democratic decision-making by emphasizing the existence of a mythical and singular people's will'. The other position highlights the need for referendums as a means for correcting the elitist character of political constitutionalism. Bellamy's position is that 'referendums can play a valid constitutional role as part of a system of checks and balances on executive authority so long as they are appropriately embedded with a system of representative democracy'. Bellamy therefore sees referendums as complementary to representative democracy. The *Handbook* ends with a 'postscript in the guise of a conclusion'. Kalypso Nicolaïdis reflects on many of the narratives of Brexit and on the role of the scholar in studying it. One, already difficult, role is just to make sense of what has happened 'when the moment under scrutiny is so pregnant with historical resonance and yet so entwined with everyday life'. Yet the study of Brexit may also have a role in contributing to the 'exceptional synthesis' that would be needed for 'the British tribes (of leave and remain) to learn again to walk together'. When our world keeps coming back to the same 'globally recurring dilemmas' doesn't it reveal that behind many differences is a shared ambivalence? Many of us are ambivalent on 'fundamental questions of cooperation and control. Who truly is simply sovereigntist or cosmopolitan?' So, 'perhaps then Brexit boils down to the contrasting connotation of one word: bond. Bond as bondage or servitude for some, bond as the ties that bind for others. Shackles vs Sharing.'

NOTES

1. The research that went into this chapter has received support from the EU's Horizon 2020 programme (Societal Challenges 6: 'Europe in a Changing World – Inclusive, Innovative and Reflective Societies') under Grant Agreement No. 822419).
2. See, for example, the UK Government's White Paper, The United Kingdom and the European Communities, Command 4715 of 1971. Also, various speeches by the Minister in charge of the Negotiations, Geoffrey Rippon, in the RIIA (Chatham House) press collection.
3. UK Government (2016) *Alternatives to Membership. Possible Models for the United Kingdom outside the European Union*, London, UK Government.

REFERENCES

Ashcroft, Lord (2016) 'How the United Kingdom voted on Thursday and why', available at http://www.lordashcroftpolls.com/2016.06. Accessed 9 March 2022.

Bickerton, C. (2012) *European Integration. From Nation States to Member States*, Oxford: Oxford University Press.

Bickerton, C. (2019) '"Parliamentary", "popular" and "pooled": Conflicts of sovereignty in the United Kingdom's exit from the European Union', *Journal of European Integration*, 41(7): 887–902.

Bickerton, C. and Tuck, P. (2017) A Brexit proposal by Christopher Bickerton and Richard Tuck, available at https://www.briefingsforbritain.co.uk/a-brexit-proposal-by-christopher-bickerton-and-richard-tuck/. Accessed 4 January 2021.

Blythe, M. (2021) 'Economics and populism', in *Brexit and Beyond: Economy, UK in a Changing Europe*, available at https://ukandeu.ac.uk/research-papers/brexit-and-beyond-economy/. Accessed 8 March 2022.

Bogdanor, V. (2019) *Beyond Brexit, Britain's Unprotected Constitution*, London: Tauris.

Cummings, D. (2017) 'On the referendum, branching histories of the 2016 Referendum and 'the frogs before the storm', Dominic Cummings's Blog, available at https://dominiccummings.com/2017/01/09/on-the-referendum-21-branching-histories-of-the-2016-referendum-and-the-frogs-before-the-storm-2/. Accessed 7 March 2022.

De Vries, C. (2017) 'Benchmarking Brexit. How the British decision to leave shapes European public opinion, *Journal of Common Market Studies*, 55(Suppl. 1): 38–53.

Dunn, J. (2000) *The Cunning of Unreason. Making Sense of Politics*, London: Harper Collins.

Eriksen, E.O. and Fossum, J.E. (2015) *The European Union's Non-Members. Independence under Hegemony?*, London: Routledge.

Fossum, J.E., Garcia Quesada, M. and Zgaga, T. (2021) 'The EU's non-members: Key principles, underlying logics and types of affiliation', ARENA Report, EU3D Report 1/20, Oslo: UiO, availabe at https://www.eu3d.uio.no/publications/eu3d-reports/report-1-20-fossum-et-al.pdf. Accessed 21 September 2021.

Garben, S. (2019) 'Competence creep revisited', *Journal of Common Market Studies*, 57(2): 205–22.

George, S. (1998) *An Awkward Partner: Britain in the European Community*, Oxford: Oxford University Press.

Gstöhl, S. (2015) 'Models of external differentiation in the EU's neighbourhood: An expanding economic community?', *Journal of European Public Policy* 22(6): 854–70.

Hillion, C. (2015) 'Accession and withdrawal in the law of the European Union', in A. Arnull and D. Chalmers (eds), *The Oxford Handbook of European Union Law*, Oxford: Oxford University Press, pp. 126–53.

Hirschman, A. (1970) *Exit Voice and Loyalty: Response to Decline in Firms, Organisations and States*, Cambridge, MA: Harvard University Press.

Hobolt, S., Tilley, J. and Leeper, T. (2020) 'Policy preferences and policy legitimacy after referendums: Evidence from the Brexit negotiations', *Political Behaviour*, http//doi.org/10.1007/s11109-020-09639.w.

House of Lords Debates. (2016). 'Outcome of the EU Referendum', 5 July 2016.

Jones, E. (2015) 'Forgotten financial union. How you can have a Euro crisis without the Euro', in M. Matthijs and M. Blyth (eds), *The Future of the Euro*, Oxford: Oxford University Press, pp. 44–69.

Keohane, R. (2002) 'Ironies of sovereignty. The European Union and the United States', *Journal of Common Market Studies*, 40(4): 743–65.

Keohane, R. and Hoffmann, S. (1991) 'Introduction', in R. Keohane and S. Hoffmann (eds), *The New European Community*, Boulder, CO: Westview, pp. 1–40.

Legatum Institute (2016) *The Road to Brexit*, London: Legatum Institute.

Lindseth, P. (2010) *Power and Legitimacy: Reconciling Europe and the Nation State*, Oxford: Oxford University Press.

Lord, C. (1996) *Absent at the Creation. Britain and the Schuman Plan 1950–52*, Aldershot: Dartmouth, pp. 9–20.

Lord, C. (2020) 'Lessons from the Past? The 1954 Association Agreement between the UK and the European Coal and Steel Community', in M. Westlake (ed.), *Outside the EU. Options for Britain*, Newcastle: Agenda, chapter 1.
Lord, C. (2021) 'Referendums and democratic theory', in J. Smith (ed.), *The Palgrave Handbook of Referendums*, London: Palgrave, pp. 29–48.
Miller, D. (1996) 'Deliberative democracy and social choice', in D. Held (ed.), *Prospects for Democracy*, Cambridge: Polity, pp. 54–67.
Milward, A. (2002) *The Rise and Fall of a National Strategy 1945–1963. The United Kingdom and the European Community Volume 1*, London: Routledge.
Moravcsik, A. (2016). 'The Great Brexit kabuki – a masterclass in political theatre', *Financial Times*, 8 April 2016.
Nicolaïdis, K. (2019) *Exodus, Reckoning, Sacrifice. Three Meanings of Brexit*, London: Unbound.
O'Leary, B. (2018) 'The Twilight of the United Kingdom and Tiocfaidh ár lá: Twenty years after the Good Friday Agreement', *Ethnopolitics* 17(3): 223–42.
Pettit, P. (2010) 'Legitimate international institutions: A neo-republican perspective', in S. Besson and J. Tasioulis (eds), *The Philosophy of International Law*, Oxford: Oxford University Press, pp. 139–60.
Rogers, I. (2017) 'The inside story of how David Cameron drove Britain to Brexit', *Prospect Magazine*, available at https://www.prospectmagazine.co.uk/politics/the-inside-story-of-how-david-cameron-drove-britain-to-brexit. Accessed 6 October 2022.
Saunders, R. (2018) *Yes to Europe! The 1975 Referendum and Seventies Britain*, Oxford: Oxford University Press.
Schonfeld, B. and Winter-Levy, S. (2019) 'Policy or partnership in the United Kingdom? Quasi-experimental evidence from Brexit', *Journal of Politics* 83(4): 1450–61.
Sobolewska, M. and Ford, R. (2020) *Brexit Land: Identity, Diversity and the Reshaping of British Politics*, Cambridge: Cambridge University Press.
Wall, S. (2019) *The Official History of Britain and the European Community. Volume 3, The Tiger Unleashed*, Abingdon: Routledge.
Weale, A. (2017) 'The democratic duty to oppose Brexit', *Political Quarterly* 88(2): 170–81.
Zürn, M. (2018) *A Theory of Global Governance. Authority, Legitimacy and Contestation*, Oxford: Oxford University Press.

PART I

THE UK AND BREXIT

2. Why did the UK leave the EU? The state of the science of explaining Brexit

James Dennison

INTRODUCTION

Explaining why the United Kingdom (UK) left the European Union (EU) has become something of a cottage industry since 2016. Not only was the outcome a notable electoral upset, a constitution rupture for the UK and a clear vote of no confidence for the EU, but the campaign exposed seemingly hitherto hidden forces in society, existential questions for Britain and, arguably, advanced post-industrial democracies elsewhere. Moreover, the UK's long and difficult relationship with 'Europe' and the myriad dramatic political and economic events in the decade prior to the referendum offer observers a large choice of potential causal explanations for why Brexit happened. In this chapter I attempt to critically overview and connect this literature. I argue that there are roughly four categories of explanation for Brexit, each of which includes multiple distinct theoretical contributions.

First, historical and identitarian explanations have explained Brexit as the result of Britain's long-term discomfort with integration resulting from a lack of European identity, Eurosceptic political and media elite and, ultimately, a distinct political history, culture and geography. Second, socio-political explanations have focused on social transformations in the UK and beyond, notably in terms of immigration, the so-called 'losers of globalisation' or 'left behind' and an emerging 'value divide' and 'cultural backlash' based on tertiary education, amongst other things. Third, a range of explanations have argued that the vote was a proxy for discontent over other issues beyond Britain's relationship with the EU, primarily opposition to austerity, anti-establishment sentiment, non-political psychological motivations and English nationalism. Fourth, more proximate explanations have focused on the campaign itself – notably the weaknesses of the Remain campaign and the strengths of the Leave campaign. Despite being theoretically distinct, the numerous mechanisms within each category tend to have common strengths and weaknesses. Finally, I argue that, despite a rich literature that includes robust advances, there are important shortcomings to our understanding of why the UK left the EU, particularly (1) in terms of understanding over-time variation in British attitudes to membership and (2) in considering retrospective voting towards the object of the referendum, the EU itself.

HISTORICAL AND IDENTITARIAN EXPLANATIONS

The first group of explanations for Brexit focuses on the UK's long-term, anomalous character within the EU. Many of these explanations directly build on observations about the UK public's attitudes to and relationship with the EU prior to Brexit, or even to accession. Indeed, the UK had long been characterised as a country of 'reluctant Europeans' (Gowland and Turner,

1999) and an 'awkward partner' (George, 1998) within the European project. This has been explained primarily as either a result of the UK's anomalous lack of popular European identity or the UK's anomalous Eurosceptic media and political class and, more profoundly, its distinct constitutional and legal system, trading and migratory patterns, and historic trajectory, not least in terms of its Second World War experience.

Survey evidence, such as that from the Eurobarometer, clearly supports the notion that British scepticism towards the EU was deeper and more long-standing than that of other member states. Put most simply, as shown in Figure 2.1, optimism towards the effects of EU membership was consistently lower in the UK than across the EU. Furthermore, over the course of the UK's membership, the British public were the least likely of all member state publics to believe that EU membership had been a good thing. In 45 per cent of the Eurobarometer's (typically biannual) pan-EU surveys, the UK was bottom on this measure, and in 83 per cent it was in the bottom two, with British respondents typically offering anomalously Eurosceptic responses on a range of other questions (Carl et al., 2019). In terms of actual voting intentions, data from the 2016 European Social Survey further supports the view that the UK was particularly Eurosceptic. Whereas a slight majority supported withdrawal in the UK, in every other member state large majorities stated that they would vote Remain in a hypothetical referendum (Dennison et al., 2021; though this is liable to contagion effects), underscoring the fact that the UK's exceptional decision was not simply the result of being the only country to have a referendum on the subject. Furthermore, as Carl et al. (2019) point out, the UK's unique post facto referendum reflected rather than caused uniquely Eurosceptic pressures from the electorate on politicians.

However, the genuine anomalousness of the UK may have been exaggerated or, at the very least, such a narrative is simplistic. After all, in the 1970s the term 'reluctant Europeans' was used to describe the Nordic countries (Miljan, 1977; see also Gstöhl's 2002 application of the term to the Swiss), demonstrating, first, how such 'reluctance' need not be set in stone: by 2016, Denmark, Finland and Sweden had become more integrated than the UK and showed greater public support for membership. Moreover, the UK was a relatively *early* joiner to the then European Economic Community (EEC), being the primary motivation and driver of the organisation's first enlargement and the UK was, and possibly remains, less reluctant than other countries that never joined, such as Iceland, Norway or Switzerland. Finally, there are important differences between member states in how attitudes to European integration have evolved.

The notion of the UK's 'awkwardness' as a participant has also come under scrutiny from historians of European integration. Ludlow (2019, p. 35) characterises Britain's participation as simultaneously 'awkward' and 'an active – and successful – partner', notably in terms of the creation of the single market and enlargement. Ludlow goes on to explain the popular and academic emphasis on 'awkwardness' as the result of the UK's direct, confrontational approach vis-à-vis the EU and other member states and popular and media allusions to the Second World War and other historical 'continental' threats, as well as 'kith and kin' beyond Europe (for similar argument see Daddow and Oliver, 2016; though see Thompson's 2021 geopolitical interpretation of British 'awkwardness').

Social scientific attempts to theoretically explain this reluctance in the UK and elsewhere have typically built on social identity theory. Social identity theory predicts that identifying as 'a European' is a key cause of support for one's country's membership of the EU (McLaren, 2004; Hooghe and Marks, 2005), with national variation seen as rooted in history

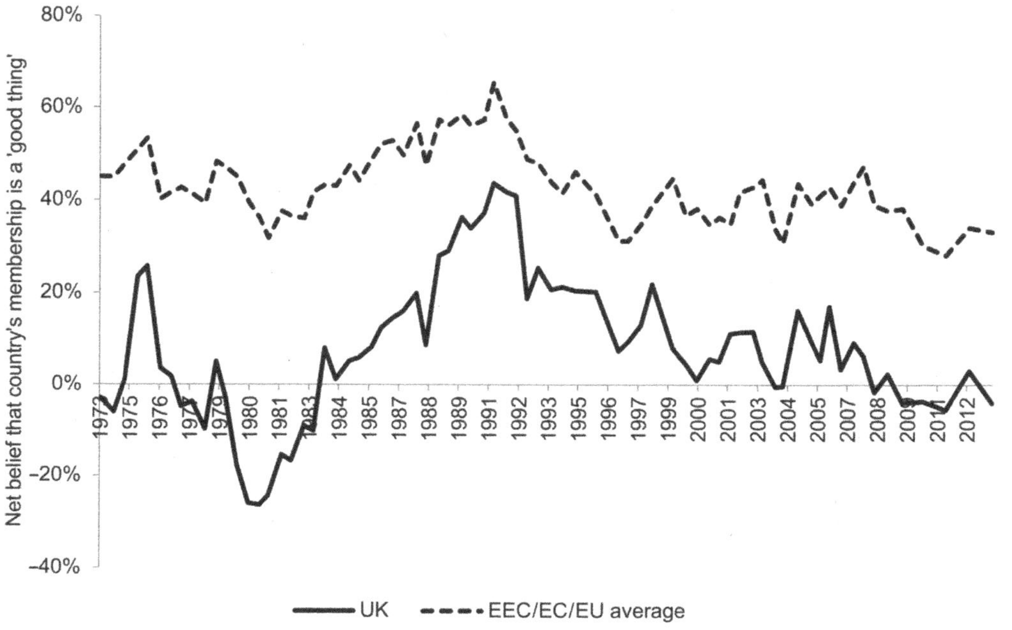

Source: Eurobarometer (1973–2013).

Figure 2.1 *Net belief that membership of the EU has been a good thing for one's country, 1973–2013*

and Second World War experience (Díez Medrano, 2000). In terms of the vote itself, Carl et al. (2019; see also Curtice, 2017; Evans et al., 2017) argue that the UK public was, in identitarian terms, 'European but not European Enough' for post-1992 levels of European integration and post-2004 rates of immigration. They highlight its anomalous and long-term lack of a European identity, showing that European identity explains a far greater proportion of national-level variation in support for membership than socio-economic, values-based or 'losers of globalisation' accounts, and that the UK is not an outlier on these alternative explanations *anyway*. They speculate on the deeper causes of this lack of European identity, which might be summarised as geographic isolation, a distinct legal and political system, a national-church (e.g. Kolpinskaya and Fox, 2021), notable constitutional and social links with former colonies outside of Europe (with some academics arguing about the effect of 'imperial nostalgia', e.g. Beaumont, 2018), and its Second World War experience, as well as its contemporary trading patterns, capital flows and emigration rates – all of which were the least Europeanised of any member state.

There are, however, good reasons to be sceptical of a purely identitarian explanation. First, as is shown in Figure 2.1, British attitudes to Europe experienced considerable variation, albeit in the form of secular trends, suggesting that, in some circumstances, Britons could be *overwhelmingly* pro-European. Second, European identity is unlikely to be entirely exogenous to attitudes to European integration. Although the former remained relatively stable in the UK in the 30 years prior to Brexit, it experienced an uptick after the referendum in the UK and had been on the rise consistently across the rest of the EU, both of which suggest that such responses are more labile than 'social identity theory' might presume. Third, as Carl et al. (2019) point out, the UK had been 'European enough' for membership for 43 years so any explanation must also explain 'why now?'. They can only speculate on four important over-time explanations: (1) the 1992 Exchange Rate Mechanism crisis; (2) greater integration from the 1992 Maastricht Treaty onwards; (3) the Eurozone crisis and post-2004 enlargement; and (4) subsequent high levels of immigration.

On the latter point, Dennison and Geddes (2018) build on identitarian arguments to show how immigration to the UK became increasingly 'Europeanised' in legal, economic and demographic terms, ultimately clashing with Britons' stubborn lack of European identity. This resulted in an unwillingness to see fellow European citizens as anything but immigrants, which coupled with a public and elite-level consensus that effective immigration policy necessitates a balance between control and numbers. These trends made 'the Europe question' electorally difficult for Conservative politicians to ignore both as a threat and opportunity, particularly as it became linked to broader patterns of prejudice (Hutchings and Sullivan, 2019) and anti-immigration sentiment (Evans and Mellon, 2019).

A second set of explanations for the UK's long-term reluctance focuses instead on the UK's anomalously Eurosceptic print media and political class. The British print media had long before the referendum been noted as Eurosceptic, emphasising the threat to Britain posed by EU institutions and integration (Hawkins, 2012). Daddow (2012) shows how the British print media became more Eurosceptic at the end of the 1980s, arguably preceding the popular turn against Europe in 1992 and potentially explaining the divergent trajectory between the British public and other West European publics. Gavin (2018) furthermore argues that the media may have increased attitudinal uncertainty over the years prior to the referendum. Hinde (2017, p. 81) notes the unusually political nature of the British press and that calls for a referendum on membership were made by tabloids as early as 1990, though is resigned to the effect of the media 'preparing the ground' for the referendum being 'impossible to calculate'. Although Carl et al. (2019, p. 299) offer reasons to doubt the causality and magnitude of the effect of media Euroscepticism on Brexit (notably in terms of the decline of print media), Foos and Bischof (2020) use the quasi-experiment of the widespread boycott of *The Sun* newspaper in Liverpool after 1989 to argue that avoiding this newspaper had an immediate negative effect on Euroscepticism in the city, lasting until the referendum.

Just as Britain's print media was probably an outlier in terms of its Euroscepticism, so was its political class, with sizable minorities of British MPs and MEPs advocating withdrawal in the years prior to the referendum. Moreover, a cursory glance through party election manifestos shows just how common and long-standing the use of referendums was across the political spectrum in attempting to appeal to an electorate of 'reluctant Europeans'. In the two general elections of 1974, the Labour Party promised (and then delivered) a referendum on membership. In 1979 and 1983 the Scottish National Party also promised such a referendum, while at the latter contest Labour promised immediate withdrawal. Only at the 1987 and 1992 general elections did no major party offer any form of referendum on Europe.

From 1997 onwards, however, the referendum manifesto pledges came thick and fast: that year, each of the Conservatives, Labour and the Liberal Democrats promised a referendum on Euro membership while the Referendum Party secured 2.6 per cent of the vote on the single issue of a vote. UKIP promised immediate withdrawal and would do so again at every subsequent election. At the 2001, 2005 and 2010 general elections, the Conservatives promised a referendum on any treaty change or joining the single currency, while Labour and even the 'pro-European' Liberal Democrats promised a referendum before joining the Euro at every election prior to 2015, with the latter *also* promising a referendum on membership in 2010. Finally, at the 2015 general election, the Conservatives, Liberal Democrats and Greens each promised a vote on membership. Though the increasing promises of a referendum partially reflect electoral expedience, it may also be that Britain's post facto 1975 referendum on membership set a precedent (enabled by an uncodified constitution) that, uniquely, left its participation in European integration as the subject of legitimate questioning and reliant on a popular majority rather than being a fait accompli.

Overall, these historical and identitarian explanations for Brexit have several strengths. Most importantly, they explain the national-level phenomenon of Brexit – and the UK's long-standing relative 'discomfort' with membership – with various national-level factors on which the UK was indeed anomalous: popular identity and a Eurosceptic print press and political class. However, they thus far only speculate on, first, the deeper historical, constitutional, cultural and geographic causes for British deviation and, second, on the over-time variation in the UK's membership, begging the question of 'why now?'. Finally, they may be wrong to assume that the vote to Leave was a genuine reflection of a desire to leave, overlooking, first, the expansive findings on the complex determinants behind voting in referendums and, second, the similar socio-political forces transforming other western countries at the time of the referendum.

SOCIO-POLITICAL EXPLANATIONS

Perhaps the most voluminous set of explanations for Brexit are those that see it as one result of socio-political changes to Britain over preceding decades. Most of these explanations share the suppositions that: (1) the referendum reflected issues far deeper than the UK's membership of the EU; (2) it presented a unique opportunity for changing societal divides to be articulated in a way that had been previously concealed and constrained by the British party system; and (3) that these emerging societal divides are found across other advanced democracies, manifesting in the rise of populist radical right parties in Europe and the 2016 election of Donald Trump, to which Brexit is interpreted as analogous.

Hobolt (2016, p. 1260) argues that 'the sentiments that led to this outcome are by no means a distinctively British phenomenon' and reflect a 'divide between those who feel left behind by the forces of globalisation and mass immigration and those who welcome such developments'. Goodwin and Heath (2016, p. 331) use district-level analysis to conclude that:

> [T]he vote for Brexit was delivered by the 'left behind' – social groups that are united by a general sense of insecurity, pessimism and marginalisation, who do not feel as though elites ... share their values, represent their interests and genuinely empathise with their intense angst.

Sobolewska and Ford (2020, p. 2) describe the Brexit vote as 'a moment when the social and political processes long underway finally became obvious, and the different groups of voters finally recognised themselves as two distinct and opposed camps', tracking the development of these groups – defined and exacerbated by educational expansion and demographic change, in ethnic and immigration terms from the post-war period onwards. They argue that these groups were activated by:

> [T]he gradual erosion of links between the traditional political parties and the electorate, the return of conflicts over immigration to the top of the political agenda and the emergence of a new party (UKIP) mobilising one pole of the identity divide. (Sobolewska and Ford, 2020, p. 3)

In this sense, they also take a historical and identitarian approach, albeit one focused on social groups within Britain.

These explanations are influenced by and align neatly with cleavage theory (Lipset and Rokkan, 1967) and the applications of that theory to explaining Europe's transforming party systems in the years prior to (and after) the Brexit referendum, notably in terms of the 'winners and losers of globalisation' and the expansion of higher education (e.g. Hutter and Kriesi, 2019). Indeed, Sobolewska and Ford (2020) contribute to this literature by measuring 'Brexit identities' and how they endure after the vote.

These explanations share considerable empirical strengths. First, a variety of sources show that 'Europe' was hardly at the forefront of the British public's mind in the years prior to the referendum (Figure 2.2). Indeed, the proportion of British citizens listing it as one of the most important issues affecting the country declined quickly as membership of the Euro became a distant prospect. By contrast, 'immigration', typically assumed to be the defining issue of the emerging globalisation cleavage, chief lament of the 'left behind' and lightning rod of the radical right, soared in the years prior to the referendum. Second, the referendum's unexpectedly high turnout added further plausibility to the notion that it exposed social

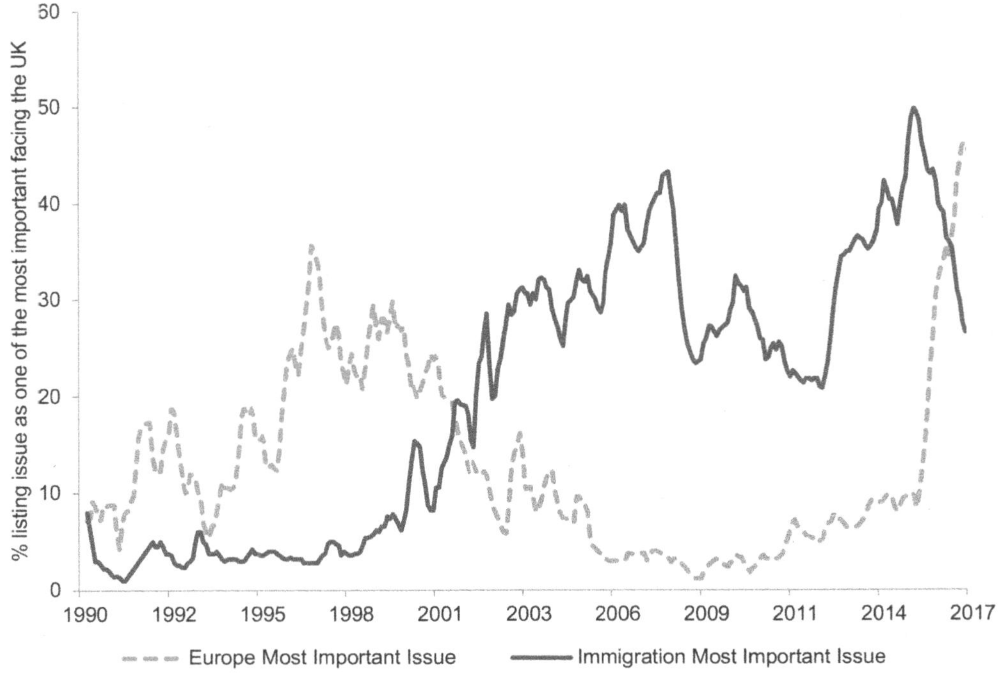

Source: Ipsos Mori, 'What are the three most important issues facing Britain today?' (from Dennison and Geddes, 2018, p. 1144).

Figure 2.2 *Public issue salience of immigration and Europe*

cleavages usually not expressed in general elections. Third, the proposed analogies between Brexit and other contemporary political events are by no means arbitrary – Euroscepticism, anti-globalisation and, particularly, anti-immigration rhetoric were all shared by analogous contemporary radical right parties and candidates.

However, evidence that Leave voters can genuinely be conceptualised as being 'left behind' or 'losers of globalisation' (both often conceptually underspecified) remains mixed (Chan et al., 2020). In Table 2.1, we can see how Britons who would go on to vote Leave and Remain, respectively, compare on variables that can be thought of as forming a basis for the 'winners and losers of globalisation', measured a few months before the vote (Fieldhouse et al., 2020). On objective measures of income and social grade, as well as self-described social class, Remain voters do appear more well off. However, in terms of economic pessimism, worsening financial circumstances, risk of unemployment and risk of poverty, there are only marginal differences between those who would go on to vote Leave and Remain.

Moreover, Green and Pahontu (2021) show that voters who have little wealth were far *less* likely to vote Leave, highlighting the importance of considering wealth – including home ownership – rather than just social grades and current income in any test of the 'losers of globalisation' thesis. This underscores a potential lack of conceptual clarity: how exactly have the 'losers of globalisation' lost from globalisation? Why have younger generations – in an arguably worse position in terms of home ownership, debt and an ability to start a family – not 'lost' from globalisation? Moreover, Carl et al. (2019) show that although some 'losers of globalisation' measures (e.g. views of globalisation, bad or worsening job situation, lack of trust in politicians) correlate positively with Euroscepticism at the national level, the UK low scores relative to the rest of EU member states suggest it would be one of the *least* likely countries to withdraw.

Table 2.1 *Differences between Leave and Remain voters according to the measures of key theories of referendum voting*

Measures of key theories (with date at which the question was asked)	Leave voters	Remain voters
'Losers of globalisation'/'left behind' measures		
% household finances situation will get 'a lot' or 'a little' worse over next 12 months (June 2015)	32.8	32.4
% household finances got 'a lot' or 'a little' worse over last 12 months (May 2016)	33.6	31.0
% risk of unemployment over next year 'very' or 'fairly' likely (May 2016)	15.4	15.1
% receiving unemployment benefit (from May 2015)	1.8	1.4
% risk of poverty over next year ('won't have enough money') described as 'very' or 'fairly' likely (from May 2016)	21.0	19.0
Mean gross household income (£000s; May 2016)	27.0	33.0
Social class/Grade		
% self-describe as 'working class'	49.6	36.4
% social grade A-C1	55.4	72.4
% social grade C2-E	44.6	27.6
'Calculation, cues, community' (all from May 2016)		
% leaving EU will make personal financial situation 'better' or 'much better'	15.6	1.8
% who received and read the Government's official pro-Remain leaflet	51.2	50.0
Mean European identity (1–7 scale from 'not at all' to 'very strongly')	2.4	4.6

Source: British Election study, Fieldhouse et al. (2020).

Following Hooghe and Marks's (2005) classic theory of attitudes to the EU as based on 'calculation, cues and community', in Table 2.1, we also see how Leave and Remain voters varied across measures of each of their three factors. Only a small minority of 15.6 per cent of Leave voters thought that Britain leaving the EU would make them personally more well off, though this is far more than the percentage of Remainers who thought similarly. In terms of cues, Leave voters were actually slightly more likely to have read the government's pro-Remain official pre-referendum leaflet, though there was only a tiny difference between the two groups. Finally, in terms of community, we see that Leave voters had a far lower sense of European identity than Remain voters.

Though less clearly in the vein of cleavage theory, Evans et al. (2017) and Evans and Menon (2017) similarly see Brexit as resulting from previous concealed social divides. However, rather than viewing the social divides as particularly new, they see the key divide as a long-standing class division concealed by the party system, which had seen the working class electorally marginalised as the mainstream parties converged on a socially liberal consensus from the 1990s onwards, abetted by Britain's first-past-the-post electoral system. In this view, the referendum was a chance for long-standing working-class attitudes on immigration and Europe to be articulated for the first time since Labour took on a pro-European position – and the higher immigration and more modest European integration in the meantime – reflected in the high turnout of the referendum compared to recent low turnout general elections.

However, one of the major changes in British attitudes to the EU was the sharp drop in pro-European attitudes amongst the highest social grades. In Figure 2.3, we see how those in 'professional' and 'manual' occupations changed their preferences regarding European integration between 1993 and 2013. Manual workers have consistently been less pro-European than professional workers, however, in 1993 there was considerable enthusiasm amongst this group for either greater integration (21 per cent) or the creation of a single European state (10 per cent) – with the two figures falling to 4 and 2 per cent, respectively, by 2013. At first glance, the 'losers of globalisation' thesis stands up based on this decline. Yet almost the exact same fall in support happened amongst professional groups, albeit from a higher constant. Whereas in 1993, 21 per cent of professionals wanted further integration and another 19 per cent wanted a single European state (!), by 2013 these figures had fallen to 7 and 4 per cent, respectively. The major class divide by 2013 was not about positivity or negativity to European integration, but whether it should be reduced (57 per cent of professionals and 36 per cent of manual workers) or Britain should withdraw altogether (15 per cent of professionals and 36 per cent of manual workers). This all goes to show, however, that amongst all social grades, support for *outright* withdrawal from the EU was a minority position in the years prior to the referendum. How, then, did this change after 2013? This is discussed in the next section on proxy explanations and cleavage effects.

However, a further, final set of socio-political explanations also frame Brexit as the result of an emerging political cleavage common to many 'western' countries, but place less emphasis on the social underpinnings of this cleavage and more on its psychological basis, primarily in terms of values. Norris and Inglehart (2019) argue that Brexit was one manifestation of a 'cultural backlash' against the earlier 'silent revolution' in values, with the referendum seeing 'populist' values pitted directly against 'cosmopolitan' ones (see also Chan et al., 2020). Other scholars have similarly argued that 'all told, the Brexit story is mainly about values, not economic inequality' (Kaufmann, 2016) and claimed that the referendum reflects an increasingly important value divide (Goodwin and Heath, 2016; Evans and Menon, 2017; Ford and

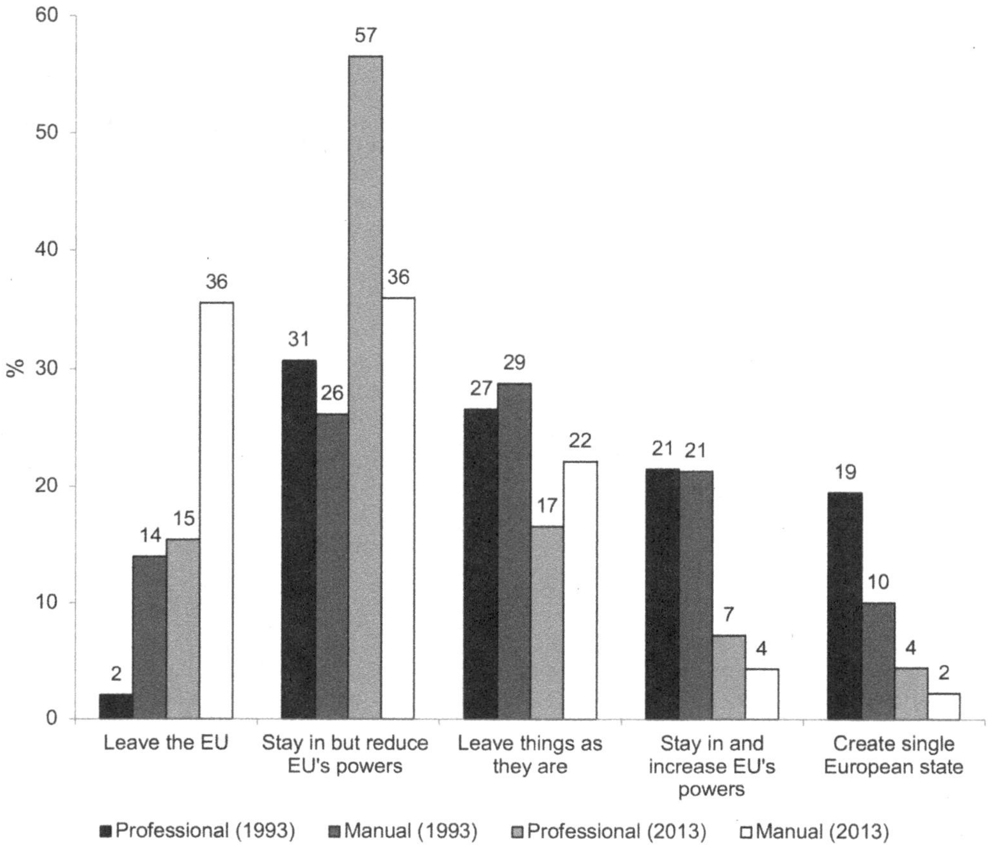

Source: British Social Attitudes (1993, 2013).

Figure 2.3 *Attitudes to the relationship between the UK and EU, professionals and manual workers in 1993 and 2013*

Goodwin, 2017; Koch, 2017; Arnorsson and Zoega, 2018; Andreouli et al., 2019), operationalising values as political attitudes towards social issues such as the death penalty. Dennison et al. (2021) also take a values-based approach to explaining individual-level voting variation, however, instead of using political values or attitudes, they introduce a non-political, personal psychological schema – Schwartz's theory of basic human values, 'one's guiding motivational goals in life'. They show that, of these, valuing universalism increased the chance of voting Remain whereas valuing conformity, security and tradition increased one's chance of voting Leave, with the effects primarily indirect, via attitudes to immigration and European identity (see Dennison et al., 2021 for comparison with dynamics in other member states).

PROXY EXPLANATIONS AND CAMPAIGN EFFECTS

Several explanations for Brexit argue that the referendum was not actually fought over Britain's relationship with the EU, but instead the referendum was a proxy for other issues. While these accounts offer insights into how an outright majority for Leave was attained, they tend to share common shortcomings in terms of underspecification of the causal mechanism and considerably smaller effect sizes than the factors mentioned above (see Chan et al., 2020). The first set of explanations – relating to anti-austerity sentiment, inequality and poverty – saw widespread popularity in the aftermath of the referendum, not least in the popular press. Indeed, poorer areas of the UK were found to be more supportive of Brexit (Becker et al., 2017), while later dynamic analyses at both the individual and district levels found a positive effect of austerity-induced welfare reforms on support for Leave (Carreras et al., 2019; Fetzer, 2019). That said, Carl et al. (2019) point out that measures of inequality and austerity show little relationship with support for the EU at the national level, while surveys of voters that directly asked why citizens voted as they did found little evidence that 'austerity' or 'inequality' were driving factors (Prosser et al., 2016).

Second, some academics and pundits interpreted the vote as a reflection of widespread anti-incumbent or anti-establishment sentiment (e.g. Iakhnis et al., 2018). Again, this interpretation received widespread popularity in the immediate aftermath of the vote but also receives considerable theoretical and empirical support from past referendums on European integration across Europe (e.g. Franklin et al., 1994; Frankin et al., 1995; Hobolt, 2009). It also aligns with UKIP's clearly anti-establishment messaging in the years and decades prior to the referendum: a tactic that worked particularly well after the Conservatives moved to the centre under David Cameron's leadership from 2005 onwards (Goodwin and Dennison, 2018).

Third, a range of psychological predictors have been applied to predicting voting in the referendum, aside from values as discussed above, not all of which can be overviewed in this chapter. For example, the personality trait of 'openness' (one of the Big Five) has been shown to predict voting Remain (Garretsen et al., 2018), while unhappiness (Liberini et al., 2019) has been shown to predict Leave voting. Although at risk of pathologising opposition to British membership of the, at that point, crisis-beleaguered EU, there are several psychoanalytic explanations (see Nielsen and Capelos, 2018) and ethnographic-based findings, for example, regarding 'apathy, anger and frustration' (Mckenzie, 2017) or 'anger, hate and passion' (Manners, 2018) as drivers of the vote to Leave. Aside from political psychological and psychoanalytic approaches are a number of cognitive studies that find that both Remainers and Leavers held similarly widespread and ideologically informed misperceptions about the EU, though the magnitude of misperceptions may have been greater among Leavers (Stoeckel et al., 2021).

The fourth and final proxy-based explanation argues that the vote to Leave was an expression of English nationalism (Henderson et al., 2016; Henderson et al., 2017), as evidenced by (1) England being one of two of the four 'home nations' in which a majority voted Leave and (2) the repeatedly demonstrated effect that English identity was positively associated with support for Leave. However, others have offered caution about the plausibility of this explanation (Kenny, 2016). Indeed, a majority in Wales (52 per cent, the same as England) and large minorities in Scotland (38 per cent) and Northern Ireland (44 per cent) voted in favour of Brexit, few of whom are likely to be English nationalists. Moreover, few, if any, voters surveyed since the referendum have listed English nationalism as a motivation for their vote decision. Indeed, it seems more likely that British nationalism, which is most prevalent in England, Wales and amongst Northern Irish unionists, though existing to various extents across all four home nations, explains support for Leave. Henderson and Wyn Jones (2021), building on earlier work, show that Britishness has different meanings in different parts of the UK and that support for Leave in England is associated with grievances about England's treatment in the Union. All that said, Hobolt (2016) shows the effect size of European identity on vote choice was at least four times larger than either English or British identity. Chan et al. (2020) add further nuance by showing that British identity predicts greater Leave support when considered on its own, but greater Remain support when juxtaposed against English identity.

A second group of explanations that seek to explain Britain's turn towards a pro-Leave majority in the final years before the referendum focus on dynamics during the referendum campaign and the preceding renegotiation. During and after the referendum, commentators have argued that the Leave campaigns actively misled the public, summarised succinctly as 'the lies we were told' (Wren-Lewis, 2018; see also Cooper, 2021 on misinformation and populist rhetoric during the campaign). These arguments build on earlier works regarding Britain's long-term anomalously Eurosceptic media that primed and legitimised a campaign based on 'strategies of fear, resentment and empowerment' (Zappettini, 2021, p. 277). Glencross (2016, p. 35) argues that '[n]othing was inevitable about the Brexit vote: the campaign mattered profoundly' and that the campaign was undermined by the Remain campaign's focus purely on economics at the expense of positive arguments about integration or identity issues (see also Goodwin et al., 2020). Clarke et al. (2017) show how the renegotiation did little to absolve Eurosceptic fears so that when polls are compared using dynamic factor analysis (Clarke et al., 2016), Leave had the lead throughout the entire campaign. Others (e.g. Williamson, 2019) have argued that the lack of an emphatically pro-EU, social democrat political leader outside of Scotland during the campaign undermined Remain, with David Cameron leading a divided Conservative Party and the historically Eurosceptic Jeremy Corbyn leading Labour. Moreover, Shaw et al. (2017, p. 1020) argue that Leave won because its campaign 'focused on a more consistent and tightly focused set of campaign themes, provided more explanation of those themes, and focused more on their own core issues than Remain'.

THE STATE OF THE SCIENCE OF EXPLAINING BREXIT

In the years following the referendum, a wealth of explanations has been offered to explain voting dynamics and, ultimately, why Britain voted to Leave the EU, something that had seemed an unlikely prospect only a few years earlier. All of these have strengths and weaknesses, and many are beginning to be incorporated into the wider literature on Euroscepticism in the UK and beyond (e.g. Gastinger, 2021).

Historical and identitarian explanations have linked Britons' evident long-term 'reluctance' to integrate with the 2016 result, pinpointing it as the primary reason for Brexit and explaining it either, with external validity, as the result of an anomalously low popular sense of European identity or, less robustly, as the result of a particularly Eurosceptic media and political class. However, neither of these explanations can explain the considerable variation across time in attitudes to the EU throughout membership, including periods of high levels of support even for further integration. Indeed, over-time explanations so far have been speculative, focusing on high-profile events related to the EU – the 1992 ERM crisis, treaty change (particularly Maastricht and Lisbon), the Eurozone crisis and post-2004 immigration from Central and Eastern European countries. Similarly, the roots of this lack of European identity have also been postulated but less commonly tested. Furthermore, the extent to which variation in European identity is genuinely exogenous to attitudes to the EU is debatable (although this is probably even more the case for explanations based on a Eurosceptic media or political class) while other EU member states have seemingly resolved early worries about sovereignty to become comfortable with membership, highlighting the shortcomings of any deterministic accounts.

Socio-political accounts see Brexit as just one political result of ongoing changes to British society and other 'western' democracies, particularly in terms of globalisation and its economic and migratory effects, but also the expansion of higher education. According to this explanation, the victory of Leave was the result of 'those who feel left behind by the forces of globalisation and mass immigration' outnumbering 'those who welcome such developments' (Hobolt, 2016, p. 1260). Indeed, the referendum secured an unexpectedly high vote share amongst those with less education and those in social grades C2 to E. That said, Leave voters have also been shown to have relatively *higher* wealth and there is little difference between the Leave and Remain voters in self-described financial or employment worries, despite Leave voters being far more likely to self-describe as 'working class'. Moreover, Britons in professional positions turned against Europe in a similar fashion to those in manual occupations in the 25 years prior to the vote, albeit from a higher constant, begging the question of how exactly people had lost from globalisation, if at all and when. Other scholars have similarly framed Brexit as the result of socio-political divisions, but in terms of the social psychology of values, rather than the threat of globalisation. However, it remains unclear why moves to post-material values, greater higher education or otherwise should make the UK *more* Eurosceptic over time and, more pressingly, why it was the UK that voted to Leave rather than one of the numerous other member states in which the (ever more conceptually stretched) 'losers of globalisation' are more prevalent by reasonable measures.

Several theoretically distinct explanations have seen the referendum as a proxy vote for other issues, so that Brexit was caused by, respectively, austerity, anti-establishment sentiment, numerous psychological indicators or English nationalism. These explanations, alongside those focusing on the effects of the campaign, share the strength that up until the years before the referendum there was no overwhelming appetite for outright withdrawal, with reducing the powers of the EU instead a considerably more popular position. Similarly, some of the findings about the local or individual-level effects of austerity do seem robust, if somewhat small. That said, they still cannot explain why the UK, rather than another member state, left, given far harsher austerity, higher inequality and more prevalent deprivation elsewhere. The same is the case for the explanatory plausibility of anti-establishment (or anti-incumbent) voting – why not elsewhere? It may be, then, that these proxy explanations were enough to push Britain over the edge, while more fundamental factors did the causal heavy lifting. One analytically distinct approach focuses on the four 'home nations' of the UK and argues that widespread frustrations over national identity in one – England – caused Brexit. While it is true that English identity is positively associated with Leave voting, its explanatory power is still far weaker than that of European identity and it remains a theoretical stretch given the majority for Leave in Wales and large minorities in Northern Ireland and Scotland, as well as the lack of an obvious causal mechanism.

Finally, one of the more considered factors in the months after the referendum was the controversial and even violent nature of the campaign, which has been portrayed as misleading and 'to blame' for the victory of Leave. However, evidence about the effect of the campaign remains mixed and certainly insufficient, thus far, to label it as the cause of Brexit, even if its unprecedented and eventful nature give scholars plenty of causes to point the finger at and primary accounts from those involved in respectively managing the Remain, and especially Leave campaigns argue for this notion (Blanchard, 2021).

With all of this in mind, I argue that, despite a rich literature, there are still important shortcomings to our understanding of Brexit and two in particular. First, while the differences between voters are well known, if not over-determined (a weakness in itself), and the UK's various anomalous characteristics are at least analysed, the temporal dimension of the UK's departure remains overlooked. This is a crucial shortcoming given the clear, secular trends in support for the EU throughout membership – which, to an extent, were common across the EU – suggesting important causes of over-time variation that, at the very least, are currently underexplored. Second, the object of the referendum – the EU – has almost entirely escaped analysis for what was, after all, a successful vote of no confidence (though see de Vries, 2019 for relative assessments of national and EU government, and Vasilopoulou, 2016 for pre-referendum consideration of the likely importance of retrospective voting). This is all the more stark given the numerous crises affecting the EU at the time of the referendum and the importance of 'retrospective voting' across other areas of electoral studies (Healy and Malhotra, 2013). Scholars hoping to better understand Brexit should consider these as two pressing areas of research, while integrating the theories listed above and, hopefully, building on their strengths and overcoming their weaknesses. Doing so would further improve the already rich state of the science of explaining Brexit.

REFERENCES

Andreouli, E., Kaposi, D., and Stenner, P. (2019). Brexit and Emergent Politics: In Search of a Social Psychology. *Journal of Community and Applied Social Psychology*, *29*(1), 6–17.

Arnorsson, A., and Zoega, G. (2018). On the Causes of Brexit. *European Journal of Political Economy*, *55*(1), 301–23.

Beaumont, P. (2018). Brexit, Retrotopia and the Perils of Post-colonial Delusions. *Global Affairs*, *3*(4–5), 379–90.

Becker, S.O., Fetzer, T., and Novy, D. (2017). Who Voted for Brexit? A Comprehensive District-level Analysis. *Economic Policy*, *32*(92), 601–50.

Blanchard, J. (Host.) (2021, 18 June). How to Spin a Referendum: The Inside Story of the Brexit Campaign [Audio podcast episode]. In *POLITICO's Westminster Insider*. POLITICO. https://www.politico.eu/podcast/how-to-spin-a-referendum-the-inside-story-of-the-brexit-campaign/?utm_source=RSS_Feed&utm_medium=RSS&utm_campaign=RSS_Syndication (accessed 29 September 2022).

British Social Attitudes (1993, 2013). Survey NatCen Social Research. [data collection]. 2nd edn. *UK Data Service*.

Carl., N., Dennison, J., and Evans, G. (2019). European But Not European Enough: An Explanation for Brexit. *European Union Politics*, *20*(2), 282–304.

Carreras, M., Irepoglu Carreras, Y., and Bowler, S. (2019). Long-Term Economic Distress, Cultural Backlash, and Support for Brexit. *Comparative Political Studies*, *52*(9), 1396–424.

Chan, T.W., Henderson, M., Sironi, M., and Kawalerowicz, J. (2020). Understanding the Social and Cultural Bases of Brexit. *The British Journal of Sociology*, *71*(5), 830–51.

Clarke, H.D., Goodwin, M., and Whiteley, P. (2016, 5 July). Leave Was Always in the Lead: Why the Polls Got the Referendum Result Wrong. *LSE British Politics and Policy Blog*. https://blogs.lse.ac.uk/politicsandpolicy/eu-referendum-polls/ (accessed 29 September 2022).

Clarke, H.D., Goodwin, M., and Whiteley, P. (2017). *Brexit: Why Britain Voted to Leave the European Union*. Cambridge University Press.

Cooper, G. (2021). Populist Rhetoric and Media Misinformation in the 2016 UK Brexit Referendum. In H. Tumber and S. Waisbord (eds), *The Routledge Companion to Media Disinformation and Populism* (pp. 397–410). Routledge.

Curtice, J. (2017). Why Leave Won the UK's EU Referendum. *Journal of Common Market Studies*, *55*(1), 19–37.

Daddow, O. (2012). The UK Media and 'Europe': From Permissive Consensus to Destructive Dissent. *International Affairs*, *88*(6), 1219–36.

Daddow, O., and Oliver, T. (2016, 15 April). A Not so Awkward Partner: The UK Has Been a Champion of Many Causes in the EU. *LSE Brexit Vote Blog*. https://blogs.lse.ac.uk/brexit/2016/04/15/a-not-so-awkward-partner-the-uk-has-been-a-champion-of-many-causes-in-the-eu/ (accessed 29 September 2022).

De Vries, C. (2019). *Euroscepticism and the Future of European Integration*. Oxford University Press.

Dennison, J., and Geddes, A. (2018). Brexit and the Perils of 'Europeanised' Migration. *Journal of European Public Policy*, *25*(8), 1137–53.

Dennison, J., Davidov, E., and Seddig, D. (2020). Explaining Voting in the UK's 2016 EU Referendum: Basic Human Values, Attitudes to Immigration, European Identity and Trust in Politicians. *Social Science Research*, *92*(1), Article 102476.

Dennison, J., Seddig, D., and Davidov, E. (2021). The Role of Human Values in Support for EU Membership. *Journal of Cross-Cultural Psychology*, *52*(4), 372–87.

Díez Medrano, J. (2000). *Framing Europe: Attitudes to European Integration in Germany, Spain and the United Kingdom*. Princeton University Press.

Eurobarometer (1973–2013). Kantar Public [producer]. *GESIS Data Archive, Cologne*.

Evans, G., and Menon, A. (2017). *Brexit and British Politics*. Polity.

Evans, G., and Mellon, J. (2019). Immigration, Euroscepticism, and the Rise and Fall of UKIP. *Party Politics*, *25*(1), 76–87.

Evans, G., Carl, N., and Dennison, J. (2017). Brexit: The Causes and Consequences of the UK's Decision to Leave the EU. In M. Castells, O. Bouin, J. Caraca, G. Cardoso, J. Thompson and M. Wieviorka (eds), *Europe's Crises*. Polity, pp. 380–404.

Fetzer, T. (2019). Did Austerity Cause Brexit? *American Economic Review*, *109*(11), 3849–86.

Fieldhouse, E., Green, J., Evans, G., Mellon, J., Prosser, C., De Geus, R., Bailey, J., Schmitt, H., and Van der Eijk, C. (2020). British Election Study Internet Panel Waves 1–20. https://www.britishelectionstudy.com/data-objects/panel-study-data/ (accessed 29 September 2022).

Foos, F., and Bischof, D. (2020, 15 August). *Tabloid Media Campaigns and Public Opinion: Quasi-Experimental Evidence on Euroscepticism in England*. Working Paper. https://doi.org/10.31235/osf.io/mqahj.

Ford, R., and Goodwin, M. (2017). Britain after Brexit: A Nation Divided. *Journal of Democracy*, *28*(1), 17–30.

Franklin, M., Marsh, M., and McLaren, L. (1994). Uncorking the Bottle: Popular Opposition to European Unification in the Wake of Maastricht. *Journal of Common Market Studies*, *32*(4), 455–72.

Franklin, M., Van der Eijk, C., and Marsh, M. (1995). Referendum Outcomes and Trust in Government: Public Support for Europe in the Wake of Maastricht. *West European Politics*, *18*(3), 101–17.

Garretsen, H., Stoker, J.I., Soudis, D., Martin, R.L., and Rentfrow, P.J. (2018). Brexit and the Relevance of Regional Personality Traits: More Psychological Openness Could Have Swung the Regional Vote. *Cambridge Journal of Regions, Economy and Society*, *11*(1), 165–75.

Gastinger, M. (2021). Introducing the EU Exit Index Measuring Each Member State's Propensity to Leave the European Union. *European Union Politics*, *22*(3), 566–85.

Gavin, N.T. (2018). Media Definitely Do Matter: Brexit, Immigration, Climate Change and beyond. *The British Journal of Politics and International Relations*, *20*(4), 827–45.

George, S. (1998). *An Awkward Partner: Britain and the European Community*. Oxford University Press.

Glencross, A. (2016). *Why the UK Voted for Brexit: David Cameron's Great Miscalculation.* Palgrave Macmillan.
Goodwin, M., and Dennison, J. (2018). The Radical Right in the United Kingdom. In J. Rydgren (ed.), *The Oxford Handbook of the Radical Right* (pp. 521–44). Oxford University Press.
Goodwin, M.J., and Heath, O. (2016). The 2016 Referendum, Brexit and the Left Behind: An Aggregate-Level Analysis of the Result. *The Political Quarterly*, *87*(3), 323–32.
Goodwin, M., Hix, S., and Pickup, M. (2020). For and Against Brexit: A Survey Experiment of the Impact of Campaign Effects on Public Attitudes toward EU Membership. *British Journal of Political Science*, *50*(2), 481–95.
Gowland, D., and Turner, A. (1999). *Reluctant Europeans: Britain and European Integration 1945–1998.* Routledge.
Green, J., and Pahontu, R.L. (2021). *Mind the Gap: Why Wealthy Voters Support Brexit.* Working Paper. https://dx.doi.org/10.2139/ssrn.3764889.
Gstöhl, S. (2002). *Reluctant Europeans: Norway, Sweden and Switzerland in the Process of Integration.* Lynne Rienner Publishers.
Hawkins, B. (2012). Nation, Separation and Threat: An Analysis of British Media Discourses on the European Union Treaty Reform Process. *Journal of Common Market Studies*, *50*(4), 561–77.
Healy, A., and Malhotra, N. (2013). Retrospective Voting Reconsidered. *Annual Review of Political Science*, *16*(1), 285–306.
Henderson, A., and Wyn Jones, R. (2021). *Englishness: The Political Force Transforming Britain.* Oxford University Press.
Henderson, A., Jeffery, C., Liñeira, R., Scully, R., Wincott, D., and Wyn Jones, R. (2016). England, Englishness and Brexit. *The Political Quarterly*, *87*(2), 187–99.
Henderson, A., Jeffery, C., Wincott, D., and Wyn Jones, R. (2017). How Brexit Was Made in England. *The British Journal of Politics and International Relations*, *19*(4), 631–46.
Hinde, S. (2017). Brexit and the Media. *Hermès, La Revue*, *77*(1), 80–86.
Hobolt, S.B. (2009). *Europe in Question: Referendums on European Integration.* Oxford University Press.
Hobolt, S. (2016). The Brexit Vote: A Divided Nation, a Divided Continent. *Journal of European Public Policy*, *23*(9), 1259–77.
Hooghe. L., and Marks, G. (2005). Calculation, Community and Cues: Public Opinion on European Integration. *European Union Politics*, *6*(4), 419–43.
Hutchings, P.B., and Sullivan, K.E. (2019). Prejudice and the Brexit Vote: A Tangled Web. *Palgrave Communications*, *5*(1), Article 5, 1–5.
Hutter, S., and Kriesi, H. (eds) (2019). *European Party Politics in Times of Crisis.* Cambridge University Press.
Iakhnis, E., Rathbun, B., Reifler, J., and Scotto, T.J. (2018). Populist Referendum: Was 'Brexit' an Expression of Nativist and Anti-Elitist Sentiment? *Research & Politics*, *5*(2), 1–7.
Kaufmann, E. (2016, 7 July). It's NOT the Economy, Stupid: Brexit as a Story of Personal Values. *LSE British Politics and Policy Blog.* https://blogs.lse.ac.uk/politicsandpolicy/personal-values-brexit-vote/ (accessed 29 September 2022).
Kenny, M. (2016, 23 June). The Idea That English Nationalism Has Powered Support for Brexit Is Unduly Simplistic and Requires Re-examination. *LSE British Politics and Policy Blog.* https://blogs.lse.ac.uk/politicsandpolicy/the-idea-that-english-nationalism-has-powered-support-for-brexit-is-unduly-simplistic-and-requires-re-examination/ (accessed 29 September 2022).
Koch, I. (2017). What's in a Vote? Brexit beyond Culture Wars. *American Ethnologist*, *44*(2), 225–30.
Kolpinskaya, E., and Fox, S. (2021). *Religion and Euroscepticism in Brexit Britain.* Routledge.
Liberini, F., Oswald, A.J., Proto, E., and Redoano, M. (2019). Was Brexit Triggered by the Old and Unhappy? Or by Financial Feelings? *Journal of Economic Behavior & Organization*, *161*(1), 287–302.
Lipset, M.S., and Rokkan, S. (1967). *Cleavage Structures, Party Systems, and Voter Alignments: An Introduction.* Free Press.
Ludlow, P. (2019). The Historical Roots of the 'Awkward Partner' Narrative. *Contemporary European History*, *28*(1), 35–8.

Manners, I. (2018). Political Psychology of European Integration: The (Re)production of Identity and Difference in the Brexit Debate. *Political Psychology*, *39*(6), 1213–32.

Mckenzie, L. (2017).'It's Not Ideal': Reconsidering 'Anger' and 'Apathy' in the Brexit Vote among an Invisible Working Class. *Competition & Change*, *21*(3), 199–210.

McLaren, L. (2004). Opposition to European Integration and Fear of Loss of National Identity: Debunking a Basic Assumption Regarding Hostility to the Integration Project. *European Journal of Political Research*, *43*(6), 895–912.

Miljan, T. (1977). *The Reluctant Europeans: The Attitudes of the Nordic Countries towards European Integration*. McGill-Queen's University Press.

Nielsen, J.H., and Capelos, T. (2018). Editors' Preface to the Special Issue The Political Psychology of European Integration: Brexit and Beyond. *Political Psychology*, *39*(6), 1207–12.

Norris, P., and Inglehart, R. (2019). *Cultural Backlash: Trump, Brexit, and Authoritarian Populism*. Cambridge University Press.

Prosser, C., Mellon, J., and Green, J. (2016). What Mattered Most to You When Deciding How to Vote in the EU Referendum? *British Election Study*. https://www.britishelectionstudy.com/bes-findings/what-mattered-most-to-you-when-deciding-how-to-vote-in-the-eu-referendum/#.YRzFUYgzYdU (accessed 29 September 2022).

Shaw, D., Smith, C.M., and Scully, J. (2017). Why Did Brexit Happen? Using Causal Mapping to Analyse Secondary, Longitudinal Data. *European Journal of Operational Research*, *263*(3), 1019–32.

Sobolewska, M., and Ford, R. (2020). *Brexitland: Identity, Diversity and the Reshaping of British Politics*. Oxford University Press.

Stoeckel, F., Lyons, B., and Reifler, J. (2021) Public Misperceptions of European Integration in the UK. *Journal of Elections, Public Opinion and Parties*. https://doi.org/10.1080/17457289.2021.1945612.

Thompson, H. (2021). The European Geopolitical Space and the Path to Brexit. *Government and Opposition*, *56*(3), 385–404.

Vasilopoulou, S. (2016). UK Euroscepticism and the Brexit Referendum. *The Political Quarterly*, *87*(2), 219–27.

Williamson, A. (2019). *Europe and the Decline of Social Democracy in Britain: From Attlee to Brexit*. Boydell & Brewer.

Wren-Lewis, S. (2018). *The Lies We Were Told: Politics, Economics, Austerity and Brexit*. Bristol University Press.

Zappettini, F. (2021). The Tabloidization of the Brexit Campaign: Power to the (British) People? *Journal of Language and Politics*, *20*(2), 277–303.

3. The Brexit referendum

Julie Smith

INTRODUCTION

Referendums were still a relatively uncommon phenomenon in the United Kingdom (UK) when Conservative leader and Prime Minister David Cameron proposed holding an In/Out referendum on British membership of the European Union (EU). This would be the second chance for UK voters to opine on the question, and only the third-ever UK-wide referendum, although it would become part of a pattern of direct consultation with the voters during Cameron's premiership.[1] It came after two referendum victories (on electoral reform in 2011 and Scottish independence in 2014), though he could not have known the Scottish referendum would go his way in 2013 when he made the Bloomberg Speech proposing a renegotiation of the UK's terms of membership and a subsequent referendum. There were many lessons to be learned from the first two referendums but also some differences that would turn Cameron's pledge into more of a gamble than he anticipated (Glencross, 2016; Smith, 2018). The print media had been strongly behind Cameron's commitment to maintaining the UK in the 2014 independence referendum in Scotland, in marked contrast to their views regarding the EU for example. His assumption of support and of being on the right side of history was misguided on the European question, which would ultimately destroy his premiership and any legacy to which he aspired.

The rationale for the proposed referendum was essentially the same as in 1975: political parties were divided and the prime ministers of the day felt the best course of action, at least for themselves and their divided parties, was to allow citizens to decide for themselves on the thorny question of membership of the EU or, as it tended to be known in the 1970s, the Common Market. Prime Minister Harold Wilson decided to waive Cabinet responsibility in 1975, meaning that ministers would not be expected to campaign to stay in the Common Market, despite the official government stance to do so. David Cameron did likewise in 2016, just one of many examples of the way he sought to emulate Wilson's success. This chapter looks especially at the reasons why the Brexit referendum was called and how and why it played out as it did, highlighting many of the key themes covered in more detail elsewhere in Part I of this *Handbook*. It starts by putting the UK's relations with the EU into historical perspective.

BACKGROUND

The UK opted not to join the European Communities (EC) at their inception, believing it retained both a global role as leader of the nascent Commonwealth and a 'special relationship' with the United States (US). Successive governments, Labour and Conservative alike, rejected the opportunity for the UK to be a founder member of the European Coal and Steel Community in 1951 and the Atomic Energy and Economic Communities in 1957, preferring to retain national sovereignty and a global rather than a regional role. Yet, after the Suez Crisis of 1956, the UK's position seemed less secure: at odds with the US and let down by Commonwealth partners, it needed to rethink its place in the world and, especially, its place in Europe. As its economy declined in the 1960s, while those of the six EC states boomed, the Communities became more attractive to British leaders. After almost a decade when membership was thwarted by French President Charles de Gaulle, by the early 1970s a change of President in France coupled with the election of a passionately Europhile British Prime Minister, Edward Heath, the UK was finally willing and able to join the Communities. Or, more accurately, the Six enabled the UK to join and the ruling Conservative Party was willing to do so. However, the opposition Labour Party had turned against membership and the public were not asked for their views.

The UK was the only country in the first wave of EU enlargement not to hold an accession referendum. The formal decision to accede was taken by Parliament, not the people directly. Opinion polls indicated that citizens were not supportive of membership in the early 1970s and it is not clear that British electors would have opted to join if they had been asked to decide in advance of accession. Even the parliamentary route to membership was heavily contested; the main opposition party, Labour, opposed membership at the time and some Tories went against their party line to vote against. However, thanks to some rebel Labour MPs, agreement was reached on joining and the 1972 European Communities Act passed, enabling the UK to join the EC on 1 January 1973.

The Labour Party remained divided on the issue, however. In order to try to resolve the matter, party leader Harold Wilson pledged at the February 1974 general election to renegotiate the terms of membership ('Tory terms' as he called them) and allow citizens to have their say either at another general election or in a referendum. Since that election resulted in a hung parliament, leading to a minority Labour government and another election in October the same year, there was no appetite for a further general election on the European question. Thus, the way was paved for the first UK-wide referendum to be held on 5 June 1975, following a renegotiation that made some relatively minor changes to the UK's terms of membership. Wilson claimed that the changes were sufficient for him to recommend staying in the Common Market. He did not campaign actively during the referendum and could plausibly have remained in office had it gone the other way, as he had not staked his reputation on the issue, unlike Cameron.

The vote in 1975 was confirmatory, and hence, somewhat different from the accession referendums held in most other latecomers, including Denmark, Ireland and Norway, which all voted on the question of whether to join in 1972. In the first two cases, the referendums were constitutionally required and both led to a popular decision to join. The Irish vote reflected elite and popular support for European integration, so the decision was relatively uncontroversial and clearly legitimated accession. The Danish political situation was rather closer to the British, with the Social Democrats divided on the question of membership. The referendum allowed the issue to be resolved by the public rather than Parliament, preventing the Social Democrats splitting over the issue and giving an element of democratic legitimacy that was perhaps lacking in the UK.

One should always beware the counterfactual, but opinion polls from the time do seem to suggest that the UK, like Norway but unlike Denmark and Ireland, would not have voted to join the Common Market in 1972 if citizens had been invited to vote *before* rather than *after* accession. By the time British citizens were invited to express their views on membership, the

UK had already been inside the EC for nearly two and a half years. They were not voting on whether to *join* but on whether to *stay in* the Common Market, creating a slightly different dynamic from accession referendums and one that might perhaps have been expected to lead to a status quo decision, as indeed occurred. The rhetoric in that referendum was actually quite similar to that in Norway, a country where the naysayers prevailed in 1972 (and indeed in 1994). However, whereas for Norway the vote would be about prospective membership, for the UK it was subtly different: whether to stay. The assumption was that voters would take the status quo approach. Norwegian voters did take this conservative approach on both occasions, which for them meant staying out of the EU in order to retain their national sovereignty. That said, when Norway voted in 1994, it was already closely linked to the EU via the European Economic Area Agreement, which gave access to the internal market without membership of the EU institutions. The referendum did nothing to weaken this relationship, even though the dynamic legal incorporation it set in motion infringes Norwegian sovereignty much more than was envisaged at the time the agreement was entered into.

Just as sovereignty was the decisive factor for the Norwegians, so 'rule from Brussels' did not seem attractive to many of those who advocated the UK leaving 'Europe' because they wanted to regain the sovereignty and sense of independence which they believed integration jeopardised. In 1975 the British voters took the status quo approach to stay, not because of an idealistic vision of European integration – British voters and indeed political elites have tended to be at best pragmatic about the issue – but rather because the prevailing international and economic situation was such that membership at least temporarily seemed to be beneficial for the UK. At the time of that first referendum, high global food prices meant there was a temporary benefit vis-à-vis food prices from the Common Agricultural Policy (CAP), normally the *bête noire* of Eurosceptics: for once European (and hence British) prices were lower than global prices. That sense of a cheaper shopping basket helped persuade some voters to say 'Yes' in 1975 (see Smith, 1999). There was also an element of deference prevailing during that referendum as voters were still willing to listen to leading politicians and vote according to their recommendations, something which would be noticeably lacking in 2016.

The referendum was meant to put paid to the question of membership. It did not. True, the undercurrent of widespread scepticism arose only slowly, but those who rejected the outcome of the 1975 referendum began to mobilise again quite quickly after the referendum. Over the next 20 years, European integration was usually low salience, certainly for the public. The UK seemed set to remain and successive Prime Ministers even sought to take a leading role in the Communities in the hope of putting Britain 'at the heart of Europe'. Voters were not expected to be asked for their views again.

Yet as European integration deepened and other states began to voice their opinions on treaties (for example Denmark on the Treaty on European Union (TEU), which it initially rejected), calls arose for UK citizens also to have a say. Such calls initially came from the media rather than the grassroots and they eventually found a hearing from leaders of the three main political parties in the 1990s – Labour, Conservative and Liberal Democrat – all of whom pledged a referendum on membership of the common currency, the Euro, should the UK consider joining. (An opt out from that aspect of the TEU ensured that unlike other EU member states, there was no expectation that the UK or Denmark should join.) These commitments to direct democracy on European issues would be the first of many such promises that came to nought. By contrast, domestically the Labour government triggered a series of referendums in the nations and regions of the UK in pursuit of its policies on devolution, the most significant being on devolution to Scotland and Wales in 1997 and a new settlement in Northern Ireland after the Good Friday Agreement in 1998. No such polls were called on European matters. As EU treaties came and went, so politicians made pledges to hold referendums that never materialised: the main parties may have talked of a referendum before joining the Euro, but that scenario never arose. Tony Blair pledged to hold a poll on the Constitutional Treaty and David Cameron on ratifying the Lisbon Treaty, while the Liberal Democrats even called for an In/Out referendum at the time of Lisbon ratification. For those anxious to debate the issue this emerging pattern of parties holding out the prospect of a vote that would never be delivered merely increased their frustration. Eurosceptics felt politicians were reluctant to allow people a say. If the French, Dutch, Danes and Irish could vote, why should the British be denied the same opportunity? Such frustration contributed to the rise of the United Kingdom Independence Party (UKIP), which increasingly took votes from the Conservatives. In turn it contributed to the increasing Tory Euroscepticism ahead of the 2010 general election, a scepticism that would ultimately lead the Prime Minister to call a referendum on leaving the EU, which would not technically have been possible until the Lisbon Treaty.[2]

OPPOSING LISBON

Since its inception, the EU (and its predecessor bodies) has had a provision that any European state can apply to be a member. Accession was never as straightforward as the simple treaty article implied, but it was a genuine possibility for several states including the UK during the Cold War, and for many more after the collapse of Communism in Europe in 1989–91. However, accession provided a one-way route into the European project. No provision was envisaged for states that were dissatisfied with membership subsequently to leave again. Only with the Lisbon Treaty was an article added to the TEU that formally allowed for departure. Ironically, a treaty that paved the way for states to leave was greeted with profound dissatisfaction by the British Conservative Party, which demanded a referendum on it. The incumbent Labour Prime Minister, Gordon Brown, was determined not to concede such a poll. He argued that the treaty, unlike the Constitutional Treaty which had been defeated by French and Dutch voters, did not represent a fundamental change and could thus be ratified by normal parliamentary procedures. It was duly ratified in 2009.

Nonetheless, the possibility of a poll and frustration at the failure of successive governments to deliver began to gain traction. Frustration first emerged around the time of the Maastricht Treaty, when the Irish and the Danes were being invited to offer their opinion on European integration while Britons were forced to remain silent. As already discussed, party leaders pledged to hold referendums at various times but none was called. In particular, Tony Blair had committed to holding a referendum on the Constitutional Treaty, a decision that had led to the French and others pledging similarly to hold referendums on ratifying it. Thus it was that in 2005 the French and the Dutch voted within a matter of days of each other to reject the Constitutional Treaty. The British referendum was quietly dropped. Two years on, an initiative under the German EU presidency of 2007 resulted in a further attempt at treaty reform. Crucially, the new Lisbon Treaty made no pretence to be a constitution, although several leading figures, most notably former French President Valéry Giscard d'Éstaing, highlighted the marked similarities in the substance of the two treaties. Both Nicolas Sarkozy and Gordon

Brown, who had replaced Chirac and Blair, respectively, declined to offer referendums on the Lisbon Treaty.

Brown's decision may have shaped British history irrevocably. Ratifying a treaty by referendum can be profoundly difficult and unpredictable as Denmark, Ireland, France and the Netherlands have all shown at different times (see Smith, 2021, Introduction). Had Brown followed the path set by Blair and demanded by Cameron and allowed a referendum on Lisbon (or indeed on any other European question), it is highly likely that it would have been lost. However, a vote against a treaty does not prefigure departure from the whole European construct.[3] Indeed, some countries have seen that the very danger of being forced out of the EU in the event of repeated No votes as a reason to vote Yes the next time around (see Laffan, 2021).[4] By not allowing citizens of the UK to vote on Lisbon, Brown missed an opportunity to provide what might have proved to be a safety valve. A 'No to Lisbon' would have meant a treaty not ratified, not the departure of a member state and a potentially an unwelcome precedent, should a successful departure have inspired the disaffected in other member states to seek in turn to leave. Assuming the situation had been resolved (as in the cases of deals to placate Denmark and Ireland after previous No votes, with positive ramifications for public opinion) the question of a popular vote would have been resolved. The Eurosceptic boil could have been lanced.

By failing to do so, Brown secured safe passage for the Lisbon Treaty but left the wider European question for Cameron and Clegg to resolve. Both main opposition parties had called for a referendum over Lisbon. In the case of the Liberal Democrats, party leader Nick Clegg called for an In/Out referendum, ostensibly on the grounds that no one under the age of 50 had had a chance to vote on the question of membership. That no one had had a say on membership of the North Atlantic Treaty Organization (NATO), the monarchy or the established church/church-state relations for even longer did not seem to feature in such deliberations and argumentation, perhaps reflecting the contested nature of UK membership of the EU even among the most Europhile of politicians. A further reason for the call – and a more political one – was the fact that the Liberal Democrat MPs were divided over whether or not to support the Lisbon Treaty. A referendum pledge was Nick Clegg's way of trying to get all his MPs on board. He did not manage to do so and, moreover, upset his colleagues in the House of Lords and the party's European Working Group, who were broadly opposed to the idea of another referendum believing little good could come of it. The Conservative preference was for a vote on the Treaty itself and party leader David Cameron committed to hold a referendum if the Treaty had not come into effect by the time that the Conservatives entered government (not a given but seen as likely at the time the Lisbon Treaty was being debated in Parliament). By the time of the 2010 election, the Treaty had been ratified in all 27 member states and had come into effect. An *ex post* referendum was deemed by Cameron to be unfeasible. The situation contributed to backbench frustration during the 2010–15 Parliament, especially among disgruntled MPs who believed that the creation of a coalition with the Liberal Democrats was depriving them of the chance of preferment and moving the government in a too pro-European direction. 'Europe' became the favoured topic for these MPs to challenge Cameron, not least because by 2010 the party grassroots had become extremely hostile to EU membership. Thus, at selection meetings for parliamentary candidates, would-be Tory MPs were asked a question along the lines of 'If there were one piece of legislation you could repeal, what would it be?' The expected answer, and the one that most would-be Tory MPs proffered, was 'The 1972 European Communities Act', that is, the legislation through which the UK had entered the-then EC in January 1973. The 2010 election thus brought a strongly Eurosceptic group of

MPs into Parliament. The die was cast for years of intra-Conservative wrangles, which would eventually spill over into wider British politics and, ultimately, impact the whole EU.

Lisbon was ratified before the coalition government took office, thus it was too late to hold the referendum that Cameron and many in his party had wanted and some still demanded. The European question was now highly salient and increasingly toxic within his party. The European Union Act 2011 agreed on by the two coalition partners did not go far enough to resolve the growing tensions within the Conservative Party, despite including a requirement to hold a referendum before any significant future transfer of power to Brussels. Following a petition led by *The Daily Express*, the House of Commons held a debate on 24 October 2011 on a proposal to hold a three-way referendum that could broadly be summarised as offering a choice of stay, leave or renegotiate the terms of membership (Smith, 2017, p. 66). The leaders of all three main parties imposed a three-line whip on their MPs to vote the proposals down as they felt a three-way referendum was unworkable; 81 Conservative rebels voted in favour of a referendum, the vast majority of them Eurosceptics who hoped such a poll would lead to the UK's departure from the EU. A few pro-Europeans also supported an early referendum, which they assumed could be won, thereby putting the European question to bed for another generation. The proposal was massively defeated in the Commons. However, the party leaders' success in averting a referendum was short-lived. Just 15 months later, the Prime Minister who famously did not want Europe to dominate his premiership made the fateful decision to offer the European referendum that would prove his downfall and would overshadow any legacy he might otherwise have enjoyed.

BLOOMBERG AND BEYOND

On 23 January 2013 David Cameron, then Prime Minister of the UK, gave a landmark speech at Bloomberg Corporation, henceforth known as the Bloomberg Speech. Cameron gave his views on the UK's relations with the EU and pledged to seek to reform the EU, to alter the UK's terms of membership and then to hold a referendum on whether or not to remain. This proposition had the benefit for Cameron of enabling him to hold his own political party together for the next two and a half years through the 2014 European Parliament elections and until after the general election of May 2015. Conservatives who favoured leaving the EU or who were deeply unsatisfied in whatever way with European integration felt that finally a political leader had listened to them and might now be willing to take the UK out of the EU if that was what citizens wanted. By contrast, pro-Europeans in the Conservative Party assumed, perhaps complacently, that any referendum would result in a vote to remain in the EU and were therefore not too perturbed by Cameron's proposition. Labour and the Liberal Democrats were rather more concerned by the prospect of a referendum, although Liberal Democrat leader Nick Clegg's earlier advocacy for an In/Out referendum meant he could scarcely object to the proposal. He did subsequently declare that he had been 'utterly nonplussed' by Cameron's decision, however (Clegg, 2016, p. 206).

From January 2013 until May 2015 the question of 'Europe' to some extent dropped off the political agenda. UKIP remained a significant force in British politics, topping the polls in the 2014 European Parliament elections with 27 per cent of the vote and securing almost four million votes in the 2015 general election. However, the vagaries of the UK electoral system ensured that UKIP only won one seat, despite its significant electoral showing. What was far more significant in the outcome of the general election was the small outright Conservative victory giving Cameron a majority of 12 seats. His erstwhile coalition partners, the Liberal Democrats, saw their support collapse and they were reduced to just eight MPs. The Labour Party also performed poorly, notably in Scotland where the Scottish National Party (SNP) swept the board, winning 56 of the 59 parliamentary seats available in Scotland. This was in large part a result of the 2014 independence referendum that the SNP had technically lost yet which gave it an electoral boost as voters turned against both Liberal Democrats and Labour for their perceived treachery in working with the Conservatives in coalition or during the referendum. The electoral landscape had dramatically changed and Cameron now had to deliver on his pledge to reform, renegotiate and then hold a promised referendum (Smith, 2017, chapter 6).

Whether because of the shock of winning or because of concerns over rising Euroscepticism, Cameron rushed into the referendum and did not leave adequate time to prepare either the renegotiation or the referendum campaign, or indeed to soften up the public on the issue. Cameron had originally committed to holding a referendum by the end of December 2017. The logic behind that date was to give the longest possible time between the general election of 2015, the date of which was already known because of the Fixed-term Parliaments Act 2011, the elections for the French Presidency that were due in spring of 2017 and the German general election due in the autumn of 2017. In addition, if the UK were to vote to leave the EU, the two-year process envisaged under Article 50 of the TEU would conclude in 2019, if triggered right after the referendum. This would have presented a potential departure date around the end of the five-year institutional cycle of the EU, although of course Cameron was not expecting such a scenario. Almost as soon as the results of the general election were known it became clear that the Prime Minister wished to hold the referendum in June 2016, rather than at a later date as originally envisaged. The SNP, and indeed politicians from across Scotland and Wales, pointed out that this would not be wise because Scottish and Welsh elections were due to be held in May, as were local elections in London and some other parts of England. Moreover, school holidays begin in late June in Scotland meaning people might well have been away and hence turnout reduced in a summer poll, even though postal votes are easily available in the UK. All of these factors would inevitably detract from the necessary campaigning for Remain, since Labour, Liberal Democrat, SNP and Plaid Cymru activists were all expected to play a key part, yet were all likely to focus on the local and national rather than European polls until May. Cameron was insistent, however, owing to fears that a repetition or an extension of the migrant crisis which had seen people dying in the Mediterranean Sea in spring 2015 could cause hostility towards the EU among voters ahead of the referendum. On a more parochial level, he was also anxious to ensure that the European question would not overshadow yet another Conservative Party Conference in the autumn of 2016.

PREPARING FOR THE REFERENDUM

The Prime Minister needed to start two parallel processes: creating the legislative framework to allow the referendum to take place and negotiating with the other 27 member states to try to establish a more favourable package to put to the electorate in the promised poll. What he did not do was begin to engender wider popular support for the EU. The government introduced the bespoke legislation for the referendum in June 2015. The legislation was quite straightforward, but many hours were spent scrutinising proposals, including the rules for funding and spending limits, as well as the wording of the question. The wording, 'Should the United Kingdom remain a member of the European Union or leave the European Union?' was recommended by the Electoral Commission and was intended to be as unbiased as possible.[5] The outcome of the referendum would not be legally binding (arguably the voice of the people could not countermand a Parliament that was minded to ignore it, although the legislation permitting the 2011 referendum on electoral reform *had* stated that the outcome of the poll would be implemented). It was clear, however, that the outcome would be politically binding.

As soon as the European Union Referendum Bill was introduced into the House of Commons, Parliament began a debate on the pros and cons of membership which would set the pattern for the referendum itself and the bitter post-referendum recriminations. This was especially the case for the Leave side, which had already begun to organise itself quite effectively within the cross-party Vote Leave organisation by October 2015. By contrast, the Remain side's umbrella organisation, Britain Stronger in Europe, seemed to lack vision and purpose, perceptions that were merely compounded by the chairmanship of Tory peer, Lord Rose. Their campaign got off to a bad start from which it never really recovered. The problems for the Remain side were compounded by the fact that David Cameron had asked Conservative MPs not to state their preference for Remain or Leave until he had completed the renegotiation and made a recommendation. While many pro-European MPs obeyed the request, there were enough Leavers to set the agenda very effectively well ahead of the recommendation from the Prime Minister which finally came in February 2016, even though their own organisation got off to a rocky start, in part due to the role of the divisive figure of Dominic Cummings.

By bringing forward the date of the referendum the Prime Minister had effectively reduced the amount of time available to renegotiate the UK's terms of membership of the Union (the idea of reforming the Union had already slipped off the agenda). Whereas the original timing would have allowed a two-year period for the negotiations ahead of a referendum, it was now crucial for the Prime Minister to complete any renegotiation well ahead of the summer of 2016. One might have expected the Prime Minister immediately to tell the other members of the EU, henceforth the EU-27, what the UK wished to achieve in the renegotiation but he did not. In fact, he spent the six months from May 2015 until November that year seemingly trying to work out what he could ask for and what he might be able to achieve in his renegotiation, arguing that if people were unclear about his aims they should look at his Bloomberg Speech and the 2015 Conservative Party manifesto. This was not the ideal way to win the necessary support among his EU counterparts. Only in mid-November did it become clear precisely what the UK sought. The Prime Minister wrote a letter to the European Council President, Donald Tusk, and also gave a speech at the Royal Institute of International affairs (Chatham House) in which he talked about four 'baskets' of changes that would form the core of the required renegotiation: (1) economic governance; (2) competitiveness; (3) sovereignty, including an enhanced role for national parliaments; and (4) immigration, meaning limiting access to social security benefits for EU citizens (Smith, 2016).

Any change to the UK's terms of membership required the agreement of the EU-27. By making clear that he wanted the referendum over and done with by mid-2016, Cameron had made himself a hostage to the 27 who knew that any British demands would be constrained by the looming deadline. This gave the EU the upper hand. Moreover, Cameron further boxed himself in by trying to ascertain what he could get before making his demands explicit, which is not the way to maximise gains in negotiations.

He was further hampered by the legacy of Harold Wilson and James Callaghan and their renegotiation ahead of the 1975 referendum. Wilson's claims to have secured reform was subsequently undermined by figures such as erstwhile German Chancellor Helmut Schmidt, who would go on to call it a 'cosmetic operation' (quoted in Young, 1998, p. 283). While Wilson and Callaghan had a fresh canvas, Cameron's apparent attempt to replicate the renegotiation and let the people decide, complete even with the decision to waive collective Cabinet responsibility, fell victim in part to the fact that the precedent itself had been flawed. Moreover, Cameron had assumed that the model used in 1975 would work for him but he neglected to learn the lessons of history and was, perhaps, ignorant of the fact that that renegotiation of 1975 was viewed by many to have been quite minimal. Opponents would repeatedly talk of Cameron asking for little and getting less and of a 'so-called renegotiation'.

What Cameron did, and indeed what Theresa May would subsequently do when seeking to negotiate a Brexit withdrawal agreement, was attempt to find out the other side's bottom line before stating their own case. This essentially left the UK on the back foot, as became all too clear in the months and years after the end of the renegotiation and subsequent referendum. Boris Johnson, then a backbench MP, in his regular newspaper column made very clear that one important aspect of negotiations is a willingness and an ability to walk away from the negotiating table. By contrast, Cameron had left himself and the UK in a situation where that was not possible. By pledging to renegotiate and then hold a referendum he had effectively tied his own hands and given the advantage to the EU-27 who were acutely aware that the negotiations mattered far more for the UK than they did for the EU. David Cameron wanted to get a deal that he could sell to British voters and he wanted to do it as quickly as possible, ideally by the end of February 2016.

THE REFERENDUM

David Cameron did indeed secure agreement with the 27 in February 2016, announced late in the evening at a press conference in Brussels when, like Harold Wilson before him, he claimed that now he was able to recommend to the British people that the UK should vote to remain in the EU. The Prime Minister rushed back to London to chair a Cabinet meeting during which it was agreed that the official government position would be to recommend staying in the EU. Yet, the divisions within the ruling party were clear to everyone; barely had Cameron made his announcement when five Cabinet members appeared at the Vote Leave headquarters. The Leavers included Cameron's friend Michael Gove, who had originally told him that he would not play an active part in the campaign (Cameron, 2019). Gove went on to co-chair the Leave campaign alongside Labour MP and former Europe Minister, Gisela Stuart. Also actively supporting the Leave side was Boris Johnson, a long-time Eurosceptic, who had been responsible for many 'Euromyths' published in the *Daily Telegraph* while he was their Brussels correspondent. Johnson's intervention proved crucial; a charismatic politician with clear political ambitions, his enthusiastic campaigning alongside Gisela Stuart gave a dynamism to Leave, whereas the Remain side seemed rather more technocratic and lacked inspirational leaders. The assumption had been that once the negotiations were over, Cameron himself would play a leading role in the campaign – quite unlike Wilson in 1975, who stayed aloof and could thus have deflected blame if the result had gone the wrong way. Cameron threw himself body and soul into the Remain campaign – or at least so he believed. Yet his interventions were rather late and could scarcely overcome the damage done at the outset by Lord Rose's launch event for Britain Stronger in Europe – nor the unfortunate abbreviation of 'BSE' and its echoes of 'mad cow disease', which had overshadowed the UK's relations with Europe in the 1990s.

The Remain campaign did not get going until the renegotiation was over – and, as discussed above, for many started in earnest only after local and Scottish and Welsh elections in early May – by which time the opponents of the EU had both stolen a march in the campaign and belittled the outcome of the renegotiation. The fact that the Remain side also virtually ignored the deal during the referendum campaign suggests that David Cameron's victory in securing it was Pyrrhic. Perhaps too much effort was put into negotiating with the 27 and not enough into preparing the referendum campaign itself and negotiating with citizens at home, or indeed within the Conservative Party.

The general framework for the referendum was the Political Parties, Elections and Referendums Act 2000 (PPERA), augmented by specific provisions and amendments made in the European Union Referendum Act 2015. This included provisions on permitted expenditure and donations, as well as certain rules on literature that could be circulated, although such rules did not apply to social media. In addition, PPERA mandates a period of 'purdah' ahead of referendums and elections, that is, a few weeks during which public bodies, in this case especially the government, cannot be seen to do anything 'political' that might influence the poll. Thus, in the immediate weeks before 23 June 2016, the government machine could no longer advocate Remain as the Treasury in particular had being doing. From the moment purdah kicked in, the Leave side could relax to some extent, safe in the knowledge that the government could not directly engage in any rebuttals to its arguments.

The franchise chosen was that used in British general elections, namely, British, Irish and Commonwealth citizens aged over 18. Attempts to widen the franchise to include 16- and 17-year-olds and EU nationals, both of whom had been allowed to vote in the 2014 Scottish independence referendum, were rejected by the government. The House of Lords voted to reduce the voting age to 16, but the Commons subsequently rejected the proposal.[6] The issue of enfranchising EU citizens was not pressed to the vote in the Lords thanks in part to confusion among the signatories to the relevant amendment. There was, inevitably, hostility from Brexiteers to any potential extension to the franchise, which they assumed would be to the benefit of the Remain side.

Advocates of the two sides in the referendum were encouraged to work on a cross-party basis in order to secure the designation as the leading umbrella organisation, which brought with it both financial benefits and certain rights to television broadcasts. On the Remain side, Britain Stronger in Europe was the main campaign body from the outset and was unchallenged to be designated by the Electoral Commission as the umbrella organisation for Remain. The Leave side was more fragmented, with leading Eurosceptic and UKIP leader Nigel Farage leading a hard-line Leave movement known as Leave.EU as the main challenger to Vote Leave. The latter was able to claim greater cross-party support, thanks to the high-profile role played by Gisela Stuart, alongside senior Conservatives and even a former Liberal Democrat MP, Paul Keetch. In addition, a third Leave organisation, Grassroots Out unsuccessfully sought the designation. The fragmentation of the Leave side could have been a disadvantage. In reality, it was a strength, as Leave.EU could whip up support from passionate Leavers, helping increase turnout, while the designated Vote Leave campaign could shrug off some of their more offensive messages. A case in point was the 'Breaking Point' poster featuring Nigel

Farage, which showed a vast queue of mostly young men seemingly queuing – perhaps to enter the UK, and certainly intended to suggest the EU allowed unfettered immigration.

The assumption on all sides was that the electorate was split roughly into thirds: Remain, Leave and those who were undecided, the so-called 'don't knows'. This was broadly the finding of the academic pollsters as well as those making strategic decisions on behalf of the two campaigns. Initially, about 10 per cent were assumed to be hard Remainers and about ten per cent hard Leavers (i.e. not likely to be swung by the campaigns on either side) with many more tending towards Remain or Leave (these groups growing during the course of the campaigns). The remainder were swing voters whose voices and votes were expected to make all the difference in the final referendum outcome. The binary nature of the majoritarian referendum as enshrined in the European Union Referendum Act 2015 ensured that in order to win either side required merely 50 per cent plus one of the total vote across the whole of the UK. Although votes were counted regionally and nationally, the final outcome would be determined by the UK-wide vote, with no veto for any of the four nations, as might occur in a federal state such as Switzerland. The referendum campaigns thus became very polarised with a particular focus on swing voters, especially on the Remain side where the official Britain Stronger in Europe campaign focused more on those swing voters who might make all the difference to the campaign rather than shoring up support among those they believed were already more likely to vote Remain. Given that in a referendum every vote counts quite unlike British general elections, this was a misguided tactic, ignoring as it did the importance of differential turnout in referendums. In practice, the turnout was very high by British standards and this ultimately was to benefit the Leave side.

The Leave side played their cards rather better and perhaps had an advantage, although they did not see it that way before the referendum. As seen in referendums on treaty reform in other European member states, 'No' campaigns have some advantages, precisely because those advocating 'No' can deploy myriad specific reasons for a No vote. (In Ireland, on one occasion, a successful strategy was 'if you don't know, vote No'; while the play on words would not work in other languages, the gist was important – voters in referendums may not have fixed or deep preferences, so they can be swayed perhaps more easily than in elections.) By contrast, Yes campaigners may need to persuade voters of the merits of the whole package. The proxies for No and Yes were Leave and Remain, respectively, with Leave focusing clearly and cleverly on framing their main message as 'take back control'. They also provided a wide range of ways in which citizens voting to leave might indeed take back control – of laws, money and borders, thereby giving many voters who had perhaps not previously focused much on what the European question meant a reason or reasons to vote to leave. Sovereignty per se did not matter to all Leave voters, but it mattered to some. Immigration did not matter to all Leave voters – hence the insinuations by some disappointed Remainers in the wake of the referendum that all Leavers were racist was clearly ill founded as well as misguided – but it mattered to some. The debate was not quite as straightforward as it might have appeared. For example, Vote Leave referred to the EU's 'racist immigration policy' as it sought to win over voters from Commonwealth countries. The inference, if not a direct pledge, was that leaving the EU with its rights of 'free movement of people' – the right of all EU citizens to live, study and work elsewhere in the EU, which many millions of UK and EU citizens have taken up and whose numbers feed into the UK's net migration figures – would allow the UK to take more third country nationals, thereby, perhaps allowing non-EU family members to join their relations. That net migration figures excluding EU nationals were already higher than the Conservative government's manifesto pledge to keep net migration figures in the tens of thousands meant that this vague hope was unlikely ever to be fulfilled in practice. However, the key point was that people believed it – or some people believed it, while others were soon won over by other promises of the Leave side.

In particular, the cost of membership, long a sore point in EU-UK relations, was a clear and present challenge for the Remain side, even though objectively the UK's contribution to the EU's coffers was only a very small percentage of national expenditure (about 1 per cent of GNI and 2 per cent of government spending). Vote Leave thus set the agenda on the budget. By headlining the UK's purported financial contribution, alleged by Vote Leave to be £350 million a week, and emblazoning that figure on the side of a bus, Leave campaigners ensured that the cost was a major talking point. They also guaranteed that the Remain side was constantly on the back foot, typically trying to assert that the figure was wrong, ignoring as it did both receipts from the EU and the rebate, long ago secured by Margaret Thatcher.[7] Regardless of the factual accuracy or otherwise of the claims, the Leavers could always close down debate on the matter very effectively by stating, 'Well, it's still a lot of money' – a point that usually generated a wry smile in debates during the referendum. Remainers were unable effectively to refute such points, despite the fact that as a percentage of GNI and of government expenditure the contribution to the EU was relatively small – rarely was a pie chart used to highlight this fact, leaving numbers to be read out instead, not a very effective way of transmitting information to a sceptical electorate.

Opinion poll data presented by Matthew Goodwin and John Curtice at Chatham House in December 2015 showed at an early stage that two issues were likely to dominate –immigration and the economy, with the Leave campaign stronger on the former issue, Remain on the latter. It was assumed by pollsters and campaigners alike that the Remain side would be at an advantage on the economy, in part because Remain was the official government position and also because the Treasury under George Osborne was strongly backing Remain and because the economic benefits of EU membership were deemed to be positive. Public opinion was thus likely to swing behind Remain – that issue was the Remain side's to lose. Moreover, anecdotally, the BBC did not focus so much on this side of the membership question because it felt that Remain had already won the argument. Nor did the Leave side really try to press this issue. Yet the Treasury's long-term projections for likely financial consequences of Brexit backfired somewhat, as the attempt at precision seemed implausible, not least because the Treasury's record of forecasting is poor. Remain had squandered a potential campaigning strength and attempts by the Treasury to put forward the horror stories of the economic impact of Brexit simply failed to gain traction.

By contrast, the question of immigration was always set to be the Achilles' heel of the Remain side. In particular, following the Big Bang enlargement of the EU in 2004 free movement of nationals from the new member states had contributed to significant growth in the size of the resident population in the UK and led to considerable public hostility to an extent that mainstream politicians tended to ignore. Their complacency about the impact of free movement, alongside a failure to understand many voters' sense that they had been left behind by European integration (in reality serving as a proxy for globalisation) and their interests overlooked by political elites, ensured that leading advocates of Remain found it difficult to persuade undecided voters of the merits of EU membership. Their efforts were further hampered by the Leave-leaning print media, notably the Murdoch press, which had in fact done much to foster British – or more correctly English – Euroscepticism for a quarter of a century.

Where David Cameron could rely on the press to support his efforts to reject two forms of constitutional change – electoral reform in 2011 and Scottish independence in 2014 – when it came to Brexit he could not rely on the fourth estate to give its support to the status quo option.

OUTCOME

Against all the odds, the insurgent Leave movement overturned decades of European integration and secured a narrow victory of 52 per cent to 48 per cent. Leave had mobilised their supporters effectively and the die had been cast. However, a majority of voters in both Scotland and Northern Ireland had voted to Remain in the EU – had the count been done by nation rather than the whole UK, the result would almost certainly have been to Remain. As it was, on 24 June 2016, it was announced that the UK had voted to leave the EU. A shell-shocked Prime Minister immediately tendered his resignation. The equally shell-shocked leaders of Vote Leave gave a press conference. Yet, while Nigel Farage was quick to celebrate a victory for which he could claim much credit, Michael Gove and Boris Johnson looked less ebullient. After all, Vote Leave had a strategy for the referendum; it did not have a plan for delivering its outcome. Indeed, its leading lights had outlined differing preferences for life outside the EU, ranging from a 'hard Brexit' – taken to mean departure from the Single Market and the Customs Union and minimal ongoing cooperation with the EU-27 – to ongoing membership of the European Economic Area, alongside Norway, Iceland and Liechtenstein. The impact on the fabric of the UK would become a leading theme of British politics for the following five years, alongside fraught negotiations with the UK's spurned European partners. The June 2016 referendum did not mark the end of EU-UK relations, so much as herald a new, unpredictable and thorny phase in the relationship.

NOTES

1. Referendums were historically eschewed at the national level in the UK, although there were some local polls. In 1973 there was a 'border poll' in Northern Ireland (see Hayward, 2021); the first UK-wide referendum was the 1975 vote on membership of the Common Market, while various votes on devolution became increasingly prevalent from 1979 onwards.
2. It is unclear what would have happened in the event of a 'No' vote in 1975 but one assumes that the eight other member states would have created a way to deal with the situation.
3. Nick Clegg's preference for an In/Out referendum would of course have been another matter entirely and, indeed, the fact that the Liberal Democrats had previously called for such a poll at the time of the Lisbon Treaty was to create problems for a party that was so keenly wedded to remaining in the EU.
4. The fact that the EU has no provision to expel a member state means such a threat is meaningless at one level but at times of economic crisis it can be effective in winning over some wavering voters.
5. In Wales the question was asked in both English and Welsh.
6. On the issue of the franchise, see also Richard Bellamy's Chapter 28 in this volume.
7. The Community Budget was a source of considerable aggravation to the UK from the time of accession negotiations onwards. Harold Wilson's renegotiation did little to solve the problem but after almost five years of lobbying, Margaret Thatcher managed to resolve the issue with a 'rebate'. Years later, Tony Blair ceded part of the rebate as the EU looked to enlarge eastwards. The political fallout from that decision ensured that politicians would be increasingly hawkish on the budget, an issue that Vote Leave tapped into very effectively.

REFERENCES

Cameron, D. (2019). *For the Record.* HarperCollins Publishers.

Clegg, N. (2016). *Politics.* Bodley Head.

Glencross, A. (2016). *Why the UK Voted for Brexit: David Cameron's Great Miscalculation.* Palgrave Macmillan.

Hayward, K. (2021). The 1998 Good Friday (Belfast) Agreement Referendums in Northern Ireland and the Republic of Ireland. In J. Smith (ed.), *The Palgrave Handbook of European Referendums* (pp. 247–65). Palgrave Macmillan.

Laffan, B. (2021). Referendums on EU Treaty Reform: Revisiting the Result in Second Referendums. In J. Smith (ed.), *The Palgrave Handbook of European Referendums* (pp. 563–81). Palgrave Macmillan.

Smith, J. (1999). The 1975 Referendum. *Journal of European Integration History*, *5*(1), 41–56.

Smith, J. (2016). Reform, Renegotiation and Referendum, *Policy Brief.* Oslo: NUPI.

Smith, J. (2017). *The UK's Journeys into and out of the EU – Destinations Unknown.* Routledge.

Smith, J. (2018). Gambling on Europe: David Cameron and the 2016 referendum. *British Politics*, *13*(1), 1–16.

Smith, J. (2021). *The Palgrave Handbook of European Referendums.* Palgrave Macmillan.

Young, H. (1998). *This Blessed Plot – Britain and Europe from Churchill to Blair.* Macmillan.

4. Parties[1]

Andrew Glencross and Monika Brusenbauch Meislová

INTRODUCTION

This chapter examines the complicated period between the general election of 2015 and the entry into force of the Withdrawal Agreement between the United Kingdom (UK) and the European Union (EU) in 2020, which marked the end of the UK's EU membership. As befits the protracted policy process of Brexit, the party politics of leaving the EU was a rather messy affair. During this time, UK politics was buffeted by multiple crises as the aftermath of the 2016 referendum led to two Prime Ministerial casualties, two snap general elections, unexpected participation in a European Parliamentary election, and an influential – if unsuccessful – grassroots campaign to hold a second referendum.

We analyse this sequence of events by reflecting on how UK parties defined themselves in relation to Brexit: not just for or against, but what end form it should take. In particular, this chapter explores how the ensuing internal tensions, especially within the two main Westminster parties, the Conservatives and Labour, came to dominate the political process. Although the referendum itself was fought by competing cross-party coalitions, the labels, slogans, and identities of this campaign lived on well after voting ended on the evening of 23 June 2016. Little did anyone realise at the time the extent to which the two tribes of Leave and Remain would transform the landscape of UK politics for years to come (Sobolewska and Ford, 2020).

Brexit automatically brought the future of the UK back into question because it foisted an English (and Welsh) constitutional preference upon Scotland and Northern Ireland, where 62 per cent and 56 per cent of voters, respectively, chose to remain in the EU. Hence, the analysis also emphasises the way that party politics in the post-referendum era were bound up with UK territorial politics. The Scottish National Party (SNP) had anticipated this dilemma. However, its suggestion of a double-majority voting system, requiring a majority of individual voters and of the four UK nations for any result to stand, fell on deaf ears in London. As a result of overlooking the territorial implications of Brexit, the status of Northern Ireland came to bedevil the UK-EU negotiations at a time when from June 2017 to December 2019, the Conservative government depended on the support of the Democratic Unionist Party (DUP) for its Commons majority. The key to breaking the parliamentary deadlock over Brexit was Boris Johnson's decision to fight a general election on the premise that he had a new deal ready for ratification. This was a stretch of the political imagination, but it worked.

THE 2016 BREXIT REFERENDUM CAMPAIGN

By 2013, Prime Minister David Cameron was very attuned to the electoral threat posed by the anti-EU United Kingdom Independence Party (UKIP). Nigel Farage's UKIP was gaining traction in the polls by linking EU membership to immigration concerns and the spectre of economic instability in the Eurozone. In the 2013 UK local elections, UKIP received 20 per cent of the votes before topping the national vote in the European Parliament (EP) elections of 2014 with 27 per cent. Since the Liberal Democrats were in a coalition with the Conservatives and Labour was still reeling from the political fallout of the 2008 financial crisis, UKIP assumed the mantle of the challenger party able to pick up the votes of the disaffected (Copsey and Haughton, 2014). Such was the context for Cameron's signature promise, in January 2013, to hold an in/out referendum on EU membership if his party won the coming general election.

This announcement was met with delight by the long-standing Eurosceptic wing of the Conservative Party inside Parliament. These were the heirs of the 'bastards' that had disrupted John Major's time in office; MPs who harboured doubts about the Prime Minister's own stance on the EU. They had good reason to be sceptical as Cameron had committed himself to holding a referendum on ratifying the 2009 Lisbon Treaty, but reversed course when he entered Downing Street in 2010 (Dorey, 2017). The in/out referendum was also a product of the crisis of the neoliberal policy paradigm characterised by the shift from 'responsive' to 'responsible' party government (Mair, 2014). As argued by Jennings and Lodge (2019, pp. 777–8), this meant 'credibility and prudence were seen as electoral vote-winners and seemed to have displaced the politics of redistribution' in the wake of Tony Blair. In this sense, the referendum pledge was political responsiveness to populist criticism of representative politics and a protest of voters against the 'responsible', as it 'undercut appeals to "responsible" party government … and instead pushed politicians to more populist styles of decision-making' (Jennings and Lodge, 2019, p. 776).

Winning a majority of seats in the 2015 general election meant Cameron could forge ahead with an in/out referendum, conditional on first renegotiating the terms of UK membership in line with the strategy he had set out in 2013. He was confident in this gambit of letting the people decide, having successfully seen off the alternative vote proposal backed by the Liberal Democrats (2011), as well as the Scottish independence referendum (2014). He eventually decided on an early vote, in the summer of 2016, in order to give less time for opponents of his new deal with the EU – agreed at a meeting of European leaders in February 2016 – to mobilise (Glencross, 2016). A relatively poor showing by UKIP in the general election made it seem as if the best moment to win the vote was early in Cameron's term of office.

The referendum campaign formally began on 15 April 2016. The government line was to back remaining in the EU, although David Cameron had to contend with a split Cabinet as 6 of his 30 ministers opted to support EU withdrawal, most notably future Prime Minister Boris Johnson. All the main parties were in the Remain camp except the Conservatives, who took a strategic decision not to use the party organisation to campaign for either side (Lynch and Whitaker, 2018). The Labour Party membership was strongly in favour of staying in the EU, but its new leader, Jeremy Corbyn, was far more ambivalent. His thinly concealed convictions – deemed mistaken by most experts (Tarrant and Biondi, 2017) – that re-nationalising public utilities and supporting a bold industrial strategy were incompatible with Brussels' competition agenda made him an unreliable partner in the pro-EU campaign. Labour also drew the lesson that participation in the cross-party campaign to prevent Scottish independence had proved electorally costly given the collapse in the Labour vote North of the Tweed (Fieldhouse and Prosser, 2018). Labour had gone from winning 41 of the 56 Scottish seats at Westminster in 2010 to clinging on to only a single seat in 2015 as opposed to the SNP's 53. Thus, the new Labour leadership explicitly wanted to minimise their involvement in an electoral contest they perceived as a tool for managing internecine Conservative Party strife (Shipman, 2016).

UKIP were naturally hostile to the EU, but they suffered an initial blow by failing in their attempt to lead the official Leave campaign. Instead, Vote Leave was the designated campaign group promoting UK withdrawal from the EU (Shipman, 2016). Its master strategist was Dominic Cummings who, as campaign director, devised the 'take back control' slogan at the heart of their political messaging. The genius of this line of attack was that it linked together criticism of the EU's lack of democracy with voters' desire for a fundamental change of direction on a number of policy issues. For instance, the Leave campaign's political advertisements made it seem that Turkey was on the brink of joining the EU. The strategy was to query the democratic legitimacy of this supposed fait accompli and connect it to the consequences a rise in immigration would have on the state of the National Health Service. The overall effect was a very powerful one because it created a narrative of a loss of control over two of the most sensitive areas of public policy, which supposedly could only be remedied by leaving the EU.

The ability to put the Remain camp on the defensive by portraying the EU as an undemocratic monolith constraining UK policy-making was a characteristic of the entire referendum debate. In the case of the message about looming Turkish membership of the EU, David Cameron was particularly discomfited because, as was successfully highlighted by Vote Leave in a number of campaign advertisements, he was on the record as publicly advocating Turkish membership of the EU (Ker-Lindsay, 2018). The stump speeches of Michael Gove and Boris Johnson for Vote Leave in effect replicated core UKIP arguments about immigration and sabotaged the government's economic message about the risks of leaving the EU (Clarke et al., 2017). Time and again, therefore, Remain campaigners would be trapped in the position Ronald Reagan famously warned against: 'if you're explaining, you're losing'.

The campaign was dominated by rather reckless promises on both sides. There was the doom and gloom of Cameron and his Chancellor George Osborne who claimed Brexit would cause a DIY recession. This relentless messaging about the economic cost of EU withdrawal messaging, dubbed Project Fear by its opponents, was the foil for the almost parodic optimism of Boris Johnson's post-Brexit vision of sunlit uplands. Reflecting on his decision to hold the referendum, which cost him his job as he resigned the very day the result was announced, Cameron insisted it was the right move 'because this issue had been poisoning British politics for years' (Phipps, 2017). What he really meant was that his own party had been deeply divided over EU issues for decades with pressure coming to a head during the coalition years (2010–15). In this period there were multiple backbench rebellions by Tory Eurosceptics, the most significant of which was in 2011, when 81 Conservative MPs defied a three-line whip and voted in favour of an in/out referendum on EU membership (Cowley and Stuart, 2012). Cameron had expected to heal these divisions by winning the referendum, which is why even with the polls narrowing at the end of the campaign he forbad 'blue-on-blue' attacks on the credibility of Johnson. So instead of bringing catharsis, the referendum created a damaging fault line, personal as well as political, in British party politics.

At the same time, politicians and political parties faced great difficulties in adapting to a new environment in which traditional party loyalty was suddenly much less relevant. MPs in Westminster were conscious that while the national result was tight, 52 per cent for Leave, a much larger majority of parliamentary seats voted Leave: 63 per cent. This discrepancy was down to the fact that Remain voters tended to cluster in large cities, as opposed to Leave voters that were more evenly distributed across England. The breakdown by party was even more telling: 74 per cent of Conservative-held seats from 2015 voted Leave, as did 64 per cent of Labour ones. Similar figures applied after the 2017 general election (Hanretty, 2017).

These figures go a long way in explaining Labour's chronic indecision, in the aftermath of the referendum, over how far to contest Brexit as well as the natural attraction of a pivot towards Brexit at all costs for the Tories.

Historically speaking, British Euroscepticism had excelled at finding flaws in the EU system, but as a reactive and negative creed it never articulated a coherent template for life outside supranational integration (Usherwood, 2018). Thus, given that no concrete alternative to EU membership was offered on the ballot, it was left to UK political parties to interpret how to respect the referendum result itself. However, these parties were in a tight bind because traditional party identification took a back seat to the affective polarisation between Remainers and Leavers. The persistence of this cleavage after the referendum was not just a reflection of the tightness of the 52 per cent majority in favour of EU withdrawal. What made these two tribal identities take on a special, lasting significance was a combination of grassroots mobilisation and elite opportunism unleashed by the referendum. Both major parties had to adapt to a reality in which voters, especially those most emotionally invested on one side or the other, wanted their predictions about the consequences of Brexit to be vindicated. Zadie Smith captured the national mood perfectly in her Brexit Diary, written shortly after the vote, where she rued a political culture in which 'being right was always the most important thing' (Smith, 2016). It was in this context that the new Prime Minister, Theresa May, sought to provide a supposedly unifying vision for a post-Brexit Britain. In her words, the rejection of EU membership was a 'quiet revolution': one in which 'millions of our fellow citizens stood up and said they were not prepared to be ignored anymore' (May, 2016).

THERESA MAY'S FIRST CABINET

Following the UK's decision to leave the EU, Theresa May and her Conservative government became responsible for the task of delivering Brexit, that is, transforming the 'will of the people' into a feasible withdrawal process. The government's intention was to lead a process that would culminate in a Withdrawal Agreement, negotiated with the EU and approved by the UK Parliament. As it turned out, however, withdrawing from the EU presented the Westminster establishment and its political institutions with 'their greatest challenge of modern times' (McConnell and Tormey, 2020, p. 685). Initially, Theresa May rode a wave of popularity as David Cameron stepped down as Prime Minister and Member of Parliament. Her strong devotion to the task of delivering Brexit won praise from the right wing of the Conservative Party, its media outriders, and was reflected in strong polling numbers. She was, for instance, applauded for her January 2017 Lancaster House speech in London, which outlined the UK government's priorities for Brexit and which professed a tough stance on Brexit ('no deal is better than a bad deal'), while simultaneously acknowledging the importance of maintaining close ties with the EU (McConnell and Tormey, 2020, p. 693).

On 29 March 2017, the British government invoked Article 50 of the Treaty of the EU, which served as formal notification of its intent to leave the EU. By this point, Brexit-related strains on the UK constitution had already become apparent. The parliamentary vote to start exit negotiations went against the wishes of the Prime Minister. The government was forced to concede the point that the executive could not use Royal prerogative to start the Brexit process after losing a judicial review in the Supreme Court initiated by Gina Miller. As part of these proceedings, the Court also had to rule on whether the devolved legislatures could block Westminster's right to proceed with Brexit (Raitio and Raulus, 2017). The UK's highest court decided there was no such veto power, a decision Scottish First Minister Nicola Sturgeon interpreted as contrary to the Sewel Convention specifying that UK legislation affecting devolution normally requires express consent from devolved institutions. Thereafter, the SNP government in Scotland continually opposed the Conservative government's negotiating stance with the EU, advocating instead the softest type of Brexit and sought allies in Westminster to that effect.

Once the Commons gave the green light by a majority of 498 to 114 to start the formal exit process, the clock started ticking on a two-year negotiating window as mandated by the relevant treaty article. This meant the UK was originally supposed to leave on 29 March 2019 – a deadline, however, that was never met. Hence the entire period until the UK's actual withdrawal became characterised by a 'pathological combination of chaos, gridlock, constantly unravelling negotiations, serial failures to find a way forward, and intensely adversarial intra and inter-party divisions' (McConnell and Tormey, 2020, p. 686). These divisions were apparent across the whole political spectrum, from the Westminster elite to the wider British public (Gifford, 2021; McConnell and Tormey, 2020, p. 686).

In April 2017, shortly after triggering Article 50, Theresa May called, very unexpectedly, an early general election. The first post-Brexit election was constitutionally unnecessary given the Fixed-term Parliaments Act and took place on 8 June 2017, less than two years after the previous one. Justified on the grounds of overcoming parliamentary opposition to Brexit, May's surprising decision was motivated by her desire to get a strong popular mandate for her vision of Brexit (and her premiership more generally), strengthen her hand in the withdrawal process (Hobolt, 2018, p. 39) and enable the unproblematic passage of the Brexit legislation (Heath and Goodwin, 2017, p. 345).

Yet, what happened was the very opposite of what Theresa May had hoped for. The dramatic election of 2017, dubbed 'the revenge of the Remainers' (Bogdanor, 2017, p. 371), did not settle the European issue. Quite the contrary, it reopened the divisions of 2016 as the election campaign exposed deep fault lines over how to approach Brexit within the Conservative and Labour Parties. Having resulted in a hung Parliament, the election confounded most expectations and weakened Theresa May's position both within her party and the Parliament (Hobolt, 2018, p. 39; Vasilopoulou, 2020, p. 81). Instead of an increased majority, the Conservative Party lost the small majority it already enjoyed in the House Commons, formed a minority government and became dependent on ten MPs from Northern Ireland's Democratic Unionist Party (DUP) to pass legislation on a confidence and supply basis (Gamble, 2019, p. 177).

Essentially, it was an election in which 'almost everybody lost' (Bogdanor, 2017, p. 370). The incumbent Conservatives – whose 2017 campaign is now generally considered to have been badly run by a coterie of powerful and out-of-touch advisers (Vaccari et al., 2020, p. 587) – adopted a retro manifesto, which included calls to restore fox hunting, support for a hard Brexit, grammar schools and changes to social care payments (dubbed the 'dementia tax', but this was quickly abandoned after causing much controversy) (Heath and Goodwin, 2017, p. 357; Prosser, 2018, p. 1229). They also emphasised May's leadership ('strong and stable' as compared to a 'coalition of chaos' led by Corbyn) instead of the party brand which turned out to be a mistake, as May was a rather poor campaigner (Prosser, 2018, p. 1229). Conservative strategy was rather narrow, counting on keeping support from the more middle-class and pro-Remain wing of the Conservative Party while seeking support in the more pro-Brexit, left behind and Labour areas of the country (Heath and Goodwin, 2017,

p. 357). The party gained popularity in more economically left behind, heavily white and older areas which had expressed strong support to Nigel Farage's UKIP in 2015, but was much less successful in more high skilled areas that had expressed lower support for UKIP two years ago (Heath and Goodwin, 2017, p. 357). This said, the number of votes that Theresa May attracted (13,636,684) was higher than, for instance, the number that Tony Blair won in his landslide victory in 1997 (13,518,167), and quite close to John Major's post-war 1992 record of 14,093,007 (Cooper and Cooper, 2020, p. 752).

The only real winner in the 2017 election was radical left-winger Jeremy Corbyn, whose position as Labour leader was significantly strengthened (Bogdanor, 2017, p. 371). With 262 seats won (an increase of 30 on 2015 results), Labour experienced the largest increase in the vote for any party between one electoral contest and another since 1945 (Bogdanor, 2017, p. 373). Labour advanced a suitably ambiguous 'jobs first Brexit' designed to appeal to the broadest constituency regardless of the referendum vote. The Labour Party was largely silent on the practical questions surrounding how to implement Brexit (Vaccari et al., 2020, p. 589), but promised to secure 'managed immigration' and, at the same time, keep the advantages of the single market and Customs Union, in order to attract both Leave and Remain votes (Avril, 2020, pp. 340–42; Bogdanor, 2017, p. 372). What should not go unnoticed in this respect is the paradox of Remainers looking to Jeremy Corbyn, a lifelong critic of the EU who voted Leave in the 1975 referendum and against the Maastricht and Lisbon Treaties, to avoid Brexit, and Brexiteers looking to Theresa May, who supported the Remain side in the 2016 referendum, to secure a 'hard' Brexit (Bogdanor, 2017, p. 373). Labour's remarkable electoral gains can be attributed not only to its ability to attract support from a broader coalition of voters but also to the increase in turnout. The turnout was higher in younger and more ethnically diverse areas with a greater proportion of graduates, having changed the composition of voters in favour of Labour (Heath and Goodwin, 2017, p. 357).

The Liberal Democrats, 'the one national UK party with an uncomplicated and unwavering commitment to Europe' (Gamble, 2019, p. 183), by contrast, struggled to attract support, having won eight seats. Remainers had probably calculated that a vote for Liberal Democrats was a wasted one and that the best way how to avert Brexit (or at least mitigate its adverse implications) was to support Labour (Bogdanor, 2017, p. 372).

The avowedly pro-EU SNP lost ground in the 2017 election and the chances of holding a second independence referendum were diminished. The party won 35 of the 59 Scottish constituencies, which was a massive drop of 21 seats from 2015 result. Yet, it did remain the largest party in Scottish politics (Prosser and Fieldhouse, 2017; Simpkins, 2018). UKIP, which was the third largest party in 2015 by number of votes, lost its only seat, with its vote share having decreased from 12.6 per cent to 1.8 per cent (Tournier-Sol, 2021, p. 385; Usherwood, 2019, p. 1223).

Overall, the 2017 election demonstrated quite clearly the cleavages in British politics. The whole country was at least as divided as the House of Commons itself, including on the generational, cultural and meritocratic fronts, and on the toxic issue of Brexit (Bogdanor, 2017, p. 370). Indeed, voters' split over whether leaving the EU was the right decision was especially important as Brexit-based identity polarisation was as strong or stronger than political party consolidation (Duffy et al., 2019, p. 16). On paper, the outcome strengthened the UK two-party system, with both Labour and the Conservatives having gained votes at the expense of smaller parties, especially UKIP. Together they accounted for more than 80 per cent of the overall vote – for the first time since 1979 (Gamble, 2019, p. 180; Kavanagh, 2018). The evidence also suggests that Brexit produced a significant electoral realignment (Gamble, 2019, p. 186) and delivered a more polarised two-party system and electorate, with centre-right and centre-left traditions well weakened (Gamble, 2019, p. 185).

FROM ONE SNAP ELECTION TO ANOTHER

The subsequent two years were highly challenging for the government fraught with intractable internal divisions on Brexit. Theresa May's handling of Brexit was widely criticised – not least for lacking any coherent and credible vision, adopting a too hard Brexit stance, poor execution of the withdrawal negotiations, and inadequate planning thereof (Brusenbauch Meislová, 2019, p. 681). In this period there were 42 ministerial resignations over Brexit, which reflected internal party divisions exacerbated by May's apparent shift over time from a hard Brexit to closer alignment with EU customs rules. The key reason behind the fluctuation in policy and personnel lay in the government's (flawed) approach to delivering Brexit and the biased assumptions in its negotiating strategy (Figueira and Martill, 2020). The source of this failure can be located in erroneous assumptions about the EU's interests, compounded by a lack of decision-making openness as well as a lack of EU expertise and informal contacts within the EU (Dunlop et al., 2020; Figueira and Martill, 2020).

The Conservative government tried to put pressure on the EU to come up with a formula that would combine frictionless trade with the EU (especially in order to avoid a hard border between Northern Ireland and the Republic of Ireland), on the one hand, and exit from the single market, end of the free movement and control over national borders, on the other. These two goals were largely irreconcilable though, and led to an acute political impasse with the EU (McConnell and Tormey, 2020, p. 693). Relatedly, the British government also hoped that the EU would offer the UK a highly bespoke relationship, that EU27 member states would respond positively to the UK-induced bilateral initiatives, and that EU unity would dissolve if push came to shove as the negotiations went to the wire. None of these expectations came to fruition, however (Figueira and Martill, 2020), and the negotiations were slow, arduous and frustrating.

What further contributed to the Brexit political paralysis was the confidence and supply agreement with the DUP, which gave the party 'an unprecedented opportunity to exercise power in British politics' (Vasilopoulou, 2020, p. 89), making it 'the kingmakers at Westminster' (Gamble, 2019, p. 184). This significantly narrowed the government's options and tied its hands, as the DUP opposed any 'backstop' that would limit the effect of Brexit in Northern Ireland by creating a special customs status that in turn would create East-West trade friction across the Irish sea (McConnell and Tormey, 2020, p. 693). With a different arrangement for Northern Ireland compared to the rest of the UK being unacceptable for the DUP, irrespective of the fact that Northern Ireland has been treated differently since the 1920s (Gamble, 2019, p. 184), the party consistently undermined the government's Brexit negotiation proposals.

To overcome DUP obstinacy, the UK government and the EU agreed in December 2017 a joint report specifying that a hard border on the island of Ireland should be avoided by virtue of the future UK-EU trade relationship, to be settled after the withdrawal negotiations. Failing this, paragraph 49 committed the UK to 'maintain full alignment with those rules of the Internal Market and the Customs Union which, now or in the future, support North-South cooperation, the all-island economy and the protection of the 1998 Agreement' (European Commission, 2017, p. 8). This compromise bought a temporary peace within the government and DUP ranks and allowed the Article 50 talks to progress further.

However, May's communication strategy inspired substantial levels of exasperation among both her domestic and European partners. Trapped in short-term and reactive thinking designed to solve one political problem at a time, the Prime Minister resorted to appeasing different camps – the DUP, hard Brexiters, those wanting frictionless trade – in a way that generated expectations that were impossible to fulfil. The flurry of ministerial resignations, especially those of David Davis, Secretary of State for Exiting the EU, and Foreign Secretary Boris Johnson in July 2018, reflected the disappointment of those who felt they had been misled. Moreover, her discursive approach to Brexit 'created a schism between her rhetoric on Brexit and reality, fostering a perception of distrust and betrayal', and her:

> [C]losed-off, secretive, and rigid approach, unresponsive to change, did very little, bordering on nothing, to inform the public bewildered by Brexit about the trade-offs inherent in any deal, or the potential consequences of the version of Brexit pursued by her government. (Brusenbauch Meislová, 2019, p. 687)

With the political landscape highly polarised and party discipline in tatters, the UK government found it both hard to maintain a majority and to establish cross-party support for its eventual Withdrawal Bill that emerged from a lengthy Cabinet debate in November 2018. Cabinet unity on this occasion belied the fact that May's Brexit lacked a strong institutional backing within the Conservative Party (Lynch and Whitaker, 2018). The draft Withdrawal Agreement was perceived as 'a fudged compromise not satisfying either camp within the Conservative Party' (Vasilopoulou, 2020, p. 89) and given May put managing the interests of the party first this document constituted a weak foundation for garnering cross-party support (Mabbett, 2019, p. 177). The EU Withdrawal Bill was opposed by the majority of Labour Party, Liberal Democrat, SNP, Green Party and Plaid Cymru MPs. As a result, the British Parliament was unable to resolve the Brexit issue, rejecting Theresa May's Withdrawal Bill on three separate occasions (15 January, 12 March and 29 March 2019) by 230, 149 and 58 votes, respectively. A significant number of Conservative MPs defied party whips and voted against their own government (115, 75 and 34, respectively) (Prosser, 2021, p. 451; Vasilopoulou, 2020, p. 89), with the defeat of 15 January 2019 constituting the largest House of Commons loss of any British government in modern history (Prosser, 2021, p. 451).

May 2019 brought another unexpected challenge: an election that was not supposed to happen (Martill, 2020, p. 368). The lack of agreement in the British Parliament on the Withdrawal Bill resulted in the government having to request an Article 50 extension, thereby delaying the UK's withdrawal from the EU. Notwithstanding previous protestations to the contrary, Theresa May announced on 7 May 2019, at a relatively short notice, that since the UK was still effectively an EU member state, it was legally obliged to hold the EP elections.

European elections were held across the UK on 23 May 2019 and turned into 'a proxy for a second referendum' (Vasilopoulou, 2020, p. 82). Small parties outside of government ran on unambiguous Brexit platforms and became the main beneficiaries of a debate that recycled the Leave/Remain dichotomy of the 2016 referendum (Martill, 2020, p. 368). The brand-new Brexit Party, founded by Nigel Farage in November 2018, whose only purpose was to ensure that the UK leaves the EU, ran for the first time in an electoral contest and triumphed, winning 29 seats and the largest share of the national vote (30.5 per cent) (Tournier-Sol, 2021, p. 386).

With 16 seats and 19.6 per cent, Liberal Democrats that campaigned on the promise of a second referendum came second and scored their highest electoral result at any EP election.

The Labour and Conservative Parties, by contrast, recorded the lowest ever combined share of the vote not only since the first EP election in 1979 (Vasilopoulou, 2020, p. 89), but since they became the main representatives of the two-party system (Cutts et al., 2019, p. 496). Both of them promised to respect the referendum result but were riven by infighting. The Labour Party suffered from the so-called 'pincer movement', meaning that it lost support in its mainly white, working-class left behind heartlands, but also in younger cosmopolitan areas where Labour had polled strongly at the 2017 general election (Cutts et al., 2019, p. 496). The Conservative Party lost votes both to the Brexit Party and the Liberal Democrats (Cutts et al., 2019). Last but not least, with its votes absorbed by the Brexit Party, UKIP lost all its seats in the EP, declining from 27.5 per cent in the 2014 EP elections to 3.3 per cent in 2019 (Tournier-Sol, 2021, p. 386).

On 24 May 2019, only one day after the vote and before the official results were declared, Theresa May, whose Brexit legacy was to go down in history as weak and wobbly rather than strong and stable (Brusenbauch Meislová, 2019, p. 687), announced her resignation. This paved the way for Boris Johnson, former London Mayor and Foreign Secretary, to win a convincing victory over Jeremy Hunt in the Conservative Party leadership race on 23 July 2019 and succeed Theresa May as the UK's next Prime Minister the following day. As he had promised his backbenchers, Johnson negotiated a revised Withdrawal Agreement at the end of the summer. His goal was to revise the Irish backstop provision by – to the immense displeasure of the DUP – committing to a special customs status for Northern Ireland so that the rest of the UK could leave the entire architecture of the single market and Customs Union. The text of the associated Political Declaration was also modified to water-down promises about future commitments on labour standards. This new deal, which reflected the EU's original preference to have specific arrangements for Northern Ireland rather than a customs deal for the whole of the UK, met the joint opposition of Labour, Liberal Democrat, Green and DUP MPs. Consequently, Johnson paused the legislative process and, three months after becoming Prime Minister, decided to call for a snap election – the third general election in four years, the ninth major electoral contest in a decade and the second snap election in a row (Prosser, 2021, p. 451).

2019 GENERAL ELECTION AND ITS AFTERMATH

The election was held on 12 December 2019 and marked a watershed moment in the post-referendum period. As Cutts et al. (2020, p. 20) rightly remark, it delivered 'what over the course of the previous three years their elected representatives had proven unable to deliver: an answer to Brexit'. The election produced a decisive result for the Conservative Party which won 365 seats (a net gain of 47 seats), providing a majority of 80 seats. Even though the overall Conservative share of the vote went up only by 1.4 per cent, a minor improvement compared to May's 2017 result, it was the Conservative's largest majority since 1987 and the largest for any party since New Labour's second victory in 2001 (Cutts et al., 2020, p. 7; Norris, 2019). It was also their fourth consecutive increase since entering power in 2010. These results were all the more impressive given the 'years of austerity cuts by successive Tory governments, doubts about Johnson's flamboyant character, and fratricidal internal party division over Britain's membership of the EU' (Norris, 2019). Put bluntly, the Conservatives were very successful in 'convincing voters that they could clean up a mess which the Conservatives themselves had created' (Richardson and Rittberger, 2020, p. 662).

Compared to Theresa May, Boris Johnson communicated his case more clearly and comprehensively, pledging to leave the EU on the basis of the revised Withdrawal Agreement negotiated in October 2019 (Cooper and Cooper, 2020, p. 755). Conservative campaign strategy was rather 'unconventional' and 'leftist', having promised to 'level up Britain', 'unleash Britain's potential', 'break with austerity' and, perhaps most importantly, 'get Brexit done' (irrespective of how ultra-vague this message was) (Cooper and Cooper, 2020, p. 756). Johnson's disciplined and highly focused message promised change, was populist in nature and focused on the crisis in the Parliament and its failure to deliver Brexit (Cooper and Cooper, 2020, p. 754). Overall, this approach, masterminded by the 2016 Leave guru Dominic Cummings, was successful in capturing three-quarters of the Leave-voting electorate (Curtice, 2020).

As Curtice (2020, p. 11) shows, it was the much stronger concentration of the Leave vote behind the Conservative Party that explains why, under the UK's single-member-constituency first-past-the-post electoral system (which generally tends to marginalise minority parties and deliver substantial majorities), the Conservatives won their biggest majority since the 1980s. In tandem with this Vote Leave strategy redux, the Conservatives also concentrated on a small but electorally significant group of potential swing voters within the former 'red wall' seats (Cooper and Cooper, 2020, p. 760). All but three out of the 47 gained seats were captured from the Labour Party, including traditional Labour heartlands in the so-called 'red wall', such as Bolsover (which is a seat that Labour had never lost when contesting) and Leigh and Don Valley (Labour seats since 1922) (Cutts et al., 2020, p. 7). Cooper and Cooper (2020, p. 753) identify three heuristic groups that Johnson successfully consolidated in his 2019 coalition: (1) the Brexit hardliners, those who supported a no-deal Brexit and wanted the sharpest possible split in relations between the UK and the EU; (2) the Brexit compromisers, those willing to support May's deal; and (3) Remain compromisers, comprising voters who were prepared to accept Johnson's Brexit.

For Labour, the election produced a historic defeat. The party suffered its worst election defeat since 1935, winning only 202 seats and losing 60 of them. It was also left with only one seat in Scotland. Labour did not sustain the loyalty of its 2017 electorate and lost massively despite the fact that it was competing with the incumbent Conservative Party. As Cutts et al. (2020, p. 22) summarise, between 2015 and 2020, under Jeremy Corbyn, the party experienced 'its worst ever result in elections to the Scottish Parliament, its worst ever share of the vote at any EP election, the worst sets of local election results for any opposition party in recent times, and two consecutive general election defeats'. Labour's poor election performance owed much to the unpopularity of Jeremy Corbyn's leadership, his radical economic agenda, scandals over the issue of antisemitism and, crucially, the Party's notorious vagueness and ambiguity on Brexit (Norris, 2019; Prosser, 2021, p. 452). Corbyn had been forced to accommodate internal pressure to back a second referendum, or 'people's vote' on Brexit. Although he promised to hold such a vote if elected, he fudged the issue of how he would vote, claiming it would depend on what kind of withdrawal agreement his government would be able to negotiate. Corbyn sought to campaign on traditional Labour issues such as the NHS, but this meant neglecting the Brexit question, which was the most important issue from the electorate's perspective (Norris, 2019). This ambiguous stance allowed the party to pick up only a half of the Remain-voting electorate with one in five backing the Liberal Democrats (Curtice, 2020).

The election was nevertheless a disappointment for challenger parties, the Brexit Party and the Liberal Democrats too. It produced disastrous results especially for the Liberal Democrats, with few Liberal Democrat (and Liberal) election results in history as calamitous as these (Sloman, 2020, p. 35). Having started the campaign with opinion poll ratings as high as 20 per cent, they campaigned on a clear anti-Brexit card. Even though they increased their overall vote share by more than 4 per cent (as well as their vote share in Remain seats), they obtained only 11.6 per cent, having won 11 seats (a loss of one seat on 2017). The party's new leader, Jo Swinson, even lost her own seat in East Dunbartonshire to the SNP. Much blame has been cast on misfiring campaign strategy as well as structural difficulties which the party has been facing in an increasingly polarised political environment (Sloman, 2020, p. 35). As Sloman (2020, p. 35) argues, the polarisation of public opinion along multiple fronts, including austerity and polarised opinions on Jeremy Corbyn and Brexit has broken the broad coalition of support which the Liberal Democrats gained during the 1990s and 2000s.

Further to this, to avoid splitting the Leave vote, the Brexit Party stood only in opposition seats and asked its candidates to stand down in seats held by Conservatives (Norris, 2019). The Brexit Party did well in some target seats, such as Barnsley, Doncaster and Hartlepool, but overall gained only 2 per cent of the vote and no seats at all. Yet, according to Norris (2019), its strategy might have as much as doubled the Conservative parliamentary majority, with the role of Nigel Farage therefore being 'one of kingmaker in terms of both the predominance of the Brexit agenda and the size of the Conservative majority' (Norris, 2019). UKIP did even worse, obtaining 0.1 per cent and only 22,817 votes. Both electorally wiped-out parties are thus 'seemingly consigned to become a footnote of modern history and the occasional doctoral thesis' (Norris, 2019). The SNP gained 13 seats on 2017 result, having won 48 of 59 Scottish seats and 45 per cent of the Scottish vote share. Interestingly, Scotland also experienced a different pattern of Conservative support, compared to England and Wales, with the Conservatives vote share recording a decline of 3.5 per cent (Prosser, 2021, p. 456).

CONCLUSION

Viewed with hindsight, the 2019 election was not just a by-product of Brexit. Rather, it marked a continuation of longer-term trends in the dealignment and realignment of political loyalties in British politics, rather than a radical departure from the past (Cutts et al., 2020, p. 21). The election also signalled 'a return to the "normal" functioning of British democracy' (Prosser, 2021, p. 450) by ending the deadlock in Parliament, which had empowered backbenchers and frustrated the executive. In this sense, the Brexit interlude of weak Westminster government was over. The return of strong government allowed for an orderly departure from the EU, while still leaving the lingering impression, as recounted in Michel Barnier's memoirs of the Brexit negotiations, of what might have been had Parliament united to hold a second referendum (Barnier, 2021).

Thanks to its comfortable 80-seat parliamentary majority, Boris Johnson's government introduced a bill to ratify the Withdrawal Agreement, which passed its second reading in the House of Commons on 20 December 2019 by 358 votes to 234 and became law on 23 January 2020 as the European Union (Withdrawal Agreement) Act 2020 (Baines et al., 2020, p. 756). The EP gave its consent to the Withdrawal Agreement on 29 January 2020 and the Council of the European Union adopted, by written procedure, the decision on the conclusion of the

Withdrawal Agreement the following day. On 31 January 2020 at 11 pm GMT, the UK left the EU, after 47 years of membership. Boris Johnson can thus be viewed as 'the first Conservative leader to triumph over the Europe question, an issue that had undermined Margaret Thatcher, John Major, David Cameron and Theresa May' (Cutts et al., 2020, p. 20). Yet, the extraordinary political turmoil over Brexit was not about to end just yet.

NOTE

1. In Monika's case, the writing of this chapter was supported by the Masaryk University project 'Perspectives of European Integration in Context of Global Politics V' (MUNI/A/1196/2022).

REFERENCES

Avril, E. (2020). Labour and the Interplay of Brexit and Electoral Politics. *Journal of Contemporary European Studies*, *29*(3), 335–50.

Baines, D., Brewer, S., and Kay, A. (2020). Political, Process and Programme Failures in the Brexit Fiasco: Exploring the Role of Policy Deception. *Journal of European Public Policy*, *27*(5), 742–60.

Barnier, M. (2021). La grande illusion. *Journal secret du Brexit*. Gallimard.

Bogdanor, V. (2017). 2017: The Election of the Trojan Horses. *The Political Quarterly*, *88*(3), 370–74.

Brusenbauch Meislová, M. (2019). Brexit Means Brexit – or Does It? The Legacy of Theresa May's Discursive Treatment of Brexit. *The Political Quarterly*, *90*(4), 681–9.

Clarke, H.D., Goodwin, M.J., and Whiteley, P. (2017). *Brexit: Why Britain Voted to Leave the European Union*. Cambridge University Press.

Cooper, L., and Cooper, C. (2020). Get Brexit Done: The New Political Divides of England and Wales at the 2019 Election. *The Political Quarterly*, *91*(4), 751–61.

Copsey, N., and Haughton, T. (2014). Farewell Britannia? 'Issue Capture' and the Politics of David Cameron's 2013 EU Referendum Pledge. *Journal of Common Market Studies*, *52*(1), 74–89.

Cowley, P., and Stuart, M. (2012). The Cambusters: The Conservative European Union Referendum Rebellion of October 2011. *The Political Quarterly*, *83*(2), 402–6.

Curtice, J. (2020). Brave New World: Understanding the 2019 General Election. *Political Insight*, *11*(1), 8–12.

Cutts, D., Goodwin, M., Heath, O., and Milazzo, C. (2019). Resurgent Remain and a Rebooted Revolt on the Right: Exploring the 2019 European Parliament Elections in the United Kingdom. *The Political Quarterly*, *90*(3), 496–514.

Cutts, D., Goodwin, M., Heath, O., and Surridge, P. (2020). Brexit, the 2019 General Election and the Realignment of British Politics. *The Political Quarterly*, *91*(1), 7–23.

Dorey, P. (2017). Towards Exit from the EU: The Conservative Party's Increasing Euroscepticism Since the 1980s. *Politics and Governance*, *5*(2), 27–40.

Duffy, B., Hewlett, K., McCrae, J., and Hall, J. (2019). *Divided Britain? Polarisation and Fragmentation Trends in the UK. King's College London*. The Policy Institute at King's College London. https://www.kcl.ac.uk/policy-institute/assets/divided-britain.pdf (accessed 11 June 2021).

Dunlop, C., James, S., and Radaelli, C. (2020). Can't Get No Learning: The Brexit Fiasco through the Lens of Policy Learning. *Journal of European Public Policy*, *27*(5), 703–22.

European Commission. (2017, 8 December). Joint report from the negotiators of the European Union and the United Kingdom Government on progress during phase 1 of negotiations under Article 50 TEU on the United Kingdom's orderly withdrawal from the European Union (TF50 (2017) 19). https://ec.europa.eu/info/publications/joint-report-negotiators-european-union-and-united-kingdom-government-progress-during-phase-1-negotiations-under-article-50-teu-united-kingdoms-orderly-withdrawal-european-union_en (accessed 11 June 2021).

Fieldhouse, E., and Prosser, C. (2018). The Limits of Partisan Loyalty: How the Scottish Independence Referendum Cost Labour. *Electoral Studies*, *52*(1), 11–25.

Figueira, F., and Martill, B. (2020). Bounded Rationality and the Brexit Negotiations: Why Britain Failed to Understand the EU. *Journal of European Public Policy*. https://doi.org/10.1080/13501763.2020.1810103.
Gamble, A. (2019). The Realignment of British Politics in the Wake of Brexit. *The Political Quarterly*, *90*(2), 177–86.
Gifford, C. (2021). Brexit and Trump: Contesting New Cleavage Formation. *Journal of Contemporary European Studies*, *29*(3), 309–21.
Glencross, A. (2016). *Why the UK Voted for Brexit: David Cameron's Great Miscalculation*. Palgrave Macmillan.
Hanretty, C. (2017). Areal Interpolation and the UK's Referendum on EU Membership. *Journal of Elections, Public Opinion and Parties*, *27*(4), 466–83.
Heath, O., and Goodwin, M. (2017). The 2017 General Election, Brexit and the Return to Two-Party Politics: An Aggregate-Level Analysis of the Result. *The Political Quarterly*, *88*(3), 345–57.
Hobolt, S.B. (2018). Brexit and the 2017 UK General Election. *Journal of Common Market Studies*, *56*(1), 39–50.
Jennings, W., and Lodge, M. (2019). Brexit, the Tides and Canute: The Fracturing Politics of the British State. *Journal of European Public Policy*, *26*(5), 772–89.
Kavanagh, D. (2018). Brexit, the Conservatives and the General Election 2017. *Revue Française de Civilisation Britannique*, *23*(2), 1–11.
Ker-Lindsay, J. (2018). Turkey's EU Accession as a Factor in the 2016 Brexit Referendum. *Turkish Studies*, *19*(1), 1–22.
Lynch, P., and Whitaker, R. (2018). All Brexiteers Now? Brexit, the Conservatives and Party Change. *British Politics*, *13*(1), 31–47.
Mabbett, D. (2019). A Crisis for Both Parties. *Political Quarterly*, *90*(2), 177–9.
Mair, P. (2014). Representative Versus Responsible Government. In P. Mair (ed.), *On Parties, Party Systems and Democracy* (pp. 581–96). CECPR Press.
Martill, B. (2020). The 2019 European Parliament Election in the UK. *Italian Political Science Review/Rivista Italiana di Scienza Politica*, *50*(1), 368–81.
May, T. (2016). *Speech to the Conservative Party Conference* [Transcribed speech]. British Political Speech. http://britishpoliticalspeech.org/speech-archive.htm?speech=364 (accessed 11 June 2021).
McConnell, A., and Tormey, S. (2020). Explanations for the Brexit Policy Fiasco: Near-Impossible Challenge, Leadership Failure or Westminster Pathology? *Journal of European Public Policy*, *27*(5), 685–702.
Norris, P. (2019, 16 December). Was Farage the Midwife Delivering Johnson's Victory? The Brexit Party and the Size of the Conservative Majority. *LSE BPP Blog*. https://blogs.lse.ac.uk/politicsandpolicy/ge2019-brexit-party-impact/ (accessed 11 June 2021).
Phipps, C. (2017, 30 March). David Cameron: I Was Right to Hold EU Referendum. *The Guardian*. https://www.theguardian.com/politics/2017/mar/30/david-cameron-i-was-right-brexit-referendum.
Prosser, C. (2018). The Strange Death of Multi-Party Britain: The UK General Election of 2017. *West European Politics*, *41*(5), 1226–36.
Prosser, C. (2021). The End of the EU Affair: The UK General Election of 2019. *West European Politics*, *44*(2), 450–61.
Prosser, C., and Fieldhouse, E. (2017, 2 August). A Tale of Two Referendums – the 2017 Election in Scotland. The British Election. *British Election Study*. https://www.britishelectionstudy.com/bes-findings/a-tale-of-two-referendums-the-2017-election-in-scotland/#.YHFym68zaqk (11 June 2021).
Raitio, J., and Raulus, H. (2017). The UK EU Referendum and the Move towards Brexit. *Maastricht Journal of European and Comparative Law*, *24*(1), 25–42.
Richardson, J., and Rittberger, B. (2020). Brexit: Simply an Omnishambles or a Major Policy Fiasco? *Journal of European Public Policy*, *27*(5), 649–65.
Shipman, T. (2016). *All out War: The Full Story of How Brexit Sank Britain's Political Class*. HarperCollins.
Simpkins, F. (2018). The 2017 General Election in Scotland: A Return to Multi-Party Politics? *Revue Française de Civilisation Britannique*, *23*(2), 1–13.
Sloman, P. (2020). Squeezed out? The Liberal Democrats and the 2019 General Election. *The Political Quarterly*, *91*(1), 35–42.

Smith, Z. (2016). Fences: A Brexit Diary. *New York Review of Books*, *63*(13), 24–6.
Sobolewska, M., and Ford, R. (2020). *Brexitland: Identity, Diversity and the Reshaping of British Politics*. Cambridge University Press.
Tarrant, A., and Biondi, A. (2017). Labour's Programme and EU Law. *Renewal: A Journal of Labour Politics*, *25*(3/4), 66–89.
Tournier-Sol, K. (2021). From UKIP to the Brexit Party: The Politicization of European Integration and Disruptive Impact on National and European Arenas. *Journal of Contemporary European Studies*, *29*(3), 380–90.
Usherwood, S. (2018). The Third Era of British Euroscepticism: Brexit as a Paradigm Shift. *The Political Quarterly*, *89*(4), 553–9.
Usherwood, S. (2019). Shooting the Fox? UKIP's Populism in the Post Brexit-Era. *West-European Politics*, *42*(6), 1209–29.
Vaccari, C., Smets, K., and Heath, O. (2020). The United Kingdom 2017 Election: Polarisation in a Split Issue Space. *West European Politics*, *43*(3), 587–609.
Vasilopoulou, S. (2020). Brexit and the 2019 EP Election in the UK. *Journal of Common Market Studies*, *58*(1), 80–90.

5. Brexit and the nations

Michael Keating

THE TWO UNIONS[1]

At the heart of the case for Brexit is the idea that the United Kingdom's (UK) constitutional order, based on the sovereignty and supremacy of the Westminster Parliament, is incompatible with the sharing of sovereignty in the European Union (EU). From another perspective, however, UK devolution and European integration are complementary processes of functional and political rescaling and transformation. The EU provided an external support system for the devolution programme, which transformed the UK into a differentiated state with quasi-federal features. Brexit destabilizes the devolution settlement and has increased centrifugal pressures, including movements for secession in Scotland, Northern Ireland and, to some extent, Wales. These are exacerbated by moves to recentralize power within the UK. Such a programme of recentralization faces formidable obstacles, but so does the fragmentation of the UK into its constituent nations.

UNDERSTANDING THE UK

There have long been two interpretations of the UK as a polity. One has seen it as a homogeneous nation-state, without significant territorial variations (Blondel, 1974; Finer, 1974). It was often presented as the archetype of the modern state, created through territorial integration and functional differentiation. The foundation of the constitution was the doctrine of the absolute sovereignty and supremacy of the Crown-in-Parliament, underpinned by the 'Whig' interpretation of British history as the march of progress and liberalism (Butterfield, 1968). It was, of course, the insistence on this particular doctrine of sovereignty that was at the root of the UK's troubled relationship with the EU during its almost five decades of membership (Gros-Fitzgibbon, 2016). Parliamentary sovereignty, however, was always an intellectual puzzle. As famously articulated by A.V. Dicey (1959), it was presented as a simple fact, not requiring any historical or normative justification. This made it a powerful doctrine but at the same time a rather empty one, resting ultimately on a tautology. Parliament was sovereign because, by virtue of its sovereignty, it had said that it was. Yet the doctrine long bedevilled ideas of federalizing the state, adopting a written constitution or, in due course, resolving its relationship with Europe.

Another interpretation sees the UK as a plurinational union, created in stages and leaving intact elements of its pre-union components, as in Rokkan and Urwin's (1983) 'union-state'. The unions of Scotland (1707) and Ireland (1801) with England took the form of negotiation and pactism, rather than absorption, and this was also true of continued constitutional evolution (Jackson, 2012). In defiance of Westphalian principles, by 1921 Scotland and England had different established churches, while Ireland/Northern Ireland and Wales did not have established churches at all. Key elements of classic nation-building, including the legal and educational systems, were never harmonized across the UK. The issue of sovereignty was never resolved because, as Scottish jurists noted from time to time, the union of 1707 created a new Parliament of Great Britain, which could not simply have inherited all the prerogatives of the English Parliament and none of the Scottish Parliament, which itself had not established absolute sovereignty.

These issues remained largely confined to legal circles, except in times of high tension, such as the Irish Home Rule crises of the late nineteenth and early twentieth centuries. It was these crises that led Dicey himself into intellectual contortions when he tried to argue that Parliament was not in fact competent to set up a subordinate legislature in Ireland (McLean, 2010). After the First World War, the secession of the larger part of Ireland and the consignment of the other part to a unionist-dominated Parliament in Belfast took the Irish issue of out British politics. Agitation for Home Rule in Scotland and Wales died down amid economic depression as politicians there turned their attention to gaining help and support from the British state (Jones and Keating, 1985). It was not until the late twentieth century that the territorial question returned with force, leading to the establishment of devolved legislatures for Scotland, Wales and Northern Ireland.

The official Westminster view of devolution is that power is merely lent to Scotland, Northern Ireland and Wales and can be taken back at any time. The matter of the union is reserved to the centre, and Westminster retains the authority to override the devolved legislatures, change their powers and even abolish them at will. The only constraint is the 'Sewel Convention' under which it will not 'normally' legislate in devolved matters or change the settlement itself without the consent of the devolved bodies. Again, however, there is another interpretation, which sees devolution as the outcome of referendums in the three territories and so as an act of self-determination. Linking to early ideas about the nature of the union, it sees devolution as a significant constitutional change, which requires a reconsideration of the nature of sovereignty. While the courts have never upheld this idea, many academic commentators and even judges, when speaking *obiter dicta* or in academic settings (e.g. Arden, 2015), have concurred (Keating, 2021). The issue remains unresolved and devolution remains an ambiguous concept, subject to interpretation as decentralization in a unitary state, quasi-federalism or a pact among nations (Casañas Adam, 2017; Tierney, 2018).

Brexit is postulated on the most radical interpretation of parliamentary sovereignty, in which membership of the EU, with its supremacy provisions, is seen as incompatible with the fundamental principles of the constitution. As Prime Minister Theresa May (2017) put it, 'supranational institutions as strong as those created by the EU sit very uneasily in relation to our political history and way of life'. From the second perspective, however, there is a close affinity between the UK union and understandings of the EU. Both are political orders lacking consensus on four key elements: *demos*, the nature of the people; *telos*, the purpose of the union; *ethos*, or governing values; and sovereignty, the location of ultimate authority (Keating, 2021). We could describe them as uncompleted political orders but that might imply that they are lacking in something. Instead, they might be seen as examples of post-sovereignty, in which sovereignty has not disappeared but is dispersed and shared (MacCormick, 1999; Keating, 2001). They exemplify modern understandings of sovereignty, in which it is not a fixed characteristic of any given institution but rather a set of relationships (Loughlin, 2003). They are open-ended polities, in which consensus on foundational principles is not only lacking but probably unnecessary. Searching for them can merely provoke division.

DEVOLUTION AND EUROPE

The EU has thus provided a discursive space for ideas of shared and divided sovereignty. There are also more specific connections. The devolution statutes work on the 'reserved powers' model, meaning that only the powers reserved to the centre are specified. Anything else is devolved. Yet they also stipulated that the devolved governments and legislatures must operate within EU law as well as within the provisions of the European Convention on Human Rights of the Council of Europe. This provided a transversal limitation on devolved competences, which altered according to the extensions of EU law. Most devolution jurisprudence in the courts has involved these provisions rather than the alleged encroachments on powers reserved to the UK under the statutes.

The European provision meant that many competences were in practice shared between the EU and the devolved governments, with the UK Government entering the process only in the negotiation of policies within the Council of the EU. This included agriculture, fisheries, environmental policy, regional development and (in Scotland and Northern Ireland) justice and home affairs. Education, which occasionally comes into the EU's purview, is wholly devolved although research is shared. Devolved governments then exercised the same degree of discretion in transposition of directives and implementation that was available to member states, leading to significant divergences in matters including agricultural and rural policy. More broadly, it was the EU Internal Market regime that assured an effective internal market with the UK itself. The only reference to the internal market in the devolution statutes is a clause in the Northern Ireland Act, which never seems to have been invoked.

The EU framework also effected the management of borders within and beyond the UK, most obviously in the case of Northern Ireland. As early as the (failed) Sunningdale Agreement of 1973, hopes had been expressed that the new position of the UK and Ireland within the European Economic Community might facilitate the management of the conflict (Dorr, 2017). The regular meetings of British and Irish ministers in the Council of the EU[2] and European Council has also been credited with improving relations between the two states (Coakley and Todd, 2020). The eventual 1998 settlement, based on the Good Friday Agreement (GFA), had two aspects. The first concerns power-sharing within Northern Ireland between the unionist and nationalist communities. The second concerns the external relations of the province, with both Great Britain (east-west) and the Republic of Ireland (north-south). The GFA led to the removal of security controls at the border across the island of Ireland. Combined with the European Single Market programmes, this allowed the removal of all border infrastructure so that the border became invisible. The joint membership of the UK and Ireland in the EU also permitted the development of all-Ireland markets in matters including energy and programmes of cross-border cooperation. While the internal aspects of the settlement have been rather unstable, the border itself had, by 2016, largely disappeared from debate. Although nationalists still had long-term aspirations to the reunification of the island, polls since 2009 had consistently shown that, within the Catholic community, power-sharing under the GFA was a more popular option than unification (Keating, 2021).

Europe also affected the constitutional debate in Scotland because the Scottish National Party had, in the 1980s, changed its policy to independence-in-Europe, suggesting a willingness to share sovereignty. This meant that an independent Scotland would not have a hard border with the rest of the UK. In the 2014 Scottish independence referendum, the SNP were even able to argue that Scotland would remain within five unions: the European; monarchical;

monetary; defence; and social. It would withdraw only from the political one with England and Wales (and Northern Ireland if it was still in the union itself) (Keating and McEwen, 2017). Their opponents were reduced to arguing that Scotland could be excluded from Europe if it voted for independence – an ironic argument in the light of subsequent events.

THE BREXIT VOTE

The constituency for the EU referendum of 2016 was the UK and Gibraltar and a simple majority of all voters was required. Demands from the Scottish Government that withdrawal should require a concurrent majority across the nations were dismissed. Yet the campaign was highly differentiated. All the parties represented in the Scottish Parliament (SNP, Conservative, Labour, Liberal Democrat and Green) were in favour of Remain, although there were some dissidents. In Wales, Labour, Plaid Cymru (nationalist) and Liberal Democrats were for Remain, the Conservatives were divided and UKIP (UK Independence Party) was also present in the Assembly (now called the Senedd). Northern Ireland's moderate nationalists in the Social Democratic and Labour Party (SDLP) are historically strongly pro-Europe as is the cross-community Alliance Party. The radical nationalists in Sinn Féin are historically Eurosceptic but supported Remain to avoid the 'repartition of Ireland'. The Ulster Unionist Party supported Remain, at least until the vote, but the larger and more radical Democratic Unionist Party (DUP), historically anti-European, came out for Leave.

The referendum outcome reflected these divisions. While England and Wales both voted by 53 per cent to leave, Scotland voted to remain by 62 per cent. This is not to be attributed simply to nationalism – voters for all the parties were more pro-European than their English counterparts. This has been the case since the 1990s, although the strongest supporters both of Scottish independence and of British unity tend to be more Eurosceptic; the post-sovereigntists favouring devolution and moderate pro-Europeanism predominated (Keating, 2009). In spite of the SNP linking independence to Europe, the proportions voting for Brexit were similar among those voting Yes and No in the 2014 independence referendum (Prosser and Fieldhouse, 2017). Northern Ireland voted to remain by 56 per cent but there was a large difference between the communities. Catholics and nationalists[3] voted by almost 90 per cent to remain while unionists voted by two to one to leave (Garry, 2017). SDLP voters supported Remain by 95 per cent, while 75 per cent of DUP voters went for Leave. One of the most striking features was in England, where voting to leave the EU is strongly linked to feeling more English than British (Ashcroft, 2019; Future of England, 2019; Henderson and Wyn Jones, 2021). If anti-EU feeling is impelled by nationalism in the UK, it is not the nationalism of the state but that of its largest part.

These differing voting patterns raised the question of what is the relevant *demos* for the decision to leave the EU. The Scottish Government had earlier argued that concurrent mandates among the four nations would be required. The UK Government disagreed although English Brexiters might have had a different view had England's Leave vote been small enough to be overridden by the votes of Scotland and Northern Ireland. Prime Minister Theresa May (2019) declared that: 'There can and must be no false choice between honouring the solemn commitments of the Belfast Agreement and delivering on the decision of the British people in the EU referendum.' Yet the Belfast (Good Friday) Agreement was negotiated with the involvement of the Government of Ireland and endorsed by referendums in both parts of Ireland. The

'British people' that voted for Brexit was an altogether different *demos*, dominated by English voters.

Yet, while Scotland, Northern Ireland and England voted differently on Brexit, it was difficult to translate this straightforwardly into distinct mandates for internal constitutional change. In Scotland, there was no majority for any combination of Yes/No to independence and Remain/Leave to Europe. Northern Ireland did not have anything like the cross-community consensus required for further change. England does not have an obvious 'exit' option from the UK, nor does it have a parliament to give expression to its wishes. In the aftermath of the Brexit referendum, however, there were significant changes, with rise in secessionist sentiment across the smaller nations. Support for Scottish independence increased from the 45 per cent it had gained in the 2014 referendum, to somewhere in the mid-50s as a small but crucial section of the 2014 No voters prioritized the EU (Curtice, 2019). Attitudes towards independence and Europe began to align as Scotland was marked by increasing political polarization between the pro-independence/pro-Europe option and the anti-independence referendum/pro-Brexit option, with the former comprising around half of the electorate and the latter a quarter (McCrone and Keating, 2021). Polarization also increased in Northern Ireland. While Protestants and unionists have never shown more than negligible support for Irish unity, many Catholics can be persuaded either way, depending on what the alternative is. So, after 2016, among Catholics and nationalists, support for reunification once again overtook support for the GFA and power-sharing (Keating, 2021).[4] Even in Wales, there was some interest in independence and polls indicating support from a quarter or third of the population (Trystan, 2019). Surveys in England, meanwhile, showed that a majority of Leave voters were determined to press ahead with Brexit even it if meant the secession of Scotland and/or Northern Ireland (Ashcroft, 2019; Future of England Survey, 2019). While it was never expressed this way, that would mean the effective secession of England from the UK.

TAKING BACK CONTROL

In the immediate aftermath of the referendum, there were suggestions that there might be a differentiated Brexit, with parts of the UK remaining in the EU one way or another. There was some talk of a 'reverse Greenland', referring to Greenland's decision in 1979 to leave the EU[5] but remain with Denmark. Another proposal was for England and Wales to leave, allowing Scotland and Northern Ireland to retain the UK's EU membership (O'Leary, 2016). These raised numerous practical difficulties but, in any case, did not even enter into the negotiations.

Instead, the narrow referendum result – 52 per cent across the UK to leave – was taken by the UK Government as a mandate to leave not only the EU but also the Internal Market and the Customs Union, ruling out intermediate options such as the European Economic Area (EEA) (May, 2017). While the original premise of Eurosceptics had been the defence of parliamentary sovereignty, the referendum aftermath saw an effective shift to the idea of popular sovereignty, in the slogan 'the British people have voted for Brexit'. The implications of this were less evident in England than in Scotland and Northern Ireland, where the idea of a unitary British *demos* is widely questioned. Indeed, the GFA expressly accepts a plurality of political identities and provides for their realization.

The UK Government proclaimed that there would be a 'red, white and blue Brexit', with the whole of the UK leaving together (Elgot, 2016). To this end, the central government was the sole negotiator, with no presence for the devolved administrations in the British team. Instead, a Joint Ministerial Committee (European Negotiations) was created, with a consultative role. Devolved ministers regularly complained that this was inadequate and that they were not given advance notice of matters or timely sight of relevant papers. As the Northern Ireland devolved institutions were out of operation between January 2017 and January 2020, there was no political input from there.

An early constitutional test was provided in the celebrated Miller case. Gina Miller had gone to court to obtain a ruling that parliamentary approval was needed to trigger Article 50, starting the withdrawal provision; the UK Government had claimed that it could be done under prerogative powers, as a matter of foreign policy and treaties. The Scottish Government, joined when the matter reached the Supreme Court, by litigants from Northern Ireland, argued that, because Brexit would affect devolved competences, the Sewel Convention applied. So the devolved legislatures should be asked to consent – it was not argued that they had a veto. The Supreme Court could have ruled that Brexit was a reserved matter or that the situation was not 'normal'. Instead, it chose, following the argument of the UK Government (Case for Her Majesty's Attorney General and Her Majesty's Advocate General, 2018), to rule that Sewel was merely a 'political' convention and thus no business of the courts (R v Secretary of State for Exiting the European Union, 2017). While strictly this did not alter the constitution, it did remove the essential uncertainty about the status of the convention and allowed the UK Government to override it in subsequent Brexit legislation. It did, thus, have constitutional implications (Douglas-Scott, 2019).

The next argument concerned what would happen to those competences that were devolved to Scotland, Wales and Northern Ireland but also subject to EU law. The UK Government argued that, because these had been subject to EU law, they were not really devolved at all. After Brexit, therefore, they should revert to Westminster (Department for Exiting the European Union, 2017). This was to confuse the reservations to Westminster in the devolution statutes with the transversal obligation work within EU law. In fact, were nothing to be done, the powers would revert to the devolved bodies. In order to bring the powers back to the centre, the first draft of the EU Withdrawal Bill provided to bring all 'retained EU law' back to Westminster, with provision for the powers to be 'released' to Scotland, Wales and Northern Ireland should reservation prove unnecessary. The argument proved embarrassing even to some Conservatives and the bill was subsequently amended to allow Westminster effectively to centralize competences selectively for a period of time, after which they could be released. Taking the powers back is subject to a consent mechanism analogous to the Sewel Convention but this one is more specific. It provides that if the measure is approved by the devolved legislatures, or it is not approved by them, or if they say nothing, then it will go ahead.

In a further move, in 2020 the UK Government published a White Paper and Bill on the UK Internal Market (Department of Business, Energy and Industrial Strategy, 2020). The rationale was that, after leaving the EU Internal Market, measures would be needed to sustain a UK internal market. This was accompanied by the claim that a UK internal market had existed since the unions with Scotland and Ireland, which rather contradicted the first argument, as that implied that the internal market was only in place because of the EU. The subsequent Internal Market Act relied on two principles, non-discrimination and mutual recognition. Any trader is allowed to appeal to the courts if a good that is legal in one part of the UK is not allowed to be sold in another part because of regulatory differences. This includes goods imported into a part of the UK. There are exceptions to the principle, covering matters where regulations already differ, health and social services, and a list of specific exceptions. These are much narrower than the broad public policy exceptions allowed under the EU Internal Market regime. Items can be added to or removed from the list at the discretion of the UK Government, using a statutory instrument. After pressure in Parliament, this was subject to a consent mechanism but that provides that if the devolved legislatures have not approved within 28 days then the measure goes ahead anyway.

There were widespread objections to the UK Internal Market Act on two grounds. First, it was argued that it would undermine the regulatory capacity of the devolved governments as their regulations could be undermined by goods brought in from elsewhere. As England is by far the largest market among the nations, its standards would, by default, prevail everywhere. Second, the analogy with the UK Internal Market is not accurate. In the EU, measures are proposed by the Commission, approved by the Council by qualified majority vote and subject to the principles of subsidiarity and proportionality. None of these features in the UK devolution settlement.

The Internal Market Act thus represents a further centralizing measure, which will work asymmetrically, constraining the devolved territories but not England. As Scotland and Wales have consistently been under centre-left government since devolution, they are also more likely to be affected by deregulatory pressures coming from England. The Act also contained clauses allowing UK ministers powers to spend on devolved competences in Scotland, Wales and Northern Ireland. EU Structural Funds were previously administered by the devolved administration. Their replacement will be controlled by the UK Government, reinforcing other measures of direct spending intended to bypass the devolved administrations.

THE IRISH CONUNDRUM

One of the most difficult aspects of Brexit has been the Irish border, which has several aspects. There is a jurisdictional border, which is guaranteed by the GFA, unless referendums in both parts of Ireland demonstrate a will to unify. There is an economic border, almost eliminated by the EU Internal Market. The security border was largely attenuated by the peace process, which allowed the removal of checks and patrols. There is also the imagined border in the minds of both nationalists and unionists, the former favouring an all-Ireland and the latter a pan-UK framework. The border also shapes relationships among people living in border communities, who daily negotiate around it (Hayward, 2017; Todd, 2018).

In another sense, the basic issue around the border after Brexit is quite simple. If the UK is outside the Single Market and Customs Union and Ireland inside them, then there will be an economic and regulatory border between the two, which includes the border between the two parts of Ireland. This could be avoided only by placing a border between Northern Ireland and Great Britain, so dividing the UK. The first is unacceptable to nationalists in Northern Ireland and the second to unionists. Either would go against the spirit, if not the letter of the GFA, which was intended to respect the identities and aspirations of both communities, including their territorial projection. Yet UK Governments have, since the Brexit vote, refused to accept this logic, seeking instead a series of wishful solutions that would make the issue disappear.

In the aftermath of the Brexit vote, two developments served to make the issue more acute. First, the Irish Government, which had cooperated closely with the UK during the peace process and the GFA, made a strategic decision to act as a loyal European and trust the EU to look after its interests (Connelly, 2017). Unlike the UK Government, the Irish Government had made advance preparations for Brexit (Murphy, 2018). This paid off, as the EU made agreement on the Irish border one of the three conditions, along with finance and citizens' rights, for the opening of substantive talks on withdrawal. Second, in the snap General Election of June 2017, the Conservative Government lost its parliamentary majority and entered into a confidence and supply arrangement with the DUP, which had set itself against any border in the Irish Sea.

The outcome, after elaborate negotiation, was the first Irish Protocol, part of Theresa May's withdrawal agreement of 2018. This proposed three solutions. First, it was hoped that the final trading agreement between the UK and the EU would deal with the problem. Second, there could be technical solutions such as locating border controls at some distance from the border and using electronic surveillance. Pending these, there would be a 'backstop' in which Northern Ireland would be subject to EU regulations in so far as necessary to sustain the GFA (Connelly, 2018). The first version of the backstop would have kept Northern Ireland in the Customs Union but that was vetoed by the DUP. Instead, the whole of the UK would remain in a customs arrangement with the EU, a suggestion on which May's government later proposed to build in its 'Chequers Plan'.

There were problems with all three options. The first would require that the final agreement include all the items in the backstop, so was wishful thinking. The second relied on non-existent technology and in any case an electronic border is still a border, dividing two regulatory zones.[6] The third was highly ambivalent. The GFA contains little about the EU but, arguably, the EU Single Market has been essential to its development over time. So, the UK Government clung to a narrow interpretation of the implications of the GFA, while the Irish Government believed that it effectively committed Northern Ireland to the Single Market rules. The DUP could not accept the Protocol and, after Boris Johnson had resigned from government over the Chequers Plan, he addressed the DUP conference to assure them that no British Prime Minister could accept a border in the Irish Sea.

Theresa May's deal failed to gain parliamentary approval and she resigned with effect from June 2019. Her successor, Boris Johnson, having gained a majority at another snap election in December, abandoned the DUP and did a deal with the Irish Government. The final withdrawal deal entailed Northern Ireland remaining in the EU regulatory zone for most purposes and in both the EU and UK customs zone. There was to be an effective border in the Irish Sea. This new arrangement was not agreed with the parties in Northern Ireland but there was provision for the Northern Ireland Assembly to break with it after a period of time and at intervals thereafter. The fact that the Protocol was supported by the nationalist and non-aligned parties, as well as the Irish Government, meant that this was extremely unlikely to happen. The backstop had, in effect, been eliminated by being made permanent.

Like the overall withdrawal agreement, there is much to be negotiated in practice and in detail and interpretations differ. There were some arcane discussions about the difference between regulatory alignment and absence of regulatory divergence. Boris Johnson declared that an Irish Sea trade border would only be over his dead body; there would be no checks at the border (ITV, 2020); EU negotiators insisted that there would be checks (O'Carroll, 2020). Johnson later admitted that there would (Colston, 2020). Experience proved that the EU was correct. The deal proved fragile from the start and both sides undermined it in the early stages. The UK Government introduced a provision in its UK Internal Market Bill in late 2020, allowing it to disapply any controls on movements between Northern Ireland and Great

Britain, while conceding that this violated the withdrawal agreement and international law, as the Secretary of State for Northern Ireland put it, 'in a very specific and limited way'. This was clearly not going to help the UK's negotiations for a trade agreement with the EU (although some ministers seemed to think it would enhance their negotiating position) and, after the relevant bill was amended by the House of Lords, the Government dropped the provision. In January 2020, the EU Commission announced that it would override part of the Protocol in order the control the movement of Covid vaccines out of the EU via Northern Ireland. They, too, had to back down after an outcry united the Irish and British Governments and all the parties in Northern Ireland. In March 2021, the UK Government announced that it would unilaterally delay introducing controls between Great Britain and Northern Ireland.

SCOTTISH DIFFERENTIATION

The response of the SNP Government in Scotland to Brexit was set out in a paper in 2016 (Scottish Government, 2016). This stated that its policy was for Scotland to be an independent state within the EU. The differential Brexit vote, it argued, provided the material change of circumstances that, in its election manifesto, it had said would provide the justification for a second independence referendum. Failing that, it would prefer the whole of the UK to remain within the Single Market and Customs Union. If that was not possible, then it proposed that Scotland alone remain within the Single Market, using the machinery of the EEA, while also remaining within the UK's regulatory space. The idea received short shrift from the UK Government, which insisted that the whole UK should leave together, although some of the measures proposed bore a resemblance to those eventually adopted in the Northern Ireland Protocol.

The Scottish Government then introduced its own Legal Continuity Bill. Although the first foundered on a technicality,[7] it was followed by another, which was enacted. This gives Scottish ministers powers, but not the obligation, to maintain dynamic alignment with EU regulations. One motive is to retain the *acquis communautaire* as far as possible in Scotland pending an independence vote. Another is to continue using Brussels, rather than London, as an inspiration for policy development. It is likely, however, that use of this power would be undermined by the provisions of the UK Internal Market Act, which allow products meeting English or Welsh regulations to come into the Scottish market from outside, undercutting Scottish producers.

Another concern in Scotland has been freedom of movement. There has long been a cross-party consensus in the Scottish Parliament that freedom of movement, and migration more generally, is needed in Scotland for economic and demographic reasons. The 2016 proposals would have allowed EU workers to come to Scotland freely, but not to move to England. Other proposals have involved territorially differentiated migration and working rights, similar to those in Canada. None of these has been admitted by the UK Government.

The Scottish and Welsh Governments also requested the right to participate in the Erasmus student exchange programme, in return for making the standard financial contribution. Although the request was supported by 145 MEPs, Commission President Usula von der Leyen ruled it out on the grounds that only independent countries could participate; this is despite the fact that higher education is fully devolved to Scotland and Wales (Gallardo,

2021). Students in Northern Ireland, on the other hand, can participate in the Irish Erasmus programme funded by the government of the Republic.

INTERNATIONAL AGREEMENTS

After Brexit, many matters that were previously handled by the EU became matters of foreign policy. This includes trade agreements, including the new Trade and Cooperation Agreement with the EU. During EU membership, there was a system to allow an input from the devolved governments into EU policy making via the Joint Ministerial Committee (JMC) (Europe), the only one of a series of JMCs that regularly met. Ministers and civil servants from the devolved administrations could, by invitation, participate in UK delegations to the Council of the European Union. While devolved ministers would regularly complain that this was inadequate, it did provide an input to policy and a forum for discussion. There is no corresponding provision for devolved participation in the new Partnership Council. Nor is there provision for devolved input into international trade negotiations, although 'consultation' is promised. Similarly, the devolved governments have no role in international negotiations on climate change or other matters falling within their competences.

THE END OF THE UNION?

The EU served as an important external support system for UK devolution and Brexit has profoundly destabilized the settlement. By forcing issues of sovereignty, it has made explicit the abeyances, 'silences' (Foley, 2012) and ambiguities that made possible the management of the union and membership of the EU. The debate over Europe has also hastened the process of discursive reconstruction of the nations and the national movements, which has been underway for some years. So, while in the European referendum of 1975, Scotland revealed itself as less pro-European than England, that had been reversed since the 1980s. Although the SNP's formula of independence-in-Europe had failed to turn Scots from reluctant Europeans into Euro-enthusiasts, the Brexit debate and its aftermath did serve to forge such a link. By championing EU membership, the nationalists were able to take a place on the European stage as pro-Europeans, contrasting themselves with the narrow nationalists in the Brexit camp. Radical nationalism in Northern Ireland, which had been slowly abandoning its Euroscepticism, now joined moderate nationalism in embracing Europe and, thereby, interdependence and constrained sovereignty. Although Wales voted to leave, the Labour-led Welsh Government sought to remain as close to the EU as possible. The nationalists of Plaid Cymru, also pro-European, were able to move back to a policy of national independence by assuring the public that this would be in the context of Europe. The emerging English political identity, by contrast, was strongly marked by Euroscepticism although it is not yet clear whether Brexit will serve to appease and still this English nationalism or to unleash it.

These centrifugal tendencies might point to the disintegration of the UK through the secession of its constituent nations. Yet there are formidable obstacles to this. The rise in support for secession created by Brexit is clear but not enough on its own to produce convincing majorities. Independence became the critical cleavage in Scottish politics but divided the country rather than uniting it. Northern Ireland Catholics moved back towards Irish unity but Protestants were unmoved. Outside of Sinn Féin, there is little support in the Republic of Ireland for unity in the short term, given the cost of supporting the North and the need to adapt the institutions and practices of the Republic to accommodate the Protestant/unionist population. The stirring of interest in Welsh independence did not amount to a coherent political movement as in Scotland. English discontent with the union did not produce a clear question let alone an answer. Fragmentation of the UK, moreover, would create economic borders between the nations, reproducing those created by Brexit but in enhanced form, given that trade volumes across the UK are much greater than those between the UK and the EU.

In the years since devolution, surveys have consistently shown majority support in Scotland and Wales for deepening it. In Northern Ireland, power-sharing has been the most popular option and the only one commanding cross-community support. Considerable additional powers have been handed to the three nations since 1998 as devolution is seen as a rolling programme. As nationalism has risen, there has been a constant search for a new compromise short of secession, sometimes known as maximum devolution or 'devo-max'. Many people argued that it should feature as a second question on the ballot in the Scottish independence referendum. There has also been a renewed interest in federalism. While in the EU context, the British political class has always seen federalism as centralizing, in the domestic context it is seen as a form of radical decentralization. Although it has been discussed since the territorial crises of the late nineteenth century (it earlier featured in the Scottish debates on the Union of 1707), it has never adequately been defined. Federalists have often been reluctant to accept that it would entail curtailing the supremacy of the Westminster Parliament. The territorial crisis provoked by Brexit has brought back the search for a 'third way' between devolution and secession but at the same time may have rendered it irrelevant. Brexit has polarized opinion in Scotland and Northern Ireland and, to some extent, Wales as the middle ground is shrinking. Neither federalism nor any version of devo-max, moreover, resolve the critical question of Europe. It has proved possible for a constituent part of a member state to be outside the EU, as with Greenland and the Faroes. It is not possible for a constituent part of a non-member state to be inside. There is no reverse Greenland and there is no political will to reproduce the Northern Ireland Protocol elsewhere.

It is not clear whether Eurosceptism and the search for sovereignty will be sated by Brexit. There have long been voices on the Eurosceptic right advocating repeal of the Human Rights Act, which entrenched the European Convention on Human Rights (ECHR) in the UK and these will not be stilled. What is often not appreciated here is that the ECHR is incorporated into the devolved settlement in a distinct way, through the devolution statutes. While laws of the Westminster Parliament can be challenged in the courts on ECHR grounds, they cannot be struck down. Instead, there is a fast-track procedure allowing Westminster to put matters right. Laws of the devolved legislatures can, and have been, struck down. Repeal of the Human Rights Act would not affect this, and there is almost no constituency to repeal the ECHR provisions of the devolution statutes. The favoured replacement for the Human Rights Act and, in some versions, for ECHR itself, is a British Bill of Rights. This would link human rights to British national citizenship and identity, serving as a unifying theme for the nation. The problem is that many people in Scotland and Northern Ireland do not feel British at all and would reject such a nationalizing move. The House of Lords and House of Commons Joint Committee (2008) preferred the title 'UK Bill' rather than 'British Bill' on the grounds that some people do not consider themselves British, but English, Scottish, Irish or Welsh. This merely begs the question of what 'UK' covers and whether it is intended as a reference to national identity; they do write that

> there is an inevitable and entirely appropriate link with national identity. A national bill of rights is an expression of national identity and the process of drawing one up deliberately invites reflection on what it is that 'binds us together as a nation,' what we regard as of fundamental importance, and which values we consider to guide us. It is potentially a moment of national definition. (House of Lords and House of Commons Joint Committee on Human Rights, 2008)

JUSTICE (2007) excluded Northern Ireland from its proposed bill, which is defined as British, but it says nothing about the implications in Scotland and addresses only the English legal system. The Constitution Reform Group (2018) similarly suggests a 'charter of the union', as does the Bingham Centre's (2015) proposal. If the UK survives as a union, this may be the next terrain of conflict.

Before the Brexit referendum, it was possible to see the UK as a site for experimentation in new forms of union and statehood, embedded in an overarching post-sovereign order. There was no blueprint or final destination as the two unions evolved and adjusted. Brexit has resulted in the reassertion of traditional ideas of sovereignty as well as a recentralization of state functions. The Brexit process involved two attempts to assert executive authority over Parliament, first, when Theresa May sought to trigger Article 50 without parliamentary sanction and second, when Boris Johnson sought to prorogue Parliament in order to avoid it getting in the way of Brexit. Both were struck down by the Supreme Court. The devolution settlement, however, has no such protection in UK law.

The prospect is for new measures to integrate the UK as Brexit unfolds, along with measures to strengthen executive powers. Proposals limit judicial review of actions of the UK Government and represent further extensions of executive dominance. At the same time, Scotland, Northern Ireland and Wales will continue to be drawn into the European orbit. These centripetal and centrifugal pressures will continue to strain the union.

NOTES

1. The research on which this is based was supported by the project *Differentiated Integration in the European Union* (InDivEU), European Commission Research Grant, 822304.
2. For continuity, I use EU throughout.
3. These two largely coincide but not perfectly.
4. The data are from the Northern Ireland Life and Times survey.
5. It was not then called the European Union but I use this terminology for consistency.
6. It should be noted that Michel Barnier had also advocated an electronic border, this time in the Irish Sea, downplaying its significance (Randerson, 2018).
7. The Supreme Court found that, while it was constitutional at the time it was introduced, the provisions of the EU Withdrawal Act had subsequently rendered parts of it unconstitutional.

REFERENCES

Arden, M. (2015). *Common Law and Modern Society*. Oxford University Press.

Ashcroft, L. (2019, 21 October). England and the Union. *Lord Ashcroft Polls*. https://lordashcroftpolls.com/2019/10/england-and-the-union/ (accessed 5 October 2022).

Bingham Centre for the Rule of Law. (2015). *A Constitutional Crossroads: Ways Forward for the United Kingdom.*

Blondel, J. (1974). *Voters, Parties, and Leaders. The Social Fabric of British Politics* (revised edn). Penguin.

Butterfield, H. (1968). *The Whig Interpretation of History.* Penguin (first published Bell, 1931).

Casañas Adam, E. (2017). An Unanswered or Unanswerable Question? The Scottish Parliament's Competence to Legislate for an Indendence Referendum for Scotland. *Revista Catalana de Dret Públic, 54*, 81–99. https://doi.org/10.2436/rcdp.i54.2017.2982.

Case for Her Majesty's Attorney General and Her Majesty's Advocate General, U.K.S.C. 0080 (2018). https://assets.publishing.service.gov.uk/government/uploads/system/uploads/attachment_data/file/728147/Applicants__Written_Case.pdf (accessed 5 October 2022).

Coakley, J., and Todd, J. (2020). *Negotiating a Settlement in Northern Ireland, 1969–2019.* Oxford University Press.

Colston, T. (2020, 11 February). Boris Johnson Promised Frictionless Trade after Brexit But Now His Government Admits New Border Checks Are 'Inevitable'. *Business Insider.* https://www.businessinsider.com/boris-johnson-michael-gove-admits-brexit-border-checks-are-inevitable-2020-2?r=US&IR=T (accessed 5 October 2022).

Connelly, T. (2017). *Brexit & Ireland. The Dangers, the Opportunities, and the Inside Story of the Irish Response.* Penguin Ireland.

Connelly, T. (2018, 20 October). Brexit: A Brief History of the Backstop. *RTE.* https://www.rte.ie/news/brexit/2018/1019/1005373-backstop-tony-connelly/ (accessed 5 October 2022).

Constitution Reform Group. (2018). *Act of Union Bill.* http://www.constitutionreformgroup.co.uk/publications/ (accessed 5 October 2022).

Curtice, J. (2019, 1 July). Could Brexit Yet Undermine the Future of the British State? *What Scotland Thinks.* http://blog.whatscotlandthinks.org/2019/07/could-brexit-yet-undermine-the-future-of-the-british-state/ (accessed 5 October 2022).

Department for Exiting the European Union. (2017). *Legislating for the United Kingdom's Withdrawal from the European Union* (Cm 9446).

Department of Business, Energy and Industrial Strategy. (2020). *Internal Market Bill, 2020: Policy Statements.* https://www.gov.uk/government/publications/uk-internal-market-bill-2020-policy-statements (accessed 5 October 2022).

Dicey, A.V. (1959). *Introduction to the Study of the Law of the Constitution.* Macmillan.

Dorr, N. (2017). *Sunningdale: The Search for Peace in Northern Ireland.* Royal Irish Academy.

Douglas-Scott, S. (2019). *The Constitutional Implications of the EU (Withdrawal) Act 2018: A Critical Appraisal* (Research Paper No. 299/2019). Queen Mary School of Law Legal Studies. https://papers.ssrn.com/sol3/papers.cfm?abstract_id=3316710 (accessed 5 October 2022).

Elgot, J. (2016, 6 December). Theresa May Calls for 'Red, White and Blue Brexit'. *The Guardian.* https://www.theguardian.com/politics/2016/dec/06/theresa-may-calls-for-red-white-and-blue-brexit (accessed 5 October 2022).

Finer, S. (1974). *Comparative Government.* Penguin.

Foley, M. (2012). *The Silence of Constitutions: Gaps, 'Abeyances' and Political Temperament in the Maintenance of Government.* Routledge Revivals.

Future of England Survey. (2019). https://www.cardiff.ac.uk/__data/assets/pdf_file/0010/1708624/Copy-of-Wales-16-Oct-AH.pdf (accessed 5 October 2022).

Gallardo, C. (2021, 16 February). EU Rejects Call to Readmit Scotland to Erasmus Scheme. *Politico.* https://www.politico.eu/article/ursula-von-der-leyen-rejects-calls-to-readmit-scotland-in-erasmus-scheme/ (accessed 5 October 2022).

Garry, J. (2017). The EU Referendum Vote in Northern Ireland: Implications for Our Understanding of Citizens' Political Views and Behaviour (Knowledge Exchange Seminar Series 2016–17). *Northern Ireland Assembly.* https://www.qub.ac.uk/brexit/Brexitfilestore/Filetoupload,728121,en.pdf (accessed 5 October 2022).

Gros-Fitzgibbon, B. (2016). *Continental Drift: Britain and Europe from the End of Empire to the Rise of Euroscepticism.* Cambridge University Press.

Hayward, K. (2017). *Bordering on Brexit: Views from Local Communities in the Central Border Region or Ireland/Northern Ireland.* Queen's University Belfast. http://go.qub.ac.uk/bordering (accessed 5 October 2022).

Henderson, A., and Wyn Jones, R. (2021). *Englishness: The Political Force Transforming Britain.* Oxford University Press.

House of Lords and House of Commons Joint Committee on Human Rights. (2008). *A Bill of Rights for the UK? Twenty-ninth Report of Session 2007–08* (HL Paper 165-I, HC 150-I).

ITV. (2009, 14 August). Johnson Says Irish Sea Trade Border 'over My Dead Body'. https://www.itv.com/news/utv/2020-08-13/irish-sea-trade-border-over-my-dead-body-says-johnson (accessed 5 October 2022).

Jackson, A. (2012). *The Two Unions: Ireland, Scotland and the Survival of the United Kingdom, 1707–2007.* Oxford University Press.

Jones, B., and Keating, M. (1985). *Labour and the British State.* Oxford University Press.

JUSTICE. (2007). *A British Bill of Rights: Informing the Debate.*

Keating, M. (2001). *Plurinational Democracy: Stateless Nations in a Post-Sovereignty Era.* Oxford University Press.

Keating, M. (2009). *The Independence of Scotland. Self-Government and the Shifting Politics of Union.* Oxford University Press.

Keating, M. (2021). *State and Nation in the United Kingdom: The Fractured Union.* Oxford University Press.

Keating, M., and McEwen, N. (2017). The Scottish Independence Debate. In M. Keating (ed.), *Debating Scotland: Issues of Independence and Union in the 2014 Referendum.* Oxford University Press, pp. 1–26.

Loughlin, M. (2003). Ten Tenets of Sovereignty. In N. Walker (ed.), *Sovereignty in Transition.* Hart, pp. 55–68.

MacCormick, N. (1999). *Questioning Sovereignty. Law, State and Nation in the European Commonwealth.* Oxford University Press.

May, T. (2017). *Plan for Britain: The Prime Minister's Speech on Brexit* [Speech transcript]. Prime Minister's Office. https://www.gov.uk/government/speeches/the-governments-negotiating-objectives-for-exiting-the-eu-pm-speech (accessed 5 October 2022).

May, T. (2019). *PM Speech on the Union: 4 July 2019* [Speech transcript]. Prime Minister's Office. https://www.gov.uk/government/speeches/pm-speech-on-the-union-4-july-2019 (accessed 5 October 2022).

McCrone, D., and Keating, M. (2021). Questions of Sovereignty: Redefining Politics in Scotland. *The Political Quarterly, 92*(1), 12–22. https://doi.org/10.1111/1467-923X.12958.

McLean, I. (2010). *What's Wrong with the British Constitution?* Oxford University Press.

Murphy, M.C. (2018). *Europe and Northern Ireland's Future: Negotiating Brexit's Unique Case.* Agenda.

O'Carroll, L. (2020, 24 January). Revealed: Complex Post-Brexit Checks for Northern Irish Traders. *The Guardian.* https://www.theguardian.com/politics/2020/jan/24/revealed-complex-post-brexit-checks-for-northern-irish-traders (accessed 5 October 2022).

O'Leary, B. (2016). *The Dalriata Document: Towards a Multinational Compromise That Respects Diversity in the United Kingdom.* Queen's University. https://www.qub.ac.uk/Research/GRI/mitchell-institute/FileStore/Filetoupload,756968,en.pdf (accessed 5 October 2022).

Prosser, C., and Fieldhouse, E. (2017). A Tale of Two Referendums – the 2017 Election in Scotland. *British Election Study.* http://www.britishelectionstudy.com/bes-findings/a-tale-of-two-referendums-the-2017-election-in-scotland/#.WeoCaDb9O7M (accessed 5 October 2022).

R (on the application of Miller and another) (Respondents) v Secretary of State for Exiting the European Union (Appellant), U.K.S.C. 5 (2017). https://www.supremecourt.uk/cases/uksc-2016-0196.html (accessed 5 October 2022).

Randerson, J. (2018, 6 July). Michel Barnier: EU Won't Break the Single Market for Brexit UK. *Politico.* https://www.politico.eu/article/michel-barnier-brexit-customs-eu-wont-break-the-single-market-for-brexit-uk/ (accessed 5 October 2022).

Rokkan, S., and Urwin, D. (1983). *Economy, Territory, Identity: Politics of West European Peripheries.* Sage.

Scottish Government. (2016). *Scotland's Place in Europe* (Corporate Report).

Todd, J. (2018). *Identity Change after Conflict: Ethnicity, Boundaries and Belonging in the Two Irelands*. Palgrave.

Trystan, D. (2019, 22 June). Indycurious and Curiouser: New Poll Shows Support for Welsh Independence on the Rise. *Nation Cymru*. https://nation.cymru/opinion/indycurious-and-curiouser-new-poll-shows-support-for-welsh-independence-on-the-rise/ (accessed 5 October 2022).

6. Brexit and economic ideas

Craig Parsons

INTRODUCTION: THE PURSUIT OF 'GLOBAL BRITAIN'

Now that Brexit is achieved, British leaders are eager to build a future free of constraints from the European Union (EU). In particular, the Conservative government seeks 'to prove that Brexit was not a "Little England" pipe dream but a platform for a new global Britain', as the *Financial Times* paraphrased advisers to Prime Minister Boris Johnson in January 2021 (Parker, 2021). As Johnson himself put it a month earlier, the goal is an 'open, generous, outward looking, internationalist and free trading global Britain' (Prime Minister's Office, 2020).

Given that the 2016 vote for Brexit is more easily interpreted as a 'Little England' rejection of openness, these goals beg explanation. Pro-'Leave' voting patterns have been widely analysed as a 'mutiny against the cosmopolitan elite' (Calhoun, 2016) combining reactions of 'economic have-nots and cultural backlash' (Norris and Inglehart, 2019), and drawing disproportionate support from 'areas with deprivation in terms of income, education, and employment' (Becker et al., 2017). Prominent scholars explain the vote mainly as a reaction against market openness, with references to Karl Polanyi's notion that market liberalisation inherently harms societies and generates opposition (Polanyi, 1944). Neoliberal policies went quite far in Britain after the 1970s, threatening people in disadvantaged positions. Much of that openness was framed in the EU, so the Leave vote reflected 'a protective counter-movement to subordinate the market to political constraints' (Hopkin, 2017, p. 466; also Schmidt, 2018; Vail, 2020). But if some of the post-2016 Brexiteer agenda makes sense in such terms, like adoption of a more restrictive immigration system and plans for more free-handed dispersal of state aids, its 'Global Britain' elements do not. Conservative leaders have loudly and consistently proclaimed that leaving the EU will bring more deregulation and free trade, not less.[1]

A growing body of scholarship addresses this odd mix of anti- and pro-openness discourse around Brexit, and this chapter builds on its contributions to understand the role of economic ideas in the story. As Ben Rosamond puts it (2019, p. 414), 'the referendum result was delivered through an alliance between hyperglobalist neoliberals and nativist economic nationalists'. Quinn Slobodian, Dieter Plehwe and Lars Cornelissen have traced the development of 'neoliberals against Europe' in ways that help us see how Thatcherite free-marketeers came to see departure from the world's largest single market as the linchpin of their agenda (Slobodian, 2018; Slobodian and Plehwe, 2020; Cornelissen, 2021). Owen Worth makes the strongest claim that 'the major driving force behind Brexit was ideological, rather than the result of any "anti-establishment" backlash and was drawn from economic neoliberal ideals …' (Worth, 2017, p. 105). Drawing on these sources, but also making some modifications to their insights, the chapter advances two main arguments about the origins and role of distinctive economic ideas in the Brexit story.

First, where widespread lore portrays Margaret Thatcher and other Conservatives as supporting European institutions to pursue 'single market' liberalisation but then becoming hostile over steps towards a 'social Europe' and monetary union in the late 1980s, I emphasise that Thatcherites consistently rejected the notion that robust European institutions were desirable, *even for liberalisation.* More than being betrayed by a Europe that turned away from pro-market goals, Thatcher and some of her closest allies never endorsed the logic of the 'Single Market 1992' plan to begin with.

Second, I explore the roots of this early and consistent antipathy to EU institutions. Where other accounts often cast Brexiteers as especially committed neoliberals – most fully prioritising 'free market purity', as Worth puts it (2017, p. 104) – I portray them more as a peculiar, non-obvious variety of neoliberalism. To see the goal of open markets across European states as remotely plausible without strong supranational rules requires a very particular view of markets. The view that informed Thatcher's antipathies, and that her powerful leadership magnified into the dominant view of British Conservatives, developed in the intellectual and political context of mid-to-late-20th-century Anglo-American economic theory. Relative to other strands of neoliberalism, it stands out for emphasising that market openness can and should come about with little central authority.

Further highlighting the distinctiveness of such thinking, as I note in concluding, is the EU response to Brexit. Its insistence on the single market's 'indivisible freedoms' of goods, services, labour and capital seems powerfully neoliberal itself. At the core of Brexit, then, was a clash between two varieties of neoliberal ideas. Defenders of the highly institutionalised and central rule-focused EU openness regime confronted an Anglo-American neoliberalism centred on antipathy to federal authority.

In sum, this chapter modestly modifies other work on neoliberalism and Brexit with emphasis on more consistent Thatcherite rejection of EU authority and more distinctiveness of these ideas within neoliberalism. By highlighting these ideational roots of Brexit, we can better explain how a nationalist and nativist-tinged vote inaugurated 'Global Britain' as the key frame for the United Kingdom's (UK) economic future.

THATCHER'S CONSISTENT OPPOSITION TO EUROPEAN AUTHORITY *FOR LIBERALISATION*

Most observers of the EU or British politics know that the British Right began turning against Europe in the late 1980s. The Conservatives had been 'the party of Europe' into the 1980s, especially relative to a more anti-European Economic Community (EEC) Labour Party. They generally welcomed the liberalising 'Single Market 1992' programme codified in the Single European Act (SEA) of 1986. According to Thatcher herself and many later Brexiteers, Europe then 'betrayed' them (Spicer, 1992; Thatcher, 1993, p. 536; Cornelissen, 2021). As Gabriel Siles-Brügge summarises (2017, p. 12):

> Having empowered supranational institutions with the Single European Act in 1985 as a means of deregulating the European economic space, many [Conservatives] were incensed at then European Commission President Jacques Delors's rhetoric and measures in pursuit of a 'social Europe'.

In particular, Delors – a French Socialist – gave two speeches in 1988 that trumpeted a flood of Europe-level legislation and announced goals for European-level social policy. The UK's watershed moment came when Thatcher took the opportunity of a September 1988 speech in Bruges to respond with a phrase oft-invoked by Brexiteers: 'We have not successfully rolled back the frontiers of the state in Britain, only to see them re-imposed at a European level with a European super-state exercising a new dominance from Brussels' (Thatcher, 1988). Even some of the most sophisticated scholars of neoliberalism, like Slobodian and Plehwe, echo the core narrative that Thatcherites and other neoliberals basically supported the European project through the SEA, when it advanced 'the causes favored by neoliberals themselves', but turned against 'when it appeared that the French Socialist Delors … might take Europe in a more social democratic and redistributive direction' (Slobodian and Plehwe, 2020, p. 92).

Though this chapter does not aspire to test competing theories of European integration, it is worth noting that leading theories also implicitly support something like the 'betrayal' narrative. Andrew Moravcsik's 'liberal intergovernmentalism' (LI) posits that governments form preferences for certain policy outcomes that lead functionally to their preferences for certain European institutions (Moravcsik, 1998). LI's main rivals from 'neofunctionalist' or institutionalist theory share the same expectation – governments pursue certain substantive policy goals, typically to satisfy interest groups, and endorse supranational rules that help achieve them – while adding that European-level agents often play a brokering or persuading role to achieve integrative deals (Sandholtz and Sweet, 1998). These theories agree that national leaders delegate power to European institutions when they see it as serving their policy goals, but disagree over whether governments arrive at European deals on their own or through persuasion by supranational agents. Both schools encourage us to expect that the Thatcher government would support European institutional authority for liberalisation but would turn against it when a social policy agenda came on the table.

Some commentators further exaggerate this logic, seeing British neoliberals eager to bind Europe into an institutional cage of deregulation and market openness. Evoking the famous call to bind the continent into an open-market federation from Friedrich Hayek, a founding father of neoliberalism, Philippe Van Parijs (2018) describes 'Thatcher's plot' to build 'Hayek's trap':

> If there is one person who understood Hayek's message perfectly, it was Margaret Thatcher. She campaigned for her country to confirm its membership of the European Economic Community in 1975. When in office between 1979 and 1990, she strongly supported both the further unification of the common market – particularly through the 1986 Single European Act – and later its further expansion, made possible by the collapse of the Iron Curtain in 1989. In accordance with Hayek's argument, the increased mobility created by the deepening of the common market further disempowered Member States, while the increased heterogeneity created by the post-1989 enlargements further undermined the potential for the federation to take over the regulatory and redistributive powers that Member States were increasingly unable to exercise. This is Hayek's trap: member states disabled by their immersion in the single market, combined with a Union disabled by its heterogeneity. (van Parijs, 2018, p. 254)

There are two major problems, however, with British Conservatives' 'betrayal' narrative and its echoes from other observers. One is that it was and is strange to perceive much of a European turn away from Thatcher's own policy priorities in the late 1980s. In 1988 the liberalising '1992' agenda was in full swing, including high-salience steps like the capital liberalisation directive. It would continue to roll on well into the 1990s and beyond, with a flood of strongly liberalising legislation and also major developments in European jurisprudence that leaned massively in the direction of market openness (Armstrong and Bulmer, 1998; Grin, 2003; Jabko, 2006; Howarth and Sadeh, 2013; Schmidt, 2018). This liberalising trajectory of European policy-making had been roughly predicted by the British Foreign Office, whose analyses in the lead-up to the SEA argued that expanded majority voting on internal market issues would favour British policy preferences more often than not (Wall, 2008, p. 51). Though Delors and other continental actors certainly ramped up discourse about 'social Europe' around 1988, most observers saw and still see actual substantive steps on this agenda as very modest relative to internal market liberalisation (Höpner, 2018). Indeed, by the later 1990s, left-leaning European scholars were complaining that the whole EU architecture was fundamentally skewed towards market liberalisation (as Van Parijs emphasises in his language about 'Hayek's trap') (Scharpf, 1999). Additionally, even if the European agenda had actually turned more towards major steps in social policy, Britain had ways to limit or avoid them, as it did later in opting out of the still-quite-modest 'social chapter' of the Maastricht Treaty. This is not to dispute that around 1988, Thatcher and other Conservatives felt genuinely threatened by prospects of the European Commission (EC) developing significant powers in social policies. The point is just that this perceived threat was far from an obvious read of anything that was actually happening or likely to happen on the ground. It tells us more about these actors' prior beliefs about the nature of the European project.

It was more plausible for Thatcher's turn against Europe in the late 1980s to be motivated by concerns about steps in monetary integration, where much more significant movement was developing, but here the problem for the 'betrayal' narrative is that it is not obvious how much someone with Thatcher's substantive economic policy views should have perceived these developments as departing from her preferences. The most active terrain for debate inside Thatcher's government at the time concerned whether or not to join the Exchange Rate Mechanism (ERM) of the European Monetary System. Foreign Secretary Geoffrey Howe and Chancellor Nigel Lawson, who eventually forced Thatcher to accept joining the ERM by threatening to resign, were neoliberal economic 'dries' who saw this step as the best option for British economic goals (Lawson, 1992; Howe, 1994).[2] Also contested at the time was how Britain should approach emerging continental ambitions for monetary union. In Thatcher's government, only Howe saw much appeal in a single currency, but Lawson, diplomats like Stephen Wall and others shared Howe's concern that Thatcher hampered effective diplomacy on the topic by combining increasingly harsh anti-Brussels language with dismissive over-confidence that single currency talk would come to nothing (Lawson, 1992, p. 898; Howe, 1994, pp. 573–80; Young, 1999, p. 342; Wall, 2008, pp. 77–107). In other words, many of Thatcher's colleagues thought that Britain might still see gains or exert influence on its neighbours in these monetary discussions, and perceived that Thatcher preferred immediate self-exclusion from this terrain – not that monetary integration veered uncontrollably away from British interests.

The other problem with the 'betrayal' narrative, which is amply documented in the best-informed accounts (and for which I will add some evidence), is that it is flatly wrong historically to suggest that Thatcher and her most similarly minded colleagues ever accepted that European institutional empowerment was functionally necessary or even clearly good for their liberalisation agenda. As we can read in accounts by scholars like Mark Aspinwall (2004), journalists like Hugo Young (1999), politicians like Lawson (1992) or Howe (1994) or diplomats like Wall (2008), Thatcher resisted any change to the European treaties and repeatedly rejected the notion that the SEA reforms (and majority voting in particular) were necessary to advance her preferred policy agenda. She was eventually persuaded by her colleagues to *accept* SEA institutional reforms – most importantly expanded majority voting on internal market issues – but consistently characterised them as unfortunate elements of European bargaining about liberalisation. Her own words could not be more explicit. In March 1985, after the first European Council that touched on both the liberalising 'White Paper on Completion of the Single Market' and proposals for EEC institutional reform, she said:

> Now, needless to say, we in the UK are enthusiasts for the completion of the common market and will be working very hard for that ... We are not interested in changing the Treaty as far as majority voting is concerned ... But there are quite a number of things that can be done with the present treaty. Europe is not a Community designed to manufacture more and more regulations, but a Community to free up markets and not, in fact, to put increasing shackles on them. (Thatcher, 1985a)

In July 1985, after Thatcher was outraged by an Italian-led move at the Milan European Council to convene an intergovernmental conference to discuss treaty reforms relating to both the White Paper and institutional reforms (De Ruyt, 1987, p. 62), she told the House of Commons:

> I do not think that an intergovernmental conference is necessary. We could have agreed great improvements in decision-making on the matters that were on the table, and that we had circulated well before the meeting. Some of us wished to; others wanted to go further than that, and they called an intergovernmental conference ... One of those proposed treaty amendments at the intergovernmental conference would change the unanimity rule, and I think most of us – I certainly – would wish to keep the unanimity rule on directives which could be quite vital to many of our industries ... It is important that the internal market be completed, but I think it can be completed keeping the unanimity rule. (Thatcher, 1985b)

In December 1985, at a midnight press conference immediately after final SEA negotiations where she reluctantly accepted expanded majority voting and some other institutional reforms, she said:

> We could have done a great many of the things which have been done here with treaty changes, we could have done without treaty changes, had we agreed to go about it that way. Now, people very much wanted an intergovernmental conference, so they had one ... I think we could have done what we have done ... that we could have done by agreement without it ... but if they wanted to do it this way, so be it. (Thatcher, 1985c)

A few days later she explained the deal to the Commons in the same terms:

> We could have done it by agreement among the same people, who would be called a European Council instead of an intergovernmental conference. If one belongs to a Community, one has to take into account other people's views, particularly if one wants some of the changes that are being made to enable some of our people to establish themselves in the Community, which they cannot now do. We wanted something from our European partners and they wanted something from us. It seemed a reasonable compromise. (Thatcher, 1985d)

It is difficult to imagine more direct evidence that Thatcher did not think that EC majority voting was functionally necessary or even helpful for her substantive goals of liberalisation. In her 1993 memoir she changed her tune slightly to fit the bargaining outcome, writing that 'more majority voting' was 'the price ... we had to pay' to get over other member states' resistance to liberalisation (Thatcher, 1993, p. 541), but otherwise she was quite forthright that this was not what actually happened. It was those other member states who insisted on expanding majority voting, not Britain, and she never wavered in the view that formal institutional empowerment of the EC was the wrong approach. Importantly, while some of her colleagues shared these views, like Norman Tebbit or Nicholas Ridley, equally neoliberal Conservatives like Howe or Leon Brittan consistently defended the SEA reforms as pragmatic and helpful to achieve liberalisation.

The record is unambiguous, then, that Thatcher consistently opposed substantial European authority even for her liberalising agenda. She did not want anyone to be 'caged' into European institutions, whether those institutions were making deep new commitments to liberalisation or not. This point should alter our understanding of the 'betrayal' narrative to which she later contributed. Again, that she and other anti-EC Conservatives *did* feel increasingly betrayed by EC developments after the mid-1980s is not in doubt. As she put it in her 1995 memoir (p. 473), '[t]he Single European Act, contrary to my intentions and my understanding of formal undertakings given at the time, provided new scope for the European Commission and the European Court to press forward in the direction of centralisation.' But in recognising that her dislike for European institutional authority always applied to areas of liberalisation as well, we see this objection to SEA 'centralisation' in a different light. Rather than objecting mainly to steps in social policy (where, again, little had happened and only modest steps were even plausibly imaginable), or to other European policies that the British disliked, like in agriculture (where considerable centralisation had long been achieved), Thatcher and her like-minded colleagues were reacting largely to centralisation within the Single Market 1992 programme itself. They certainly played up threats of a socialistic Europe or a German-dominated monetary zone, but most of the European action at the time was about empowerment of central institutions *for liberalisation*. Like many other observers, Thatcher was surprised at how far the single market project succeeded at shifting regulatory authority to Brussels in the late 1980s and 1990s. She had never wanted that to happen, and regretted allowing it.

THE ANGLO-AMERICAN SOURCES OF ANTI-FEDERAL NEOLIBERALISM

From Thatcher's hostility to internal market majority voting in the SEA to the Brexiteers' 'Global Britain' discourse runs a very straight ideational line. Thatcherite neoliberalism always rejected the notion that European-level authority could be good for markets, even given strong mandates to use that authority to advance liberalisation. It was this distinctive belief about economic governance that eventually allowed certain British neoliberals to ally with anti-openness hostility to the EU. To explain the larger Brexit story, we must back up further to consider the sources and logic of this belief.

The relatively simple part of this genealogy concerns the nationalist attachments of Thatcher and like-minded allies to British sovereignty. Such *souverainiste* views were well established in an anti-EEC minority of Conservatives when she appeared on the scene, and were rooted in old discourse about Britain's indivisible parliamentary sovereignty and ostensibly 'pragmatic' rejection of utopian (and socialist) continental institutional projects (Forster, 2002; Daddow, 2013). As Howe remarked in his memoirs about the 1988 Bruges speech, at that point, he 'began to see her as a natural member of the gallant but misguided back-bench group of Enoch Powells, Robin Turtons and Derek Walker-Smiths who had fought so long and hard against the European Communities Bill in 1971' (Howe, 1994, p. 538). Though Thatcher campaigned for EEC membership in the 1970s, some sources from the time already hint that she held relatively nationalistic views (Denham and Garnett, 2001, p. 323). The record holds no frank discussion of her decision-making at this time, but her outwardly pro-EEC position makes the most sense as driven by tactical politics: for a previously minor political figure (and first woman) to consolidate leadership of the 'party of Europe', she probably had to take this stance (Fontana and Parsons, 2015). Her early pro-EEC stance was also useful to signal a broad commitment to Western-alliance cohesion that Labour could not be trusted to sustain.[3]

The more mysterious components fall on the neoliberal side: why did it make sense to Thatcher and some colleagues to see hardline sovereignty views as consistent with the radical new discourse they came to champion on market openness? The previous section offered a proximate answer: Thatcher and many of her compatriots believed that 'the single market did not require supranational regulation' (to use Andrew Gamble's apt phrase about Thatcher's views on the SEA: Gamble, 2012, p. 227). If European liberalisation could be achieved without supranational institutional authority, it was not in tension with British sovereignty. But on the deeper question of why that belief took hold among certain British Conservatives, when many pro-market Europeans came to the opposite view – that much liberalisation in their region would come about through stronger European authority – the scholarly literature is not very clear.

Slobodian's magisterial history of neoliberalism (2018) draws a key distinction between anti- and pro-EU strands, but focuses mainly on central European figures and does not explore why British neoliberals ended up so strongly in the former group. As neoliberalism consolidated in the mid-20th century, he shows that most of its champions positioned themselves as 'universalist' proponents of broad frameworks for free trade. When the EEC proposal came along, the universalists interpreted it mainly as a dangerous compromise with French-led interventionism. However, their circles also included a minority of 'constitutionalists' – especially some German-speaking figures who were trained as lawyers rather than as economists – who thought the EEC could be a powerful tool for neoliberal goals. In this view, the movement for supranational European institutions might support a stronger set of open-market commitments than could be achieved otherwise. When the EEC format won out politically, many universalist neoliberals came to tolerate it, and in the 1980s welcomed the '1992' agenda (though many still disliked its institutions, as we have seen). In the 1990s, to which Slobodian has given additional recent attention in work with Plehwe, this account sees practically all neoliberals becoming broadly critical of the EU, mainly over issues relating to the euro. They also note, but do not explain, that leading British neoliberals mostly remained universalists and soon gravitated to especially sharp rejection of Europe:

> If the constitutionalist contingent of Euroskeptic neoliberals, with a preponderance of German-speaking and southern European participants, leaned toward internal reform, the British members of the Bruges Group [the first anti-EU think tank, founded by British arch-neoliberal Ralph Harris in 1988] edged toward rejection of the EU through the 1990s. (Slobodian and Plehwe, 2020, p. 97)

Cornelisson's recent article focuses more squarely on the British and Brexit, but he too observes British neoliberal hostility to Europe more than he explains it. Besides displaying their self-narrative of post-SEA betrayal, he highlights the 'bitter – but not altogether unexpected – disappointment' of both British and many continental neoliberals at the failure of a 'common currency' alternative to the euro (Cornelissen, 2021, p. 13). This proposal, which drew on Hayekian ideas about competition between parallel currencies, was floated by the British government several times from 1988 to 1990. But if it is surely true that many British neoliberals were unhappy at the other member states' quick rejection of this idea – first in January 1989, then repeatedly thereafter when the British brought it up – this complaint, like the Delors-social-policy-betrayal narrative, is not easy to interpret as a major reason to eventually call for Brexit. British neoliberals' dislike for the Eurozone certainly gave them further reasons for discomfort with the EU overall, but there was no question that they could remain in the single market without joining the euro. As I have begun to suggest by emphasising Thatcher's hostility to European authority for liberalisation itself, there is more of a story to tell about why Thatcherite neoliberals consistently (but also increasingly) disliked the EU's core single market project – not just the limited social policies, horse-traded agricultural and regional side payments or optional single currency zone that arose alongside it.

I now make a brief attempt to fill in that story. First, I highlight some old ambiguities in neoliberal thought about single market regulation. Then, I sketch conditions that contributed to the salience of a distinctively universalist and 'anti-federal' resolution of those ambiguities in Britain. We will see that some major threads of the story pass through America.

The ambiguities in question concern how much liberalisation in a single market requires supranational authority. They are nicely illustrated, if unconsciously, in the most famous neoliberal text on the topic: Hayek's 1939 proposal for a European federation. Hayek argued that a certain form of multi-level governance optimises economic liberty and dynamism. Markets flourish in a federal-style arena where central institutions ensure that 'goods, men and money can move freely over the [subunit] frontiers', but are otherwise limited to this function (plus defence). Mobility and competition across the subunits deters interventionism at their level, generating 'less government all round' (Hayek, 1939, pp. 133, 140).

At first glance, Hayek's design emphasises strong supranational rules, envisioning the 'cage' noted by Van Parijs. Alongside commitments to something like the EU's 'four freedoms', Hayek's vision in 1939 included a single currency (though later he came to prefer competing parallel currencies). At the same time, however, Hayek pictured that states in his federation retained considerable economic authority. Rather than achieving 'less government' at the state level through direct central prohibitions on state regulation, he thought that outcome would arise largely as a consequence of interstate mobility and competition. Consider the range of powers that Hayek's states would retain:

> While the states could, of course, exercise control of the qualities of goods and the methods of production employed, it must not be overlooked that, provided the state could not exclude commodities produced in other parts of the Union, any burden placed on a particular industry by state legislation would put it at a serious disadvantage as opposed to similar industries in other parts of the Union. As has been shown by experience in existing federations, even such legislation as the restriction of child labor or of working hours becomes difficult to carry out for the individual state ... Not only would the greater mobility between the states make it necessary to avoid all sorts of taxation which would drive capital or labor elsewhere, but there would also be considerable difficulties with many kinds of indirect taxation ... The whole armory of marketing boards and other forms of monopolistic organizations of individual industries will cease to be at the disposal of state governments. If they still want to assist particular groups of producers, they will have to do so by direct subsidies from funds raised by ordinary taxation. (Hayek, 1939, p. 134)

The main image here is one where mobile factors and competition put pressure on regulatory choices by states that still have the authority to regulate products, production processes or labour conditions, tax as they please, and even favour their constituents with discriminatory state aid. The only central rule implied in these passages is that 'states could not exclude commodities produced in other parts of the Union', and other language in the essay about free movement for 'goods, money and men' implies similar rules against explicit interstate protectionism in services, labour and capital. Overall, the idea seems to be that states would be legally barred from tariffs, quotas and other egregious interstate discrimination (except state aids?), and that these central rules would encourage enough mobility and competition to discipline the states' other interventionist temptations.

Then, however, Hayek points out that these relatively modest central requirements might not be sufficient to generate or protect the desired dynamics of mobility and competition:

> It is in fact likely that, in order to prevent evasions of the fundamental provisions securing free movement of men, goods, and capital, the restrictions it would be desirable for the constitution of the federation to impose on the freedom of the individual states would have to be even greater than we have hitherto assumed and that their power of independent action would have to be limited still further ... The experience in [the American and Swiss] federations makes it appear that ... it is scarcely sufficient to prohibit tariffs and similar obvious impediments to interstate commerce ... [A]ll the effects of protection can be achieved by means of such provisions as sanitary regulations, requirements of inspection, and the charging of fees for these and other administrative controls. In view of the inventiveness shown by state legislators in this respect, it seems clear that no specific prohibitions in the constitution of the federation would suffice to prevent such developments; the federal government would probably have to be given general restraining powers to this end. This means that the federation will have to possess the negative power of preventing individual states from interfering with economic activity in certain ways, although it may not have the positive power of acting in their stead. (Hayek, 1939, pp. 135, 141)

This second theme suggests much further-reaching central rules. These passages still envision selective (not complete) limits on state regulation – picturing the federation 'preventing individual states from interfering with economic activity *in certain ways*' – but Hayek now seems to envision stronger federal bans. These would presumably prohibit state policies that most obstruct free movement of economic factors, while leaving other 'interferences' to be disciplined by mobility.

I do not mean to suggest that Hayek's overall argument is flatly contradictory, but it is certainly ambiguous. A good Hayekian could be forgiven for asking: how much federal authority am I being told to support? The second theme seems to hint that the federation might need to directly forbid (and police?) different safety standards for goods, different qualifications for professional service providers, different labour rules or different regimes for financial-firm oversight. If it were forbidding these sorts of things, would it really allow states to favour their residents with discriminatory aid? How about procurement: if states could subsidise their residents, could they prefer locals for public contracts too?

Two developments after 1939 raised the stakes around these ambiguities. One was the vast expansion of state regulation everywhere in the 1960s and 1970s, magnifying questions about how much a neoliberal federation should directly prune it back. The other, a bit later, was that the world's two largest single markets came to display different resolutions of these questions.

The American federation displayed major features of Hayek's first image in 1939, and still does. It bars its states from engaging in 'purposeful discrimination', with exceptions for state aids and procurement, where US states systematically favour their citizens. While the federation has since come to set many standards or rules for goods, services, labour and capital – which Hayek would have regretted – these are mostly regulatory 'floors' that still allow states to experiment with (and perhaps compete over) additional requirements as they see fit. The federation pays little active legislative attention to single market issues, exercises practically no central administrative oversight of the states – no requirements that states inform the federation of their regulations, for example – and leaves arbitration of conflicts almost entirely to passive enforcement by courts. As Cass Sunstein summarised in an early comparison to Europe's single market project, America's internal market rests on a background architecture of governance that limits most protectionism, but does not substantively pursue free trade (Sunstein, 1988). In principle, it relies more on mobility and competition to limit state-level interventionism.

In Europe, meanwhile, Hayek's second theme seems to have been taken much more seriously. The EU construes as potential treaty violations any state rules or actions that 'hinder or make less attractive' interstate market access – a far stronger legal standard than America's. This includes state aids and procurement, where anti-discrimination rules are actively policed. Like the US, its courts play a powerful role in resolving conflicts, but unlike the US, the EU also pursues an active legislative and administrative project to require openness. Across the 'four freedoms' the EU attempts to enact and enforce the same general principles: default rules of centrally required 'mutual recognition' – meaning market access for goods, services, labour and capital mainly under country-of-origin regulation – with more elaborately negotiated regulatory 'harmonisation' where states balk at that default. This means that EU standards and rules are generally not floors: member states may set additional requirements only for their *own* citizens or firms, not for those from other states. Administratively, the EU requires notification of all relevant state regulation, tracks state respect of its rules with threats of infringement proceedings and shaming in a 'Single Market scoreboard', and commandeers states into systems like a central e-procurement framework and 'single digital gateways' to facilitate interstate mobility (Parsons et al., n.d.).

This EU-US contrast is relevant because it fleshes out different models of single market regulation that might both claim Hayekian-neoliberal inspiration. I want to argue that Thatcherite neoliberalism developed with intellectual and political ties to one of them and partly in contrast to the other. In the 1960s and 1970s, Anglo-American neoliberals steadily resolved neoliberalism's ambiguities in favour of Hayek's initial emphasis on less central authority, which also fit roughly with the American internal market model. Though I can only tell this story very briefly, I believe they did so because this interpretation of neoliberalism dovetailed with political-coalitional considerations in American politics and deep discursive traditions in the British domestic arena.

As a point of departure, Hayek himself contributed to this Anglo-American trajectory, though it was mostly carried forward by others. His presence from 1931 to 1950 at the London School of Economics (LSE), where he wrote *The Road to Serfdom* (1944), contributed to its emergence as the main British pole of neoliberal thought. His move to America from 1950 to 1962 was related to the even stronger consolidation of neoliberal influence at the University of Chicago. During his American years, his thinking moved further away from the Austrian and Germanic strands of neoliberalism, much of which emphasised a strong state as the backbone of market openness, towards the minimisation of central rules. He became best known for advocating dynamic 'evolutionary' processes of change, with a strong emphasis on decentralised interjurisdictional policy competition (Streit and Wolgemuth, 2000).

The main arc of Anglo-American neoliberal thought in this period was led by Americans, whose ascendancy in economics worldwide was supported by wealthy universities, superpower status, and the transition they led to mathematical social science. All the most salient contributions of conservative American economists from the 1950s to the 1990s effectively argued for decreasing central/federal economic authority and relying on interstate policy competition to discipline local interventionism. For Milton Friedman, who became the world's best-known neoliberal thinker in the 1960s, the main 20th-century threat to markets was big, distant government. Even if markets suffered from local protectionism or private monopoly, central government fixes were worse than these diseases. As his 'Chicago School' colleague George Stigler theorized, regulation is subject to business capture 'as a rule' (Stigler, 1971). But the bigger the jurisdiction, Friedman argued, the less easily citizens can move to escape bad governance, so '[i]f government is to exercise power, better in the county than in the state, better in the state than in Washington' (Friedman, 1962, p. 3). James Buchanan's 'Virginia School' of public choice centered on the same idea about fiscal competition, echoing Hayek that '[t]otal government intrusion into the economy should be smaller … the greater the extent to which taxes and expenditures are decentralized' (Brennan and Buchanan, 1980, p. 216). Richard Posner led the incorporation of these theories into legal debates with seminal contributions to the 'law and economics' literature (Posner, 1973). A growing complex of think tanks nurtured these ideas into policy proposals, like Stanford's Hoover Institution, the American Enterprise Institute, the Heritage Foundation and the Cato Institute (Teles, 2008).

To my knowledge, nowhere in this vast literature did Hayek's second theme receive substantial attention.[4] This is striking, given that a leading original motivation for the US Constitution was to empower the federation to ensure the free flow of interstate commerce, and also that especially by the later 20th century, there was no shortage of interstate regulatory barriers to which American neoliberals might have objected. When they finally achieved major federal power with Ronald Reagan in 1980, the US states were actively protectionist in procurement and state aids, generally did not recognise each other's professional licensing, routinely set varying standards for goods (either on top of federal 'floors' or in their absence), and maintained a complex patchwork of varying financial rules. All these things are still true, because American neoliberals were uninterested in them. Rather than invoking federal commerce authority to promote internal market openness, Reagan and his political descendants from Newt Gingrich to Paul Ryan focused on 'returning power to the states' with a 'new federalism', a 'devolution revolution', and the notion that in regulation, federal government should step back and 'states should be encouraged to take the lead' (Scheiber, 2000; Kousser, 2014; Ryan, 2016). In parallel, an increasingly powerful 'federalist' movement in conservative jurisprudence 'frequently seem[ed] preoccupied with protecting state autonomy as an end in itself' (Halberstam, 2004, p. 795).

Why did American neoliberals play up antipathy to federal authority and minimise state-level impediments to free-flowing markets? For one thing, their home arena featured unusually high geographic mobility and interstate exchange, despite the undeniable presence of interstate regulatory barriers (not, as many people assume, because there were no such barriers). That presumably made Hayek's first image seem especially plausible. Even today, American interstate trade is roughly twice as dense as that across EU countries, and interstate mobility is 10–20 times as high as in Europe (Bonin et al., 2008; Pacchioli, 2012; Kaplan and Schulhofer-Woll, 2015). Another broad context that favoured this interpretation was the Cold War. American anti-communism was especially virulent, and the USSR kept the evils of big government front and centre. The most important and proximate causes, however, were two features of the domestic political landscape.

First, American neoliberalism was largely a reaction to Roosevelt's New Deal (Nash, 1976). FDR revolutionised the role of the federal government, vastly expanding federal authority to pursue progressive agendas – including a legal revolution in which the constitutional Commerce Clause was reinterpreted to authorise this expansion by arguing that practically any activity could affect interstate commerce (Friedman and Deacon, 2011). Post-New Deal conservatives perceived federal authority, including the commerce authority itself, as something to restrain. Second, and most concretely, the 'Reagan revolution' was the result of a long-developing alliance that strongly foreshadowed the Brexit neoliberal-nativist coalition, connecting neoliberal economics with a southern movement for 'states' rights' (Carmines and Stimson, 1989; Schickler, 2016). Southern racists reacted bitterly against the incorporation of Blacks into the New Deal coalition and the subsequent civil rights movement. It took time to forge their alliance with pro-business Republicans (their old enemies), but the two eventually found common cause against progressive federal authority. The first national-level fusion came in Senator Barry Goldwater's failed presidential candidacy in 1964, which combined a Friedman-advised economic programme with opposition to civil rights. As they worked out this realignment, which finally consolidated with Reagan, conservative Americans thus had powerful reasons to favour Hayek's first image. Given that federal authority seemed so inclined to dangerous expansion, it should only police the most egregious state protectionism. Otherwise states should be free to compete to attract mobile firms and people – even including some rather odd kinds of 'competition', like excluding each other's licensed professionals or disbursing preferential contracts.

In Britain, meanwhile, similar ideas percolated more slowly and through somewhat different mechanisms. Several British economists contributed to the early days of neoliberalism, most famously LSE's Lionel Robbins. He drafted the programme for the Hayek-initiated Mont Pelerin Society, whose annual meetings became the key forum for neoliberal thinking worldwide. Though Robbins and most other pro-market economists participated in government planning during World War II, many came to interpret those efforts as the lead-in to Labour's major expansion of the welfare state after 1945 – informing calls for restraining interventionism much like American reactions to the New Deal (Tribe, 2009). Deepening Anglo-American academic integration encouraged this parallel development, above all at LSE, to the point that some accounts of the postwar economics profession in Britain characterise it as 'economics in mid-Atlantic' (Baumol, 1995; Backhouse, 2000). In terms of policy advocacy, however, British academics were more integrated with political elites than their American colleagues, and Conservative Party loyalism seems to have muted their critiques during the 'postwar consensus' period of alternating Conservative and Labour governments (Tribe, 2009, p. 88). Instead, neoliberalism incubated mainly in the new setting of the Institute for Economic Affairs (IEA), created in 1955 by free-market entrepreneur (and chicken farmer) Anthony Fisher, economist Ralph Harris, and LSE-trained pamphleteer and editor Arthur Seldon. As Richard Cockett chronicles best, the IEA's events and publications cultivated neoliberal ideas for figures like Sir Keith Joseph and the young Thatcher, including frequent connections to Friedman and other Americans (Cockett, 1995). Later the IEA's think tank role was complemented by the Centre for Policy Studies (CPS, created by Joseph in 1974) and the Adam Smith Institute (created in 1977 by Scottish free-marketeers after several years in American think tanks). Economic journalists Samuel Brittan and Peter Jay were other key vectors for the introduction of these ideas, especially Friedman's monetarism.

When Thatcher won the 1979 election, then, she and her closest allies had been steeped in American-tinged neoliberalism for some time. A Friedman stop in London in early 1980, to promote his television miniseries *Free to Choose*, was treated 'almost as a state visit', according to the Margaret Thatcher Foundation's account (Margaret Thatcher Foundation, 2021). Unlike Reagan's administration, though, Thatcher's government did not come in with strong agreement around its economic agenda – and especially not around how its American-inflected economic ideas related to Europe. The economic policy tussles between Conservative 'wets' and 'dries' are well known (Holmes, 2019). Even Thatcher, Howe and other leading 'dries' were still working out their agenda – both what they wanted to do and what they could get past their internal skeptics – and received much criticism from Friedman for insufficient zeal (Frazer, 1982). On the EEC in particular, British neoliberals in the 1970s had studiously avoided discussion. Cockett (1995, p. 329) describes Europe as 'the issue that dared not speak its name' at the IEA, which issued no substantial publications on the EEC after one in 1972 (a well-informed and largely pro-EEC paper by an economist who had worked in Brussels: Lewis, 1972). Though I do not know of evidence from the period that offers much direct insight into this non-barking dog, the absence of EEC discussions within circles who were otherwise eager to provoke the Conservative establishment suggests to me that divisions on the topic were already substantial among the 'dries' themselves. Going forward from 1979, further evidence of those divisions becomes increasingly clear in the record, and unsurprisingly consolidated in the SEA process that raised newly concrete questions of EEC reform. Howe became the most prominent neoliberal to interpret EEC institutions mainly as pragmatically useful for British policy goals. Thatcher clarified her rejection of that view. A few years later, the European divergences between these two figures would be the immediate reason for Thatcher's ouster.

Still to be explained, though, are why Thatcher and certain other British free-marketeers were drawn so strongly to American-style anti-federal neoliberalism, and why this strand eventually dominated Britain despite Thatcher's ejection by Howe and other more pro-EC Conservatives.

On the first point, as I hinted at the beginning of this section, conventional wisdom about sources of British Euroscepticism provides plausible answers. Thatcher did not rely as Reagan did on racist allies implacably opposed to federally enforced civil rights, but her political context provided powerful rationales to filter neoliberal ideas in ways that foregrounded opposition to European-level authority: the profoundly anti-federal tradition of parliamentary sovereignty, and ostensibly 'pragmatic' mistrust of continental rationalism in the land of common law, the unwritten constitution, and gradual change. Of course these traditions did not *have* to be interpreted to reject European authority so strongly, as we see in the different views of staunch neoliberals like Howe or Brittan. On Europe they stuck with the interpretation of most Conservatives since the late 1960s, who had decided that the 'pragmatic' course was to participate in the EEC, whatever its flaws, and steer it towards liberalisation. Explaining precisely why Thatcher, Ridley or Tebbit rejected that turn would take us into idiosyncratic individual biographies. But as Jon Elster notes in a famous treatment of visible but non-deterministic causal mechanisms, '[w]e cannot tell ahead of time what will become of the child of an alcoholic, but if he or she turns out either a teetotaler or an alcoholic, we may suspect that we know why' (Elster, 1998, p. 45). British Conservatives could read their late 20th-century heritage into various positions on European institutions, but we can see the powerful discursive conditions that encouraged anti-federal neoliberalism.

On the second point, Cary Fontana and I have traced how Thatcher personally generated powerful mechanisms that amplified British Euroscepticism and led towards Brexit, with an important catalytic role for her fall itself (Fontana and Parsons, 2015). In all scenarios, I should note, Britain's relationship with Europe would presumably have been difficult in the 1990s and beyond. The politics of the ERM were especially problematic, and a monetary union opt-out was likely in any case. Support for European integration dropped everywhere in the 1990s amid economic recession and Eastern enlargement. Nonetheless, a Thatcher heart attack before 1988 would have weakened many of the mechanisms that turned the Conservatives to hard Euroscepticism. New generations of Conservatives defined themselves in Thatcher's image, inspired both by her ideological boldness and the boom growth and Cold War 'victory' in the late 1980s. Her high-profile turn against Europe in 1988 and subsequent turfing-out by her party's grandees then defined Euroscepticism as a litmus test of faithfulness to the Iron Lady. (Nigel Farage left the party at this point.) Thatcher reinforced this test from retirement, actively encouraging the biggest rebellion in party history over the Maastricht Treaty.[5] Furthermore, though this acrimony contributed to the Conservative's electoral wipeout in 1997, Tony Blair's landslide ironically reinforced the hardliners: more centrist pro-European Conservatives lost as the party was truncated back to safe seats held mostly by Thatcherite diehards. In the Conservative leadership selection of 1997, though most party constituency chairpersons supported the notably pro-EU Kenneth Clarke, the parliamentary party ruled him out and accepted Lady Thatcher's endorsement of William Hague, a slick 36-year-old who promised supporters to reject euro membership. While the party floundered over the next two electoral cycles, activist carriers of the Thatcher flame made Euroscepticism the main constituency-level selection mechanism for parliamentary candidates (Parsons and Weber, 2011). By the time that David Cameron retooled the 'nasty party' towards the centre and greater electoral success after 2008, the Brexit scene was set. Cameron eventually floated a referendum in hopes of silencing his rebellious ultra-Eurosceptical wing and weakening the electoral challenge from Farage's UK Independence Party (UKIP). We know what followed.

There is much more to the Brexit story, of course, but I have now traced key threads of it that relate to economic ideas. Though the eventual 'Leave' vote skewed towards a Polanyi-esque reaction against markets, Owen Worth is right that the main impetus to this process came from a certain form of neoliberalism. Politicians who saw themselves as the political heirs of Margaret Thatcher demanded the referendum to begin with. Their distinctively Anglo-American, anti-federal form of neoliberalism allowed them to make common cause against the EU with opponents of openness. While there is no small dose of ideological flexibility and opportunism in this tale – personified by Boris Johnson – its main lines and the current government's 'Global Britain' discourse and policies derive from this Thatcherite heritage.

CONCLUSION

This chapter has focused on the logic and historical sources of Thatcherite neoliberalism as they relate to the EU, but the full case for the distinctiveness of these economic ideas requires a contrast to other forms of pro-market thinking. By way of conclusion, let me note how sharply Britain's negotiations to exit the EU highlight that contrast.

The basic goal of Britain's Brexit negotiators was to liberate themselves from EU authority while retaining as much access as possible to the EU single market. This made good sense to them: far from leaving the EU to close themselves off from their neighbours, Thatcherite Brexiteers were seeking to shed the EU legal system, centralised regulatory processes, budget contributions and various side payments that they had long believed to be unnecessary (and actively unhelpful) for healthy markets in the neighbourhood. After all, as the IEA's Director of Public Policy, Ryan Bourne, explained just before the referendum, today's EU is simply 'not a free market institution'. Disputing the view of a Spanish neoliberal that the EU had largely implemented Hayek's federation, he emphasised that the EU's centralising approach 'has simply ignored Hayek's later works in opposition to constructive [*sic*] order and in favor of the evolution of institutions' (Bourne, 2016).

When we look at the main lines of the EU response to Brexit, however, it seems very odd to describe it as 'not a free market institution'. The EU negotiating position sounded like a direct manifestation of the second theme in Hayek's 1939 essay. Britain could not 'cherry pick' selective internal market access, explained EU negotiator Michel Barnier, due to the 'indivisibility' of the 'four freedoms' guaranteed by the single market (Barnier, 2017). Importantly, this position was not strongly rooted in legal limits, economic feasibility or electoral appeals. There was no legal reason why the EU and Britain could not negotiate distinct arrangements across various aspects of the single market (Barnard, 2017). Economists noted that in many ways the freedoms of goods, services, labour and capital make more sense as substitutes than as necessary complements (Koller and Müller, 2017). Nor were the 'four freedoms' especially popular at this point in any EU member state. Instead it reflected a defence of the core institutional commitments in the treaties, reinforced by EU leaders' concern about the precedent of allowing members to renegotiate selective deals. As Wolfgang Münchau explained in the *Financial Times*, 'the logic of the four freedoms is not based on economic but political reasoning'. The 'very essence' of the EU is a political commitment to these strong, centrally defined rules for openness (Münchau, 2017).

Is the Brexiteer position in this confrontation the 'more' neoliberal one, reflecting a more radical and 'purer' commitment to markets? Anglo-American neoliberals like to characterise their stance in this way, as do many of their progressive critics, but their claim to that status is not exactly obvious. Relative to EU doctrine, they certainly argue for more decentralised political authority and more reliance on interstate competition and mobility to achieve economic liberty and dynamism. On the other hand, in so doing they downplay the first economic problem that Hayek's federation (and the American constitution) sought to solve: *state*-level temptations to obstruct free-flowing markets. Moreover, they routinely ally themselves with state-level opponents of openness, both economically and socially in terms of immigration, cultural issues and racial equality. Meanwhile the EU's neoliberal 'four freedoms' project makes its own set of compromises with other goals, allowing a variety of market-mitigating logics into its central architecture of regulations and transfers, but still attempts to require and enforce interstate market access far more systematically than any other polity in history. Today it is hard to say on which side of the English Channel we see more 'real' faith in markets, but we can see that these distinct economic ideas lead to very different politics.

NOTES

1. For an excellent compilation of speeches and other materials, see the 'Global Britain reading list' published by the House of Commons Library (2020). Perhaps the most aggressive frame is an image of London as 'Singapore-on-Thames', though this phrase emerged in the media, not directly from Conservatives. Wikipedia offers a surprisingly good genealogy of the phrase, see Wikipedia (2021).
2. Lawson did resign in October 1989 over policy fights with Thatcher's economic adviser Alan Walters, making it near-impossible for Thatcher to resist a call for her next Chancellor, John Major, to join the ERM a year later.
3. Thanks to Christopher Lord for this point.
4. Some relatively less conservative participants in debates over American federalism touch on related issues, like Inman and Rubinfeld (2020), but still only lightly. Their book has no direct discussion of the strength of single market rules despite featuring a chapter on regulatory federalism and one on the EU.
5. Note that this rebellion was an internal ideological fight, not an electoral strategy. As John Major put it (1999, p. 697): 'The notion that Britain in 1997 was racked by anxiety over Europe is pure nonsense. Conservative politicians were. The electorate was not.' Voters shifted massively to a Labour Party that was more pro-EU than ever.

REFERENCES

Armstrong, K. and Bulmer, S. (1998). *Governance of the Single European Market*. Manchester University Press.

Aspinwall, M. (2004). *Rethinking Britain and Europe: Plurality Elections, Party Management and British Policy on European Integration*. Manchester University Press.

Backhouse, R. (2000). Economics in Mid-Atlantic: British Economics, 1945–95. In A.W. Coats (ed.), *The Development of Economics in Western Europe since 1945* (pp. 19–39). Routledge.

Barnard, C. (2017). Brexit and the EU Internal Market. In F. Fabbrini (ed.), *The Law and Politics of Brexit* (pp. 201–18). Oxford University Press.

Barnier, M. (2017). *Protecting Citizen's Rights in the Negotiations with the UK* [speech]. Speech by Michel Barnier at the 7th State of the Union Conference, Florence, Italy, 5 May 2017. https://ec.europa.eu/commission/presscorner/detail/en/SPEECH_17_1236 (accessed 4 September 2021).

Baumol, W. (1995). What's Different about European Economics? *Kyklos*, *48*(2), 187–92.

Becker, S.O., Fetzer, T., and Novy, D. (2017). Who Voted for Brexit? A Comprehensive District-Level Analysis. *Economic Policy*, *32*(92), 601–50.

Bonin, H., Eichhorst, W., and Florman, C. (2008). Geographic Mobility in the European Union. *IZA Research Report*, No. 19. https://www.iza.org/publications/r/111/geographic-mobility-in-the-european-union-optimising-its-economic-and-social-benefits (accessed 4 September 2021).

Bourne, R. (2016, 18 March). Hayek Would Have Been a Brexiteer. *Institute of Economics Affairs Blog*. https://iea.org.uk/blog/hayek-would-have-been-a-brexiteer (accessed 4 September 2021).

Brennan, G., and Buchanan, J. (1980). *The Power to Tax: Analytic Foundations of a Fiscal Constitution*. Cambridge University Press.

Calhoun, C. (2016). Brexit Is a Mutiny against the Cosmopolitan Elite. *New Perspectives Quarterly*, *33*(3), 50–58.

Carmines, E., and Stimson, J.A. (1989). *Issue Evolution: Race and the Transformation of American Politics*. Princeton University Press.

Cockett, R. (1995). *Thinking the Unthinkable: Think-tanks and the Economic Counter-Revolution 1931–1983*. HarperCollins Publishers.

Cornelissen, L. (2021). Elements of Neoliberal Euroscepticism: How Neoliberal Intellectuals Came to Support Brexit. *British Politics* (online), 1–18. https://doi.org/10.1057/s41293-020-00155-3.

Daddow, O. (2013). Margaret Thatcher, Tony Blair and the Eurosceptic Tradition in Britain. *The British Journal of Politics and International Relations*, *15*(2), 210–27.

De Ruyt, J. (1987). *L'Acte unique européen*. Editions de l'Université de Bruxelles.

Denham, A., and Garnett, M. (2001). *Keith Joseph*. Routledge.
Elster, J. (1998). A Plea for Mechanisms. In P. Hedstrom and R. Swedberg (eds), *Social Mechanisms: An Analytical Approach to Social Theory* (pp. 45–73). Cambridge University Press.
Fontana, C., and Parsons, C. (2015). 'One Woman's Prejudice': Did Margaret Thatcher Cause Britain's Anti-Europeanism? *JCMS: Journal of Common Market Studies*, *53*(1), 89–105.
Forster, A. (2002). *Euroscepticism in Contemporary British Politics: Opposition to Europe in the Conservative and Labour Parties since 1945*. Routledge.
Frazer, W. (1982). Milton Friedman and Thatcher's Monetarist Experience. *Journal of Economic Issues*, *16*(2), 525–33.
Friedman, M. (1962). *Capitalism and Freedom*. University of Chicago Press.
Friedman, B., and Deacon, D. (2011). A Course Unbroken: The Constitutional Legitimacy of the Dormant Commerce Clause. *Virginia Law Review*, *97*(8), 1877–938.
Gamble, A. (2012). Europe and America. In B. Jackson and R. Saunders (eds), *Making Thatcher's Britain* (pp. 218–33). Cambridge University Press.
Grin, G. (2003). *The Battle of the Single European Market*. Routledge.
Halberstam, D. (2004). Of Power and Responsibility: The Political Morality of Federal Systems. *Virginia Law Review*, *90*(3), 731–834.
Hayek, F. (1939). The Economic Conditions of Interstate Federalism. *New Commonwealth Quarterly*, *5*(2), 131–49.
Hayek, F. (1944). *The Road to Serfdom*. Routledge.
Holmes, M. (2019). *The First Thatcher Government, 1979–1983: Contemporary Conservatism and Economic Change*. Routledge.
Hopkin, J. (2017). When Polanyi Met Farage: Market Fundamentalism, Economic Nationalism, and Britain's Exit from the European Union. *British Journal of Politics and International Relations*, *19*(3), 465–78.
Höpner, M. (2018, 19 November). Social Europe Is a Myth: Why a More Social EU Sometimes Needs Protection against Too Much Europe. *International Politics & Society*. https://www.ips-journal.eu/regions/europe/social-europe-is-a-myth-3037/ (accessed 4 September 2021).
House of Commons Library. (2020, 29 January). Brexit Reading List: Global Britain. *UK Parliament*. https://commonslibrary.parliament.uk/research-briefings/cbp-8338/ (accessed 4 September 2021).
Howarth, D., and Sadeh, T. (eds) (2013). *The Political Economy of Europe's Incomplete Single Market*. Routledge.
Howe, G. (1994). *Conflict of Loyalty*. Palgrave Macmillan.
Inman, R., and Rubinfeld, D. (2020). *Democratic Federalism: The Economics, Politics, and Law of Federal Governance*. Princeton University Press.
Jabko, N. (2006). *Playing the Market: A Political Strategy for Uniting Europe, 1985–2005*. Cornell University Press.
Kaplan, G., and Schulhofer-Woll, S. (2015). Understanding the Long-Run Decline in Interstate Migration. *Federal Reserve Bank of Minneapolis*, Working Paper No. 697.
Koller, W., and Müller, G. (2017, 8 November). Brexit, the Four Freedoms and the Indivisibility Dogma. *Voxeu.org*. https://voxeu.org/article/brexit-four-freedoms-and-indivisibility-dogma (accessed 4 September 2021).
Kousser, T. (2014). How America's 'Devolution Revolution' Reshaped Its Federalism. *Revue francaise de science politique*, *64*(2), 265–87.
Lawson, N. (1992). *Memoirs of a Tory Radical*. Bantam.
Lewis, W.R. (1972). *Rome or Brussels…?* Institute for Economic Affairs.
Major, J. (1999). *John Major: The Autobiography*. HarperCollins.
Margaret Thatcher Foundation. (2021). Thatcher, Hayek and Friedman. https://www.margaretthatcher.org/archive/Hayek.
Moravcsik, A. (1998). *The Choice for Europe: Social Purpose and State Power from Messina to Maastricht*. Cornell University Press.
Münchau, W. (2017, 12 November). Europe's Four Freedoms Are Its Very Essence. *Financial Times*. https://www.ft.com/content/49dc02dc-c637-11e7-a1d2-6786f39ef675 (accessed 4 September 2021).
Nash, G. (1976). *The Conservative Intellectual Movement in America since 1945*. Intercollegiate Studies Institute (ISI).

Norris, P., and Inglehart, R. (2019). *Cultural Backlash: Trump, Brexit, and Authoritarian Populism*. Cambridge University Press.

Pacchioli, C. (2012). Is the EU Internal Market Suffering from an Integration Deficit? *CEPS Working Documents* No. 348.

Parker, G. (2021, 3 January). Johnson Prepares 'Global Britain' Relaunch in Wake of Brexit. *Financial Times*. https://www.ft.com/content/a377fbc1-df1c-4de9-8660-5862b51ecd7f (accessed 4 September 2021).

Parsons, C., and Weber, T. (2011). Cross-Cutting Issues and Party Strategy in the European Union. *Comparative Political Studies*, *44*(4), 383–411.

Parsons, C., Matthijs, M., and Springer, B. (n.d.). Why Did Europe's Single Market Surpass America's? [Manuscript submitted for publication].

Polanyi, K. (1944). *The Great Transformation*. Beacon.

Posner, R. (1973). *Economic Analysis of Law*. Little Brown.

Prime Minister's Office. (2020, 31 December). Prime Minister's New Year's Message: 31 December 2020. *Gov.uk*. https://www.gov.uk/government/news/prime-ministers-new-years-message-31-december-2020 (accessed 4 September 2021).

Rosamond, B. (2019). Brexit and the Politics of UK Growth Models. *New Political Economy*, *24*(3), 408–21.

Ryan, P. (2016). *A Better Way: Our Vision for a Confident America*. https://web.archive.org/web/20181224224320/https://abetterway.speaker.gov/ (accessed 4 September 2021).

Sandholtz, W., and Sweet, A.S. (eds) (1998). *European Integration and Supranational Governance*. Oxford University Press.

Scharpf, F. (1999). *Governing in Europe: Effective and Democratic?* Oxford University Press.

Scheiber, H. (2000). Devolution and Federalism in Historical Perspective. In L. Levy and K. Karst (eds), *Encyclopedia of the American Constitution* (pp. 775–8). Palgrave Macmillan.

Schickler, E. (2016). *Racial Realignment: The Transformation of American Liberalism, 1932–1965*. Princeton University Press.

Schmidt, S. (2018). *The European Court of Justice and the Policy Process: The Shadow of Case Law*. Oxford University Press.

Siles-Brügge, G. (2017). Taking back Control? The Discursive Constraints on Post-Brexit Trade Policy. In Scott Lavery, Lucia Quaglia, and Charlie Dannreuther (eds), *The Political Economy of Brexit and the UK's National Business Model*, SPERI Paper No. 41 (pp. 11–16). Sheffield Political Economy Research Institute.

Slobodian, Q. (2018). *Globalists: The End of Empire and the Birth of Neoliberalism*. Harvard University Press.

Slobodian, Q., and Plehwe, D. (2020). Neoliberals against Europe. In W. Callison and Z. Manfredi (eds), *Mutant Neoliberalism: Market Rule and Political Rupture* (pp. 89–111). Fordham University Press.

Spicer, M. (1992). *A Treaty Too Far: A New Policy for Europe*. FourthEstate.

Stigler, G. (1971). The Theory of Economic Regulation. *Bell Journal of Economics and Management*, *2*(1), 3–21.

Streit, M E., and Wohlgemuth, M. (2000). The Market Economy and the State: Hayekian and Ordoliberal Conceptions. In P. Koslowski (ed.), *The Theory of Capitalism in the German Economic Tradition: Historism, Ordo-Liberalism, Critical Theory, Solidarism* (pp. 224–71). Springer.

Sunstein, C. (1988). Protectionism, the American Supreme Court, and Integrated Markets. In R. Bieber, R. Dehousse, and J. Weiler (eds), *1992: One European Market?* (pp. 127–50). Nomos.

Teles, S. (2008). *Rise of the Conservative Legal Movement: The Battle for Control of the Law*. Princeton University Press.

Thatcher, M. (1985a, 30 March). Press Conference after Brussels European Council. https://www.margaretthatcher.org/document/106004 (accessed 4 September 2021).

Thatcher, M. (1985b, 2 July). Commons Sitting of 2 July 1985, vol. 82, col. 187-8. https://api.parliament.uk/historic-hansard/commons/1985/jul/02/european-council-milan (accessed 4 September 2021).

Thatcher, M. (1985c, 4 December). Press Conference after Luxembourg European Council [speech]. *Margaret Thatcher Foundation*. https://www.margaretthatcher.org/document/106187 (accessed 4 September 2021).

Thatcher, M. (1985d, 5 December). Commons Sitting of 5 December 1985, vol. 88, col. 431. https://api.parliament.uk/historic-hansard/commons/1985/dec/05/european-council-luxembourg (accessed 4 September 2021).

Thatcher, M. (1988, 20 September). Speech to the College of Europe ('The Bruges Speech') [speech]. *Margaret Thatcher Foundation*. https://www.margaretthatcher.org/document/107332 (accessed 4 September 2021).

Thatcher, M. (1993). *The Downing Street Years*. Harper.

Thatcher, M. (1995). *The Path to Power*. Harper.

Tribe, K. (2009). Liberalism and Neoliberalism in Britain, 1930–1980. In P. Mirowski and D. Plehwe (eds), *The Road from Mont Pèlerin: The Making of Neoliberal Thought Collective* (pp. 68–97). Harvard University Press.

Vail, M. (2020). A Cautionary Tale: 'Brexit', Economic Citizenship, and the Political Perils of Neoliberalism. In S. Greer and J. Laible (eds), *The European Union after Brexit* (pp. 18–37). Manchester University Press.

Van Parijs, P. (2018). Fair Brexit for a Just Europe. In B. Martill and U. Staiger (eds), *Brexit and beyond: Rethinking the Futures of Europe* (pp. 251–7). UCL Press.

Wall, S. (2008). *A Stranger in Europe: Britain and the EU from Thatcher to Blair*. Oxford University Press.

Wikipedia. (2021). Singapore-on-Thames. *Wikipedia*. Retrieved 11 October, 2021, from https://en.wikipedia.org/wiki/Singapore-on-Thames (accessed 4 September 2021).

Worth, O. (2017). Reviving Hayek's Dream. *Globalizations*, *14*(1), 104–9.

Young, H. (1999). *This Blessed Plot: Britain and Europe from Churchill to Blair*. Overlook.

7. Brexit and Europe's political economy

Amy Verdun

INTRODUCTION[1]

On 31 January 2020 the United Kingdom (UK) left the European Union (EU). In the European Parliament (EP), Members of the European Parliament (MEPs) cried together and folded flags. It marked the end of an era. At the end of that year, after much agony, the EU-UK Trade and Cooperation Agreement (TCA) was signed on 24 December 2020 and the ratification was completed in April 2021. The TCA allows both entities tariff-free, quota-free access to markets for goods. Services are not part of the TCA. Part of the agreement are also fishing rights as well as cooperation in the area of security (e.g., in the area of information sharing security related to matters of internal security), but no mention of security and defence collaboration. There are still many unresolved issues. Some of these issues involve fishing matters (Reuters, 2021). But collaboration in security and defence matters is also crucial as demonstrated by the need to deal with the war in Ukraine that erupted following the Russian invasion on 24 February.

The arrangements made with the EU have left the situation internal to the UK not fully settled. The Northern Irish Protocol allows, for the time being, that customs and immigration matters are decided in a way that gives Northern Ireland a special status. Clearing of customs and immigration is done prior to the goods entering Northern Ireland. It avoids having to impose a hard border between Northern Ireland and the Republic of Ireland. This agreement has effectively produced a border in the Irish Sea and has made many unionists unhappy.

Besides the situation in Northern Ireland also the Scottish situation is not fully stable. Nationalists are musing about another independence referendum in Scotland (Politico, 2021a). Of the almost four million votes cast in the Brexit referendum in Scotland only 38 per cent were cast for 'leave' whereas 62 per cent voted for 'remain'. In 2014 an independence referendum took place that was narrowly lost (55 per cent voted no to independence with 45 per cent voting in favour of independence). At that time, within only a few days to hold the referendum, as it looked though a majority might vote in favour of independence, there was a lot of uncertainty about whether Scotland would have to leave the EU if it became independent from the UK.[2] Brexit has reinvigorated these nationalist sentiments in Scotland.

This chapter explores the relationship between Brexit and Europe's political economy in the post-Brexit era. It does so in the following way: How does the UK remain linked to the European political order? How is the UK related to the EU institutions? The chapter pays particular attention to economic, monetary and financial matters as well as the Single Market. Its bottom line is that the EU and the UK are bound to stay in close contact with one another and may find ways to keep close relations. The two entities will have both formal ties and informal ways to stay together. The challenge for the EU is to enable the UK to be close, but not to make rules that enable the UK effectively to benefit from the EU without being a member. The UK by contrast needs to signal domestically that it is able to decide alone, whilst avoiding major disruption to its economy. This strategy has been part and parcel of the UK Brexit strategy. To discuss these questions the chapter is structured as follows. The next section discusses briefly the path towards Brexit. The third section examines the most contentious issues from a political economy perspective, thereby covering the usual political economy issues, but also others that have an impact on the political economy dimension. The fourth section reviews the possible options for future relations. The final section concludes.

BREXIT IN THE MAKING

Five years before the UK left the EU, it was not at all clear that the referendum on the UK leaving the EU (held on 23 June 2016) would be one where a majority would favour 'leave' (Cini and Verdun, 2018). In part, the surprise came because most of the elites were in favour of 'remaining'. Even the majority of the Conservative government and the at the time main opposition parties (Labour and Liberal Democrats) were on the whole still more or less in favour of remaining, as were most people in the City of London as well as business owners – those who would be the typical 'Conservative' voter (James and Quaglia, 2019). Political economy issues, such as the overall economic well-being related to the UK membership of the EU were part of the rationality of why elites favoured remaining. Early assessments of why the Brexit referendum even occurred pointed to the choices made by then Prime Minister David Cameron who used the referendum to try to discipline Conservative backbenchers and his overly risky strategy to poach voters away from the UK Independence Party (Glencross, 2018). Another challenge was the paucity of the UK constitutional system that did not meet the needs for these kinds of situations (Eeckhout, 2018; Weale, 2018). Effectively, a slight majority of voters (52–48 per cent) were able to determine the course of the future of the UK, even if the referendum itself was formally only an advisory one.

In fact, right away, one of the main concerns was that it was unclear what UK voters actually wanted to get out of Brexit; no one really knew what Brexit would look like. More than anything, Brexit was an idea (see Parsons, Chapter 6 in this volume). Even though in the run-up to the referendum, it was not clear what would be done if a referendum was close. Numerous reports indicated that a second referendum was possible, especially because whether or not to hold a second referendum lay squarely in the hands of Parliament (Institute for Government, 2019). Yet, once the results came in, and in the ensuing months, a second referendum seemed not to be feasible. The arguments made were both legal and political, although as Richard Bellamy argues, from a philosophical point of view it is unclear why such a referendum was impossible (see Bellamy, Chapter 28 in this volume).

What was clear, however, was that the majority of UK voters were uneasy with the path that the EU was on. Looking at Eurobarometer statistics, UK voters had been for years the least enthusiastic about European integration and shared few ambitions for deeper integration. In spring 2016, as the UK prepared for the referendum, the UK scored the lowest on a number of questions on EU achievements. On the question 'Which of the following do you think is the most positive result of the EU? Firstly and then?' EU citizens as a whole identified 'the free movement of people, goods and services within the EU' and 'peace' as the two most important ones (at 55 per cent) and the euro in third place (32 per cent). Of those interviewed in the UK, 44 per cent chose 'the free movement of people, goods and services within the EU', 52 per cent chose peace, and only 5 per cent chose the euro (Standard Eurobarometer 85 'European citizenship', in European Commission, 2016a: 7). Likewise, if asked whether they felt a citizen of the EU, in the UK, only 28 per cent answered 'yes definitely' and 25 per cent yes to some extent, with 25 per cent and 20 per cent, respectively, responding 'no not really' or 'no definitely not' (Standard Eurobarometer 85 'European citizenship', in European Commission, 2016a: 16). UK citizens were the only ones of the 28 member states who had a score higher than 50 per cent to the question whether they saw themselves as their nationality only (in the UK 62 per cent) – not as European. All other member states had 50 per cent or lower answers to the same question; in other member states, the identity was to national and European (only Cyprus and Bulgaria had rates slightly below 50 per cent, see Standard Eurobarometer 85 'European citizenship', in European Commission, 2016a: 22). The UK was a clear outlier when it comes to attitudes towards the euro and Economic and Monetary Union (EMU) (Figure 7.1).

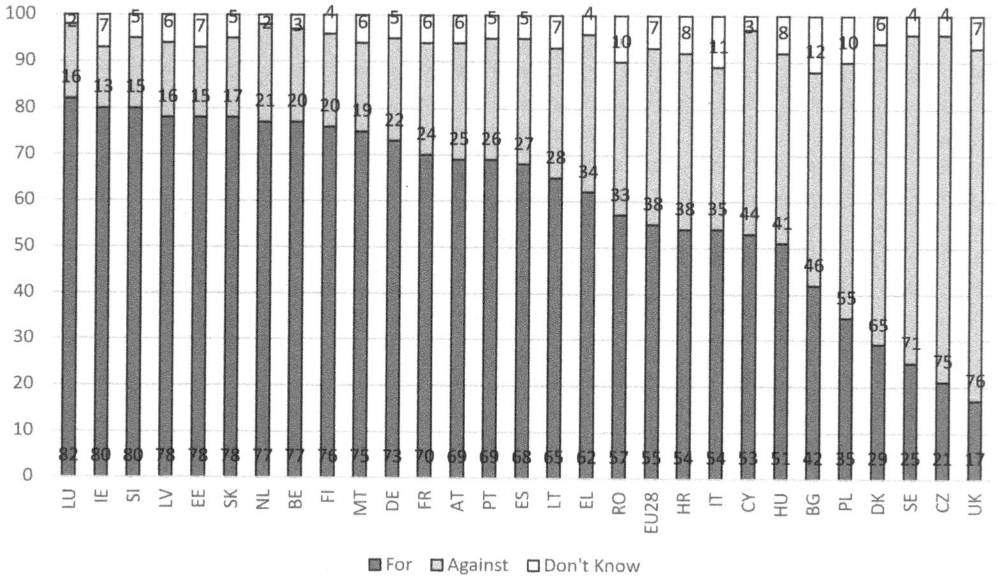

Source: European Commission (2016b: 14).

Figure 7.1 *Attitudes for and against EMU*

Another element that was emotional but salient in the Brexit debates was UK voters' concern with immigration (Staiger, 2018). Research on migration in the UK highlights that a number of UK voters have expressed dissatisfaction with their own lives, and have blamed change in the community on the increase in numbers of immigrants (Burrell and Hopkins, 2020). The UK was, however, quite well integrated into the EU economy. Many of the workers in the UK were from the EU and many UK citizens worked abroad. Eurobarometer data of spring 2016 indicated that 63 per cent of respondents found that 'Immigrants contribute a lot to our country', a much higher amount than the EU average at 40 per cent (QD4.2) (Standard Eurobarometer 85 'European citizenship', in European Commission, 2016a: 48). Similarly, in the UK there was in that same timeframe a high level of willingness to support refugees (75 per cent in the UK compared to 63 per cent in the EU average (QD4.5) (Standard Eurobarometer

85 'European citizenship', in European Commission, 2016a: 49). It is remarkable, though, that areas with high percentages of 'leave' voters also showed a higher turnout level, and correlated with lower levels of education as well as with areas in decline – often areas that did not actually feature high levels of migrant populations (Goodwin and Heath, 2016). Some analyses on why people voted leave have indicated that UK elites had not been paying much attention to those voters who were so-called 'losers of globalisation' (cf. Hobolt, 2016).

The Brexit debacle did not emerge in a vacuum, but rather followed a range of crises (Nugent, 2018). The referendum in June 2016 came on the heels of a major migration crisis that affected all of Europe during 2015–16, when more than a million migrants arrived in Europe seeking refuge and a better life. The EU was unable to conjure up a collective response (Scipioni, 2018). Prior to that, the EU experienced a financial crisis (including a banking crisis) and shortly after that, the sovereign debt crisis. Many EU member states had a difficult time in those years; the UK was no exception. The perception among some UK voters, however, about the link between the problems and the solutions of the global financial crisis, the banking crisis and the sovereign debt crisis may not have been clear. After all, the UK had stayed outside of Europe's monetary union. The UK was not part of the euro and chose to stay outside the Banking Union and opposed the so-called fiscal compact (Treaty on Stability, Coordination and Governance in the Economic and Monetary Union or 'TSCG', 2012) – an intergovernmental treaty that stipulated a need for balanced budgets. EMU has been asymmetrical from the outset (Verdun, 1996) meaning that its monetary union is managed by a supranational institution, the European Central Bank, whereas fiscal policies are national. Many EU policy makers realise that this incomplete EMU needs deepening and that this deepening will only occur when the time is right (Schure and Della Posta, 2021). Therefore, in the aftermath of the sovereign debt crisis, and reflecting on 60 years since the signing of the Treaty of Rome that created the European Economic Community, the EU issued a number of reflection papers about the future of the EU (European Commission, 2017a, 2017b. 2017c). Even though the exact path was not clear, the EU was still in search of the next steps to complete Europe's monetary union. The felt need, in this domain, was different for UK voters than for most of the EU member states.

Eventually the UK left the EU. This outcome prevailed not only because its electorate voted to leave. In fact, there was an extended period of heated parliamentary debates about what the next steps would be to digest the referendum results. The internal domestic political establishment was unable to find a path that would satisfy the need to find a different relationship with the EU, a clear communication strategy to articulate such a path and a political vision that competed with that of the Conservative Party (Lynch, Whitaker and Cygan, 2019). The domestic ordeal that the UK went through in 2016–20 was painful. Political observers disagree on many things regarding the substance of the policies and possible paths that could have been taken. But few disagree about the sheer frustration and difficulties that the UK political system went through during those years (Farrell and Suiter, 2019; McConalogue, 2019). Ironically, by the end of 2020 it was still not fully clear what the relationship would be between the EU and the UK. But the COVID-19 pandemic that erupted in its full severity in March 2020 worked as a lightning rod to reorient the political debate (Harvey, 2021).

CONTENTIOUS ISSUES

One of the most difficult matters in the Brexit dossier, during the negotiations before the UK formally left, remained that the UK was hoping to have access to the Single Market whilst remaining outside it. The government wanted to find a way to be exempt from the legal provisions that would make it a member of the Single Market. Norway, Iceland and tiny Liechtenstein, for instance, are not EU member states. Yet they are connected to the Single Market through the European Economic Area (EEA) (Eliassen and Sitter, 2003; Fossum, Chapter 21 and Frommelt, Chapter 22 in this volume; Frommelt and Gstöhl, 2011; Kristjánsson and Kristjánsson, 2000). Similarly, Switzerland, although not a member of the EEA, has made bilateral agreements with the EU that allows that country to be part of the Single Market. Choosing to be heavily integrated into the EU means that in some areas the Swiss have had to implement more laws from the EU than others, even though they do not have a say over the details of the original EU law (Linder, 2013: 191–2). Having those provisions has, however, enabled EEA countries and the Swiss the same rights to live, work and travel in the EU as EU citizens. But the downside of this arrangement is that the Swiss have not had any say over EU laws during the legislative process. Instead, once laws have been adopted, the Swiss subsequently have had to take it as a basis for their own laws (see also Lavenex and Veuthey, Chapter 20 in this volume). In this way one could argue that the TCA has features that resemble the trade relations between the EU and Canada, the Comprehensive Economic Trade Agreement (CETA) (see also Neuwahl, Chapter 23 in this volume).

The freedom of movement of people and their rights was one of the factors the UK government was keen to control: it wanted to curtail EU flows of people and migration. At the same time, it had the desire to maintain full access to a market of 450 million consumers and 22.5 million small and medium-sized enterprises. However, in deciding to withdraw from the Single Market and the Customs Union, the UK needed to reintroduce customs and the accompanying formalities for products imported and exported between the EU and the UK. This red tape is a major nuisance for importers and exporters, which led to long delays at the border (Morris, 2022). The reason was that goods that were crossing into the UK had to be entered into a so-called HMRC Goods Vehicle Movement Service (GVMS) in order to determine if further inspection would be needed.[3] The effect of the delays at the border has a larger impact on the UK than on its EU partners as the UK does a larger percentage of its trade with the EU than individual member states do with the UK (Figures 7.2 and 7.3).

Trade was likely going to be affected in the short-run (Figure 7.4). Adjustments would be taking place, but there were still also questions as to whether trade would pick up in the medium run (Thissen, van Oort, McCann, Ortega-Argilés and Husby, 2020). In terms of the balance between trade in goods and services, in 2020, the UK exported £251 billion in goods and services to EU member states, which is 42 per cent of total UK exports. In terms of imports from the EU, the total amount in goods and services imports was £301 billion (50 per cent of total UK's imports). These movements led to a trade deficit for the UK with the EU of −£49 billion (but it did have a surplus with non-EU countries of £54 billion). In terms of the balance between goods and services, the UK had a deficit in goods with both the EU and non-EU countries (of −£86 billion and −£43 billion, respectively). By contrast, in terms of services, it had a trade surplus with both the EU and non-EU countries (£37 billion and £96 billion, respectively). These amounts in terms of percentages show a significant share for the continent: 47 per cent of UK goods exports and 36 per cent of services exports went to the EU

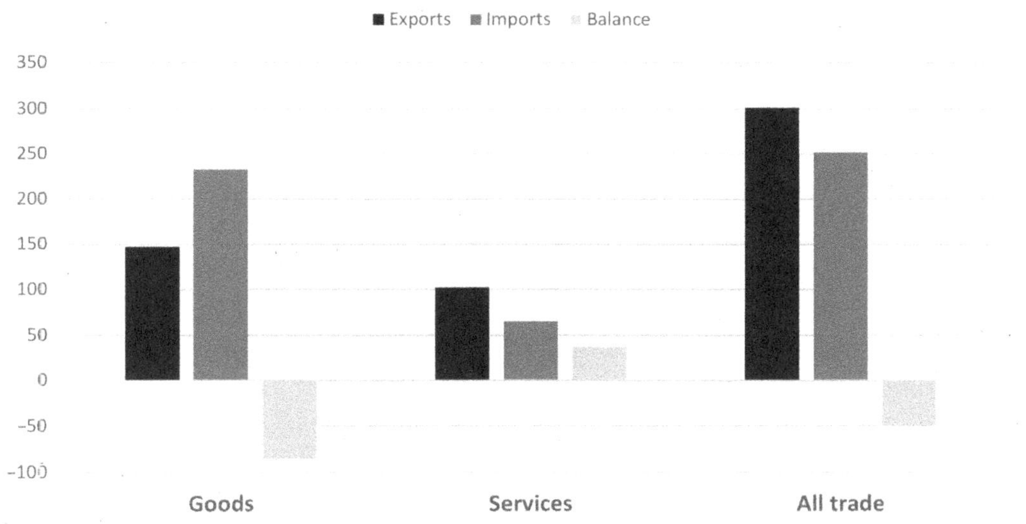

Source: UK Parliament (2021 4).

Figure 7.2 *UK trade with the EU*

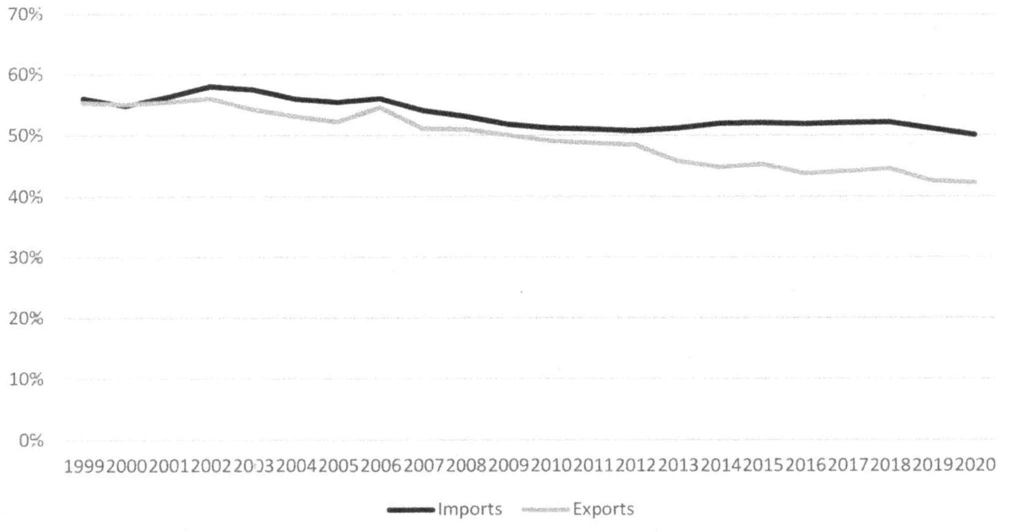

Source: UK Parliament (2021: 4).

Figure 7.3 *Share of UK trade with EU (1999–2020)*

whereas 53 per cent of the UK's imported goods and 43 per cent of imported services came from the EU (UK Parliament, 2021: 5).

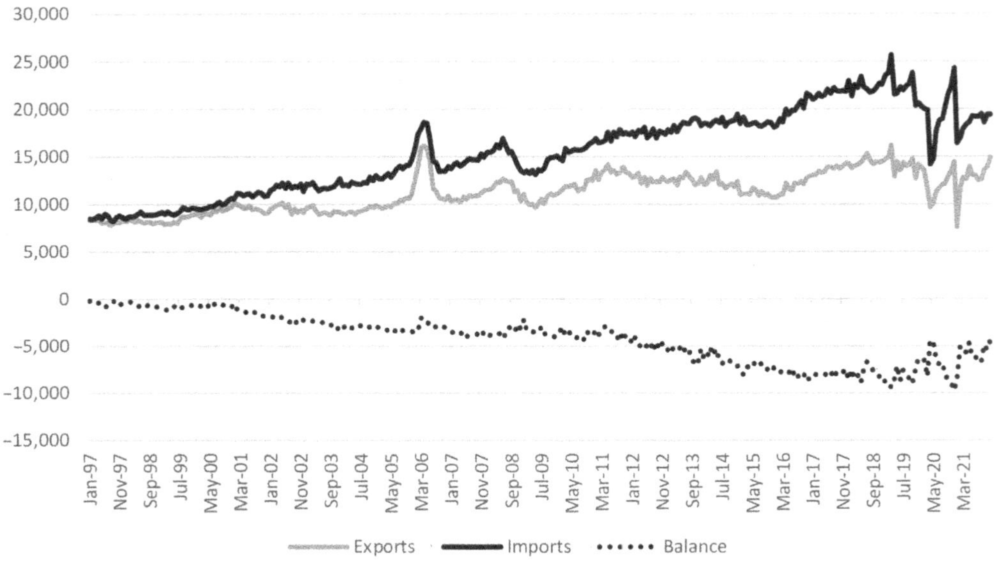

Source: Statista (2022).

Figure 7.4 *Value of trade in goods with the EU in the UK from January 1997 to November 2021 (in million GBP)*

For services Brexit means the end of what is known as 'financial passporting rights' for the UK services sector. Not covered by the TCA are financial services. These make up 7 per cent of UK GDP (The Economist, 2021). The TCA agreement states:

> the Trade and Cooperation Agreement does not cover any decisions relating to equivalences for financial services, the adequacy of the UK data protection regime, or the assessment of the UK's sanitary and phytosanitary regime for the purpose of listing it as a third country allowed to export food products to the EU. Indeed, these are unilateral decisions of the EU and are not subject to negotiation.[4]

It also means that the UK no longer benefits from Community preference. UK product certification will not be automatically recognised in the EU. The immediate result of these non-tariff barriers has been long lines of lorries at the EU-UK borders, restrictions on immigration and disruption of supply chains.

One anomaly has been Northern Ireland. When the negotiations started, few observers, indeed few members of the general public, appreciated the situation on the island of Ireland. The relationship between the UK and Ireland was always going to be a tricky one, due to the interconnection of the two countries, but in particular given the 'troubles' in Northern Ireland: the ethno-nationalist conflict in Northern Ireland that took place from the late 1960s until the Good Friday Agreement in 1998. The latter solved the Northern Irish issues but it was linked to the EU rules and institutional structures. When they were to fall away it meant that any change was inevitably going to pose a major challenge to the Agreement (Wright, 2018). As has been extensively discussed in more detail elsewhere (e.g., Duparc-Portier and Figus, 2021; see also in particular Chapter 5 by Keating, Chapter 8 by Piris and Chapter 14 by Laffan in this volume), the Northern Ireland protocol places the de facto border of the EU and the UK in the Irish Sea. Customs and other formalities are done prior to goods entering into Great Britain. Northern Ireland therefore is treated as if it is still in the Customs Union with the EU. A system of rebates has been set up for Northern ireland. The Northern Ireland Assembly will decide every four years whether to keep the Protocol. In summer 2021 the UK government expressed concern about the feasibility of the Northern Ireland Protocol, seeking to change the way the border between Great Britain and Northern Ireland was managed – 'as if it were one between two sovereign states' (Menon and Rutter, 2021).

Not only the situation in Ireland but also the capital city had a special position in the Brexit vote. Although a majority of those in England who voted in the referendum voted 'leave', the City of London did not vote 'leave'. Only 25 per cent of people who worked in the financial sector voted 'leave' and only 19.4 per cent of investment bankers voted to leave (Clarke, 2016) (Figure 7.5). Furthermore, those with higher salaries in the City of London voted in larger numbers to 'remain' than those on the lower end of the salary spectrum (Figure 7.6).

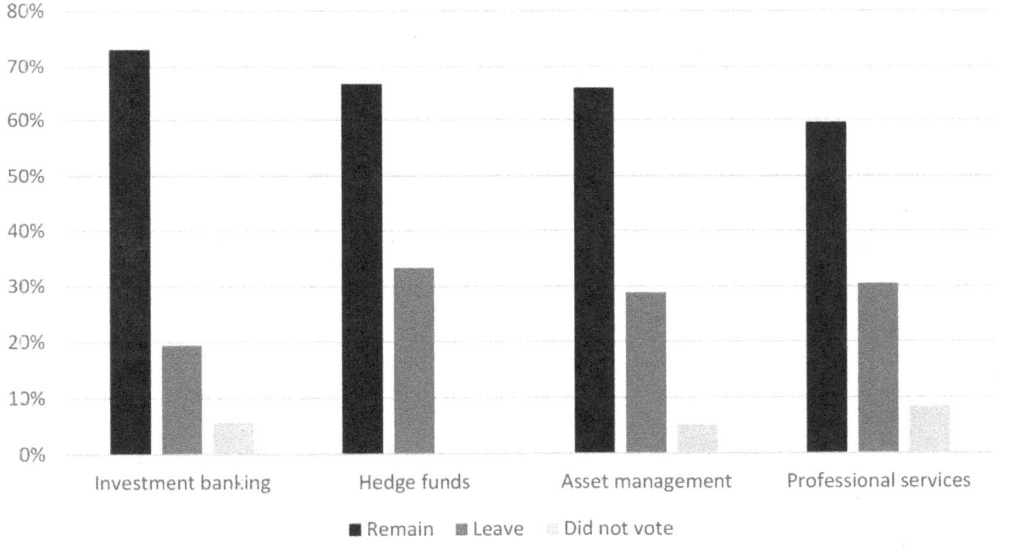

Source: Clarke (2016).

Figure 7.5 *How the City of London voted on Brexit by sector*

In fact, the City of London has been the financial capital of Europe for decades. The notification of Brexit has led to numerous companies (such as Panasonic and Sony) moving their headquarters to within the EU (Financial Times, 2018, 2019). During the COVID-19 pandemic it is difficult to know the exact outcome. Most of the analyses suggest that on the whole more companies have left (or are due to leave) than have come (or will be coming) (MoneyWeek, 2020; Investopedia, 2021). Having said that, in some cases, the reverse has happened. For instance, Unilever (a Dutch/UK company that a few years ago was planning to become fully Dutch) changed to fully British, in part to be listed on the London Stock

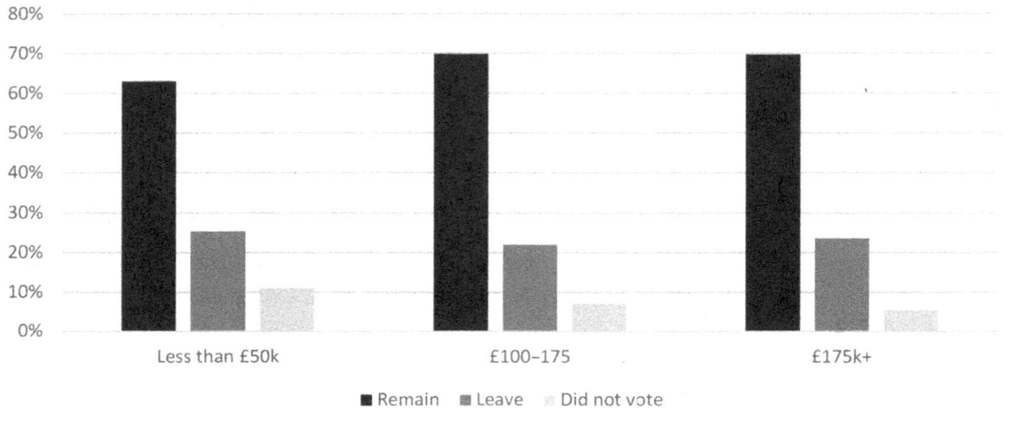

Source: Clarke (2016).

Figure 7.6 How the City of London voted on Brexit by earning power

Exchange. British shares are, however, still listed on the Dutch Stock Exchange (NL Times, 2020). Political economists Scott James and Lucia Quaglia examined early on the risks the City of London's financial sector would face. They found that the City of London was unable to influence the government stance on Brexit proportional to its impact on the UK economy (James and Quaglia, 2019).

US-American economist Barry Eichengreen, writing before the formalities were complete, argued that the effects of the implications of Brexit would be 'potentially far-reaching' (Eichengreen, 2019). Seeing that London is the financial centre of Europe, he argues that the impact of the change is potentially significant. Focusing on capital flows and international finance, he finds that governance and institutional structures might change in the post-Brexit period, some of it due to regulatory changes. Prior to Brexit more than 90 per cent of the euro-denominated interest rate swaps of euro area banks, and the vast share (three-quarters) of foreign exchange transactions and about half of bank lending and securities transactions took place in London (Eichengreen, 2019). By February 2022, the share of euro-denominated derivatives handled by the London Stock Exchange had remained unchanged. Eichengreen in 2019 forecast that European regulators might impose rules that could change the status quo, for instance, by requiring that UK banks would not be permitted to trade currencies and securities for European account holders. In fact, UK banks wrote to European customers asking them to close their accounts. Some banks moved some of their business to the EU (Barclays moved some business to the Republic of Ireland; and some clearing houses already exist in continental Europe that are as of yet fully integrated into the UK financial market; Sapir, Schoenmaker and Veron, 2017). In terms of the inflow of foreign direct investment (FDI), the literature prior to Brexit actually happening suggested that the UK would most likely experience a reduction in FDI inflows, and possibly government responses to these risks, for instance, by reducing corporate taxation (Welfens and Baier, 2018). Indeed, in February 2022 the European Commission started a four-week consultation period to examine how to provide incentives to firms so that they would move their business away from London to one of the EU financial centres (Frankfurt, Amsterdam, Milan and Paris) (Financial Times, 2022b). Brexit will no doubt eventually have a negative effect on the dominance of the City of London as the main financial centre of Europe, but the fact that various centres on the European continent are competing for a share of the pie is an obstacle to change. Only small changes have been observed: in terms of equity trading, Amsterdam has outpaced London in average daily value, but is still ahead of Paris and Frankfurt (Financial Times, 2022a) (Figure 7.7).

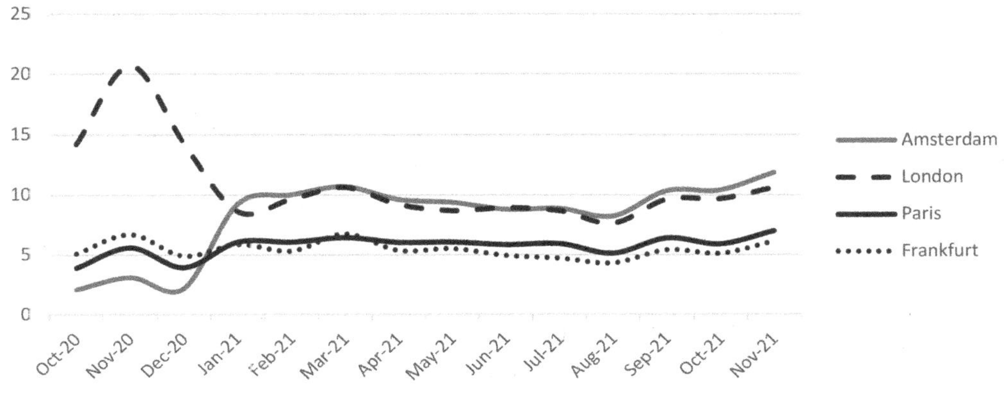

Source: Financial Times (2022a).

Figure 7.7 *Equity trading: average daily value (€bn)*

The influence of the City of London is much older than either the creation of the Single Market or the start of EMU (Strange, 1988). In fact, it can be argued that as much as the UK will suffer from Brexit, the EU also loses out. Some of the major financial institutions (such as the London Stock Exchange) are now outside the EU. The European institutions will not be able to influence the development of the City of London as much as when the UK was still in the EU (Politico, 2020).

Another major area of contention surrounding Brexit was in Scotland. As mentioned above, a significant majority of the Scottish vote was in favour of 'remain'. Given the situation around the Scottish independence referendum in 2014, this Brexit referendum result may foreshadow another independence referendum. If there was a vote in favour of independence, it could affect the UK constitutional settlement. The 1707 Act of Union brought the Scottish and English Parliaments together to form Great Britain. Wales had formally joined the Kingdom of England in 1536. Ireland was added with the Act of Union in 1801, uniting Great Britain (England and Scotland) and Ireland to become the United Kingdom of Great Britain and Ireland. In 1922 Catholic Ireland seceded and Northern Ireland joined the UK again. By 1927 the formal name was the United Kingdom of Great Britain and Northern Ireland. Devolution in the UK occurred in the 20th century in different stages. Most of this devolution process was built on the principles of being part of the EU. The referendum on membership in the EU was not voted upon in the same way in all four nations (or 'countries') of the UK. Northern Ireland and Scotland voted 'remain' and Wales and England 'leave'. The referendum results, and the lack of consideration of these different realities in each of these nations, has further triggered nationalist tendencies in each of these nations – especially in Scotland where 62 per cent voted to remain (BBC News, 2016). At the end of November 2021, First Minister of Scotland, Nicola Sturgeon, announced the start of the planning for a referendum due to take place by the end of 2023 (Financial Times, 2021). The situation in Scotland is considerably different in a post-Brexit period. Scotland is much more closely tied to the rest of the UK than to the EU. Scottish business exports three times as much to other parts of the UK than it does to the EU. Should Scotland be independent there could also be checkpoints and border controls. The UK government argued during the Brexit negotiations that technology could be used to avoid physical checks, but to date this issue remains a challenge as argued above with reference to the situation in Ireland (Reuters, 2022). The matter of the currency is also a major challenge. If Scotland were to become independent would it introduce its own currency and if so would it be tied to the pound? But then, after some time, it would presumably replace the new currency with the euro. Given the significant trade between the two nations, such a choice would not be immediately obvious. Barry Eichengreen (2020) highlighted that in addition there would be other political economy issues that would need to be settled such as the income from North Sea Oil (would it be based on regional distribution or per capita for instance), how to divide up the national debt of the UK and so on. These are not minor issues and would have to be negotiated.

The situation is even more extreme in the tiny overseas territory Gibraltar where 96 per cent voted to remain. This small piece of land at the tip of Spain is still a part of the UK but has become closer to the EU (Mardell, 2021). Negotiations were still ongoing in early 2022 to find an agreement in a treaty between the UK and the EU so that Gibraltar could become part of the Schengen area, so that there would not need to be border checks between Gibraltar and Spain (Politico, 2021b).

FUTURE OPTIONS FOR THE EU-UK RELATIONS

With the UK having left the EU, the challenge for the EU has been how to facilitate good relations between the EU and the UK whilst avoiding giving the impression that the UK is given a special deal. The EU has needed to signal that there are benefits of being a member of the EU that cannot be obtained by making side deals. This principle has been at the heart of the relationship between the EU and Switzerland as well as between the EU and the EEA countries. The EU has tried to ensure this outcome by ensuring that the Single Market would not be undermined and also that the Court of Justice of the EU would have jurisdiction over the Single Market and the rules with these third countries pertaining to Single Market access. The UK demanded that the Court of Justice of the EU (CJEU) not have jurisdiction anymore in the UK. Thus the CJEU only plays a role in Northern Ireland as part of the Northern Ireland Protocol; the CJEU does not oversee the TCA. Article COMPROV.13(3) of the TCA specifically states: 'For greater certainty, an interpretation of this Agreement or any supplementing agreement given by the courts of either Party shall not be binding on the courts of the other Party.' British negotiators were at first keen to remove the CJEU jurisdiction over Northern Ireland, but more recently the negotiators have moved to more practical considerations (Irish Times, 2021).

On the side of the UK, the political establishment has tried to signal that as Theresa May had stated repeatedly 'Brexit means Brexit', namely, that it would matter that the UK is no longer in the EU. Repeated analyses of the various models that the UK could choose from, whether it be the Norway model or the Canada model confirmed that the UK needed to signal to its domestic constituency that it was able to 'take back control'. There is a clear paradox in the situation. The best access to the EU Single Market and access to rule-making is by being part of the EU. Leaving the EU effectively means becoming a rule-taker in so far as access to the Single Market is concerned, or simply not have access to that market.

A number of other elements of the relationship between the EU and the UK will be less straightforward. As we mentioned above, given the dominance of the City of London, it is as of yet unclear whether the UK will lose influence or the EU will lose influence in the role of financial centre. Some reorientation and adjustments are to be expected. But a priori, without seeing the politics of regulation play out, it is unclear whether the UK will come out much weaker in the post-EU era. The EU does have the power to reduce the ability of the UK to remain the dominant financial centre, or at least, it has the power to weaken it. It is not immediately clear if that is in the interest of the EU. Although, as mentioned above, the Commission in February 2022 is seeking ways to entice business to move their euro-swaps to EU financial centres, away from London. Again, the EU needs to signal the relative value of being a member of the EU and try to find ways to keep some form of jurisdiction over the financial market, that with Brexit has now moved outside the reach of EU law. But it also needs to keep a good relationship with the UK as one of its most important neighbours.

As the line-ups at UK borders and shortages persist, some might think that Brexit is only doom and gloom. Experience from other forms of economic collaboration across the globe suggest otherwise. The relatively sudden departure of the UK from the EU and the 11th-hour negotiations have not given the UK economy time to adjust. Over time new rules will be made and the UK will adjust. What is perhaps more disturbing is that UK citizens have not had a chance to have a good discussion about exactly what Brexit entailed in the run-up to the referendum. Few understood exactly what Brexit meant. The government did not do a careful study of the costs and benefits of leaving the EU, nor did it offer careful scenarios with analyses. Even the Scottish referendum of 2014 was better prepared in that regard (Scottish Government, 2013; Constitution and Cabinat Directorate, 2017). Finally, if the constitutional set-up of the UK changes, parts of the UK might consider joining the EU again. Whether this is a real prospect remains to be seen, as all four countries in the UK trade more with one another than separately with the EU.

CONCLUSION

This chapter explored the relationship between Brexit and Europe's political economy in the post-Brexit era. It reviewed the path that the UK took that ended up in its departure from the EU. Even though the dust has not yet settled on the TCA, we can already start thinking about the question of how the UK will remain linked to the European political order. In terms of the UK link to EU institutions, the UK has tried to put distance between itself and the process of deepening of European integration. In particular in the area of EMU, the UK has lacked enthusiasm (both government and its electorate).

With reference to financial matters, as well as the Single Market, the UK government, but also the business community and voters, have been keen to stay closer to the EU. The situation with the Northern Ireland Protocol remains a bit unstable. It is as of yet unclear whether it would need to change sooner rather than later. Brexit itself may also change the constitutional make-up of the UK, which in turn could lead to separate countries of the British Isles one day joining the EU again. The EU managed to keep a single voice in the negotiations. Brexit has been an example that has given Eurosceptics moments to pause. However, when the time comes that the adjustment has occurred it is not clear that the UK will only have negative effects from being outside the EU. The EU will then need to ensure that the relationship that the EU has with the UK is not so comfortable that Eurosceptics may more easily point to the UK situation as one that is desirable. Therefore, for the foreseeable future, both sides have some incentive in demonstrating that the relationship with the EU and the UK will remain somewhat rocky.

NOTES

1. An earlier version was presented at the 117th American Political Science Association's Annual Meeting & Exhibition, virtually from 28 September to 3 October 2021. The author thanks James A. Caporaso, Sergio Fabbrini, John Erik Fossum, Chris Lord, Craig Parsons and Vivien Schmidt for comments on earlier versions of this chapter. She is grateful to Malcolm Thomson for research assistance and for Zoey Verdun for assistance with the figures and graphs. Some of the research funding was provided by the Social Science and Humanities Research Council (SSHRC) of Canada.
2. At the time European Commission President Barosso spelled out: 'If part of the territory of a member state would cease to be part of that state because it were to become a new independent state, the (EU) treaties would no longer apply to that territory.' Barosso (2013) quoted in European Parliament (2013). Various scholars did, however, indicate that Scottish membership of the EU should not be too difficult, but the general public was a bit concerned (Douglas-Scott, 2014). But no matter how one looks at it, the UK has left the EU, which in turn has lost one of its largest member states.
3. https://www.fleetpoint.org/logistics/distribution/customs-clearance/new-border-rules-trigger-long-queues-of-trucks-in-calais/, accessed 11 February 2022.
4. https://ec.europa.eu/info/strategy/relations-non-eu-countries/relations-united-kingdom/eu-uk-trade-and-cooperation-agreement_en, accessed 11 February 2022.

REFERENCES

BBC News (2016) 'UK votes to leave the EU', https://www.bbc.co.uk/news/politics/eu_referendum/results.

Burrell, Kathy and Peter Hopkins (2020) 'Introduction: Brexit, race and migration', *Environment and Planning C: Politics and Space*, 37(1): 4–7, https://doi.org/10.1177/0263774X18811923a.

Cini, Michelle and Amy Verdun (2018) 'The implications of Brexit for the future of Europe', in B. Martill and U. Staiger (eds), *Brexit and Beyond: Rethinking the Futures of Europe* (pp. 63–71). London: UCL Press, https://doi.org/10.2307/j.ctt20krxf8.12.

Clarke, Paul (2016) 'The Brexit divide: How the City of London voted in the EU referendum', efinancialcareers, https://www.efinancialcareers-canada.com/news/2016/07/this-is-how-city-of-london-workers-voted-in-18 July, last accessed, 11 February 2022.

Constitution and Cabinet Directorate (2017) 'Cost of 2014 Scottish Independence Referendum: FOI release'. Information request and response under the Freedom of Information (Scotland) Act 2022. FOI reference FOI/17/02858 (date received 24 November 2017; date responded 28 November 2017).

Douglas-Scott, Sionaidh (2014, July) 'How easily could an independent Scotland Join the EU?', *Oxford Legal Studies Research Paper* No. 46/2014, Available at SSRN: https://ssrn.com/abstract=2462227 or http://dx.doi.org/10.2139/ssrn.2462227.

Duparc-Portier, Geoffroy and Gioele Figus (2021) 'The impact of the new Northern Ireland Protocol: Can Northern Ireland enjoy the best of both worlds?', *Regional Studies*, doi: 10.1080/00343404.2021.1994547, last accessed, 11 February 2022.

Eeckhout, Piet (2018) 'The Emperor has no clothes: Brexit and the UK constitution', in Benjamin Martil and Uta Staiger (eds), *Brexit and Beyond: Rethinking the Futures of Europe* (pp. 165–73), London: UCL Press, http://www.ucl.ac.uk/ucl-press, accessed 11 February 2022.

Eichengreen, Barry (2019) 'The international financial implications of Brexit', *International Economics and Economic Policy*, 16: 37–50.

Eichengreen, Barry (2020) 'Scotland needs a plan for a new currency if it wants independence', *The Guardian*, 13 October, https://www.theguardian.com/business/2020/oct/13/scotland-new-currency-independence-sterling-euro, accessed 11 February 2022.

Eliassen, Kjell A. and Nick Sitter (2003) 'Ever closer cooperation? The limits of the "Norwegian Method" of European integration', *Scandinavian Political Studies*, 26(2): 125–44, https://doi.org/10.1111/1467-9477.00082.

European Commission (2016a) 'Standard Eurobarometer 85 report. European citizenship – Publication Reports – EN', Spring.

European Commission (2016b) 'Standard Eurobarometer 85 report – Europeans' views on the priorities of the European Union – Publication Reports – EN', Spring.

European Commission (2017a) 'White paper on the future of Europe: Reflections and scenarios for the EU27 by 2025', Directorate-General for Communication, Publications Office, 26 April, https://data.europa.eu/doi/10.2775/042301, accessed 11 February 2022.

European Commission (2017b) 'Reflection paper on the deepening of the Economic and Monetary Union', Directorate-General for Communication, Publications Office, 31 May, https://data.europa.eu/doi/10.2775/321289, accessed 11 February 2022.

European Commission (2017c) 'Reflection paper on the future of EU finances', Directorate-General for Communication, Publications Office, 26 October, https://data.europa.eu/doi/10.2775/451158, accessed 11 February 2022.

European Parliament (2013) 'Answer given by Mr Barroso on behalf of the Commission', Parliamentary question – E-011023/2013(ASW) 20.11.2013.

Farrell, David M. and Jane Suiter (2019) *Reimagining Democracy: Lessons in Deliberative Democracy from the Irish Front Line*, Ithaca, NY: Cornell University Press.

Financial Times (2018) 'Panasonic blames Brexit for moving European headquarters', by Leo Lewis and Robin Harding in Tokyo, 30 August, https://www.ft.com/content/b4e11b6e-ac53-11e8-94bd-cba20d67390c, accessed 11 February 2022.

Financial Times (2019) 'Sony to shift European domicile from UK on Brexit risk', by Kana Inagaki and Leo Lewis in Tokyo and Henry Mance in London, 23 January, https://www.ft.com/content/e11ddf32-1edb-11e9-b126-46fc3ad87c65, accessed 11 February 2022.

Financial Times (2021) 'Planning for second Scottish independence vote to start next year, says Sturgeon', by Mure Dickie, 29 November, https://www.ft.com/content/2fb045a9-31d5-482b-8ac4-c19ac40c87ef, accessed 11 February 2022.

Financial Times (2022a) 'The EU vs the City of London: A slow puncture', by Sam Fleming, Philip Stafford and Laura Noonan, 9 January, https://www.ft.com/content/f83ddf05-e7a1-4c9b-83ad-e82a54c71afa, accessed 11 February 2022.

Financial Times (2022b) 'Brussels aiming to move derivatives clearing from London to EU' by Sam Fleming in Brussels, 8 February, https://www.ft.com/content/6fb09fcd-f392-43dd-b3f4-0ea79bd3d335#post-dec1d55c-7988-4e49-806a-fa533bb4c92b, accessed 11 February 2022.

Frommelt, Christian and Sieglinde Gstöhl (2011), 'Liechtenstein and the EEA: The Europeanization of a (very) small state', *Europautredningen*, Report 18, 67 pages.

Glencross, Andrew (2018) 'Cameron's European legacy: How Brexit demonstrates the flawed politics of simple solutions', in Benjamin Martil and Uta Staiger (eds), *Brexit and Beyond: Rethinking the Futures of Europe* (pp. 22–7), London: UCL Press, http://www.ucl.ac.uk/ucl-press, accessed 7 October 2022.

Goodwin, Matthew and Oliver Heath (2016) 'The 2016 Referendum, Brexit and the left behind: An aggregate-level analysis of the result', *The Political Quarterly*, 87(3): 323–32.

Harvey, Darren (2021) 'Brexit and Covid-19', *King's Law Journal*, 32(1): 26–36, doi: 10.1080/09615768.2021.1891617.

Hobolt, Sara B. (2016) 'The Brexit vote: A divided nation, a divided continent', *Journal of European Public Policy*, 23(9): 1259–77.

Institute for Government (2019), 'How would a second referendum on Brexit happen?', https://www.instituteforgovernment.org.uk/explainers/second-referendum-brexit, accessed 11 February 2022.

Investopedia (2021) 'Brexit: Winners and losers', by Michelle P. Scott, https://www.investopedia.com/news/brexit-winners-and-losers/#citation-10, updated 22 August, accessed 7 October 2022.

Irish Times (2021) 'Britain drops demand for removal of ECJ role from NI protocol', 10 December, https://www.irishtimes.com/news/world/uk/britain-drops-demand-for-removal-of-ecj-role-from-ni-protocol-1.4752375, accessed 11 February 2022.

James, Scott and Lucia Quaglia (2019) 'Brexit, the City and the contingent power of finance', *New Political Economy*, 24(2): 258–71, doi: 10.1080/13563467.2018.1484717.

Kristjánsson, Svanur and Ragnar Kristjánsson (2000) 'Delegation and accountability in an ambiguous system: Iceland and the European Economic Area (EEA)', *The Journal of Legislative Studies*, 6(1): 105–24, doi: 10.1080/13572330008420615.

Linder, Wolf (2013) 'Switzerland and the EU: The puzzling effects of Europeanisation without institutionalisation', *Contemporary Politics*, 19(2): 190–202, doi: 10.1080/13569775.2013.785830.

Lynch P., R. Whitaker and C. Cygan (2019) 'Brexit and the UK Parliament: Challenges and opportunities', in T. Christiansen and D. Fromage (eds), *Brexit and Democracy: European Administrative Governance*. Cham, Switzerland: Palgrave Macmillan, https://doi.org/10.1007/978-3-030-06043-5_3.

Mardell, Mark (2021) 'Is Brexit driving Gibraltar into Europe's arms?', 10 March, https://foreignpolicy.com/2021/03/10/is-brexit-driving-gibraltar-into-europes-arms/, accessed 11 February 2022.

McConalogue, Jim (2019) *The British Constitution Resettled. Parliamentary Sovereign before and after Brexit*, Cham, Switzerland: Palgrave Macmillan.

Menon, Anand and Jill Rutterl (2021) 'Protocol on Northern Ireland: If Britain wants to resolve it this is not the way to do it', *UK in a Changing Europe*, 27 July, https://ukandeu.ac.uk/protocol-northern-ireland/, accessed 11 February 2022.

MoneyWeek (2020) 'Winners and losers from a hard Brexit', *MoneyWeek*, 9 February, https://moneyweek.com/economy/uk-economy/brexit/600778/winners-and-losers-from-a-hard-brexit, accessed 11 February 2022.

Morris, Chris (2022) 'Dover queues: The firms struggling with Brexit red tape', *BBC News*, 28 January, https://www.bbc.com/news/business-60161094, accessed 11 February 2022.

NL Times (2020) 'Unilever officially no longer Dutch company', 29 November, https://nltimes.nl/2020/11/29/unilever-officially-longer-dutch-company, accessed 11 February 2022.

Nugent, Neill (2018) 'Brexit: Yet another crisis for the EU', in Benjamin Martil and Uta Staiger (eds), *Brexit and Beyond: Rethinking the Futures of Europe* (pp. 54–62), London: UCL Press, http://www.ucl.ac.uk/ucl-press, accessed 7 October 2022.

Politico (2020) 'Brexit has crippled EU's soft power over financial rules. Losing rule-setting power over London will erode Europe's global sway', by Matei Rosca, 23 December, https://www.politico.eu/article/uk-brexit-takes-with-it-much-of-the-eu-soft-power-in-finance/, accessed 11 February 2022.

Politico (2021a) 'Scotland's Nicola Sturgeon continues push for independence referendum by end of 2023', by Andrew McDonald, 29 November, https://www.politico.eu/article/scotland-nicola-sturgeon-independence-referendum-2023, accessed 11 February 2022.

Politico (2021b) 'Post-Brexit talks on Gibraltar's future drag into 2022', 16 December, https://www.politico.eu/article/post-brexit-talks-on-gibraltars-future-drag-into-2022/, accessed 11 February 2022.

Reuters (2021) 'French fishermen disrupt UK trade routes over fishing licence row', by Layli Foroudi and Manuel Ausloos, 26 November, https://www.reuters.com/world/europe/french-fishermen-block-boat-st-malo-brexit-protests-begin-2021-11-26/, accessed 11 February 2022.

Reuters (2022) 'Scotland faces border checks with England if it rejoins the EU – think tank', by Andrew Macaskill, 3 February, https://www.reuters.com/world/uk/scotland-faces-border-checks-with-england-if-it-rejoins-eu-think-tank-2022-02-03/, accessed 11 February 2022.

Sapir, André, Dirk Schoenmaker and Nicolas Veron (2017, February) 'Making the best of Brexit for the EU-27 financial system', Policy brief 17–18, Peterson Institute for International Economics.

Schure, P. and P. Della Posta (2021) 'An expert survey on fiscal solidarity in the Euro Area', Paper presented at the Nederlandse Politicologenetmaal (Annual Political Science Workshops of the Low Countries), 3–4 June.

Scipioni, Marco (2018) 'Failing forward in EU migration policy? EU integration after the 2015 asylum and migration crisis', *Journal of European Public Policy*, 25(9): 1357–75, doi: 10.1080/13501763.2017.1325920.

Scottish Government (2013, 26 November) *Scotland's Future*. https://www.gov.scot/publications/scotlands-future/, accessed 11 February 2022.

Staiger, Uta (2018) 'The heart of the matter: Emotional politics in the new Europe', in Benjamin Martil and Uta Staiger (eds), *Brexit and Beyond: Rethinking the Futures of Europe* (pp. 230–38), London: UCL Press, http://www.ucl.ac.uk/ucl-press, accessed 7 October 2022.

Statista (2022) 'Value of trade in goods with the European Union in the United Kingdom from January 1997 to December 2021', https://www.statista.com/statistics/284750/united-kingdom-uk-total-eu-trade-in-goods-by-trade-value/, accessed 11 February 2022.

Strange, Susan (1988) *States and Markets: An Introduction to International Political Economy*. London: Pinter Publishers.

The Economist (2021, 4 February) 'Access to the EU financial-services market is not worth the price'.

Thissen, Mark, Frank van Oort, Philip McCann, Raquel Ortega-Argilés and Trond Husby (2020) 'The implications of Brexit for UK and EU regional competitiveness', *Economic Geography*, 96(5): 397–421, doi: 10.1080/00130095.2020.1820862.

Treaty on Stability, Coordination and Governance in the Economic and Monetary Union (TSCG) (2012, 2 March) Council of the EU, https://www.consilium.europa.eu/media/20399/st00tscg26_en12.pdf, accessed 11 February 2022.

UK Parliament (2021) Statistics on UK-EU Trade. House of Commons Library by Matthew Ward, 3 December, https://researchbriefings.files.parliament.uk/documents/CBP-7851/CBP-7851.pdf, accessed 11 February 2022.

Verdun, Amy (1996) 'An "asymmetrical" Economic and Monetary Union in the EU: Perceptions of monetary authorities and social partners', *Revue d'Integration Européenne/Journal of European Integration*, 20(1), Autumn: 59–81.

Weale, Albert (2018) 'Brexit and the improvised constitution', in Benjamin Martil and Uta Staiger (eds), *Brexit and Beyond: Rethinking the Futures of Europe* (pp. 28–36), London: UCL Press, http://www.ucl.ac.uk/ucl-press, accessed 7 October 2022.

Welfens Paul, J.J. and Fabian J. Baier (2018) 'Brexit and foreign direct investment: Key issues and new empirical findings', *International Journal of Financial Studies*, 6: 1–21.

Wright, Nicholas (2018) 'Brexit and Ireland: Collateral damage?', in Benjamin Martil and Uta Staiger (eds), *Brexit and Beyond: Rethinking the Futures of Europe* (pp. 105–13), London: UCL Press, http://www.ucl.ac.uk/ucl-press, accessed 7 October 2022.

PART II

BREXIT AND THE EUROPEAN UNION INSTITUTIONS

8. The making of Brexit: legal aspects of the 2016–20 negotiations

Jean-Claude Piris

INTRODUCTION

The United Kingdom (UK) left the European Union (EU) on 1 February 2020, the day when the *Withdrawal Agreement* (WA) (2019) entered into force: Brexit was legally done. The UK was no longer an EU member state. It benefited, however, from a transition period until 31 December 2020,[1] during which it continued to have most rights and duties of an EU member state. Both parties had to negotiate another agreement as a basis for their future relations, in particular in order to avoid World Trade Organization (WTO) rules to be immediately applied to their mutual trade on 1 January 2021. They had to negotiate it during the 11 months left of 2020, thus in a very short time, given the difficulties. On 24 December, they agreed in extremis the *Trade and Cooperation Agreement* (TCA) (2021), about 1,500 pages long.[2] In order to avoid a gap after the end of the transition period, they decided to apply the TCA on a provisional basis on 1 January 2021, before its ratification and entry into force. The effects of Brexit began to be felt on 1 January 2021, taking into account that agreement. This chapter aims at presenting the most important legal disagreements between the UK and the EU during the negotiations of both the WA and the TCA. During the first years of the period from June 2016 to December 2020, the UK's policy on its future relations with the EU, inexistent at the time of the referendum, remained hesitant and unclear. British policy developed by successive steps. At first it aimed at keeping a close relationship with the EU's single market. It later aimed at a weak relationship and a hard Brexit. Under the leadership of Prime Minister (PM) Johnson, political ideology ('sovereignty first') became much more important than economic interests.

THE POINT OF DEPARTURE: WHILE AN EU MEMBER STATE, THE UK DID NOT HAVE THE SAME RIGHTS AND DUTIES AS THE OTHERS

The UK never had the same political vision of the EU as the other member states. Britons even speak about 'Europe' as a geographical entity to which they do not belong. History books and the media often celebrate Britain's national identity and values, without showing its close links with continental Europe. Most Britons feel more cultural links with Australia and New Zealand than with France and Germany. When invited by the Six to participate in the making of the 1950 Treaty on Coal and Steel, and later the 1957 European Economic Community (EEC), the UK did not participate, or left before the end of the diplomatic conference. It even tried to establish a rival organisation with the creation of the EFTA (European Free Trade Association) in 1960.[3] Realising, however, that EEC was a clear success, it applied to be a candidate in 1963 and 1967. These applications were both rejected by de Gaulle, who regarded the

UK as having *deep-seated hostility* to any pan-European project. Finally, on 1 January 1973, along with Denmark and Ireland, the UK acceded the EEC, often presenting it to its population as *a mere trading block*, with no political objective.[4]

The UK did not wait long after its accession to make EEC life difficult. It requested a substantial budgetary rebate and insisted on establishing a principle of *juste retour* between what a member state contributes to the budget and how much money it obtains directly from it, without taking account actual economic and other benefits. Meanwhile, jealous of its sovereignty, Britain slowed or refused more coordination of the member states' economic and fiscal policies, of their foreign policies, as well as of cooperation for defence and internal security, police and justice. In 1992, when the Maastricht Treaty on the EU was adopted, it used its veto right to opt out from the creation of a common currency, the cooperation in justice and home affairs and social policy provisions. It was enthusiastic only about the single market, opening external trade and welcoming new members.

With others, the UK encouraged the accession of new member states. For the UK, it was a win-win strategy: stabilising the security of the continent, helping the Central and Eastern European countries to economically progress and open to trade, as well as diluting the EU into a less coherent community. The EU, trying not to be diluted by members benefiting from opt outs copied from the UK's major derogations (*half a member state*), made its enlargement policy stricter. New members could no longer get permanent major opt-outs: they would have to accept the four freedoms, the common currency and Schengen. The EEA-EFTA (European Economic Area-European Free Trade Association) states participate in most of the single market without being EU members, but at the price of following EU law without participating in its decision-making. This made the EU more rigid, without solving the main issue, which was the necessity to reform its institutions and their decision-making process, for them to remain efficient. This was not recognised by some members, led by the UK. As a result, successive enlargements, not accompanied by institutional reforms, led to a weakening of the EU. Having grown from six to 28 members, with every member supposed to follow the same path, the EU's major decisions still require common agreement or unanimity.[5] Common agreement to amend EU Treaties and ratification by every member state make any major revision virtually impossible (Closa, 2013). Besides, over the years, the United Kingdom Independence Party (UKIP), as well as fractions of the Conservative and the Labour Parties, helped by the infamous but influential tabloid press, convinced a part of the British public that the EU was becoming a federal state. That state would have its own currency, its economic and fiscal policies, its diplomacy and its army, it would decide on most issues, emptying the powers and sovereignty of its member states, which Turkey would soon join, and it is already costing a lot of money, especially to the UK. These lies were at the heart of the campaign before the 23 June 2016 referendum. The UK's policy persistently and efficiently opposed the EU becoming a political actor in the world, both to preserve its national sovereignty and because it feared that such a union would be dominated by Germany and France. During its 47-year membership, while participating in the development of the EU, it was constantly struggling to preserve what it regarded to be its major national interests.

As 51.89 per cent voted *Leave* in the 23 June 2016 referendum, Brexit happened paradoxically at a time when most, if not all, of these British interests had been successfully preserved:[6]

- enlarging the EU (from 9 to 28), without adapting enough the decision-making of its institutions to the fact that this increased number would increase difficulties to adopt the many decisions to be adopted either by unanimity or by common agreement;
- getting better control of EU powers (subsidiarity[7]) and eliminating federalist symbols (Piris, 2010, pp. 47–8);
- keeping the internal market benefits, despite derogations from other EU core policies, in particular the euro and Schengen, and a permanent rebate on its contribution to the EU budget;
- preserving a veto on decisions related to foreign and defence policies, police and judicial cooperation and internal security, and affecting in any way possible what it regarded as its sovereignty. On these matters, the UK did not believe in a European interest, but only in a national one.

Traditionally a trading country, the UK loved the EU's single market (SM).[8] The SM was built, with the blessing of Mrs Thatcher, based on the White Paper produced in June 1985 by Lord Cockfield, then a British Commissioner.[9] During and after the referendum campaign, the leaders of Brexit promised, perhaps in good faith, probably not, that leaving the EU would not mean that the UK would leave the SM. They pretended to be able to build special links with the EU, exiting the EU as a potential political entity, but keeping full access to its SM. At the same time, they rejected any option which would oblige the UK to follow the EU's legislation regulating the SM and its future evolution without participating in its decision-making, such as is the case of the three EEA-EFTA countries in the EEA framework.[10] This illusion of being able to exit the EU while keeping frictionless trade with its market deeply affected the negotiations. British ministers were certainly correctly briefed by the civil service, but they either suspected it to be hostile to Brexit or decided that politics obliged them to lie. Whether due to ignorance or to lies, this might explain many misunderstandings and disputes between the EU and the British government throughout the negotiations.

1. THE FIRST DISAGREEMENTS BETWEEN THE TWO PARTIES: THE PROCEDURES FOR THE NEGOTIATIONS

Both parties agreed that there was no legal way to exit other than following the procedure set out in Article 50 TEU,[11] as modified by the Lisbon Treaty. Despite a few lawyers' opinions, no other exit mechanism was either legally possible (for example, Article 54(b) of the 1969 Vienna Convention on the Law of Treaties (VCLT))[12] or politically wise (in the case of a national law purporting to withdraw without an agreement with the EU). However, the British side had several illusions, due either to lack of knowledge about the functioning of the EU or to a pretended belief that the EU could circumvent its rules. The government wanted to apply rules of general international law to the negotiations, while knowing that the EU, not being a state, is bound by the *principle of conferral*.[13] It asked the EU's institutions to begin negotiating before having followed the correct EU legal procedure,[14] or to immediately negotiate their future relations while it was still an EU member, before the ratification of the WA.[15] The UK also tried to bypass the EU by speaking to its member states. This was a legal mistake, given that the 27 were not a party to the negotiation. It was above all a political error, as the EU had strong mechanisms to ensure that, as in any negotiation, the positions taken by its negotiators were known, approved and trusted by the 27 members of the EU Council. In the current case, this pushed the 27 to strengthen even more the position of the EU institutions. The UK finally admitted that the EU had to respect its 'constitutional' rules,[16] but this provoked delays and reduced trust.

2. THE LEGAL RIGHT OF THE UK TO UNILATERALLY WITHDRAW THE NOTIFICATION OF ITS INTENTION TO EXIT, UNTIL THE ENTRY INTO FORCE OF THE WITHDRAWAL AGREEMENT

A legal debate took place in 2016–17 as to whether the UK would have the right to unilaterally withdraw the notification of its intention to exit, despite having already sent it to the EU. The British government believed that the notification was final. The EU institutions thought that to withdraw its intention, the UK would need the unanimous consent of the EU 27. Both opinions looked legally wrong (Eeckhout and Frantziou, 2016; Peers and Weatherill, 2018; Piris, 2016a; Smismann, 2016). First, the decision to invoke Article 50 is a unilateral act that does not depend on what other member states think. Second, Article 50 provides for notification by the interested state of its *intention* to leave: it is not an irreversible decision. Third, according to Article 50, only one of two events may lead to Brexit: either the entry into force of a WA with the EU or the failure to conclude such a WA two years after the triggering of Article 50. If the intention to leave is withdrawn before one of these events is happening, the process is interrupted, the status quo ante prevails, and the UK remains an EU member. Fourth, Article 50(5) confirms this interpretation: an ex-EU member can be a candidate to rejoin, but only after having exited.

In December 2017, a petition for judicial review was lodged in the Court of Session (Scotland) by members of the British, Scottish and European Parliaments, to determine whether the notification could be revoked unilaterally before the end of the two-year period. The Court of Session referred this question to the EU Court of Justice for a preliminary ruling. In December 2018, in its *Wightman* judgment, the Court of Justice of the European Union (CJEU) judged that the UK was free to decide, in accordance with its constitutional requirements, to revoke the notification of its intention to exit (*Andy Wightman and Others v Secretary of State for Exiting the European Union*, 2018). The sovereign nature of the right of withdrawal supports the conclusion that the member state concerned keeps its unilateral right to revoke its notification. That revocation, which must be *unequivocal and unconditional*, may be decided unilaterally, in accordance with the UK's constitutional requirements. The status of the UK as an EU member state was neither suspended nor altered by the notification. To subject the British right to revoke its intention to the European Council's unanimous approval, as the Commission and the Council proposed, would transform a unilateral sovereign right into a conditional one.

3. AFTER HAVING NOTIFIED ITS INTENTION TO EXIT, THE UK COULD HAVE DELAYED THE ACTIVATION OF ARTICLE 50

Article 50 TEU created a unilateral right for a member state to withdraw from the EU.[17] Thus, the exiting state is the only one that can decide when to exercise its withdrawal right and when to notify its intention to the EU (for a different opinion, see Gatti, 2017). In the British case, the referendum was not legally binding: it had to be followed by a legal decision. Given that the UK has no written Constitution, it was not sure if the government had the authority to take that decision without the Parliament's approval, and this had to be settled by the UK's Supreme Court (*Miller v Secretary of State*, 2017).[18]

The government had chosen to organise the referendum without any planning as to what to do in case *Leave* would win. Actually, no one knew what relationship the UK would want to try to build with the EU. The British Parliament was divided, and mainly composed of *Remainers*. David Cameron, the Prime Minister who decided the referendum, resigned after the results. Theresa May, who voted to *Remain*, was appointed in July by the Conservative Party as his successor. She promised to respect the *Leave* majority in the referendum. Then, she had to take a major decision: the date when she would send the EU the intention of the UK to withdraw. According to Article 50, that date would be the point of departure of the two-year period for the WA negotiations. A further extension of that period would not be in the hands of the UK: it could only be decided by the UK *and the EU 27 unanimously*. If the WA entered into force before, or at the latest on that date, the exit would take place. Should no WA enter into force, the exit would automatically take place two years after that date.

After having stated that the referendum was politically acted, May said that the government decided to implement it. She could have added that, as there was no consensus either in the government or in the House of Commons, all possible options had to be examined first. She could have explained that the UK was thus not ready to negotiate, but that it could avoid doing it under time pressure, given its legal right to decide on the starting date. It is true that the 27 put pressure on May to do it quickly, but they had no legal right to force the UK when to decide:

- on the time necessary to prepare its negotiating position,
- on the best time for British interests to begin the negotiations.

However, May decided not to take that path. Moreover, in her speech given at Lancaster House on 17 January 2017,[19] without any study about the available options and their possible effects, she made several *red lines* public. This had the effect of closing many ways forward, before even evaluating them: no CJEU, no single market and no free movement of people. She added that 'no deal for Britain is better than a bad deal' (May, 2017a). Following the *Miller* Supreme Court judgment (24 January) (*Miller v Secretary of State for Exiting the European Union*, 2017), she requested the Parliament's green light (16 March) and decided to trigger Article 50 on 29 March 2017.[20] This meant that the WA would have to be negotiated, signed and ratified, at the latest, on 29 March 2019. This was not a wise decision, knowing that the government, the Parliament and the two main political parties were internally deeply divided. Nobody knew how the negotiating position of the UK could be defined and how to reconcile the different views within the British political authorities. On top of that, the PM decided to have general elections three years earlier than necessary, to try and get a larger majority. Unfortunately for her, the Conservative Party won the 8 June 2017 elections, but lost the slight absolute majority that it had before: the PM would now need the votes of the Democratic Unionist Party (DUP, Northern Ireland) to get a majority in the House of Commons. That would make a possible compromise more difficult to get.

Therefore, May entered in a two-year negotiation with the EU in a hurry, as her country was divided, unprepared and under time pressure. On the other side, the EU was well prepared and had a clear and united negotiating position.[21]

4. THE POWERS OF THE EU'S INSTITUTIONS OVER THE NEGOTIATION, SCOPE AND ADOPTION OF THE WITHDRAWAL AGREEMENT

Article 50 was criticised as legally unclear. Its wording is, however, the result of lengthy discussions during the 2001–03 Convention and was kept unchanged in the Lisbon Treaty. It gives exceptional powers to the EU institutions. Contrary to a treaty of accession of a new member state (Article 49 TEU) as well as a treaty revising the EU Treaties (Article 49 TEU), neither a common accord, nor a ratification by member states, is required to agree on a WA. The authors of the Treaties, aware of the difficulties involved, but also of the political necessity for the EU not to procrastinate in case one member would want to leave, tried not to complicate the way forward.

The WA belongs to the exclusive powers of the EU. The WA is negotiated by the Commission and adopted by a qualified majority of votes in the Council, with the consent of the European Parliament (EP) (Articles 50(2) TEU and 231 TFEU). The Council must work in the light of Guidelines adopted by the European Council by consensus (Articles 50(2) and 15(4) TEU). In addition to the WA, a short revision treaty will be needed to delete the UK from the list of members given in Article 52 TEU, but its temporary absence would have no legal effect.

Thus, the WA is an international law treaty concluded by the EU: it is not EU primary law (the EU basic Treaties, the TEU and the TFEU, are the primary law, i.e. the EU constitutional law). It thus may be subject to the jurisdiction of the CJEU, which could be seized of any incompatibility with the EU Treaties. It may deal with all areas covered by the EU Treaties and EU law, without any limit other than not violating these, as emphasised by the Council in the Directives for Negotiation:

> The Agreement will be negotiated and concluded by the Union. In this respect, article 50 TEU confers on the EU an exceptional horizontal competence to cover in this Agreement all matters necessary to arrange the withdrawal. This exceptional competence is of a one-off nature and strictly for the purpose of arranging for the withdrawal from the EU. (Council of the EU, 2017, p. 3)

The aim and the content of the WA, described briefly as: 'setting out the arrangements for [the UK's withdrawal], taking account of the framework for its future relationship with the Union' (Withdrawal Agreement, 2019, p. 178), would consist in giving answers to many complex questions:

- According to which calendar would the UK stop its participation in ongoing EU policies and activities?

- What would the follow-up to the administrative and judicial cases concerning the UK and pending in the Commission and the CJEU be?
- How the three preliminary questions would be solved: the rights of EU citizens, the budgetary issues and the avoidance of a hard land border within the island of Ireland?
- What kind of governance, with which mechanisms for the settlement of disputes, was to be foreseen?

5. ARTICLE 50 DOES NOT CONFER ON THE EU THE POWER TO NEGOTIATE AN AGREEMENT ON ITS FUTURE RELATIONS WITH A WITHDRAWING STATE

Article 50(3) TEU provides that the WA must take account of the framework of the future relationship. It does not permit substantive provisions on what this future relationship shall be, because that must be based on other legal EU Treaty provisions. As to the shape and content of the framework, it was up to the UK to present its wishes, but, during a long period, internal divisions prevented its government from adopting a position. Despite this situation, the government asked the EU to engage immediately in a parallel negotiation on the agreement on future relations (May, 2017a, 2017b).[22] It was, however, not possible for the EU to engage in such a negotiation at that stage: it had no legal power to do it. The legal base for an agreement with a third country (Articles 216 to 219 TFEU) is to be used to negotiate with a third country, not with an EU member. Negotiating with a third state must use different procedures than those specific to Article 50. An ordinary FTA (Free Trade Agreement) may be concluded by a qualified majority in the Council and a simple consultation of the EP (Article 218(6)(b) and (8) TFEU). In case of an association agreement, they would require unanimity in the Council, and the consent of the EP (Article 218(6)(a) TFEU). In case of a mixed agreement concerning areas where powers belong to the member states, each member state would have to conclude it, according to its constitutional requirements.

The UK finally admitted that the EU had to follow its constitutional rules.

6. THREE ISSUES OF THE WITHDRAWAL AGREEMENT, REGARDED BY THE EU AS PRELIMINARY, WERE NEGOTIATED BEFORE THE OTHERS

Negotiations began in June 2017. The EU insisted that they should be divided in two stages. It explained that some issues were preliminary, as compared with those linked with the future relationship. Right from the beginning, it was stressed in the Guidelines of the European Council (European Council, 2017a) and in the Negotiating Directives (Council of the EU, 2017) addressed to the Commission[23] that the EU would not accept debating other questions before settling these three issues:

(a) *The protection of the rights of EU citizens living in the UK and of UK citizens living in the EU 27:* many Britons were living, working or were retired as EU citizens in other EU countries before Brexit, while millions of EU citizens of the 27 were living in the UK. Both parties agreed that most rights of these individuals[24] had to be preserved after the transition period. This issue was considered as essential by the EP. It was finally solved rather generously in Part Two of the WA *Citizens' Rights*. It gives the right of residence and employment without discrimination for those who arrived before the end of the transition period (TP), and their family. It opens the possibility of legal challenges against a violation of their rights and to preliminary rulings by the CJEU, up to eight years after the end of the transition period (Article 158 WA). The WA also provides that a British independent authority shall monitor the implementation in the UK of that Part Two (Article 159 WA).[25] After the end of the transition period, the normal settlement of disputes, through an arbitration mechanism, will apply, except on pending cases.

(b) *The past budgetary commitments of the UK:* any WA would have to determine the amount and the conditions of payment of the British budgetary commitments taken before its exit. All budgetary consequences of decisions made when the UK was a member state, including the cost of pensions of EU staff, or of multi-year programmes or projects, had to be fairly shared. Negotiations started based on a Commission paper that listed the commitments and proposed a methodology to calculate the UK's debt. A reasonable result was also agreed in the Joint Report of 8 December 2017 (European Commission, 2017), and then formalised in the draft WA (European Commission, 2018, Articles 133–157), including on spreading the British payments (between 35 to 39 billion euros) over a number of years.

(c) *The absence of controls at the Irish border:* last, but not least, the issue on how to avoid re-establishing a hard border between the two parts of the Irish island was the most complex. How to ensure that Northern Ireland, as a part of the UK and thus a third country vis-à-vis the EU, belonging neither to the EU's single market nor to its customs union, could continue to have no control at its border with the Irish Republic (an EU member state), as prescribed by the Good Friday Agreement (GFA) (1998)? This solution was desired by all but how to obtain it? How could goods go from a third state to an EU state without being checked at a border? What about possible different customs duties, or different standards and norms? It was like trying to square a circle.

Initially, the UK did not agree that these three issues had to be preliminary. Why should it be legally required to distinguish them from the others? The EU argued that, given that they were independent from the framework for the *future* UK-EU relations, they should be dealt with first and independently, given that they pertained to the *past*. Was this EU position legally defensible? It was true that the budgetary issue was linked only to the period prior to the Brexit date, thus independent from any future relations. As for the rights of the citizens, they had to exist before the withdrawal.

However, the EU's position on the issue of the Irish border was legally debatable, although politically understandable. The EU insisted that, regardless of what the future UK-EU relations would be, the GFA should integrally be respected and protected (European Council, 2017a).[26] This was true, but the UK could have argued that a link with future relations existed, because a result could be more or less easy to reach, according to what the participation of the UK – or at least of Northern Ireland – would be in the EU's customs union or in its single market. Whatever the legal value of the respective arguments, the EU won the case, which it considered to be essential, as it was imperative that the GFA, a complex and delicate agreement, should be protected from any risk of destabilisation.

On 8 December 2017, the 'Joint Report from the negotiators of the EU and the UK government on progress during phase 1 of the negotiations under Article 50 TEU on the UK's orderly withdrawal from the EU' included a compromise[27] according to which there would be a regulatory alignment between Northern Ireland and the Republic of Ireland (i.e. the EU), to avoid controls on trade in goods (European Commission, 2017). On this basis, the European Council decided on 15 December 2017 that sufficient progress had been made on the preliminary issues: negotiations could continue with the other issues (European Council, 2017b). However, the Irish border problem was far from having been solved.

7. THE ATTEMPT OF THE UK GOVERNMENT TO KEEP THE EU SINGLE MARKET BENEFITS

When the negotiations began, one year after the referendum, the British government was continuing its internal debate on the shape of the future relations with the EU. Several ministers had still illusions, well illustrated by the famous formula: 'let's have the cake and eat it'. Some argued that the UK should be able to leave the EU only as 'a would-be political entity'. They believed, or at least they said, that the EU needed to continue trading with the UK and would thus allow it to continue to participate in the EU's single market. There was probably a lack of understanding, during that period, between politicians and civil servants in the UK, as the excellent British civil service could not have had any illusion as to what the EU's answer to such a request would be.

May noted that the EU had offered, in December 2017, that if NI continued to respect the pertinent EU legislation, it could stay in its customs union and benefit from its single market. As mentioned earlier, this offer was refused by the UK, because it saw it as 'constitutionally' difficult to accept. May thought that, given that the EU had accepted such an option for Northern Ireland, it could as well accept it for the whole of the UK. She proposed to work on that basis. She had difficulties to convince her Cabinet, but finally got a majority to agree to her suggestion, during a difficult meeting at Checkers on 6 July 2018. Two members of the government resigned (Johnson and Raab). May presented her offer to the EU in a summit held in Salzburg in September 2018. The UK would remain in the EU's customs union and commit itself to align, in a so-called 'common rulebook', to EU's single market rules. This would apply neither to services, nor to the freedom of movement of persons. The principles of EU law and the role of the CJEU were not mentioned.

The EU's answer in Salzburg was negative. An exceptional solution benefiting a small territory (Northern Ireland), subject to extraordinary circumstances (GFA) (1998) and 'the unique circumstances on the island of Ireland' (European Commission, 2017, p. 7), was not acceptable for the whole of the UK. It could not be a model for the broader UK-EU issues. It was not conceivable for a third country to get similar single market benefits to those of a member state, in exchange for a promise to partly align its domestic law to relevant EU law, while not accepting the jurisdiction of the CJEU and the principles of EU law (primacy, direct effect, exclusive final power of interpretation by the CJEU, etc.). A country not bound by the same rules as an EU member could not get similar single market access. That would affect the homogeneity, credibility and legal security of the single market. As regards goods, participating states must respect common norms and standards. Timely and full implementation of EU law is not only checked by the Commission and national administrations. Individuals, consumers and economic operators may demand its correct and timely application. They may get compensation in case of damage, through their national courts, which in turn get the legal interpretation of EU law by the CJEU. Moreover, 'If the Court finds that the Member State concerned has not complied with its judgment it may impose a lump sum or penalty payment on it' (Article 260(2), second subparagraph TFEU).

The single market's credibility depends on the strength of that full and coherent system, based on an identical playing field. Opening loopholes benefiting a third state would jeopardise this strength and reduce the trust of economic operators, as well as the trust of countries negotiating trade agreements with the EU. Despite early warnings (Piris, 2017b), especially by the EU's Chief negotiator Michel Barnier, the EU's refusal of the British offer in Salzburg was a shock for some in the UK. The meaning of Brexit became clearer in London. The EU would not accept to weaken its single market.

That was the end of the illusion of 'having the cake and eating it', and of the belief that there was a possible agreement which would be, at the same time, better for the British economy than the Canada type and more acceptable politically to the UK than the Norway type. The illusion of a possible 'soft Brexit' was waning. By refusing to follow current and future EU rules on the single market, the free movement of persons and the CJEU's jurisdiction, the UK had closed all doors to a 'soft Brexit' or a similar arrangement such as the EEA. A hard Brexit was the only way, with different options but with no participation in the EU single market.

8. LEGAL ASPECTS OF THE POSTPONEMENTS OF THE EXIT DATE[28]

Taking that into account, May negotiated with the EU a new version of the WA and of a Political Declaration (PD) on future relations. Both were agreed on 8 December 2018. A Protocol on Ireland/Northern Ireland (2019) provided for common regulations in Northern Ireland and in Ireland, and a 'backstop'[29] for the Irish border. But the PM had difficulties getting a majority in the Parliament, and 'the clock was ticking'. Article 50(3) TEU allows the European Council, acting unanimously[30] and in agreement with the exiting state, to extend the negotiating period of the WA. The number and duration of extensions are not limited by the Treaty. As a result, the time left to negotiate the agreement on future relations would be automatically reduced. Given that a cliff edge would also have been bad for itself, the EU was accommodating to the British wishes.

The parties agreed to several postponements of the 29 March 2019 exit date, which had first been chosen by May. The UK requested and got a first extension until 12 April (or 22 May) 2019, a second one until 31 October 2019, and finally a third one until 31 January 2020. No condition is foreseen in Article 50. However, the EU recalled some existing obligations of the UK during the extensions. It had especially 'to act in a constructive manner and responsible manner throughout the extension period' (European Council, 2019, p. 5), and to hold EP elections when the day would come.

During the ten-month duration of the extensions, May managed to get a consensus of her Cabinet three times on different versions of a WA draft agreed by the EU, all versions keeping the 'backstop' concept. The House of Commons refused these proposals, once in January and twice in March 2019. Those voting against included the DUP MPs and many MPs of her own party. May resigned and was succeeded by Johnson, who had become the most popular *hard leaver* and called new elections on 12 December 2019. The Tories won with 43.6 per cent of the votes (1.2 per cent more than in June 2017) and a majority of more than 80 seats. A new WA version was promptly agreed with the EU and approved by the House of Commons. The WA was then approved on 29 January 2020 by the EU (EP and Council) and entered into force on 1 February 2020. Brexit was done, with a transition period of 11 months, finishing on 31 December 2020.

9. THE CHANGES TO THE FINAL VERSION OF THE WITHDRAWAL AGREEMENT OBTAINED BY PM JOHNSON

The 'backstop' included in the Ireland-Northern Ireland Protocol, first accepted by May, but refused by the House of Commons, was unacceptable to Johnson. He declared that this was establishing a separation between two parts of the UK, Great Britain (GB) and Northern Ireland (NI), with a risk of becoming permanent. He proposed another mechanism, which he discussed during a private meeting with the Irish PM. This apparently *new* option was, in a different form, the option suggested previously by the EU in December 2017, but then rejected by May (see Section 7 above). Only Northern Ireland, as opposed to the rest of the UK (Great Britain), would benefit from the EU's single market and customs union, while continuing to follow the corresponding EU rules. May thought that 'no British PM would ever accept that'. Johnson accepted it, on the condition that while Northern Ireland would follow the EU's customs union rules, it would simultaneously remain part of the UK's customs union.

Thus, Northern Ireland is part of the customs territory of the UK (Protocol on Ireland/ Northern Ireland, Article 4). However, in order to get a regime of *no duties-no quotas* for its trade with the EU, Northern Ireland would have to respect the EU rules as if it was still part of the EU's customs union. In order to allow for no hard border, Northern Ireland would also be bound by many of the EU's single market rules. This would be the case for at least four years[31] after the end of the transition period, then subject to a decision of the Northern Ireland democratic authorities. Changes were also made to the Political Declaration, which was meant to be the basis for negotiations on the future agreement. However, when negotiations began, the UK refused to use it as that basis. This caused a serious weakening of trust by the EU. Moreover, soon after having signed the WA, Johnson stated publicly several times that the UK government will not exercise a control over goods traded between Britain and Northern Ireland. Negatively surprised, the EU stressed that this would be a violation of the Irish Protocol, given that, according to that text, goods going from one customs territory to another (between GB and the EU) should be controlled. The UK also refused the EU's request to have an office in Northern Ireland (see Section 15 below). These positions had further negative impacts on the EU's trust.

Finally, the UK reluctantly admitted that it would exercise controls as provided for in the Irish Protocol, but without being monitored by the presence of EU staff. This situation raised concerns in the EU about the sincere will of the UK to implement the Protocol fully and in good faith. These concerns increased considerably when, on 9 September 2020, the British government proposed a British Internal Market Bill (2020), which explicitly put aside some of the Protocol's articles (see Section 14 below). This violation of international law was explicitly acknowledged in the Parliament by the government.[32]

10. THE PARTICIPATION OF THE UK IN THE ELECTIONS OF THE EUROPEAN PARLIAMENT AND THE ABSENCE OF A BRITISH NATIONAL IN THE COMMISSION BEFORE THE EXIT

When the British government asked for a postponement of its exit until after the date of the elections (23/26 May 2019) of the EP, the Commission recalled that it would be legally required to organise these elections on its territory. The 2018 European Council Decision establishing the composition of the EP provided appropriate options for the two possible cases: an EP with or without MEPs elected in the UK (European Council Decision (EU) 2018/937, 2018). The UK was reluctant to organise elections, but for the EU[33] this was a *sine qua non* condition, for three legal reasons:

(i) British nationals, as well as other EU citizens living in the UK, had a legal right to participate; they could go to court if their right was not respected;[34]
(ii) the legality of any act adopted with the participation of the EP (even for a consultation), when required by the Treaties, could be questioned in court, if UK nationals were not represented;
(iii) if the UK used its right to revoke its Article 50 notification, British nationals would have to be represented in the EP.

Thus, the EP elections took place in the UK on 23 May. The participation rate was low (37 per cent) and UKIP got 30 per cent of the votes. The very poor results of the Tories (less than 9 per cent of the votes) encouraged May to resign in June. In July 2019, Johnson was appointed PM by the members of the Conservative Party. When the time came for the British government to propose a candidate for a post of Commissioner,[35] the Commission reminded the UK government that it had a legal obligation to do so. Johnson refused. He argued that general elections were to take place on 12 December 2019 and that this kind of decision could not be taken during an electoral campaign. He implied that the date of Brexit would become certain after that, as he hoped to win the elections and thus to ratify the WA quickly. The Commission was not happy, but events confirmed the wishes of Johnson. The new Commission took office at the normal date, with 27 Commissioners instead of 28, and worked in this composition for one month. This did not raise any legal or political problem.[36]

11. THE LEGAL BASE FOR THE ESTABLISHMENT OF A TRANSITION PERIOD IN THE WITHDRAWAL AGREEMENT

In case of success of the negotiations of the WA, both parties would have to formally ratify that Agreement before 29 March 2019. How could a *cliff edge* be avoided at that date, should the parties (or one of them) not have accomplished their constitutional procedures? If nothing was done, Brexit without a WA would automatically entail the application of WTO rules.[37] In the absence of any explicit legal base in the EU Treaties for the adoption of transition measures by the EU's institutions, how could that be avoided?

The only legal basis for an EU action appeared to be in Article 50(2) TEU, according to which the WA should set out the arrangements for the withdrawal, 'taking account of the framework of (the) future relationship'. Was it legally possible to establish a transition period on the basis of these few words? This was not obvious. Some lawyers thought that it would violate the EU Treaties, because these Treaties do not confer on the institutions the power to establish *ex nihilo* a status for *a semi-membership status* (Craig, 2017, p. 66). Others stressed that this would be possible only if the framework for the future relationship was known, because it should be a transition towards that aim.[38] However, most people regarded Article 50(2) as opening the possibility of transition measures, in order to help smooth progress towards post-exit arrangements. But which measures? Which advantages – normally reserved for EU members – could the EU's institutions agree to permit the UK, which would have then become a third state, to continue to benefit from, during a transition period? Many suggestions which were made would have been either insufficient or too difficult to negotiate. The idea of the UK becoming a *short-term member of the EEA*, for example, raised difficult problems. It would require delicate negotiations, including to reform the EEA institutions, followed by ratifications by the EU and 32 states (including Switzerland). The option to allow the UK to participate during a few years only in the EU's customs union would have been insufficient. To try to design a custom-made treaty through opening long negotiations for each EU policy was unrealistic.

Finally, the UK requested a full transition (implementation) period on the whole range of UK-EU relations. The EU agreed. It decided that an interim semi-membership status, limited in time, could be established in the WA in order to progress towards the withdrawal. This was a bold interpretation of the EU Treaties, taking also into account the possible contradiction with democratic principles (Armstrong, 2020, p. 182). The limited duration of the transition period was the *sine qua non* condition of its legality, because, except that interpretation of Article 50 TEU, there was no other legal basis which could be envisaged, either in the TEU or the TFEU. The WA, which entered into force on 1 February 2020, provides for its termination at the end of 2020,[39] after 11 months, which is quite reasonable.

The option chosen was simple enough to avoid lengthy discussions. It was a 'Full Monty' option (Piris, 2017a): the UK would keep *all* benefits and duties as if it was still a member state:

- First, '[u]nless otherwise provided for in this Agreement, Union law shall be applicable to and in the UK during the TP' (Art 127(1) WA);
- Second, '[d]uring the TP, the institutions, bodies, offices and agencies of the Union shall have the powers conferred upon them by Union law in relation with the UK …' (Article 131 WA).

Thus, all rules applicable to EU members would apply to the UK,[40] while respecting its existing derogations (euro, Schengen, Justice and Home affairs). The EU institutions would continue to exercise, vis-à-vis the UK, their powers to legislate and decide, as well as their tasks of interpretation, supervision and enforcement. The principles of primacy and of direct effect of EU law would be preserved (Article 4(1)-(3) WA). No British national would participate in EU institutions, bodies, offices and agencies and in their decision-making process. During the transition period, nothing would change for individuals and companies. One of the difficulties was to make third countries accept to continue to apply to the UK the legal obligations they have vis-à-vis the EU (especially for trade) and its 27 member states during this period. That worked in most cases. Besides, the UK would be allowed to engage in trade negotiations with third countries for the future.

12. THE LIMITED LEGAL[41] POSSIBILITIES TO AMEND THE WITHDRAWAL AGREEMENT AFTER ITS ENTRY INTO FORCE

This issue was discussed ad nauseam in social media, especially as regards the length of the transition period. Three possibilities were put forward:

1. *A modification by the Joint Committee.* Actually, the power of the Joint Committee to amend the WA exists but is limited to 'the cases provided for in this Agreement' (Article 164(4)(f) WA). Similarly, decisions the Joint Committee is permitted to take are only those enumerated in the WA (Articles 164(4)(e) and 166 WA). Some political commentators thought that, despite that, if no extension of the transition period was decided before 1 July, 'one may find a legal way' to extend the transition period if the Parties decided to do so before 31 December. The author of this chapter disagrees with this opinion. An extension of the transition period could only have been decided based on Article 132(1) WA, according to which 'the Joint Committee may, before 1 July 2020, adopt a single decision extending the transition period for up to 1 or 2 years'. The Joint Committee should have decided on an extension at the latest on 30 June 2020. Given the curious formulation of the provision 'for up to 1 or 2 years', there was a hesitation: was the extension possible for one or two years, or could it be less than one, or less than two? The words 'up to' must have a legal meaning, so it might have been either one or two years, or less than one of these durations. It could not go beyond 31 December 2022.[42]
2. *An EU decision based on Article 352 TFEU.* According to its own terms, Article 352 TFEU can be used only if the action envisaged 'should prove necessary, within the policies defined in the Treaties, to attain one of the objectives set out in the Treaties and the Treaties have not provided the necessary powers … Thus, it would not be legally correct to use it in the present case: first, because the withdrawal of a member state is not one of the policies or objectives of the EU (see Article 3 TEU) and second, because Article 50 does provide the necessary powers for the EU to confront that situation. Besides, two Declarations no. 41 and 42 concerning Article 352 were unanimously agreed and published in the Lisbon Intergovernmental Conference (IGC) Final Act (2007) when the Lisbon Treaty was signed. They clarify even more the limits of Article 352. The first one stresses that 'the reference in Article 352(1) to objectives of the Union refers to the objectives as set out in Article 3(2) and (3) of the TEU …' (Lisbon IGC Final Act, 2007, p. 262). The second one recalls that Article 352:

   > [B]eing an integral part of an institutional system based on the principle of conferred powers, cannot serve as a basis for widening the scope of Union powers beyond the general framework created by the provisions of the Treaties as a whole and, in particular, by those that define the tasks and the activities of the Union. (Lisbon IGC Final Act, 2007, p. 263)[43]

3. *A new UK-EU treaty, based or not by the EU on Article 50.* The EU basic Treaties do not provide any substantive legal base other than Article 50 TEU to deal with a request for withdrawal of a member state. On 1 February 2020, the EU Treaties ceased to apply to the UK, with the entry into force of the WA, concluded by the EU on that basis. Since then, the EU can no longer use Article 50 as a legal basis to conclude an agreement with the UK, as the UK is now a third country. The EU has no legal basis to amend the WA, neither

Article 50 nor any other article. Some international lawyers argue that, in any case, any international treaty may be amended freely by the parties (Repasi, 2020). They stress that Article 39(1) of the 1969 Vienna Convention on the Law of Treaties, which mostly reflects customary international law, provides that '[a] treaty may be amended by agreement between the parties' (VCLT, 1969, Article 39(1)). But this Vienna Convention concerns only the treaties *between states*. It could not be applicable to the EU, which is not a state.

There is another Vienna Convention dealing with the law of treaties when at least one of the parties is an international organisation (1986). However, this Convention is not in force and the EU did not sign it. Moreover, the corresponding Article 39 of this Convention provides in a paragraph 2 that 'The consent of an international organization to an agreement provided for in paragraph 1 shall be governed by the rules of that organisation.' In our case, the treaty in question, i.e., the WA, expressly limits the possibilities to amend it: its Article 164(4) provides that 'the Joint Committee shall: … (f) adopt amendments to this Agreement in the cases provided for in this Agreement'. There is no provision giving such power to the Joint Committee on the duration of the transition period.

Thus, the EU has no power to modify the institutional provisions of the WA, even if the UK had agreed to do so. More than any EU Treaty in the past, the Lisbon Treaty insists on 'the principle of conferral'.[44] This is probably the most important EU principle: contrary to states, the EU has not an unlimited treaty-making power. It has not the competence to extend its competences. Thus, institutional provisions of the WA were frozen, including the duration of the transition period. In any case, this became an academic issue when the British government confirmed its decision that the transition period would not be extended, and that the EU took note of that.

13. REMEDIES IN CASE OF BREACHES OF THE WA'S OBLIGATIONS OTHER THAN IN THE IRISH PROTOCOL

During the Transition Period

During the transition period, EU law remained applicable to and in the UK with the same legal effects as for the member states (Article 127 WA), with some precise exceptions. Article 131 WA deals briefly with supervision and enforcement and the powers of the EU's institutions during that period:

> During the transition period, the institutions, bodies, offices and agencies of the Union shall have the powers conferred upon them by Union law in relation to the United Kingdom and to natural and legal persons residing or established in the United Kingdom. In particular, the Court of Justice of the European Union shall have jurisdiction as provided for in the Treaties. The first paragraph shall also apply during the transition period as regards the interpretation and application of this Agreement.[45]

Thus, the UK was subject to the same controls as the member states and to the same decisions of the EU institutions. This is precisely what happened when the British Internal Market Bill (2020) was considered in September 2020, and the Commission began an infringement procedure under Article 258 TFEU.[46] In any case, it was obvious that any breach of the WA's obligations by a party during the transition period would immediately entail political consequences on the position taken by the other party in ongoing negotiations on their future relations.

Since the Transition Period

Since the end of the transition period, beginning on 1 January 2021, most EU law no longer applies to and in the UK, despite a few exceptions, especially in Northern Ireland. On top of that exception, EU institutions keep the limited powers conferred on them in a few explicit provisions of the WA. This is the case, for instance, in the Protocol on British bases in Cyprus (2019), where, because the British bases remain part of the EU's customs union, pertinent EU law is still applicable, including EU law on excise tax and VAT and rules to avoid fraud, and the CJEU has jurisdiction. In the Protocol on Gibraltar (2019), Article 1 on citizens' rights continues to apply. On administrative procedures, Commission infringement cases on state aid granted before the transition period's end, as well as OLAF (EU European Anti-Fraud Office) procedures, will still be possible for four years after the end of the transition period, regarding decisions made or procedures begun before that date (Article 93 WA). The judgments of the CJEU are no longer binding in the UK, but UK courts and authorities have 'due regard for' these judgments. There are two exceptions:

- regarding most rights of EU citizens, which will continue to be interpreted by the CJEU during eight years after transition period's end;[47]
- regarding infringement actions and preliminary rulings over cases concerning references to the EU budget in Part Five (Financial Settlement).

Part Six of the WA deals with 'Institutional and final provisions' and lists provisions which remain in force after 1 January 2021. The Joint Committee is the most important body for governance, with six specialised committees: Citizens' Rights; Other Separation Provisions; Implementation of the Irish Protocol; Protocol on Cyprus; Protocol on Gibraltar; and Financial Provisions.

As for the 'normal' (excluding Northern Ireland issues) settlement of disputes, it provides that consultations in the Joint Committee are always the first step. If no solution is found after three months, the dispute may go to an arbitration panel (Articles 167 to 181 WA),[48] to which individuals have no direct access. The rulings of the arbitration panel shall be binding for the parties. In case of no compliance after a period agreed by the parties or decided by the panel, the panel may impose a lump sum or penalty payment. If the party concerned does not pay, the complainant shall be entitled to suspend some of its obligations (but not for citizens' rights). Temporary remedies are allowed for a party if and when the other party does not comply with an arbitration ruling. Counterbalancing measures are possible. Any of these measures will have to be temporary and respect the principle of proportionality. If the arbitrators must decide on an issue raising a question of interpretation of a concept of EU law to settle a dispute, they will have to request a ruling by the CJEU. The ruling of the court shall be binding on the panel.

The TCA contains a provision on '*Essential elements*'[49] which mentions three issues as being '*essential elements of the partnership*' established by the TCA: (i) democracy, rule of law and human rights, (ii) fight against climate change, and (iii) countering proliferation of weapons of mass destruction. This means that, if a party violates one of these elements, the other one may suspend or terminate the agreement after following the applicable procedure.[50]

14. THE SEPTEMBER 2020 BRITISH INTERNAL MARKET BILL, ITS CONSEQUENCES AND ITS WITHDRAWAL IN DECEMBER 2020

On 9 September 2020, the incredible happened: the British PM presented to the British Parliament a Bill on the British Internal Market (2020). One of the aims of this proposed legislation was to authorise the government to ignore provisions of a signed and ratified treaty by taking measures 'notwithstanding' some provisions of the WA. This obvious violation of international law was publicly recognised in the House of Commons by a member of the British government (see Section 9 above). This provoked outrage in the legal professions in the UK, as well as in the House of Lords. Two senior British officials involved decided to resign. However, the House of Commons approved the government's position and voted in favour of the bill with a majority of well over 80 votes.

The PM explained that the WA was drafted hastily, and one realised only later that it was bad for the UK. This is not convincing. From the beginning, the UK did not like some parts of the WA, but realised that they were necessary to get the deal on Brexit swiftly accepted by the EU. The PM needed that deal to be done in order to hold national elections rapidly 'with a deal done'.

The EU institutions and the 27 member states were flabbergasted. The trust they still had was sharply reduced. Their determination to demand that the TCA include precise provisions on the level playing field (LPF) and on a robust governance was strengthened. On 1 October, the Commission began a legal procedure of infringement (Article 258 TFEU) against the UK, given that the CJEU was still competent during the transition period. It argued that the UK was violating the WA and the principle of good faith.[51] The reactions in third countries were bad, with strong reactions in the US Congress, due to the link with the Irish problem. The UK's long-standing reputation as a state respecting law and its legal commitments was damaged. In the future, it would have a problem requesting others to respect international law, be it China in Hong Kong or Russia in Ukraine.

The EU thus insisted even more on a single global agreement providing for the possibility of unilateral cross-measures in case of breach of its legal obligations by the other party. Such measures could be taken, for example, after a refusal of a party to execute the ruling of the arbitration tribunal and include suspension of some parts of the agreement in any area (cross-sector retaliation). These are classic possibilities offered by international law, which generally remain unused ('deterrent').

Apart from the damage done to the UK, this might have been dangerous in Ireland, as it could have entailed a hard border for trade of goods between the Republic of Ireland and Northern Ireland. Given that the logic of the Good Friday Agreement and Peace Process would be incompatible with such checks to be carried out at the land border, where could they take place, if the WA provisions which permit that had not been respected by the UK's new legislation? There would be no other way than controls on land. In that case, who would be bold enough to be certain that it would not cause any troubles?

It is true that the wording of the Protocol on Ireland/Northern Ireland is complicated and sometimes ambiguous, but it was democratically accepted by both parties. The British tactic was dangerous, especially when legal means existed, as the WA and the Protocol were offering different possible procedures:

a) Each party may refer to the Committee on the Protocol on Ireland/Northern Ireland and to the Joint Committee of the WA, any issue relating to the implementation, application and interpretation of the Agreement or of the Protocol (Articles 164–166 WA; Article 14 Protocol on Ireland/Northern Ireland).
b) If the Joint Committee of the WA cannot settle differences in interpretation, the WA also provides for reasonable means to settle these disputes, including an arbitration procedure (Articles 167–181 WA).
c) Moreover, article 16 of the Protocol (with its Annex 7 on Procedures) allows each party to 'unilaterally take appropriate safeguard measures', which 'shall be restricted with regard to their scope and duration to what is strictly necessary in order to remedy the situation' in case of the application of the Protocol leading to 'serious economic, societal or environmental difficulties that are liable to persist, or to diversion of trade'. The same article however allows the other party to take proportional rebalancing measures.

Finally, in December 2020, the Committee on Ireland/Northern Ireland found an agreement on all the issues discussed.[52] Immediately, the UK government declared that the criticised provisions of the Internal Bill would be withdrawn, as well as similar provisions in the Taxation Bill.

15. THE PROTOCOL ON IRELAND/NORTHERN IRELAND (I/NI): DIFFERENCES OF INTERPRETATION; THE AGREEMENT OF THE JOINT COMMITTEE I/NI IN DECEMBER 2020; REMEDIES IN CASE OF A DISPUTE

The Ireland/Northern Ireland Protocol 'shall apply as from the end of the transition period' (Article 185 WA). There are some exceptions where it was already applied from the date of the WA's entry into force. Article 12(4 and 5) of the Protocol on Ireland/Northern Ireland (2019) provides that EU bodies, including the CJEU, have competence to apply or interpret the provisions according to which most EU rules continue to apply in Northern Ireland, making it a de facto part of the EU's single market (Articles 7 to 10), as well as the provisions of Article 5 on 'Customs, movement of goods'. This includes state aid, including aid decided by the UK's government which 'affect' trade in goods between Northern Ireland and the EU (Article 10(1)).

The Differences of Interpretation

The specialised Committee on issues related to the implementation of the Ireland/North Ireland Protocol (2019, Article 14) met to prepare its application after the end of the transition period. Disagreements over the interpretation of two sets of provisions appeared: (1) the presence of EU officials on the Northern Ireland territory and the legal status to be given to their office, as well as (2) the necessity or not to control goods going from GB to Northern Ireland and from Northern Ireland to GB.

According to Article 12, 'the authorities of the UK shall be responsible for implementing and applying' in Northern Ireland the provisions of EU law made applicable by the Protocol. EU 'representatives shall have the right to be present' during the related activities of the UK's authorities' activities and 'the UK shall facilitate such presence of Union representatives'. On this basis, the EU requested to exercise this right and expressed the wish to open an official EU representation in Belfast. The UK refused, arguing that it was not necessary.

The second problem appeared to be more difficult, given several statements made by Johnson, according to which there will not be any control on goods going between Northern Ireland and GB. He stressed that, according to Article 6(1) of the Protocol, '[n]othing in this Protocol shall prevent the UK from ensuring unfettered access for goods moving from Northern Ireland to other parts of the UK's internal market'. But he forgot to mention that it remains mandatory for the UK to implement the relevant EU customs code in respect of all goods leaving Northern Ireland to go to a third country, including GB. All EU norms and standards, regulations on security and health, etc. shall be applicable, as prescribed by EU law. As to these controls, both parties accepted the WA precisely because its provisions do not provide for customs controls at the Irish land border, while they do foresee effective controls which are necessary between the EU and a third country outside its single market and its customs union (Wheaterill, 2020). This means, implicitly but necessarily, that these controls must be done in the Irish Sea, between Britain and Northern Ireland. After the end of the transition period, Northern Ireland remained part of the customs territory of the UK (Article 4, first sentence) but became also simultaneously part of the EU's customs territory, given the application of all EU rules concerning the EU customs union according to the Protocol: Article 5 (paragraphs 3 to 5) and Annex 2, which is a list of EU Acts of more than 20 pages.[53] The presumption is that any goods going from Britain to Northern Ireland shall automatically be considered at risk of going to the EU and thus duties must be paid, unless proof of the contrary is established. Would it appear later that duties were not to be paid, the Protocol provides that they must be reimbursed. Moreover, Northern Ireland has to apply EU rules and legislation on product regulation, environmental standards, sanitary and phytosanitary rules, and state aid; value-added tax and excise tax shall also follow EU rules. On all these matters, EU laws have the same effect as in an EU member state. This means that, for goods going from GB to Northern Ireland, controls must in principle be established, applied and implemented by the British authorities, in the presence of EU representatives, and that this presence must be facilitated by the UK. In opposition to that, the British *command paper* from 27 May 2020 setting out the UK's position on the implementation of the Protocol had expressed a hard line. It provided neither a permanent EU presence in Northern Ireland nor enough adequate controls in ports.

The Joint Committee Agreement in December 2020

Discussions went on in the Joint Committee on Northern Ireland and, finally, after the melodramatic episode of the British Internal Market Bill in September 2020,[54] a global agreement '*in principle*' on discussed issues was politically reached on 8 December 2020, and confirmed legally on 17 December. The British government agreed then to withdraw the British Internal Market Bill, as well as the further Taxation Bill – which was going to be introduced in the House of Commons and would also have violated the WA. There was also an agreement about the possibility for the EU (the Commission) to be present in Northern Ireland when UK officials are applying EU law.

The main points agreed are as follows:

- *On goods going from Northern Ireland to Great Britain:* Arrangements permit the UK to allow 'unfettered access' to the UK internal market for qualifying Northern Ireland businesses. No export or exit declarations shall be required on qualifying goods moving between Northern Ireland and GB. Instead, British authorities will collect data through other sources and share it with the EU. Other goods will be accompanied by an exit summary declaration.
- *On goods going from GB to Northern Ireland:* If they can be shown to remain in Northern Ireland, they will be controlled by British authorities through a UK Trader Scheme (UKTS), reserved for businesses established in Northern Ireland.
- *On goods directly entering Northern Ireland:* Goods entering Northern Ireland from the rest of the world will also come under the scheme.
- *Emergency brake:* The UKTS will be subject to safeguards, including an emergency brake in 2024 'in the event of significant diversion to trade, fraud or other illegal activities' (Article 9).
- *Agri-food:* Supermarkets and trusted suppliers identified by Northern Ireland authorities shall benefit from a grace period until 1 April 2021. Some products shall be allowed to move between GB-NI for six months. Longer term, the UK and EU agreed to try and minimise checks, but if they don't succeed, the temporary measures shall end and the full agri-food controls shall apply.
- *State aid:* EU state aid law shall apply to measures which 'affect trade' between NI and EU, but only if there is a 'genuine and direct link' to Northern Ireland. Agricultural support shall be exempted from state aid rules up to £380 million, as well as fisheries aid, for a lesser amount (Article 1).
- *Internal Market Bill:* The UK withdrew the disputed provisions from this bill, as well as those contained by the Taxation Bill. What remedies are there in case of a party breaching its obligations under the Protocol?

On matters covered by EU law: Article 12(4 and 5) of the Protocol on Ireland/Northern Ireland (2019) provides that, regarding some provisions, including Articles 5 on *Customs, movement of goods* and 10 on *state aid*, the EU institutions, including the CJEU, shall, in relation to the UK, have the powers conferred upon them by EU law, with the same legal effects as in the EU. After the end of the transition period, the Commission shall thus retain its capacity to pursue infringement cases against the UK, and the CJEU to interpret applicable EU law, including in preliminary rulings. Individuals adversely affected by incorrect application of this part of the Protocol may also complain to their national authorities and tribunals and request compensation.[55]

On matters not governed by EU law, since the end of the transition period, the 'normal' WA procedure applies: a dispute should first be discussed in the Joint Committee; after three months, an arbitration panel might be established; the CJEU shall be competent regarding interpretation of EU law only.

16. THE VALUE OF THE POLITICAL DECLARATION AS THE BASIS FOR THE TRADE AND COOPERATION AGREEMENT (TCA)

Political declarations are frequently attached to international treaties. They are not legally binding, but are regarded as political commitments taken in good faith. Parties negotiate and sign them simultaneously with their legal commitments. It is rare that the parties decide to make cross references to both texts in a treaty and in a declaration, because their value is different. In the current case, the parties stressed the importance of the Political Declaration (2020) by making such cross references. In the WA's preamble, they noted 'that in parallel with this Agreement, the Parties have made a Political Declaration setting out the framework for the future relations between the EU and the UK' (Withdrawal Agreement, 2020, recital 15 of the preamble). Article 184 WA on the negotiation of the future relationship further provides that:

> The EU and the UK shall use their best endeavours, in good faith and in full respect of their respective legal order, to take the necessary steps to negotiate expeditiously the agreements governing their future relationship referred to in the Political Declaration of 17 October 2019. (Withdrawal Agreement, 2020, Article 184)

One of the parties, acting in good faith, might, after reflection, change its mind on some issues, especially if a political declaration is long (141 paragraphs in this case). The UK went further, by stressing, soon after having accepted the Political Declaration, that it was not legally binding and that it had no intention of transforming some of its provisions into legal commitments. The UK stated its determination to ignore such important issues as: aiming at a wide-ranging and comprehensive agreement; having provisions for foreign policy, security and defence; building an overarching institutional framework; and having commitments to ensure a level playing field (LPF) for open and fair competition.

The EU saw this British position as a breach of the principle of good faith and its trust was further seriously affected.

17. THE DIVERGENCES ON THE GENERAL FRAMEWORK OF THE TCA AND ON THE SETTLEMENT OF DISPUTES

On the EU side, the negotiating directives given by the Council to the Commission[56] took the Political Declaration as *the* basis for the negotiations. The aim was 'to develop an ambitious, wide-ranging and balanced economic partnership' (Political Declaration, paragraph 17). An Association Agreement[57] was suggested by the EU, which requires the consent of the EP and unanimity in the Council (Article 218(6)(a) and Article 218(8) TFEU). If the TCA had covered matters going beyond the EU's competences, it would also have needed to be concluded by the member states (*mixed agreement*). The EU wanted a single agreement and the whole agreement to be provided by 'an overarching institutional framework' (Political Declaration, paragraph 118), with 'robust, efficient and effective arrangements for its management, supervision, implementation, review and development over time, and for the resolution of disputes and enforcement' (paragraph 122). This implied that commitments in all matters would be linked and that the violation of one part of the Agreement might entail a suspension or unilateral measures of retaliation concerning other parts ('*cross retaliations*').

Immediately after the entry into force of the WA, the UK government, while admitting that 'the parameters for that future relationship are set out in the Political Declaration' (HM Government, 2020), said that the negotiations should essentially aim at an FTA. It suggested that this FTA should copy FTAs recently agreed by the EU with non-European countries (Canada, Japan, Singapore, South-Korea), with weak provisions on governance and no or weak dispute resolution mechanisms. The UK further suggested that this FTA might be supplemented by about ten separate agreements,[58] each with its own governance arrangements.

This made clear that the aims of the UK government had radically changed. This change was due either to its new government or to the fact that it had now become clear that participation in the EU's single market was not possible for the UK if it did not accept the same constraints as an EU or an EFTA-EEA member state. In any case, the UK had reduced its ambitions for the future agreement to a *hard Brexit*. Closing the doors on rule of law mechanisms would further reduce its ambitions for possible cooperation in other domains, in particular justice and police cooperation and access to data.

On its side, the EU insisted on the general structure of a single agreement and on strong governance arrangements, while recalling the Political Declaration: 'In order to ensure the proper functioning of the future relationship, the Parties commit to engage in regular dialogue and to establish robust, efficient and effective arrangements for its management, supervision, implementation, review and development over time, and for the resolution of disputes and enforcement, in full respect of the autonomy of their legal orders' (paragraph 122).

The EU also wanted to follow the Political Declaration on dispute settlement (paragraphs 129 to 132): a discussion in the Joint Committee, a possible flexible mediation mechanism and, in case of a disagreement continuing after a given period, an independent arbitration panel or tribunal whose decisions would be legally binding for the parties. A reference by the panel to the CJEU would only happen if a dispute raised a point of law on the EU's side. The agreement should also provide for the conditions under which remedies could be taken by a party, in case of non-compliance by the other. These measures should include the possibility of a unilateral suspension of parts of the agreement, on the model of the temporary remedies contained in Articles 178 and 179 of the WA. This EU position was strengthened after the British Internal Market Bill of 9 September 2020 which violated the WA (see Section 14 above).

The final text of the TCA, about 1,400 pages long, and which shall be authentic in the 24 EU official languages, partly corresponds to these EU wishes.[59] A Joint Partnership Council (having the right to make decisions by common agreement of both parties) is substituted by the Joint Council, with about 20 Committees, each competent for a specific area. In conformity with the UK's wishes, the TCA stresses that the sovereignty of both parties is respected. The agreement is based on classic public international law (Article 4 TCA), and does not create direct rights for individuals (Article 5 TCA). Either party may terminate the agreement with a one-year notice, but the EU demanded that terminating the fisheries part of the TCA would automatically terminate the trade, aviation and road transport parts of the TCA. In that case, trade on fish will remain free of tariffs and quotas. The parties may review the agreement after five years. The UK will be consulted if a third state applies to accede the EU. In such a case, the EU 'shall endeavour to … (b) take into account any concerns expressed by the United Kingdom' on this issue (Article 781).[60] The TCA may be amended to take new EU accessions into account.

The CJEU will have no jurisdiction in Britain,[61] but only in Northern Ireland (on the basis of the WA). An independent arbitration tribunal will be established. It will be convened for each dispute and will have 160 days to give a ruling. In case a party does not comply with a ruling, the other party may suspend parts of the TCA, including in other areas. The parties cannot refer disputes to the arbitration tribunal over some areas, especially fisheries, competition, state aid controls, or justice and home affairs. In case of disputes concerning these areas, the parties can use temporary trade remedies or rebalancing measures. Any serious breach of commitments by one party in respect of democratic values, fundamental rights, climate change and non-proliferation may lead to suspension of part or whole of the TCA by the other party.[62]

The TCA does not apply to Gibraltar. Only Article 1 (on citizens' rights) of the WA's Protocol on Gibraltar still applies at the end of the transition period (Article 185 WA). On 31 December 2020, the last day of the transition period, both Spain and the UK announced that their discussions were successful, particularly on a proposal to make Gibraltar 'a part of Schengen', with border controls entrusted to the EU Agency Frontex, apparently with participation of the Spanish police. If it is confirmed, the details of that informal 'non-paper' on free movement of persons between Gibraltar and Spain (which will need the approval of the authorities of the Schengen area, and at least the political agreement of Gibraltar) should, in principle, have been developed in six months into an agreement between the UK and the EU. However, at the end of 2021, the negotiations had not yet succeeded.

18. THE DIVERGENCE ON THE CORE OF THE TCA: FREE TRADE (NO TARIFFS, NO QUOTAS) AND THE LEVEL PLAYING FIELD

Both parties agreed from the beginning of the negotiations that their future relations should be based on a FTA providing for no tariffs and no quotas on goods, including on agriculture and fish products. Up to now, the EU has never accepted such a large scope for a FTA, even in the EEA.[63] To reach that aim, and following the Political Declaration, the EU demanded rules on a LPF to exclude any kind of dumping, given the UK's geographical proximity to the EU and its economic size.

The EU's initial requests were extremely demanding. It requested the UK to follow the EU's existing and future legislation and the rules on state aid and competition, as interpreted by the CJEU, as well as the EU's standards for protection of environment, climate change, social and employment matters. The UK refused these – excessive – requests. It asked to be treated in the same way as non-European countries in the recent FTAs agreed by the EU. The EU stressed that the UK's economic weight, its geographical situation and its links with the EU 27 make it a different case than remote non-European countries with which trade is much less important. It recalled the strong wording of paragraph 77 of the Political Declaration on a LPF for open and fair competition, accepted by the UK: 'given the Union and the United Kingdom's geographic proximity and economic interdependence'. It insisted that this wording should be translated into treaty provisions. In place of continued CJEU jurisdiction, the EU requested a mandatory arbitration, which the UK refused. The EU recalled that the UK is guaranteed that each of the EU 27 members will remain bound by its state aid regime, under independent surveillance and possible sanctions. The risk was thus asymmetrical, the UK having benefits without obligations (with the exception of Northern Ireland), while a large part of its trade is done with the EU.

It was only during the month of December 2020 that rumours were heard on discussions rapidly progressing on what had to be called now 'managing divergences', thus announcing progresses towards an agreement.

The main results of the final agreement were the following:

- On state aid (subsidies): the TCA contains weaker provisions than the initial wishes of the EU, but much stronger than those contained in recent FTAs concluded by the EU, like with Canada and others. Most provisions are actually similar to the TFEU provisions, including on exceptions. They commit both parties 'to establish or maintain an operationally independent authority or body' (Article 371 TCA) and to accept a robust internal control, enforceable in domestic courts. In case of disputes not solved diplomatically, the parties shall have the right to take remedial unilateral measures (Article 374 TCA).[64] There is an option for an arbitration to assess if there was a breach of the Agreement. The arbitration ruling may authorise the complainant to suspend parts of the TCA, including on fish. One may wonder how the UK will soon be able to implement its obligations, given that it currently has no domestic law on state aids and that the EU Treaties ceased to apply to and in the UK.
- On competition: commitments are similar to those contained in FTAs concluded recently by the EU.
- On taxation: the parties commit not to lower standards below those agreed in the Organisation for Economic Co-operation and Development (OECD) before 2021. There is no dispute settlement mechanism.
- On the protection of labour and social standards, as well as on the overall level of environment and climate protection: the parties have the right to establish their desired level of protection, but they commit not to '*weaken or reduce*' that protection in a way that would impact trade or investment. Proportional counter measures, including tariffs, are allowed in case of unfair competitive advantages, but may be subject to arbitration.
- Finally, a 'rebalancing mechanism' allows a party to ask for a review of the agreement after four years, if there are significant divergences in the LPF that are impacting trade or investment (Article 411 TCA).

19. THE DISAGREEMENTS ON THE ACCESS OF EU FISHERMEN TO BRITISH WATERS AND ON TRADE IN FISH

On the issue of the access of EU fishermen to British waters, and on trade in fish, the difference between the parties was extremely wide (Senior European Experts, 2020). For both the UK and EU, its economic importance is a tiny part of their GDP, but it is politically equally sensitive. On the UK side, it was presented by the UK as a question of *sovereignty* of its waters. Actually, the issue was not that EU fishermen asked to be allowed to fish in the UK's sovereign territorial waters, but mainly in its Economic Exclusive Zone (EEZ).[65] Eight EU member states wanted their fishermen to continue benefiting from the so-called *historic rights* which they have been exercising for centuries, long before the EEC's creation. The Law of the Sea was not what it is today, especially since the United Nations Convention of the Law of the Sea was signed in Montego Bay in 1982. With the exception of some specific international agreements, fishermen of all countries were free to fish in all waters beyond a limit of six nautical miles off the coasts, that is, beyond the territorial sea. Nowadays, all countries have exclusive rights to fish (or to sell these rights) within a limit of 200 nautical miles from their coasts, in the EEZ. After the accession of the UK to the EU and the development of the EU common fisheries policy (see Title III of Part Three of the TFEU), there was no problem, given that there was an EU common policy on fisheries. Therefore, EU fishermen continued to fish in the British EEZ, as well as in the British waters from 6 to 12 nautical miles.

Given its withdrawal from the EU, and in conformity with its legal rights, the UK wanted to exercise in full its exclusive rights to the resources of its waters and in the EEZ and to negotiate and sign annual agreements with the EU. The EU tactically linked the subject to the trade issue, given that the UK needs to sell a large part of its catch of fish to the 27 member states.[66] The EU stated that it could decide to raise customs duties on the import of this fish, or even not to accept an FTA, in case of no agreement on access to waters. Despite the parties having endeavoured to reach a deal on this issue on a priority basis,[67] a deal looked far from done as late as a few days before 31 December 2020. It was the very last one to be solved. As a result of a difficult compromise, the UK[68] will be free to manage its resources in the EEZ, but only after five and a half years (and not three). During this period, the catches of the EU fishing boats will gradually be reduced to 75 per cent of their pre-Brexit catches (and not 25 per cent).

Thus, in June 2026, the UK's share of fishing quotas will be only 25 per cent of the catches in its territorial and EEZ waters. After that date, the UK will have sovereignty over the fish resources in its EEZ and will be able to negotiate with the EU, in principle on an annual basis. Fish trade will remain free of tariffs and quotas, which was considered as important by the UK (apparently not taking sufficiently into account the non-tariff obstacles). If, after June 2026, the UK reduces the access of EU fishing boats in UK waters, the EU will have the right under certain conditions to impose 'compensatory' tariffs on imports of British fish products (Article 501 TCA). This part of the TCA was criticised by the fishery industry in the UK, especially in Scotland.

20. THE DISAGREEMENT ON FINANCIAL SERVICES

The other priority of the negotiations was on financial services, which have a huge economic importance for the UK.[69] But the future agreement, like all FTAs, aimed at trade in goods, not services. Thus, the EU 'financial passport rights' was to be lost for firms based in the UK at the end of the transition period. This meant that the future relationship should be settled by each party deciding whether the other one qualifies for access rights, through unilateral 'adequacy decisions' or 'equivalence frameworks'. By taking such a decision, a party recognises that the other party's legal requirements are to be regarded as equivalent to its own rules. This is not a single decision but multiple decisions for different market activities (almost 30 sectors). On the EU side, these decisions may be taken and withdrawn (with one-month notice), including in the light of political or economic interests, by the Council on the basis of the Commission's proposals, without justification. EU legislation does not permit these decisions to be taken in all sectors: for instance, they are possible for some areas of investment banking and insurance, but not for retail banking and reinsurance. Sometimes, it is necessary for individual companies to get an additional approval from the EU regulators.

The issue did not progress as hoped. The UK wanted some stability. It did not wish that the Commission would remain free, at any moment and unilaterally, to withdraw its decisions of equivalence. The EU rejected that request. According to the EU negotiators, 'the UK demands ... to be able to co-decide with the Union on decisions relating to the withdrawal of equivalences for financial services, when they know they are – and must remain – our own, autonomous decisions' (Barnier, 2020). The EU said also that the Commission could not finish its analysis of the British regulations because the UK did not provide sufficient information and did not answer some questions (European Commission, 2020).[70] It stressed, in particular, that the UK was not clear about the degree of divergence from EU rules that it was envisaging.

Thus, the TCA was signed while the EU had taken only two decisions of equivalence. The EU gave the UK a temporary equivalence only in the two areas where it was beneficial for the 27 (derivatives clearing and settling Irish securities). The EU position can be explained by its political will to become more independent from the City of London, and its concerns about opening its markets to a country which might diverge from its rules in the future.

21. THE DIVERGENCES ON UK'S PARTICIPATION IN THE EU'S JUSTICE AND HOME AFFAIRS COOPERATION AND ACCESS TO DATA

The cooperation on justice and home affairs (JHA) among member states was given its first legal base in the 1992 Maastricht Treaty. This legal base was later strengthened in the 1997 Amsterdam Treaty, which incorporated the intergovernmental Schengen cooperation in the EU and made the JHA an EU policy. The UK decided then, along with Ireland (given their Common Travel Area[71]), not to participate in Schengen. Both countries negotiated protocols on opt-outs, permitting them to choose not to participate in some other JHA policies.

When the Lisbon Treaty provided that most JHA measures would be subject to the CJEU jurisdiction in the future, the UK requested to opt out from all EU policies in that field and to be able to opt back in only for those of its choice. Actually, the British government opted back into the 35 most important ones, among them:

- Europol, the agency for police cooperation,
- the European Arrest Warrant (EAW), which facilitates quick extradition of criminals among member states,
- Eurojust, the agency for cooperation between national courts and prosecuting authorities,
- the Passenger Name Recognition (PNR) which helps to identify criminals on flights, and
- the Schengen data bases on exchange of information to help member states to protect their borders.

The British administrations and agencies working in this field wanted the UK to continue to participate as much as possible after Brexit. However, the will of the government not to be obliged to follow pertinent EU laws and to refuse the jurisdiction of the CJEU were two huge obstacles. The EU was also insisting that the UK should accept, in relation to these issues, the EU's high standards for data protection, on human rights, and a clear commitment to uphold the European Convention on Human Rights (ECHR). Given the high priority given by the British government to its 'sovereignty', this could not include retention of the jurisdiction of the CJEU,[72] but the commitment to human rights, including remaining bound by the ECHR, is stressed in the TCA.

The main agreements were as follows:

- As for *Europol*, a membership is excluded for non-EU member states, but a partnership agreement was retained, on the model of the agreements that the EU concluded with Norway, Switzerland, the USA and other countries (Title V, Part Three TCA). Such an agreement will allow exchange of information, but will not give the UK direct access to the EU data bases, including the Secure Information Exchange Network Application which facilitates the exchange of sensitive or classified data[73] and the European Information System, a criminal information and intelligence data base on serious crimes including terrorism.
- As for *Eurojust*, the UK will also have a cooperation agreement like other third countries (Title VI, Part Three TCA), not permitting close cooperation. For example, third countries do not have access to the Eurojust Case Management system and to Joint Investigation Teams.
- On the *EAW*, the UK and the EU decided to conclude provisions similar to the Agreement concluded by the EU with Iceland and Norway, which does not involve the CJEU (Title VII, Part Three TCA). It is narrower than the EAW, but better than the only other option available, which would have been for the UK and the EU to go back to the application between them of the slower and less efficient 1957 Convention of the Council of Europe. The loss of the EAW will have significant effects for the UK, because it used it frequently.
- As to *the UK's access to EU data bases*, difficulties prevented the UK from accessing some security data bases, such as the important Schengen ones (Schengen Information System). However, the EU and the UK will continue to apply two useful instruments to fight terrorism: the transfer of Passenger Name Records (PNR) (Title III, Part Three, TCA)[74] and the cooperation based on the Prüm Convention (Title II, Part Three TCA)[75] allowing the sharing of DNA, fingerprint data and vehicle registration data, though it will no longer be systematic real-time transfers for the UK.
- The TCA contains also other provisions on mutual assistance, anti-money laundering, etc. However, the close cooperation which existed among the 28 on police and judicial cooperation in the fight against criminality (including terrorism) and to ensure the security of Europeans, although continuing, will be weaker in the future, given that the UK is no longer an EU member. Moreover, civil law cooperation and the Lugano Convention on recognition and enforcement of judgments in civil and commercial cases are not mentioned in the TCA.
- *As to the termination or suspension of this Part Three of the TCA*, this part contains specific provisions (Article 692-693 TCA) permitting its termination at any moment in writing with an eight-month notice, or immediately if the UK or an EU member state denounces the European Convention on Fundamental Rights, or its suspension 'in the event of serious and systemic deficiencies within one Party as regards the protection of fundamental rights or the principle of the rule of law' (Article 693(1) TCA).
- On access to data, *as regards transmission of data* from the EU to the UK, according to Article 45 of the General Data Protection Regulation (GDPR) (2016), the EU could in theory take an adequacy decision[76] on the UK's rules, with the possibility to withdraw it unilaterally. It could also accept transfers on the basis of appropriate safeguards. The

UK asked for an adequacy decision. However, the CJEU has proven to be very protective of the EU system of data protection. Despite the huge practical and political problems it would provoke, the Court invalidated the decision of the Commission on the adequacy of the protection provided by the USA-EU Data Protection Shield (C-362/14 *Schrems*, 2015; C-311/18 *Facebook Ireland*, 2020), a decision which enabled data transfers between the EU and the USA. A third country is required 'in fact to ensure, by reason of its domestic law or its international commitments, a level of protection of fundamental rights and freedoms that is essentially equivalent to that guaranteed within the European Union' (C-311/18 *Facebook Ireland*, 2020, paragraph 94).

Besides, in the recent past, UK domestic legislation and practice were found to respect EU law less than it did before. At the time of agreeing the TCA, the EU refused to adopt an adequacy decision for the UK's rules. This might also have an effect on trade, when transfer of data is necessary. There is, however, a temporary arrangement to allow data to continue to be transferred for four months (extendable to six), as long as the UK does not change its legislation, waiting for a possible stable EU adequacy decision in the future. There is also a separate agreement concerning Security Procedures for Exchanging and Protecting Classified Information.

22. WHAT HAPPENED ON 1 JANUARY 2021, WITH THE PROVISIONAL APPLICATION OF THE TCA

As early as June 2020, the British PM had decided that the UK did not want the transition period to be extended. The parties agreed to intensify the talks in order to try and finish an agreement in time for it to be in force on 1 January 2021. The end of October was mentioned by some as a final date for initialling a deal, in order to have time for translations into the EU's 23 official languages other than English, legal verifications and ratifying procedures. However, the Covid-19 pandemic had stopped actual meetings for a while, substituted by videoconferences. As this was not compatible with an efficient negotiation, actual meetings took place from July to December 2020, alternatively in London and in Brussels.

At the time of the 15–16 October 2020 meeting of the European Council, even if there was some progress, the three most difficult issues remained unsolved: LPF, settlement of disputes and fisheries. This had not changed when the European Council met on 11–12 December. Johnson, who had said successively that these two dates would be the final dates for reaching a deal, was disappointed by the tough position taken by the 27 leaders on both occasions. He declared that the negotiations had failed. However, after telephone calls between the two chief negotiators and between the PM and the President of the Commission, negotiations went on. They concentrated on an FTA (and on fish) and thus on LPF, while the settlement of disputes became a major problem, as the British Internal Market Bill had been seen by the EU as a sign that the UK could conclude a treaty without respecting it. However, after the Joint Committee on Ireland/North Ireland agreed on a solution, the atmosphere improved. Progress was rapidly made on LPF and on other subjects going beyond trade.

For the UK, it was absolutely essential that the agreement would be seen as respecting the 'sovereignty' of the UK[77] on its laws, on its borders and on its waters, avoiding any reference to EU law and to the CJEU, and not mentioning either foreign policy or defence. For the EU, a *sine qua non* condition was to preserve the credibility of the single market and to associate the LPF with a legally binding arbitration system and possible unilateral cross-sector retaliations, in case an arbitration tribunal's ruling would not be respected. A solution for retaining the access of EU fishermen to British waters during a transition period was also necessary, as the EU linked it with any agreement on trade. This was solved in the end, Johnson having to concede ground on this delicate issue[78] in order to avoid adding a *cliff edge* to the Covid-19 crisis and to end the UK's participation in the EU single market. The agreement was initialled by the negotiators on Christmas Eve, one week before the end of the transition period.

Important changes happened on 1 January 2021. The transition period ended. Provisions of the WA permitting the UK to be treated in the same way as an EU member state ceased to apply. UK thus effectively became a third country vis-à-vis the EU. According to its choice, it was no longer bound either by EU law or by the CJEU, it stopped benefiting from the EU's single market and customs union (except for Northern Ireland), and it no longer participated in EU policies. The trade in goods would still be without tariffs, but with many more non-tariff barriers, and trade in services would become much more difficult for British economic actors. Borders were re-established and controls at the borders implemented in the same way as between the EU and any third country not participating in the EU single market.

The main results of the TCA are resumed below:

- *On mobility of persons:* British citizens, no longer being EU citizens,[79] lost their right to move freely to any of the EU 27 member states to reside, study, work, open a business, have health care, etc. Their (visa free) stay in the EU is now limited to three months during any six-month period. Travellers must obey the other party's rules when transporting products or accompanied by a pet. There are provisions on social security coordination (Protocol on Social Security Coordination, 2021).
- *On services:* While services represent nearly 80 per cent of the UK's economy, the provisions of the TCA for services are very weak, comparable to classic FTAs, such as those concluded by the EU with Canada or Japan. It contains customary principles, like national treatment, most-favoured nation, market access for services with no requirement for a local subsidiary. These principles look good, but they are in fact subject to long lists of exceptions (in Annexes), which vary with sectors and with each EU member state.

  UK firms and individuals lost the right of establishment and the right to deliver some services in the EU. Existing mutual recognition of professional qualifications have ended. The EU did not accept the derogations desired by the UK for the free movement of British individuals providing services in the 27. British operators lost the financial services passports. The legal services look to be better treated, but there are many variations according to EU member states. Thus, British firms, which provide services to the 27, either financial, legal or of any other kind, linked or not with trade in goods, will now have a more difficult task. Moreover, for people who used to travel for work for short periods, such as musicians and actors, the travel and visa provisions are restrictive. In the future, equivalent rights might be accepted by the EU for some British regulations.[80]
- *On transport:*
  - Air transport: UK and EU airlines lost traffic rights inside each other's territory, but will continue to be able to carry passengers and cargo between points in the EU and in the UK (third and fourth freedoms) (Kassim, 2021).
  - Road haulage: a transition period was agreed for nine months to allow full access for road haulage operators licensed in the UK for the carriage of goods by road between

the UK and the EU. They lost the right to carry out cabotage for more than two operations. High standards on safety and working conditions apply.
    - There were no problems for train and maritime transports.
- *On trade in goods:* As the TCA covers all goods, it should be more beneficial to the EU than to the UK, given the EU huge surplus trade of nearly £100 billion with the UK. The non-tariff obstacles to trade increased significantly for exporters and importers of both parties, but are heavier for the UK. The most important and probably the most expensive for businesses are the complex *rules of origin.*[81] They reduce the possibility, for economic operators from one party, to export their products tariff-free to the other party, if a given part or ingredient of their products came from a third country. As a result of the UK no longer participating in the EU single market, all goods coming from the UK, as imported from a third country, shall (in principle) stop at the EU external border. This is because, although not paying customs duties, they must be checked for their conformity with EU sanitary and phytosanitary rules, with norms and standards and with the rules of origin.[82] British importers and exporters from and to the EU must also fulfil administrative and tax declarations. The UK left the EU VAT system and adopted a new system on imported goods from the EU, beginning also on 1 January 2021, which is a further change.

  All these new rules have an impact on trade. This will still be the case even if British exporters continue – for the time being at least – to implement the EU single market legislations, because these were incorporated into British domestic law and will remain applicable until modified. Besides, even if the UK changes its norms and standards, British economic operators might choose to continue to follow EU norms and standards, which will be necessary if they wish to export their goods to the EU. Finally, the UK lost the benefits of all FTAs concluded by the EU with almost 70 countries, but the UK negotiated roll-over bilateral agreements with almost 60 of them.
- *On intellectual property:* The TCA contains provisions to protect intellectual property rights (copyrights, patents, trademarks, designs).
- *On energy and climate policies:* Both parties will have their own independent policy, but will cooperate. The UK will continue to have access to the EU internal energy market, but not as an EU member state. Cooperation on connectivity for the furniture of gas and electricity will continue. There is also a separate agreement on nuclear energy between the UK and Euratom for cooperation on the Safe and Peaceful Uses of Nuclear Energy (2021).
- *On EU programmes:* The UK will cease to benefit from multiple cooperation organised by the EU between the member states, whether managed by the Commission or by EU agencies, in particular on some policies aimed at internal security and judicial cooperation in civil and criminal matters (see Section 21), on environment, on foreign and defence policy, etc. There are a few exceptions foreseen in the TCA, such as scientific research, Horizon Europe (2021–2027), Copernicus, the fusion Test Facility ITER, the EU Satellite Surveillance and Tracking (SST), North Ireland Peace Process. A committee on participation in EU programmes has been established to finalise agreements. Cooperation, with financial contributions, in the same way as other third countries, will be organised later and protocols added to the TCA. A role might be conferred on the CJEU in some cases (Article 728(2)-(3) TCA). Finally, and sadly, the UK decided no longer to participate in the EU programme on exchange of students (Erasmus).

CONCLUSION

The strategic, political and economic effects of Brexit, especially for the UK, but also for the EU – and more generally for Europe – will be important and negative, both in the short and in the long term. It was already known before the referendum that Brexit could not lead to good economic results for the UK (Piris, 2014, 2015a, 2015b, 2016c, 2016d). It was a politically and ideologically driven move, actually not aiming at economic results, but at more national independence and sovereignty. Thus, the aim of the TCA was not, as it is usual for a FTA, to reduce obstacles to trade, but to try and reduce the obstacles to trade created by the exit of the UK from the EU. The possibility of an economically *soft Brexit* was an illusion. The only way to reach such a result would have been for the UK to accept the freedom of movement of persons, the jurisdiction of the CJEU and the dynamic and continued application of EU law, without being part of the EU's decision-making, which was politically excluded by the UK government.

With the WA and the TCA, the UK and the EU managed to solve the following urgent problems:

- to keep a no tariff, no quotas trade of goods between them,
- to avoid as much as possible problems at the border on the island of Ireland, and
- to find a compromise for fish.

At the same time, major concerns of both parties ('*red lines*') were fully respected:

- The UK succeeded in getting its red line on 'sovereignty': it no longer has to follow EU law and EU policies, including the freedom of movement of persons. It is no longer bound by judgments of the CJEU. Its sovereignty over its EEZ and freedom to negotiate agreements with other countries, including but not only on trade, are fully recognised. It has no obligation to consult anybody else before taking decisions on foreign policy.
- The EU also got its red lines. It preserved the solidity and credibility of its single market. It obtained some rules on a level playing field for open and fair competition, a single agreement with a governance arrangement, which will allow it to react, should the UK not apply some of its provisions correctly. It got a good agreement on trade in goods while almost nothing on services, as well as a good result for its fishermen.

Moreover, the TCA is based on the respect for the rule of law, on the protection of fundamental rights, including an obligation not to denounce the ECHR, and on other *essential elements*.[83] It provides for future cooperation. It contains some transitional periods to make adaptation to new rules easier. It mentions domains for which unilateral decisions of equivalence or agreed cooperation could be developed in the future. It implies bilateral negotiations continuing, especially if the impact on the British economy happens to be significant in the short and medium term, including with regard to the volume of foreign investments that it used to attract. Negotiations between the UK and the EU, friends, allies and economically intertwined, did not finish on 31 December 2020. It is important that they continue on a myriad of issues. Let's hope that these negotiations begin as soon as possible, on the basis of the TCA, which, for the EU, creates an association with its most important and close neighbour.

* * *

What is happening now on our planet, with the earthquake of the Covid-19 pandemic, puts however the UK-EU relations into a new perspective. The tsunami following the earthquake, that is, the economic crisis which is already accompanying the pandemic and which will follow it for years, is just beginning. Its social and political effects in the world, including in Europe, are unknown and probably underestimated. At the same time, the world is no longer dominated by one super power, the USA, the friend, ally and faithful protector of Europe and of other so-called *Western* countries:

- First, this situation was modified by US policy, in particular by the Trump administration, and will not come back completely to the *ex ante* situation.
- Second, China grows economically, scientifically and militarily at an impressive pace. Before long, it will be speaking on equal terms with the USA.
- Third, some powerful regional countries, Brazil, Indonesia, Russia, Turkey, governed by populist leaders, might generate uncertainty and increase international instability.
- Fourth, the neighbourhood of the EU is not exempt from risks of crisis, from Ukraine and Belarus to the Western Balkans, Iran, the Middle East or Africa.

Given that geopolitical context, what could be done by the EU? Should all Europeans together, EU members or not, try to be less dependent on the external world, for instance, as a first step on medicines, health products and other goods and products necessary to protect them in case of a possible natural or man-made catastrophe? Should the EU open itself to non-member states and offer more possibilities of cooperation in these and other domains? Should any further EU enlargement, including for the Western Balkan countries, be preceded by a revision of the EU basic Treaties? Will the Conference on the Future of Europe manage to find innovative suggestions? Rapid changes in the world affect the EU. This should make its leaders rethink its current architecture. They should try to find more differentiated options, which might accommodate better its neighbours.

NOTES

1. Article 132 (1) of the Withdrawal Agreement (2019) provides that the UK and the EU 'may, before 1 July 2020, adopt a single decision extending the transition period for up to 1 or 2 years'. The UK decided that this option would not be used.
2. Including two other agreements, as well as protocols, annexes, appendices and footnotes, which shall form an integral part of the Agreement. The two other agreements are one between the UK and Euratom (EU-UK Civil Nuclear Agreement, 2021) and the other between the UK and the EU on exchange and protection of classified information (EU-UK Security Information Agreement, 2021).
3. Together with the other six founding members: Austria, Denmark, Norway, Portugal, Sweden and Switzerland.
4. While informed British did know that the project was basically political. See, for example, Shonfield (1973).
5. See the list of these type of decisions in Piris (2010), pp. 47–8.
6. See in the book written by former British Ambassador to the EU, Lord Kim Darroch: '[t]he fact was that we had negotiated for ourselves a privileged form of EU membership, full of British exceptionalism: Mrs Thatcher's rebate, our unique permanent exclusion from the euro, and our partial exclusion from those bits of Schengen, "Europe without Frontiers", that we didn't like. In short, we had managed to get ourselves effectively the best of both worlds; the advantages of membership, absent the obligations we didn't like, and with a special discount on costs' (Darroch, 2020, p. 61).

7 According to Article 5 of the Treaty on the European Union (TEU), '[u]nder the principle of subsidiarity … the Union shall act only in and insofar as the objectives of the proposed action cannot be sufficiently achieved by the Member States …'.
8. The single market is the heart of the EU, aiming at the free movement of people, goods, services and capital throughout the EU. Although still imperfect, it has made the EU the largest market in the world.
9. The White Paper '*Completing the Internal Market*' is a compendium of 300 legislative proposals aiming at the elimination of physical, technical and fiscal non-tariffs barriers between the member states of the EU. With the reduction of tariff barriers in the world, the major obstacles to trade are the non-tariff ones (norms, standards, measures to protect labour and social regulation, protection of health, of the consumers or the environment, rules of origin, etc.) (European Commission, 1985).
10. Iceland, Liechtenstein and Norway. The EEA was established by an agreement with the EU in 1994. Switzerland decided not to participate, while remaining a member of the EFTA with these three countries.
11. See the full text of Article 50 TEU in the Appendix.
12. 'The termination of a treaty or the withdrawal of a party may take place: (a) in conformity with the provisions of a treaty; or (b) at any time by consent of all the parties after consultation with the other contracting States' (VCLT, 1969, Article 54).
13. According to which the powers of the EU are limited to those conferred upon it by its member states in the EU Treaties: see Articles 4(1) and 5(1 and 2) TEU.
14. Article 50 (2) TEU provides that, after the adoption of guidelines by the European Council, Article 218 Treaty on the Functioning of the European Union's (TFEU) procedure must be followed: recommendation of the Commission to the Council, decision of the Council to open negotiations, nomination of the head of the negotiating team, adoption of directives to the negotiator. The procedure for the conclusion of a WA by the EU (a decision of the Council by a qualified majority and the consent of the European Parliament) is specific, i.e. not the one used for other international agreements, which differs according to their content (Article 218(6 and 8) TFEU).
15. The WA referred to in Article 50 TEU aims at 'setting out (with the exiting State) the arrangements for its withdrawal, taking account of the framework for its future relationship with the Union'. Any agreement with an ex member state on trade and other relations may be negotiated only after its withdrawal and under the procedures applicable to relations with a third state, including for its conclusion.
16. According to the Court of Justice of the EU (CJEU) in the case of *Les Verts*, the EU basic Treaties constitute, for the EU, 'the basic Constitutional Charter of a Community based on the Rule of Law' (*Parti écologiste 'Les Verts' v European Parliament*, 1986).
17. The issue on whether it was legally possible to exit the EU before the Lisbon Treaty is not discussed in this chapter.
18. On 24 January 2017, in its judgment *Miller v Secretary of Secretary of State for Exiting the European Union*, the UK Supreme Court decided that the UK government may not initiate the UK's withdrawal from the EU by notification to the EU without a preliminary Act of the UK Parliament allowing it. Thereafter, a law was adopted to that effect: European Union (Notification of Withdrawal) Act 2017.
19. The UK's Ambassador to the EU, Ivan Rogers, resigned on 3 January 2017, given his disagreement with the Prime Minister's EU policy.
20. On the same day, the European Council adopted a statement on the application of Article 50 ('Article 50': this mention means that, in application of Article 50(4), the withdrawing State is not represented) stressing in particular that '[i]n these negotiations, the Union shall act as one and preserve its interests'.
21. See the European Guidelines of 29 April 2017 (European Council, 2017a) (modified 15 December 2017 (European Council, 2017b) and 23 March 2018 (European Council, 2018)), followed by the Council Directives for the Negotiation adopted on 22 May 2017 (Council, 2017) (modified 29 January 2018 (Council, 2018)). The European Commission published many Working Papers and even a '*Draft Withdrawal Agreement*' of 118 pages on 28 February 2018 (European Commission, 2018).

22. The Prime Minister even expressed her hope 'to have reached an agreement about our future partnership by the time the two years Article 50 process has concluded' (May, 2017a). This was again mentioned in her letter of 29 March 2017 triggering Article 50 negotiations (May, 2017b).
23. Adopted on the basis of Article 218 (4) TFEU.
24. Based on Articles 18–25 TFEU.
25. Moreover, if a Party uses temporary remedies in case of non-compliance by the other Party, it cannot suspend any obligation contained in Part Two (see Article 178(2)(b) WA).
26. '... the goal of peace and reconciliation enshrined in the GFA in all its parts ...' and 'the achievements, benefits and commitments of the Peace Process will remain of paramount importance' (European Council, 2017a, p. 6).
27. 'specific to the unique circumstances on the island of Ireland' (European Commission, 2017, p. 7).
28. For a detailed analysis, see Fabbrini and Schmidt (2020).
29. It was called 'backstop' because it would continue to be applied 'until and unless' both parties would agree on a different arrangement having the same result. In conformity with the GFA, it guaranteed no hard border (i.e. no visible controls on goods, given that persons are not controlled anyway) between Northern Ireland and the Republic of Ireland. The draft text agreed by Mrs May and the EU provided the UK as a whole would participate in the EU's customs union and de facto keeping Northern Ireland in most aspects of the EU's single market.
30. Unanimity allows abstentions, see Article 235(1) TFEU.
31. Article 18 of the Protocol on Ireland/Northern Ireland provides that, four years after the end of the transition period (these four years are *called* 'the initial period'), the UK would need a democratic consent in Northern Ireland in order to continue to apply Articles 5 to 10 of the Irish Protocol (which provide for the implementation of the EU's single market legislation and no hard controls at the land border after the end of the transition period).
32. The Northern Ireland Secretary Brandon Lewis: 'It does break international law, although in a very specific and limited way' (European Union Committee, 2020, paragraph 66).
33. According to some lawyers, an extension without an election in the UK could have lasted until 30 June. They argued that the newly elected EP would only take office on 1 July. However, this did not take account of the right of EU citizens living in the UK to vote like others. The European Council decided that no exception was possible: the UK was obliged to hold the EP elections if the extension was continuing after 22 May.
34. An extension of the mandate of the MEPs elected in the UK for a five-year term in 2014 would have been illegal, as the TEU is specific on a five-year term for MEPs (Article 14(3) TEU).
35. The text of Article 17(5) TEU provides that the Commission shall consist of a number of members 'corresponding to two thirds of Member States, unless the European Council, acting unanimously, decides to alter this number'. On 22 May 2013, the European Council decided to come back to the former rule of one Commissioner per member state. This was following a political agreement reached by the European Council in 2008 after the first Irish referendum on the Lisbon Treaty on 12 June 2008, which was negative. That agreement was regarded as having helped Ireland to successfully organise a second referendum on 2 October 2009. The text of the TEU was not formally amended.
36. This had already briefly happened several times in the past, for different reasons, equally without difficulty. The continuity of the functioning of the institutions must prevail.
37. The UK and the EU would have to manage the trade between each other according to the rules of the World Trade Organization (WTO), in particular the *Most Favoured Nation* (MFN) rule. This rule is that any WTO state must provide all concessions granted to a particular WTO member to all other WTO members, except if these concessions are part of a customs union or a free trade area (FTA) covering substantially most sectors.
38. The UK argued that it was not to be called a period *of transition*, but a period *of implementation*, just to mark politically the fact that the withdrawal would legally take place on the first day of the *transition* period, and not on its last day, which is a fact.
39. Article 126 WA states that '[t]here shall be a transition or an implementation period, which shall start on the date of entry into force of this Agreement and end on 31 December 2020'.
40. However, there are some exceptions, such as decisions on foreign and security policy (Article 129 (6) WA) and enhanced cooperation (Article 127 (4) WA).

41. It goes without saying that one of the two parties cannot unilaterally amend the WA (see below).
42. In case of an extension, Article 132 (2 and 3) WA provides that both parties would have to decide together on the 'contribution to the Union budget' to be made by the UK.
43. Besides, the German Constitutional Court decided that Article 352 TFEU could not be used unless and until a German law is adopted to allow its use: point 328 of its judgment concerning the Lisbon Treaty, dated 30 June 2009: '... With a view to the undetermined nature of future application of the flexibility clause [i.e. Article 352 TFEU], its use constitutionally requires ratification by the German *Bundestag* and *Bundesrat* on the basis of Art 23.1 second and third sentence of the Basic Law [i.e. the German Constitution]. The German representative in the Council may not express on behalf of the Federal Republic of Germany the formal approval of a corresponding legislative proposal of the Commission as long as these constitutionally required preconditions are not met' (BVerfG, 2009, point 328).
44. See particularly Article 4(1) TEU: '... competences not conferred upon the Union in the Treaties remain with the Member States'; Article 5(1) TEU: 'The limits of Union competences are governed by the principle of conferral'; and Article 5(2) TEU: 'Under the principle of conferral, the Union shall act only within the limits of the competences conferred upon it by the Member States in the Treaties to attain the objectives set out therein.' This paragraph continues: 'Competences not conferred upon the Union in the Treaties remain with the Member States.'
45. Compare with Article 12 (4 and 5) of the Protocol on Ireland/Northern Ireland.
46. See Section 14 below.
47. Part Two WA.
48. An arbitration panel shall be composed of five members, from a list of 25 to be drawn up jointly. It must give its ruling within 12 months.
49. The title of Article 771 of TCA refers implicitly to Article 60 (3)(b) of the 1969 Vienna Convention on the Law of Treaties, which provides that a Party to a treaty may terminate or suspend the operation of that treaty in case of the violation by another Party of 'a provision essential to the accomplishment of the object or purpose of the treaty'.
50. Article 771 TCA gives the list of the three essential elements of the TCA (see Article 60 VCLT). The following Article 772 TCA states that a Party may terminate or suspend the operation of the TCA in case of the violation by the other Party of one of the essential elements and describes the procedure to be followed in that case.
51. See Articles 4, 5, 127, 131 WA.
52. See Section 15 below.
53. Article 5(1) reads: First subparagraph: 'No customs duties shall be payable for a good brought into Northern Ireland from another part of the UK ... unless that good is at risk of subsequently being moved into the EU ...'. Second subparagraph: 'The customs duties in respect of a good being moved by direct transport to NI other than from the EU or from another part of the UK shall be the duties applicable in the UK ... unless that good is at risk of subsequently being moved into the Union ...'. Article 5(2) reads: 'For the purposes of the first and second subparagraphs of paragraph 1, a good brought into Northern Ireland from outside the Union shall be considered to be at risk of subsequently being moved into the Union unless it is established that the good ...'.
54. See Section 14 above.
55. This interpretation of the Protocol was to be violated by the British Internal Market Bill, but this bill was withdrawn before being adopted (see Section 14 above).
56. Council Decision (EU, Euratom) 2020, adopted on 25 February 2020 (the Directives are in an Annex, document 5870/20, Addendum 1, rev. 3). The Commission had already published a number of papers in January: Financial Services, FTA, LPF, Fisheries, Law enforcement and Judicial cooperation in criminal matters, Foreign policy, Security and Defence, Governance, UK Participation in EU Programmes, Mobility of Persons, Architecture and legal nature of the Partnership.
57. As the TCA was finally based by the EU on Article 217 TFEU, it is an Association Agreement.
58. Covering principally fisheries, law enforcement and judicial cooperation in criminal matters, transport and energy.
59. See the following paragraph in the Preamble of the TCA: 'Recognising the need for an ambitious, wide-ranging and balanced economic partnership to be underpinned by a level playing field for open and fair competition and sustainable development, through effective and robust frameworks for sub-

sidies and competition and a commitment to uphold their respective high levels of protection in the areas of labour and social standards, environment, the fight against climate change, and taxation', as well as the long (pp 179–218) Title of the TCA on 'Level playing field for open and fair competition and sustainable development'.

60. The UK will of course have no right of veto, but it shall be able to express its opinion, which would be very important if Scotland would try to be recognised by the EU as a potential candidate after a referendum regarded as constitutionally illegal by the UK. Such a consultation is not foreseen in the EEA Agreement (see its Article 128). On the obligation for a candidate state to the EU to respect the rule of law, see Articles 49 and 2 TEU and Piris (2016b).
61. Except for some EU programmes in which the UK could decide to participate, as well as for the temporary role (during eight years) on the rights of EU citizens in the UK. Moreover, the interpretation of EU law by the CJEU will always have an indirect effect when the relevant texts must be respected by economic operators of any third country in the world willing to export to the EU (Bradford, 2020).
62. See Section 13 above.
63. The EEA excludes from free trade both non-transformed agriculture products and fish.
64. On condition that there is 'a significant negative effect on trade or investment between the Parties ... based on reliable evidence and not merely on conjecture or remote possibility' (Article 374(1) TCA).
65. The EEZ goes beyond the territorial sea which is under the sovereignty of the coastal state. It is an area of the sea in which surface waters are international and free for navigation, but in which coastal states have exclusive rights on marine resources (energy, fish). It stretches from the baseline (territorial sea) to 200 nautical miles. See Part V of the United Nations Convention on the Law of the Sea, signed in Montego Bay, Jamaica, on 10 December 1982.
66. Over 70 per cent of the UK's fish exports go to the EU, especially to France. On the other side, UK is buying fish coming from the EU. This is because the catches are not the same species and do not correspond to the local consumption.
67. Paragraph 74 of the Political Declaration (2020): 'The Parties will use their best endeavours to conclude and ratify their new fisheries agreement by 1 July 2020 in order for it to be in place in time to be used for determining fishing opportunities for the first year after the transition period.'
68. The UK wished to get 80 per cent of the EU catch over a period of three years and to forbid EU boats to fish in the six to twelve miles zone from the coast.
69. Paragraph 36 of the Political declaration (2020): '... endeavouring to conclude assessments before the end of June 2020'.
70. In a document dated 9 July 2020 '*Getting Ready for Changes*', the Commission stated that 'the Commission shared with the UK questionnaires covering 28 equivalence areas. By the end of June, only four completed questionnaires had been returned' (European Commission, 2020, p. 13).
71. The Common Travel Area was established between both countries after the Irish Free State seceded from the UK in 1923.
72. The EU has about 50 agencies and other bodies to implement some of its policies, from Europol and Eurojust for JHA, to the European Chemicals Agency, the European Food Safety Agency or the European Medicines Agency. Some of them are within the jurisdiction of the CJEU. The UK refusal of the jurisdiction of the CJEU implies therefore that the UK shall have sometimes to establish its own agency (for aviation safety for example) or to develop its existing one (for medicines for example).
73. Information on ongoing cases might be allowed to continue for a given period.
74. Based on Directive 2016/681, OJ L 119/13, which permits to conclude agreements with third countries.
75. Based on the Prüm Convention on the fight against terrorism, signed on 27 May 2005.
76. Such a decision needs a proposal from the Commission, an opinion of the European Data Protection Board, an approval from representatives of EU member states in a Committee, and the adoption of the decision by the Commission.
77. See, for example, Article 1 TCA: '... respectful of the Parties' autonomy and sovereignty'.
78. See Section 19 above.

79. Despite some ongoing judicial complaints in tribunals, the EU citizenship is linked to the citizenship of a member state (Article 20(1) TFEU). Since 1 February 2020, the UK is not an EU member state anymore.
80. See Section 20 above.
81. See Chapter 2, Title One, in Heading One of Part II, Draft TCA (and Annexes, pp. 440–510).
82. A transition period of 12 months was agreed for companies exporting goods between the EU and the UK before being obliged to produce some of this paperwork, especially on the rules of origin. Moreover, a six-year phasing-in period was agreed for rules of origin requirements on electric cars and hybrid cars: from a maximum of 60 per cent of their content coming from outside the EU during four years, then decreasing to 55 per cent in the years 2023–26 and then to 45 per cent from 2027.
83. See, in Section 13 above, other '*essential elements*' of the TCA.

REFERENCES

Agreement between the European Union and the United Kingdom of Great Britain and Northern Ireland concerning security procedures for exchanging and protecting classified information (EU-UK Security Information Agreement). (2021). *Official Journal of the European Union*, L 149/2540.

Agreement between the European Union and the United Kingdom of Great Britain and Northern Ireland and the European Atomic Energy Community for cooperation on the safe and peaceful uses of nuclear energy (EU-UK Civil Nuclear Agreement). (2021). *Official Journal of the European Union*, L 150/1.

Agreement on the withdrawal of the United Kingdom of Great Britain and Northern Ireland from the European Union and the European Atomic Energy Community (Withdrawal Agreement). (2019). *Official Journal of the European Union*, C 384 I/1.

Andy Wightman and Others v Secretary of State for Exiting the European Union, CJEU, Case C-621/18, ECLI:EU:C:2018:999 (2018) (EU).

Armstrong, K.A. (2020). The transition. In Federico Fabbrini (ed.), *The Law and Politics of Brexit: Volume II: The Withdrawal Agreement* (pp. 171–90). Oxford University Press.

Barnier, M. (2020, 10 June). Speech by Michel Barnier at the European Economic and Social Committee Plenary Session. *European Commission*. https://ec.europa.eu/commission/presscorner/detail/en/speech_20_1037 (accessed 31 January 2021).

Belfast Agreement (Good Friday Agreement (GFA)), United Kingdom–Ireland, 10 April 1998. https://www.gov.uk/government/publications/the-belfast-agreement (accessed 31 January 2021).

Bradford, A. (2020). *The Brussels Effect: How the EU Rules the World*. Oxford University Press.

Bundesverfassungsgericht (BVerfG). (2009). Judgement of the Second Senate of 30 June 2009, 2 BvE 2/08. https://www.bundesverfassungsgericht.de/e/es20090630_2bve000208en.html (accessed 31 January 2021).

CJEU (2015). C-362/14 Maximillian Schrems v Data Protection Commissioner. ECLI:EU:C:2015:650.

CJEU (2020). C-311/18 Data Protection Commissioner v Facebook Ireland Limited and Maximillian Schrems. ECLI:EU:C:2020:559.

Closa, C. (2013). *The Politics of Ratification of EU Treaties*. Routledge.

Consolidated version of the Treaty on the European Union (TEU). (2012). *Official Journal of the European Union*, C 326/13.

Consolidated version of the Treaty on the Functioning of the European Union (TFEU). (2012). *Official Journal of the European Union*, C 326/47.

Council Decision (EU, Euratom) 2020/266 of 25 February 2020 authorising the opening of negotiations with the United Kingdom of Great Britain and Northern Ireland for a new partnership agreement. (2020). *Official Journal of the European Union*, L 58/53.

Council Decision (EU, Euratom) of 22 May 2017 authorising the opening of negotiations with the United Kingdom of Great Britain and Northern Ireland for an agreement setting out the arrangements for its withdrawal from the European Union and Directives for the negotiation of an agreement with the United Kingdom of Great Britain and Northern Ireland setting out the arrangements for its withdrawal from the European Union. XT 21016/17 ADD 1 REV 2 BXT 24.

Council of the European Union. (2018). ANNEX to the COUNCIL DECISION supplementing the Council Decision of 22 May 2017 authorising the opening of the negotiations with the United Kingdom of Great Britain and Northern Ireland for an agreement setting out the arrangements for its withdrawal from the European Union – and Supplementary directives for the negotiation of an agreement with the United Kingdom of Great Britain and Northern Ireland setting out the arrangements for its withdrawal from the European Union. XT 21004/18 ADD 1 REV 2 BXT 5.

Craig, P. (2017). The process: Brexit and the anatomy of Article 50. In F. Fabbrini (ed.), *The Law and Politics of Brexit* (pp. 49–69). Oxford University Press.

Darroch, K. (2020). *Collateral Damage: Britain, America and Europe in the Age of Trump*. William Collins.

Directive (EU) 2016/681 of the European Parliament and of the Council of 27 April 2016 on the use of passenger name record (PNR) data for the prevention, detection, investigation and prosecution of terrorist offences and serious crime. *Official Journal of the European Union*, OJ L 119/13.

Eeckhout, P., and Frantziou, E. (2016). *Brexit and Article 50 TEU: A Constitutionalist Reading* (UCL European Institute Working Paper, December 2016). UCL European Institute.

European Commission. (1985, 14 June). *Completing the Internal Market* (White Paper from the Commission to the European Council). COM(85) 310 final.

European Commission. (2017, 8 December). Joint report from the negotiators of the European Union and the United Kingdom Government on progress during phase 1 of negotiations under Article 50 TEU on the United Kingdom's orderly withdrawal from the European Union. TF50 (2017) 19.

European Commission. (2018). *Draft Agreement on the Withdrawal of the United Kingdom of Great Britain and Northern Ireland from the European Union and the European Atomic Energy Community*. TF50(2018)35.

European Commission. (2020, 9 July). *Getting Ready for Changes. Communication on Readiness at the End of the Transition Period between the European Union and the United Kingdom*. COM/2020/324 final.

European Council Decision (EU) 2018/937 of 28 June 2018 establishing the composition of the European Parliament (2018). *Official Journal of the European Union*, L 165 I/1.

European Council. (2017a). *Special Meeting of the European Council (Art. 50) (29 April 2017) – Guidelines*. EUCO XT 2004/17, BXT 10 CO EUR 5 CONCL 2.

European Council. (2017b). *European Council (Art. 50) (15 December 2017) – Guidelines*. EUCO XT 20011/17, BXT 69 CO EUR 27 CONCL 8.

European Council. (2018). *European Council (Art. 50) (23 March 2018) – Guidelines*. EUCO XT 20001/18, BXT 25 CO EUR 5 CONCL 2.

European Council. (2019, 28 October 2019). European Council Decision taken in agreement with the United Kingdom extending the period under Article 50(3) TEU. EUCO XT 20024/2/19, REV 2, BXT 88.

European Union (Notification of Withdrawal Act 2017). (2017, 16 March). HL Bill 103, 56/2.

European Union Committee. (2020, 16 October). The United Kingdom Internal Market Bill: Part 5. 14th Report of Session 2019-21, HL Paper 147. https://publications.parliament.uk/pa/ld5801/ldselect/ldeucom/147/14707.htm (accessed 31 January 2021).

Fabbrini, F., and Schmidt, R. (2020). The extensions. In F. Fabbrini (ed.), *The Law and Politics of Brexit: Volume II: The Withdrawal Agreement* (pp. 66–82). Oxford University Press.

Gatti, M. (2017). The Article 50 procedure for withdrawal from the EU: A well-designed secession clause. *European Papers*, *2*(1), 159–81.

HM Government (2020). *The Future Relationship with the EU: The UK's Approach to Negotiations*. https://assets.publishing.service.gov.uk/government/uploads/system/uploads/attachment_data/file/868874/The_Future_Relationship_with_the_EU.pdf (accessed 31 January 2021).

Kassim, H. (2021, 11 January). Aviation and the Brexit deal. *UK in a Changing Europe*. https://ukandeu.ac.uk/brexit-deal-aviation/ (accessed 31 January 2021).

Lisbon Intergovernmental Conference (IGC) Final Act. (2007). *Official Journal of the European Union*, C 306/231.

May, T. (2017a, 17 January). The government's negotiating objectives for exiting the EU: PM speech [speech]. *Prime Minister's Office, gov.uk*. https://www.gov.uk/government/speeches/the-governments-negotiating-objectives-for-exiting-the-eu-pm-speech (accessed 31 January 2021).

May, T. (2017b, 29 March). Prime Minister's letter to Donald Tusk triggering Article 50. *Prime Minister's Office, gov.uk*. https://www.gov.uk/government/publications/prime-ministers-letter-to-donald-tusk-triggering-article-50 (accessed 31 January 2021).

Miller v Secretary of State for Exiting the European Union, U.K.S.C. 5 (2017) (Eng.). https://www.supremecourt.uk/cases/docs/uksc-2016-0196-judgment.pdf (accessed 31 January 2021).

Parti écologiste 'Les Verts' v European Parliament, CJEU, Case 294/83, ECR I-1339, ECLI:EU:C:1986:166 (1986) (EU).

Peers, S., and Weatherill, S. (2018, 16 January). Can Article 50 notice of withdrawal from the EU be unilaterally revoked? *EU Law Analysis Blog*. http://eulawanalysis.blogspot.com/2018/01/can-article-50-notice-of-withdrawal.html (accessed 31 January 2021).

Piris, J.-C. (2010). *The Lisbon Treaty. A Legal and Political Analysis*. Cambridge University Press.

Piris, J.-C. (2014, 4 December). Future relations between the UK and the EU. *Politico*. https://www.politico.eu/article/future-relations-between-the-uk-and-the-eu/ (accessed 31 January 2021).

Piris, J.-C. (2015a, 5 May). Should the UK withdraw from the EU: Legal aspects and effects of possible options. *Fondation Robert Schuman*, European Issues No. 355. https://www.robert-schuman.eu/en/doc/questions-d-europe/qe-355-en.pdf (accessed 31 January 2021).

Piris, J.-C. (2015b, 26 October). Brexit or Britin: Is it really colder outside? *Fondation Robert Schuman*, European Issues, No. 355 Bis. https://www.robert-schuman.eu/en/doc/questions-d-europe/qe-355-bis-en.pdf (accessed 31 January 2021).

Piris, J.-C. (2016a, 1 September). Article 50 is not for ever and the UK could change its mind. *Financial Times*. https://www.ft.com/content/b9fc30c8-6edb-11e6-a0c9-1365ce54b926 (accessed 31 January 2021).

Piris, J.-C. (2016b). La Unión Europea, Cataluña y Escocia (Cuestiones jurídicas sobre las recientes tendencias secesionistas en los Estados Miembros de la UE). *Teoría y Realidad Constituciona*, *37*(1), 101–34.

Piris, J.-C. (2016c). *If the UK Votes to Leave: The Seven Alternatives to EU Membership*. Centre for European Reform. https://www.cer.eu/sites/default/files/pb_piris_brexit_12jan16.pdf (accessed 31 January 2021).

Piris, J.-C. (2016d, 12 January). Brexit is the easy bit. *Financial Times*. https://www.ft.com/content/ee4825f2-b91f-11e5-b151-8e15c9a029fb (accessed 31 January 2021).

Piris, J.-C. (2017a, 4 May). It is Europe's interest to treat Britain fairly. *Financial Times*. https://www.ft.com/content/37e7e082-2f33-11e7-9555-23ef563ecf9a (accessed 31 January 2021).

Piris, J.-C. (2017b, 17 November). The myth and delusion over single market access. *Financial Times*. https://www.ft.com/content/7a3d13ee-cabf-11e7-8536-d321d0d897a3 (accessed 31 January 2021).

Political declaration setting out the framework for the future relationship between the European Union and the United Kingdom (EU-UK Political Declaration). (2020). *Official Journal of the European Union*, L 34/1.

Protocol on Gibraltar (2019). *Official Journal of the European Union*, C 384 I/143.

Protocol on Ireland/Northern Ireland to the Agreement on the withdrawal of the United Kingdom of Great Britain and Northern Ireland from the European Union and the European Atomic Energy Community (Protocol on Ireland/Northern Ireland). (2019). *Official Journal of the European Union*, C 384 I/92.

Protocol on Social Security Coordination. (2021). *Official Journal of the European Union*, L 149/2292.

Protocol relating to the Sovereign Base Areas of the United Kingdom of Great Britain and Northern Ireland in Cyprus. (2019). *Official Journal of the European Union*, C 384 I/136.

Prüm Convention on the fight against terrorism. (2005).

Regulation (EU) 2016/679 of the European Parliament and of the Council of 27 April 2016 on the protection of natural persons with regard to the processing of personal data and on the free movement of such data, and repealing directive 95/46/ec (General Data Protection Regulation). (2016). *Official Journal of the European Union*, L 119/1.

Repasi, R. (2020, 30 January). Avoiding the next Brexit cliff-edge: Extending the transition period for the UK after 1 July 2020. *Blog on EU Law Analysis*. https://eulawanalysis.blogspot.com/2020/01/avoiding-next-brexit-cliff-edge.html (accessed 31 January 2021).

Senior European Experts. (2020, 25 February). *The UK-EU Negotiations: Fishing. Senior European Experts*. https://senioreuropeanexperts.org/paper/uk-eu-negotiations-fishing/.

Shonfield, A. (1973). *Europe: Journey to an Unknown Destination. An Expanded Version of the BBC Reith Lectures 1972*. Penguin Books.

Smismans, S. (2016, 29 November). About the revocability of withdrawal: Why the EU (law) interpretation of Article 50 matters. *UK Constitutional Law Association Blog*. https://ukconstitutionallaw.org/2016/11/29/stijn-smismans-about-the-revocability-of-withdrawal-why-the-eu-law-interpretation-of-article-50-matters/ (accessed 31 January 2021).

Taxation (Post-Transition Period) Act 2020 (Taxation Bill), c. 26.

Trade and Cooperation Agreement between the European Union and the European Atomic Energy Community, of the one part, and the United Kingdom of Great Britain and Northern Ireland, of the other part (EU–UK Trade and Cooperation Agreement). (2021). *Official Journal of the European Union*, L 149/10.

United Kingdom Internal Market Bill (British Internal Market Bill). (2020). Bill 177 2019-21, 58/1.

United Nations Convention on the Law of the Sea. (1982). No. 31363.

Vienna Convention on the Law of Treaties (VCLT). (1969, 23 May). 1115 *United Nations Treaty Series* 331.

Vienna Convention on the Law of Treaties between States and International Organisations or between International Organisations. (1986, 21 March).

Weatherill, S. (2020, 17 March). The Protocol on Ireland/Northern Ireland: What it says is not what it does. *EU Law Analysis Blog*. http://eulawanalysis.blogspot.com/2020/03/the-protocol-on-ireland-northern.html (accessed 31 January 2021).

APPENDIX

Consolidated Version of the Treaty on European Union

Title VI

Final provisions

Article 50

1. Any Member State may decide to withdraw from the Union in accordance with its own constitutional requirements.
2. A Member State which decides to withdraw shall notify the European Council of its intention. In the light of the guidelines provided by the European Council, the Union shall negotiate and conclude an agreement with that State, setting out the arrangements for its withdrawal, taking account of the framework for its future relationship with the Union. That agreement shall be negotiated in accordance with Article 218(3) of the Treaty on the Functioning of the European Union. It shall be concluded on behalf of the Union by the Council, acting by a qualified majority, after obtaining the consent of the European Parliament.
3. The Treaties shall cease to apply to the State in question from the date of entry into force of the Withdrawal Agreement or, failing that, two years after the notification referred to in paragraph 2, unless the European Council, in agreement with the Member State concerned, unanimously decides to extend this period.
4. For the purposes of paragraphs 2 and 3, the member of the European Council or of the Council representing the withdrawing Member State shall not participate in the discussions of the European Council or Council or in decisions concerning it.

   A qualified majority shall be defined in accordance with Article 238(3)(b) of the Treaty on the Functioning of the European Union.
5. If a State which has withdrawn from the Union asks to rejoin, its request shall be subject to the procedure referred to in Article 49.

9. The European Council and Brexit: from accommodating an 'awkward partner' towards managing a conflictual relationship?

Birgit Bujard and Wolfgang Wessels

INTRODUCTION[1]

Inside the European Union (EU) the European Council functions as the 'highest political authority' providing 'procedural leadership' (Wessels, 2016, p. 71). It sets out the Union's 'general political directions and priorities thereof' (Art. 15(1) TEU). Accordingly, throughout the United Kingdom's (UK) membership of the European Community (EC)/EU, the European Council was the key institution which shaped the relationship between the 'awkward partner' (George, 1998, p. 1) and the EC/EU and determined Britain's special status inside the Union. It continued to be the ultimate decision-maker once it was clear that the country would leave the Union. It determined the Brexit process and set the key parameters for the future relationship with the ex-member state. It will remain the ultimate decision-maker on the EU side, should there be any significant change to the EU-UK relationship as set out in the 2020 Trade and Cooperation Agreement (TCA) in the future and when it comes to handling sensitive issues in that relationship. To understand the evolving new relationship between the EU and its former member state and the options for a distinctive 'close partnership' (European Council, 2017b, p. 8) between the two in the future, a study of the European Council's decisions on Brexit as set out in the institution's Conclusions is essential. Using a process tracing approach, this chapter analyses the European Council's role in relation to the UK during the time of Britain's EC/EU membership and the withdrawal negotiations. It then discusses perspectives for the European Council's role in the future development of EU-UK relations.

BEFORE BREXIT: ACCOMMODATION OF AN 'AWKWARD PARTNER'

Beginning with the summit at The Hague in 1969 – which can be seen as a predecessor of the European Council – when the leaders of the six founding members agreed to the UK's accession to the Community after its first two applications had failed due to French resistance (Knipping, 2004, pp. 156–7), the European leaders repeatedly took decisions on issues of particular interest to the UK. Moreover, they set the terms of the country's special status inside the Union. In the following years the European Council regularly discussed EU budget matters and agreed to grant the UK a long-term rebate on its budget contribution. Additionally, the European leaders cemented the UK's special status inside the Union by granting the country a number of opt-outs from key EU policies such as from Economic and Monetary Union

Table 9.1 *Key decisions on the UK's special status until the 2016 referendum*

Fontainebleau Summit, 1984	Agreement of British budget rebate
Maastricht Treaty, 1991	Opt-out from Economic and Monetary Union and Social Chapter
Amsterdam Treaty, 1997	Opt-out from Schengen and Area of Freedom, Security and Justice
Lisbon Treaty, 2007	Affirmation of opt-out from Area of Freedom, Security and Justice and opt-out from Protocol on Charter of Fundamental Rights of the European Union
Brussels Summit, February 2016	Offer of special status (including opt-out from 'process of creating an ever-closer union among the peoples of Europe'), if British citizens voted to remain in the EU in the referendum

Source: Own compilation based on European Council Conclusions and Geddes (2013).

(EMU) and the Social Chapter during the Maastricht Treaty negotiations in the early 1990s as well as later from the Schengen area (Wessels, 2016, chapter 4) (Table 9.1).

When Prime Minister David Cameron demanded treaty changes after he had promised his voters a referendum on EU membership in 2013, the European Council renegotiated the terms of Britain's relationship with the Union. In February 2016 the EU leaders agreed provisions which were intended to help Cameron in the referendum campaign, but did not include any treaty changes to key elements of the Union (European Council, 2016a).

After the referendum on 23 June 2016, in which a majority of British citizens voted to leave the EU, the European Council continued its pivotal role in UK-EU relations. Immediately after the vote, it took the lead in shaping the new relationship with the UK. It did so, firstly, by organising and structuring the Brexit process itself and, secondly, in line with its treaty obligations, by setting the 'general political directions and priorities thereof' (Art. 15(1) TEU) for the EU concerning its aims for the new relationship with the soon-to-be ex-member state (Table 9.2). It framed its decisions in a narrative which focused on the EU's achievements and the differences between members and non-members. Complementary to the European Council's accession criteria, these provisions might become an 'exit doctrine' (Lippert, 2019, p. 632; von Ondarza, 2020, p. 92) eventually (Bujard and Wessels, 2021, pp. 14–15).

THE EUROPEAN COUNCIL'S KEY BREXIT DECISIONS

The European Council took key Brexit decisions particularly on the withdrawal process as well as on the framework for the future relationship with the soon-to-be ex-member state.

Providing Political and Procedural Leadership

The Treaty on European Union grants the European Council a distinct role in the withdrawal process of a member state: Firstly, the withdrawal notification has to be sent to the European Council, which then determines the guidelines for the subsequent exit negotiations. Also, the negotiation period of two years can only be extended by the European Council (Art. 50 TEU).

At 19 of its 38 meetings between the end of June 2016 and the UK's exit from the EU on 31 January 2020 the European Council discussed Brexit and the future relationship with the soon-to-be ex-member. After Britain's withdrawal from the Union, the frequency of its discus-

Table 9.2 *Key European Council decisions on Brexit*

28/29 June 2016	First decisions on the withdrawal negotiation process and framework for future EU-UK relations
15 December 2016	Further decisions on withdrawal negotiation process
29 April 2017	Adoption of guidelines for the withdrawal negotiations
15 December 2017	Agreement on sufficient progress in the 1st phase of negotiations for the 2ndphase to begin and to negotiate a stand-still transition phase
23 March 2018	Adoption of guidelines for the negotiations of the future EU-UK relationship
19/20 September 2018	Decision to agree with the UK on a Political Declaration on the future relationship to accompany the withdrawal treaty
25 November 2018	Approval of withdrawal agreement and Political Declaration
21 March 2019	Agreement of first extension of the Art. 50 period
10 April 2019	Agreement of second extension of the Art. 50 period
17 October 2019	Approval of revised withdrawal agreement and Political Declaration
29 October 2019	Agreement of third extension of the Art. 50 period
13 December 2019	Call to begin preparations for future relationship negotiations and for ratification and implementation of the withdrawal agreement
17–21 July 2020	MFF (Multiannual Financial Framework) negotiations: agreement of a 'Brexit Adjustment Reserve' for member states and sectors most affected by Brexit

Source: Own compilation based on European Council Conclusions.

sions on the issue declined. In 2020 the future relationship was only addressed at four of the 13 European Council meetings (Bujard and Wessels, 2021, pp. 15, 20). Even while Britain was still a member, the discussions about the withdrawal process and the EU's negotiation position beginning in late June 2016 were in line with the Lisbon Treaty restricted to the remaining 27 heads of state or government without any participation of the British prime minister.

The European Council meeting on 28–29 June 2016 was the first at which the EU leaders discussed the implications of the UK referendum as 27 without the British prime minister. David Cameron only attended the beginning of the summit to inform about the referendum outcome but did not stay for the discussion of it. At this meeting, the leaders took charge of the subsequent Brexit process by setting key aspects of the Union's reaction and by confirming the European Council's pivotal role in the upcoming negotiations. In their statement on the meeting, the 27 noted with regard to Britain's membership status that 'EU law continues to apply to and within the UK, both when it comes to rights and obligations' (European Council, 2016b, p. 1). They demanded that the British withdrawal from the EU would be conducted based on Article 50 TEU in an 'orderly fashion' (European Council, 2016b, p. 1). They, moreover, announced that there would be no informal negotiations outside of the framework provided by Article 50 TEU: the UK should begin the withdrawal process soon by sending its notification as there could 'be no negotiations of any kind before this notification has taken place' (European Council, 2016b, p. 1). Thus, right from the beginning of the Brexit process, the European Council confirmed the unity of member states with regard to negotiating Britain's withdrawal. In its statement the European Council also referred to the other EU institutions by stating that the European Commission and the European Parliament would both 'play their full role in accordance with the Treaties' (European Council, 2016b, p 1). Thus, the European leaders also took up the task to be the masters of the EU procedures.

Yet at the summit, the EU leaders not only determined the upcoming withdrawal process, they also discussed the implications of the referendum outcome for the EU itself. This discussion was followed up at another meeting of the 27 EU leaders in September 2016 in

Bratislava. From that point on, the European Council framed its decisions on Brexit in a narrative which focused on the EU's achievements as well as the differences between members and non-members. It continued to do so throughout the Brexit process (Bujard and Wessels, 2021). The 27 EU leaders confirmed their intention to 'remain united and work in the framework of the EU to deal with the challenges of the 21st century and find solutions in the interest of our nations and peoples' (European Council, 2016b, p. 2). In its Bratislava Declaration, the European Council stated that for the remaining members the EU was 'indispensable' (European Council, 2016c, p. 1). The 27 heads of state or government focused on the achievements of the Union and confirmed their decision to proceed with the integration process. They stated in June 2016: 'The European Union is a historic achievement of peace, prosperity and security on the European continent and remains our common framework' (European Council, 2016b, p. 2).

Despite backing continued integration, the European Council acknowledged that not everything was well and that there was a need for improvement: 'Europeans expect us to do better when it comes to providing security, jobs and growth, as well as hope for a better future. We need to deliver on this, in a way that unites us' (European Council, 2016b, p. 2). To achieve this the EU leaders in June 2016 announced a period of 'political reflection to give an impulse to further reforms, in line with our Strategic Agenda, and to the development of the EU with 27 Member States' (European Council, 2016b, p. 2). They assigned themselves an important task for the subsequent integration process which was 'to offer to our citizens in the upcoming months a vision of an attractive EU they can trust and support' (European Council, 2016c, p. 2).

With these declarations as well as those of Rome in 2017 (European Council, 2017a), Sibiu in 2019 (European Council, 2019c) and the new strategic agenda 2019–24 (European Council, 2019d) in 2019, the 27 heads of states or government clarified that to them Brexit only had a limited significance for the future integration process (Bujard and Wessels, 2021, p. 18).

On 15 December 2016 the European Council took further decisions on the Brexit process: after Britain's withdrawal notification it would set the guidelines for the negotiations. Then the Council of the EU would agree the start of the negotiations on the basis of a recommendation by the European Commission. The 27 European leaders welcomed the appointment of Michel Barnier as the EU's chief negotiator and called on the Council to confirm the European Commission as the EU's sole negotiator. They, moreover, showed that they personally intended to focus on Brexit by announcing that that they would regularly assess the state of the negotiations and that representatives of the President of the European Council would join all negotiation meetings (European Council, 2016d, p. 2). Additionally, the European Council explained how the European Parliament would be involved: it invited the President of the Parliament to attend its own summits and called on the chief negotiator 'to keep the European Parliament closely and regularly informed throughout the negotiation' (European Council, 2016d, p. 3).

After the UK government had formally notified the European Council in March 2017 of its intention to leave the EU, the institution on 29 April 2017 adopted its guidelines for the withdrawal negotiations and announced that there would be two phases of negotiations. In the first phase issues related to Britain's withdrawal from the EU would be negotiated. The negotiation on the future relationship would begin in a second phase. However, it could only be finalised once the UK was a third country. Again, taking the lead, the European Council announced that it would be the EU institution that would decide when the move to the second negotiation phase would be done (European Council, 2017b, p. 4). In addition, it identified three key issues to be negotiated during the first phase: (a) the rights of EU citizens in the UK and British citizens in the EU 27, (b) a financial settlement and (c) the Irish border question. To secure the peace process on the island of Ireland a way needed to be found to keep the border between Northern Ireland and the Republic open (European Council, 2017b, pp. 5–6).

In the guidelines the European Council, moreover, confirmed its aim to create a 'close partnership' (2017b, p. 8) with the UK and to cooperate on trade, the fight against crime and terrorism and foreign, security and defence policy (2017b, p. 8). However, the European Council went on to clearly differentiate between member states and non-members: 'a relationship between the Union and a non Member State cannot offer the same benefits as Union membership' (2017b, p. 8). In addition, it noted that any future treaty with the UK needed to 'be based on a balance of rights and obligations, and ensure a level playing field' (2017b, p. 3). This was not new as the 27 heads of state or government had already stated this in June 2016 at their first meeting after the referendum (European Council, 2016b, p. 2).

On the future trade relationship, the European Council announced its willingness to conduct negotiations about a free trade agreement. However, such an agreement could not 'amount to participation in the Single Market or parts thereof, as this would undermine its integrity and proper functioning' (European Council, 2017b, p. 8). Again, this was something the 27 EU leaders had already said at their first meeting to discuss Britain's EU exit, when they had stated: 'Access to the Single Market requires acceptance of all four freedoms' (European Council, 2016b, p. 2).

Additionally, the 27 heads of state or government referred in their guidelines to the Court of Justice of the European Union's autonomous role as well as to the autonomous decision-making by the Union. They, moreover, rejected separate agreements on individual issues with the UK as well as bilateral negotiations with the country (European Council, 2017b, p. 3). With this they reaffirmed their unity with regard to the soon-to-be ex-member state.

The withdrawal negotiations, which began in June 2017, were difficult. The Irish border question was the most complicated as well as the dominant issue of these negotiations. For the EU solving this problem was important, because it was essential for its member state Ireland which shared a land border with the UK and would be the country among the 27 most severely affected by the economic impact of Brexit because of its close trading links with the UK (European Parliament, 2017, p. 32). Despite the difficulties, in December 2017 the European Council confirmed that progress of the first negotiation phase was adequate to move to the second. It, moreover, agreed to negotiate a stand-still transition period as part of the withdrawal agreement after the British EU exit, in which the country would remain subject to EU rules, yet without being part of the Union's decision-making (European Council, 2017c, pp. 1–2). In addition, it announced that it would publish supplementary guidelines in March 2018 which would particularly focus on the future relationship (2017c, p. 3).

In these additional guidelines, published on 23 March 2018, the European Council specified the potential shape of a future free trade agreement. It reiterated 'that the four freedoms are indivisible and that there can be no "cherry picking" through participation in the Single Market based on a sector-by-sector approach, which would undermine the integrity and proper functioning of the Single Market' (European Council, 2018a, p. 3). The EU leaders instead offered zero tariffs and zero quotas on goods, as long as the agreement would include adequate rules of origin. There should also be provisions on trade in services. The scope here, however, would be more limited taking into account that the UK would be a third country.

On fisheries, the European Council proposed retaining current levels of access to waters and fishing quotas (2018a, p. 4). In addition, the EU leaders argued for cooperation in the areas of law enforcement as well as in combating criminal matters. Here again they noted that it needed to be considered that Britain would be a third country and, moreover, not a member of the Schengen area. They also reiterated their aim to secure 'strong EU-UK cooperation in the fields of foreign, security and defence policy' (2018a, p. 6).

When Prime Minister Theresa May in 2018 presented her Chequers Plan for the future relationship which envisioned an EU-UK free trade area for goods with a common rule book of the EU and the UK, which would have meant for the EU to accept that the Single Market was divisible (Bujard, 2019, p. 551; Owen, 2020), the European Council at its meeting in Salzburg on 19–20 September 2018 clarified that this was not an option. After the summit the President of the European Council, Donald Tusk, explained that 'while there are positive elements in the Chequers proposal, the suggested framework for economic cooperation will not work. Not least because it risks undermining the Single Market' (Tusk, 2018).

Further negotiations followed and in November 2018 the two sides reached a withdrawal agreement and agreed on a Political Declaration on the future relationship. The European Council endorsed both on 25 November 2018 (European Council, 2018b, p. 2). The Political Declaration was new: at its Salzburg meeting the 27 EU leaders had further structured the negotiation process by deciding that an outline of the EU-UK future relationship would be set out in a non-binding Political Declaration to be agreed with the UK (Tusk, 2018).

The withdrawal treaty included a safeguarding provision to keep the Irish land border open: the 'backstop'. It would be applied if no other solution to keep the border open would be agreed by the time the UK left the EU (Institute for Government, 2020). It was highly controversial in Britain and therefore the treaty ratification was difficult. Over the course of 2019, three attempts to ratify the treaty failed in the Westminster Parliament and two extensions of the Article 50 negotiation period had to be agreed by the European Council (Bujard, 2019, pp. 553–6; European Council, 2019a, 2019b). As a consequence of her failure to achieve the treaty ratification, Theresa May resigned as prime minister. Boris Johnson succeeded her in July 2019. Boris Johnson, who already during the Tory leadership campaign had stated that Britain should leave the EU on 31 October 2019 with or without a deal, at first campaigned for the scrapping of the 'backstop' (Bujard, 2019, pp. 557–8). Upon realising that the EU would not agree to this, he went on to campaign for a renegotiation of the provisions on the Irish border and in October 2019 signed up to a revised Northern Ireland Protocol as part of the withdrawal agreement. To keep the border open, Boris Johnson had agreed to a special solution for Northern Ireland which meant that it would continue to follow EU customs regulations and Single Market rules on goods. The consequence would be a customs and regulatory border between Northern Ireland and Great Britain in the Irish Sea. Its depth would depend on how far the UK would diverge from EU regulations after leaving the EU Single Market and Customs Union. This arrangement resembled the EU's 2018 proposal of a special solution for Northern Ireland, which then Prime Minister Theresa May had rejected as unacceptable (Bujard, 2020, p. 430). On 17 October 2019, the European Council endorsed the revised withdrawal agreement and approved the also revised Political Declaration (European Council, 2019e, p. 1). Soon after, it decided on the third British request to extend Article 50 (Guardian, 20 October 2019). It agreed another extension until 31 January 2020 (European Council, 2019f). On 13 December 2019, a day after the Conservatives won a majority in the UK general election, the European Council began preparations for the negotiations on the future relationship: it called on the European Commission to send a draft negotiating mandate to the Council and on the Council to adopt this as soon as Britain would have left the EU (European Council, 2019g, p. 1).

Once more, the negotiations between the EU and the UK, which had formally left the EU on 31 January 2020, were difficult. But in December 2020 – shortly before the end of the transition phase the Boris Johnson government had not wanted to extend (Financial Times, 12 June 2020) – both sides agreed on the EU-UK TCA. As offered in 2018 by the European Council, it was a free trade agreement with zero tariffs and quotas, but rules of origin for goods. These provisions were supplemented by level playing field rules which went beyond provisions the EU had included in other trade agreements it had so far negotiated (Melo Araujo, 2021). The agreement also included provisions for trade in services, but they did not go far (Lowe, 2021, p. 1). Thus, without accepting its four freedoms participation in the Single Market is no longer possible for the former member state. The two parties also agreed to cooperate on police and judicial issues which – as the European Council had suggested in its guidelines – illustrates Britain's third country status outside the Schengen area (Institute for Government, n.d.). Additionally, the treaty did not include longer-term decisions on the equivalence of financial services and data protection, as these are taken unilaterally and the EU had not done so by the end of 2020 (Bille and Morin, 2021).

In some areas, however, the European Council did not achieve what it set out in 2017 and 2018. On fisheries, for example, the European Council's maximalist position as stated in its guidelines was not acceptable to the UK. But the agreement that was eventually reached turned out to be closer to the EU's starting position than the UK's (Stewart, 2020). There is, moreover, no role for the Court of Justice of the European Union in the treaty's governance and dispute settlement structure as is the case in the withdrawal agreement (Fella et al., 2020, p. 15). In addition, the TCA does not cover foreign and defence policy as the UK had rejected any treaty-based cooperation with the EU on this (Kassim, 2021, p. 149).

The European Council as a Collective Actor

One of the unexpected developments in the Brexit process was the unity the 27 heads of state or government displayed throughout the negotiations up until their end in December 2020. This is particularly surprising considering how often member states take different views on key questions of European integration. On Brexit, the EU leaders maintained their common position and – as they had stated in their guidelines – did not negotiate bilaterally with the UK. This was also the case with the larger member states. For instance, when Boris Johnson in summer of 2019 visited Berlin and Paris and demanded the scrapping of the 'backstop', neither Angela Merkel nor Emmanuel Marcon negotiated with him unilaterally but maintained the EU position on the issue (Guardian, 21 August 2019). The solidarity the member states displayed on Brexit was striking. They showed it with Ireland and only the Irish Taoiseach Leo Varadkar unilaterally negotiated with Boris Johnson in the autumn of 2019 about the Irish border question, which allowed the finalisation of a withdrawal agreement with Boris Johnson (Financial Times, 18 October 2019). This solidarity was again displayed in 2020 when the EU leaders – as part of the new Multiannual Financial Framework – agreed on a 'Brexit Adjustment Reserve' of five billion euros to help countries and sectors in the EU most affected by Brexit. With this decision they clarified that no country would be expected to compensate losses due to Britain's exit from the EU completely on their own (European Council, 2020a, p. 59).

Once the withdrawal treaty was agreed a more fragile European unity was expected, because the 27 would to different degrees be affected by new arrangements, for instance, on trade or fisheries as part of the future relationship settlement. But once more, they remained united. However, in contrast to the negotiations on the UK's withdrawal, the European Council no longer focused intensively on the future relationship negotiations. There were a number of reasons for this. For one, there were more urgent issues. There was, firstly, the impact of the COVID-19 pandemic on public health and the economy. Also, agreements of the Multiannual Financial Framework for 2021–27 and on the establishment of the Next Generation EU Recovery Fund were urgently needed. These were difficult issues whose final adoption was only achieved in December 2020 after Hungary and Poland ended their refusal to accept an agreement due to the new rule of law mechanism (Siebenhaar, 2020; Wessels and Hopp, 2021). However, it also appears to be the case that the 27 EU leaders did not see any necessity over the course of 2020 to adapt their guidelines for the future EU-UK relationship, which they had set early in the negotiation process and had not even revised when Boris Johnson succeeded Theresa May as prime minister and it became clear that he would pursue a different form of Brexit than his predecessor had done. Despite spending less time discussing the relationship with the UK internally, the EU leaders did take measures to keep their discussions confidential. An example was the meeting on 15–16 October 2020, where the members of the European Council were not allowed to have mobile phones or other devices with them in the room while the issue was debated (Eder, 2020).

In autumn of 2020, differences between the 27 with regard to the negotiations came into view. On fisheries, for instance, particularly France took a tough stance saying that it would not agree to a deal with the UK at the cost of its own fishing sector. The Netherlands, Denmark and Belgium were also concerned (Financial Times, 3 December 2020). Yet, as before, no member state broke unity. And also, after the first of several high-level discussions in December 2020 between the President of the European Commission Ursula von der Leyen and Boris Johnson, the latter again attempted to circumvent the Commission by calling for direct negotiations with Angela Merkel and Emmanuel Macron. Both declined (The Irish Times, 2020).

The low attention the European Council gave to Brexit in its final phase – at least publicly – might signal that the EU leaders were sufficiently satisfied with the way the negotiations were going and perhaps also that the shaping of relations with the UK had lost some of its political relevance.

PERSPECTIVES ON FUTURE NEIGHBOURLY RELATIONS AND THE EUROPEAN COUNCIL'S ROLE IN IT

The conclusion of the EU-UK TCA did not mark the beginning of a process of identifying and discussing new areas of cooperation between the EU and the UK. Instead, it appeared as if the agreement of December 2020 was the high point of engagement between the two with both sides being happy not to engage much with each other for a while. Despite the fatigue to find a formal agreement, however, the mutual relationship's final state has not yet been reached. There are issues which offer the potential for future cooperation but also for conflict. Many issues could be handled in a pragmatic way inside or outside the agreement. If this were the case, the European Council would not be involved. However, some might be sufficiently politically sensitive to reach its agenda. Although this key institution might be less inclined to formulate a specific vision or narrative for the EU's relations with the UK, some of its conclusions on individual issues of mutual interest might add up to a framework for the new relationship: will we observe the European Council's framing of some kind of informal 'close partnership' (European Council, 2017b, p. 8) between the EU and 'Global Britain' based on trust as good neighbours leading perhaps to a form of 'privileged partnership' (Gstöhl and Phinnemore, 2019, p. 5), or will there be more ad hoc, transactional and conflictual relations?

The lack of trust between the two, which has developed since the 2016 referendum, has made cooperation more difficult. Particularly the Boris Johnson government's often confrontational approach to the negotiations with the EU and the threat in September 2020 of passing domestic legislation breaching the withdrawal agreement it had only ratified a few months earlier added to the impression on the part of the EU that this was not a government to be trusted (Kassim, 2021, p. 150). Additionally, the UK's initial refusal to grant the EU ambassador in London the diplomatic status given to representatives of states did not help smooth the relationship with the Union (BBC, 2021). Meanwhile, the European Commission's near application of Article 16 of the Northern Ireland Protocol in January 2021 as part of its export authorisation regulation on vaccines was severely criticised in the UK (Connelly, 2021a). When the UK government in March 2021 announced the unilateral extension of grace periods for the export of goods from Great Britain to Northern Ireland (Connelly, 2021b), the EU reacted with dismay (European Commission, 2021). Moreover, the Boris Johnson government's attempts to ignore the EU as an interlocutor and thereby questioning its role as a global player – such as on the issue of the EU's diplomatic status – made cooperation even on issues of mutual interest more difficult.

The European Council will remain the ultimate decision-maker on issues of high sensitivity or political relevance in the EU-UK relationship. The implementation of the Northern Ireland Protocol is of such sensitive nature. The Protocol unlike other areas of their new relationship means that the UK and the EU share a common responsibility to make this unique situation work on the ground in Northern Ireland. At the same time, member states apart from Ireland might fear that the European Commission in looking for a solution to implement the Northern Ireland Protocol might allow the UK a backdoor into the Single Market. There will also be other matters of high sensitivity, for instance, distribution problems such as the pandemic-related question of vaccine exports between the EU and the UK in early 2021. This issue – as it was highly contested among member states – did eventually reach the European Council. The 27 heads of state or government discussed it on 25 March 2021, although they did not directly refer to the UK in their statement on the summit (European Council, 2021a).

The TCA itself might also be a source for future engagement of the European Council in EU-UK relations. It includes several revision clauses – most importantly the one on the treaty itself, which will come up firstly in 2025 and then every five years (Usherwood, 2021). Depending on the state of EU-UK relations by then, the European Council might be the forum in which the 27 member states discuss the Union's position on the future relationship. This might be the case if the then UK government (by 2025 there will have been a regular UK general election) takes a different view on the relationship to the EU and, for instance, looks for a closer partnership, or if the EU-UK relationship has become even more fractious and difficult. In addition, there are elements of the treaty which are set to come up for renegotiation in the next few years. In 2026, for example, the transition phase on fisheries expires and annual negotiations between the EU and the UK begin (Bevington, 2021). As mentioned, several member states – particularly France – have strong views on this issue.

There are, moreover, matters on which both sides have a mutual interest such as health policy (e.g., combating pandemics) as well as fighting climate change. Prime Minister Boris Johnson and the President of the European Council Charles Michel identified both in a phone call on 28 December 2020 as issues that the United Kingdom and the European Union would look to intensify cooperation on (European Council, 2020b).

A major subject area on which Boris Johnson and Charles Michel in December 2020 said they wanted to 'continue exchanging views and seek cooperation on specific issues' (European Council, 2020b) is foreign policy. This includes relations to countries around the world such as China, Russia or Turkey. It might be helpful that the Joe Biden administration has an interest in cooperating on these matters with the EU and the UK together. Yet with the UK aspiring to be 'Global Britain' and the EU's goal of 'strategic autonomy' and its development of a 'strategic compass', this might lead to rivalry between the two on the world stage. As a consequence of the UK's refusal of a contractual arrangement with the EU on foreign, security and defence policy, there is no regular format in which both sides discuss such matters. In line with its attempts to extend Britain's global influence while refusing to directly cooperate with the EU (Major and von Ondarza, 2021, p. 3), the Boris Johnson government tended to coordinate its foreign policy cooperation with EU member states through informal arrangements such as bilaterally or the E3 with Germany and France (Bond, 2020, p. 5). Other members, however, have previously criticised the E3 format for bypassing EU processes and for excluding them. There could again be opposition from them to expand cooperation in this format (Billon-Galland et al., 2020, pp. 4–5). They might prefer a relationship with the UK which includes more members (Bond, 2020, p. 7). Yet without a formal arrangement for EU-UK cooperation in these areas, it might prove to be a good format to keep Britain engaged and an option to enhance European influence on security and foreign policy (Billon-Galland et al., 2020, p. 6). Including the EU High Representative in a E3 + EU format might help in giving the other member states a voice as well as stave off criticism they might have (Major and von Ondarza, 2021, p. 6). There are also other suggestions for cooperation in parallel to NATO and the EU that could include the UK such as the already existing European Intervention Initiative (E2I). In addition, the long-standing German-French proposal of a European Security Council (ESC), if finally realised, could be a perspective to embed the UK in an EU-related format (Billon-Galland et al., 2020, pp. 8–10). Another area with the potential to lead to a more formal collaboration is military cooperation in the Permanent Structured Cooperation (PESCO) framework. The Council of the EU in May 2021 invited the United States, Canada and Norway to join the PESCO project 'Military Mobility', making them the first third countries to join PESCO (Council of the European Union, 2021). The UK followed suit and in early October 2022 24 EU member states unanimously agreed that the country should also be allowed to join this PESCO project (Hernandez, 2022).

In any case, as the Lisbon Treaty grants the European Council the power to 'identify the Union's strategic interests, determine the objectives of and define general guidelines for the common foreign and security policy' (Art. 26(1) TEU), questions of foreign, security and defence policy are bound to reach the European Council in the context of future EU-UK relations.

In the future, an informal procedural way forward might be to install a high-level dialogue between the EU leaders and the British prime minister on foreign policy issues as well as on others. This would mean more direct involvement of the European Council in the management of the EU-UK relations. At least while Boris Johnson was prime minister there appeared to be no incentive for such a course. For instance, unlike it did with US President Joe Biden, the European Council had not invited Johnson to attend one of its summits (Michel, 2021).

On 24 May 2021 the European Council discussed EU-UK relations for the first time after the end of the transition period. In the Conclusions it signalled that Britain's move to third country status was complete: relations to the UK were mentioned after the institution's conclusions on Belarus and Russia and before the Middle East and Mali. The EU leaders also clarified that they had no intention of continuing negotiations with the UK, for instance, on the Northern Ireland Protocol as they stated that the TCA 'together with the Withdrawal Agreement and its Protocols, provides the framework for our relations with the UK. Both Agreements should be fully and effectively implemented and their governance structures made operational' (European Council, 2021b, p. 4). Contentious matters such as fisheries, rights of EU citizens and the level playing field were specifically mentioned (2021b, p. 4). The European Council showed a tough and defensive line on EU-UK relations as it did not offer any 'carrots' to Britain to implement the treaties. It, instead, called on the European Commission to make sure that the agreements were fully implemented also by using all instruments available (2021b, p. 4). The EU leaders once more confirmed their unity on EU-UK relations as well as the European Council's continued lead role on the EU side by announcing that it would 'remain seized of the matter' (2021b, p. 4).

The Russian invasion of Ukraine in early 2022 and the subsequent war also impacted on EU-UK relations. On 6 October 2022 the first meeting of the European Political Community, which the European Council had discussed at its meeting in June 2022 (European Council, 2022, p. 1) was conducted in Prague. The heads of state or government of 44 countries, including the 27 EU member states and the United Kingdom as well as the Presidents of the European Council and the European Commission, attended the meeting to particularly discuss the war in Ukraine as well as the energy crisis (European Council and Council of the European Union, 2022). It remains to be seen whether this forum will become a successful format for the members of the European Council to discuss and possibly agree common action on urgent issues with leaders from neighbouring countries in general and with the United Kingdom in particular. Yet irrespective of possible joint decisions, the European Political Community offers the opportunity for an informal exchange of views between the EU leaders and the British prime minister away from media and public attention.

CONCLUSION

On Brexit, the European Council – as it has done during the UK's EC/EU membership – functioned as the 'highest political authority' and provided 'procedural leadership' (Wessels, 2016, p. 71). Through its provisions since June 2016, framed in a narrative which focused on the achievements of the Union and the differences between members and non-members, the European Council not only determined the Brexit process as well as the bloc's future relationship with the UK but also an 'exit doctrine' (Lippert, 2019, p. 632; von Ondarza, 2020, p. 92; Bujard and Wessels, 2021, p. 21). Thus, there is now a counterpart to the European Council's accession doctrine from the 1993 Copenhagen summit (European Council, 1993, p. 13). The

UK's withdrawal might serve as a model should other members wish to leave the Union in the future. Key elements of this exit doctrine are:

- A non-member cannot be better off than a member state and having rights means also fulfilling obligations.
- Any form of partial membership or opt-ins of non-members into selected EU policy areas are not possible.
- The integrity of the Single Market has the highest priority: participation in it is only possible if all of its four freedoms are accepted and sectoral participation is not.
- The solidarity among member states (in this case with Ireland) is a key principle.
- Decisions on the negotiation procedure as well as the relationship with the withdrawing member are reserved for the political leaders of the member states as the masters of the legal provisions set out in Article 50 TEU (Bujard and Wessels, 2021, p. 21).

The European Council reaffirmed these decisions in May 2021 when it stated that the two EU-UK treaties meant that the EU would have 'as close as possible a partnership with the UK, while recognising that a non-member of the EU cannot enjoy the same benefits as a member and that the relationship must be based on a balance of rights and obligations at all times' (European Council, 2021b, p. 4). The European leaders also noted that the EU-UK relationship 'should remain mutually beneficial and can under no circumstances undermine the integrity of the Single Market, the Customs Union or the EU's decision-making autonomy' (2021b, p. 4). This illustrates the continuity of the European Council's decisions on relations with the former member state.

With regard to the UK, the European Council has confirmed its role as the ultimate decision-maker on the Union side. While the country was a member, the European Council chose to accommodate the 'awkward partner' (George, 1998, p. 1) by granting it a special status inside the Union. After the 2016 EU referendum, accommodating British interests was no longer relevant to the European Council. It instead focused on setting out the possible framework for the UK's place fully outside the Union, thereby clarifying that a special status for the UK in the form of an opt-in to Union policies as a non-member, similar to its previous opt-outs as a member, was not on offer.

On the traditional dichotomy of supranational versus intergovernmental features of the EU's institutional architecture, the European Council's role on Brexit cannot be seen as evidence of a purely intergovernmental approach. Although the EU leaders determined the procedural provisions of the withdrawal process by taking the key decisions and formulating mandates and instructions, they then delegated the power to negotiate to the European Commission, while at the same time refusing to negotiate bilaterally at nation state level. They, moreover, set out clearly the role of the European Parliament in the process. Therefore, the Brexit case confirms existing trends of 'horizontal fusion' in which several EU institutions have to share responsibilities (Wessels, 2016, pp. 19–20). The EU leaders reiterated the sharing and division of responsibilities in May 2021 when they called on the European Commission to secure the full implementation of the existing EU-UK agreements and to do so in cooperation with the Council of Ministers (European Council, 2021b, p. 4).

At the time of writing, it remains unclear whether the UK and the EU will in the coming years manage to develop a 'close partnership' (European Council, 2017b, p. 8) based on mutual trust or whether we will see more distant and possibly conflictual neighbourly relations between the two. As outlined, there are several issues on which both sides could cooperate –

formally and informally – and over time rebuild trust that has been eroded since 2016. The European Council's part in this is pivotal, because inside the EU this key institution will continue to be the ultimate decision-maker exercising political as well as procedural leadership when it comes to shaping EU-UK relations. The kind of relationship the European Council will be motivated to frame will much depend on whether the European leaders perceive the UK as a reliable potential partner on matters of mutual interest and whether they feel cooperation with the former member state provides added value to the EU. While Britain was a member, the European Council spent much time and energy accommodating the UK inside the Union by granting it a special status, because the other leaders felt it was important to keep the country on board. Yet the Brexit process has shown that the European Council very quickly adapted to the UK being outside the EU framework. It might need the UK to demonstrate again why forging a closer relationship with the 'awkward partner' (George, 1998, p. 1) is beneficial to the European Union.

NOTE

1. Parts of this chapter are based on Bujard and Wessels (2021).

REFERENCES

BBC. (2021). UK and EU in row over bloc's diplomatic status. *BBC News*, 21 January. https://www.bbc.co.uk/news/uk-politics-55742664 (accessed 2 October 2021).

Bevington, M. (2021). What does the Brexit deal mean? *UK in a Changing Europe*, 20 January. https://ukandeu.ac.uk/explainers/what-does-the-brexit-deal-mean (accessed 2 October 2021).

Bille, B. and Morin, N. (2021). The TCA is the start of the UK-EU future relationship. *UK in a Changing Europe*, 12 January. https://ukandeu.ac.uk/the-tca-is-the-start-of-the-uk-eu-future-relationship (accessed 2 October 2021).

Billon-Galland, A., Raines, T. and Whitman, R.G. (2020). The future of the E3: Post-Brexit cooperation between the UK, France and Germany. Research Paper. *Chatham House*. https://www.chathamhouse.org/sites/default/files/2020-07-28-future-e3-post-brexit-cooperation-billon-galland-raines-whitman.pdf (accessed 12 October 2021).

Bond, I. (2020). Post-Brexit foreign, security and defence co-operation: We don't want to talk about it. *Centre for European Reform*. https://www.cer.eu/sites/default/files/pbrief_brexit_forpol_26.11.20.pdf (accessed 2 October 2021).

Bujard, B. (2019). Vereinigtes Königreich [United Kingdom]. In W. Weidenfeld and W. Wessels (eds), *Jahrbuch der Europäischen Integration 2019* [*Yearbook of European Integration*] (pp. 551–8). Nomos Verlagsgesellschaft.

Bujard, B. (2020). Die Europäische Union und das Vereinigte Königreich [The European Union and the United Kingdom]. In W. Weidenfeld and W. Wessels (eds), *Jahrbuch der Europäischen Integration 2020* [*Yearbook of European Integration 2020*] (pp. 429–36). Nomos Verlagsgesellschaft.

Bujard, B. and Wessels, W. (2021). Der Brexit-Prozess und die Austrittsdoktrin: Die Führungsrolle des Europäischen Rats [The Brexit Process and the Exit Doctrine: The European Council's Leadership Role]. *Zeitschrift für Außen- und Sicherheitspolitik*, *14*(1), 13–24.

Connelly, T. (2021a). Fear and loathing: Return of the Northern Ireland Protocol. *RTE News*, 6 February. https://www.rte.ie/news/2021/0205/1195326-tony-connelly-analysis/ (accessed 2 October 2021).

Connelly, T. (2021b). The NI Protocol: The EU's legal action and a roadmap to a deal. *RTE News*, 20 March. https://www.rte.ie/news/2021/0320/1205052-northern-ireland-protocol-brexit/ (accessed 2 October 2021).

Council of the European Union. (2021). PESCO: Canada, Norway and the United States will be invited to participate in the project Military Mobility. Press Release, 6 May. https://www.consilium.europa.eu/en/press/press-releases/2021/05/06/pesco-canada-norway-and-the-united-states-will-be-invited-to-participate-in-the-project-military-mobility/ (accessed 2 October 2021).

Eder, F. (2020). POLITICO Brussels Playbook: Signed, sealed, delivered – Brexit deadline dud – Plenary ping-pong. *Politico*, 16 October. https://politico.eu/newsletter/brussels-playbook/politico-brussels-playbook-signed-sealed-delivered-brexit-deadline-dud-plenary-ping-pong (accessed 2 October 2021).

European Commission. (2021). Statement by Vice-President Maroš Šefčovič following today's announcement by the UK government regarding the Protocol on Ireland/Northern Ireland, STATEMENT/21/1018, 3 March. https://ec.europa.eu/commission/presscorner/detail/en/STATEMENT_21_1018 (accessed 12 October 2021).

European Council. (1993). Conclusions of the Presidency, 21–22 June, SN 180/1/93 REV 1. https://www.consilium.europa.eu/media/21225/72921.pdf (accessed 2 October 2021).

European Council. (2016a). European Council meeting (18 and 19 February 2016) – Conclusions, EUCO 1/16. https://www.consilium.europa.eu/media/21787/0216-euco-conclusions.pdf (accessed 2 October 2021).

European Council. (2016b). Informal meeting at 27 Brussels, 29 June 2016 Statement. https://www.consilium.europa.eu/media/20462/sn00060-en16.pdf. (accessed 12 October 2021).

European Council. (2016c). The Bratislava Declaration. 16 September. https://www.consilium.europa.eu/media/21250/160916-bratislava-declaration-and-roadmapen16.pdf (accessed 2 October 2021).

European Council. (2016d). Informal meeting of the Heads of State or Government of 27 Member States, as well as the Presidents of the European Council and the European Commission, 15 December. https://www.consilium.europa.eu/media/24173/15-euco-statement.pdf (accessed 2 October 2021).

European Council. (2017a). The Rome Declaration, 25 March. https://www.consilium.europa.eu/en/press/press-releases/2017/03/25/rome-declaration/ (accessed 2 October 2021).

European Council. (2017b). Special meeting of the European Council (Art. 50) (29 April 2017) – Guidelines, EUCO XT 20004/17. https://data.consilium.europa.eu/doc/document/XT-20004-2017-INIT/en/pdf (accessed 2 October 2021).

European Council. (2017c). European Council (Art. 50) meeting (15 December 2017) – Guidelines, EUCO XT 20011/17. https://www.consilium.europa.eu/media/32236/15-euco-art50-guidelines-en.pdf (accessed 2 October 2021).

European Council. (2018a). European Council (Art. 50) (23 March 2018) – Guidelines, EUCO XT 20001/18. https://www.consilium.europa.eu/media/33458/23-euco-art50-guidelines.pdf (accessed 2 October 2021).

European Council. (2018b). Special meeting of the European Council (Art. 50) (25 November 2018) – Conclusions, EUCO XT 20015/18. https://www.consilium.europa.eu/media/37101/xt20015-en18.pdf (accessed 2 October 2021).

European Council. (2019a). Special meeting of the European Council (Art. 50) (21 March 2019) – Conclusions, EUCO XT 20004/19. https://data.consilium.europa.eu/doc/document/XT-20004-2019-INIT/en/pdf. (accessed 12 October 2021).

European Council. (2019b). Special meeting of the European Council (Art. 50) (10 April 2019) – Conclusions, EUCO XT 20015/19. https://www.consilium.europa.eu/media/39042/10-euco-art50-conclusions-en.pdf. (accessed 12 October 2021).

European Council. (2019c). The Sibiu Declaration, 9 May 2019. https://www.consilium.europa.eu/en/press/press-releases/2019/05/09/the-sibiu-declaration/ (accessed 2 October 2021).

European Council. (2019d). A new strategic agenda 2019–2024, 20 June. https://www.consilium.europa.eu/en/press/press-releases/2019/06/20/a-new-strategic-agenda-2019-2024/ (accessed 2 October 2021).

European Council. (2019e). Special meeting of the European Council (Art. 50) (17 October 2019) – Conclusions, EUCO XT 20018/19. https://www.consilium.europa.eu/media/41087/17-10-euco-art50-conclusions-en.pdf (accessed 2 October 2021).

European Council. (2019f). EUROPEAN COUNCIL DECISION taken in agreement with the United Kingdom extending the period under Article 50(3)TEU, 28 October 2019, EUCO XT 20024/2/19

REV 2. https://data.consilium.europa.eu/doc/document/XT-20024-2019-REV-2/en/pdf (accessed 2 October 2021).

European Council. (2019g). European Council (Art. 50) meeting (13 December 2019) – Conclusions, EUCO XT 20027/19. https://www.consilium.europa.eu/media/41796/13-euco-art50-conclusions-en.pdf (accessed 2 October 2021).

European Council. (2020a). Special meeting of the European Council (17, 18, 19, 20 and 21 July 2020) – Conclusions, EUCO 10/20. https://www.consilium.europa.eu/media/45109/210720-euco-final-conclusions-en.pdf (accessed 2 October 2021).

European Council. (2020b). Read out of the phone call between President Charles Michel and UK Prime Minister Boris Johnson. Press Release, 28 December. https://www.consilium.europa.eu/en/press/press-releases/2020/12/28/read-out-of-the-phone-call-between-president-charles-michel-and-uk-prime-minister-boris-johnson/ (accessed 2 October 2021).

European Council. (2021a). Statement of the members of the European Council, 25 March 2021, SN 18/21. https://www.consilium.europa.eu/media/48976/250321-vtc-euco-statement-en.pdf (accessed 2 October 2021).

European Council. (2021b). Special meeting of the European Council (24 and 25 May 2021) – Conclusions, EUCO 5/21. https://www.consilium.europa.eu/media/49791/2425-05-21-euco-conclusions-en.pdf (accessed 2 October 2021).

European Council. (2022). European Council meeting (23 and 24 June 2022) – Conclusions, EUCO 24/22. https://www.consilium.europa.eu/media/57442/2022-06-2324-euco-conclusions-en.pdf (accessed 16 October 2022).

European Council and Council of the European Union. (2022). Meeting of the European Political Community, 6 October. https://www.consilium.europa.eu/en/meetings/international-summit/2022/10/06/ (accessed 16 October 2022).

European Parliament. (2017). An Assessment of the Economic Impact of Brexit on the EU27. Directorate-General for Internal Policies. Study for the IMCO Committee. https://www.europarl.europa.eu/RegData/etudes/STUD/2017/595374/IPOL_STU(2017)595374_EN.pdf (accessed 2 October 2021).

Fella, S., Ferguson, D., Webb, D., Jozepa, I., Ares, E. and Kennedy, S. (2020). The UK-EU trade and cooperation agreement: Summary and implementation. Briefing Paper No. 09106. House of Commons Library. https://researchbriefings.files.parliament.uk/documents/CBP-9106/CBP-9106.pdf (accessed 12 October 2021).

Financial Times. (2019). Can Johnson 'get Brexit done'?, 18 October. https://www.ft.com/content/c7bb3a3a-f1a8-11e9-ad1e-4367d8281195 (accessed 2 October 2021).

Financial Times. (2020). UK formally rejects Brexit transition extension, 12 June. https://www.ft.com/content/f92e799d-7bac-4432-bb3f-9b21a6b0af85 (accessed 2 October 2021).

Financial Times. (2020). Tough Macron stance leaves Brexit deal hanging in balance, 3 December. https://www.ft.com/content/7a679982-abef-4f9a-8a55-e06588e7b770 (accessed 2 October 2021).

Geddes, A. (2013). *Britain and the European Union*. Palgrave Macmillan.

George, S. (1998). *An Awkward Partner: Britain in the European Community*. Oxford University Press.

Gstöhl, S. and Phinnemore, D. (eds). (2019). *The Proliferation of Privileged Partnerships between the European Union and Its Neighbours*. Routledge.

Guardian. (2019). Merkel gives Johnson 30 days to find solution to avoid no-deal Brexit, 21 August. https://www.theguardian.com/politics/2019/aug/21/merkel-gives-johnson-30-days-to-find-solution-to-avoid-no-deal-brexit (accessed 2 October 2021).

Guardian. (2019). Brexit: Johnson sends unsigned letter asking for delay, and second arguing against it, 20 October. https://www.theguardian.com/politics/2019/oct/19/eu-will-grant-brexit-extension-if-johnson-sends-letter-says-brussels (accessed 2 October 2021).

Hernandez, A. (2022). POLITICO Brussels Playbook: Gas cap tango in Prague – talkin' WWIII blues – Council Sec-Gen Saga. *Politico*, 7 October. https://www.politico.eu/newsletter/brussels-playbook/gas-cap-tango-in-prague-talkin-wwiii-blues-council-sec-gen-saga/ (accessed 16 October 2022).

Institute for Government. (n.d.). UK-EU future relationship: The deal. Law and justice. https://www.instituteforgovernment.org.uk/publication/future-relationship-trade-deal/law-justice (accessed 2 October 2021).

Institute for Government. (2020). Irish Backstop, 24 February 2020. https://www.instituteforgovernment.org.uk/explainers/irish-backstop (accessed 2 October 2021).

Kassim, H. (2021). Relations with the EU. In UK in a Changing Europe (ed.), *Brexit and Beyond* (pp. 149–50). https://ukandeu.ac.uk/wp-content/uploads/2021/01/Brexit-and-Beyond-report-compressed.pdf (accessed 6 October 2022).

Knipping, F. (2004). *Rom, 25. März 1957: Die Einigung Europas* [*Rome, 25 March 1957: Europe's unification*]. Deutscher Taschenbuch Verlag.

Lippert, B. (2019). Beitritt, Auvstritt und europäische Assoziierung – Vertragsgrundlagen und politische Praxis der Europäischen Union [Accession, Withdrawal and European Association – Treaty basis and political practice in the European Union]. In P. Becker and B. Lippert (eds), *Handbuch Europäischen Union* [*European Union Handbook*] (pp. 619–43). Springer VS.

Lowe, S. (2021). The EU-UK trade and co-operation agreement: A platform on which to build? CER Insight. *Centre for European Reform*. https://www.cer.eu/sites/default/files/insight_SL_12.1.21.pdf (accessed 2 October 2021).

Major, C. and von Ondarza, N. (2021). Die EU und Global Britain: So nah, so fern. Wie 'Global Britain' nach dem Brexit außen- und sicherheitspolitisch eingebunden werden kann. [The EU and Global Britain: So close, so far away. How 'Global Britain' after Brexit can be included in foreign and security policy]. *SWP-Aktuell*, *35*, 1–8. https://www.swp-berlin.org/publications/products/aktuell/2021A35_EU_GlobalBritain.pdf (accessed 1 October 2021).

Melo Araujo, B. (2021). Brexit trade problems: What's gone wrong and can it be fixed? *The Conversation*, 14 January. https://theconversation.com/brexit-trade-problems-whats-gone-wrong-and-can-it-be-fixed-153270 (accessed 2 October 2021).

Michel, C. (2021). Speech by President Charles Michel at the European Parliament on the inauguration of the new President of the United States, 20 January. https://www.consilium.europa.eu/en/press/press-releases/2021/01/20/speech-by-president-charles-michel-at-the-european-parliament-on-the-inauguration-of-the-new-president-of-the-united-states/ (accessed 2 October 2021).

Owen, J. (2020). Theresa May's Brexit Deal: Chequers plan. *Institute for Government*, 17 February. https://www.instituteforgovernment.org.uk/explainers/theresa-may-brexit-chequers-plan (accessed 2 October 2021).

Siebenhaar, H-P. (2020). Die Lösung des EU-Haushaltsstreits ist eine Meisterleistung Merkels [The solution of the EU's budget dispute is a master stroke by Merkel]. *Handelsblatt*, 10 December. https://www.handelsblatt.com/meinung/kommentare/kommentar-die-loesung-des-eu-haushaltsstreits-ist-eine-meisterleistung-merkels/26708252.html (accessed 12 October 2021).

Stewart, B. (2020). What does the trade deal mean for fisheries? *UK in a Changing Europe*, 27 December. https://ukandeu.ac.uk/fisheries-trade-deal (accessed 2 October 2021).

The Irish Times. (2020). Merkel and Macron refused approaches from Johnson and opted for united front, 11 December. https://www.irishtimes.com/news/world/europe/merkel-and-macron-refused-approaches-from-johnson-and-opted-for-united-front-1.4434419 (accessed 2 October 2021).

Tusk, D. (2018). Remarks by President Donald Tusk after the Salzburg informal summit, 20 September. https://www.consilium.europa.eu/en/press/press-releases/2018/09/20/remarks-by-president-donald-tusk-after-the-salzburg-informal-summit/ (accessed 2 October 2021).

Usherwood, S. (2021). Mapping the next period of Brexit. *Politics at Surrey*, 7 January. https://politicsatsurrey.ideasoneurope.eu/2021/01/07/mapping-the-next-period-of-brexit/ (accessed 2 October 2021).

Von Ondarza, N. (2020). The Methode 'Barnier' – Lehren aus der Verhandlungsführung der EU beim Brexit [The 'Barnier' Method – learnings from the EU's Brexit negotiation]. *Integration*, *43*(2), 85–100.

Wessels, W. (2016). *The European Council*. Palgrave Macmillan.

Wessels, W. and Hopp, L. (2021). The European Council's financial mega deal: An unprecedented challenge for the political and academic world. TRACK Policy Brief Series Part III. Cologne: *CETEUS*. https://track.uni-koeln.de/sites/track/user_upload/Track_Policy_Brief_3_-_Corona_Krise.pdf (accessed 2 October 2021).

10. The European Parliament and Brexit[1]

Christopher Lord

INTRODUCTION

The Lisbon Treaty made Brexit possible. Article 50 created, for the first time, a mechanism for a member state to withdraw from the European Union (EU). But other, less well-known, aspects of the Lisbon Treaty also shaped Brexit. Amongst them are the treaty arrangements for negotiating international agreements (Article 218) and for special legislative procedures (Article 289 (2)). Together with Article 50, those other provisions meant that the consent of the European Parliament (EP) was needed for any withdrawal agreement (WA). If the United Kingdom (UK) was to leave with an agreement and not crash out with a 'no-deal Brexit' that would partly depend on the EP. The approval of the EP was also needed for the Trade and Cooperation Agreement (TCA) settled at the end of 2020. That agreement, for now, sets the framework for relations between 'Brexit UK' and the EU. And so it is likely to go on: the EP's approval will also be needed for further treaties with the Union.

Yet, formally speaking, the EP only had veto powers and not agenda-setting powers over those treaties defining of Brexit. The consent procedure only gave the EP the power to accept or reject the WA or the TCA. The EP had no power to amend either of the two agreements. Still, awareness that the EP can veto can be incentive enough to amend and adjust agreements during their negotiation to positions taken in the EP. The EP can, therefore, be an informal agenda-setter and an informal source of amendments even where it has neither of those powers formally. As Bressanelli et al. (2021) have nicely put it, the EP has been a 'quasi-negotiator' in the WA and TCA.

For sure, the EP felt the need at one point to remind the European Council of its power to veto if it was not sufficiently included in discussions throughout the negotiation of the WA. Yet, it was probably always in the interest of the Commission and European Council to include the EP. As well as minimising the risk of laboriously negotiated agreements falling at the last hurdle to a parliamentary veto, the participation of the EP in international agreements is likely, as we will see, to shift outcomes closer to the preferences of the Commission and European Council and away from preferences of third parties. Indeed, one suspects the consent procedure was designed with such an effect in mind and not just to give some democratic legitimation.

Much depended on the structure of preferences: were the preferences of the EP closer to the Commission and European Council than the UK? Almost certainly, yes, on essentially all questions raised by Brexit. Much also depended on the credibility of the threat: would the EP really carry through on a threat to veto agreements on a matter as important as Brexit? Maybe also, yes, on such issues so deeply affected by Brexit as Northern Ireland and Citizens' Rights. Both involved difficult questions of obligation and right. Those included obligations that the EU – as much as the UK – had accumulated through the UK's membership of the EU. They included rights that had been accorded to all EU citizens and to all UK citizens through their EU citizenship. They also included rights that had been accorded to communities and citizens of Northern Ireland with at least the implicit guarantee of the EU. The strategic and the normative – bargaining and legitimation – interacted in interesting ways in the EP's role in Brexit. I will come back to that.

The role of the European Parliament was also affected by the other parliaments with powers over agreements defining of Brexit. Between June 2016 and the UK election in December 2019, the UK Parliament was a far larger obstacle to any WA than the EP. Especially in the 2017–19 House of Commons there was no clear majority for any form of Brexit. The WA negotiated by the Theresa May Government was famously rejected three times by majorities of 232, 149 and 58 votes, respectively. Much changed with the election in December 2019 of a new UK Government with an overall parliamentary majority of more than 80. The role of parliament in the UK political system reverted to one of 'heckling a steamroller' (Weir and Beetham, 1999, p. 405). A renegotiated withdrawal agreement passed the House of Commons with a majority of 330 to 231 on 10 January 2020. Only three days were then needed to complete the remaining stages in the House of Commons. Barely a year later the UK Government published the bill enacting the TCA (29 December), before the legislation passed through all its stages the next day (30 December), all in the interval between Christmas and New Year's Day 2020.

Hence, the EP was, arguably, the only source of parliamentary veto or even scrutiny of the WA in its final form and throughout the negotiation of the TCA. The latter was somewhat surprising. It had been widely expected that two parliaments – the EP and the UK Parliament – would have vetoes and influence over the WA. Yet, it had also been assumed that those two Parliaments would then have to share influence and veto powers over any subsequent trade agreement. In January 2017, Sir Ivan Rogers had famously resigned as the UK's Permanent Representative when his advice that Brexit could take ten years undermined his relationship with Downing Street. Rogers's calculation was simple: the UK needed a trade agreement. But trade agreements are mixed agreements. They involve the powers of member states and therefore require the agreement of national parliaments and even some sub-national ones. The EU's trade agreement with Canada (CETA), for example, had taken more than five years to negotiate in the shadow of multiple parliamentary vetoes. A trade agreement with the UK could be expected to be more complex and contentious than the CETA: allow two years to negotiate a withdrawal agreement, five to seven years to negotiate a trade agreement and then one had to add in a bit of time before invoking Article 50. It seemed a fair bet that the negotiation and ratification of Brexit would cover the best part of ten years. That would, amongst other uncertainties, have involved three different European Parliaments – the 2014–19, 2019–24, 2024–29 European Parliaments – in the negotiation of Brexit.

That parliamentary marathon was, however, avoided by the decision of the Commission to not propose the TCA as a trade agreement under Article 207, but rather to propose it as an association agreement under Article 217 (Van Der Loo and Chamon, 2021) and to classify it accordingly as a 'European-only agreement'. The Commission's decision avoided huge economic disruption. But it was contentious. Perhaps the TCA is, more accurately, both an association agreement and a trade agreement. In its latter role, it treads on national competence and ought, therefore, to have been agreed upon by all national parliaments.

Yet, even if the EP was the only likely source of a parliamentary veto over the final version of the WA and throughout the TCA, it was still constrained by the huge difficulties of concluding either of the two agreements. Both turned into games of chicken that could only be concluded at the last moment before breakdowns damaging to both sides. Time for parliamentary ratification was, therefore, squeezed. Despite promises to leave the EP three months to scrutinise, deliberate and decide, its public debate of the WA was largely limited to a discussion in the Constitutional Affairs Committee on 23 January 2020 and a plenary debate on 29 January. Time for ratification of the TCA disappeared altogether. The TCA came into force as a provisional agreement pending EP ratification. The lack of time put the EP in the difficult position of only being able to use its veto if it was prepared to overturn an agreement that was already beginning to be implemented on the ground.

The chapter proceeds as follows. The second section considers the EP's role in the attempt by the UK to renegotiate its EU membership prior to the Brexit referendum in 2016. The third section discusses the internal organisation and politics of the EP's response to the WA and TCA. The fourth section analyses the EP's role as a strategic actor eager to contribute to the EU's overall bargaining power in shaping Brexit. The fifth section discusses the EP's role as a normative player with a responsibility for helping to shape a justified form of Brexit. The sixth section considers some implications of Brexit for the EP: for its composition and for an understanding of what kind of a parliament the EP is and can be when dealing with a complex problem in the EU's political order.

THE EP AND THE UK 'RENEGOTIATION'

Brexit has been a part of the politics and work of two European Parliaments: the 2014–19 and the 2019–24 ones. Whilst, though, David Cameron committed the British Conservative Party to an 'in-out' referendum on the UK's continued membership of the EU in January 2013, it was by no means certain at the start of the 2014–19 European Parliament that it would have to deal with a UK withdrawal. Brexit only grew in importance during the 2014–19 Parliament.

Between European elections in June 2014 and the UK elections in May 2015 a British referendum seemed unlikely. Opinion polls suggested the UK Conservatives would not be re-elected with an overall majority. Except in the improbable event of the United Kingdom Independence Party (UKIP) securing enough seats for a minority Conservative Government to depend on its support, it seemed unlikely there would be a majority for a referendum. Between May 2015 and June 2016, the unexpected re-election of the Conservatives with an overall majority made an in-out referendum all but certain. Yet, many assumed the UK would vote to remain an EU member. That period created two challenges for the EP: one for its British members and one for the EP as a whole.

The 73 Members of the European Parliament (MEPs) from the UK – around 10 per cent of the 751 MEPs – began to fight the referendum from May 2015 onwards. Most aligned predictably: the Labour, Liberal and Green MEPs all seem to have campaigned to remain, as did the Scottish Nationalist and Plaid Cymru MEPs. All 22 UKIP MEPs obviously campaigned to leave. They were not part of the official leave campaign, however, which calculated that the leave vote would be maximised by distancing itself from UKIP, whilst leaving the latter, nonetheless, to mobilise its own voters in its own way. Only the Conservative MEPs split: 13 seemed to have voted to remain[2] and seven for leave.

For the wider EP, the main challenge before June 2016 was how to respond to the demand by the David Cameron Government to 'renegotiate' the UK's membership. Here David Cameron was attempting to follow a clear historical script. The UK had renegotiated its membership before. It had also voted to remain in a referendum before. Those were both amongst the first things the UK did as a member. The first change of Government after UK accession in 1973 brought in a Labour Government (1974–79) committed to do exactly what David Cameron was now proposing: namely, renegotiate the terms of UK membership and then put the result to a referendum with a recommendation from the government. The earlier 'renegotiation' was widely assumed to have played some role in turning public opinion around from net opposition to a clear endorsement of the UK's continued membership of the European Communities, by a two-thirds majority in the referendum of 1975. Yet there was a difficulty repeating that 'choreography' in 2016. Unlike the 1975 renegotiation, the 2016 renegotiation would also require the support of the EP.

A further difficulty was that the European Council decided in February 2016 that the EU would not even start implementing the renegotiation unless the UK voted to remain in the referendum. Hence, if David Cameron was to convince the British public throughout the four months of a referendum campaign that the renegotiation had substance, he would need to be able to claim some kind of a commitment from the EP to vote for future legislation that had not yet even been drafted. David Cameron met with the Conference of Presidents of each party group in the EP (European Parliament, 2016, p. 22). The BBC then reported that a 'Downing Street Source' had indicated that 'the three largest groups [the European Peoples Party, the Socialist and Democrats and the Liberals with a combined membership of two-thirds of the EP] had "made clear their support" for the UK's EU deal' and told David Cameron that 'they would take any "necessary legislation" through the [European] Parliament quickly' (BBC, 2016).

That, however, may have been disingenuous. A promise to pass legislation quickly through the EP did not imply a commitment to pass it without amendment. Nor, as the President of the EP, Martin Schulz, told David Cameron could such a 'guarantee' be given (Shipman, 2017, p. 135). Parliaments cannot commit themselves to future legislation without even seeing a draft of that legislation. Piris has argued that David Cameron's renegotiation agreement risked circumventing all the following: (1) any decision by national parliaments and/or electorates that would have to ratify treaty change; (2) the Commission's exclusive right to initiate ordinary legislation; and (3) the EP's scrutiny, amendment and veto powers (Piris, 2015). That, in turn, created an interesting puzzle. Had the UK voted to remain it would have been after a renegotiation that was, in turn, the basis of the UK Government's recommendation to vote to remain. But the EP was not under any obligation to adopt the legislation in the exact form agreed by the UK and the European Council (Peers, 2016).

Another curiosity was that David Cameron's claim to have reached an understanding with the three largest groups in the EP did not include the UK Conservatives' own group, the European Conservative and Reform Group (ERC). The Conservatives' largest partner in the ERC was the governing Law and Justice Party from Poland that, at the level of the European Council, had most opposed David Cameron's proposals for an emergency brake to free movement and for limits to the remission to other EU countries of social security benefits earned in the UK.

THE WITHDRAWAL AGREEMENT AND THE TCA: INTERNAL POLITICS AND ORGANISATION OF THE EP

From 24 June 2016 to the UK's formal withdrawal on 31 January 2020, 10 per cent of the EP consisted of representatives from a member state that had voted to withdraw from the

Table 10.1 *The Brexit Steering Group within the European Parliament*

Original group formed on 6 April 2017	
Guy Verhofstadt, Chair	Renew Europe Group, Flemish Liberal Party, Ex-Prime Minister of Belgium
Danuta Hübner	European Peoples Party, Civic Platform (Poland), Former European Commissioner
Philippe Lamberts	Co-President of the Group of the Greens/European Free Alliance, Écologistes (Belgium)
Elmar Brok	The European Peoples Party, Christian Democrat EU (Germany)
Roberto Gualtieri	Group of Socialists and Democrats, Partito Democratico (Italy), Chair of the Economic and Monetary Committee of the EP
Gabriele Zimmer	Chair of the Confederal Group of the United European Left, Die Linke (Germany)
Replacements for original members after 2019	
Pedro Silva Pereira	Group of Socialists and Democrats, Partido Socialista (Portugal), Former Government Minister, Vice President of EP
Martin Schirdewan	The Left Group of the European Parliament, Die Linke (Germany)
Antonia Tajani	The European Peoples Party, Forza Italia (Italy), President of the EP, Former European Commissioner

EU. That presented an obvious challenge: the EP wanted to maximise its participation in the negotiation of the WA. Yet some of its members were elected in the country on the other side of the negotiating table. How should the EP combine its roles as a representative institution and a quasi-negotiator? The EP could conceivably have taken the view that all representatives are equal and even representatives from the UK should have had an equal right to participate in the discussion and formulation of the EP's position. But that would have been at an obvious cost to the EP's role as a quasi-negotiator and therefore at a cost to the representation of MEPs and their voters from continuing member states in an inter-institutional formulation of the EU's overall negotiating position. The European Council and Commission were unlikely to share information – and especially not information about their bottom lines in bargaining – that anyone in the EP could pass on to the UK Government. Another challenge was that the EP needed to prevent Brexit overwhelming the rest of its regular duties. It needed to compartmentalise Brexit.

The main party groups in the EP responded to both challenges with a certain ruthlessness. The EP is normally doubly fastidious: (1) first, in representing all party groups in all decisions and discussions in exact proportion to their overall strength in the EP; (2) second, in constructing reports and resolutions through careful negotiation between all affected committees. In complete contrast, five party groups used their majority to appoint a Brexit Steering Group (BSG) which excluded three other groups: namely, the ERC; the European Freedom and Democracy Group (EFD) and the Europe of Nations and Freedom Group (ENF) (Table 10.1). The ERC was excluded because it included the British Conservatives, the EFD because it included UKIP and the ENF because it too was a far-right and a pro-Brexit group.

Meanwhile, EP committees provided inputs to reports and resolutions, but discussions with the Commission and European Council of what the EP was prepared to support in formulating the EU's overall negotiating position were restricted to the BSG (Bressanelli et al., 2021, p. 17). This allowed for secrecy, but at a cost to inclusiveness (p. 17) and, conceivably, to expertise from more reflective scrutiny within and between the EP's committees. Once, then, the British left and there was less need for secrecy, the EP reverted to normal practices for influencing and evaluating the TCA. The BSG was replaced by a 'UK Coordination group' on which all party groups were represented. The EP's position on the TCA was built bottom up from the committees (p. 19). The EP's substantive positions on the WA and TCA were set out in resolutions passed between 2017 and 2020. Votes on those resolutions, as well as on the WA and TCA themselves, are shown in Tables 10.2 and 10.3.

Both agreements passed by overwhelming majorities. Only 12 MEPs from other member states than the UK voted against the WA on 29 January 2020. As shown in Table 10.4, the remaining 37 who opposed the agreement were all pro-remain MEPs from the UK determined to use one last opportunity to indicate their opposition to Brexit. Many votes on the resolutions prior to the WA and TCA were more contested. As is often the case in the EP, it was able to agree positions on Brexit that were acceptable to the centre right, the Social Democrats, the liberals in the Renew Europe Group, the Greens and even the far left. Most disagreements were limited to the far right and Eurosceptics.

Table 10.2 *European Parliament votes on the Withdrawal Agreement (WA)*

Date	Voting item	Yes	No	Abstain
29 January 2020	Withdrawal Agreement (Complete Text)	621	49	13
14 January 2020	Resolution on Citizenship	610	29	68
18 September 2019	Resolution on the State of Play of the UK's Withdrawal	544	126	38
14 March 2018	Guidelines on future EU-UK Relations	544	110	51
13 December 2017	State of Play of Negotiations	556	62	68
3 October 2017	State of Play of Negotiations	557	92	29
5 April 2017	Negotiations with the UK	516	133	50

Table 10.3 *European Parliament votes on the Trade and Cooperation Agreement (TCA)*

Date	Voting item	Yes	No	Abstain
28 April 2021	TCA (Complete Text)	660	5	32
28 April 2021	TCA (EP Resolution)	578	51	68
18 June 2020	TCA Recommendations for Partnership with UK	527	34	91
18 February 2020	TCA Mandate for Negotiations	543	39	69

Table 10.4 *How UK Members of the European Parliament voted on the Withdrawal Agreement 29 January 2020*

	Yes	No	Abstain
All British MEPs	33	37	0
Conservative	7	0	0
Green	0	7	0
Labour	0	10	0
Liberal	1	16	0
Plaid Cymru	0	1	0
Scottish Nationalist Party	0	3	0
Brexit Party	24	0	0
DUP	0	1	0
Sinn Fein	1	0	0

THE EP AS STRATEGIC ACTOR

Immediately after the 2016 referendum there appears to have been a brief struggle within the Commission-European Council-EP triangle over who should negotiate with the UK and what the EP's role should be. The European Council created its own task force. Since the UK would remain a member state right up to the moment of leaving, it was at least arguable that any WA would be a negotiation between member states, properly handled by the European Council. The Commission, however, disputed that analysis. In its view, Article 50 treated a withdrawing state as a third state that could not be involved in any way in the European Council discussions and decisions on the negotiations (Heath and Eder, 2016). The EP sided with the Commission. However, the EP also had to fight for its own involvement. The European Council seemed at first to anticipate the EP would only be informed rather than consulted during the negotiation (Closa, 2020, p. 637).

Several factors had to be considered in distributing negotiating roles between the Commission, the European Council and the EP:

1. First, the Brexit negotiations were full of perils for the EU (Schuette, 2021). A European Council-led negotiation would be more likely to supply the UK with information on disagreements between member states. That information might then be used to tempt some member states into supporting proposals that privileged particular sectors (such as finance) or into prioritising their own bilateral relations with the UK over a strong multilateral agreement that safeguarded all member states from the collateral of Brexit.
2. Second and closely related to the previous point, the EU-27 wanted a negotiation that defended core principles: notably, the autonomy of EU institutions; the integrity of the internal market, and the indivisibility of the four freedoms of capital, labour, goods and services. The EU-27 would need to reach an agreed understanding of just what each of those principles would require of their new relationship with the UK. Each principle would then need to be coherently applied across two huge and complex agreements. All that would then need to be consistent with all other EU policies, laws and treaties, internal as well as external. Specifying core principles required the participation and control of member states. Ensuring coherence and feasibility required the expertise of the Commission.
3. Third, the Brexit negotiations were a mixed-motive game 'in which the goals of the players are partially coincident and partially in conflict' (Gallo and McClintock, 1965, p. 68). It may be the first rule of negotiations that the parties should understand what kind of a game – cooperative or competitive – they are playing. But that is not so easy where the negotiation is a bit of both. The EU and UK had many reasons for cooperating over Brexit. Among the most prominent ones was the need to avoid a breakdown in the peace process in Northern Ireland or disruption to supply chains. Yet questions such as fish or settling the UK's outstanding financial liabilities to the EU were more conflictual. Still other questions – such as level playing fields in environmental and labour standards or in state aids, as well as the practicalities of avoiding a border on the island of Ireland – resembled a game of prisoners' dilemma. Both the UK and EU might be better off reaching an agreement. Either, though, might be still better off if there were a few gaps or opportunities for non-compliance, or if the agreement was one-sided in its constraints.

Yet, Brexit was also a negotiation unlike any other. General concepts from negotiating and game theory cannot capture all that was at stake in the WA and TCA. As De Vries (2017) has argued, Brexit creates a unique counterfactual to European integration. Arguments for or against European integration have long been limited by the difficulty of knowing exactly what things would be like without the EU. In contrast, Brexit creates a kind a real-world experiment in just how well a one-time member can manage outside the EU. In so far as Brexit is understood in that way, it may not even matter that the experiment is imperfect or limited in its generalisability from what is involved in the UK leaving, to what would be involved in any other member doing so. Even if it had no wish to 'punish' the UK, the EU had an interest in highlighting, rather than concealing, the costs of withdrawal (Barnier, 2021). Things were the other way round for those in the UK Government whose reputations were heavily invested in demonstrating that the decision of the 2016 referendum was the right one. A struggle over the meaning and interpretation of Brexit would be as much a part of the negotiation of the WA and TCA as any cooperation or conflict of interests.

In sum, the EU needed to find some way of distributing negotiating roles between the Commission, European Council and EP that could:

1. Keep member states at 'arms-length'. To obtain the full benefits of operating as a bloc negotiator and to avoid any fragmentation in their position, member states would need to avoid direct contact with the UK in the negotiations.
2. Make full use of the expertise of the Commission in ensuring the compatibility of the WA and TCA with the EU's negotiating principles and with all other EU policies, laws and treaties.
3. Involve the EP sufficiently for it to improve agreements through informed scrutiny and for its veto powers to work to the EU's advantage.
4. Ensure, nonetheless, the participation and control of member states.

The EU responded by adapting to the case of Brexit with practices it commonly follows in international negotiation (European Council, 2016). The Commission was designated as the EU's negotiator. The Commission, in turn, assembled a 'task force' led by Michel Barnier, himself a former European Commissioner and Foreign Minister of France. Yet, the Commission was required to negotiate to a mandate agreed by the member states. The Committee of the Permanent Representatives (*Coreper*) of member states convened as often as needed – and often at short notice – to discuss with the Commission how it should respond to developments in the negotiations. Representatives of the President of the European Council participated in all negotiation sessions alongside the Commission (Bressanelli et al., 2021, p. 17). Hence, member states exercised oversight and control throughout. But they did not come into direct contact with the UK during the negotiations themselves.

As for the EP, it was, on Brexit matters, included in the preparation of European Councils. The President of the EP was 'invited to be heard' at the start of the European Council meetings. Above all, the European Council allowed the Commission discretion in involving the EP: 'The [EU] negotiator will be invited to keep the [EP] closely and regularly informed throughout the negotiation' (Bressanelli et al., 2021, p. 18). The EP was heavily involved because Barnier wanted it that way.

Two interview-based studies, namely, by Bressanelli et al. (2021) and Closa (2020), concur that Barnier's team and the EP cooperated closely to their mutual advantage. As Bressanelli et al. (2021, p. 18) put it, the 'EP and the Commission developed a well-oiled mechanism of sending out mutually reinforcing political signals, usually arriving at a strong coherence of tactics and strategy'. That even extended to:

> Commission officials ... often coordinating with the EP political groups on what and how the latter should report to the press. There were moments in the withdrawal agreement negotiations where the BSG decided to tactically intervene publicly in support of a certain position, after consulting with [Michel] Barnier. (Bressanelli et al., 2021, p. 18)

Or as Closa (2020, p. 631) puts it, the EP 'repeatedly signal[ed] its willingness to transform the vote into a veto of both the contents of the agreement and the scope of its own procedural role in the negotiations'. Since the preferences of the EP and Commission were largely aligned and since both institutions could benefit from strengthening the EU's bargaining power relative to the UK, it made sense for the EP to include Commission priorities in its own resolutions. Positions taken by the Commission could be reinforced by the implicit threat of a parliamentary veto; in return, the EP could expect the Commission to listen to its own concerns. The Commission could borrow the EP's veto powers. The EP could access the Commission's informal agenda-setting powers as one of the few players in the game with some ability to supply everyone else's need for workable solutions in limited time. The following are three examples of how EP resolutions signalled Commission priorities:

1. The EP backed the Commission on sequencing the withdrawal and future agreements. The UK wanted to link the two negotiations so that the future agreement would, in part, be negotiated at the same time as the WA. That, the UK hoped, would help it use leverage on security cooperation to obtain a better deal on market access and on matters covered by the WA. The EP simply adopted the Commission's view that it would be contrary to EU law for the UK to begin negotiations with third countries on trade agreements before it had completed its withdrawal from the EU (European Parliament, 2017a).
2. The EP warned against attempts to conclude bilateral agreements in areas of EU competence. Again, the EP claimed that would be contrary to EU law. An interesting implication was that the EP's veto powers did not just have the likely effect of shifting outcomes closer to the EU's preferences. They also worked as a commitment technology for member states: the EP could credibly threaten to veto deals that deviated from core principles or which seemed to be based on special understandings between the UK and particular members. The EP could shore up the EU's ability to negotiate as a bloc and reduce the risks of any member 'defecting' from agreed positions.
3. The EP warned it would it 'not consent to' any agreement that allowed 'a state withdrawing from the [European] Union' to enjoy similar benefits to those of an EU member state (European Parliament, 2017a, p. 4). For good measure, the EP added that 'a third country must not have the same rights and benefits as a Member State of the European Union, or a member of the European Free Trade Association (EFTA) or EEA' (European Parliament, 2018). The EP especially objected to any 'cherry picking' that would give privileged access to UK-based financial institutions (European Parliament, 2017a) or allow access to the single market without 'acceptance of the four freedoms, the jurisdiction of the Court of Justice of the European Union, general budgetary contributions and adherence to the European Union's common commercial policy' (European Parliament, 2017a, p. 4).

On both the WA and TCA, the EP also insisted on voting last after the UK Parliament (European Parliament, 2019, p. 7). That conserved its veto powers until the end. However, in the case of the TCA, the EP, as seen, was forced to choose between ratifying between 24 and 31 December 2020 or ratifying only after the TCA came into force as a provisional agreement.

Both seemed to indicate constraints on the EP's veto powers: the EP could be forced into a position in which it would either have no time to scrutinise or it would be faced by a fait accompli. Yet even then the threat of a parliamentary veto was not without all credibility. In March 2021, the EP postponed setting a date to ratifying the TCA as more than a provisional agreement after the UK delayed implementation of its commitment under the WA to introduce checks between the rest of the UK and Northern Ireland on agricultural and food products.

THE EP AS NORMATIVE ACTOR

As well as being a strategic player in Brexit, the EP had a normative role in shaping what would be a justified form of Brexit. Parliaments have a special importance in specifying the obligations, values and rights that policy, laws or treaties need to respect. Only parliaments can ensure that: (1) representatives elected on a basis of one person, one vote can (2) demand justifications for laws or treaties during the process of law or treaty-making themselves within (3) a public forum where all views can be tested in relation to one another (Mill, 1861 [1972]). All that can, in turn, be backed up (4) by parliamentary powers of scrutiny and control over the subsequent administration of laws and treaties (see Habermas, 1992, p. 171 for a discussion on the 'parliamentary principle'). The following examples on citizens' rights, Northern Ireland and governance illustrate how the EP scrutinised obligations, rights and standards involved in the WA and TCA.

Citizens' Rights

It was widely accepted that the EP should have a special role in ensuring a form of Brexit that respected citizens' rights. At least four million citizens of the EU-27 were resident or employed in the UK and at least one million UK citizens lived or worked in the EU-27. Finding a form of Brexit compatible with those rights was the responsibility of the EU as well as the UK. EU-27 citizens in the UK and UK citizens in the EU had made 'life choices' to live, work, retire or have families in another member state using rights and a citizenship status created by the EU. All that required the EP to consider the normative questions involved in individuals losing rights covered by EU citizenship: what was it about EU citizenship that would need to be protected in any withdrawal process? The EP indicated it would not give its consent to any WA incompatible with the Charter of fundamental rights of the EU (European Parliament, 2017a).

The EP also set an ambitious goal of no 'reduction in rights' (European Parliament, 2018). However, some reduction of rights was hard to avoid, given the nature of EU citizenship and the nature of Brexit. For example, the EP called on the EU-27 to do everything it could for 'British citizens' who have 'expressed strong opposition to losing the rights they currently enjoy'. Yet, in the same breath, the EP acknowledged that solutions would need to be 'within the treaties' and observe 'principles of reciprocity, equity, symmetry and non-discrimination' (European Parliament, 2017b, 2020). The treaties limited EU citizenship to citizenship of member states. Loss of membership, therefore, meant loss of citizenship. Nor was there much hope of some new status on a basis of reciprocity. The UK Government was busy framing Brexit as a recovery of British identity. It had limited interest in exploring, with the very grouping it was leaving, some special status for those 'citizens of nowhere' who sought forms of citizenship not linked to states. Hence, the principle of no reduction of rights was narrowly defined as ensuring those who were exercising their rights of residency or employment in another member state on 23 June 2016 should be able to do that after Brexit. Protection from loss of rights became an administrative exercise in registering those with a 'right to rights' they had used continuously since before the Brexit referendum. Here, the EP was sharply critical of the UK's settlement scheme. The EP pressed – with limited success – for the UK to allow EU citizens to just 'declare' their eligibility to settle without needing to document it and for the UK authorities to have the burden of proof in cases of doubt (European Parliament, 2020).

Northern Ireland

The EP also noted 'there are 1,8 million citizens born in Northern Ireland who, by virtue of the Good Friday Agreement, are entitled to Irish citizenship and are thereby entitled to EU citizenship and to EU citizenship rights where they reside' (European Parliament, 2019, p. 3). Likewise, the EU was an implicit guarantor of the Good Friday Agreement (GFA) and, therefore, of the peace process. All that, as O'Leary has put it, 'presupposed a European roof' (2018, p. 229). When, in 2019, the Johnson Government insisted on renegotiating the WA to remove the 'all-UK backstop' aimed at keeping the UK in a customs union if that was necessary to avoid a border between Ireland and Northern Ireland, the EP indicated that it would support a 'Northern Ireland only backstop' but it would veto a WA 'without any backstop' (European Parliament, 2019). The EP had also indicated that it would veto any future treaties with the UK until the latter honoured its commitments and responsibilities on citizens' rights, the financial settlement and the GFA in all its parts (European Parliament, 2017a).

Governance

From early on, the EP supported a joint EU-UK body to regulate relations after Brexit. Yet the EP was wary. If non-members were not to have advantages unavailable to members, any dispute resolution mechanism would need to offer 'equivalent guarantees of independence and impartiality' to the EU's own Court (European Parliament, 2018). The EP also needed to safeguard its own institutional interests. Ensuring that any joint EU/UK body should 'preserve the autonomy of EU decision-making and its legal order' included a need to protect the 'legislative prerogatives of the EP' (European Parliament, 2018). The problem is that the EP mainly uses its law-making powers by amending legislation, not by blocking it. Would the EP de facto lose its powers of amendment if many future proposals for legislation turned out to be negotiated in an EU-UK body, whose agreements the EP would then be expected to adopt on a more or less 'take it or leave it' basis? The Partnership Council established under the TCA may also need watching, given that it has some self-amending powers to 'deepen commitments' and 'broaden' its own 'scope' (Van der Loo and Chamon, 2021). The TCA establishes a joint parliamentary assembly of the EP and UK, though as with Brexit itself, the EP's influence will probably depend on how far it can establish a working relationship with the Commission on matters covered by the Partnership Council (Van der Loo and Chamon, 2021).

WHAT DOES BREXIT MEAN FOR THE EP?

The EP was a player in Brexit. But Brexit also had implications for the EP. Most obviously it raised the question of what to do with the 73 seats in the EP left vacant by the UK's withdrawal. Some – including Emmanuel Macron – saw an opportunity to create a pool of seats that would be allocated in proportion to votes received across the entire EU. It was hoped that it would help move EP elections away from 'second-order' contests (Reif and Schmitt, 1980) on domestic issues that do little to structure voter choice around questions relevant to the EU's own powers. Allocating seats at the EU level would help Europeanise EP elections by requiring parties to form European lists. Those heading up the lists could also be the lead candidates (*Spitzenkandidaten*) of each European party for the Presidency of the Commission. Would that have made the UK's withdrawal a catalyst in the development of the EU's own political order and democratic politics?

In the event, 27 of the UK seats were allocated to 14 other member states (European Council, 2018). That moved the EP closer to the treaty requirement that it should be elected on the principle of degressive proportionality whereby each member state receives a minimum of seats (currently six) and further seats are then added in proportion to population. Beyond that, the European Council decided not to decide. The remaining 46 of the UK seats were left empty and available either for allocation to new member states or for the creation of a pool of seats contested at the EU level.

Finally, its role in the WA and TCA can help us understand what kind of parliament the EP is. Weber (1994, pp. 176–7) famously argued that parliaments should not just be public forums (cf. Mill, 1861 [1972]). They should also 'continuously share in the work of government'. Modern government is based on information. Modern parliaments need to 'share in the work of government' if they are to overcome asymmetries of information (Krehbiel, 1991). The EP often shares in the work of the Commission and the European Council. But a focus on building inter-institutional compromise can lead to secluded forms of decision-making (Bressanelli et al., 2016, pp. 91–2; Reh, 2014). It can be at a cost to a continuous interaction with the represented in ways that promote public debate and public control (Lord, 2018). For certain, the EP worked with the Commission on Brexit. However, Barnier was probably far more publicly visible than the EP.

CONCLUSION

We will probably never know to what extent the EP influenced Brexit. The preferences of its main party groups were, in any case, largely aligned with those of the Commission and the European Council (Bressanelli et al., 2021, p. 17). The EP sought to coordinate and not differentiate itself from positions taken by other EU institutions. But we can observe the behaviours of the EP on Brexit if not their consequences. Strategically the EP sought to shore up the EU's position as a bloc actor and to reduce risks of cutting special deals. Normatively it sought to insist on a form of Brexit that respected citizens' rights, obligations to the peace process in Northern Ireland and governance standards in any bodies set up to coordinate or arbitrate future EU-UK relations.

NOTE

1. The research that went into this chapter has received support from the EU's Horizon 2020 programme (Societal Challenges 6: 'Europe in a Changing World – Inclusive, Innovative and Reflective Societies') under Grant Agreement No. 822419).
2. This calculation is based on an article in the *Guardian* from 8 March 2016 which reported 11 out of 20 had declared form remain with four still undeclared. Two of the four (Jacqueline Price and Geoffrey Van Orden) seem to have voted remain.

REFERENCES

Barnier, M. (2021). *La Grande Illusion. Journal Secret du Brexit 2016–2020*. Gallimard.

BBC News. (16 February 2016). EU referendum: David Cameron deal 'gets backing of Euro MPs'. *BBC UK Edition*. https://www.bbc.com/news/uk-politics-eu-referendum-35584189 (accessed 4 October 2022).

Bressanelli, E., Koop, C. and Reh, C. (2016). The impact of informalisation: Early agreements and voting cohesion in the European Parliament. *European Union Politics*, *17*(1), 91–113.

Bressanelli, E., Chelotti, N. and Lehmann, W. (2021). Managing disintegration: How the European Parliament responded and adapted to Brexit. *Politics and Governance*, *9*(1), 16–26.

Closa, C. (2020). Inter-institutional co-operation and intergroup unity in the shadow of the veto: The construction of the EP's institutional role in the Brexit negotiations. *Journal of European Public Policy*, *27*(4), 630–48.

De Vries, C.E. (2017). Benchmarking Brexit. How the British decision to leave shapes European public opinion. *Journal of Common Market Studies*, *55*, 38–53.

European Council. (2016). Informal meeting of the Heads of State or Government of 27 Member States, as well as the Presidents of the European Council and the European Commission, 16 September 2016. https://www.consilium.europa.eu/media/24173/15-euco-statement.pdf (accessed 4 October 2022).

European Council. (2018). EUROPEAN COUNCIL DECISION establishing the composition of the European Parliament. https://data.consilium.europa.eu/doc/document/ST-7-2018-REV-1/en/pdf (accessed 24 June 2021).

European Parliament. (2016). The UK's 'new settlement' in the European Union. Renegotiation and Referendum. https://op.europa.eu/en/publication-detail/-/publication/1e8d4675-e4fa-11e5-8a50-01aa75ed71a1 (accessed 24 June 2021).

European Parliament. (2017a). European Parliament resolution of 5 April 2017 on negotiations with the United Kingdom following its notification that it intends to withdraw from the European Union (2017/2593(RSP)). http://www.epgencms.europarl.europa.eu/cmsdata/upload/b9a0c645-21c2-4117-b933-04689cf7cb46/European_Parliament_Resolution_5_April.pdf (accessed 15 March 2021).

European Parliament. (2017b). European Parliament resolution of 13 December 2017 on the state of play of negotiations with the United Kingdom (2017/2964(RSP)). http://www.epgencms.europarl.europa.eu/cmsdata/upload/e845eb9c-8326-44b6-b70e-461d5602d0a9/EP_REsolution_13_December_2017_State_of_Play.pdf (accessed 24 May 2021).

European Parliament. (2018). European Parliament resolution of 14 March 2018 on the framework of the future EU-UK relationship (2018/2573(RSP)). https://www.europarl.europa.eu/doceo/document/TA-8-2018-0069_EN.html (accessed 4 May 2021).

European Parliament. (2019). European Parliament resolution of 18 September 2019 on the state of play of the UK's withdrawal from the European Union (2019/2817(RSP)). https://www.europarl.europa.eu/doceo/document/TA-9-2019-0016_EN.pdf (accessed 15 March 2021).

European Parliament. (2020). European Parliament resolution of 15 January 2020 on implementing and monitoring the provisions on citizens' rights in the Withdrawal Agreement (2020/2505(RSP)). http://www.epgencms.europarl.europa.eu/cmsdata/upload/692e5800-e0b0-4e4c-a04c-2a86e140b1e9/TA-9-2020-0006_EN.pdf (accessed 24 May 2021).

Gallo, P.S. and McClintock, C.G. (1965). Cooperative and competitive behaviour in mixed-motive games. *Journal of Conflict Resolution*, *9*(1), 68–78.

Habermas, J. (1992). *Between Facts and Norms*. Polity.

Heath, R. and Eder, F. (2016). Brussels power struggle over Brexit negotiations. Commission and Council both want to be in charge of British divorce talks. *Politico*, 28 June. https://www.politico.eu/article/brussels-power-struggle-over-brexit-negotiations/ (accessed 4 October 2022).

Krehbiel, K. (1991). *Information and Legislative Organisation*. University of Michigan Press.

Lord, C. (2018). The European Parliament: A Parliament Without a Public? *Journal of Legislative Studies*, *24*(1), 34–50.

Mill, J.S. (1861). *Utilitarianism, on Liberty and Considerations on Representative Government*. Dent. Reprinted in 1972.

O'Leary, B. (2018). The twilight of the United Kingdom and Tiocfaidh ár lá: Twenty years after the Good Friday Agreement. *Ethnopolitics*, *17*(3), 223–42.

Peers, S. (2016). Explaining the EU deal: is it legally binding?' *Full Fact*, 17 February. https://web.archive.org/web/20160514173344/https:/fullfact.org/europe/explaining-eu-deal-it-legally-binding/ (accessed 4 October 2022).

Piris, J.-C. (2015). Constitutional pathways: Which institutional and constitutional adjustments for the United Kingdom? In *United Kingdom's Renegotiation of its Constitutional Relationship with the EU: Agenda, Priorities and Risks*. European Parliament. https://www.europarl.europa.eu/RegData/etudes/STUD/2015/536489/IPOL_STU(2015)536489_EN.pdf (accessed 4 October 2022).

Reh, C. (2014). Is informal politics undemocratic? Trilogues, early agreements and the selection model of representation. *Journal of European Public Policy*, *21*(6), 822–41.

Reif, K. and Schmitt, H. (1980). Nine second-order national elections, a conceptual framework for the analysis of European election results. *European Journal of Political Research*, *8*(1), 3–44.

Schuette, L.A. (2021). Forging unity: European Commission leadership in the Brexit negotiations. *Journal of Common Market Studies*, 1–18.

Shipman, T. (2017). *All out War. The Full Story of Brexit*. William Collins.

Van Der Loo, G. and Chamon, M. (2021). The European Parliament Flexes its Muscles on the EU-UK Trade Deal. *European Policy Centre*, 5 March. https://epc.eu/en/Publications/The-European-Parliament-flexes-its-muscles-on-the-EUUK-trade-deal~3c43bc (accessed 4 October 2022).

Weber, M. (1994). Parliament and government in Germany under a New Political Order. In P. Lasman and R. Speirs (eds), *Weber. Political Writings* (pp. 130–271). Cambridge University Press.

Weir, S. and Beetham, D. (1999). *Political Power and Democratic Control in Britain. The Democratic Audit of the United Kingdom*. Routledge.

11. The European Commission and the Brexit negotiations[1]

Hussein Kassim

That the European Commission played a central role in the Brexit negotiations is well known. The Commission constructed the European Union's (EU) negotiating position based on member state concerns. It supplied the technical expertise on the EU side, and as Union negotiator, it represented the EU at the table. As chief negotiator and head of the Task Force, Michel Barnier won the trust and respect of EU political leaders. Behind the scenes, he and his colleagues were in constant contact with the national capitals. The Task Force cooperated closely with the European Council, Council and the European Parliament (Kassim 2017), and helped to create and sustain unity among the EU27 (Laffan 2019; Scheutte 2021). In public, Barnier offered a continuous commentary on the negotiations. As well as reminding the United Kingdom (UK) of the EU's position, he pointed out the implications of the UK's red lines, highlighted problems in the UK's approach, and referred repeatedly to the ticking clock.

The Commission's relationship with the European Council, as well as the structure and functioning of the institutional architecture devised for the Brexit negotiations, are, however, less well understood (though see Bujard and Wessels, this volume). As a result, the Commission's influence has been exaggerated, decisions taken by the EU27 have been mistakenly ascribed to the Commission, and insistence on EU 'red lines' by national capitals has been interpreted as bureaucratic inflexibility on the part of the Commission, when it was the Commission that sought to find the leeway among the positions of the EU27 that made agreement possible. Overlooking the European Council's primacy in decision making concerning the withdrawal of a member state is especially problematic. Under Article 50 the European Council has the power to decide the EU's approach in relation to a withdrawing state, to choose the Union negotiator, and to define the negotiating guidelines, which include the institutional arrangements. In the wake of the UK referendum vote, it used this authority to insist that Council representatives sat alongside the Commission, and to ensure close and continuous interaction between the Commission and national governments throughout the negotiations.

This chapter examines the role played by the European Commission in negotiating Brexit. Drawing on scrutiny of official documents and more than 80 interviews conducted by the author on a non-attributable basis between 2017 and 2022 with members of the Commission Task Force, senior officeholders in the European Commission as well as the Council Secretariat, officials in the Secretariat of the European Parliament, and delegates from the permanent representations of seven member states, the chapter discusses the system of governance put in place by the EU to handle the negotiations and the position of the Commission therein. It looks at how the Commission and the European Council prepared the EU's response to the UK referendum, how they interacted in shaping the EU's negotiating position, and their respective roles in the negotiations on the UK's withdrawal and its post-Brexit relationship with the EU.

The discussion below is organised into four parts. The first covers the period between the negotiation of the UK's 'new settlement' and the UK referendum. The second examines how the EU responded to the referendum outcome, the system of governance it created to handle the unprecedented withdrawal of a member state, and the role of the European Council, the EU27 and the Commission in defining the EU's negotiating guidelines and objectives. Negotiations with the Theresa May government are discussed in the third, and those with the administration of Boris Johnson, which saw the conclusion of the Withdrawal Agreement and the EU-UK Trade and Cooperation Agreement are considered in the fourth.

FROM THE 'NEW SETTLEMENT' TO THE UK REFERENDUM

In what Derek Beach and Sandrino Smeets (2019) have characterised as 'collaborative leadership', the Commission worked closely with the European Council in the renegotiation of the UK's relationship with the EU. As the issue was *chefsache* – that is, a matter of high-level political importance such that decision making was reserved to political leaders – the European Council took the lead. The process of negotiation was initiated by UK PM David Cameron at the July 2015 summit, shortly after the Conservative Party's general election victory. It followed a commitment that Cameron made in his speech at Bloomberg in January 2013, where he had pledged that a future Conservative government would negotiate a 'new settlement' with the EU, on the basis of which the British people would then be invited to cast their vote in an 'in'/'out' referendum.

Commission President Jean-Claude Juncker set up a Task Force under senior Commission official Jonathan Faull to undertake preparations for the strategic issues related to the UK referendum and asked the Commission think-tank, the European Political Strategy Centre, to consider what form a fair deal for Britain might take. The process and timeframe for negotiating the new settlement were decided by President of the European Council, Donald Tusk, and Juncker, together with senior officeholders from the two institutions. They agreed that the EU would follow the precedent set by the Edinburgh summit where heads of state and government had responded to the Danish 'no' vote on the Maastricht Treaty by adopting a binding protocol rather than undertaking full treaty reform (interview, senior Commission official, 29 April 2019).

The EU's response to Cameron's requests for changes on sovereignty, fairness, competitiveness and immigration was developed by a small group, chaired by the Secretary General of the Council, Jeppe Tranholm-Mikkelsen, that included the Commission President's chef de cabinet Martin Selmayr, senior officeholders from both sides of the rue de la Loi, and involving the two Legal Services. The UK and the EU reached an agreement on the new terms at the February 2016 European Council (European Council 2016a; Ludlow 2016a). Although the EU side believed that it had gone as far as it could in meeting the UK's demands,[2] there was little optimism that the terms would be sufficient to turn the tide of UK domestic opinion. 'We gave the agreement about a week' was the judgement of one senior Council official (interview, 25 July 2017). Indeed, there were very few references to the 'new settlement' in the referendum campaign.

At Cameron's request, the institutions kept a low profile during the referendum campaign.[3] In the background, the Commission and European Council each considered the effects on the EU of the possible eventualities and worked on a joint statement for when the results of the referendum were known. Then, in the 48 hours leading up to the vote, Tusk cleared both yes and no drafts texts with the national capitals of the EU27. At 7:22 a.m., shortly after the outcome of the vote had been confirmed, Tusk issued a press release, in which he expressed regret at the outcome, but promised that the future relationship between the EU and the UK would be close. The text made clear that business in Brussels would continue as usual (European Council 2016b). In a joint statement later the same day, the Presidents of the Commission, the European Council, the European Parliament and the Council of the European Union issued a common statement with a similar message (European Council 2016c). While expressing regret, they noted their readiness to ensure the UK's orderly departure. They also ruled out the possibility of a further renegotiation in case London believed that the referendum result may have strengthened the UK's negotiating hand and that it could return to the table (European Council 2016b).

PREPARING FOR THE NEGOTIATIONS

Although the Commission was closely involved, the European Council took the lead in defining the EU's approach. On 29 June at an informal European Council called by Tusk, the leaders of the EU27 set out the four principles that would guide EU policy throughout the two sets of negotiations (European Council 2016b). First, the EU would not open negotiations with the UK until London had formally notified the EU of its decision to withdraw. As well as casting the UK as *demandeur*, the principle of 'no negotiation without notification' was intended to discourage national capitals from opening their own bilateral talks with London. Anticipating that the UK would try to 'divide and rule' member governments, EU leaders sought to ensure that the EU27 took a collective approach. Second, negotiations would be sequenced as set out by the Treaty. While Article 50 stated that a framework of the future relationship should accompany the withdrawal arrangements, it noted that trade talks could only begin once the terms of the UK's departure had been agreed. The UK would not be allowed to 'cherry-pick' was the third principle. Any future relationship would involve a balance of rights and obligations, and the EU would rebuff any attempts at 'cake-ism' – a term that entered common parlance after a photo showed an aide to a Conservative MP leaving 10 Downing Street with notes on the single market that read 'what's the model? Have your cake and eat it' (BBC 2016). Fourth, single market access would require 'acceptance of all four freedoms', which the leaders of the EU27 regarded as indivisible.

The 29 June Statement quickly became the key reference point for EU leaders and the leaders of the EU27. It would be constantly invoked over the following four years. The Statement was constructed in terms that were intended to be self-explanatory in deference to the perception of the UK government as a 'formidable spinner' (interview, senior Council official, 25 July 2017). There was also an introspective element. Recognising that in the face of rising Euroscepticism the Union needed 'to do better', heads of state and government signed up to a 'leaders' agenda', an active review process, where they committed themselves to working to find a common approach to issues that mattered most to EU citizens. Furthermore, when the question arose as to the process of negotiating with the UK, EU27 leaders made it clear in the course of their discussions that governments would need to be closely and continually involved (Ludlow 2016b). Negotiating the UK's departure was both politically sensitive and quasi-constitutional, so could not be handled in the same way as a traditional trade negotiation, where the Commission undertakes negotiations on the basis of a Council mandate, but only reports back periodically to the member states.

Both the Council Secretariat and the Commission moved quickly to set up internal coordinating bodies. The Secretary General of the Council appointed Didier Seeuws, a senior official and former Belgian diplomat who had served in Herman van Rompuy's private office, to head a Task Force to coordinate action in the Council Secretariat. The Task Force worked on questions relating to the withdrawal process, the implications of Brexit, and likely negotiating issues. It asked Directors General to profile EU regulations on a sector-by-sector basis, identify what was at stake for the EU, and set out the EU's defensive and offensive interests (interview, senior Council official, 25 June 2019). More broadly, to help Tusk prepare his draft European Council guidelines, the Tusk cabinet and Secretary General met leaders of the EU27 individually throughout November 2016. As well as seeking views on substantive matters and the organisation of negotiations, the meetings were used to explain the implications of Article 50 to the member states.

Despite reassurances from the Council Secretariat that the responsibilities of the Task Force were intended to be merely internal, some officeholders in the Commission reacted strongly to what they saw as a 'power grab' (Heath and Eder 2016).[4] Although, since the Commission alone had the necessary expertise and human resources, there was little doubt that the European Council would use its power under Article 50 to designate the Commission as the Union negotiator, leaders of the EU27 insisted on creating a system that would allow them an active role. As part of their preparation for the European Council guidelines, members of Tusk's cabinet and senior Council officials invited Barnier and other members of the Task Force to discuss the design of these arrangements over the course of the autumn (Barnier 2021).

The plans were unveiled at the 15 December 2016 informal European Council (European Council 2016d). In their Statement, the leaders announced their decision to name the European Commission as the Union negotiator and welcomed the Commission's nomination as chief negotiator of Michel Barnier, whom Jean-Claude Juncker had appointed to head the Commission's Brexit Task Force in July. The Statement underlined that representatives of the President of the European Council (PEC) and the rotating Council President would be present 'in all negotiation sessions, alongside the European Commission', albeit 'in a supporting role'. The Union negotiator would be required to 'systematically report to the European Council, the Council and its preparatory bodies', including a new ad hoc Council Working Party (the 'Brexit Working Group'). The Brexit Working Group would monitor the negotiations and offer guidance to the Union negotiator. To ensure continuity over the course of the negotiations, the Council Secretariat rather than the rotating Presidency would provide the chair – Didier Seeuws would later be appointed to this position. The European Parliament would also be closely associated with the negotiations. Its representatives would attend preparatory meetings of the European Council and the Union negotiator was called upon to keep the Parliament informed about progress of the talks.

The system, which only came into operation in May 2017 once the UK had formally notified and the Council had adopted the negotiating mandate for the Commission, was designed to encourage fluid and continuous interaction between the Commission and the member states. Since the Brexit Working Group allowed any of the EU27 to voice its concerns and the chief negotiator to address all governments simultaneously, it allayed suspicions that conversations were going on elsewhere, or that Berlin and Paris were working on a 'stitch-up' (interview, senior Council official, 25 July 2017). Information-sharing was also intended to mitigate efforts by London to 'divide and rule'. Since, in addition, the UK continued to participate in Council bodies, shifting discussion on Brexit matters into a parallel system would prevent the UK from obstructing normal policy making and Brexit from interfering in day-to-day EU business.

As the Commission as an institution was designated Union negotiator, its internal procedures and hierarchy applied to decision making on the negotiations. Decisions were taken by the College of Commissioner, to which the chief negotiator reported every six to eight weeks. The Commission President held overall responsibility for the negotiations, which Juncker and Ursula von der Leyen delegated to Barnier as their personal representative. Major changes in the EU's negotiating position would require presidential approval. The Commission President also represented the EU in talks with the UK PM and at key points became personally involved in the negotiations. Juncker and later von der Leyen were kept informed of the negotiations by designated cabinet members, and the chief negotiator, who submitted a weekly report. This arrangement allowed the Commission President to monitor developments, while continuing to work on other business. For his part, President Juncker sought to implement a broad post-Brexit agenda that would strengthen the EU, which included trade talks with third countries and the EU's future development (interview, senior Commission official, 29 April 2019).

A two-step procedure for the negotiations was clarified by the Statement of 15 December 2016. First, under Article 50, the European Council would adopt the guidelines that provided the framework for the EU's position and internal organisational arrangements. The guidelines would include not only the terms of withdrawal, but also an outline of the future partnership. The draft guidelines were circulated by the PEC to the EU27 and discussed by the General Affairs Council and the Sherpas before political leaders agreed a final text. In the second step, under Article 218, the Council authorised the opening of negotiations and adopted the negotiating directives or mandate, which set out negotiating objectives in detail. Although the mandate was based on a Commission recommendation, the Commission's agenda-setting power was limited, first because the negotiating directives had to be aligned with the European Council's guidelines and second, because the draft text was scrutinised and amended by COREPER before their adoption in the General Affairs Council. The Statement noted that the negotiating directives could be 'amended and supplemented as necessary throughout the negotiations' by the European Council to reflect the guidelines as they evolved.

Laying the Groundwork

Although shortly after his appointment in July 2016 Barnier and his aides had paid informal visits to several European capitals, including Berlin and Paris, the Commission's Article 50 Task Force formally began operations on the fifth floor of the Berlaymont building on 1 October 2016, where it was supported by the Secretariat General (interview, senior Task Force member, 27 July 2017). Barnier had been given rein by Commission President Juncker to handpick staff from across the Commission. He moved quickly to recruit Sabine Weyand, a trade expert and German national, who would become his deputy and a key figure on the EU side, and Stefanie Riso, an economist and French national, who would also play a crucial role in the negotiations. It was established early on that Barnier, Weyand and Riso would discuss and decide all issues (interview, senior Task Force member, 9 March 2021).

A staff of ten initially grew quickly to 30 (Barnier 2016), organised into four technical directorates, with a fifth responsible for strategy, coordination and communication (European Commission 2016). The Task Force, which had core specialisms in single market and customs, EU budget and citizens' rights, was given authority to draw directly on the expertise of the

Commission services. It also established links with the European Central Bank, European Investment Bank, Europol and the European Court of Justice, and received visits from national delegations – notably, the Irish government, as part of significant diplomatic effort to communicate its concerns, especially in relation to the border with Northern Ireland – and spoke to stakeholders from across the Union.

Finding out the main concerns of the member states was an immediate priority. With a view to drafting the negotiating directives, Barnier embarked on a tour of the EU27 in autumn 2016, where he met prime ministers in their national capitals to discuss the principles that should guide the EU approach (Barnier 2016; interview, senior Task Force official, 17 July 2017). In addition, the Task Force undertook a detailed sector-by-sector screening of the legal and technical aspects of the UK's withdrawal and their implications. This exercise enabled the Task Force to develop a comprehensive overview of the rights and obligations associated with membership, to 'map scenarios' for 'the cost of different Brexit options for the UK and the EU' (Barnier 2016), to identify key negotiating points, and to identify how to ensure legal certainty for governments, businesses and citizens (interview, senior Task Force member, 9 March 2021).[5]

By the end of November, Barnier was ready to share the Task Force's understanding with experts from the EU27 (Rankin 2016). A week later, in his first public speech on Brexit, Barnier warned that the process would be complex and difficult. Emphasizing that, 'Time will be short', he estimated that if London made its formal notification in March 2017, agreement before October 2018 would be necessary in order to allow sufficient time for ratification of a withdrawal deal and negotiation of the new partnership to be completed within the two-year deadline. He called on the UK to 'tell us what they want' – a phrase that would soon develop into a mantra.

On the eve of the negotiations, Barnier (2017a) commented in an address to the Committee of the Regions on the UK objective that the British PM Theresa May had outlined at Lancaster House in January 2017 (May 2017a). The PM had announced the UK would leave the single market, cease to pay 'huge sums' to Brussels, and end the free movement of persons as well as the jurisdiction of the European Court of Justice over the UK. London would seek tariff-free access to EU markets *and* the power to negotiate trade deals. Barnier made clear that although the EU was willing to negotiate a free trade agreement with the UK, it would not allow it à la carte participation in the single market. Moreover, the scope for UK regulatory divergence would be limited. Barnier questioned whether the UK had been listening to the EU, especially on sequencing, and indeed whether the government had yet come to terms with the consequences of leaving the EU.[6] He also challenged May's publicly stated preference for 'no deal' above a 'bad deal' which he believed severely underestimated the costs of the former. Juncker took an even harder line and expressed broader concerns. Despite voicing hope for an amicable relationship with the UK, he spoke of the need to dissuade other capitals from following London's example (Agence Europe 2017a).

The EU Negotiating Position

The EU's preparation was methodical, and delivered on schedule. As Tusk had promised in September 2016, the EU side was ready in March to receive the UK's notification. Based on their consultations with EU27, and drawing on in-house expertise, as well as input from the Commission Task Force, the Tusk cabinet and Council Secretariat had prepared a draft of the

European Council guidelines. Among the ideas proposed by the Task Force was a review of 'sufficient progress' to determine whether to proceed to talks on the framework of the future partnership (interview, senior Task Force official, 15 March 2021). In anticipation of UK notification, Tusk convened a special European Council (Article 50) for 29 April 2017. When presenting the draft on 31 March, Tusk highlighted the need to minimise disruption, repeated that the EU27 would decide when progress on withdrawal issues was sufficient to warrant the opening of trade discussions, and warned that fair conditions for competition would have to be included in any trade agreement with the UK. He noted that the EU would be prepared to consider a transition period. Tusk also underlined that, although Barnier would be the single point of contact for the UK, he (Tusk) would remain in regular contact with May.

Discussed by the General Affairs Council on 27 April in advance of the informal European Council on 29 April, the guidelines identified three issues for the first phase of negotiations: the protection of citizens' rights, settlement by the UK of its financial liabilities, and the avoidance of a hard border between Northern Ireland and Ireland, which would support the Good Friday Agreement, while ensuring the integrity of the Union's legal order (mainly the single market). Other issues included UK Sovereign Base Areas in Cyprus, UK obligations under international agreements signed as part of the EU, the relocation of EU agencies from the UK, as well as future arrangements to ensure legal certainty, and dispute settlement mechanisms in relation to the Withdrawal Agreement. The EU's position was further toughened following input from the Sherpas – the personal representatives of the heads of government of the EU27. On citizens' rights, they called on London to grant permanent resident status to EU nationals present in the UK before Brexit day, and to make the process smooth and simple. On the financial settlement, they averred that the UK's outstanding financial liabilities should include the European Investment Bank, the European Development Fund and the European Central Bank, and cover the full period of the Multiannual Financial Framework (MFF), 2014–20.

Regarding the framework for the future relationship, EU leaders underlined that a free trade agreement would require a level playing field in competition and state aid, as well as tax, social and environmental regulation, and appropriate enforcement and dispute settlement mechanisms. They signalled that single market access for UK financial services could not be assumed. At the same time, the text expressed hope that the partnership could cover security, defence, foreign policy and the fight against terrorism and international crime. It also endorsed the procedural arrangements set out on 15 December 2016. In a testimony to the thoroughness with which the meeting had been prepared, the European Council (Article 50) took less than ten minutes to endorse the text (European Council 2017a).

With the guidelines in place, the Commission's Task Force fleshed out its recommendation for the negotiating directives. Presenting his draft text at COREPER on 3 May, Barnier called on the UK to provide clear and specific commitments on the divorce terms, including assurances for the rights of EU27 citizens in the UK and UK citizens in the rest of the EU, and guarantees covering labour market access, education, healthcare and the recognition of educational qualifications. He noted that the European Court of Justice's opinion would play a part in dispute resolution, and reiterated the European Council's position on the financial settlement and the Irish border. He promised to report after three months on whether sufficient progress had been made to warrant opening negotiations on the outline of the new partnership, which would include trade.

The General Affairs Council gave effect to the negotiating directives at its meeting on 22 May (Council 2017). Ministers formally nominated the Commission as Union negotiator and set up a Brexit Working Group. Going further than the Commission's draft on citizens' rights and the financial settlement,[7] they called for strict conditions to apply to any transition period. Following COREPER's endorsement, the Commission adopted a transparency policy, committing itself to making its texts publicly available. These would include the negotiating documents it shared with EU member states, the European Council, the European Parliament, the Council, national parliaments and the UK, as well as agendas for negotiating rounds, EU position papers, non-papers and EU text proposals (European Commission 2017a).

NEGOTIATING WITH THE MAY GOVERNMENT

With the opening of negotiations, the Commission Task Force took centre stage. It negotiated on the basis of position papers (European Commission 2017b) it had prepared to reflect the concerns and demands of the EU27. The drafts were tested with governments before the final versions were sent to the UK and published on the Commission website. The level of technical input needed from member governments varied. While the position paper on citizens' rights had required intensive interaction with national capitals, work on the financial settlement had been mainly an internal Commission matter. The Irish border, meanwhile, in the words of one senior Task Force official 'required time to get our minds around' since it could not simply be read off from EU law (interview, 15 March 2021). Barnier had visited Dublin in October 2016 to understand the issues, and the Task Force continued to liaise with the Irish government on the question of the border.

During the negotiations, Barnier or a senior member of his team met with officials from the EU27 in the Brexit Working Group (or COREPER) before and after each negotiating session, and also gave a briefing to the European Parliament's Brexit Coordination Group. Barnier also attended the European Council whenever Brexit featured on the agenda. He met Tusk frequently, notably before meetings of the European Council. At official level, there were constant meetings between Weyand and Seeuws, as well as other members of the two Task Forces. Moreover, Barnier held a press conference after each negotiating round, which enabled him to summarise proceedings, explain the EU's stance, and comment on the UK's position.

The European Council monitored negotiations, intervening at key points to take decisions relating directly or indirectly to the UK's departure. At its meeting on 22 June 2017, for example, it endorsed the procedure for the relocation of UK-based agencies – the European Banking Authority and the European Medicines Agency. Inside the Commission, the Secretariat General of the Commission was given the task of handling practical arrangements (European Council 2017b).

From the Opening of Negotiations to the Joint Report

Negotiations with the May government are best considered in three phases. The first began with the opening session on 17 June, when Barnier and Weyand agreed the timetable and the format of the talks with their UK counterparts, David Davis, Minister for Exiting the EU, and Olly Robbins, senior civil servant and UK chief negotiator. The 'row of the summer' that Davis had threatened over sequencing did not materialise, although this did prevent the UK from continuing to press the EU to progress to a discussion of trade. Negotiations were organised in four-weekly cycles, culminating in a fifth round in the week of 9 October, with a review in October when the European Council would determine whether 'sufficient progress' had been made. Three tables dealt respectively with citizens, financial aspects and other separation issues, while talks on the Irish border were conducted by senior members from each side.

In the first period, progress was slow, and the Task Force was frustrated by what it saw as a lack of realism and insufficient preparation on the UK side. London clearly wanted to open trade talks, and the Task Force found UK negotiators unwilling or unable for political reasons to engage on the withdrawal issues. On citizens' rights, the EU wanted legal certainty and far-reaching rights for EU citizens. Although May had offered what she believed to be a generous package,[8] and by October several issues had been resolved, differences remained on family reunion and the UK export of social security benefits. On the financial settlement, while the Task Force worked on a method for calculation of the UK's liabilities, the UK was unwilling to make an offer. In her Florence speech in September 2017, May had confirmed UK preparedness to pay its fair share, which she linked to the transition period, but two months later the UK had still not indicated how much it was prepared to pay.

On the Irish border, although agreement was reached quickly between the two sides on the Common Travel Area and, importantly, keeping the border open in line with the Good Friday Agreement, London could not explain how it planned to keep the border open with no physical infrastructure or how customs formalities and regulatory standards would be observed for goods entering Ireland from Northern Ireland. The Task Force rejected as 'magical thinking' the UK's proposals for the use of untested technology to monitor movements of goods along a 500 kilometre border with 208 crossings. Although the two sides did begin to compile a list of affected sectors, the EU negotiating team suspected that the UK was holding out for the Irish border to be negotiated alongside trade, so as to increase London's bargaining leverage (interview, senior Task Force official, 1 February 2018).

With the failure to achieve significant progress at the fourth and fifth rounds of negotiations in late September and early October, it became increasingly clear that the October European Council deadline would not be met. Meeting on 20 October, the European Council (Article 50) decided to postpone until December its review of 'sufficient progress', while starting its own internal preparations for the trade talks and a transition period. The Commission also stepped up work on EU contingency plans for no deal. A further (sixth) round of negotiations concluding on 10 November produced little progress. While Davis urged the EU to open trade talks, Barnier (2017b) held firm on the December deadline. Emphasising the work needed on all three withdrawal issues, he underlined that the UK had only two weeks before the December summit. A week later, the Irish Taoiseach Leo Varadkar increased the pressure by calling for the UK to bring forward its plan to keep the Irish border open.

With the approach of the December deadline, and a meeting between Juncker and May scheduled for 4 December, intense behind-the-scenes negotiations brought the two sides closer. By 28 November, media reports suggested that, although issues remained, agreement on the financial settlement and citizens' rights was within sight. On the Irish border too, compromise appeared to have been reached only for talks between Juncker and May to break up without an agreement following a call to the PM from DUP leader, Arlene Foster. Foster declared her opposition to a solution that would maintain EU rules on the island of Ireland on the grounds that Northern Ireland would be treated differently from other parts of the UK.

After Barnier told member states on 7 December that the UK had two days to agree a text in advance of the European Council meeting, the two teams worked intensely to make progress on the Irish border. Under the terms of a rapidly revised text, Northern Ireland and Ireland would remain in regulatory alignment, and there was agreement that no new obstacles to trade between Northern Ireland and the rest of the UK would be introduced. Either London would negotiate a trade deal with the EU that would make a hard border with Ireland unnecessary or it would propose an alternative solution. Should neither materialise, a backstop would come into operation, according to which: 'the United Kingdom will maintain full alignment with those rules of the internal market and the customs union which, now or in the future, support north-south cooperation, the all-island economy and the protection of the 1998 agreement'.[9] Although this three-level solution was widely recognised as a fudge and both sides accepted that further negotiation was necessary on all three of the withdrawal issues, the agreement made it possible to proceed to talks on a framework for the new relationship. The Joint Report, signed by Juncker and May, was formally endorsed by the European Council (Article 50) on 15 December 2017 (European Commission 2017c).

From the Joint Report to the Withdrawal Agreement and Political Declaration

The institutional division of labour on the EU side remained unchanged in the second phase. The European Council (Article 50) adopted guidelines to move to negotiations on the transition and the future partnership at its 12 December 2017 meeting – the occasion on which Barnier presented his famous 'step diagram' of the range of options remaining to the UK. The guidelines outlined the need for a level playing field and a balance of rights and obligations as part of the economic relationship, and repeated the EU's desire for a close partnership with the UK in areas beyond. They made it clear that the EU would consider a transition period, but only on condition that '[a]ll existing Union regulatory, budgetary, supervisory, judiciary and enforcement instruments and structures', as well as trade policy, continued to apply. The European Council set March as the start date for negotiations on the future partnership, which EU27 leaders hoped would give the UK time to prepare its position.

In its draft negotiating directives for this new phase, which were published five days later, and adopted by the Council on 19 March, the Commission proposed a transition period that would last until 31 December 2020. With the scope of the negotiations now extending to the whole acquis, the Task Force hosted a series of seminars for experts from the EU27 that covered virtually every policy sector.[10] As well as detailing the legal and practical dimensions of the UK's withdrawal, they spelt out the implications of third country status for the UK.

The Task Force also continued its work on the outstanding withdrawal issues. In an effort to speed up the talks, the Task Force published a full draft text of the Withdrawal Agreement on 28 February (European Commission 2018b). A traffic light system, updated after each round, showed where agreement had been reached and where further progress was necessary. Although mainly based on the Joint Report, the draft covered areas including Euratom and intellectual property that had not yet featured in the talks, and included provisions on a transition period.

The draft agreement's most controversial provisions concerned the Irish border. In an effort to 'de-dramatise' the border, the text proposed regulatory alignment between Northern Ireland and Ireland in animal health, phytosanitary standards and the environment in order to avoid the need for customs checks. Although Barnier emphasised that the backstop would only come into operation if not superseded by the future relationship or a solution proposed by the UK, he declared himself ready to work on any proposal tabled by the UK government. May, however, rejected the provisions as an arrangement to which 'no UK prime minister could ever agree' (BBC 2018), since it treated Northern Ireland differently from the rest of the UK.

At the same time that the 'Irish backstop' became a totemic issue for Brexiters, the EU linked progress on the future relationship to finding a solution for the Irish border. Although the two sides announced on 19 March that they had reached agreement, the issue was still not fully resolved. Presenting the draft Agreement to the General Affairs Council on 20 March, Barnier reported that the two parties had agreed that a legally operative version of the backstop solution, based on the Joint Report, 'would form part of the legal text of the Withdrawal Agreement'. In the guidelines it adopted three days later, the European Council (Article 50) called for intensified efforts to resolve the outstanding withdrawal issues. With an October deadline looming for the final deal, the Taoiseach stated his hope that the Irish Protocol could be agreed in June.

When in an attempt to break the impasse May moved in June 2018 to extend the backstop to the whole of the UK, however, the EU rejected her proposal. Although it would resolve the customs issue, inclusion of the whole UK would make it much more difficult for the EU to protect the integrity of the single market. While the EU could accept a unique solution, Barnier argued that a UK-wide arrangement would amount to cherry-picking, since the UK would keep the benefits of the single market, but not be subject to its rules. Serious differences on the Northern Ireland Protocol remained despite the Joint Statement signed by the two sides in June (HM Government 2018b). The standoff continued through July and August.

The two sides were also at some distance from each other over the new relationship. When Tusk met May on 1 March, he warned that London should not entertain any illusions. London's own red lines left a free trade agreement as the only option (Barnier 2018). Although May had retreated from the position she had adopted the year before in Florence when she had rejected existing models, including Norway and Canada (May 2017b), the PM was still calling in her Mansion House speech in 8 March for a customs partnership between the EU and the UK in order to keep trade in goods as 'frictionless as possible' (May 2018b). She also wanted UK membership of EU agencies in aviation, chemicals and medicines (HM Government 2018a).

The draft guidelines for the future partnership circulated by Tusk on 7 March underlined once more that a free trade agreement was the only option, since the EU could not

> agree to grant the UK the rights of Norway with the obligations of Canada. No Member State is free to pick only those sectors of the Single Market it likes, nor to accept the role of the ECJ only when it suits their interest. By the same token, a pick-and-mix approach for a non-member state is out of the question. (Tusk 2018)

Warning that 'this will be the first FTA in history that loosens economic ties, instead of strengthening them', he noted that 'agreement will not make trade between the UK and the EU frictionless or smoother. It will make it more complicated and costly than today, for all of us.'

At their meeting on 23 March, leaders of the EU27 agreed to open negotiations on the future relationship and a transition period, and adopted the guidelines (European Council 2018a). Though expressing hope for a close partnership, they noted that friction in trade would be inevitable. Specific negotiating objectives included: zero tariffs or quotas for goods, reciprocal access to fishing waters, customs cooperation with appropriate safeguards, trade in services, and access to public procurement markets, investment and the protection of intellectual property rights. They emphasised that 'the UK's geographic proximity and economic interdependence with the EU27' would necessitate 'robust guarantees' to 'ensure a level playing field'.

The 'unfair competitive advantage that the UK could enjoy through undercutting of levels of protection' would have to be prevented by 'a combination of substantive rules aligned with EU and international standards, adequate mechanisms to ensure effective implementation domestically, enforcement and dispute settlement mechanisms in the agreement as well as Union autonomous remedies'.

The guidelines also foresaw EU-UK cooperation on climate change, an open approach to the movement of people, action to ensure continued transport connectivity, and UK participation in programmes in research, innovation and culture. They were less clear on the UK's participation in European agencies. Cooperation between law enforcement and legal authorities, and judicial cooperation was envisaged, but personal data would be subject to an EU decision on adequacy. More generally, the governance of the future relationship with the UK would 'have to address management and supervision, dispute settlement and enforcement, including sanctions and cross-retaliation mechanisms'.

The text concluded with a request to the Commission and the member states to 'work on preparedness at all levels for the consequences of the UK withdrawal, taking into account all possible outcomes' including no deal. This task, which involved a review of the entire acquis by the services to identify areas where disruption was possible, to adapt legislation where necessary, and to undertake contingency planning with member state administrations on practical consequences was entrusted to the Secretariat General of the Commission (interview, senior Commission official, 17 July 2018). In practice, in December 2017 the Secretariat General had already begun to work with Commission services to prepare for the UK's departure from the EU, either with or without an agreement (interview, senior Commission official, 29 April 2019), but it stepped up its preparations in 2018 (European Commission 2018a).

The June European Council (Article 50) noted that important aspects of the Withdrawal Agreement, including a solution for the Irish border, remained outstanding, and work on a political declaration was still necessary. After a showdown meeting at Chequers, where May tried to secure collective Cabinet backing for her approach (Menon and Wager 2021), the UK set out its position in a White Paper. Retreating from earlier more ambitious aims, it proposed a common rulebook for goods, where UK legislation would be aligned with EU regulations to allow 'frictionless trade', and it conceded a role for the European Court of Justice. The White Paper proposed facilitated arrangements, which would treat the UK and EU 'as if a combined customs territory', where the UK would apply the EU's tariffs on goods intended for the EU, but its own tariffs for goods heading into the UK. It also proposed a policy of 'managed divergence'.

EU reaction to the Chequers Plan was negative. Barnier rejected the common rulebook as 'cherry picking', since it separated one single market freedom from the others. He also rejected the idea that the UK could collect customs duties on the EU's behalf. When May attempted an appeal to her counterparts at an informal European Council summit in Salzburg, they rejected her calls as an attempt to renegotiate the guidelines and bypass the Union negotiator. Reminding the PM of the October deadline, and reiterating their support for Barnier, as EU chief negotiator, they repeated that there would no Withdrawal Agreement without an operational and legally binding Irish backstop.

In an effort to break the deadlock, and following a suggestion made by Weyand and agreed by ambassadors, a core group of negotiators from the two sides entered a 'tunnel' on 5 October, where they could hold intense negotiations outside the public eye. The first set of talks ended in failure, with the leaders of the EU27 announcing at the October European Council that not enough progress had been made. With the clock ticking, they agreed to hold a special summit in November. In the meantime, the negotiators re-entered the 'tunnel'. In a significant concession, the Commission gave way on the possibility of a UK-wide customs union, albeit with safeguards, which opened up the possibility of agreement with the UK.

However, the concession created anxiety in the capitals of the EU27. Governments feared that the EU would lose leverage over other issues, including especially access to UK fishing grounds. Weyand was able to assuage these concerns by persuading EU ambassadors that the introduction of level playing requirements at this stage would in fact set a baseline for talks on the future relationship (Boffey 2018), which would be very useful for the EU. Although the Task Force carried the day on the broader issue, it faced anger from Madrid when the Spanish government complained that Gibraltar had been overlooked – one of the few occasions where a member government considered that the Task Force had not properly represented its interests.[11]

On 12 November Barnier told the Council that key issues remained. With the prospect of a no deal looming, the Commission adopted a contingency plan on 13 November, which was again coordinated by the Secretariat General (European Commission 2018c). However, following the efforts of the negotiating teams in the 'tunnel', Barnier was able to report decisive progress three days later, including agreement on a UK-wide backstop. The draft Withdrawal Agreement and outline of the Political Declaration were discussed by EU foreign ministers on 19 November, sent to the national capitals on 22 November, and endorsed by the European Council (Article 50) on 25 November.

At the meeting, EU leaders initiated the steps for formal approval by the EU institutions so that the Agreement could enter force on 30 March 2019 and allow for the UK's orderly withdrawal (European Council 2018b). In their Statement, leaders restated the EU's desire for a 'close as possible partnership with the UK' and reaffirmed the positions and principles set out in previous guidelines. They also thanked Barnier 'for his tireless efforts as the Union's chief negotiator and for his contribution to maintaining the unity among EU27 Member States throughout the negotiations'. The Commission began the approval process on 5 December and the EU27 leaders confirmed their decision of 25 November at a special European Council (Article 50) on 13 December (European Council 2018b). They underlined also that the Agreement was 'not open for renegotiation'. The Council approved the texts on 11 January 2019 and forwarded to the European Parliament.

From the Withdrawal Agreement to May's Resignation

With negotiations apparently complete and May attempting to secure parliamentary approval for her deal, the EU shifted to a different mode. The European Council and the Commission kept a close eye on developments in the UK, and both Tusk and Juncker remained ready to respond to the PM. In the meantime, Barnier toured national capitals with senior members of the Task Force to discuss preparedness and explain the state of play with the UK and the EU's position. According to one Task Force official, in looking for ways to progress the negotiations, 'No one said: shall we give [the UK] more flexibility?' (interview, 24 May 2019).

Following the postponement of a House of Commons vote on the deal that had been scheduled for 11 December, May requested clarification on the backstop from Tusk and Juncker. The PM sought a guarantee that the backstop would be time-limited and that the UK could unilaterally trigger a release. In a joint letter, the two Presidents confirmed the temporary nature of backstop, but only to the extent that it was superseded by a future trade agreement. They repeated that the EU would not reopen the Withdrawal Agreement. Although the European Council (European Council 2018c) offered some assurances at its special meeting on 13 December, they fell short of what May requested.

After the government's heavy defeat in the delayed vote on 15 January, May met Tusk and Juncker on 7 February. The meeting with Tusk achieved little, while Juncker again rejected the PM's call for legally binding changes to the backstop. After delaying a second vote initially planned for 14 February, May met Juncker on 20 February, again seeking to secure written assurances that the backstop would never come into force. The two sides agreed to work on an interpretive document, and UK Attorney General, Geoffrey Cox, whose affirmation May considered essential to securing support among Conservative MPs, held exploratory talks with Task Force members. Following difficult discussions, agreement was reached on 11 March on a 'joint legally binding instrument' which confirmed that the backstop could not become permanent and a Joint Statement supporting the Political Declaration. Cox was able to signal that the risk that the UK would be 'indefinitely and involuntarily detained' in the backstop had been reduced, but he could not state that the UK had an 'ultimate unilateral right' to leave. A second heavy government defeat followed on 12 March.

With the 29 March deadline approaching May requested an extension of the Article 50 extension period. Although EU leaders were divided about whether more time would improve the chances of successful passage through the Commons,[12] they nevertheless agreed to prolong the period until 22 May 2019 – the eve of elections to the European Parliament – in the event that the Withdrawal Agreement passed through the Commons before 29 March 2019, but 12 April 2019 if not. They also echoed earlier assurances given by Juncker to May.

When the government lost a third meaningful vote on 29 March, Tusk called an emergency European Council for 10 April. The idea was to allow the UK time to develop an approach based on indicative votes in the House of Commons. However, when no option commanded a majority, May sought to develop a cross-party approach. Although the Labour leader Jeremy Corbyn entered talks, progress moved slowly. On 5 April, May requested a second extension until 30 June. She committed to holding elections to the European Parliament if a longer extension proved to be necessary. This second extension request was debated more intensively than the first. Although leaders again took different views, the European Council decided to grant a flexible extension until 31 October 2019, or earlier, if the UK were to ratify the Withdrawal Agreement sooner.

May's announcement of a fourth vote in early June was, however, to prove ill-fated. After receiving fierce criticism for a series of concessions to Brexiters, the PM cancelled the vote. Then following the Conservative Party's poor showing (9 per cent) in the European elections, May announced her resignation, and stepped down from the leadership on 7 June.

NEGOTIATIONS WITH BORIS JOHNSON

When Boris Johnson became PM, expectations of a deal were low on the EU side. A leader of the Leave campaign, Johnson had been critical of May's approach to the negotiations, telling the EU, for example, in relation to the financial settlement that it could 'go whistle'. In addition to his calls for the UK's 'liberation', pleas to 'let my people go', and demand for the return of full regulatory autonomy to the UK, he argued that no deal could be positive for the UK.

Following his leadership victory, Johnson called for the replacement of the Irish backstop with 'alternative arrangements' and threatened to withhold the UK's 'divorce payment'. Barnier reiterated that while amendment of the Political Declaration was possible, the Withdrawal Agreement could not be renegotiated, to which Johnson replied that he would not negotiate with the EU27 until it changed its red line. The impression on the EU side over the summer was that the UK PM had little interest in a deal (senior Council official, 27 September 2019).

When Johnson announced his intention to prorogue Parliament from 9 September to 14 October – less than three weeks before the scheduled Brexit date of 31 October 2019 – many suspected that his plan was to stop MPs from preventing a no deal Brexit. However, after MPs passed the Benn Bill, which stopped the PM from simply allowing the deadline to expire, Johnson signalled that he might be interested in a deal. He wanted an open Irish border, but with a Northern Ireland-specific solution and democratic consent. This solution was not only different from May's, but it allowed for regulatory divergence on the UK's part. Avoiding Brussels in the first instance, Johnson consulted Berlin, Dublin and Paris to ascertain the scope for agreement. He then met Juncker, and two weeks later forwarded his plan for an 'all-island regulatory zone' to the Commission President. Northern Ireland would remain in the single market for agricultural and industrial goods, and sanitary and phytosanitary controls would apply to traffic between Northern Ireland and the rest of the UK, but the UK would leave the customs union (HM Government 2019a). However, in a telephone conversation, Angela Merkel reportedly informed the PM, first, that Northern Ireland must remain in the customs union in order to preserve the open border with Ireland and, second, that a technological solution to controls would not be acceptable to the EU. Since it had committed itself to no new checks or infrastructure at the Irish border when it signed up to the Joint Report, the UK had a choice: a border in the Irish Sea or remaining in the single market and customs union.

Although some observers believed that the talks had broken down, Johnson held informal talks over the following days with Varadkar, then Juncker. He agreed that Northern Ireland could remain aligned to a limited number of EU rules and stay in the UK's customs territory, and that Northern Ireland should be able to decide every four years on whether to continue to apply EU rules. These elements were incorporated in a new Irish Protocol (HM Government 2019b). The revised EU Withdrawal Bill passed the Commons on 22 October by 329 to 299 votes, although the government suffered a defeat on confirming 31 October as the exit date, which forced Johnson to request an extension. At its October meeting, the European Council acceded, giving the UK until 31 January 2020 (European Council 2019). In a Declaration (European Council 2019), the leaders of the EU27 endorsed the Withdrawal Agreement, but excluded the reopening of negotiations, and requested the UK not to take any action that would hamper the implementation of the Agreement. Claiming that Brexit was 'oven ready', Johnson called a general election in which he won in December 2019 with an 80-seat majority. The Withdrawal Agreement was signed by the EU leaders on 24 January, approved by the European Parliament on 29 January, and ratified by the EU the following day. The UK left the EU on 31 January 2020.

The EU had already begun its preparation for negotiations on the new partnership. Once the Withdrawal Agreement had been agreed, Juncker, in consultation with President-elect von der Leyen in October 2019, created the Task Force for Relations with the UK from a merger of the Article 50 Task Force and the Brexit preparedness unit of the Secretariat General. With the broader scope of the negotiations, the Task Force was expanded and reorganised into six units. It worked with a greater number of Commission services and more closely with them. With the appointment of Weyand to head DG TRADE, Stéphanie Riso's departure and replacement by Pauline Dejmek, and the appointment of Clara Martinez Alberola, who had been Juncker's chef de cabinet, as deputy Director General of the Task Force, Barnier accepted the invitation from the new Commission President, Ursula von der Leyen, to continue as chief negotiator, a decision welcomed by the European Council (European Council 2019). In an early intervention, Barnier highlighted the importance of implementing the Withdrawal Agreement effectively, as well as reaching a deal on the future relationship.

After some debate, where supporters of continued centralisation prevailed over advocates of a more sectorally based approach, the European Council (Article 50) decided at its 13 December 2019 meeting to keep the same organisation in place for the new negotiations. The ad hoc Working Party on Article 50 TEU became the Working Party on the UK, and retained its permanent chair until the end of the transition period. Seeuws was re-appointed to the role. EU political leaders also decided to carry over its approach to transparency. On the substance, the European Council recalled the commitment to the close relationship the EU had agreed with the UK in the Political Declaration, reaffirmed its previous guidelines, statements and declarations, and highlighted the importance it assigned to achieving a balance of rights and obligations, as well as a level playing field.

The Commission's draft negotiating directives, presented by Barnier following consultation with national capitals on 3 February, reiterated these elements. Barnier identified three component parts: an economic partnership based on a level playing field; a security partnership; and a robust governance framework. COREPER tightened the language on the level playing field, with the aim of ensuring that UK businesses would not benefit from an unfair competitive advantage as the EU continued to raise its regulatory standards, and establishing effective mechanisms in each area of concern (Agence Europe 2020). They committed to parallelism 'among the various sectoral tracks of the negotiation' to prevent the UK from concentrating negotiations on issues it favoured, while leaving those most salient to the EU until last.[13] Foreign ministers required barely a minute to adopt the mandate on 25 February.

On the UK side, there was a marked change in rhetoric (see Frost 2020). Sharply differentiating itself from the previous administration, the Johnson government declared that its main goal was to 'restore economic and political independence' and chief negotiator, David Frost, underlined repeatedly that the UK and EU were negotiating as 'sovereign equals'. Retreating both from the broad aims of the May administration (HM Government 2020) and commitments in the Political Declaration that it had signed only a few months previously, the government warned that it would 'not negotiate any arrangement in which the UK does not have control of its own laws'. It presented its trade ambitions as no more than a Canada-style agreement with 'zero tariffs, zero quotas', though it also sought 'supplementary agreements on fisheries, judicial cooperation on criminal matters', and rejected checks on food and animals moving between the UK and EU. Calling for a 'broad outline' to be finalised by September, the UK indicated that it would prepare for a no deal if sufficient progress had not been made.

Battlelines between the EU and UK were drawn in five main areas: the level playing field, where against the EU's insistence on 'regulatory coherence', the UK demanded regulatory autonomy, 'its own regime of subsidy control', the right to 'adopt or modify its labour laws', and environmental standards'; fish, where the EU wanted EU fishers to retain access to UK waters with a multiannual agreement on quota shares, while the UK declared that it would become a sovereign coastal state at the end of the transition period and would accept only annual negotiations; governance, where the EU wanted a single institutional framework, while the UK preferred a series of agreements; on internal security, the UK wanted access to EU databases, but the EU required it to submit to the role of the European Court of Justice; and a system of arbitration mechanism, where the UK insisted the European Court of Justice should play no role. The talks began amidst deepening tensions after the UK government failed to implement checks on trade between Northern Ireland and the rest of the UK as agreed under the Withdrawal Agreement. As a result, the EU became only more concerned to negotiate strong implementation and enforcement provisions.

The talks began on 2 March, but following the outbreak of the Covid pandemic, a new schedule was agreed, with three rounds in April, May and June, followed by a high-level meeting to take stock in June 2020. Discussions took place around 11 tables. Teams were co-chaired by the head of unit or deputy from the Task Force and an official from the Commission services. All staff involved on the EU side, which grew to 180 persons at some points, attended a briefing at 18:00 every day or every other day, either virtually or face-to-face where they discussed developments table by table to make sure that information was shared, issues considered, and all members were on the same page.

The negotiations proved slow and difficult. While the defence, foreign policy and external security aspects remained a dead letter after the UK indicated it was not interested in institutionalised cooperation, Barnier complained about the UK's failure to engage (Barnier 2020a), challenged Frost's claim that the UK was looking for no more than a Canada-style agreement (Barnier 2020b), and asked how the UK's demands were to be reconciled with the Political Declaration to which the two sides had signed up only a matter of months previously. Although the Task Force repeated its strategy of producing a full draft text (18 March), which it based this time on the Council's 25 February mandate (European Commission 2020), the fourth round of talks saw no significant advance on the main issues.

As the high-level review meeting approached, but with little progress on the main issues, Barnier suggested that the EU might soften its approach on state aid and require only that the UK adopted a system of subsidy control rather than essentially emulate the EU model. On fish, he had already described the EU position as 'maximalist', and looked to the eight member states with strong fishing interests to offer some leeway. On the eve of the review, the two sides signed a Joint Statement called for 'new momentum' and agreed an intensified schedule of meetings in July, August, and September.

At the high-level meeting on 15 June, which involved the British PM and the Presidents of the Commission, the Council and the Parliament, the EU moved to accommodate the UK's red lines on fair competition, fisheries and governance, including the European Court of Justice. To the EU's frustration, however, the UK did not reciprocate on the level playing field or fish, and although progress was made elsewhere, they remained deadlocked on these two central issues. With only five months until the end of the transition period, the Commission published a preparedness communication and updated the 102 readiness notices that it had originally drafted in 2018, while the European Council agreed a 5 billion euro Brexit adjustment reserve to assist member states and sectors most affected by the UK's departure.

Following the eighth round in the early autumn, Barnier (2020c) remarked that the UK was still failing to respond to the flexibility shown by the EU on the core issues or to engage on several others. At the same time, trust in the UK on the EU side fell when the government introduced an Internal Market Bill that threatened to override parts of the Withdrawal Agreement and violate international law. Commission Vice President Maroš Šefčovič's response was immediate, while von der Leyen invited the government to remove the problematic provisions, before initiating infringement proceedings in early October.

Against this background, the ninth round proved more productive, even if there was still no progress on the topics that mattered most to the EU – the level playing field, governance and fish (Barnier 2020d). With time running down, some member states were anxious about the trade-offs that they could be asked to make in order to secure a deal, especially in the light of concessions already made by the EU. At a meeting on 7 October, Barnier gave his reassurance to the eight EU member states with major fishing interests that though he would need some flexibility if a trade agreement was to be reached, he was not about to sell out them out. The message was reinforced by Tusk's successor as PEC Charles Michel, who after a call to the British PM tweeted: 'The EU prefers a deal, but not at any cost.'

With the clock ticking, von der Leyen and Johnson agreed on 3 October following the conclusion of the ninth round to a further month of talks and called on their chief negotiators to work to close gaps on fisheries, the level playing field, and governance. They also agreed to talk regularly. The Task Force was therefore taken by surprise when Johnson reacted to the call by EU political leaders at the 15 October European Council meeting for the UK to make the necessary moves to reach agreement possible with a threat to end the talks, even more so when Frost told Barnier not to bother to come to London for the next round (Barnier 2021). Following Barnier's statement to the European Parliament, which gave explicit recognition of the UK's sovereign status, the talks were resumed. Indeed, as one senior Task Force member recalled (interview, 1 April 2022), 'we negotiated every single day' from October to 24 December.

Fisheries and state aid remained the key issues until the end of the negotiations. When von der Leyen applied pressure to the UK, there was again some concern among the EU27 ambassadors that the UK would be allowed to cherry pick. Barnier sought to calm nerves about the effects of the EU's decision to relax its position on state aid and UK alignment with EU rules by incorporating a retaliatory mechanism in the draft text. 'Rebalancing', the right to apply immediate tariffs in the event of a breach, would allow the EU to respond if the UK sought to benefit from an unfair competitive advantage. As the mechanism would be available to both sides, London also found the proposal acceptable.

Fish remained the outstanding issue. While some member states raised the possibility of a separate later deal, Barnier insisted that fisheries should be included in the agreement. While recognising its symbolic importance, Barnier was able to persuade member states that it was not worth sacrificing the entire agreement for this one sector, especially since the alternative was no access to UK waters. Both the Commission President and her cabinet and the Task Force were involved in the negotiations that took place in December, which required repeated calls to London, Paris and Berlin, and involved agreeing quotas for each species of fish. A compromise on fisheries enabled the two sides to announce on 24 December that they had reached a deal. EU leaders signed the document on 30 December, and the Trade and Cooperation Agreement was published in the *Official Journal* on 31 December.

CONCLUSION

As the above discussion shows, the Commission played a central role in the Brexit negotiations. It represented the EU side at the negotiating table, its technical expertise was a crucial resource at all stages, and Michel Barnier played a key role as the public face of the Union. The Task Force provided a link to the national capitals, to other EU institutions, and to the rest of the Commission, including the thirteenth floor of the Berlaymont. It consulted extensively, but also received representatives of member governments, and it provided an important pedagogical service, explaining the legal and technical complexities and implications of the UK's departure to a wide range of stakeholders.

The Task Force model allowed the rest of the Commission to continue its work in other areas, while Barnier and his team focused on the negotiations. This role included not only constructing the EU's position on the basis of consultations with the EU27, but developing new concepts to overcome impasses in the talks and assuaging anxieties in the national capitals. Juncker's choice of Barnier to head the Task Force – a politician with the administrative status of a Director General – was a 'master stroke' (interview, senior Council official, 21 September 2018). Barnier brought to the role experience as a former Commissioner for regional policy, and the internal market and services, but also the communication skills of a senior politician. His status enabled him to interact as a peer with government ministers, including his UK opposite number.

At the same time, the Task Force was not the only part of the Commission involved in the negotiations. The Task Force drew extensively on the expertise of the services, including the Legal Service, and the Directorates General sat alongside members of the Task Force in the negotiations on the new partnership, while the Secretariat General handled preparedness and contingency over both sets of negotiations. The Secretary General, initially Alexander Italianer, then Martin Selmayr, also played an important part in shaping the Commission's approach and liaised closely throughout with the Council Secretariat. The Commission President remained a key decision maker during the negotiations. Both Juncker and von der Leyen were in regular contact with the UK PM. They also intervened personally in the negotiations – Juncker in the months following the agreement signed with May, and von der Leyen with Johnson in the autumn and winter of 2020.

As has been argued above, however, it is important not to overstate the role of the Task Force or to see the Commission as the lead institution, despite the significance of the part that they played. The Task Force and the Commission operated within an institutional architecture that was put in place largely at the behest of the European Council and the shape of which was strongly influenced by the Secretary General of the Council and the President of the European Council. The Task Force functioned against the background of a shared concern about and appreciation of the significance of the challenge presented by the UK's decision to leave the EU. In the face of this unprecedented situation, the political leaders of the EU27 placed a premium on close collaboration among themselves, with the Council and the European Council, and between the EU institutions. The European Council decided the Union's overall approach, which included the creation of a system that gave the Commission responsibility for conducting the negotiations, alongside observers from the Council and with structures in place that allowed the governments of the EU27 to monitor talks and input their concerns. The arrangements made it possible to mobilise the Commission's technical expertise and negotiating know-how, while ensuring that the Task Force both remained aware of member state priorities and concerns, and was seen to be acting on their behalf. The challenge for the Task Force and the Commission more broadly was to calculate where member state positions left leeway for trade-offs to advance the talks with the UK and at what point in the negotiations.

Despite initial reluctance on the part of the Commission, there was widespread agreement that the arrangements worked well. According to one senior Council official, expressing a view that was repeated by national officials in interviews throughout the process, there were rarely real differences on substance (interview, 25 June 2019), even if there were occasional tensions concerning tactics. In contrast to other challenges that the EU faced during this time, the relationship between the Commission and the Council was cordial and collaborative. One Commission, commenting on the very different atmosphere, remarked that Commission-Council relations were transformed. 'We're in this together. We don't have to defend the Commission in the Council. [It's] not like trade negotiations, not like changing policy' (interview, senior official, Task Force, 17 July 2017).

In this experimentation with a newly devised system of governance specifically to manage the negotiations, the Task Force and Michel Barnier were the most consistently visible actors on the EU side. However, despite the success of what has been christened 'the Barnier method', it is important not to overlook the role played by the European Council and the part played by the Council working party. Through their combined efforts, and with a unity that surprised even insiders, the EU institutions and the national governments of the EU27 collectively mobilised in response to the challenge posed by the UK's decision to leave the Union.

NOTES

1. The research for this chapter was carried out under ESRC grants no. ES/R001626/1 and ES/T000961/1 as part of the author's Senior Fellowship under 'The UK in a Changing Europe' initiative. The author would like to express his gratitude to the ESRC. He is also most grateful to all the officials who agreed to be interviewed as part of the research.
2. Indeed, many on the EU side believed they had barely stayed within the bounds of the treaty and thought that they had conceded too much (interview, senior Council official, 21 September 2018).
3. Juncker later expressed regret that the Commission did not speak out to correct misleading claims (Gotev 2019).
4. Senior officeholders on both sides of the rue de la Loi were very keen in interviews to downplay any sense of rivalry or discord.
5. The Task Force in the Council Secretariat also carried out screening. The two Task Forces kept in close touch (interviews).
6. Similarly, the press carried reports that Juncker had called German Chancellor Angela Merkel the day after a dinner with the PM on 26 April to tell her that May was deluding herself that the negotiations would be simple or quick (Agence Europe 2017b; Boffey 2017).
7. On the first, it asked for more detail on rights for students, family members, and those whose rights 'are in the process of being obtained', and for healthcare rights and free movement; on the second, it referred to pensions and the use of 'past data' to determine the financial settlement.
8. While member states considered that the UK was making 'lavish promises' at the same time as a series of domestic reports were casting doubt on the competence of the Home Office and the evidentiary basis of its policies (BBC 2017), members of the Task Force expressed doubt in the face of the 'fantasy things, new systems and processes that will happen overnight, efficient, quick, costless' that UK negotiators were promising (interview, senior Task Force member, 14 November 2019).
9. 'The fruit of mapping the difficulties over months' by the Task Force, in the words of one senior official (interview, 27 April 2021).
10. The slides were published on the Task Force website, https://ec.europa.eu/info/brexit-negotiations/negotiating-documents-article-50-negotiations-united-kingdom_en#slides. Accessed 13 October 2022.
11. Interviews with national officials and senior members of the Task Force.

12. Some EU leaders thought that an extension would give the UK time to reflect, or even to rescind Brexit; others that a deadline was the only way to achieve a result. 'We looked at the House of Commons numbers and concluded that there was little we could do. With the mess in the UK, we needed to protect our own interests through no deal preparation' (interview, senior Task Force official, 27 April 2021).
13. Although the idea of parallelism apparently originated in the Task Force (interview, senior Task Force member, 18 March 2021).

REFERENCES

Agence Europe (2017a) 'Brexit will cost London around €58 billion, says Juncker', *Europe Daily Bulletin* No. 11753, 24 March, accessed 8 April 2022.

Agence Europe (2017b) 'Broad consensus in favour of Brexit negotiating guidelines', *Europe Daily Bulletin* No. 11776, 27 April, https://agenceurope.eu/aewebsite_dev/en/bulletin/article/11776/2, accessed 8 April 2022.

Agence Europe (2020) 'EU ministers invited to endorse an ambitious negotiating mandate on respect of fair competition rules', *Europe Daily Bulletin* No. 12432, 25 February, accessed 8 April 2022.

Barnier, M. (2016) 'Introductory comments by Michel Barnier', 6 December, https://ec.europa.eu/info/news/introductory-comments-michel-barnier-2016-dec-06_en, accessed 8 April 2022.

Barnier, M. (2017a) 'Speech by Michel Barnier, Chief Negotiator for the Preparation and Conduct of the Negotiations with the United Kingdom, at the plenary session of the European Committee of the Regions', SPEECH/17/723, 24 March.

Barnier, M. (2017b) 'Speech by Michel Barnier following the sixth round of Article 50 negotiations with the United Kingdom', 10 November, https://ec.europa.eu/commission/presscorner/detail/en/SPEECH_17_4545, accessed 8 April 2022.

Barnier, M. (2018) 'Speech by Michel Barnier at BusinessEurope Day 2018', https://ec.europa.eu/commission/presscorner/detail/en/SPEECH_18_1462, accessed 8 April 2022.

Barnier, M. (2020a) 'Press statement by Michel Barnier following the second round of future relationship negotiations with the United Kingdom', 24 April, https://ec.europa.eu/commission/presscorner/detail/en/STATEMENT_20_739, accessed 8 April 2022.

Barnier, M. (2020b) 'Remarks by Michel Barnier following Round 3 of negotiations for a new partnership between the European Union and the United Kingdom', 15 May, https://ec.europa.eu/commission/presscorner/detail/en/speech_20_895, accessed 8 April 2022.

Barnier, M. (2020c) 'Statement by Michel Barnier following Round 8 of negotiations for a new partnership between the European Union and the United Kingdom', 10 April, https://ec.europa.eu/commission/presscorner/detail/en/STATEMENT_20_1612, accessed 8 April 2022.

Barnier, M. (2020d) 'Statement by Michel Barnier following Round 9 of negotiations for a new partnership between the European Union and the United Kingdom', 9 October, https://ec.europa.eu/commission/presscorner/detail/en/statement_20_1817, accessed 8 April 2022.

Barnier, M. (2021) *La grande illusion: Journal secret du Brexit* (2016–2020), Gallimard.

BBC (2016) '"Have cake and eat it" Brexit notes played down by government', https://www.bbc.co.uk/news/uk-politics-38134859, accessed 8 April 2022.

BBC (2017) 'UK overestimates non-EU students staying illegally, data suggests', 24 October, https://www.bbc.com/news/uk-politics-41030304, accessed 8 April.

BBC (2018) 'Theresa May: No UK PM could ever agree with EU draft', https://www.bbc.com/news/av/uk-politics-43228485, accessed 8 April 2022.

Beach, D. and Smeets, S. (2019) 'The unseen hands: Collaborative instrumental leadership in the British renegotiation case', *European Journal of Political Research*, 59, doi:10.1111/1475-6765.12354.

Boffey, D. (2017) 'Juncker rejects claim May begged for help at dinner meeting', *Guardian*, https://www.theguardian.com/politics/2017/oct/22/mays-ex-policy-chief-claims-juncker-aide-leaked-brexit-dinner-details, accessed 8 April 2022.

Boffey, D. (2018) 'How the draft Brexit agreement emerged from the "tunnel"', *Guardian*, 14 November, https://www.theguardian.com/politics/2018/nov/14/how-the-draft-brexit-agreement-emerged-from-the-tunnel, accessed 8 April 2022.

Cameron, D. (2013) 'EU speech at Bloomberg', https://www.gov.uk/government/speeches/eu-speech-at-bloomberg, accessed 8 April 2022.

Council (2017) Directives for the negotiation of an agreement with the United Kingdom of Great Britain and Northern Ireland setting out the arrangements for its withdrawal from the European Union, https://www.consilium.europa.eu/media/21766/directives-for-the-negotiation-xt21016-ad01re02en17.pdf, accessed 8 April 2022.

European Commission (2016) 'Task Force for the Preparation and Conduct of the Negotiations with the United Kingdom under Article 50 TEU (TF50)', https://ec.europa.eu/info/sites/default/files/organisation_charts/organisation-chart-tf50_en.pdf, accessed 8 April 2022.

European Commission (2017a) 'The European Commission's approach to transparency in the Article 50 negotiations', 22 May with the United Kingdom, https://wayback.archive-it.org/11980/20201224120114/https://ec.europa.eu/commission/brexit-negotiations/european-commissions-approach-transparency-article-50-negotiations-united-kingdom_en, accessed 8 April 2022.

European Commission (2017b) Position papers, Article 50 negotiations, https://ec.europa.eu/info/publications/article-50-negotiations-united-kingdom_en, accessed 8 April 2022.

European Commission (2017c) Joint Report from the negotiators of the European Union and the United Kingdom Government on progress during phase 1 of negotiations under Article 50 TEU on the United Kingdom's orderly withdrawal from the European Union, 8 December, https://ec.europa.eu/info/publications/joint-report-negotiators-european-union-and-united-kingdom-government-progress-during-phase-1-negotiations-under-article-50-teu-united-kingdoms-orderly-withdrawal-european-union_en, accessed 8 April 2022.

European Commission (2018a) 'Preparing for the withdrawal of the United Kingdom from the European Union on 30 March 2019', Communication, COM(2018) 556 final/2, Brussels, 27 August.

European Commission (2018b) Draft Agreement on the withdrawal of the United Kingdom of Great Britain and Northern Ireland from the European Union and the European Atomic Energy Community, 19 March, https://ec.europa.eu/info/publications/draft-agreement-withdrawal-united-kingdom-great-britain-and-northern-ireland-european-union-and-european-atomic-energy-community-0_en, accessed 8 April 2022.

European Commission (2018c) 'Preparing for the withdrawal of the United Kingdom from the European Union on 30 March 2019: A Contingency Action Plan', COM(2018) 880 final, Strasbourg, 13 November.

European Commission (2020) Draft text of the Agreement on the New Partnership with the United Kingdom, 18 March, https://ec.europa.eu/info/sites/default/files/200318-draft-agreement-gen.pdf, accessed 8 April 2022.

European Council (2016a) 'European Council meeting (18 and 19 February 2016) Conclusions', 19 February, https://www.consilium.europa.eu/media/21787/0216-euco-conclusions.pdf, accessed 8 April 2022.

European Council (2016b) 'Press statement by President Donald Tusk on the outcome of the referendum in the UK', 24 June, https://www.consilium.europa.eu/en/press/press-releases/2016/06/24/tusk-statement-uk-referendum/, accessed 8 April 2022.

European Council (2016c) 'Statement by the EU leaders and the Netherlands Presidency on the outcome of the UK referendum', 24 June, accessed 8 April 2022 https://www.consilium.europa.eu/en/press/press-releases/2016/06/24/joint-statement-uk-referendum/, accessed 8 April 2022.

European Council (2016d) 'Statement after the informal meeting of the 27 heads of state or government 15 December 2016', https://www.consilium.europa.eu/media/24173/15-euco-statement.pdf, accessed 8 April 2022.

European Council (2017a) 'European Council (Art. 50) guidelines for Brexit negotiations', 29 April, https://www.consilium.europa.eu/en/press/press-releases/2017/04/29/euco-brexit-guidelines/, accessed 8 April 2022.

European Council (2017b) 'Procedure leading up to a decision on the relocation of the European Medicines Agency and the European Banking Authority in the context of the United Kingdom's

withdrawal from the Union', 22 June, https://www.consilium.europa.eu/media/21503/22-euco-conclusions-agencies-relocation.pdf, accessed 8 April 2022.
European Council (2018a) 'European Council (Art. 50) (23 March 2018) – Guidelines', 23 March, https://www.consilium.europa.eu/media/33458/23-euco-art50-guidelines.pdf, accessed 8 April 2022.
European Council (2018b) 'Special meeting of the European Council (Art. 50) (25 November 2018) – Statements for the minutes', https://www.consilium.europa.eu/media/37102/xt20017-en18.pdf.
European Council (2018c) 'Special meeting of the European Council (Art. 50) (13 December 2018) – Conclusions', 13 December, https://data.consilium.europa.eu/doc/document/XT-20022-2018-INIT/en/pdf.
European Council (2019) 'Brexit: European Council adopts decision to extend the period under Article 50', 29 October, https://www.consilium.europa.eu/en/press/press-releases/2019/10/29/brexit-european-council-adopts-decision-to-extend-the-period-under-article-50/, accessed 8 April 2022.
Frost, D. (2020) 'David Frost lecture: Reflections on the revolutions in Europe', No. 10 Blog, 17 February, https://no10media.blog.gov.uk/2020/02/17/david-frost-lecture-reflections-on-the-revolutions-in-europe/, accessed 8 April 2022.
Gotev, G. (2019) 'Juncker regrets not intervening in Brexit referendum campaign', *Euractiv*, 8 May, https://www.euractiv.com/section/uk-europe/news/juncker-regrets-not-having-interfered-in-brexit-referendum-campaign/, accessed 8 April 2022.
Heath, R. and Eder, F. (2016) 'Brussels power struggle over Brexit negotiations', *Politico*, 28 June, https://www.politico.eu/article/brussels-power-struggle-over-brexit-negotiations/, accessed 8 April 2022.
HM Government (2018a) 'The future relationship between the United Kingdom and the European Union', 12 July, https://www.gov.uk/government/publications/the-future-relationship-between-the-united-kingdom-and-the-european-union, accessed 8 April 2022.
HM Government (2018b) 'Joint statement on Withdrawal Agreement – 19 June 2018', 19 June, https://www.gov.uk/government/publications/joint-statement-on-withdrawal-agreement-19-june-2018, accessed 8 April 2022.
HM Government (2019a) 'UK proposals for a new Protocol on Ireland/Northern Ireland', 2 October, https://www.gov.uk/government/publications/uk-proposals-for-a-new-protocol-on-irelandnorthern-ireland, accessed 8 April 2022.
HM Government (2019b) 'New Withdrawal Agreement and Political Declaration', 19 October, https://www.gov.uk/government/publications/new-withdrawal-agreement-and-political-declaration, accessed 8 April 2022.
HM Government (2020) 'The future relationship with the EU. The UK's approach to negotiations', February, CP211, https://assets.publishing.service.gov.uk/government/uploads/system/uploads/attachment_data/file/868874/The_Future_Relationship_with_the_EU.pdf, accessed 8 April 2022.
Kassim, H. (2017) 'The European institutions', in H. Kassim and S. Usherwood (eds), *Negotiating Brexit: What Do the UK's Negotiating Partners Want*, https://ukandeu.ac.uk/wp-content/uploads/2017/10/Negotiating-Brexit-book-NEW.pdf, accessed 8 April 2022.
Laffan, B. (2019) 'How the EU27 Came to Be', *Journal of Common Market Studies*, 51(S1), 13–27.
Ludlow (2016a) 'David Cameron's deal with the EU', *Eurocomment*, Commentary 2016/2.
Ludlow (2016b) 'June and September 2016', *Eurocomment*, European Council Briefing Note 2016/4-5.
May, T. (2017a) 'The government's negotiating objectives for exiting the EU', 17 January, https://www.gov.uk/government/speeches/the-governments-negotiating-objectives-for-exiting-the-eu-pm-speech, accessed 8 April 2022.
May, T. (2017b) 'PM's Florence speech: A new era of cooperation and partnership between the UK and the EU', 22 September, https://www.gov.uk/government/speeches/pms-florence-speech-a-new-era-of-cooperation-and-partnership-between-the-uk-and-the-eu, accessed 8 April 2022.
May, T. (2018a) 'PM speech on our future economic partnership with the European Union', 2 March, https://www.gov.uk/government/speeches/pm-speech-on-our-future-economic-partnership-with-the-european-union, accessed 8 April 2022.
May, T. (2018b) 'Theresa May: No UK PM could ever agree with EU draft', 28 February, https://www.bbc.com/news/av/uk-politics-43228485, accessed 8 April 2022.
Menon, A. and Wager, A. (2021) 'The Long Goodbye: Brexit', in R. Ford and T. Bale (eds), *The British General Election of 2019*, Springer, pp. 29–68.

Rankin, J. (2016) 'EU's chief divorce negotiator to make first Brexit statement', 6 December, https://www.theguardian.com/politics/2016/dec/06/eus-chief-divorce-negotiator-michel-barnier-to-make-first-brexit-statement, accessed 8 April 2022.

Scheutte, L.A. (2021) 'Forging unity: European Commission leadership in the Brexit negotiations', *Journal of Common Market Studies*, 59(5), 1142–59.

Tusk, D. (2018) 'Statement by President Donald Tusk on the draft guidelines on the framework for the future relationship with the UK', 7 March, https://www.consilium.europa.eu/en/press/press-releases/2018/03/07/statement-by-president-donald-tusk-on-the-draft-guidelines-on-the-framework-for-the-future-relationship-with-the-uk, accessed 8 April 2022.

12. EU agencies and Brexit: assessing the implications of Brexit for EU agencies

Michael Kaeding

INTRODUCTION

This chapter considers implications of Brexit for a set of actors which are often neglected, but without whom the future of Europe has become unthinkable: the European Union's (EU) decentralised agencies. Currently there are 34 EU decentralised agencies,[1] dispersed over 22 EU Member States. EU agencies have not only grown in numbers since the beginning of the European integration process, but their remits have multiplied. They are (semi-)independent EU bodies (Rittberger and Wonka, 2011; Busuioc et al., 2012) which perform specific tasks[2] for the EU and its Member States by assisting in designing and implementing EU policies. On the one hand, EU agencies relieve the burden on the European institutions, in particular the European Commission, and, on the other hand, strengthen cooperation between the Member State governments and the European Commission in many policy areas[3] by bundling the specialist and expert knowledge available at European and national level, facilitating Europe-wide cooperation between stakeholders and efficient and flexible implementation of EU legislation (Kelemen, 2002; Mastenbroek and Martinsen, 2018). Despite the fact that they remain a practical and theoretical challenge in the EU constitutional landscape (Curtin and Dehousse, 2012; Genschel and Jachtenfuchs, 2013; Vos, 2018), more than ever, EU agencies stand for solutions to European problems and promoter of European integration and Europe's future.

EU agencies not only play an important role in European governance, and raise important constitutional questions, but they have direct relevance for third countries. In fact, there is a growing body of scholarship dedicated to the study of the international dimension of EU agencies (Hofmann et al., 2019). However there are still significant gaps that need to be filled (Egeberg and Trondal, 2017). Third country participation in EU agencies, for example, has attracted little academic interest[4] despite the fact that participation of third countries in EU agencies figures potentially an important element of external differentiation in the EU (Lavenex, 2015, 2022).

In recent years there have been studies looking into the participation and influence of third countries in the EU agencies focusing predominantly on the European Economic Area (EEA)/European Free Trade Agreement (EFTA) and European Neighbourhood Policy (ENP) countries (Lavenex, 2015). For Turkey and the Western Balkans region only a preliminary mapping has been done so far (Milenkovic, 2018; Kaeding and Milenkovic, forthcoming), for the United Kingdom (UK) even less (Mustert et al., 2019; Volpato and Wright, 2020; Lavenex, 2022). This chapter will take up this regional challenge and start filling the gap by inquiring whether the UK not only represents a 'new category of state in Europe: that of an EU ex-member', but whether and how the UK also represents a new category of its own when cooperating with EU agencies.

This chapter is structured as follows: Drawing on official documents from European and UK negotiators, the UK Government White Paper on the future relationship between the UK and the EU (2018), the various versions of the Withdrawal Agreement (WA) and respective Political Declarations (2018, 2019) and the final 2020 EU-UK Trade and Cooperation Agreement (TCA), this chapter assesses the EU agencies' role during the Brexit negotiations and those on the future EU-UK relations. It will show how the UK moved from a decisive and respected EU decision maker during 47 years of full EU membership in all EU agencies to one of many rule takers with the status of 'just another third country' – despite geographical proximity and considerable EU-UK sector-specific interdependencies. The chapter will show that the set of EU agencies selected for some future cooperation with the UK kept on changing during the three years of EU-UK negotiations. Also, the selection of EU agencies for cooperation with the UK has, so far, followed predominantly a top-down 'foreign policy' rationale (Lavenex, 2011) of serving the general interest of the EU and supporting 'the European Commission in promoting its core foreign policy agenda ...' (Rimkutė and Shyrokykh, 2017). Hence, accordingly, it is the country's status that determines the level of cooperation between the EU agency and the third country. At the end of this contribution, the chapter discusses the next steps involved in giving effect to the provisions of the EU-UK TCA on EU agencies and their future relationship with the UK, bearing in mind that 'uncertainties and contestation about Brexit are only beginning to be resolved'.[5] To conclude, the chapter summarises the findings and elaborates on their implications for the future of Europe as one of external differentiated integration (Schmidt, 2019), in which non-member states of the EU may participate in shaping future policies.

ANALYSIS: WHAT DOES BREXIT MEAN FOR UK'S POTENTIAL ROLE IN EU AGENCIES? FROM AN EU RULE MAKER TO JUST ANOTHER THIRD COUNTRY

The analysis is divided into three temporal blocks in which EU agencies have played very different roles illustrating whether and how the UK represents a new category of its own when cooperating with EU agencies: the (1) first period runs from formal notification of the UK's wish to leave the EU in March 2017 to ratification in January 2020 of the revised WA and Political Declaration on the UK's orderly departure; the (2) second period covers the Transition period from February to December 2020; (3) the third covers early experiences in operating the EU-UK TCA since January 2021.

First Period from 29 March 2017 to 30 January 2020: 34 Months of UK's Power and Control over EU Agencies Slipping Away

The UK made a significant and in many areas leading contribution to the work of EU agencies during the period of its 47-year-long EU membership lasting until 30 January 2020. Before leaving the EU, the UK representatives had voting rights and a seat on each management board of all EU agencies. British experts took part in the decision-making of all EU agencies' internal bodies (such as executive boards, boards of appeal and/or scientific committees). They led risk assessments, examinations, approvals and authorisation – especially those carried out in the most powerful regulatory agencies, such as the Community Plant Variety Office (CPVO),

European Chemical Agency (ECHA), European Food Safety Agency (EFSA), European Medicine Agency (EMA) and European Maritime Safety Agency (EMSA).

In a number of agencies, in particular, UK experts represented a significant pool of trusted know-how: '[i]n fact, 12,5% of [EFSA] scientific panel experts came from the UK in the period 2009–18 – for certain panels the percentage rising even to 23,81%' (Volpato and Wright, 2020, p. 2).

But then with the Brexit vote in June 2016, and with the formal notification of its intention to leave the EU in March 2017, the picture began to change. The UK's power and control over EU agencies slipped slowly, but steadily away over those 34 months.

Relocation of London-based EU agencies

The first obvious step in UK's loss of power and influence over EU agencies manifested itself through the relocation of the two London-based EU agencies. As a direct consequence of the 2016 Brexit referendum and the UK's decision to leave the EU, as notified to the European Council on 29 March 2017, a decision to relocate the UK-based EU agencies, the EMA and the European Banking Authority (EBA), was deemed essential by the governments of the 27 Member States.

The EMA, important to the functioning of the single market for medicines in the EU, had been based in London since it was established in 1995. It employed 900 staff members at its headquarters in Canary Wharf, London, with responsibilities for scientific evaluation, supervision and safety monitoring of medicines in the EU. Its main tasks include to facilitate development and access to medicines, to evaluate applications for marketing authorisation, to monitor the safety of medicines across their lifecycle, and to provide information to healthcare professionals and patients (EMA, 2021).

The EBA, responsible for prudential regulation and supervision of the European banking sector, maintaining financial stability and safeguarding integrity and efficiency, had been based in its headquarters in Canary Wharf, London, since 2011 (replacing the so-called Committee of European Banking Supervisors). The EBA employed 150 staff working to ensure effective and consistent prudential regulation and supervision across the European banking sector. The EBA, inter alia, assesses risks and vulnerabilities in the EU banking sector through EU-wide stress tests (EBA, 2021).

After the heads of state and government of 27 Member States voted on the relevant procedure in the margins of the European Council on 22 June 2017, there were eight bids to host the EBA and 19 bids to host the EMA shortly afterwards. On 20 November 2017, EU-27 ministers then voted on the relocation of the two UK-based EU agencies. The selected new seat of the EMA is Amsterdam and the new location of the EBA is Paris, unlike London the capital of a Eurozone country.

Both agencies had just over 16 months to prepare for the move and take up its operations. But EBA's departure well in advance of Brexit, for example, was symbolic for 'European banking shifting away from London', and Paris, Luxembourg, Frankfurt and Dublin becoming its home months before the UK eventually exiting the EU. Even if Brexit had not gone ahead as a result of a second referendum, presumably the UK would still have lost these agencies. Yet, studies suggest that the location and relocation of agencies have few consequences for their actual operation (Egeberg and Trondal, 2018).

Role of EU agencies during the negotiations of the first WA and Political Declaration (under Prime Minister Theresa May)

During the early negotiations of the WA which were formally launched in June 2017, the UK expressed in its 2018 White Paper on 'The Future relationship between the United Kingdom and the European Union' its wish to continue structured cooperation after leaving the EU, not with all, but with a few EU agencies.

In particular, the UK proposed active UK participation in 'those EU agencies that provide authorisation for goods in highly regulated sectors – namely the European Chemical Agency, the European Aviation Safety Agency, and the European Medicines Agency' (HM Government, 2018, pp. 12, 25 and 96), Europol and Eurojust, on the basis that 'it is in the mutual interests of the UK and the EU for the UK to continue close cooperation with EU law enforcement and criminal justice agencies' (ibid., p. 66), and bilateral cooperation with EU agencies in a number of other policy areas, namely: EMSA (ibid., p. 45), European Defence Agency (EDA) (ibid., pp. 71, 85) and EU Agency for Network and Information Security (ENISA) (ibid., p. 75).

When the EU and UK negotiators (under Prime Minister May) reached an agreement on the WA and on a Political Declaration on the future relationship in November 2018, it foresaw the possibility of UK cooperation with nine EU agencies, with specific reference to the EMA, ECHA, EASA. Furthermore, the texts underlined possibilities of working 'together to identify the terms of the United Kingdom's cooperation via Europol and Eurojust' (ibid., p. 88), cooperation and information exchange with the EMSA (ibid., p. 65) and Frontex (ibid., p. 116), collaboration in projects of the EDA (ibid., p. 104), and possible participation in certain activities of the ENISA (ibid., p. 111), excluding the possibility, though, of UK participation in the decision-making of EU agencies. Finally, it envisaged possible limited UK national expert participation in EU agencies during a so-called Transition period.

In the end, however, this first WA and the Political Declaration would no longer be valid a few months later. With Theresa May's resignation in July 2019 and Boris Johnson's coming to power, both texts were revised during autumn 2019 with a final agreement on a revised WA and Political Declaration reached in October 2019, in which EU agencies – old and new – again played some important roles.

Second Period from 1 February 2020 to 31 December 2020: 11 Months Caught between the Chairs

Following the UK's withdrawal from the EU on 31 January 2020 based on the October 2019 revised WA and Political Declaration (under Prime Minister Boris Johnson), the UK was no longer an EU member and its role within EU agencies became severely reduced to one of a rule taker, rather than an active rule maker.

As a third country, the UK did not only lose its voting rights, but in fact no longer participated in the EU's decision-making processes at all in order to safeguard the 'decision making autonomy of the Union and its legal order' (Volpato and Wright, 2020, p. 2). The UK was no longer represented in the EU agencies and the supervisory boards and respective working groups, although during the so-called Transition period until 31 December 2020 it would still be bound by EU law, EU agencies' acts and contribute to agencies' budgets.

Next to arrangements for outstanding commitments (House of Lords, 2020, p. 96) and further payments after 31 December 2020 by the UK to agencies (ibid., pp. 116–17), the revised WA and Political Declaration (under Prime Minister Boris Johnson) made references to nine EU agencies, including special arrangements for UK access to data and information from various EU agencies, such as Eurojust (ibid., pp. 47–8), European Environment Agency (EEA) (ibid., p. 71), Intellectual Property Office (EUIPO) and CPVO (ibid., p. 42). It included provisions of information on previous marketing authorisation procedures for medicinal products by UK to EMA (ibid., p. 33) and rules on representation in ongoing proceedings before the EUIPO (ibid., p. 72).

It is noteworthy, though, that not all nine EU agencies mentioned in the 'first' WA and Political Declaration (under Prime Minister May) 'survived' and made it into the revised WA and Political Declaration (under Prime Minister Boris Johnson), such as those covering the policy areas of transport (EASA and EMSA), chemicals (ECHA), defence (EDA), cybersecurity (ENISA) and border control (Frontex).

Instead, the Boris Johnson administration included 'new' EU agencies covering the policy areas of financial services (EBA, EIOPA and ESMA), environment (CPVO and EEA) and intellectual property (EUIPO). But again, not all nine of them would make it into the final EU-UK TCA.

Third Period from 1 January 2021: EU-UK TCA Starts to Apply Provisionally – The UK as an Ex-EU Member State Treated as Just Another Third Country

On 1 January 2021 the UK left the EU Single Market and Customs Union, as well as all EU policies and international agreements. With the provisional application of the TCA, the free movement of persons, goods, services and capital with the EU is put to an end. The EU and the UK start to form 'two separate markets; two distinct regulatory and legal spaces'.

In the end, (only) seven EU agencies are mentioned in the TCA (2020), namely: ENISA, Agency for the Cooperation of Energy Regulators (ACER), the EU Agency for the Operational Management of Large-Scale IT Systems in the Area of Freedom, Security and Justice (eu-LISA), EASA, Eurojust, Europol and EUIPO. More specifically the arrangements concern the following:[6]

- EASA and the UK Civil Aviation Authority may participate as observers in each other's oversight activities (TCA, 2020, p. 260).
- Strengthening institutional cooperation between the intellectual property offices of the UK and the EU (EUIPO) (ibid., p. 262).
- Arrangements for cooperation with ACER (ibid., pp. 182–3).
- Cooperation and arrangements for the exchange of information with Europol and Eurojust (ibid., pp. 310–11, 321–31) to ensure robust capabilities in tackling serious cross-border crime.
- Exchange of information and experience between ENISA and the UK on a voluntary and reciprocal basis (ibid., p. 384). Effective and swift (but no longer direct, real-time access to) data sharing in the fight against serious international crime, terrorism and cybercrime.
- Commitments by the UK to ensure common communication infrastructure, national software meets technical requirements set by eu-LISA (ibid., p. 1033); transmission of statistics and various information to eu-LISA (ibid., p. 1036).

The following five aspects are noteworthy:

1. First, Eurojust and Europol had been part of the Brexit negotiations from the beginning and feature also prominently in the TCA, while EMA did not make it in the end, despite the fact that EMA was mentioned in both versions of the WA under Prime Minister Theresa May and Boris Johnson (going beyond relocation matters).
2. Second, two agencies (ACER and eu-LISA) entered the TCA at the last minute, without having been identified previously as important to future cooperation, neither in the 2018 White Paper and 2018 WA negotiated under Prime Minister May, nor in the 2019 revised WA negotiated under Prime Minister Boris Johnson (Table 12.1).
3. Third, two agencies reappeared in the TCA from the 'Prime Minister Theresa May times', EASA and ENISA, after having been temporarily disregarded in the revised WA under Prime Minister Johnson.
4. Fourth, at the UK's request, the TCA does not cover cooperation on foreign policy, external security and defence, even though this was initially foreseen in the 17 October 2019 Political Declaration (Table 12.1). Consequently, the EDA and the EU Satellite Centre (SatCen) are not mentioned in the TCA.
5. Fifth and last, the TCA does not cover any decisions relating to explaining equivalence for financial services (EBA, European Insurance and Occupational Pensions Authority (EIOPA), the European Securities and Markets Authority (ESMA), nor possible decisions pertaining to the adequacy of the UK's data protection regime (ECHA, EMA), or the assessment of its sanitary and phytosanitary regime for the purpose of listing it as a third country allowed to export food products to the EU (EEA). These are and will remain unilateral decisions of the EU and are not subject to negotiation.

DISCUSSION: TCA SELECTION OF EU AGENCIES DRIVEN BY AN EU FOREIGN POLICY RATIONALE

To understand why EU agencies are selected for cooperation between third countries and the EU, Lavenex (2011, 2015)[7] identifies two[8] main motivations: a foreign policy rationale and a sector specific interdependence logic.

According to the top-down foreign policy rationale one expects EU agencies to act politically, serving the general interest of the EU by supporting 'the European Commission in promoting its core foreign policy agenda …' (Rimkutė and Shyrokykh, 2017, p. 5). In this way, the country's integration status determines the level of cooperation between the EU agency and the third country. Hence, patterns of cooperation through agencies 'mimic' the general level of integration between a third country and the EU.

According to the opposing bottom-up sector-specific interdependence logic, one might expect EU agencies to have functionalistic, rather than political, priorities. In other words, they serve functional (not political) needs of the EU stemming from sector-specific interdependences and externalities involved in not cooperating with third countries. In this way, EU agencies cooperate with third countries' regulators 'with whom they have strong sectoral interdependence' (Rimkutė and Shyrokykh, 2017, p. 6). '… EU agencies working in fields marked by higher interdependencies will be more involved in the external dimension of EU governance' (ibid., p. 7).

Table 12.1 *The role of EU agencies in the Withdrawal Agreements, Political Declarations and the final EU-UK TCA*

	UK EU membership 1979–2020	PM Theresa May WA (November 2018)	PM Boris Johnson WA (October 2019)	EU-UK TCA (December 2020)
EU agencies	Full membership in all decentralised EU agencies	x	x	ACER
		x	CPVO	x
		EASA	x	EASA
		x	EBA	x
		ECHA	x	x
		EDA	x	x
		x	EIOPA	x
		x	EEA	x
		EMA	EMA	x
		EMSA	x	x
		x	ESMA	x
		ENISA	x	ENISA
		x	x	eu-LISA
		Eurojust	Eurojust	Eurojust
		Europol	Europol	Europol
		Frontex	x	x
		X	EUIPO	EUIPO
Total number	34	9	9	7

Note: x = 'not mentioned' in respective document.
Source: Collected information retrieved from the 2018 UK Government White Paper, the 2018 Withdrawal Agreement and Political Declaration (under Prime Minister May), the 2019 revised Withdrawal Agreement and Political Declaration (under Prime Minister Boris Johnson) and the 2020 EU-UK TCA.

To understand the driving logic of action behind the selection of EU agencies in the final version of the TCA defining future EU-UK relations, I use the so-called 'Brexit salience concept' defined as 'the extent to which Brexit may affect EU agencies' internal workings, how important their role may be in ensuring maintenance of regulatory standards, and how closely they are connected to key areas of the UK economy' (Mustert et al., 2019, p. 2). The tripartite framework for assessing Brexit salience in EU agencies ranks all EU decentralised agencies along three dimensions: (1) connections internally with British staff, (2) UK agencies' capacity to maintain regulatory standards, and (3) economic interconnectedness. While EASA and EMA score highest (eight out of nine), the CPVO, Frontex, ACER, EIGE (European Institute for Gender Equality) and Cepol (European Union Agency for Law Enforcement Training) score lowest (with three out of nine).

While Mustert et al. (2019) identify a total of 14 agencies operating in policy areas with high sector-specific interdependence Brexit scores (six and above out of nine), only four of the 14 agencies are addressed in the TCA: EASA (eight mentions), ENISA, Eurojust and Europol (six mentions each) (Table 12.2).

The comparatively low number of EU agencies selected for cooperation with the UK after Brexit that are characterised by high interdependences may imply that the dominant logic of action behind the selected EU agencies in the TCA was less sector-specific interdependence trade-offs, but a foreign policy rationale. This becomes even clearer when taking into consid-

Table 12.2 Selected EU agencies – comparing the EU-UK TCA with the 'Brexit salience concept'

	EU-UK TCA (December 2020)	'Brexit salience concept' (five or higher out of nine)
EU agencies	ACER	x
	EASA	EASA
	x	EBA
	x	ECHA
	x	EEA
	x	EFCA
	x	EFSA
	x	EMA
	x	EMCDDA
	x	EMSA
	ENISA	ENISA
	x	Eurofound
	eu-LISA	x
	Eurojust	Eurojust
	Europol	Europol
	EUIPO	x
	x	FRA
Total number	7	14

Note: x = 'not mentioned' in respective document.
Source: Own compilation with information from Mustert et al. (2019).

eration the full text of the TCA stressing 'broad economic, social and environmental cooperation in areas of mutual interest' (European Commission, 2021), such as:

- *Environmental protection and climate change:* All UK goods entering the EU will still have to meet the EU's high regulatory standards, including food safety (e.g. sanitary and phytosanitary standards) and product safety. Yet, there is no reference to the CPVO and its role in upholding common high standards across the EEA in ensuring environmental protection.
- *Fisheries:* The TCA sets out new arrangements for the joint management of more than 100 shared fish stocks in EU and UK waters, preserving the activities and livelihoods of fishing communities reliant on those waters and resources. Hence, it is striking that there is no provision for cooperation with the European Fisheries Control Agency (EFCA).
- *Transport:* In order to ensure continued road, and maritime connectivity, supporting trade flows and passengers with high levels of transport safety, workers' and passenger rights, and environmental protection it is remarkable to find no provisions to EMSA and the EU Agency for Railways (ERA).

All in all, it is remarkable that the EU-UK TCA refers to only seven EU agencies considering that the TCA 'goes well beyond traditional free trade agreements and provides a solid basis for preserving [the] longstanding friendship and cooperation going forward' (European Commission, 2021), which might imply the predominant logic of action behind the selection of EU agencies following a foreign policy rationale, which might also fit with the current EU's point of view vis-à-vis the implementation of the TCA and its EU agency-specific provisions.

WHAT NEXT? IMPLEMENTATION OF THE TCA AND ITS EU AGENCY-SPECIFIC PROVISIONS

From the EU's point of view, the TCA and its implementation stresses two general commitments, which underlines the predominant foreign policy rationale behind the EU agencies selected for inclusion in the TCA:

1. 'EU membership matters': the UK has deliberately chosen the least ambitious model and therefore the EU should not be defensive or try to be flexible with regard to the implementation of the agreement.
2. 'TCA is final': the TCA 'constitutes a single rulebook and agreement', which needs to be implemented. It is not a plug-in model, not just a basis for years of future negotiations with the UK.

Consequently, the presence of UK experts is not excluded, provided that they do not take part in the agencies' governance and that EU legislation allows for the participation of experts from third countries. EU agencies would need to liaise with their European Commission partner DGs and the European Commission UKTF/UK Service before agreeing with the UK on future relations, and to apply a test based on the following three 'integration status related' questions ('three-questions-test'):

1. Whether the future cooperation with the UK is provided for in the legislation.
2. What the precedents are for the agency's relations with third countries which do not have a specific relation with the EU, meaning that the UK should be compared with countries like Japan, South Korea or Canada, not with Norway/EEA, Switzerland/EFTA or Turkey/Customs Union.
3. Whether the cooperation could influence the governance of EU systems, potentially making the UK a '28th partner', which would not be acceptable.

Eventually, all seven EU agencies mentioned in the TCA will have to establish working arrangements with the UK. All seven EU agencies' respective founding acts contain the following standard provision stating that the

> agency shall be open to the participation of third countries which have concluded agreements with the EU which provide for the adoption and application by these countries of Community law in the area covered by the basic act. Under these agreements, arrangements shall be made specifying, in particular, the nature and the manner in which these countries will participate in the agency's work, including provisions on participation in certain internal bodies, financial contributions and employment of staff.[9]

These working arrangements with the UK will have to follow different procedures (Table 12.3). Analysing the founding acts of all seven EU decentralised agencies mentioned in the TCA, future working relations between EU agencies and the UK will be decided following different procedures, that is, involving the European Commission or the Council and/or the Management Board, exclusively or sequentially.

While Eurojust will 'only' have to consult the European Commission on arrangements for cooperation with the UK, ENISA requires the approval of the European Commission, whereas

Table 12.3 *EU agencies – UK: future working relations requiring different procedures*

Procedure	EU agencies mentioned in TCA
After European Commission approval	ENISA
After European Commission opinion	eu-LISA, EUIPO
After Council approval	Europol
After Management Board approval and European Commission consultation	ACER, EASA
After consulting European Commission	Eurojust

Source: Own compilation based on information from EU agencies' founding acts.

EASA will have to obtain the approval of its Management Board after consultations with the European Commission.

The next few months will show whether, how quickly and which aspects the working arrangements between the seven selected EU agencies and the UK will cover.

CONCLUSION

EU agencies have existed since the beginning of the European integration process,[10] have evolved in different waves,[11] and eventually have become an indispensable feature of executive governance in the EU and its future shape (Dehousse, 1997; Busuioc, 2009). Today, in fact, it is practically impossible to imagine running the Union without them (Chiti, 2013; Everson, 2014, p. 53; Egeberg and Trondal, 2017).

This chapter illustrates that EU agencies have played some role during the Brexit negotiations, the Transition period, and will do so in the future EU-UK relations as laid down in the TCA. From a scholarly point of view, this chapter addresses an often neglected feature of the differentiation literature (Holzinger and Schimmelfennig, 2012; Leruth and Lord, 2015; Bátora and Fossum, 2019; Schimmelfennig and Winzen, 2020): the growing involvement of third countries in EU agencies as a form of external differentiation. Overall, third country participation beneath core EU decison-making institutions, such as decentralised EU agencies, represents an important 'external face of differentiated integration' (Lavenex, 2011, 2015, 2022).

In practical terms, the TCA addresses seven EU agencies eventually covering policy areas of shared interest explicitly: energy (ACER), transport (EASA and EMSA), the areas of freedom, security and justice (eu-LISA, Eurojust, Europol) and intellectual property (EUIPO). However, the TCA does not, at the UK's request, cover cooperation on foreign policy, external security and defence, even though this was initially foreseen in the Political Declaration. Furthermore, it does not cover any decisions relating to equivalences for financial services, nor possible decisions pertaining to the adequacy of the UK's data protection regime, or the assessment of its sanitary and phytosanitary regime for the purpose of listing it as a third country allowed to export food products to the EU.

This lack of engagement with EU agencies covering policy areas defined by high interdependencies implies that the driving force behind the TCA followed predominantly a foreign policy rationale (i.e. EU agencies) where third country involvement in EU agencies serves the general interest of the EU by supporting 'the European Commission in promoting its core foreign policy agenda ...' (Rimkutė and Shyrokykh, 2017).

'The most difficult challenge in the future of EU agencies may be the loss of expertise that the disengagement of UK experts will bring' (Vopato and Wright, 2020, p. 2). EMA executive director Guido Rasi described the problem as follows: 'Our activities will be impacted and we need to plan for this now to avoid the creation of gaps in knowledge and expertise' (EMA, 2017). This is widespread feeling.

> It remains to be seen how far the UK will choose to actively diverge from preserved EU rules already on its statute book, and whether it chooses to act to minimise future differences with its biggest trading partner in the interests of the economy and the union. (Spisak and Britto, 2021, p. 3)

Since, in the end, the 'EU's democratic coping mechanisms are configured along EU membership lines, not along the territorial reach of EU policies' (Fossum, 2015, p. 811), this is something to be closely watched by the UK.

All in all, implementing the TCA will very likely lead to working arrangements between the seven EU agencies and the UK. The EU will make sure, however, being in line with its predominant foreign policy logic of action, that the 'TCA is not a plug-in model but final', and that 'EU membership matters'.

NOTES

1. For a list of decentralised agencies see Table 12A.1 in the Appendix. For a more detailed description of all EU decentralised agencies (formerly referred to as regulatory agencies) see European Commission, 'Agencies and other EU bodies'. Available at https://europa.eu/european-union/about-eu/agencies_en (accessed 3 August 2021).
2. Their tasks concern legal, administrative, scientific, technical issues and regulatory tasks. Agencies have an important task in identification, preparation and evaluation of specific measures in different regulatory implementation (see Groenleer et al., 2010).
3. In fact, there is hardly a policy area of EU engagement without an agency being involved with increasing numbers in EU agency staff (7,578 in 2019) and respective budgets with EU contribution to agencies steadily increasing from EUR 0.1 billion (0.1 per cent of the total EU budget) in 2000 to EUR 1.8 billion (1.5 per cent of the total EU budget) in 2020; see Kaeding (2019) for more descriptions.
4. Exceptions to the rule are Lavenex (2015) mapping third country participation in seven agencies (EASA, ECHA, EEA, EFSA, EMA, Europol, Frontex); Öberg (2019) focusing on the EEA and EFTA's possibilities to influence the content of the EU acquis via their involvement in a selected number of EU agencies. Egeberg and Trondal (2018) address the constitutional questions for the EEA countries in the sense that EU agencies intervene directly in affiliated states also. Furthermore, there is an issue of how to incorporate such measures as ACER's role in the EU's fourth energy market package for example; see also Langford and Berge (2019).
5. See Fossum and Lord's introductory chapter in this volume.
6. For a more detailed summary of the scope of all seven EU agencies see Table 12A.2 in the Appendix.
7. Later tested systematically for ENP and EEA/EFTA country by Rimkutė and Shyrokykh (2017, 2019).
8. Other factors such as path-dependencies, organisational capacities (within agencies as well as within the core-executive) might play important roles. See Copeland and Minto (2021) for a recent illustration.
9. See further 'Analytical Fiche No. 18 International Relations' Detailed analytical papers (2010). Available at https://europa.eu/european-union/about-eu/agencies/overhaul_en (accessed 9 February 2021).
10. For the first analysis of these bodies in the EU legal system see Lauwaars (1979).

11. Most authors distinguish four generations of agencies, the first created in the 1970s, the second created in the 1990s, the third-generation agencies created in the early 2000 onwards, and the fourth generation agencies that emerged in response to the EU's financial and sovereign debt crisis.

REFERENCES

Bátora, J. and Fossum, J.E. (2019). *Towards a Segmented European Political Order: The European Union's Post-Crises Conundrum* (1st edn). Routledge.

Busuioc, M. (2009). Accountability, Control and Independence: The Case of European Agencies. *European Law Journal*, *15*(5), 599–615.

Busuioc, M., Groenleer, M. and Trondal, J. (eds) (2012). *The Agency Phenomenon in the European Union. Emergence, Institutionalisation and Everyday Decision-making*. Manchester University Press.

Chiti, E. (2013). European Agencies' Rulemaking: Powers, Procedures and Assessment. *European Law Journal*, *19*(1), 93–110.

Copeland, P. and Minto, R. (2021). European Networks, Domestic Governance and the Second-order Effects of Brexit. *British Politics*. https://doi.org/10.1057/s41293-020-00156-2.

Curtin, D. and Dehousse, R. (2012). EU Agencies: Tipping the Balance? In M. Busuioc, M. Groenleer and J. Trondal (eds), *The Agency Phenomenon in the European Union. Emergence, Institutionalisation and Everyday Decision-making* (pp. 193–206). Manchester University Press.

Dehousse, R. (1997). Regulation by Networks in the European Community: The Role of European Agencies. *Journal of European Public Policy*, *4*(2), 246–61.

EBA. (2021). Missions and Tasks. https://www.eba.europa.eu/about-us/missions-and-tasks (accessed 27 October 2021).

Egeberg, M. and Trondal, J. (2017). Researching European Union Agencies: What Have We Learnt (and Where Do We Go from Here)? *JCMS: Journal of Common Market Studies*, *55*(4), 675–90.

Egeberg, M. and Trondal, J. (2018). *An Organizational Approach to Public Governance Understanding and Design*. Oxford University Press.

EMA. (2017). EMA to Relocate to Amsterdam, the Netherlands. https://www.ema.europa.eu/en/documents/press-release/ema-relocate-amsterdam-netherlands_en.pdf (accessed 27 October 2021).

EMA. (2021). Homepage. https://www.ema.europa.eu/en (accessed 19 April 2021).

European Commission. (2021). EU-UK Trade and Cooperation Agreement: A New Relationship, with Big Changes. https://ec.europa.eu/info/sites/default/files/brexit_files/info_site/6_pager_final.pdf (accessed 27 October 2021).

Everson, M. (2014). European Agencies: Barely Legal? In M. Everson, C. Monda and E. Vos (eds), *European Agencies in between Institutions and Member States* (chapter 3). Kluwer Law International.

Fossum, J.E. (2015). Democracy and Differentiation in Europe. *Journal of European Public Policy*, *22*(6), 799–815.

Genschel, P. and Jachtenfuchs, M. (2013). *Beyond the Regulatory Polity? The European Integration of Core State Powers*. Oxford University Press.

Groenleer, M., Kaeding, M. and Versluis, E. (2010). Regulatory Governance through Agencies of the European Union? The Role of the European Agencies for Maritime and Aviation Safety in the Implementation of European Transport Legislation. *Journal of European Public Policy*, *17*(8), 1212–30.

HM Government. (2018). The Future Relationship between the United Kingdom and the European Union. https://www.gov.uk/government/publications/the-future-relationship-between-the-united-kingdom-and-the-european-union (accessed 28 October 2021).

Hofmann, H., Vos, E. and Chamon, M. (eds) (2019). *The External Dimension of EU Bodies and Agencies: Law and Policy*. Edward Elgar Publishing.

Holzinger, K. and Schimmelfennig, F. (2012). Differentiated Integration in the European Union: Many Concepts, Sparse Theory, Few Data. *Journal of European Public Policy*, *19*(2), 292–305.

House of Lords. (2020). Brexit: the Revised Withdrawal Agreement and Political Declaration. 1st Report of Session 2019–20. European Union Committee. https://publications.parliament.uk/pa/ld5801/ldselect/ldeucom/4/4.pdf (accessed 27 October 2021).

Kaeding, M. (2019). Europäische Agenturen – ein Forschungsfeld im Werden. *integration*, *42*(1), 55–66.
Kaeding, M. and Milenkovic, M. (forthcoming). External Differentiation: Turkey's Role in EU Agencies. RSC 2021, Integrating Diversity in the European Union. *EUI*.
Kelemen, R.D. (2002). The Politics of 'Eurocratic' Structure and the New European Agencies. *West European Politics*, *25*(4), 93–118.
Langford, M. and Berge, B.K. (2019). Norway's Constitution in a Comparative Perspective. *Oslo Law Review*, *6*(3), 198–228.
Lauwaars, R.H. (1979). Auxiliary Organs and Agencies in the E. E. C. *Common Market Law Review*, *16*, 365–87.
Lavenex, S. (2011). Concentric Circles of Flexible 'EUropean' Integration: A Typology of EU External Governance Relations. *Comparative European Politics*, *9*(4–5), 372–93.
Lavenex, S. (2015). The External Face of Differentiated Integration: Third Country Participation in EU Sectoral Bodies. *Journal of European Public Policy*, *22*(6), 836–53.
Lavenex, S. (2022). Third Country Participation in EU Agencies: Towards 'condominio'?. In B. Leruth, S. Gänzle and J. Trondal (eds), *Routledge Handbook of Differentiation in the European Union* (pp. 248–63). Routledge.
Leruth, B. and Lord, C. (2015). Differentiated Integration in the European Union: A Concept, a Process, a System or a Theory? *Journal of European Public Policy*, *22*(6), 754–63.
Mastenbroek E. and Martinsen, D.S. (2018). Filling the Gap in the European Administrative Space: The Role of Administrative Networks in EU Implementation and Enforcement, *Journal of European Public Policy*, *25*(3), 422–35.
Milenkovic, M. (2018). The Western Balkans and Differentiated Integration – the Potential Role of the European Union Agencies. *TARN Workshop*, Brussels, 12 April.
Mustert, L., Strauss, B., Scholten, M. and Wood, M. (2019). Brexit and the Ways Forward for the UK and EU Agencies. *Renforce Blog*. http://blog.renforce.eu/index.php/nl/2019/03/05/brexit-and-the-ways-forward-for-the-uk-and-eu-agencies/ (accessed 27 October 2021).
Öberg, M.-L. (2019). Third Countries in EU Agencies: Participation and Influence. In H. Hoffmann, E. Vos and M. Chamon (eds), *The External Dimension of EU Agencies and Bodies* (pp. 204–22). Edward Elgar Publishing.
Rimkutė, D. and Shyrokykh, K. (2017). The Role of EU Agencies in the Acquis Transfer: The Case of the European Neighbourhood Policy Countries. Working Paper Series 14. *TARN*. https://dx.doi.org/10.2139/ssrn.3063194.
Rimkutė, D. and Shyrokykh, K. (2019). Transferring the Acquis through EU Agencies: The Case of the European Neighbourhood Policy Countries. In H. Hoffmann, E. Vos and M. Chamon (eds), *The External Dimension of EU Agencies and Bodies* (pp. 183–203). Edward Elgar Publishing.
Rittberger, B. and Wonka, A. (2011). Introduction: Agency Governance in the European Union. *Journal of European Public Policy*, *18*(6), 780–89.
Schimmelfennig, F. and Winzen, T. (2020). *Ever Looser Union?: Differentiated European Integration*. Oxford University Press.
Schmidt, V.A. (2019). The Future of Differentiated Integration: A 'Soft-Core,' Multi-clustered Europe of Overlapping Policy Communities. *Comparative European Politics*, *17*(2), 294–315.
Spisak, A. and Britto, D. (2021). After Brexit: Divergence and the Future of UK Regulatory Policy. *Tony Blair Institute for Global Change*. https://institute.global/sites/default/files/articles/After-Brexit-Divergence-and-the-Future-of-UK-Regulatory-Policy.pdf (accessed 27 October 2021).
Trade and Cooperation Agreement. (TCA). (2020). OJ L 444. https://eur-lex.europa.eu/legal-content/EN/TXT/PDF/?uri=CELEX:22020A1231(01)andfrom=EN (accessed 27 October 2021).
Volpato, A. and Wright, K. (2020). EU Agencies after BREXIT: Adapting to the New Scenario. 10 March. *TARN*. https://tarn.maastrichtuniversity.nl/new-tarn-blog-post-annalisa-volpato-and-kathryn-wright-eu-agencies-after-brexit-adapting-to-the-new-scenario-10-march-2020/ (accessed 30 March 2021).
Vos, E. (2018). EU Agencies on the Move: Challenges ahead. Report No. 1:2018. *SIEPS*. https://www.sieps.se/globalassets/publikationer/2018/sieps-2018_1-web.pdf (accessed 27 October 2021).

APPENDIX

Table 12A.1 Overview of all 34 decentralised EU agencies

Abbreviation	Name	Location	Founding year
ACER	European Union Agency for the Cooperation of Energy Regulators	Ljubljana (Slovenia)	2009
CdT	Translation Centre for the Bodies of the EU	Luxembourg (Luxembourg)	1994
Cedefop	European Centre for the Development of Vocational Training	Thessaloniki (Greece)	1975
CEPOL	European Union Agency for Law Enforcement Training	Budapest (Hungary)	2005
CPVO	Community Plant Variety Office	Angers (France)	1995
EASA	European Aviation Safety Agency	Köln (Germany)	2002
EASO	European Asylum Support Office	Valletta (Malta)	2010
EBA	European Banking Authority	Paris (France)	2011
ECDC	European Centre for Disease Prevention and Control	Stockholm (Sweden)	2005
ECHA	European Chemicals Agency	Helsinki (Finland)	2007
EFCA	European Fisheries Control Agency	Vigo (Spain)	2005
EFSA	European Food Safety Agency	Parma (Italy)	2002
EIGE	European Institute for Gender Equality	Vilnius (Lithuania)	2010
EIOPA	European Insurance and Occupational Pensions Authority	Frankfurt am Main (Germany)	2011
ELA	European Labour Authority	Bratislava (Slovak Republic)	2019
EMA	European Medicine Agency	Amsterdam (The Netherlands)	1995
EMCDDA	European Monitoring Centre for Drugs and Drug Addiction	Lisbon (Portugal)	1993
EMSA	European Maritime Safety Agency	Lisbon (Portugal)	2002
ENISA	European Union Agency for Cybersecurity	Heraklion (Greece)	2004
ERA	European Railway Agency	Valenciennes (France)	2004
ESMA	European Securities and Markets Authority	Paris (France)	2011
ETF	European Training Foundation	Turin (Italy)	1994
EEA	European Environment Agency	Copenhagen (Denmark)	1990
EUIPO	European Union Intellectual Property Office	Alicante (Spain)	1994
eu-LISA	European Union Agency for the Operational Management of Large-Scale IT Systems in the Area of Freedom, Security and Justice	Tallinn (Estonia)	2011
EU-OSHA	European Agency for Safety and Health at Work	Bilbao (Spain)	1994
EUROFOUND	European Foundation for the Improvement of Living and Working Conditions	Dublin (Ireland)	1975
Eurojust	European Union Agency for Criminal Justice Cooperation	The Hague (The Netherlands)	2002
Europol	European Law Enforcement Agency	The Hague (The Netherlands)	1999
FRA	Fundamental Rights Agency	Vienna (Austria)	2007
Frontex	European Border and Coast Guard Agency	Warsaw (Poland)	2004
BEREC	Body of European Regulators for Electronic Communications	Riga (Latvia)	2010
GSA	EU Agency for the Space Programme	Prague (Czechia)	2004
SRB	Single Resolution Board	Brussels (Belgium)	2015

Source: https://europa.eu/european-union/about-eu/agencies_de (accessed 1 August 2021).

Table 12A.2 Overview of EU agencies covered by the TCA: mandate, objectives and legislative basis

EU agency	Mandate and objectives	Legislative basis
ENISA	• actively supporting Member States, Union institutions, bodies, offices and agencies in *improving cybersecurity* • providing its independent opinion and analysis as well as carrying out *preparatory work* • *assisting Member States to implement the Union policy* and law regarding cybersecurity consistently • will play a crucial role in the *development of the EU Cybersecurity certification framework*	• established in 2004: Regulation (EC) No. 460/2004 of the European Parliament and of the Council of 10 March 2004 establishing the European Network and Information Security Agency replaced in 2019: Regulation (EU) 2019/881 of the European Parliament and of the Council of 17 April 2019 on ENISA (the European Union Agency for Cybersecurity) and on information and communications technology cybersecurity certification and repealing Regulation (EU) No. 526/2013 (Cybersecurity Act)
ACER	• promotes the *integration and completion of the European internal energy market* for electricity and gas • complements and coordinates the work of national regulatory authorities • *advises the EU institutions on energy issues* • monitors and reports on developments in the electricity and gas markets • monitors wholesale energy markets to identify and prevent market abuse in close cooperation with national regulators	• established in 2009: Regulation (EC) No. 713/2009 of the European Parliament and of the Council of 13 July 2009 establishing an Agency for the Cooperation of Energy Regulators • recast in 2019: Regulation (EU) 2019/942 of the European Parliament and of the Council of 5 June 2019 establishing a European Union Agency for the Cooperation of Energy Regulators (recast)
eu-LISA	• supports the implementation of EU justice and home affairs strategies through the *management of large-scale IT systems* • *manages the three main IT systems* (for visas, asylum applications and information exchange) which ensure the security of the Schengen area	• established in 2011: Regulation (EU) No. 1077/2011 of the European Parliament and of the Council of 25 October 2011 establishing a European Agency for the operational management of large-scale IT systems in the area of freedom, security and justice • replaced in 2018: Regulation (EU) 2018/1726 of the European Parliament and of the Council of 14 November 2018 on the European Union Agency for the Operational Management of Large-Scale IT Systems in the Area of Freedom, Security and Justice (eu-LISA), and amending Regulation (EC) No. 1987/2006 and Council Decision 2007/533/JHA and repealing Regulation (EU) No. 1077/2011
EASA	• ensures *safety and environmental protection in civil aviation* in Europe • promotes European and international *safety standards*	• established in 2002: Regulation (EC) No. 1592/2002 of the European Parliament and of the Council of 15 July 2002 on common rules in the field of civil aviation and establishing a European Aviation Safety Agency

EU agency	Mandate and objectives	Legislative basis
EASA *(cont.)*	• approves companies that design, manufacture or maintain aeronautical products	• replaced in 2018: Regulation (EU) 2018/1139 of the European Parliament and of the Council of 4 July 2018 on common rules in the field of civil aviation and establishing a European Union Aviation Safety Agency, and amending Regulations (EC) No. 2111/2005, (EC) No. 1008/2008, (EU) No. 996/2010, (EU) No. 376/2014 and Directives 2014/30/EU and 2014/53/EU of the European Parliament and of the Council, and repealing Regulations (EC) No. 552/2004 and (EC) No. 216/2008 of the European Parliament and of the Council and Council Regulation (EEC) No. 3922/91
Eurojust	• supports EU countries in the *fight against terrorism and serious organised crime* (affecting more than one EU country) • *cordination of investigations and prosecutions* • establishment and implementation of EU-wide remedies • organises coordination meetings, finances and provides expertise for joint investigation teams and establishes coordination centres	• established 2002: Council Decision of 28 February 2002 setting up Eurojust with a view to reinforcing the fight against serious crime (2002/187/JHA) • replaced in 2018: Regulation (EU) 2018/1727 of the European Parliament and of the Council of 14 November 2018 on the European Union Agency for Criminal Justice Cooperation (Eurojust), and replacing and repealing Council Decision 2002/187/JHA
Europol	• assists national law enforcement agencies in *combating serious international crime and terrorism* • provides *information exchange* on criminal activities and *enables law enforcement operations* • produces long-term analyses of crime and terrorism	• Europol Convention was signed in 1995 (commenced its full activities in 1999): Council Act of 26 July 1995 drawing up the Convention based on Article K.3 of the Treaty on European Union, on the establishment of a European Police Office (Europol Convention) (95/C 316/01) • current legal basis: Regulation (EU) 2016/794 of the European Parliament and of the Council of 11 May 2016 on the European Union Agency for Law Enforcement Cooperation (Europol) and replacing and repealing Council Decisions 2009/371/JHA, 2009/934/JHA, 2009/935/JHA, 2009/936/JHA and 2009/968/JHA
EUIPO	• manages EU trademark and design rights applicable throughout the EU • receives and examines new registrations • promotes the harmonisation of the procedures of the national intellectual property offices in the EU	• established in 1993: Council Regulation (EC) No. 40/94 of 20 December 1993 on the Community trademark • repealed and replaced by: Regulation (EU) 2017/1001 of the European Parliament and of the Council of 14 June 2017 on the European Union trademark

13. Brexit: the sub-national dimensions from the vantage point of the European Committee of the Regions

Justus Schönlau

INTRODUCTION[1]

The process of a Member State withdrawing from the European Union does not have just one, but several 'regional' or rather 'sub-national' dimensions, both in the country leaving the European Union (EU), and as regards the effect it has on the remaining countries and their sub-national structures. The multi-level nature of European integration is such that the first-ever withdrawal of a Member State, especially of one such as the United Kingdom (UK), with a very distinct set of relationships between its sub-national components, is bound to affect the dense network of vertical and horizontal relationships that common EU membership has fostered between sub-national entities and within the EU institutional system. This chapter will therefore look at the sub-national dimension of Brexit from the vantage point of the European Committee of the Regions (CoR), as the most visible expression of institutionalised multi-level governance in the EU (Piattoni and Schönlau, 2015).

In doing so, the chapter will focus on three distinct dimensions of how the 'wicked problem of Brexit' (Fossum, 2019) has affected, and continues to affect, the roles and views of sub-national entities in the EU 27 and in the UK, and how sub-national actors have tried to influence the process of Brexit, notably through the CoR. The first dimension in this respect is the impact of Brexit on the relationship between the different kinds of sub-national entities in the UK itself, and how this has been perceived and reflected in the political debates in the EU arena. With the causes and effects of Brexit at economic, political and constitutional level being so clearly differentiated along sub-national territorial lines, that is, the situations of Northern Ireland and Scotland in comparison to England and Wales (Keating, 2021), and given the political sensitivities surrounding these questions not just in the UK, it was inevitable that this would affect the debate about the relations between sub-national entities and 'their' respective Member States, as well as with the EU as a whole. Yet, while the political impact of this particular issue is potentially very far-reaching, and has already developed into a very serious challenge to the constitutional and political order in the UK (Rahmatian, 2018; Fossum, 2019; Tierney, 2021), at the EU level the political sensitivity of both the Northern Ireland and the Scottish issue have meant that the emphasis has been primarily on 'containing' any possible spill-over effects on other EU Member States of internal divisions being deepened by Brexit. The first section of the chapter therefore gives a brief account of how (little) this particular aspect of Brexit has been discussed, with the EU system highlighting the importance of the European integration framework in managing conflicts arising from the internal regional dynamics of the Member States, while at the same time trying to steer clear of any direct involvement.

The second key element of Brexit from a sub-national point of view is related to the EU's cohesion policy. The EU's activities in the pursuit of 'economic, social and *territorial* [emphasis added] cohesion …' (Article 3 of the Treaty on European Union (TEU)) are an important element of understanding the sub-national significance of Brexit because of the close link between the related policies and the concept of multi-level governance both as an analytical tool and as a normative category (Piattoni, 2016). In this perspective, the origins of political Euroscepticism, as well as lingering feelings of estrangement between EU citizens (not just in the UK) and the European Union as a project, as well as its processes and institutions, have been discussed at some length in the context of regional divergences within EU Member States (Dąbrowski et al., 2021). This angle, labelled recently as the 'geography of EU discontent' (Dijkstra et al., 2018), has been stressed repeatedly by the European CoR as an institutional champion of EU cohesion policy. In its first reaction to the Brexit vote in 2016, the CoR stated that 'the outcome of the UK referendum highlights the need for the EU to promote better conditions to improve the lives of our citizens by reducing inequalities and increasing territorial cohesion' (CoR, 2016b). Brexit was thus also to be understood as a warning to the remaining EU Member States and the Union as a whole, in the context of the challenge of achieving territorial cohesion within the Union, as a pre-condition for political stability and the persistence of the Union's unique system of multi-level governance.

The relevance of this sub-national element of Brexit is compounded by the differentiated economic and social impact that the uncertainty about relations with the UK has on different regions in the EU 27 Member States. The manifold repercussions of Brexit across a range of dimensions were raised by individual regions as well as by their associations and, not least, by their EU-institutional representative, the CoR, from early in the process. The Committee has continuously called on the EU institutions and the Member States to assess and predict as much as possible the vulnerabilities of particular sub-national entities, both in the UK and in the EU 27, and to provide adequate protection or compensation mechanisms (CoR, 2021a, 2021b, see below). These debates coincided in 2018–20 with the discussions about the EU's next Multi-annual Financial Framework (MFF) and notably about the support to EU regions in the context of cohesion policy. The second section of the chapter will therefore present some of these issues and highlight the permeating effects of Brexit in this context.

The third section will look at how the Committee of the Regions as an institution has been affected by Brexit and has sought to develop its own activity in response to it. Most obviously, the loss of the 24 UK members (plus the same number of alternate members) on 1 January 2020 has changed the overall membership, and to a degree the internal balances within the CoR. Since three of the CoR seats formerly allocated to representatives of UK local and regional government were redistributed to other national delegations (Estonia, Luxembourg, Cyprus), the CoR membership now stands at 329. Yet arguably the political conflicts that eventually led to the Brexit referendum had begun to affect the CoR long before the UK withdrawal, notably with the creation, in 2013, of a political group of European Conservatives and Reformists (ECR), following the exit of the British Conservatives from the European Peoples' Party in the European Parliament in 2009.

The European Committee of the Regions, created with the Maastricht Treaty in 1993 to advise and 'assist' the EU institutions alongside the Economic and Social Committee (Article 300 of the Treaty on the Functioning of the European Union (TFEU)) understands itself as the political assembly of locally and regionally elected representatives from the EU Member States. Through the opinions it adopts on policy proposals for which the respective Treaty bases require consultation of the CoR, or on its own initiative, but also through a host of other political activities, the Committee tries to act as the platform and mouthpiece of sub-national interests in EU policy and decision making (Schönlau, 2017) and frequently refers to its role in 'representing 1 million regional and local elected politicians' (CoR, 2021c).

The Committee itself reflects the enormous diversity of state organisations and levels of sub-national governance across the EU, bringing together representatives of small local authorities, intermediate levels such as provinces or districts, as well as regional ministers or parliamentarians, according to each Member State's decision. It also has members from the executive branches, and from the parliamentary assemblies or councils at the different levels. All of these representatives (and the corresponding number of alternate members) have to hold elected office or be accountable to elected assemblies (Article 300(3) TFEU). The CoR has to transform these diverse and sometimes divergent views of the sub-national levels into coherent political messages across territories, state structures and political views, and in this sense provides a focalisation point also for the variety of interests at play on the complex impact of Brexit.

In this context, it is important to recall that Article 50 of the Treaty on European Union, which is the basis for the withdrawal of a Member State, refers to the procedures of Article 218 of the Treaty on the functioning of the European Union governing the conclusion of international agreements – and these procedures to not foresee any formal involvement of the advisory Committee of the Regions. This institutional-legal position has not been challenged by the CoR as such, but the CoR has tried to use the other means at its disposal to try to influence the Brexit process from a sub-national point of view, and the third section will thus look at some of the Brexit-induced developments and their possible implications for the CoR's role and action in the wider debates about the future of the Union and its particular model of governance.

The concluding section of the chapter will then draw together the different effects of the Brexit process on the EU as a system of multi-level governance in which the sub-national levels are seeking to define their role. While it is yet too early to evaluate conclusively how exactly Brexit and its territorially differentiated consequences will impact specific regions or the wider debates about the role of local and regional authorities in European integration in the long run, it is clear that any full picture of the effects of the momentous change in EU membership needs to include the perspective 'from below' the nation state level.

BREXIT AND THE REGIONAL IDENTITY QUESTION

The Brexit referendum result, and in particular its territorial distribution within the UK constitutional context, has put the issue of devolution and territorial governance under the spotlight in the context of a particularly sensitive political conflict. By emphasising the differences in political status, and in electoral preferences, between the constituent elements of the United Kingdom, the Brexit referendum and the ensuing drama have also highlighted a constitutional oddity of the European construction. Namely, the tension between the concept of subsidiarity as a general principle, that is, that decisions should be taken 'as close as possible to the citizen' with specific reference to the regional or local levels (recital 13 of the TEU preamble and Article 5(3) TEU), on the one hand, and the commitment to respect the Member States' 'national identities, inherent in their fundamental structures, political and constitutional, inclusive of regional and local self-government' (Article 4(2) TEU), on the other. This provision is frequently cited to explain why the EU does not take sides in disputes between sub-national entities and 'their' respective EU Member States, despite the fact that subsidiarity at its conceptual origins in post-reformation ecclesiastical law is clearly a principle biased in favour of the autonomy of the 'lower' or 'weaker' levels vis-à-vis a central authority (Schönlau, 2020). The tension between these two interpretations of 'subsidiarity' in the EU context has been noted for a long time (De Búrca, 1999) and have become even more evident in the discussions on whether the Scottish Parliament or the Welsh Assembly would have a vote on Brexit (Rahmatian, 2018; Keating, Chapter 5 in this volume), but the EU structures have largely remained silent in this debate.

Moreover, as Pazos-Vidal notes, the subsidiarity principle is suffering from another major inherent tension, namely, that between understanding it as a normative concept of 'proximity' to citizens, on the one hand, and/or as an argument about 'scale' and 'effect' and therefore about the efficiency of decision making, on the other (2019, p. 24). These two differing understandings of this key concept of the European debate find their echoes in the UK debate (often without an explicit reference to subsidiarity) between national sovereignty and identity issues, as opposed to the economic and geopolitical arguments in favour of EU membership. Partially due to the unclear distinction between different aspects of these debates, and resulting disagreements about the political consequences, the attempt to bolster the remain side in the impending referendum by a 'reform agreement' between the EU and the UK in 2015, including aspects of subsidiarity, did not achieve its intended objective (Pazos-Vidal, 2019, p. 222). Thus, despite the potentially important role of subsidiarity in addressing some of the underlying problems of UK membership in a supranational European Union, and despite the fact that the concept is central to the EU debates in some other, notably federal EU Member States, subsidiarity did not become very prominent in the UK debate prior to the referendum (Walzenbach and Alleweldt, 2021).

Given how sensitive the issues of internal Member State structures and 'minority nationalism' (Anderson and Keil, 2016) are at the EU level, it is also not surprising that they were not at the forefront of debates in the EU either, even though Brexit clearly has implications for the theory and practice of 'multi-level governance' (Fossum, 2019). In the first instance, of course, for the UK sub-national entities and their relations with the 'centre', with very specific problems for Northern Ireland and Scotland, and to a lesser extent for Wales (Keating, Chapter 5 in this volume). Yet clearly, these intra-UK issues also affect, and may continue to affect, the situation in other EU Member States by highlighting, on the one hand, the important role of the Union as a stabilisation framework that helps to manage or contain Member States' domestic constitutional conflicts or, on the other hand. by encouraging, in some of the EU 27 countries, domestic independence movements to pursue their political aim within that protective context. Thus, as Cetra and Liñeira note, the precise nature of the influence of European integration on sub-state nationalism is not clear as it 'creates incentives to both polity integration and polity segmentation' (2018, p. 717).

Against this backdrop, the Union's primary concern having a specific sub-national angle was to safeguard peace on the island of Ireland, in which the EU has invested substantial political and economic capital (Lagana, 2020). Given the region's history of internal division and bloodshed, and its geographical situation as constituting the UK's land border with the EU after Brexit, Northern Ireland has been at the centre of attention of the EU. This was reflected in the various statements of the Committee of the Regions with regard to Brexit, and by the fact that it organised a fact-finding mission of its Conference of Presidents to the Republic of Ireland and Northern Ireland in 2017. Given the significance of the Union's PEACE programme and of the financial support provided to the region under the EU's cohesion policy (Birrel and Gray, 2017), as well as the particular role of cross-border cooperation between the UK and the Republic of Ireland, the case of Northern Ireland and its development post-Brexit are particularly important test cases for the medium and long-term effects of a Member State leaving the EU.

In the separate case of Scotland, the situation is equally politically sensitive, given the multiple (though often contested) parallels between Scotland's situation and other regions in the European Union. The contentious issue of Scottish independence in the years up to 2016, and including the Scottish vote to remain a part of the United Kingdom in 2014, has long been discussed with reference to Scotland's place in the European Union. EU membership, or access thereto after a possible establishment of an independent Scottish state, have been cited on both sides of the argument, and the Scottish National Party (SNP) even before the referendum on EU membership made provisions in its 2016 Scottish election manifesto, for a new referendum on Scottish independence if there was 'a significant and material change in the circumstances that prevailed in 2014 such as Scotland being taken out of the EU against our will. (SNP, 2016)' (cited in Biagi, 2020, p. 122). Yet at the same time, for political reasons those in favour of Scotland becoming a fully-fledged EU Member State on its own had to downplay to a certain extent Scotland's participation in the EU's existing structures representing 'regional' levels of governance. For instance, while after Scottish devolution, half of Scotland's four representatives (and four alternates) in the CoR had come from the Scottish Parliament, this was changed with the arrival of an SND-led minority government in 2007, to a set of only local representatives, while the Scottish government developed in parallel its 'sub-state para-diplomacy' (Salamone, 2020). The result of the Brexit referendum being so clearly different in Scotland than in England (and Wales) has highlighted again deep divisions in the political debate linked to questions of identity.

For the CoR as the platform for debating sub-national concerns in an EU context, this has of course constituted a particular challenge. The response has been not to close off debate, but to emphasise the European (Union) framework as an essential element of trying to manage the opposing trends of (European) integration and (national) disintegration, in the light of the other EU institutions' balancing act. Thus, the CoR held a debate before the UK referendum (in February 2016) with then European Council President Donald Tusk, in which he underlined that 'real regionalism is a strong antidote to nationalism and separatism' (Tusk, 2016). After the Brexit referendum, and in a context of rising tensions around the Catalonia situation, the CoR held two separate debates during its plenary sessions. One on Catalonia and the wider issue of regional autonomy in October 2017, and another on the likely impact of the UK's intention to withdraw from the EU on local and regional authorities, in December 2017 (CoR, 2017d, 2017f). While the CoR in both cases did not adopt formal positions that would have inevitably exposed and possibly deepened internal divisions, it tried to demonstrate the importance of open debate in an EU arena, in the hope of contributing to diffusing the most acute tensions (Wassenberg, 2020, p. 189).

Yet, debates since the referendum about the legal, procedural and political elements of the process of the UK leaving the EU have also led to discussions about new forms of (regionally) 'differentiated integration' (Keating, 2021). As it became clear that special provisions would have to be made in any case for Northern Ireland in order to address the dual challenge of preserving the EU single market and leaving the Ireland-Northern Ireland (EU-UK) land border as open as possible, while the Scottish Government also sought a differentiated treatment with the aim of leaving Scotland in the EU single market. Even if this was ultimately not successful, the Northern Irish situation may be significant beyond the UK case, since it is 'the first instance of a region of [a] non-Member State having a significant opt-in [to parts of the EU single market]', while so far the EU had only allowed 'regions of some Member States to opt out, wholly or … [partially] (Faroes, Greenland, Canaries, Azores)' from specific policies (Keating, 2021, p. 10). Whether and to what extent this situation could become a precedent and promote other models of sub-national differentiation in the integration context remains to be seen. Yet it does underline that, even though 'the EU has never been an actor in the UK constitutional reform or the territorial fall-out from Brexit, except in the case of the Irish border …' and it 'has stayed out of territorial conflicts in Spain and elsewhere, insisting that these are internal matters' (Keating, 2021, p. 10), the Brexit experience may still affect the relations between different levels of governance in the EU 27. There were and still are, however, some much more immediate effects of Brexit at the sub-national levels, concerning both the UK and the EU's regions, namely, in the context of the EU's cohesion policy, which will be briefly addressed in the following section.

BREXIT AND COHESION POLICY

Notwithstanding various reforms and a small overall decrease of its share in EU expenditure, cohesion policy remains a very substantial part of the EU budget and, even more importantly, the key EU investment policy (Dąbrowski et al., 2021). Moreover, as indicated above, successive rounds of re-negotiation of cohesion policy in the context of the seven-yearly Multi-annual Financial Frameworks have increasingly focused attention on the central role of the EU's structural funds in trying to foster support for European integration and feelings of European belonging or solidarity, or at least a positive attachment to the EU and its institutions (Piattoni and Polverari, 2016). The decision of a majority of UK voters in 2016 to leave the European Union therefore called into question some of the underlying expectations of cohesion policy, not just in Great Britain, but also more generally.

Indeed, even as early research showed that it was difficult to establish clear causal correlations between the levels of EU funding for cohesion and the distribution of leave/remain votes in the Brexit referendum, the debate about the overall effectiveness of cohesion policy began to gather pace in the runup to the negotiations on the 2020–27 MFF (Huggins, 2018) under the shadow of the UK referendum. And clearly, if nothing else, the referendum results did show that EU money spent in the UK regions had not been sufficient to 'buy EU love' (Landes, 2020), and that other factors had been more significant. While Northern Ireland and Scotland (both areas with high per capita receipt of EU funding) voted by majority against Brexit, in Wales, which had the highest per capita allocation of EU funds in the 2014–20 period, 52.5 per cent of voters supported leaving the EU.

In fact, at a more granular level research points to the importance of socio-economic factors, at both individual and collective levels, where low levels of education and economic security standards seem to have led to higher support for the leave vote (Goodwing and Heath, 2016). Here there is a clear territorial element to the referendum result, as this kind of socio-economic profile is concentrated in certain geographic areas, many of which have been particularly affected by economic deprivation and/or external shocks from globalisation and labour migration, notably among the lower skilled. This exposure has therefore been identified as a possible significant explanatory factor for the Brexit vote (Becker et al., 2017). While it is clear that many other factors must also have been significant in shaping the distribution of Brexit votes throughout the UK, and commentators underline the complex interconnections between economic, cultural, psychological and political elements (Veltri et al., 2019), it is significant to note that the persistence of deep economic division and the related feelings of alienation from 'the centre' and of certain areas being 'left behind', would point at least to an insufficient effect of cohesion policy, if not an outright failure.

In this context, it is somewhat ironic to recall that the UK played a central role in the development of what was to become EU cohesion policy, since it pushed very hard for the development of a regional policy in order to 'compensate' for its comparative lack of access to Common Agricultural Policy funding and its relatively higher contribution to the EU budget (Charles, 2016). In this sense, the UK became an important promotor of the (contested) notion of a '*juste retour*' in EU budgetary debates soon after joining the EU in 1973 (Piris, 2021). Yet despite this strong interest of the UK in the creation of a cohesion policy at EU level, analysis of its effectiveness in British regions reveals a rather mixed picture. Reviewing the impact of cohesion policy in the UK for the 1989–2013 period (before the Brexit referendum, and in comparison to the situation in the Republic of Ireland), for instance, Charles notes the very uneven results of the policy for different regions. The situation differs considerably between the devolved parts of the UK (Northern Ireland, Scotland and Wales), on the one hand, and England, on the other, where the former have seen some overall positive effects of EU cohesion policy over the decades, whereas 'English regions … have suffered from the constant changes in eligibility, governance and strategy' (Charles, 2016, p. 266). He attributes the overall limited effect of cohesion policy in the UK to the complex structures and numerous changes to sub-national (and also cohesion policy) governance structures, as well as numerous shifts and consequent inconsistencies in strategy, focus and relevance of regional policy, not least in terms of national co-financing. While similar problems are probably not unique for the UK situation, they may nevertheless be part of the explanation of why EU cohesion policy has not been more relevant and visible for voters across the UK when they made up their minds on EU membership. Charles concludes that cohesion policy has not been a key element in the referendum, noting that:

> [T]he UK voted to leave the EU in a referendum in which the regional issues were barely mentioned and seemed to have played little role in the decisions of people living in English and Welsh regions which have benefited most from the Structural Funds. (Charles, 2016, p. 266)

This is even more significant taking into account the fact that some studies estimated in 2019 that, due to 'many ares of the UK … falling behind the EU in terms of regional prosperity …', the UK 'would be entitled to over 13 billion of regional development funding under EU cohesion Policy for the 2021–2027 period …' if it stayed in the EU (CPMR, 2019).

The reverse is, however, clearly the case: even if cohesion policy did not have a great impact on the Brexit vote, Brexit once decided was clearly going to have a significant impact on cohesion policy for the remaining 27 EU Member States, weakening the policy at a moment when the territorially differentiated impact of Brexit was certain to increase regional divergence, and quite significantly for some EU 27 regions. The direct impact of Brexit on cohesion policy stems mainly from the effects that the withdrawal of a relatively more affluent Member State would have on the overall EU budget. Since the UK was clearly a 'major net contributor' (Gordon, 2018, p. 1) and the shortfall in the annual EU budget after Brexit was initially expected to be around 10 billion Euro out of an annual budget of around 150 billion Euro, it was clear that some considerable effects would be felt, leading to a debate about how this loss could be compensated, a debate that began early in the process of negotiating the new financial framework 2020–27 (Haas and Rubio, 2017).

Brexit, and its impact on cohesion policy, would thus clearly have repercussions in nearly all EU 27 regions, not just in those receiving most support from EU structural funds. It is therefore not surprising that much of the focus of regions across the Union in the MFF debates was on 'protecting' as much as possible the cohesion-related budget from deep cuts, whether explicitly related to Brexit or not. In this context, the European CoR, together with a large number of associations of local and regional governments, as well as individual cities and regions beyond the CoR membership, set up in 2017 the so-called 'Cohesion Alliance' (CoR, 2019b, 2020a).[2] The aim of this initiative is to underline cohesion as a 'fundamental value' of European integration and preserve cohesion policy, not just with its overall share of the budget, but also regarding the specific governance mechanisms that have been created for it, notably the partnership principle to ensure the involvement of sub-national levels of governance in policy design and implementation (Schönlau, 2016).

As it developed, and in a new context created by the coronavirus crisis, the agreement reached by the EU leaders and the European Parliament in December 2020 did preserve the share of 'cohesion' as a percentage of the overall budget (Petzold, 2021) and foresaw an additional and unprecedented financial recovery package in response to the pandemic. The dramatically changed context of all EU policymaking in the wake of COVID-19 makes it difficult to determine precisely to what extent Brexit influenced the final result of the protracted negotiations on the MFF within the limits of this brief overview, but through the prism of the institutional responses triggered by Brexit and the activities and debates in the CoR, it is possible to outline some ways in which the UK leaving the EU is affecting sub-national authorities in the EU 27 countries. It is therefore to this element we now turn.

THE COR IN THE BREXIT DEBATE

The European CoR, in its initial reaction to the result of the UK referendum, developed a quite specific reading of Brexit, deciding not to focus at first on the details of the implications of Brexit (with many in mid-2016 still hoping for the decision to be reversed). Instead, it focused on building the presumed underlying causes of Brexit into its own narrative of multi-level governance and the need for the EU to reconnect to its citizens via the sub-national level. While first stating that it 'regretted, but respected' the outcome of the referendum, the CoR Bureau Statement of 8 July 2016 goes on to say that the CoR should 'turn this critical situation into an opportunity to reform, rebuild trust and hope' (CoR, 2016b). It then went on to invite the EU to create 'better conditions to improve the lives of our citizens by reducing inequalities and increasing territorial cohesion' and to 'urgently strengthen its efforts to communicate its benefits locally …'. Moreover, the Bureau declaration specifically insists on the need to address 'unacceptable levels' of youth unemployment (CoR, 2016b), thus implicitly linking the UK referendum results to one of the most acute lingering effects of the 2008–14 economic crisis with enormous differences between regions.

While the CoR then moved on to refine its positions with a view to defending the cohesion policy budget in the post-Brexit context (CoR, 2017c), it also addressed the wider political implications of the UK leaving the EU. In its resolution of March 2017 (CoR, 2017b), in addition to echoing many of the key Brexit-related issues for the EU as a whole (such as the need for an orderly withdrawal process, legal certainty for EU and UK citizens, protecting the level playing field and the single market, and underlining that no agreement with a non-EU country must be better than membership), a number of specific regional points are mentioned: the need to anticipate Brexit consequences at regional level (CoR, 2017b, point 5); the call to keep territorial cooperation mechanisms, notably the European Grouping of Territorial Cooperation (EGTCs) open to UK devolved administrations and local government (CoR, 2017b, point 12); the need to find solutions for the particular situations of Northern Ireland and Gibraltar and the respective bordering EU 27 regions (CoR, 2017b, points 14–15); the specific regional dimensions in various EU policy areas, that is, fisheries, CAP, research, energy, youth (CoR, 2017b, points 20–24); and finally, underlining the CoR's self-understanding as being 'best placed to devise and implement institutional mechanisms to promote regular consultation and interaction with local government and devolved parliaments and assemblies in the UK' (CoR, 2017b, point 25). Significantly, the CoR also recalls the role of some EU 27 CoR members representing their Member States in the Council, for decisions on future EU-UK relations (CoR, 2017b, point 26).

Throughout 2017, the CoR continued to develop its understanding of the implications of Brexit, including by conducting a survey among its members on their expectations for the impact of Brexit, by sending its Conference of Presidents on fact-finding missions to England, Scotland, Ireland and Northern Ireland, and by holding a debate on Brexit in its last plenary session of 2017 (CoR, 2017e). Based on these elements, a second resolution on Brexit was adopted by the CoR in May 2018, in which the CoR stressed in particular the difficulties for regional and local authorities to prepare for the expected uneven consequences of Brexit, given the protracted negotiations on the withdrawal agreement and the lack of clarity about future relations (CoR, 2018b). It recalled research it had commissioned in 2017 to identify regions in the EU 27 that were particularly vulnerable to the impact of Brexit, which had clearly shown that '*the economic and social effects of the UK's withdrawal from the EU will most likely be asymmetrical not only across different sectors of the economy, but also across regions and countries*' (CoR, 2018b, point 6, emphasis added by the CoR) and that the CoR had raised these issues in its continued exchanges with the EU negotiators. In fact, EU chief negotiator Michel Barnier had made one of his first major public speeches after the referendum vote in the CoR plenary session in early 2017 and attended at least five CoR meetings between 2017 and 2020.[3]

Moreover, the CoR linked the problem of the different exposure of particular regions to negative Brexit consequences with the ongoing debates on the MFF and reiterated in this context its:

> [D]eep concern [about] the recent proposals for the MFF by the European Commission and reiterates its conviction that a strong cohesion policy, including reinforced European Territorial Co-operation programmes such as Interreg, is essential for the local and regional authorities in the EU to address adverse consequences of the UK's withdrawal. (CoR, 2018b, point 10)

The CoR also called on 'the European Commission to assess before 29 March 2019 the possible need for a stabilisation fund for regions most adversely affected by the UK's withdrawal from the EU' (CoR, 2018b, point 10).

In this resolution, the CoR also pays particular attention to the situation of Northern Ireland and the bordering regions of the Irish Republic (informed by fact-finding mission of the CoR's Conference of Presidents (CoP) in 2017), as well as to the situation of Gibraltar and its neighbouring region of Andalusia, and of some of the EU's outermost regions and their dependence on the UK economy (CoR, 2018b, points 19–21). The CoR reiterated its hope that the future relationship would allow for the participation of UK local and regional authorities (LRAs) in different forms of cooperation with EU LRAs, including in the framework of EU macro-regional strategies, Interreg and within EGTCs, an instrument particularly promoted by the CoR (Schönlau, 2016, pp. 163–4). Finally, it called for the creation and recognition of relevant forums or platforms for direct cooperation between sub-national levels of governance, and again put itself forward as the best placed to 'promote post-withdrawal regular consultation and interaction with local government and devolved parliaments and assemblies in the UK' (CoR, 2018b, point 24).

In fact, an 'inter-regional group' on Brexit had already been set up by some CoR members in early 2018 (CoR, 2018a). Modelled on the European Parliament's 'Intergroups' which provide forums for a structured exchange of ideas between stakeholder groups and interested MEPs on a given subject, CoR inter-regional groups can be set up by at least ten CoR members, including at least four national delegations. The Brexit inter-regional group initially brought together 19 CoR members and ten alternates. The group comprised members from France, Belgium, Austria, Hungary, Poland and the Netherlands, as well as virtually the entire Irish CoR delegation, but none from the UK. It was created on the initiative of Francois Decoster (FR/Renew Europe), mayor of Saint Omer in the French Channel coast region. In a next step, the CoR decided to create more formal structures for future cooperation with UK LRAs. During a meeting of the CoR Bureau on 1 February 2019, a set of possible options was discussed for short- and longer-term cooperation with UK sub-national levels of governance, including the idea of a 'North-West-Europe Forum' in the context of a wider European macro-regional strategy, but subject to future decisions on the EU-UK relationship. In particular on the question whether 'the UK will be taking part in future programmes with a territorial cooperation dimension' (CoR, 2019a, p. 4).

In the more short term, a decision was taken to establish a so-called 'CoR-UK contact group' to ensure continuity of relations with representatives of UK LRAs. The CoR-UK delegation and the various bodies nominating CoR members for the UK had tried to lobby both the UK government and the EU side to set up a joint Consultative Committee similar to those created on the basis of association agreements with countries which have applied to join the EU (CoR, 2019a, annex). Yet, it seems that the UK did not support the creation of such a structure with the CoR, differently from the EU-UK Parliamentary Assembley, and also decided not to 'opt-in' to the Interreg programmes which were a key priority for the EU 27 regions. In this situation, the CoR set up the CoR-UK contact group unilaterally as a working group of its Bureau in February 2020 with originally 12 CoR members, to which later an observer from the newly created Green Political group was added (CoR, 2020a).

Due to the slow progress of negotiations on the withdrawal agreement, and the subsequent onset of the coronavirus pandemic, it was not until July 2020 that the CoR-UK contact group met for the first time (virtually) and adopted its work programme for five meetings over the two years until March 2022, the end of the first half of the 2020–25 CoR term of office (CoR, 2020a). Among the tasks the contact group set itself (apart from providing a channel for dialogue between EU and UK sub-national entities in general and Brexit related problems in particular) is the idea to:

> [G]ive EU LRAs and UK local government and devolved parliaments and assemblies a means of discussing European Union legislation and possible changes to EU legislation currently applicable in the UK where it would affect them even after the United Kingdom's departure from the European Union. These authorities may continue to be bound by the *acquis communautaire* during the transition period and potentially as a result of any future trade deal. (CoR, 2020a, p. 2)

thus, putting a strong emphasis on the medium to long-term impact of Brexit also on the UK's sub-national entities. The list of other priority topics then identified by the contact group are: the EU-UK trade negotiations; cross-border and territorial cooperation; movement of goods, services and persons between the EU and the UK; the Northern Ireland peace process; and awareness raising about the role of LRAs in dealing with the impact of the changes ahead.

The contact group chaired by Loïg Chesnais-Girard (FR/PES), President of Brittany, convened first in the CoR members only configuration to adopt its work programme and discuss progress with the EU chief negotiator Michel Barnier, and since then has met with invited representatives of UK sub-national levels of governance where the English, Northern Ireland, Scottish and Welsh associations of local government were represented, as well as the Gibraltar and Scottish Parliaments and the Welsh Assembly. Just weeks after the EU-UK agreement was finally signed, the CoR contingent met again in January 2021, expressing once more its 'concern about the lack of a structured regional dimension in the EU-UK deal' (CoR, 2021a). Thus, one of the key messages of the CoR in response to the UK referendum and the ensuing negotiations has consistently been that there are many ways in which Brexit will have an impact on all levels of sub-national governance, that this impact will be highly differentiated according to different territories and their specific characteristics, and that it would therefore be necessary to create EU-level structures with a direct involvement of sub-national entities, to ensure appropriate policy responses.

As a concrete consequence of this observation, the CoR has continued to lobby for a specific 'Brexit adjustment Fund' as part of the EU budget, with a clear focus on the differentiated exposure of different regions in the EU 27. When the 'Brexit Adjustment Reserve' (BAR) was proposed formally by the European Commission in December 2020 as part of the wider MFF package, it was stated that the 5 billion Euro fund would 'assist regions and local communities, including those dependent on fishing activities in UK waters' (European Commission, 2020). In the CoR opinion on the proposed regulation for the BAR (adopted by the CoR plenary in March 2021), the Committee proposed changes to the legislative text highlighting the need to broaden the focus to 'all affected regions and economic sectors' (CoR, 2021b, legislative amendment 3 to recital 3), and stressed the importance of considering not only the impact on the fisheries sector, but also on sectors such as tourism, agricultural exports, research and innovation and generally to regions particularly dependent on trade (CoR, 2021b, legislative amendment 4 to Article 5(1)).

Also, the CoR regrets that the Commission proposal does not 'reflect the partnership principle applicable to cohesion policy' to ensure that LRAs are appropriately involved in the governance of the new funding instrument (CoR, 2021b, legislative amendment 13 on Article 4(a)(11)). This is an overall concern of the Committee across policy areas, but in particular now with regard to the implementation of EU financing, be it in the context of the post-COVID recovery or of the UK's withdrawal from the EU. These concerns of the CoR were answered at least partially by the European Parliament's Regional Affairs Committee (REGI) when it adopted amendments to the Commission proposal in May 2021 in which it called specifically on the Member States to 'apply the principles laid down in the European Code of Conduct on Partnership and rely on their regional and local public entities to identify the most appropriate measures'. Moreover, the EP's Regional Affairs Committee also asks the Member States to:

> [E]stablish a multi-level dialogue with local and regional authorities and communities of regions and sectors most adversely affected, social partners and civil society, aimed at defining and implementing mutually agreed measures to be supported by the Reserve as well as a monitoring mechanism. (Committee on Regional Development, 2021)

The CoR also called for an increase in the funding foreseen for the BAR from EUR 5,370,994,000 to EUR 6,370,994,000 (CoR, 2021b, legislative amendment 12 on Article 4). While the CoR was not successful in achieving this increase at this stage, the co-legislators did include a reference to the important partnership principle in the regulation that was adopted in September 2021, thus recognising the regionally 'varied' impact of Brexit and calling indeed on Member States to engage in multi-level dialogue with the sub-national authorities concerned (Regulation (EU) 2021/1755, Article 5(3)). These examples thus underline how the CoR with its insistence on the concerns of LRAs in the Brexit process is contributing to shaping not only the debates, but also legislation at EU level.

Finally, and beyond the above-mentioned political and budgetary effects of Brexit and their repercussions for the sub-national level, Brexit has also directly affected the internal structures of the CoR. With the creation, as noted above, of the ECR group in 2013 in the CoR (ECR, 2018), a fifth political group was established,[4] which changed to a certain degree the political dynamics of the CoR where Eurosceptic or Euro-realist voices had until then only been expressed by individual, non-aligned members. With initially a very high proportion of UK members in a relatively small group (17 out of a total of 32 full and alternate members at the creation of the group in 2013),[5] the ECR was very much a channel for representatives of sub-national levels of government in the UK to voice their views and concerns leading up to and following the Brexit referendum until the end of their membership. It is probably not surprising, but still significant to note, that the vast majority of UK CoR members including those in the ECR expressed their individual opposition to Brexit, as noted by the then leader of the UK CoR delegation immediately after the UK referendum (CoR, 2016a), although many of them were arguing for a 'reform' of the EU and stronger emphasis on localism and the principle of subsidiarity.

The change in membership of the EU and thus the 'freeing up' of 24 CoR seats by Brexit also meant that certain imbalances that had existed before, notably with regard to the representation of some smaller Member States, could be corrected. Concretely, the accession of Croatia to the Union in 2013 had meant that, due to the upper limit of 350 for the number of CoR members fixed in the Treaty on the Functioning of the EU (Article 305 TFEU), Luxembourg, Cyprus and Estonia had each given up one seat in the CoR. Following the withdrawal of UK members, these losses could be compensated, while, in parallel with the situation in the European Parliament, the remaining former UK seats remain unattributed for the time being, bringing the total number of CoR members for the EU 27 to 329. Moreover, Brexit created a need to modify the Rules of Procedure of the Committee of the Regions because of the references to the UK or the number of EU Member States in the rules (for instance in defining the number of members of the CoR Bureau). This imperative to review the internal rules was also seen as an opportunity to address certain other issues, and thus constitutes another indirect impact of Brexit on the way that the EU 27 sub-national levels of governance can make their voices heard in the EU process via the CoRs.

CONCLUSION: VISIBLE AND INVISIBLE SUB-NATIONAL DIMENSIONS OF BREXIT

This chapter has sought to highlight the sub-national dimensions of the UK leaving the EU, looking at different elements of the impact of Brexit on towns, cities and regions in the UK and the EU 27, and at their institutional reflections in the EU system, notably via the Committee of the Regions. While the full repercussions of the first ever withdrawal of a Member State from the integration project will only become clear in years to come, it is obvious that they affect all levels of governance. In this sense, as outlined above, Brexit may yet affect the relations between different levels of governance in individual Member States, in the EU, and its multi-level governance system more generally. It also remains to be seen how relations between the devolved levels of authority and the UK central level will develop outside the stabilising framework previously provided by EU membership. In the immediate aftermath of the 2016 referendum, the main interest of both the UK and the EU Member States and institutions – for different political reasons – was to minimise any changes and their possible repercussions (including in order to preserve the status quo in both Ireland/Northern Ireland and Scotland). However, events in early 2021, and notably the results of the May 2021 Scottish elections showed clearly that these two specific situations are evolving, with possible complex knock-on effects on other Member States in the EU. Whether, and how this will affect the EU internal debate about subsidiarity as a principle that should govern the relations not just between nation states and the EU, but between all levels of governance, is another question to be discussed in years to come.

The second area in which Brexit was and is hugely significant from a sub-national point of view is in terms of the EU's cohesion policy, both as regards its aim and purpose of reducing territorial disparities within the Union, and more immediately as regards the effect of Brexit on the resources available under cohesion policy following the 'loss' of a major net contributor to the EU budget. In this regard, the ultimate success of the efforts undertaken by many regions, and notably the European Committee of the Regions and the Cohesion Alliance, to preserve the allocations to cohesion policy as much as possible in the MFF 2021–27 despite the missing UK budget contribution may in part be due to the wider recognition that policies to address relative regional deprivation and its underlying causes are a necessary part of a comprehensive strategy to prevent Brexit-like dynamics from emerging elsewhere.

Finally, it is important to record that the early discussions about the concrete trajectory and the possible effects of Brexit, at least in the view of many of the regions and local authorities concerned, did not adequately take account of the various sub-national dimensions of the process. As Cetra and Liñeira note in their account of the limited influence of sub-state nationalism on European integration, this bears witness to the fact that, despite all efforts to regionalise the EU and its Member States, 'the European Union continues to operate as a club of states' (Cetra and Liñeira, 2018, p. 726). In this context, the European Committee of the Regions, as the main institutional representative of sub-national interests, has made it its business to stress the message that the impact of Brexit will be territorially 'asymmetric', affecting some regions more than others, and the CoR is trying to use the various instruments at its disposal to call for the necessary sensitivity and appropriate measures to address these sub-national concerns. At this point, it is too early to assess whether, and in what form, the medium to long-term effects of Brexit will lead to more regional disparities, and whether or not the most appropriate response to this would be more regionally differentiated European integration in the EU 27, or what kind of (reformed) system of multi-level governance would be necessary to keep disintegration tendencies in check. The Conference on the Future of Europe under way at the time of writing may contribute some ideas to this discussion. Yet it is clear that leaving the European Union deeply affects not just the UK's sub-national levels of governance, but also those of the remaining EU Member States, as well as the relations between all parts in the EU's multi-level system.

NOTES

1. The views expressed in this chapter are those of the author and do not represent the official position of the European Committee of the Regions. I am grateful to Michael Collins, Matthieu Hornung and Serafin Pazos-Vidal for comments and suggestions on this chapter. All remaining errors are entirely my responsibility.
2. The Alliance is referred to as Cohesion Alliance 2.0 since May 2020 (European Committee of the Regions, 2020b). It brings together more than 11,000 signatories.
3. CoR plenary debates on 22 March 2017 (CoR, 2017a) and 6 December 2018 (CoR, 2018c), the CoR summit in Bucharest on 14–15 May 2019 (CoR, 2019c), as well as the first (virtual) meeting of the CoR-UK contact group on 22 September 2020 (CoR-UK contact group, 2020c) and the virtual CoR plenary on 6 December 2020 (with London Mayor Sadiq Khan) (CoR, 2020d).
4. Since February 2020 there is a 6th political group, with the establishment of a group of Green CoR members.
5. I am grateful to the Secretariat of the ECR group in the CoR for providing these figures.

REFERENCES

Anderson, P., and Keil, S. (2016). Minority Nationalism and the European Union: The Cases of Scotland and Catalonia. *L'Europe en Formation*, *1*(1), 40–57.

Becker, S., Fetzer, T., and Novy, D. (2017), *Who Voted for Brexit?* (ifo DICE Report). Leibniz-Institut für Wirtschaftsforschung an der Universität München, *15*(4), 3–5. http://hdl.handle.net/10419/181252 (accessed 10 May 2021).

Biagi, M.G. (2020). Brexit, the SNP and Independence. In G. Hassan and R. Gunson (eds), *Scotland, the UK and Brexit: A Guide to the Future* (pp. 122–44). Luath Press.

Birrel, D., and Gray, A.M. (2017). Devolution: The Social, Political and Policy Implications of Brexit for Scotland, Wales and Northern Ireland. *Journal of Social Policy*, *46*(4), 765–82.

Cetra, D., and Liñeira, R. (2018). Breaking-up within Europe: Sub-state Nationalist Strategies in Multilevel Polities. *Journal of Common Market Studies*, *56*(3), 717–29.

Charles, D. (2016). Cohesion Policy in the Service Economies of the North. In S. Piattoni and L. Polverari (eds), *Handbook on Cohesion Policy in the EU* (pp. 250–67). Edward Elgar Publishing.

Committee on Regional Development. (2021). Final Compromise Amendments on the proposal for a regulation of the European Parliament and of the Council establishing a Brexit Adjustment Reserve (COM(2020)0854 – C9-0433/2020 – 2020/0380(COD)). European Parliament. https://drive.google.com/file/d/1h7YuIM8OPx4Rz_XEuWBhr3AZVJ3KmJcB/view (accessed 15 May 2021).

Conference of Peripheral Maritime Regions (CPMR). (2019). *UK Allocation for Cohesion Policy for 2021–2027* (CPMR report). https://cpmr.org/wpdm-package/cpmr-report-uk-allocation-for-cohesion-policy-for-2021-2027 (accessed 15 May 2021).
Consolidated version of the Treaty on European Union (TEU). (2012). OJ C 326/13.
Consolidated version of the Treaty on the Functioning of the European Union (TFEU). (2012). OJ C 326/47.
Dąbrowski, S., Spaans, M., Fernandez-Maldonado, A.M, and Rocco, R. (2021). Cohesion Policy and the Citizens' Perceptions of the EU: The Role of Communication and Implementation. *European Planning Studies*, *29*(5), 827–43.
De Búrca, G. (1999). Re-appraising Subsidiarity's Significance after Amsterdam. *Jean Monnet Working Papers*, 1999/07. Harvard Law School.
Dijkstra, L., Poelman, L., and Rodríguez-Pose, A. (2018). The Geography of EU Discontent. *Working Paper for the European Commission*. https://ec.europa.eu/regional_policy/en/information/publications/working-papers/2018/the-geography-of-eu-discontent (accessed 10 May 2021).
European Commission. (2020, 25 December). Brexit: Commission Proposes the Creation of a Brexit Adjustment Reserve [Press statement]. https://ec.europa.eu/commission/presscorner/detail/en/IP_20_2536 (accessed 10 May 2021).
European Committee of the Regions (CoR). (2016a). UK Referendum Shows EU Must Do More to Rebuild Citizens' Trust [Press release]. CoR/16/109, 08-07-2016.
European Committee of the Regions (CoR). (2016b). Outcome of the UK Referendum [Statement of the CoR Bureau]. COR-2016-02986-05-01, 14-07-2016.
European Committee of the Regions (CoR). (2017a). 122nd CoR Plenary Session [Press release]. *European Committee of the Regions*. https://cor.europa.eu/de/events/Pages/122nd-CoR-plenary-session.aspx (accessed 10 May 2021).
European Committee of the Regions (CoR). (2017b). Resolution on the implications for local and regional government of the UK's intention to withdraw from the European Union [Resolution]. COR-2017-01049-00-01-RES, 24-03-2017.
European Committee of the Regions (CoR). (2017c). The future of Cohesion Policy beyond 2020 – for a strong and effective European cohesion policy beyond 2020 [CoR Opinion]. COR-2016-01814-00-00-AC, 11-05-2017.
European Committee of the Regions (CoR). (2017d). Minutes from the 125th Plenary Session Debate on Catalonia on 10 October 2017 [Minutes]. COR-2017-03634-04-00-PV-REF, 30-10-2017.
European Committee of the Regions (CoR). (2017e). Summary Background Document for the Debate in the 126th Plenary Session on the likely impact of United Kingdom's intention to withdraw from the EU for the local and regional authorities in the EU, 30-11-2017.
European Committee of the Regions (CoR). (2017f). Minutes from the 126th Plenary Session Debate on the likely impact of United Kingdom's intention to withdraw from the EU for the local and regional authorities in the EU on 30 November 2017 [Minutes]. COR-2018-04083-02-00-PV-REF 1/6, 22-12-2017.
European Committee of the Regions (CoR). (2018a). Setting up a Brexit Interregional Group [Bureau Decision]. COR-2017-05751-09-01-NB-TRA, 30-01-2018.
European Committee of the Regions (CoR). (2018b). Resolution on the implications of the United Kingdom's withdrawal from the European Union for the EU's local and regional authorities [Resolution]. COR-2018-01976-00-01, 16-05-2018.
European Committee of the Regions (CoR). (2018c). 132nd CoR plenary session [Press release]. *European Committee of the Regions*. https://cor.europa.eu/it/events/Pages/132nd-cor-plenary-session.aspx (accessed 15 May 2021).
European Committee of the Regions (CoR). (2019a). Bureau Discussion document on Relations with UK local and regional authorities. COR-2018-06183-06-02-NB-TRA, 01-02-2019.
European Committee of the Regions (CoR). (2019b). #CohesionAlliance: EU-wide support for a strong cohesion policy for every region [Brochure]. 28-02-2019.
European Committee of the Regions (CoR). (2019c). Speakers, (Re)New EUrope: 8th European Summit of Regions and Cities, Speakers. Bucharest. 14–15 May 2019. *European Committee of the Regions*. https://cor.europa.eu/en/summit2019/Pages/speakers.aspx (accessed 10 May 2021).

European Committee of the Regions (CoR). (2020a). CoR-UK Contact Group Working Programme [Bureau document]. COR-2020-03222-00-00, 13-07-20.
European Committee of the Regions (CoR). (2020b). #CohesionAliance: For a Strong EU Cohesion Policy 2.0. https://cor europa.eu/en/engage/Pages/cohesion-alliance.aspx (accessed 16 May 2021).
European Committee of the Regions (CoR). (2020c). European Committee of the Regions Launches UK Contact Group [Press release]. *European Committee of the Regions*. https://cor.europa.eu/en/news/Pages/European-Committee-of-the-Regions-launches-UK-Contact-Group.aspx (accessed 15 May 2021).
European Committee of the Regions (CoR). (2020d). 141st Plenary Session (Virtual meeting) [Press release]. *European Committee of the Regions*. https://cor.europa.eu/en/events/Pages/141st-cor-plenary-session.aspx (accessed 15 May 2021).
European Committee of the Regions (CoR). (2021a). News Item on Meeting of the CoR-UK Contact Group on 11 January 2021. https://cor.europa.eu/en/news/Pages/EU-UK-deal.aspx (accessed 16 May 2021).
European Committee of the Regions (CoR). (2021b). Opinion on Proposal for a Regulation Establishing a Brexit Adjustment Reserve [Opinion]. COR-2021-00718-00-01-AC, 17-05-2021.
European Committee of the Regions (CoR). (2021c). CoR Delegation Ready to Represent 1 Million Regional and Local Elected Politicians at the Plenary of the Conference on the Future of Europe [Press release]. https://cor.europa.eu/en/news/Pages/CoFoE-plenary-19-June.aspx (accessed 15 May 2021).
European Conservatives and Reformists' Group in the CoR (ECR). (2018) Guide to the ECR Group in the CoR. *ECRCOR*. https://web.cor.europa.eu/ecr/about-us/Pages/default.aspx (accessed 10 May 2021).
Fossum, J.E. (2019). Can Brexit Improve Our Understanding of 'Wicked Problems'? Reflections on Policy and Political Order. *European Policy Analysis*, *5*(1), 96–116.
Goodwin, M.J., and Heath, O. (2016). The 2016 Referendum, Brexit and the Left Behind: An Aggregate-level Analysis of the Result. *The Political Quarterly*, *87*(3), 323–32.
Gordon, N. (2018). The EU Budget after Brexit: Reform Not Revolution. *Centre for European Reform*. https://www.cer.eu/publications/archive/policy-brief/2018/eu-budget-after-brexit-reform-not-revolution (accessed 18 September 2020).
Haas, J., and Rubio, E. (2017). Brexit and the EU Budget: Threat or Opportunity? *Notre-Europe/Bertelsmann-Stiftung Policy Paper*, No. 183. Jacques Delors Institute.
Huggins, C. (2018). Did EU Regional Spending Affect the Brexit Referendum? *Regional Studies*, *5*(1), 388–97.
Keating, M. (2021). Taking Back Control? Brexit and the Territorial Constitution of the United Kingdom. *EUI Working Papers*, RSC 2021/28. European University Institute.
Lagana, G. (2020). *The European Union and the Northern Ireland Peace Process*. Palgrave Macmillan.
Landes, F. (2020). Can Money Buy Love? The Impact of EU Cohesion Policy on European Identity. In E. Donat, S. Meyer, and G. Abels (eds), *European Regions: Perspectives, Trends and Developments in the 21st Century* (pp. 129–44). Transkript Verlag.
Pazos-Vidal, S. (2019). *Subsidiarity and Multilevel Governance – Actors, Networks and Agendas*. Routledge.
Petzold, W. (2021, 17 February). Unanimity, Flexibility, Conditionality: How the EU Budget 2021–2027 Was Negotiated and What It Means for Regions and Cities [Presentation, webinar]. *European Policies Research Centre*. https://www.eprc-strath.eu/News-and-events/news/News-3161.html (accessed 15 May 2021).
Piattoni, S (2016). Cohesion Policy, Multilevel Governance and Democracy. In S. Piattoni and L. Polverari (eds), *Handbook on Cohesion Policy in the EU* (pp. 65–78). Edward Elgar Publishing.
Piattoni, S., and Schönlau, J. (2015). *Shaping EU Policy from Below: Democracy and the Committee of the Regions*. Edward Elgar Publishing.
Piattoni, S., and Polverari, L. (2016). Introduction. In S. Piattoni and L. Polverari (eds), *Handbook on Cohesion Policy in the EU* (pp. 1–15). Edward Elgar Publishing.
Piris, J.C. (2021, March). The Making of Brexit: Legal Aspects of the 2016–2020 Negotiations. *EU3D Working Paper* No. 6. ARENA.
Rahmatian, A. (2018). Brexit and Scotland: Centralism, Federalism or Independence? *European Review*, *26*(4), 616–47.

Regulation (EU) 2021/1755 of the European Parliament and of the Council of 6 October 2021 establishing the Brexit Adjustment Reserve, OJ L 357/2.
Salamone, A. (2020, 15 January). Opinion – Scottish Foreign Policy in the Brexit Era. *E-International Relations*. https://www.e-ir.info/2020/01/15/opinion-scottish-foreign-policy-in-the-brexit-era/ (accessed 10 May 2021).
Schönlau, J. (2016). The European Committee of the Regions and EU Cohesion Policy. In S. Piattoni and L. Polverari (eds), *Handbook on Cohesion Policy in the EU* (pp. 156–69). Edward Elgar Publishing.
Schönlau, J. (2017). Beyond Mere 'Consultation': Expanding the European Committee of the Regions' Role. *Journal of Contemporary European Research*, *13*(2), 1166–84.
Schönlau, J. (2020) Entry Subsidiarity. In B. Wassenberg and B. Reiteld (eds), *Critical Dictionary on Borders, Cross-Border Cooperation and European Integration*. Peter Lang.
Tierney, S. (2021, 10 May). The Scottish Parliamentary Elections and the 'Second Referendum' Debate. *U.K. Constitutional Law Association Blog*. https://ukconstitutionallaw.org/2021/05/10/stephen-tierney-the-scottish-parliamentary-elections-and-the-second-referendum-debate/ (accessed 15 May 2021).
Tusk, D. (2016, 10 February). Address by Donald Tusk to the Committee of the Regions [Transcribed speech]. *European Council*. https://www.consilium.europa.eu/en/press/press-releases/2016/02/10/tusk-address-cor/ (accessed 10 May 2021).
Veltri, G.A., Redd, R., Mannarini, T., and Salvatore, S. (2019). The Identity of Brexit: A Cultural Psychology Analysis. *Journal of Community & Applied Social Psychology*, *29*(1), 18–31.
Walzenbach, G., and Alleweldt, R. (2021, 24 January). Introducing Varieties of European Subsidiarity. *E-International Relations*. https://www.e-ir.info/2021/01/24/introducing-varieties-of-european-sub sidiarity/ (accessed 15 May 2021).
Wassenberg, B. (2020). *The History of the Committee of the Regions – 25 Years of Cities and Regions Furthering European Integration*. European Committee of the Regions.

PART III

MEMBER STATES AND BREXIT

14. Ireland and Brexit

Brigid Laffan

The decision by the Cameron Government in London to hold an in-out referendum on European Union (EU) membership was met with dismay in Ireland. Across the political spectrum there was an immediate realisation that this was an enormous political gamble by David Cameron, one that he could lose and if he did, the costs and consequences would be very significant for the island of Ireland. During the referendum campaign there was dread in Irish governmental circles about the outcome, as Irish politicians were well versed in referendum campaigns, particularly on the EU. The then Taoiseach (Prime Minister) Enda Kenny spoke on more than one occasion to David Cameron about his concerns and Irish ministers urged the Irish in Britain to vote Remain. When it became evident on 23 June 2016 that Leave had won the referendum, the Irish state elite sprang into action to minimise the consequences of Brexit for Ireland and to make Ireland Brexit ready. The objective of this chapter is to analyse the Irish response to Brexit and the way in which the geopolitical shock was handled. This is a revealing case study of how a small state deploys its limited capacity to protect and promote its interests in the EU. Moreover, given the centrality of the border on the island of Ireland to the conduct and outcome of the Brexit negotiations, it is essential to an understanding of how Brexit played out in the months and years following the earthquake referendum.

THEORISING IRELAND'S BREXIT RESPONSE

For the Irish state, Brexit was an existential matter involving high politics and geopolitics. It was central to Ireland's 'raison d'état' and 'raison de la paix'. Mackinder, the father of geopolitics, reminded us that states evolved strategies for managing what he called 'economic wants and geographical opportunities' (Mackinder, 1890, p. 84). Reflecting this, Sloan and Grey suggested that 'Geography can be described as the mother of strategy' (Sloan and Gray, 1999, p. 3). Geography and history bound the island of Ireland to its larger and more powerful neighbour, Great Britain (GB), and the island was absorbed into the United Kingdom (UK) by the Act of Union 1801. That Union endured until 26 of the 32 counties became the Irish Free State, later Republic, on 1 January 1922. The partition of the island left a highly contested border on the island, that would become an EU external border when the UK exited the EU. Partition trapped a large number of Irish nationalists in a sub-state region of the UK against their wishes. Decades of discrimination against the nationalist/Catholic community in Northern Ireland led to an outbreak of communal conflict that was tamed by the signing of the Good Friday Agreement (GFA) in 1998. The GFA created a complex set of governing arrangements for Northern Ireland that involved institutions within Northern Ireland, between the two islands and between the two parts of the island of Ireland. The conflict in Northern Ireland moved largely into a non-violent phase and everyday life both within Northern Ireland and on the border returned to a welcomed degree of normality. The combination of the GFA and the earlier EU single market rendered the border invisible. As Hayward concludes, 'The fact that the Irish border has become one of the most seamless and frictionless borders in the world had come to be taken for granted' (Hayward, 2021, p. 1). That invisible mundane border was about to re-enter the limelight as the most intractable issue between the EU and UK as Brexit took root. Brexit represented a major challenge to the working of the GFA, to relations between the communities within Northern Ireland and to relations on the island of Ireland. It also soured relations between London and Dublin after a period of normalisation. Geography inescapably meant that Ireland was the EU member state most affected by Brexit given the strength of ties between the two islands and the overriding need to protect the peace. What could Ireland, a small state, do when faced with a decision by its more powerful neighbour over which it had no control?

The literature on small states in international politics points to two strategies that small states pursue when responding to the demands of their external environment and transnational/international politics. First, Katzenstein identified what he called 'the strength of the weak', arguing that small European states sought to foster domestic elite cohesion and domestic institutions that reinforced their capacity for domestic adjustment to external conditions (Katzenstein, 1985). Here the emphasis is on domestic adjustment and readiness. Although Katzenstein concentrated on political economy, its focus on a domestic consensus extends beyond political economy. Second, there is a second equally important dimension to small state strategy which relates to their positioning within the regional and global framework. Thorhalsson defined this as the search for an external protector or 'shelter' to cope with shocks and risk (Thorhalsson, 2011, p. 325). Ireland deployed both these strategies when responding to Brexit. The Government invested heavily in developing a domestic consensus across the political spectrum and crucially with economic and other interest groups so that sectoral interests were not allowed to have greater prominence than the core geopolitical consideration, peace on the island of Ireland. Moreover, the Government invested heavily in identifying the challenges facing Irish business and supporting companies in the inevitable adjustment. This was accompanied by a coherent external strategy of uploading the Irish question to the EU level and Europeanising the issue of the Irish border by seeking the shelter and protection of the Union and Ireland's partners. The Irish Government and state elite adopted a whole of government and whole of society approach when responding to what was understood as critical to the Irish state and island.

The demands of Brexit induced multilevel politics and policy making were onerous for a small state especially given the historical asymmetry of the relationship between Ireland and the UK. The Brexit process revealed Irish state capacity in action both domestically, in the EU and in the wider international system, especially in Washington. Ireland's state capacity rested on the autonomy of the state, defined by Skocpol as the ability of states to take decisions and pursue policy lines that are not simply reflective of demands arising from the interplay of societal actors (Skocpol et al., 1999). While seeking to keep societal actors on board, the strategy was designed and delivered by a small political/administrative elite that took control of the Irish response. The Irish political and administrative class drew on Ireland's state capacity to develop a strategy to ensure that Ireland's core interests would be protected in the process. This involved doing extensive homework in Dublin, generating a domestic consensus, engaging in a diplomatic offensive across the member states, working with EU institutions, monitoring intensively what was happening in London and liaising with Washington where Irish-American politicians were a source of support. Ireland is a small state with limited political, administrative and institutional resources but the clarity of the objectives around Brexit meant that state capacity was used effectively and with agility.

MULTILEVEL POLITICS: THE DOMESTIC DIMENSION

The Irish state elite grappled with the possible costs and consequences of Brexit for Ireland well before the referendum was held and had established a Brexit Task Force in the Prime Minister's Office by 2015. Arguably there was far more analysis of Brexit in Ireland than there was across the entire UK administrative system prior to the referendum. Once the outcome of the referendum became clear, the Irish system immediately launched into action. Members of the Irish Government's Brexit team began arriving in Government Buildings in the early hours of 24 June 2016 where they assembled in Room 308 (Connelly, 2017, p. 18). The focus was on communicating an Irish response spearheaded by PM Enda Kenny including the publication of a Contingency Plan that had been worked up during the months leading to the vote. Enda Kenny wanted to reassure the Irish public that Ireland could and would manage the challenge of Brexit. A central objective of successive Governments was to reassure the Irish public that however difficult Brexit might prove to be, Ireland would deal with the challenges. On 24 June Enda Kenny's disappointment about the referendum outcome was however evident:

> I am very sorry that the result of the referendum is for the UK to leave the European Union. However, the British people have spoken and we fully respect their decision. I want to assure the Irish public that we have prepared to the greatest extent possible for this eventuality. There will be no immediate change to the free flow of people, goods and services between our islands. (Kenny, 2016a)

The PM emphasised that Ireland would remain an EU member state notwithstanding the departure of the UK. The Kenny speech identified the key issues arising for Ireland from Brexit as the potential impact on trade and the economy, Northern Ireland and the Common Travel Area between Ireland and the UK. Enda Kenny spoke of meeting with the leaders of the opposition parties to give them a full briefing later that day, underlining the Government's commitment to a political consensus on the issue. As the day wore on there were frantic meetings and calls with Irish embassies and key interest organisations. Although no one knew how Brexit would unfold, there were no illusions in Dublin about the likely complications and dangers arising from this major political event. Ireland's geopolitical and economic environment had shifted decisively.

On Monday 27 June, the PM made his first statement to the Dáil (Lower House of Irish Parliament) on the outcome. He again reiterated the view that 'I believe a cross-party approach will be valuable in the time ahead' (Kenny, 2016b). He was also encouraged by the willingness of opposition leaders to use their contacts in European political groupings to ensure that the Irish position was fully understood. The PM intended to convey a sense that Ireland was preparing and would be prepared for whatever Brexit brought. He emphasised the approach as follows:

> We have a whole-of-government contingency framework, within which we will continue to track and develop key policy issues and negotiation positions. (Kenny, 2016b)

Beyond Government, the Irish Parliament became intensively involved in discussions on Brexit; a web search in September 2021 returned 10,000 hits on the topic. Two key parliamentary committees, the Joint Committee for European Affairs and the Joint Committee on the Implementation of the Good Friday Agreement, both opened hearings on the UK's exit. This contributed to domestic deliberation on Brexit and assisted the Government in developing its strategy backed by a political consensus.

The day after the referendum, the Irish Government published its first Brexit Contingency Framework, a rolling plan that was updated throughout the Brexit process until the UK ultimately left the Union (Ireland, Government Press Release, 24 June 2016). The final Brexit Readiness Action Plan was published on 9 September 2020, just before the end of the transition period. From June 2016, a strong communications strand was developed to inform Irish economic actors of the changes to come and the need to prepare, to become Brexit ready. The Government looked to Irish state agencies to assist Irish companies to adjust. Enterprise Ireland and other state agencies developed a set of dedicated support systems to prepare the Irish economy for a post-Brexit world. Economic interest groups, always vocal on Brexit, responded with considerable urgency to PM May's January 2017 Lancaster speech when it became clear that the UK was heading for a hard Brexit. There was a growing realisation among Irish economic actors that Brexit would bring considerable disruption and that the era of frictionless trade was over.

Important though the economy was, the potential consequences of Brexit for peace on the island of Ireland was the key concern. By November 2016, the Government had established an all-island Civic Dialogue on Brexit which met multiple times and brought together interest groups and civil society organisations from both sides of the Irish border. The formal GFA institutions also began to address Brexit. The North South Ministerial Council dealt with Brexit at a meeting on 18 November 2016 (Joint Statement, 2016). The Council was attended by Northern Ireland's First and Deputy First Ministers, the PM and senior ministers. A High-Level Working Group involving officials from both administrations was established to undertake detailed technical work on issues such as free movement of people and goods, peace funding and the land border.

Throughout the Brexit process, successive Irish prime ministers and senior ministers led the political response to Brexit and never waivered in their core objectives despite the dangers of a no-deal Brexit. A small group of senior civil servants coordinated and led the administrative response across the entire governmental and state system. Enhanced institutional capacity was created and existing institutions were deployed to meet what was considered to be a profound challenge to the country and the island (Ireland, 2017). The response involved deliberative processes with key stakeholders, consistent strategic communication and preparation for all eventualities. The political consensus broadly held and the public opinion overwhelmingly supported the incumbent Government; a poll taken in February 2019 found that 79 per cent of those surveyed agreed to the statement that 'the Irish Government should hold out for a legal guarantee that there will be no hard border between Northern Ireland and the Republic of Ireland even if that risks a no-deal Brexit on March 29th' (McGreevy, 2019). The then Irish government understood that it had the backing of the Irish people and was never tempted to compromise on the core issue of the land border. The display of state capacity and the determination of the Irish political and administrative elite to minimise the damage of Brexit and protect Ireland does not diminish the uncertainty and contingency that characterised the Brexit process. In summer 2016, Dublin did not have a Brexit timeframe, nor did they know what form Brexit would take. There was deep concern that the UK would use the North to get a better deal for the whole of the UK. A senior Irish diplomat speaking in summer 2016, suggested that: 'They will try to pull us out of the EU. They'll make it hard for us to stay in. That would solve the North issue and weaken the EU. The UK is in a very weak position and they'll have to play every card they have. And we are a card' (Connelly, 2017, p. 50). In order to avoid this fate, the Irish sought the backing of EU institutions and its 26 partners. The asymmetric bilateral relationship between London and Dublin could be transformed by Europeanising the border issue.

MULTILEVEL POLITICS: THE EU DIMENSION

Bringing the border issue to the EU table required a coherent and sophisticated strategy from the Dublin Government and its strategy had to be that of a loyal member state. There was considerable paranoia in the EU in the months following the vote and a strong commitment to the 'No Negotiations without Notification' mantra. There was concern that London would try to work though the capitals and divide the member states. Irish politicians and officials were particularly sensitive to this and wanted to avoid anything that might be construed in Brussels as pre-negotiation. Yet Dublin had to maintain contact with London because of their shared responsibility for the implementation of the GFA. When asked at the Bratislava Summit in September 2016, the Irish PM acknowledged that Ireland wanted to 'maintain our cooperation with our European colleagues and, at the same time, maintain our contact and close relationships with the United Kingdom' (Connelly, 2017, p. 65). The latter relationship would be fundamentally altered by Brexit. The first task of the Irish Government was to ensure that its issues and perspectives were understood in Brussels and in the EU capitals.

This involved a determined diplomatic offensive that began in July 2016 and continued throughout the entire Brexit negotiations across different phases. On 12 July 2016, PM Kenny visited Chancellor Merkel in Berlin to begin to prepare for Brexit negotiations once the UK triggered Article 50. The emphasis from the Irish delegation was on the Common Travel Area, the border and the peace process. PM Kenny drew a map of the Irish border for the Chancellor to underline the number of border crossings and the difficulty of policing it. This was followed on 21 July by a visit from President Hollande to Dublin. In the post meeting press conference, President Hollande said that 'I do recognise that there is a special situation in Ireland. It's a special situation that has to be found a place in the negotiations' (Hollande, 2016). The distinctive impact of Brexit on Ireland was beginning to break through.

Dublin understood that although the capitals mattered, EU institutions would play a critical role in the Brexit negotiations. When Michael Barnier took up his role on 1 October, one of the first capitals he visited was Dublin where he met with the Prime Minister, his deputy and the Ministers for Foreign Affairs and European Affairs. The meetings focused on the particular challenges posed by Brexit for the island of Ireland and was part of a lengthy process of putting Ireland on the agenda. The PM said at the time that 'Michel Barnier and the European Commission will have a critically important role to play in the complex negotiations that we now know will begin next spring' ('Taoiseach meets Michel Barnier', 2016). In replying to a parliamentary question on the Barnier visit, the PM further elaborated saying that: 'During our discussion, I took the opportunity to emphasise and explain in some detail Ireland's unique set of concerns arising from Brexit, in relation to Northern Ireland, the peace process, and citizenship issues; the Common Travel Area and border issues; and the depth of our economic and trade relationship with the UK' (Dáil Éireann Debate, 2016). The appointment of Michel Barnier as Chief Negotiator was warmly welcomed in Dublin because he became acquainted with Northern Ireland when Commissioner for Regional Policy. Less than one year later, Michel Barnier addressed the Oireachtas (joint houses of the Irish Parliament), an honour that is usually reserved for heads of state or government. In his speech, Michel Barnier said: 'Today, in front of these two houses, I want to reassure the Irish people: in this negotiation Ireland's interest will be the Union's interest' (Dáil Debates, 2017). The day after this speech, Michel Barnier visited the border and met with key stakeholders who would be affected by a return to the borders of the past.

Reassurance from the EU's Chief Negotiator in such a symbolic setting was critical to the Dublin Government but they also needed to secure the backing of their 26 partners, the other member states. This involved an intensive diplomatic offensive in the period leading up to the opening of the negotiations that brought Irish ministers and officials on multiple visits to the national capitals. By May 2017, the Irish Government had held over 400 discussions on Brexit with EU institutions and Ireland's EU partners (Ireland, 2017, p. 4). This effort was relentless from June 2016 until the negotiations opened a year later. Foreign ministries across Europe were given a crash course on the GFA and its centrality to peace on the island of Ireland. Because of the no negotiation without notification mantra, the Irish diplomatic effort was not matched by an equally intensive effort from London. The Irish Government concluded that their effort was cutting through, saying in May 2017 that: 'This work – one of the largest undertakings of the Irish Government over the last fifty years – has ensured that our priority concerns are now clearly understood throughout the EU' (Ireland, 2017, p. 4). A report from the House of Lords Committee on the EU published in December 2016 had suggested that Britain and Ireland agree a bilateral agreement in parallel with the Article 50 negotiations (House of Lords, 2016). But this was not possible as the border was not just an Irish border but an EU one and Dublin could not simply pre-cook an outcome with London. Senior members of the Irish Government rejected the House of Lords recommendations because as Connelly concluded: 'Ireland had declared for the EU27' (Connelly, 2017, p. 80). Membership of the EU was Ireland's geopolitical shelter and anchor.

By April 2017, the Irish Government had succeeded in Europeanising the issue of the border on the island of Ireland when the EU's negotiating guidelines for the Withdrawal Agreement negotiations were published. Three issues – citizens, budget and Ireland – were identified as requiring resolution before the EU would proceed to negotiate a future relationship with the UK. This was a major diplomatic win for the Government as the issue of the border was no longer an Ireland-UK bilateral issue but an EU27 issue. This flowed from the fact that the Irish border was the only land border the EU would have with the departing UK and of course it was a highly contested border. The EU guidelines stated: 'In view of the unique circumstances on the island of Ireland, flexible and imaginative solutions will be required, including with the aim of avoiding a hard border, while respecting the integrity of the Union legal order' (European Council, 2017a). In response to the nature of the Irish border, the EU was prepared to be flexible and search for imaginative solutions to avoid a return of the borders of the past but only within the Union's legal order and respect for the integrity of the single market. The EU was prepared to be creative but always had two goals that were not necessarily in harmony, namely an invisible border but also integrity of the single market. The EU was fearful that the

UK would use Northern Ireland to try to get a better deal for the whole of the UK, a form of cherry-picking by the backdoor.

BREXIT: THE NEGOTIATIONS

The negotiations and ratification of the withdrawal agreement were fraught. The UK Government issued its letter of notice to the EU on 29 March 2017 (May, 29 March, 2017) and finally left the having ratified the Withdrawal Agreement on 31 January 2020, following a number of extensions. There is no doubt that the challenge of the border on the island of Ireland was the most difficult and contentious issue throughout the negotiations and subsequent ratification process in London. This is because of the intrinsic challenge of managing a contested border that is also an external border of the EU. It would have been easier for any other member state to leave the EU as it could do so whole and entire. The Brexit chosen by the UK is however the main reason that finding a set of arrangements has been so difficult. From the time PM May argued that the UK would leave the single market, the Customs Union and the jurisdiction of the Court of Justice of the European Union (CJEU) and was committed to no border on the island of Ireland, there was a trilemma as checks had to go somewhere.

The EU was determined that the exit negotiations should take place on a phased basis and used the language of 'sufficient progress' as pressure on the UK to reach agreement on the divorce issues before embarking on discussions on the future relationship. Following the formal opening of Brexit negotiations in June 2017, progress was made on citizens' rights followed by a breakthrough on the budgetary issues arising from the UK's departure. Both issues were both highly technical and politically sensitive but it was clear that there was a deal to be achieved. The Irish dossier was proving far more intractable because of the underlying trilemma and the challenge for both sides to come up with solutions that they could both agree. The UK Government issued two interrelated papers in August 2017, one on the future EU-UK Customs relationship and a second on Northern Ireland. The paper on Northern Ireland suggested that there would be 'waivers from security and safety declarations, and ensuring there is no requirement for product standards checks or intellectual property rights checks at the border' (HM Government, 2017). Fintan O'Toole, an astute commentator on Brexit writing in the *Guardian* following the publication of this paper, concluded that: 'As with the whole Brexit project, the proposals for Ireland are credible only if you accept two mutually incompatible propositions: a) The UK is creating the biggest political and economic revolution since 1973; b) pretty much everything will stay the same' (O'Toole, 2017). The EU could not and would not agree to this.

By Autumn 2017, PM May wanted the EU to signal that 'sufficient progress' had been made and move the negotiations onto the future relationship. The EU was determined that this would not happen without parallel progress on all three divorce issues. The European Council meeting on 20 October 2017 concluded that there had been some progress on Northern Ireland but called on the UK 'to present and commit to flexible and imaginative solutions called for by the unique situation of Ireland' (European Council, 2017b). The negotiations would be revisited at a December European Council meeting giving the UK a short timeframe to come up with proposals on its preferred arrangements. Meanwhile the Commission and the Irish Government were working up their proposed solution to the border on the island of Ireland. The concept of a backstop whereby Northern Ireland would remain within the EU's regulatory orbit following Brexit was the core of the solution. The concept was included in a draft joint report agreed by the EU and UK that unravelled in spectacular fashion on Monday 4 December 2017 on the 13th floor of the Berlaymont at a lunch involving the Commission President Jan-Claude Juncker and PM May. While sitting down to lunch, the UK Sherpa, Olly Robbins began to receive multiple messages on his phone that he relayed to PM May. The PM then told those at the meeting that she had a serious problem concerning the draft Joint Report because of objections from the Democratic Unionist Party (DUP) on whom she relied for a parliamentary majority. The lunch was abandoned as the prime minister returned to London (Barnier, 2021, pp. 140–41). The Brexit negotiations were in the throes of the first of many crises caused by the challenge of the border in Ireland.

Over the next week there were intensive talks between London and Brussels on the Joint Report including a visit from Olly Robbins to try to square the circle of the land border. By 6.30 am on Friday 8 December, a formula had been found that both sides could sign up to. However, the formula did not resolve the issue of the Irish border and simply kicked the can down the road. Essentially the Joint Report contained two paragraphs – 49 and 50 – on the Irish border that were not entirely consistent. Article 49 began with a robust UK commitment to 'to protecting North-South cooperation and to its guarantee of avoiding a hard border' (Paragraph 49, EU UK Joint Report, 2017). Paragraph 49 listed three ways that this would be achieved in order of preference. First, the UK wanted to achieve this via the EU-UK future relationship. Second, the UK would propose specific solutions to the unique situation on the island of Ireland and finally, third, if there were no agreed solutions, the 'UK will maintain full alignment with those rules of the Internal Market and the Customs Union which, now or in the future, support North-South cooperation, the all-island economy and the protection of the 1998 Agreement' (Paragraph 49, EU UK Joint Report, 2017). The latter commitment was a robust commitment to avoiding customs and regulatory divergence. To placate the DUP, PM May also committed to 'no new regulatory barriers develop between Northern Ireland and the rest of the United Kingdom' (Paragraph 50, EU UK Joint Report, 2017). PM May struggled and failed to reconcile the dilemma of the Irish border while at the same time adhering to her redlines set out in her Lancaster House speech in January 2017.

If the UK was to leave the EU two years after its March 2017 notification, both sides needed to agree a Withdrawal Treaty by the end of 2018 to leave sufficient time for ratification. The London Government struggled to agree politically on what the future relationship with the EU might look like. The EU on the other hand wanted to translate the Joint Report into legal language and treaty text. Because this could not be agreed jointly with the UK, the EU published a 130-page draft treaty in March 2018 but said that there was 'no agreement on the right operational approach' on the Protocol on Ireland/Northern Ireland (UK Government, 2018). Both sides had settled on the need to avoid a hard border on the island of Ireland but agreement on how to achieve this was extraordinarily complex. The UK Government sought in the Chequers proposals of summer 2018 to achieve this largely via the future relationship with the EU as a whole. However, at the Salzburg Summit in September 2018, it was clear that the EU27 would not agree to the May formula, seeing it as partial membership of the single market with bespoke customs arrangements without the scaffolding of the EU's institutional and legal edifice. With the 'clock ticking', one of the recurrent catch phrases of the Brexit negotiations, the sides entered an intensive period of negotiations in November 2018 that led to a 585-page draft Withdrawal Agreement including a backstop on Ireland/Northern Ireland. The text was endorsed by a special meeting of the European Council on 25 November 2018 (European

Council, 2018a). Speaking after the European Council meeting, President Donald Tusk prophetically said, 'Ahead of us is the difficult process of ratification as well as further negotiations' (Tusk, 2018). Ratification of this Withdrawal Agreement would prove impossible.

THE POLITICS OF RATIFICATION

The EU held the upper hand during the withdrawal negotiations but was powerless to influence the ratification process in the UK. The portends of failure were evident in the weeks following agreement on the treaty text. PM May was forced to call off the House of Commons vote on the agreement which was scheduled for 10 December because of opposition to the Northern Ireland Protocol from a significant number of Conservative MPs and the Unionist DUP. PM May went back to the EU to look for changes. Having painstakingly negotiated the Withdrawal Agreement over many months, the EU at a specially convened meeting of the European Council (Article 50 format) on 13 December, stated that: 'The Union stands by this agreement and intends to proceed with its ratification. It is not open for renegotiation' (European Council, 2018b). The Conclusions of the meeting did however say that the backstop was intended as an insurance policy to avoid a hard border in Ireland and protect the single market and that the EU was ready to search for alternative arrangements to avoid the triggering of the backstop but that if it had to be triggered, it would only be temporarily applied (European Council, 2018b). In December 2018, the EU was committed to trying to address the border on the island of Ireland in ways other than the backstop but only with the backstop as an insurance policy.

In the first half of 2019, PM May attempted to achieve the ratification of the Withdrawal Agreement but was embattled both within her own party and in the House of Commons. In January 2019, she experienced the heaviest defeat in the House of Commons of any prime minister. Opposition to the Protocol on Northern Ireland was at the core of her parliamentary travails. There was a flurry of proposals emanating from her own party, especially the European Research Group (ERG), on alternatives to the backstop. The so-called Malthouse proposals, advocating the use of technology to solve the border challenge, were endorsed by the Conservative Party and the DUP. The Malthouse proposals might have managed to bring the warring sides of the Conservative Party together but did not survive contact with Brussels. The EU was clear that it had examined international border arrangements including the EU's external borders and it was impossible to do away with all border controls and checks at this stage. PM May continued to try to find a way through the parliamentary challenge of ratification asking for and receiving from the EU further clarifications and assurances but to no avail. There was a continuous discussion during this phase that the EU26, fearing a no-deal Brexit, might break with Ireland. The level of solidarity that Ireland experienced from its partners in the EU and the unity of purpose came as a surprise to London.

By May 2019, PM May's efforts to secure ratification of the Withdrawal Agreement came to an end, after three failed attempts, when she announced her resignation. Throughout the ratification period, the Dublin Government was on high alert, aware that the Protocol was at the heart of the failure to get the deal though the House of Commons. There were concerns about the prospect of a no-deal Brexit which would have been very damaging for Ireland and concerns that the unity of the 27 would not hold. In all discussions between the UK and EU institutions, Ireland was kept fully informed and contributed to the EU response. Given the tempestuous nature of UK politics during this time, the Dublin Government felt vindicated in its approach. If it had allowed the border issue to be decided during the negotiations on the future relationship, the fear in Dublin is that London would have used Ireland as a bargaining chip. British-Irish relations were under severe stress at this time. There was little trust left between these two highly connected states and societies that shared responsibility for a vulnerable and troubled place, Northern Ireland. Following PM May's resignation as prime minister in June 2019, Dublin had to await the outcome of the leadership race in the Conservative Party.

BACK TO THE NEGOTIATIONS

Boris Johnson, a leading Brexiteer, won the leadership election and replaced Theresa May as PM under the banner of 'getting Brexit done'. Boris Johnson had famously claimed that Britain could have 'its cake and eat it' and that his 'policy on cake is pro having it and pro eating it' (Dallison, 2017). In his first speech as prime minister, Johnson anticipated a new deal saying: 'we will do a new deal, a better deal that will maximise the opportunities of Brexit while allowing us to develop a new and exciting partnership with the rest of Europe' and this would be a deal without the backstop (Johnson, 2019a). He threatened to take the UK out of the EU with or without a deal on 31 October 2019. His intent was clear in a letter he wrote to President Tusk in August where he made the case for the abolition of the backstop. PM Johnson argued that it was antidemocratic and inconsistent with the sovereignty of the UK, inconsistent with the UK's freedom to diverge from EU regulations and that the backstop risked weakening the GFA (Johnson, 2019b). The letter concluded with the bold statement that the backstop could not form part of a Withdrawal Agreement (Johnson, 2019b). PM Johnson was demanding a renegotiation of the Protocol and the abandonment of a part of the Withdrawal Agreement that the EU was committed to. The arrival of PM Johnson in power was a delicate and tense moment for the Dublin Government.

Boris Johnson began a flurry of diplomatic engagements with Brussels, Berlin, Paris and also Dublin. When in Dublin, PM Johnson refused to acknowledge the Brexit trilemma when he said:

> Can we protect the economic unity of the island of Ireland and the gains that Ireland has won through its membership of the EU single market? And again I think the answer is yes – and I think we can achieve all these things while allowing the UK to withdraw whole and entire from the EU. (Johnson, 2019c)

He wanted to suggest that there were magical solutions to the border challenge that would enable the UK leave the EU without special arrangements for Northern Ireland. This was a period of maximum pressure on Ireland as a UK departure without a deal would raise the question of what the government should do about the border and the protection of the single market. Notwithstanding immense pressure, the Dublin government held firm and continued to receive the active support of EU institutions and its 26 partners. With deadlines looming, a surprise meeting was held on 10 October between Boris Johnson and Irish PM Leo Varadkar in the UK. PM Johnson had run out of time and this meeting clearly indicated that he wanted a deal. The Irish delegation having maintained close contact with Brussels suggested transforming the backstop into a frontstop. Northern Ireland would remain in the EU single market for goods but would be part of the UK customs territory albeit treated as part of the EU customs regime for administrative purposes. In addition, a consent mechanism would be built into the agreement. This was the pathway to a deal that was endorsed by the European Council (Article 50 format) on 17 October 2019. PM Johnson succeeded in altering the backstop but only by establishing a regulatory and customs border on the Irish Sea between Northern Ireland and Great Britain. Boris Johnson achieved his 'sovereignty first' Brexit but only for part of the United Kingdom, leaving Northern Ireland within the EU's regulatory orbit. The DUP objected to the Johnson deal and refused to vote for it. This did not prove decisive as the agreement was passed by the House of Commons on 20 December 2019, enabling the UK to exit the EU on 31 January 2020, completing political Brexit. A transition period that lasted until the 31 December of the same year delayed economic Brexit and it was not until January 2021 that the Protocol and a Trade and Cooperation Agreement (TCA) would come into effect. This did not however solve the challenge of the Irish border. Throughout 2021 the Protocol remained highly contentious and its implementation a source of major friction between the EU and the UK. Once again, the island of Ireland and especially Northern Ireland was in the eye of the Brexit storm.

IMPLEMENTING THE PROTOCOL

The implementation of the Protocol was never going to be smooth or automatic for two reasons. First, it met and continues to meet with fierce resistance from the Unionist community in Northern Ireland who see it as a fundamental change in the constitutional status of Northern Ireland. Although there is a spectrum of opinion among the unionist parties, all oppose the Northern Ireland Protocol. It has already cost Arlene Foster, the leader of the DUP, her leadership when she was forced to resign as First Minister and party leader in April 2021. There was an increase in loyalist riots although not a return to outright violence. Scenes of cars burning and banners saying no to a sea border were reminiscent of an earlier more dangerous time. The second source of contestation over the Protocol was the complexity of implementing the new regime required by the Withdrawal Agreement. In July 2021, the UK asked for negotiations on a new settlement. UK proposals were contained in what was called a Command Paper which argued from the perspective that 'The impact of the Protocol has been profound economically, politically, socially, and commercially' (HM Government, 2021). The Command Paper is effectively a UK request to hollow out the existing Protocol and replace it. This is a remarkable request given that the Protocol was agreed by the UK Government and endorsed by the UK Parliament only at the end of 2019. There was an immediate response from Commission Vice-President Maros Sefcovic, who is responsible for the Protocol. His statement was clear: 'We are ready to continue to seek creative solutions, within the framework of the Protocol, in the interest of all communities in Northern Ireland. However, we will not agree to a renegotiation of the Protocol' (Sefcovic, 2021). The sides are very far apart on the future of the Protocol.

There is recognition in the Commission and in Dublin that there are issues with the Protocol and the EU is willing to engage in a process of trying to find practical solutions that would address the problems of the Protocol that relate to SPS, medicines, customs and the role of Northern Ireland actors in shaping the implementation of the agreement (Institute for Government, 2021). The member states have left it to the Commission to work out the implementation of the treaty although they keep a close eye on developments. The Commission for its part is determined to adopt a sectoral issue by issue problem-solving approach rather than be drawn into noisy contestation with the Johnson Government. The Dublin Government engages with these issues via the Commission, and they work in tandem. From an Irish Government perspective, the hollowing out of the Protocol or a unilateral decision by the UK to disapply elements of the Protocol would be very problematic. Dublin has had to manage its overriding commitment to no hard border on the island of Ireland with the need to maintain its standing in the EU single market. The best outcome from a Dublin perspective is that the Protocol is implemented in an agreed way to avoid further politicisation and a further deterioration of communal relations in Northern Ireland, North-South relations and relations between London and Dublin.

CONCLUSIONS

One hundred years after the establishment of the Irish Free State on 1 January 1921, relations between Ireland and the United Kingdom are fraught. The normalisation of relations that was symbolised by the visit of Queen Elizabeth to Ireland in 2011 has been rent asunder by the consequences of Brexit for the island of Ireland. From the perspective of the UK Government, the border on the island of Ireland proved the most challenging and contentious issue in the Brexit negotiations despite the fact that the border was not a major issue during the referendum. In fact, the Leave campaigners including Boris Johnson denied that there were any challenges at all arising from Brexit for Northern Ireland. Teresa May when prime minister was determined to protect the union of the United Kingdom and was thus willing to compromise on the kind of Brexit she sought although her redlines implied a hard Brexit. Her successor had no such qualms and signed a Withdrawal Agreement that placed a goods border on the Irish Sea. Unionist objections to this were entirely predictable but given the kind of hard Brexit favoured by London, checks and controls had to go somewhere. The contested land border would have raised even greater challenges.

There is no good Brexit for the Irish state or the island of Ireland. Working from that backdrop, the Dublin Government has sought to minimise the adverse consequences and manage the tension involved in being the EU member state with a contested border with the UK. It did so by working hard to make Ireland Brexit ready and to achieving a settlement that recognised the unique circumstances of Northern Ireland. In this process it demonstrated that the small Irish state had considerable state capacity in working the multilevelled and multi-layered politics of Brexit. For the first time in history, Ireland found itself on the stronger side of the negotiating table when dealing with London. Moreover, it received the active support of the EU and the solidarity of its partners during the entire Brexit process. This came as a major surprise to the London Government as they had tried to peel Ireland off from its 26 partners. However, the instability surrounding the Protocol is a major source of instability and concern on the island of Ireland and it is unclear what would happen if the UK breaks its treaty commitments. There remains a battle between the UK Government that wants to hollow out the Protocol, the unionists in Northern Ireland that seek its abolition and the EU27 that want the Withdrawal Agreement implemented. The nature of Brexit and its impact on territorial politics in the UK raises longer-term issues for the island including the possibility of Irish unification. Unification was a possibility under the terms of the Good Friday Agreement but it has moved onto the political agenda in both parts of the island. Hence Brexit may end up being more consequential in the longer term for the island of Ireland than Great Britain.

REFERENCES

Barnier, M. (2021). *La Grande illusion: Journal secret du Brexit*. Gallimard.

Connelly, T. (2017). *Brexit and Ireland*. Penguin.

Dáil Éireann Debate. (2016, 25 October). https://www.oireachtas.ie/en/debates/question/2016-10-25/1/?highlight%5B0%5D=brexit. Accessed 30 September 2022.

Dáil Éireann Debate. (2017, 11 May). https://www.oireachtas.ie/en/debates/debate/dail/2017-05-11/4/. Accessed 30 September 2022.

Dallison P. (2017). 'A Brief History of Having Cake and Eating it', Politico, 31 August, https://www.politico.eu/article/a-brief-history-of-having-cake-and-eating-it// Accessed 30 September 2022.

European Commission. (2017). *Joint report from the negotiators of the European Union and the United Kingdom Government*. https://ec.europa.eu/info/sites/default/files/joint_report.pdf. Accessed 30 September 2022

European Council. (2017a, 29 April). *European Council (Art. 50) guidelines for Brexit negotiation* [Press release]. http://www.consilium.europa.eu/en/press/press-releases/2017/04/29-euco-brexit-guidelines/. Accessed 30 September 2022.

European Council. (2017b, 20 October). *European Council (Art 50) conclusions meeting (20 October 2017)*. https://www.consilium.europa.eu/media/23512/20-euco-conclusions-art50.pdf. Accessed 30 September 2022.

European Council. (2018a, 25 November). *European Council (Art 50) conclusions, 25 November 2018* [Press release]. https://www.consilium.europa.eu/en/press/press-releases/2018/11/25/european-council-art-50-conclusions-25-november-2018/. Accessed 30 September 2022.

European Council. (2018b, December 13). *Special meeting of the European Council (Art. 50) (13 December 2018) – Conclusions*. https://data.consilium.europa.eu/doc/document/XT-20022-2018-INIT/en/pdf. Accessed 30 September 2022.

Hayward, K. (2021). *The Irish Border*. Sage.

HM Government. (2017), Northern Ireland and Ireland: Position Paper. https://assets.publishing.service.gov.uk/government/uploads/system/uploads/attachment_data/file/638135/6.3703_DEXEU_Northern_Ireland_and_Ireland_INTERACTIVE.pdf. Accessed 30 September 2022.

HM Government. (2021). Northern Ireland Protocol: the way forward. https://assets.publishing.service.gov.uk/government/uploads/system/uploads/attachment_data/file/1004581/CCS207_CCS0721914902-001_Northern_Ireland_Protocol_PRINT__1___2_.pdf. Accessed 30 September 2022.

Hollande, F. (2016, 21 July). Trigger Brexit 'as soon as possible', Hollande and Kenny tell UK. *The Irish Times*. https://www.irishtimes.com/news/politics/trigger-brexit-as-soon-as-possible-hollande-and-kenny-tell-uk-1.2729559. Accessed 30 September 2022.

House of Lords. (2016). *European Union Committee Brexit: UK-Irish Relations* (6th Report Session 2016/17, HL Paper 76). https://publications.parliament.uk/pa/ld201617/ldselect/ldeucom/76/7602.htm. Accessed 30 September 2022.

Institute for Government. (2021). Northern Ireland Protocol: ongoing UK–EU disagreements. Retrieved 15 October 2021 from https://www.instituteforgovernment.org.uk/explainers/northern-ireland-protocol-disagreements. Accessed 30 September 2022.

Ireland (2016) Government Press Release, 24 June 2016, https://merrionstreet.ie/en/news-room/news/government_brexit_contingency_plans_announced.html Accessed 30 September 2022.

Ireland and the negotiations on the UK's withdrawal from the European Union: The Government's Approach. (2017, May). *Merrion Street*. https://merrionstreet.ie/en/eu-uk/key_irish_documents/government_approach_to_brexit_negotiations.pdf. Accessed 30 September 2022.

Johnson B. (2019a, 24 July). *First speech as Prime Minister* [Speech transcription]. UK Government. https://www.gov.uk/government/speeches/boris-johnsons-first-speech-as-prime-minister-24-july-2019. Accessed 30 September 2022.

Johnson, B. (2019b, 19 August). *PM letter to Donald Tusk: 19 August 2019* [Letter]. UK Government. https://www.gov.uk/government/publications/pm-letter-to-donald-tusk-19-august-2019. Accessed 30 September 2022.

Johnson, B. (2019c, 9 September). *PM press statement with Taoiseach Varadkar: 9 September 2019* [Press statement]. WIREDGOV. https://www.wired-gov.net/wg/news.nsf/articles/PM+press

+statement+with+Taoiseach+Leo+Varadkar+9+September+2019+09092019134300?open. Accessed 30 September 2022.

Katzenstein, P.J. (1985). *Small States in World Markets: Industrial Policy in Europe*. Cornell University Press.

Kenny, E. (2016a). *Taoiseach on UK Vote to Leave European Union* [Speech]. https://merrionstreet.ie/en/news-room/news/government_statement_on_the_outcome_of_the_uk_eu_referendum.html. Accessed 30 September 2022.

Kenny, E. (2016b, 27 June). *Statement in the Dáil on the UK EU Referendum Result by the Taoiseach, Mr Enda Kenny TD, Monday, 27 June, 2016* [Speech]. https://merrionstreet.ie/merrionstreet/en/news-room/speeches/statement_in_the_dail_on_the_uk_eu_referendum_result_by_the_taoiseach_mr_enda_kenny_td_monday_27_june_2016.html. Accessed 30 September, 2022.

Mackinder, H.J. (1890). The physical basis of political geography. *Scottish Geographical Magazine*, 6(2), 78–84. https://doi.org/10.1080/14702549008554692.

May, T. (2017, 29 March). *Prime Minister's letter to Donald Tusk triggering Article 50* [Letter]. UK Government. https://www.gov.uk/government/publications/prime-ministers-letter-to-donald-tusk-triggering-article-50. Accessed 30 September 2022.

McGreevy, R. (2019, 8 February). Opinion poll shows majority strongly support Government stance on Brexit. *The Irish Times*. https://www.irishtimes.com/news/ireland/irish-news/opinion-poll-shows-majority-strongly-support-government-stance-on-brexit-1.3786939. Accessed 30 September 2022.

O'Toole, F. (2017, 16 August). The UK government's border proposals for Ireland are absurd. *Guardian*. https://www.theguardian.com/commentisfree/2017/aug/16/uk-government-border-proposals-ireland-brexit-position-paper. Accessed 30 September 2022.

Sefcovic, M. (2021, July 21). Statement by Vice-President Maroš Šefčovič following today's announcement by the UK government regarding the Protocol on Ireland/Northern Ireland. *European Commission*. https://ec.europa.eu/commission/presscorner/detail/en/statement_21_3821. Accessed 30 September 2022.

Skocpol, T., Evans, P., and Rueschemeyer, D. (1999). *Bringing the State Back*. Cambridge University Press.

Sloan, G., and Gray, C.S. (1999). Why geopolitics? *The Journal of Strategic Studies*, 22(2–3), 1–11. https://doi.org/10.1080/01402399908437751.

Taoiseach meets Michel Barnier. (2016, 12 October). *Marrion Street*. https://merrionstreet.ie/en/news-room/news/taoiseach_meets_michel_barnier.html. Accessed 30 September 2022.

Thorhalsson, B. (2011). Domestic buffer versus external shelter: Viability of small states in the new globalised economy. *European Political Science*, 10, 324–36. https://doi.org/10.1057/eps.2011.29.

Tusk, D. (2018, 25 November). Remarks by President Donald Tusk after the special meeting of the European Council (Art. 50) on 25 November 2018 [Statement]. *European Commission*. https://www.consilium.europa.eu/en/press/press-releases/2018/11/25/remarks-by-president-donald-tusk-after-the-european-council-art-50-meeting/. Accessed 30 September 2022.

UK Government. (2018). Draft Agreement on the withdrawal of the United Kingdom of Great Britain and Northern Ireland from the European Union and the European Atomic Energy Community. https://assets.publishing.service.gov.uk/government/uploads/system/uploads/attachment_data/file/691366/20180319_DRAFT_WITHDRAWAL_AGREEMENT.pdf. Accessed 30 September 2022.

15. Germany and Brexit

Uwe Puetter

INTRODUCTION

The departure of the United Kingdom (UK) from the European Union (EU) triggers questions of how this event may affect the roles of other member states in EU politics and in individual processes of EU policy-making. Moreover, there could be implications for the EU's wider political and legal order. The UK formed, together with France and Germany, the group of the EU's three largest member states, also referred to as 'E3'. The UK represented considerable economic weight, made substantial contributions to the EU budget and brought important resources in foreign, security and defence policy to the Union. The country was both a close partner and adversary to other member states. EU intergovernmental relations, thus, are affected by Brexit and so are policy choices and future decisions about institutional reform.

Particular attention needs to be given to the case of Germany and its interaction with Britain during the time of the latter's EU membership and thereafter. Both countries acted jointly in relation to the development of the single market, as the cornerstone of the EU economy. They have shared common security and defence interests and have advocated Atlanticism, alignment with NATO and the strengthening of European capabilities within that alliance. Together with France, the UK and Germany accounted for the largest diplomatic and military components of the EU's nascent foreign, security and defence policy. During the time of the UK's EU membership Germany and Britain opted for considerably different long-term visions of EU integration, though, with consequences for institution-building and policy choices. This was exemplified by the difficult negotiations and compromises surrounding the adoption of the Treaty of Maastricht with its focus on a novel Economic and Monetary Union (EMU), an enhanced EU social policy and closer integrated justice and home affairs policies. The UK advocated rapid Eastern enlargement and free movement without transition periods, while Germany was initially more cautious and sought to hedge its domestic labour market from the immediate influx of inner-EU migration. In the 2010s this trend was reversed. UK politics witnessed a hardening stance against inner-EU labour mobility while Germany sought to uphold freedom of movement. Whatever the commonalities and quarrels were, there is little doubt that bilateral relations between the UK and Germany have affected EU politics and governance. Brexit implies that bilateral relations between the two countries are going to evolve outside the EU's institutional framework but nevertheless may have important repercussions for EU policy-making. Moreover, Brexit affects internal EU dynamics. The UK can no longer be a partner to Germany in pursuing leadership of the Union, nor an adversary who could counterbalance German influence in EU politics, thus encouraging coalition-building between member states of different sizes. This chapter reviews how Brexit affects Germany's role in EU politics and governance and discusses what this means for EU integration more broadly.

This chapter argues that the consequences of Brexit for Germany's role in EU politics and governance should not ignore the first, and in particular, the second decades of the 2000s. Many consequences for Germany's role within EU politics, which can be linked to Brexit, started to materialise before the actual departure of the UK and continue to remain relevant thereafter. Moreover, this chapter argues that Brexit negotiations are a prominent example of Germany's contemporary EU policy: if pressed hard, German governing elites choose EU unity over unilateralism or, in this case, exclusive bilateral deals or alignments with the UK.

Brexit thus is predicted to affect Germany's role in EU governance and the country's attempts in shaping the EU's political and legal order along the lines of more recent trends in EU politics. Issues such as potential German hegemony in EU politics, the country's close alignment with other major powers within the EU, such as France, as well as Germany's individual relations with the UK have to be considered in the light of recent major events in EU integration other than Brexit. Here, it is important to distinguish between EU policy domains, notably between classical single market integration and the new areas of EU activity, such as EMU, the EU's common foreign and security policy (CFSP), and justice and home affairs.

FROM ENGAGEMENT TO DISENGAGEMENT: FROM END OF THE 1990S TO THE 2010S

How much does the actual event of the UK leaving the EU as a member state actually matter for understanding Germany's role in EU politics and governance? How important were alignments and antagonisms between the two countries in the recent past? Before discussing these questions in relation to the process of Brexit negotiations and the evolution of individual EU policy domains, this section provides a broad overview of the change from a period of closer engagement between British and German governing elites on EU issues to a period of apparent disengagement. The latter period began long before the actual event of Brexit and coincides with important changes in EU intergovernmental politics during the second decade of the 2000s.

Perhaps it was the time of UK Prime Minister Tony Blair and German Chancellor Gerhard Schröder, when both tried to lobby for a permanent president of the European Council in the context of the Convention on the Future of Europe, when German-UK intergovernmental relations could be said to have been more enthusiastic. Moreover, by the end of the 1990s the two politicians and their governments had agreed to a whole set of compromise formulas in European integration. Especially in the domain of EU socio-economic governance many issues were closely related to Tony Blair's and Gerhard Schröder's own projects of partisan renewal. The so-called Lisbon agenda and the open method of coordination were major policy initiatives, which sought to overcome the post-Maastricht hangover caused by the deep divides over the creation of EMU and EU social policy. For German pro-EU governing elites both projects had been crucial during the Helmut Kohl era. The very same projects were seen as fatal exaggerations of European integration in the eyes of most Conservatives within the UK's political class but also lacked unequivocal backing from the Labour opposition. Tony Blair had changed at least the rhetoric on the euro, even though there was no real prospect of imminent policy change. However, the EU's revamped and distinctively 'soft' (cf. among many others Jacobsson, 2004) socio-economic governance framework of the early 2000s had helped to successfully paper over some of the earlier divides between British and German governing elites. Tony Blair's drive to create New Labour and Gerhard Schröder's later attempts at pursuing the Hartz reforms to revive the German labour market certainly made them like-minded politicians who could relate to each other in new ways. From a German point of view, no previous UK government had done so much to engage with Europe constructively. Frosini and Gilbert (2020, p. 770), for example, point out that '[i]ndeed, Britain became a more "European" place in the 2000s'.

Yet, the attempt at turning the outcome of the Convention on the Future of Europe into a Constitutional Treaty already showed the limits of this reproachment. Still some years away from the first hard test of the Eurozone's still nascent economic governance framework it was apparent where the fault lines were: on the surface Germany's reluctance to touch issues, such as Eurozone fiscal transfers or the reform of the Stability and Growth Pact (SGP),[1] was compatible with UK visions under New Labour of an EU economic governance regime which relied on benchmarking and reform stimuli rather than on hard rules and transfers. However, the discussion surrounding the Constitutional Treaty in the early 2000s also revealed important differences. Governing elites in Berlin were clearly more attached, if not committed, to the long-term goal of further EU constitutionalisation and institutionalisation while British concerns about a looming federalisation of the EU had not vanished, despite Blair's novel engagement with EU politics. These differences, which later moved to the centre of the Brexit debate in the UK, were not trivial. Schmidt (2020), for example, emphasises the fundamental differences in British and German understandings of sovereignty as either parliamentary sovereignty or constitutional sovereignty. She concludes that '[f]or Germans, used to obeying their constitutional court in Karlsruhe, it is a small step to accept that the ECJ [European Court of Justice] rules instead' (ibid., p. 782) whereas she sees 'a significant institutional mismatch' (ibid., p. 780) between the ECJ's understanding of the order of competence in the EU and British conceptions of parliamentary sovereignty.

These fundamental institutional issues aside, it was the invasion of Iraq during the first half of 2003 which implied a rupture in the Blair-Schröder relationship. British Prime Minister Tony Blair sided with the US and joined a bilateral military coalition with them to pursue the military campaign while German Chancellor Gerhard Schröder aligned himself with French President Jacques Chirac to oppose the invasion. Hence, the EU's most important military powers were divided in relation to a major foreign policy issue and, thus, efforts to come to more ambitious cooperation in the domain of the EU's CFSP had received a serious blow. This was all the more important as CFSP was the only major post-Maastricht EU policy domain through which the UK, as a non-euro member state, could have aligned itself with other larger member states, notably France and Germany, to provide leadership within the wider EU.

The second half of the first decade of the 2000s was marked by the EU's difficulties to ratify the Lisbon Treaty and led policy-makers to avoid open confrontations about the EU's future institutional architecture and competences. This was different in the 2010s. In the UK Conservative Prime Minister David Cameron came to power and the EU was hit by some of its hardest crises. These crises laid bare the extent of British disengagement with core EU policies and, also, politics. At the same time, Germany and its Chancellor Angela Merkel moved centre stage in the most dramatic moments of EU decision-making in the context of the so-called euro and migration crises. Most importantly, when pressed to make unavoidable decisions on institutional reform and to safeguard EU unity and the integrity of the Eurozone, Germany moved decisively (even if with delay) while UK disengagement with EU affairs became apparent. The incident of the adoption of the Treaty on Stability, Coordination and Governance in EMU, also referred to as the Fiscal Compact or Fiscal Treaty, can be seen as a watershed in this regard. When the European Council wanted to react to the further escalating euro crisis with a set of institutional reforms, which were to be implemented through changes to the Lisbon Treaty, British Prime Minister David Cameron signalled his veto in December 2011 (Hodson and Puetter, 2019, pp. 399–400). The other European Council members wasted no time and implemented the envisaged treaty changes through an intergovernmental treaty outside the framework of EU law.[2] The episode illustrates how detached Britain had become from EU intergovernmental politics by the beginning of the second decade of the 2000s. David Cameron's move had neither influenced policy nor had altered coalition-building among other EU member states. The Prime Minister had indeed prevented formal treaty change but had had to accept de facto treaty change.

Contrasting the late 1990s, on the one hand, with the beginning of the 2010s and the adoption of the Fiscal Treaty as an intergovernmental treaty outside EU law, on the other hand, can help to frame the broader question of how Brexit affects Germany's role in EU politics. What is particularly noteworthy in this regard is that while the late 1990s and early 2000s provided examples of German-UK alignment for agreeing policy (the Lisbon agenda and related coordination projects in the sphere of socio-economic governance) or disagreement (as evident in relation to the invasion of Iraq and the question of free movement of labour in the immediate aftermath of the 2004 enlargement), the example of the Fiscal Treaty shows that the question of bilateral engagement (either alignment or opposition) is almost irrelevant from the point of view of all other EU member states. Germany and the vast majority of EU member states adopted a hard-line position in relation to the question of circumventing Britain. This suggests that Brexit, if seen as the distinct event of the eventual departure of Britain from the Union, is less relevant for changes in EU intergovernmental politics than it may be assumed. However, if Brexit is understood as a longer process of which tremors were being felt throughout David Cameron's time as UK Prime Minister and leader of the Tories, even before the referendum, then the progressive withdrawal of the UK from EU politics in the 2010s deserves attention. For Germany's role in EU politics this means that its role after the actual event of Brexit, the formal act of leaving, is likely to resemble its role in EU politics in the 2010s.

GERMANY'S ROLE IN THE BREXIT PROCESS

A first test case is the negotiation of the terms of Brexit. Did bilateral interaction between Germany and the UK matter for this in any way or rather not? This section highlights the striking absence of Germany as an independent voice in the Brexit negotiations. There is almost no evidence of the country seeking to secure particular relative advantages for its export-oriented economy. Germany's close economic ties with Britain apparently did not trigger bilateral political engagement with the aim of influencing the negotiation outcome and, thus, the EU's common position. Three plausible, and partially interrelated, explanations emerge in this regard. (1) First, Germany had an overarching interest to keep the EU united and therefore accepted that it could not use Brexit as an occasion to advance particular interests in relation to the future economic and political relations between the EU and the UK. (2) Second, the government was not seriously challenged in this position at the domestic level as there was limited to no pressure from potentially powerful lobbies. (3) Third and finally, the German government had little to no trust in any of the potential UK counterparts with whom it would have been able to forge closer bilateral ties while Brexit negotiations were unfolding because of a preceding and prolonged period of disengagement on EU politics, which could not be credibly be reverted by the Theresa May and Boris Johnson governments.

GERMANY CHOOSES EU UNITY OVER INDIVIDUAL LEVERAGE

That Germany preferred EU unity over individual leverage over the Brexit negotiations is evident in the choice of the institutional set-up. Throughout the post-Maastricht period Germany has been instrumental in giving rise to the EU's new intergovernmentalism and has preferred collective decision-making in new areas of EU activity over delegation to traditional supranational institutions (Puetter, 2014). The long reign of the Christian democratic Chancellor Angela Merkel in the first two decades of the 2000s, notably her role in the context of the euro crisis, provided ample examples for how Germany's governing elites have contributed to reinforcing and shaping the practices of the post-Maastricht intergovernmentalism. Brexit was different. In this case Chancellor Angela Merkel decided otherwise. Schuette's (2021) analysis of Commission leadership in the Brexit negotiations rightly points to the limited role member states and the European Council, in particular, played in relation to determining the particular negotiation mode. Most importantly, he argues that the Commission could exercise considerable political leadership not only with regard to handling the negotiations with the UK but also with regard to exercising political leadership inside the EU and vis-à-vis the member states. It is in this context that Schuette emphasises that the Commission's role in Brexit negotiations deviated from institutional dynamics, identified by new intergovernmentalism (Bickerton et al., 2015a; Puetter and Fabbrini, 2016) and new institutional leadership theory (Smeets and Beach, 2020).

The choice of delegation to the Commission is especially interesting as the desire of the European Council to stay in close control of UK-related EU policies was still very much detectable when the EU had sought to respond to David Cameron's initial attempt at renegotiating aspects of the UK's terms and conditions of EU membership in 2015–16. Here the European Council, according to Beach and Smeets (2020, p. 460), 'informally delegated authority to a small, informal network of EU institutional actors' instead of formally putting the Commission in charge.

Choosing delegation to the Commission over close monitoring by the European Council suggests that the Angela Merkel government, indeed, preferred to emphasise EU unity and that it also regarded the overall process of Brexit negotiations not as an instance of utmost priority or even of EU crisis management. When UK Prime Minister David Cameron had sought the renegotiation of the terms of UK membership in 2015–16 there was still some sense that it was necessary for the European Council to prevent a potential Brexit, even if only through concessions which would have been a severe test for the integrity of the EU's acquis and the so-called four freedoms.

On closer inspection, delegation to the Commission in relation to the Brexit negotiations also appears in line with new intergovernmentalist theory (Bickerton et al., 2015a; Puetter, 2014), which expects resistance to delegation to appear predominantly in new, post-Maastricht areas of EU activity, such as Eurozone economic governance, rather than in the domain of single market governance. The latter is expected to broadly follow the pattern of the classical community method. As the UK was not a member of the Eurozone, the focus in the Brexit negotiations was clearly on classical single market issues, such as privileged access, acceptance of EU rules and respect for competences of EU institutions.

Moreover, with David Cameron failing to deliver a majority for the remain campaign, the German government had little to expect from centralising Brexit negotiations within the European Council. At least there is strong evidence that the UK internally faced enormous difficulties to come up with a coherent approach towards the Brexit negotiations, which would have allowed the country's most senior political representatives to speak with authority when meeting their counterparts in other EU member states, including Germany. Nowhere was this clearer as in relation to the term of office Theresa May served as UK Prime Minister. McConnel and Tormey (2020), for example, see Brexit as a 'policy fiasco' and consider three explanations which all relate to UK domestic politics: '(i) Brexit as an impossible policy challenge, (ii) ineffectual leadership by Theresa May who took poor decisions and avoided plausible alternatives, and (iii) Westminster as a partisan-fuelled institution incapable of reaching agreement on such a bi-partisan issue' (ibid., p. 685).

To conclude, despite Germany's role as the largest EU member state, there is no evidence that the government of Chancellor Angela Merkel sought to exercise tight control over Brexit negotiations, as it did in relation to other major instances of EU decision-making in the more recent past, such as in the context of the euro crisis. Instead, delegation to the Commission was a plausible option for Germany, as it has traditionally championed the single market and respect of the four freedoms. Moreover, the domestic political situation in the UK also meant that potential bilateral high-level contacts between the UK Prime Minister and the German Chancellor could not emerge. In fact, closer high-level coordination on major EU policy issues between Germany and the UK already had been absent before Brexit, as the experience of the euro crisis and the Fiscal Treaty suggests.

DOMESTIC ECONOMIC INTERESTS AND GOVERNMENT POLICY

A potential factor that could have contributed to Germany adopting a more interventionist stance in relation to the Brexit negotiations is the country's economic relations with the UK. Germany's export dependent industry could have been expected to suffer significantly as a result of Brexit. This could have triggered potential lobbying efforts on the part of German industry or particular business sectors with the aim to achieve a soft Brexit at all costs. Such expectations would be in line with a liberal intergovernmentalist notion of EU decision-making as a two-level game. However, there is no evidence that Brexit was a two-level game for the German government. On the contrary, and as in the case of the euro crisis (Csehi and Puetter, 2021), the federal government enjoyed considerable leeway in relation to Brexit and did not face domestic pressure from interest groups and public opinion.

While Walter (2021, p. 569) quotes a 2018 study from Chen et al. (2018), which indicates a 5.5 per cent drop in German GDP as a consequence of a so-called hard Brexit, other estimates, which were available to decision-makers during the negotiations, were much less pessimistic. A 2017 study by the German economics institute 'ifo' (Felbermayr et al., 2017), which was commissioned by the German Federal Ministry of Economics and Energy, estimates that changes in German real GDP due to Brexit roughly correspond to the changes computed for the EU27 average. This applies both to a so-called hard Brexit and soft Brexit scenarios. Compared to the estimated impact on the UK's own economy the expected damage to the German economy is limited, as compensatory effects are foreseen to kick in. For example, while the study estimates a 1.73 per cent drop in real GDP for the UK in the case of the most radical hard Brexit scenario (World Trade Organization rules apply for trade with the EU and major Western trading partners), it is only minus 0.26 per cent for German GDP (Felbermayr et al., 2017, p. 69). This compares with the scenarios for soft Brexit, which predict a drop in UK GDP between 0.36 per cent and 0.65 per cent while the negative effect for Germany is between 0.07 and 0.12 per cent of GDP (ibid.). Similar figures are also quoted by a study commissioned by the European Parliament (European Parliament, 2017, p. 33). Moreover, the 'ifo' study shows that the impact of Brexit on individual sectors of the German economy is uneven. While some sectors, such as pharmaceuticals, are exposed more, others, such as electronics, are not at all. More generally, services are less exposed than industrial production (Felbermayr et al., 2017, pp. 71–5). The study even sees a potential 'minor positive effect' (ibid., p. 74) in case of a soft Brexit on the German car industry and points to potential growth in some domains, such as finance, in case of both a hard or soft Brexit (ibid., p. 75).

To summarise, German decision-makers were aware of the overall negative impact of Brexit on the German economy, but they also could expect this effect to be very similar to the impact of Brexit on the entire EU27. Most importantly, compared to the losses predicted to occur to the UK economy the damage expected to materialise for the entire EU27 and the German economy was much more contained, suggesting that the UK had a greater interest in seeking a deal with the EU than vice versa. Moreover, the estimated varied impact on the different sectors of the German economy did not suggest a particular negotiation strategy, apart from the idea that damage limitation, meaning a soft Brexit, was preferrable to outright negotiation failure. However, the – compared to the UK – much narrower gap between the different possible outcomes do not suggest that the German government must have in any way felt the need to adopt a negotiation position which would have jeopardised the EU unity.

Further explanations for the lack of domestic pressure on the German federal government to intervene on behalf of German business can be found in a case study on the financial industry, a domain which was even tipped to offer potential gains from Brexit. Lavery et al. (2019) investigate the role of Frankfurt as a financial centre in Brexit politics. They distinguish between the preferences of economic and political actors (ibid., p. 1507). In relation to the latter group they emphasise the importance of sub-national actors. The three authors caution against the notion of the German federal government being particularly focussed on the idea of attracting parts of the financial industry, which was previously based in the City of London, to Germany's financial centre, Frankfurt. Lavery et al. (2019, p. 1509) instead see evidence from their interview database that there was only 'very minimal involvement' on the part of the German federal government. The authors explain this with the federal and decentralised structure of Germany. Only the Frankfurt city government and the Hesse state government were engaged in serious promotion and lobby activities. Moreover, the research suggests that there was no coherent position among the various actors within Germany's financial industry (ibid.). While transnational banks, such as Deutsche Bank, were primarily worried about potential regulatory fragmentation within the EU due to enhanced competition between member states after Brexit, the authors only detect a primary desire for political intervention to strengthen Frankfurt as a financial centre on the part of one key local financial institution. All this suggests that direct pressure on the German government to act in a particular way in relation to Brexit, or even to break away from the objective of EU unity, was limited.

Public interventions by major German business lobby groups regarding Brexit also do suggest that economic interests were not formulated in competition with the government's policy to keep the EU together and to protect the regulatory model of the single market. The German umbrella organisation of German industry lobbies, the Bundesverband der Deutschen Industrie (BDI), even backed the government's approach to Brexit negotiations unambiguously. In a press statement in March 2017 BDI president Dieter Kempf declared: 'For policy-makers in Brussels and Berlin there needs to be only one objective: keep Europe united and reinforce it … Europe is in no way the problem but Europe rather helps us to solve problems' (Bundesverband der deutschen Industrie e.V., 2017). In an interview with *The Observer* a few months later he reiterated this message and highlighted that the 'integrity of the single market and its four freedoms' (The Guardian, 9 July 2017) were the absolute priorities for German industry. In the same newspaper article another top lobbyist of German industry, the president of the German employers' associations, Bundesvereinigung der Deutschen Arbeitgeberverbände (BDA), Ingo Kramer stated: '[t]he cohesion of the remaining 27 EU member states has highest priority' (ibid.).

Another factor that might have mattered for the positioning of the German government is public opinion. As Walter (2021) highlights, people may have worried about the consequences of Brexit. Based on her research, Walter, however, concludes that EU citizens by-and-large not only considered the economic effects of Brexit but also its political fall-out: '[t]he more they [the citizens] care about the viability of the EU, the less accommodating they are' (Walter, 2021, p. 584). Walter sees that this 'accommodation dilemma moderates Europeans' Brexit-related preferences' (ibid.). This effect may indeed explain why Brexit was not a controversial issue in German domestic discourse.

GERMANY'S ROLE IN EU POLITICS AFTER BREXIT

An obvious consequence of Brexit is that it reduces the group of the EU's largest member states. In relation to Germany's role in EU politics and in particular in relation to the EU's post-Maastricht governance practice of new intergovernmentalism, this aspect may be considered as relevant along two dimensions:

1. The first dimension concerns Germany's loss of a potentially powerful ally to push ahead with major initiatives, specifically in the domain of the EU's CFSP. France, Germany and the UK had a specific role as the E3, exemplified in the negotiations on Iran's nuclear programme. Together with Italy they formed the group of the EU's G7 members and most populated EU member states. In relation to this first dimension, the question thus arises whether and how Brexit affects Germany's role in EU politics as a potentially dominant member state as part of a small group of big member states. The discussions at the advent of the Convention on the Future of Europe and the eventual provisions on double majority voting, which were later implemented with the Treaty of Lisbon, probably reflect this notion in relation to the EU's internal political order best.
2. The second dimension of Brexit in relation to the question of how far the UK's departure matters with respect to the role of the EU's largest member states in EU politics implies the opposite scenario: the potential non-alignment of the EU's largest member states (or some of them) is also a mechanism of introducing important checks and balances in EU intergovernmental relations. Seen in this way, the departure of the UK rather contributes to an increase in Germany's individual weight in EU politics.

Even though these two dimensions seem to represent obvious points of reference when assessing the consequences of Brexit, it is important not to revert to broad-brush views of EU politics too easily. Rather it makes sense to consider EU intergovernmental dynamics, and notably German-UK bilateral interactions, according to different EU policy areas. Moreover, it is important to adopt a longer time horizon when considering the implications of Brexit for EU politics and Germany's role within them. As suggested in the section 'From Engagement to Disengagement', some of the key consequences of Brexit have been felt ever since the Cameron years. In particular, the UK's disengagement with EU politics can be traced in some of the EU's biggest crisis moments in the 2010s and early 2020s. The domains of single market policies, EMU governance, and decision-making on foreign, security and defence policy issues are considered here in turn.

SINGLE MARKET POLICIES

With regard to single market governance the evolution of post-Brexit bilateral relations between Germany and the UK could become relevant in future attempts at readjusting the EU-UK relationship. As witnessed in the Brexit negotiations, the argument that Germany and the UK, as major trading partners, have a particular interest in forging close bilateral ties in order to develop common views on regulatory issues or questions of EU-UK trade relations is unlikely to carry much weight. Seen from the experience of Brexit negotiations, Germany is unlikely to sacrifice its objective to preserve the integrity of the EU's single market and to break away from its view that EU unity is more important than uncertain and rather limited comparative advantages. Moreover, even though there is little hard data on this in terms of actual cost-benefit calculations, the German economy may have fewer problems in adjusting to changed trade relations post-Brexit than the most pessimistic scenarios implied. At least there is no evidence of major German economic lobbies pushing the federal government to deviate from its policy during the Brexit negotiations. Finally, single market governance has to be seen in the broader context of EU institutional politics. As a domain of classical community decision-making it is exposed to different dynamics than new, post-Maastricht areas of EU activity, such as EMU and CFSP. Germany does not challenge the principle of delegation of regulatory powers to supranational institutions, such as the Commission and the Court of Justice in this policy domain. It rather is eager to preserve this aspect of the EU's institutional order. The departure of the UK, nevertheless, potentially changes decision-making on single market issues among the remaining EU27 member states. However, there had been limited evidence of German-UK alignment with the aim, for example, to block decisions as a tandem of two large member states before Brexit (European Parliament, 2019, p. 14).

EMU AND EUROZONE POLITICS

EMU has become one of the most important policy domains in EU politics. Its governance structure is dominated by new intergovernmentalism (Bickerton et al., 2015b; Puetter, 2012). Member states seek to control major policy decisions through the European Council and the Eurogroup while they decide predominantly by consensus. Somewhat ironically, the impact of Brexit in this domain remains limited. In the same way, the role of Germany in EMU politics has not been substantially affected by Brexit. Eurozone member states were consistent and unanimous in their rejection of UK political influence on EMU politics since the late 1990s when they founded the Eurogroup with the objective to forge decisions among themselves

(Puetter, 2006). In the 2010s the institutional reforms linked to the euro crisis further reinforced these tendencies. The creation of the Euro Summit format during the peak period of the euro crisis (Hodson and Puetter, 2019) underlined the determination of Eurozone countries to circumvent any potential veto threats at the level of the European Council when it came to preserving the integrity of the euro crisis. For German-UK relations that means that long before the actual event of the formal departure of the UK from the EU the influence of bilateral relations on Eurozone and EU politics was limited. If anything, German Chancellor Angela Merkel's decisions in the 2010s to defend the integrity of the Eurozone also against domestic political pressure (Merkel, 2010) sent an important signal to the UK that for Germany the Eurozone had become the centre piece of EU politics, implying that the EU's overall institutional design had to follow considerations of Eurozone governance if and when needed. Germany's Eurozone policy has been consistent since then and was reconfirmed by its role in negotiating the EU's COVID-19 aid package Next Generation EU in the summer of 2020. The country is determined to defend the integrity of the Eurozone financially and politically and is likely to do so in the future. At the same time, other Eurozone governments remain dependent on Germany as a central actor in Eurozone politics. Here, alignment with other key players, notably France, is likely to continue to matter (see section 'Conclusions'). Brexit, thus, does little to affect Germany's role in Eurozone politics in the 2020s.

One particular aspect of Eurozone governance, however, which may indeed encourage closer bilateral ties between Germany and the UK, is the coordination in global and international financial institutions and forums. Here, coordinated policy responses of Eurozone countries and the UK did occur prior to Brexit (Hodson, 2011). Being both members of the G7, the G20 and important actors within the International Monetary Fund, Germany and the UK are likely to find new ways to increase bilateral information exchange in the domain of global finance and systemic stability. Yet, the scope for developing bilateral positions, which would challenge or influence EU internal decision-making, is likely to be limited. Moreover, a key question is whether the UK ultimately agrees to and engages in direct and regular exchanges with Eurozone institutions, notably the Eurogroup president, the European Central Bank and the Commission. The initial reluctance of the Boris Johnson government to establish closer coordination with EU and Eurozone representatives might be easier to overcome in relation to issues concerning the global financial institutions and forums, than, for example, in relation to issues pertaining to single market governance.

EU FOREIGN, SECURITY AND DEFENCE POLICY

The case of information exchange and coordination between German and UK finance ministers related to the work of major international institutions and coordination forums in global economic and financial governance lays bare a broader issue which matters for post-Brexit bilateral relations between Germany and the UK: prior to Brexit work in the EU institutions provided ample opportunities for bilateral exchanges between both governments. These communication channels have to be replaced by venues outside the EU institutions (cf. Mühlauer and Neudecker, 2021). A policy domain for which alternative bilateral German-UK ties are likely to matter most is the domain of foreign, security and defence policy.

Major and von Ondarza (2021, p. 8) see a set of 'goal conflicts' for Germany in its future relations with the UK in the domain of foreign, security and defence policy. Both the EU and the UK continue to remain locked into the very same conflict that characterised the Brexit process: Brussels does not want to allow the UK to have a say in EU internal decision-making. The UK, under Boris Johnson, refused cooperation with the EU categorically, as it does not want to submit itself to EU decisions. In a nutshell: Germany has to choose between EU unity or alternative bi- or multilateral arrangements, which would involve the UK but circumvent EU procedures. The authors review a range of options which all reflect this dilemma. For example, Germany could, together with France, continue to cooperate with the UK in the context of the E3 format. Yet, this format is likely to be watched with scepticism on part of other EU member states (ibid., p. 6). Major and von Ondarza suggest that this could be mitigated by inviting further selected member states to join in on specific topics and to ask for the High Representative to be part of these discussions. In a similar way the so-called Quad format, involving the E3 and the US, is considered (ibid., pp. 6–7).

A first attempt at institutionalising closer German-UK bilateral relations in the post Brexit era was marked by the signing of the UK-Germany Joint Declaration of June 2021 (Foreign Commonwealth and Development Office, 2021). The document reflects, in diplomatic language, the limbo act for Germany of forging closer bilateral ties while not compromising EU integrity. Equally, the document seeks to express common ground without submitting the UK to EU authority. For example, the declaration affirms that German-UK 'cooperation is rooted in our European [not EU] and universal values' (Foreign Commonwealth and Development Office, 2021, para 1) and equally states right in the beginning that:

> For Germany, its membership of the European Union remains a key reference point … Regarding bilateral undertakings, Germany, as an EU Member State, will ensure the highest possible level of transparency towards the institutions and Member States of the European Union. (Ibid., para 3)

Joint membership in international organisations and forums as well as within NATO is a key theme of the joint declaration. Here, overlap with EU policy priorities cannot be overlooked. At the same time, and in contrast to the domain of single market governance and Eurozone politics, some scope for bilateral cooperation is identified. The Joint Declaration states that the two countries 'will enhance cooperation on conflict-prevention including stabilisation and peace building by establishing a UK-Germany Stabilisation Partnership' (ibid., para 8). Moreover, the two countries commit to jointly support a permanent seat for Germany at the United Nations Security Council (ibid., para 9).

However, the Joint Declaration is also eager to frame future German-UK cooperation as compatible with and even conducive towards EU-UK cooperation. In relation to NATO, it is stated that the two governments 'recognise the importance of a stronger and more capable European contribution' (ibid., para 10) towards the defence alliance and that they 'remain jointly committed to NATO-EU co-operation' (ibid.). There is also a list of joint priorities for the European continent and its immediate neighbourhood which reflects so far existing EU foreign policy objectives (ibid., paras 14 and 17–20). This includes resistance against Russian interference, the protection of Ukrainian territorial integrity and cooperation with Turkey with a view to tame migration and ensure regional security in the Eastern Mediterranean. Finally, the Joint Declaration commits to close policy dialogue at all political and administrative levels in the domain of foreign, security and defence policy, including 'an annual Foreign Ministers' Strategic Dialogue' (ibid., para 28) and 'regular consultations' (ibid., para 29) among senior staff and representatives of the Foreign Office and the Federal Ministry of Foreign Affairs.

The domain of EU foreign, security and defence policy is probably affected most by how future bilateral relations between Germany and the UK evolve. There is considerable interest in both countries, but also the EU more generally, to keep direct channels of communication with the UK and the above-mentioned diplomatic networks alive. As in the past, Germany, compared to other member states and because of its diplomatic, military and financial resources, is likely to pursue close bilateral contacts with the UK in this regard. To what extent this could run counter to EU internal coordination is less clear. For example, increased bilateral communication and coordination might not imply that the two countries will seek to lay the foundations of larger projects involving more institutionalised forms of cooperation or even joint missions outside the framework of the EU. This is all the more the case as the EU's CFSP is (albeit slowly) evolving. As long as Germany pursues a further strengthening of CFSP, for example through advocating the abandoning of unanimity decision-making, it will be careful not to endanger EU unity. However, and again as prior to Brexit, other member states, which have critical stakes within this policy domain, in particular Italy, Spain and Poland, will continue to closely watch Germany's bilateral contacts with the UK with suspicion.

CONCLUSIONS

This chapter discussed the impact of Brexit on Germany's role in EU politics and governance. The implications of Brexit were considered according to three main themes.

First, assessing the consequences of Brexit for Germany's role in EU politics requires taking a longer time horizon. Notably, there has been a prolonged period of disengagement with EU politics, more broadly, and with Germany in relation to EU politics, more specifically, on the part of UK policy-making elites. This disengagement predates the event of the formal departure of the UK from the EU. This finding implies that some of the implications of Brexit can be traced already in the 2010s when Germany was central to some of the EU's most important policy decisions, including the management of the euro crisis.

Second, in order to understand Germany's future role in EU politics as far as it is affected by Brexit, it is important to closely inspect the process of negotiating Brexit. Here, Germany chose EU unity over closer bilateral ties with the UK in order to gain individual leverage over the outcome of the negotiation process. Germany also accepted far-reaching delegation to the Commission. This move diverts from Germany's practice of promoting the thriving of the EU's post-Maastricht new intergovernmentalism in other policy domains and during crisis moments. However, Brexit negotiations focussed primarily on the domain of single market governance. This policy field has largely continued to function according to the classical community method in the post-Maastricht era. Moreover, the institutional design of single market governance, including its element of delegation, is consistent with Germany's long-standing preferences in EU institutional politics.

Third, the implications of Brexit for Germany's future role in EU politics should be assessed according to the diverging characteristics of different core EU policy domains. Consistent with the experience of the Brexit negotiations, Germany's future bilateral relations with the UK are unlikely to inspire German government policy to change when it comes to the integrity of the single market. In relation to EMU and Eurozone politics, the actual impact of Brexit remains limited, as disengagement between Germany and the UK predates the event of the UK's departure from the EU. There is also little to expect from the absence of UK opposition in EU politics in relation to Germany's lead role in Eurozone politics. It was the euro crisis that reinforced the notion of Germany playing the role of a 'hegemon' in the EU (Bulmer, 2014), not Brexit. And the euro crisis equally revealed important constraints in German domestic politics which served to limit a more straightforward leadership role of the country (ibid.). The EU policy domain for which Brexit may have the most detectable repercussions for how bilateral German-UK relations may affect EU internal decision-making is the EU's foreign, security and defence policy. However, also in this case there are likely limits to potential German-UK bilateralism. Krotz and Schild (2018) consider three scenarios of Germany's post-Brexit role in EU politics: hegemony, decline of the European project and a 'rejuvenated Franco-German link at the union's centre' (ibid., p. 1174). The authors consider the latter scenario as the most likely outcome.

So, does Brexit open up the way for a duopolistic France-German hegemony?[3] Judged on the basis of the findings of this chapter, the likelihood for this to occur has not decreased or increased significantly because of Brexit. More recently, the most important trigger of Franco-German alignment has been events challenging the integrity of the Eurozone, not UK opposition. Equally, limitations to Franco-German leadership ambitions occurred mainly as a consequence of domestic politics within these two countries. This too is unlikely to change with Brexit.

NOTES

1. A notable exception was the 2005 reform of the SGP which was pursued by the Schröder government in conjunction with French president Jacques Chirac as Germany's own problems with avoiding an excessive deficit had accumulated.
2. Only the Czech president, who is not representing his country in the European Council, initially refused to sign the intergovernmental treaty. A move, which was later reverted.
3. I am grateful to Christopher Lord for alerting me to the notion of duopolistic hegemony in this context.

REFERENCES

Beach, D. and Smeets, S. (2020). The unseen hands: Collaborative instrumental leadership in the British renegotiation case. *European Journal of Political Research, 59*(2), 444–64.

Bickerton, C.J., Hodson, D. and Puetter, U. (2015a). The new intergovernmentalism: European integration in the post-Maastricht era. *Journal of Common Market Studies*, *53*(4), 703–22.

Bickerton, C.J., Hodson, D. and Puetter, U. (2015b). The new intergovernmentalism and the study of European integration. In C. Bickerton, D. Hodson and U. Puetter (eds), *The New Intergovernmentalism. States, Supranational Actors, and European Politics in the Post-Maastricht Era* (pp. 1–48). Oxford University Press.

Bulmer, S. (2014). Germany and the eurozone crisis: Between hegemony and domestic politics. *West European Politics*, *37*(6), 1244–63.

Bundesverband der deutschen Industrie e.V. (2017, 29 March). BDI-Präsident Kempf: Industrie fordert beim Brexit maximale Schadensbegrenzung, Press release, Berlin. https://bdi.eu/media/user_upload/2017-03-29_PM_08_Brexit.pdf (accessed 15 September 2021).

Chen, W., Los, B., McCann, P., Ortega-Argilés, R., Thissen, M. and van Oort, F. (2018). The continental divide? Economic exposure to Brexit in regions and countries on both sides of the Channel. *Papers in Regional Science*, *97*(1), 25–54.

Csehi, R. and Puetter, U. (2021). Who determined what governments really wanted? Preference formation and the euro crisis. *West European Politics*, *44*(3), 463–84.

European Parliament. (2017, March). An assessment of the economic impact of Brexit on the EU 27. Study for the IMCO Committee, IP/A/IMCO/2016-13 PE 595.374. *Directorate-General for Internal Policies. Policy Department A: Economic and Scientific Policy*, Brussels. https://www.europarl.europa.eu/RegData/etudes/STUD/2017/595374/IPOL_STU(2017)595374_EN.pdf (accessed 1 October 2021).

European Parliament. (2019, April). The impact of the UK's withdrawal on the institutional set-up and political dynamics within the EU, PE 621.914. *Policy Department for Citizens' Rights and Constitutional Affairs and Directorate General for Internal Policies of the Union*, Brussels. https://www.europarl.europa.eu/RegData/etudes/STUD/2019/621914/IPOL_STU(2019)621914_EN.pdf (accessed 1 October 2021).

Felbermayr, G., Gröschl, J., Heiland, I., Braml, M. and Steininger, M. (2017, 1 June). Ökonomische Effekte eines Brexit auf die deutsche und europäische Wirtschaft. Studie im Auftrag des Bundesministeriums für Wirtschaft und Energie (BMWi). *ifo Institut*, Munich. https://www.bmwi.de/Redaktion/DE/Publikationen/Studien/oekonomische-effekte-eines-brexit-auf-die-deutsche-wirtschaft.pdf?__blob=publicationFile&v=6 (accessed 1 October 2021).

Foreign Commonwealth and Development Office. (2021, 30 June). UK-Germany joint declaration, June 2021: Joint Declaration by the Secretary of State for Foreign, Commonwealth and Development Affairs of the United Kingdom of Great Britain and Northern Ireland and the Federal Minister for Foreign Affairs of the Federal Republic of Germany. *UK Government*. https://www.gov.uk/government/publications/uk-germany-joint-declaration-june-2021/uk-germany-joint-declaration-june-2021 (accessed 1 October 2021).

Frosini, J.O. and Gilbert, M.F. (2020). The Brexit car crash: Using E.H. Carr to explain Britain's choice to leave the European Union in 2016. *Journal of European Public Policy*, *27*(5), 761–78.

Hodson, D. (2011). *Governing the Euro Area in Good Times and Bad*. Oxford University Press.

Hodson, D. and Puetter, U. (2019). The euro crisis and European integration. In M. Cini and N. Pérez-Solórzano Borragán (eds), *European Union Politics* (pp. 389–405). Oxford University Press.

Jacobsson, K. (2004). Soft regulation and the subtle transformation of states: The case of EU employment policy. *Journal of European Social Policy*, *14*(4), 355–70.

Krotz, U. and Schild, J. (2018). Back to the future? Franco-German bilateralism in Europe's post-Brexit union. *Journal of European Public Policy*, *25*(8), 1174–93.

Lavery, S., McDaniel, S. and Schmid, D. (2019). Finance fragmented? Frankfurt and Paris as European financial centres after Brexit. *Journal of European Public Policy*, *26*(10), 1502–20.

Major, C. and von Ondarza, N. (2021). Die EU und Global Britain: So nah, so fern. Wie 'Global Britain' nach dem Brexit außen- und sicherheitspolitisch eingebunden werden kann. *SWP-Aktuell*, *35*, 1–8. https://www.swp-berlin.org/publications/products/aktuell/2021A35_EU_GlobalBritain.pdf (accessed 1 October 2021).

McConnell, A. and Tormey, S. (2020). Explanations for the Brexit policy fiasco: Near-impossible challenge, leadership failure or Westminster pathology? *Journal of European Public Policy*, *27*(5), 685–702.

Merkel, A. (2010, 2 November). Rede von Bundeskanzlerin Merkel anlässlich der Eröffnung des 61. akademischen Jahres des Europakollegs Brügge. https://archiv.bundesregierung.de/archiv-de/rede-von-bundeskanzlerin-merkel-anlaesslich-der-eroeffnung-des-61-akademischen-jahres-des-europakollegs-bruegge-399506 (accessed 4 October 2021).

Mühlauer, A. and Neudecker, M. (2021, July 2). Abschiedstour mit Skepsis. Angela Merkel reist zum letzten Mal als Kanzlerin nach Großbritannien – und macht das Beste draus. *Süddeutsche Zeitung*. https://www.sueddeutsche.de/politik/merkel-johnson-queen-windsor-1.5340879 (accessed 1 October 2021).

Puetter, U. (2006). *The Eurogroup: How a Secretive Circle of Finance Ministers Shape European Economic Governance*. Manchester University Press.

Puetter, U. (2012). Europe's deliberative intergovernmentalism – the role of the Council and European Council in EU economic governance. *Journal of European Public Policy*, *19*(2), 161–78.

Puetter, U. (2014). *The European Council and the Council. New Intergovernmentalism and Institutional Change*. Oxford University Press.

Puetter, U. and Fabbrini, S. (2016). Catalysts of integration – the role of core intergovernmental forums in EU politics. *Journal of European Integration*, *38*(5), 633–42.
Schmidt, S.K. (2020). No match made in heaven. Parliamentary sovereignty, EU over-constitutionalization and Brexit. *Journal of European Public Policy*, *27*(5), 779–94.
Schuette, L.A. (2021). Forging unity: European Commission leadership in the Brexit negotiations. *JCMS: Journal of Common Market Studies*. https://onlinelibrary.wiley.com/doi/abs/10.1111/jcms.13171 (accessed 1 October 2021).
Smeets, S. and Beach, D. (2020). Intergovernmentalism and its implications – new institutional leadership in major EU reforms. *Journal of European Public Policy*, *27*(8), 1137–56.
The Guardian. (2017, 9 July). German industry warns UK not to expect help in Brexit negotiations. *The Observer*. https://www.theguardian.com/politics/2017/jul/08/german-industry-warns-uk-over-brexit (accessed 1 October 2021).
Walter, S. (2021). EU-27 public opinion on Brexit. *JCMS: Journal of Common Market Studies*, *59*(3), 569–88.

16. France and Brexit

Helen Drake

INTRODUCTION

Amongst the EU27, France has loomed large in the Brexit saga. The United Kingdom's (UK) demotion from former European Union (EU) member state in 2016 to third country status by 2021 was not cushioned by the comforts of the Franco-British bilateral relationship (FBBR). On the contrary, France was an active participant in a process that erased many of the certainties built up in that relationship during the 40-plus years of shared EU membership. In comparison with other EU member states, France was seen to have driven a particularly hard bargain over the terms of the UK's departure, with expressions of emotion never far from the surface. In the words of one UK diplomatic official at the Foreign, Commonwealth and Development Office in London (interview, 8 October 2020),[1] France and the UK 'cared' too much about each other not to fall out over Brexit.

As friends and allies, the two countries had each enjoyed the status of their global reach in military, defence, diplomatic and foreign policy matters. These activities, moreover, provided an institutionalised point of contact between them, most notably in the form of the 2010 Lancaster House treaties (UK Government, 2010) and the post-Brexit Sandhurst Treaty (UK Government, 2018). These bilateral relations were both distinct from and overlapped with the EU's own provisions for European defence, security and foreign policy, and coexisted with the much broader web of policies, regulation, governance, institutions and commitments that typically bind and socialise EU member states. France and the UK were, in particular, connected by their stakes in the EU's freedom of movement provisions, which eased and extended the historical flow of French and British citizens across the Channel for various purposes. Similarly, the EU provided a legal framework for joint Franco-British provisions for ridding the Channel of the more unwanted of its migrants. Trade between these two roughly equal-sized economic partners was, moreover, facilitated by membership in the European single market. The impact of the UK's departure from the EU on these and many other dimensions of Franco-British interdependence would vary in intensity and longevity.

As rivals and competitors within the EU, France and Britain never resolved their strategic or policy differences over what we can summarise as 'political Europe': the idea that Europe is more than a single market (to paraphrase former EU Commission President Jacques Delors); and that the single European market itself has symbolic as well as economic value (a difference that contributed to the UK's ultimate 'hard' Brexit). It was a fault line with a serious historical pedigree. Former French President Charles de Gaulle, on the occasion of his rejection of the UK's second application in 1967, deemed the UK as 'incompatible' with and lacking 'interest' in the 'Common Market' as well as harbouring a 'deep-seated hostility' towards European construction (BBC, n.d.; l'INA, n.d.). Brexit in theory thus provided France, particularly under its activist President Macron (since 2017), a golden opportunity to bring about the European strategic autonomy – 'political Europe' – on which he pinned his bid for power. But by the same token, France would now be further exposed to domestic Euroscepticism, were Macron's grand schemes to actually come to fruition now that the UK could no longer object to them from within the EU.

In view of this multi-faceted setting, this chapter explores the meaning of Brexit for France and the significance of Brexit for the FBBR. Structured chronologically to span the periods before, during and after Brexit, it identifies key milestones and factors that along the way account for the shape that this history-within-a-history of Franco-British relations has taken. These include questions regarding the intersection between Franco-British relations and the multilateral EU; of France's own membership of the EU, with its contradictions and flash-points; and of domestic French politics. The chapter concludes that the net impact of Brexit on the Franco-British relationship itself is likely to be significant, the UK's exit from the EU having dealt a blow to cross-Channel certainties that will take time and political will to address. Where claims to or desires for French leadership of the EU are concerned, the picture is less distinct. France will have lost an ally within the EU on foreign policy and defence matters, but it will also have lost an opponent to federalist initiatives of the type proposed by President Macron. Domestic French politics themselves can also be expected to constrain French leadership on the EU stage.

BEFORE BREXIT: TWO 'AWKWARD' EU MEMBER STATES?

France and the UK share a long and well-documented history of tug-of-war from which each party emerged roughly equal by the start of the 21st century. Their past – of wars of religion, territory, culture, language, politics and taste – had by then left a multi-layered residue of habits and expectations, and a gradually accreting infrastructure for shared if not joint action and aims. Characterised by Tombs and Tombs (2007) as 'sweet enemies', the FBBR or *entente cordiale*, to take the name of the 1904 treaty that settled their differences at a time of colonial expansion and German threat, was a largely symmetrical, consensual, interdependent, semi-institutionalised bilateral relationship based on certain shared interests, a recognition of their differences and rivalries, and a mutual accommodation with the other's otherness (Pannier, 2018, as cited in Drake and Schnapper, 2021).

Within the EU, both France and the UK to some extent shared the label of 'awkward' member state, the UK for its so-called 'semi-detached' membership, and France for its Gaullist legacy of rhetorically resisting the notion that, as *member* states, Europe's *nation* states were less sovereign (Bickerton, 2012). But in neither case did the 'awkward' narrative bear very close scrutiny. For the UK, the label referred to its opt-outs from whole swathes of the EU *acquis* including the single currency, the Schengen zone and, for many decades, matters of justice and home affairs. In a last-ditch move designed to avert Brexit, the UK in 2015–16, under its then Prime Minister David Cameron, had indeed renegotiated the terms of its membership once more, that time to opt out of the very idea of 'ever closer union' itself, amongst other provisions (Smith, 2016). That extra dose of 'awkwardness' proved insufficient to head off Brexit itself. Yet the UK was also a 'good' member state in terms of its regulatory compliance with the EU *acquis* it had signed up to, and an active member state in driving certain strategic EU policy choices (including but not limited to the single market itself).

France, for its part, and via a succession of presidents from different political families and in different political times, repeatedly and incrementally pooled its national sovereignty apace with geopolitical, strategic shifts, despite the rhetoric of national sovereignty. The Constitution of the Fifth Republic was itself amended seven times to keep pace (Burgorgue-Larsen et al., 2019, p. 1184), with all the symbolism this implies; and the inexorable movement towards further integration did meet with domestic resistance which at key points (the European Defence Community in 1954; the Constitutional Treaty in 2005) scuppered the integration process itself. The 1992 Maastricht Treaty and its provisions for a single European currency as well as a common foreign and security policy, and visions of common defence, is the most obvious example of these French commitments to European integration; and the most striking indication of how precariously balanced were the forces in France for and against European integration (the Treaty having been approved by referendum with a '*petit oui*' of 51.04 per cent (Lewis-Beck and Morey, 2007)). With regards to the latter, 'high' politics dimension of this deepened integration – foreign policy, security and defence – France and the UK's shared membership of the EU both intensified and complicated their interactions, adding a multilateral layer to their existing bilateral connections, with implications for the impact of Brexit.

Defence, Security and Foreign Policy: Where Bilateralism and Multilateralism Collide

On the international stage the two countries, unlike their European counterparts, each vaunted a permanent seat on the United Nations Security Council (UNSC), possessed nuclear weapons, and willingly deployed their military and diplomatic capabilities far afield, for strategic ends. At this level, they were typically in relative harmony within the EU, with some obvious exceptions such as the 2003 UK-US decision to invade Iraq without UN backing (Hill, 2017). By 2010, and in the specific context of the era of international disorder that emerged from the first decade of the 21st century, marked by non-state terrorism, rogue states, global rivalry between the US and China, and global disruption from Russia, the two countries had been attracted into ever more structured collaboration, at least on paper, enshrined in and symbolised by the Lancaster House Treaties of that year (UK Government, 2010). Committing themselves to joint efforts, including nuclear cooperation, R&D, procurement and battlefield military operations, France and the UK entered the fray with the potential advantages of a strength-in-numbers approach.

Both countries were also by now full NATO members again, France having completed its reintegration in 2009 under President Sarkozy. They had drawn similar conclusions from the experience of the Balkans conflicts in the 1990s with regards to the US post-Cold War engagement in Europe, both subsequently agreeing that Europe's collective security was best served by a combination of the NATO umbrella and a form of European defence 'autonomy', a commitment that had been sealed in the Franco-British St Malo declaration of 1998. The two countries had joined forces to depose Gaddafi in Libya in 2011; and in targeting Syrian forces at certain points in that protracted conflict (Hill, 2017). A combination of Brexit and French president Macron would disrupt these arrangements and expose their inherent ambiguities, forcing France potentially to take sides, as we see below. Even though the bilateral Franco-British agreements such as Lancaster House existed independently of the EU, and thus could be expected to escape impact from Brexit, the context in which they operated had become conditioned by shared EU membership of the EU. In other aspects too, the FBBR was simultaneously strengthened and challenged by joint membership of the EU.

Trains, Tunnels and Boats: Linked, for Better or Worse

The EU's 1994 freedom of movement provisions (EU, 2004) fed the pipeline of students, workers, residents, retirees and tourists that flowed across the Channel in both directions in the 1990s and first two decades of the 21st century, fuelled by transport that was typically cheap (budget airlines), convenient (Eurostar) or both. Measuring these stocks and flows became approximate at best, irrelevant at least – until Brexit, which forced the two countries' populations onto opposing sides: EU citizen, or not. In its heyday, this *chassé-croisé* of French and UK nationals across the Channel, much as in previous centuries, also sustained friendly competition between the two countries: for their youth (appeals to French youth to 'come back' to France (Drake, 2018)); for their euro (courtesy of the 'Brits in France'); or for their labour (especially the 'London French' (Lequesne, 2020)); but by and large, it was a fact of life, taken for granted in its multiple dimensions (social, economic and political EU citizenship rights).

The 1986 Treaty of Canterbury (United Nations, n.d.) had sealed the Franco-British agreement to, finally, connect the two countries with a 'fixed' link – the Channel Tunnel – through which this exchange of citizens, business and trade could flow. The operation of the tunnel – its infrastructure – was a bilateral matter to the point where in the course of the Brexit negotiations, authority was delegated to France to negotiate directly with the UK on the extension of these arrangements, in derogation to the rule whereby the EU27 negotiated Brexit as a single unit (European Council, 2020). More broadly, with respect to the Channel, Franco-British bilateral arrangements slotted into a jigsaw alongside EU provisions for the freedom of movement, for passport-free travel in the Schengen zone, and for the 'management' of refugee and irregular migrant flows.

The 2003 Franco-British le Touquet Treaty (House of Commons, 2004) provided for 'juxtaposed' borders whereby French and UK border agencies could operate on the others' territory for the purposes of border control. This included the troubles of securing the EU's external borders with third countries, and of 'managing' the flows of third country nationals entering the EU's member states by irregular means. In the case of the Franco-British relationship this meant 'managing' the migrants risking their lives to reach the UK from the northern coast of France, especially Calais and its outskirts. The response was a steady 'securitisation' and even 'militarisation' (Tyerman and Van Isacker, 2020) of the shared sea border thanks to a series of rolling Franco-British deals (cash and equipment for patrol and control); and cooperation to implement the EU's 'Dublin III' provisions governing asylum-seeking, including provisions for the 'return' of irregular migrants from the UK to France under certain conditions. Brexit would mean finding new ways of handling Franco-British border issues without reference to the EU legal framework and the early signs, in 2020 (during the UK's 'transition' from member state to ex-member state), were that this would be a challenging area of future Franco-British cooperation.

Trade, Markets and the Political Economy: 'Anglo-Saxons' and the Rest

Beneath the sea, out of sight from the lives being risked on the surface, the Channel Tunnel was a powerfully symbolic manifestation of Franco-British political cooperation, in much the same way as the Concorde and Airbus projects before it (Glencross, 2019). It also came to highlight the contrast between the two countries' physical, economic interdependence, on the one hand, and, on the other, their political differences concerning the market, corporate governance, and in particular the role of the state. By way of example, the French state retained a 55 per cent share in the tunnel rail operator Eurostar whereas in 2014, the UK government 'sold its 40% stake to a consortium of pension funds for £757m' (Financial Times, 2021, p. 28). As majority shareholder, the French state has been reluctant to entertain ceding any control to competitor train operators (such as Deutsche Bahn; ibid.). When the company faced severe financial pressures during the period of Covid travel restrictions, the bailout came not from the UK government (where the company is based) but from bank and shareholder funds.

Elsewhere in the economy, both public and private enterprise connected the two countries with regard, for example, to nuclear power (Hinkley Points B and C); electricity 'interconnection'; energy trading; and collaboration in the steering of the EU towards renewable energy. Large French companies such as Véolia, Suez and Engie invested in critical UK infrastructure, such as water supply, waste collection and processing. For its part, the UK was (and may well remain) a key foreign direct investment (FDI) player in France (UK FDI in France in 2020 representing €103 billion: Business France, 2020); and the UK and France were key trading partners for the other. This interdependence was facilitated and conditioned by the two countries' shared membership of the EU's single market – including the internal energy market (IEM) – which eradicated so many of the previously existing barriers to trade (tariff and non-tariff) between EU member states.

At the same time, however, differences persisted between the two countries regarding in particular the politics of the waves of deregulation that so characterised the EU's neoliberal-style single market economics (in no small part a British legacy to the EU). French presidents repeatedly called for – largely without success – the EU to 'protect' itself and its 'social model'. This referred to the protection of its own workers, their rights and salaries from 'unfair' competition (some would say, competition full stop); of its production and manufacturing: 'made in France' was a well-established theme of French political discourse on the political right as well as left; and of its international supply chains which in so many sectors fuelled a distinctively French anti-globalisation pushback from the early 1990s onwards (Gordon and Meunier-Aitsahalia, 2001). On the heels of the global financial crisis of 2008–9 which highlighted the dangers of French exposure to risky financial markets, the Covid-19 pandemic that struck France in 2020 with as much force as most other places brought such perspectives into the light. These Franco-British differences over their political economy were central to the domestic challenges of France's membership of the EU which, potentially at least, rendered France vulnerable to 'Frexit' in the wake of Brexit.

Flirting with Frexit? The Domestic Politics of France's EU Membership

As a founding and erstwhile would-be leading member of the EU, France's membership and the contradictions at the heart of its 'journey to an unknown destination' (Shonfield, 1973) can be summed up in the challenge of 'making Europe without unmaking France' (*faire l'Europe sans défaire la France*).[2] The fact of France's commitment to successively deepen European integration has however, over time, created a serious fault line in its political landscape, despite 'Europe' being typically of low electoral salience for many years. Public support for membership has become unstable; and core EU policies including the Common Agricultural Policy (CAP) and competition policy (in the transport sectors for example) have encountered serious opposition (Parsons, 2017; Rozenberg, 2020).

In the mainstream

France's traditional, mainstream political parties have each been compromised by their struggle to contain and represent contradictory stances towards EU membership. For its part, on the right of the political spectrum, the party currently called les Républicains (LR) have been conditioned by their Gaullist heritage. De Gaulle himself (President 1958–69), had cloaked ambitions for common European policy (in defence, in culture) in an infamously intransigent discourse of national sovereignty and state power. LR and its predecessors were, accordingly and by way of example, viscerally resistant to the EU citizenship provisions (broadly defined) triggered by the Maastricht Treaty (Collard, 2010); and at election time, typically emphasise the perceived need to tighten national borders (to the point of suspending Schengen). For example, in the 2019 European Parliament elections, LR emphasised a need to defend national identity, 'civilisation' and values (see Lastennet, 2019). With regards to the socio-economic dimensions of European integration, the French centre-right has sought to combine Gaullist ambitions for common European action (for example, for more EU-level policies to support youth employment ('Européennes: comparez les programmes', 2014); with a somewhat schizophrenic appetite for liberal EU policy to curb French excesses (public spending, public deficits), on the one hand, and a sustained critique of the 'Anglo-Saxon' drift of EU public policy, on the other.

For the mainstream French left, European integration has without a doubt challenged notions of French national solidarity and European norms of social market economy, and the cry to 'protect' French workers, producers and products from 'Anglo-Saxon' methods has been recurrent. In the case of the French Socialist Party (PS), the struggle has been lethal to party unity, dating back to the days of François Mitterrand's presidency and the party's embrace of the single currency as a condition of being in power. Indeed, the PS was bent out of its original Eurosceptic shape by President François Mitterrand (1981–95) who by virtue of an early (1983) policy U-turn and then the 1993 Maastricht Treaty forced the party into an uneasy accommodation with, in particular, the single market and then the single currency (Hanley, 2017). This orientation has coexisted within the party with a persistent strain of idealism regarding the potential for stronger EU-level democracy (parliamentary rather than plebiscitary, as in the 2017 presidential elections); EU-level action to tackle universal challenges such as climate change and human rights; and more federal governance for the Eurozone (Parti socialiste, 2019). The 2005 referendum on the EU's Draft Constitution by and large turned into a plebiscite on just such matters, and exposed deep rifts in the PS that never healed. That tension exploded during François Hollande's presidency (2012–17) and contributed to their disastrous 2017 election results.

The movement that brought President Macron to power, la République en Marche (LREM), for its part, represents the federalist vision of its founder, Emmanuel Macron; specifically, that in such a troubled world, Europe should exercise sovereignty across virtually all policy domains including the economy, defence and migration. The message to domestic French voters is that only Europe can protect France from planetary, existential challenges (to security, to the climate); and only Europe can promote specific values (of fair markets, for example, hence proposals to tax the global tech giants). Key to Macron's message is that the route to these transformations in governance is to prioritise the democratic representation of national populations, and this in the face of strong populist pressures at French and EU levels. This stance was particularly notable in the 2019 EP elections where he was seen to pitch 'progressives' such as himself against 'nationalists' of the ilk of the Rassemblement national; the list itself was called 'Renaissance'. To date, Macron's party, LREM has overall fallen into line with the president's vision, with nevertheless specific (but to date limited in effect) rebellions over the president's lines on migration and free trade in particular.

At the extremes

On the far ends of the political spectrum too, on both right and left, the issue of France's EU membership is a source of strategic tension and division. Neither Marine le Pen's Rassemblement national (RN) nor Jean-Luc Mélenchon's la France insoumise (LFI) was able to fully or coherently commit to leaving the EU (or the Eurozone in particular) in the 2017 national elections. French membership of the Eurozone especially has in fact come to generate serious doubt amongst economists, but to publicly espouse such doubt – to question the 'Eurodoxy' (Granville, 2021) is to enter politically treacherous waters given the stranglehold of the 'rhetoric of unanimity' (Rozenberg, 2011) on French political discourse. Marine le Pen's attempt in 2017 to do just that was met with derision; in no small part, however, due to her fairly incoherent rationale on the matter, and the party subsequently muted the idea in subsequent elections (and it prompted a split in the party).

French EU membership: in limbo or in crisis? Enter Brexit

French membership of the EU by the time of Brexit thus exerted centrifugal pressure on the country: both a critical factor in the 'making' of the country – its political economy, its place in the world and so on – and in the 'unmaking' of its political stability. These opposing forces effectively placed France in political limbo. As uncomfortable as this situation was, it represented a form of certainty as opposed to the unknowns of Frexit. Macron's own fervour for more European integration was in its own way a pitch for *less* rather than more change, however disruptive of the established order his stance may have appeared. Unsurprisingly, therefore, French political leadership opted to frame Brexit as an existential threat to the status quo and entered the Brexit negotiations firmly on the side of the remaining EU27.

The response to Brexit of France's mainstream parties was thus strikingly but predictably unanimous. All mainstream parties wished for a fast Brexit. All professed to support the notion that the UK referendum result must be respected. None wished to endanger the *entente cordiale* between London and Paris, but none countenanced bespoke access to the single market (no cherry-picking). LR most explicitly instrumentalised Brexit to pursue its quest to reform the Schengen zone, calling for a 'new European treaty'. At the time of Brexit and in its immediate aftermath, then, France was not as 'eager to leave' the EU as might have been expected (van Kessel et al., 2020) despite initially jubilant reactions to the UK's referendum result on the part of Marine le Pen, for example; and despite a clear trend for French voters to express support for parties and candidates willing to espouse a sustained critique of France's EU membership, as demonstrated in the 2012 presidential elections (Reynolds, 2017). No serious political party, then, explicitly espoused Frexit in the 2017 elections. But during this before-Brexit period, moreover, on the BBC's *Andrew Marr Show*, President Macron was honest or rash enough to express the view that were France to hold a similar referendum, it could well choose to leave the EU itself: the 'Frexit' scenario (BBC, 2018). He also repeatedly expressed the view that referendum outcomes were to be respected, however inconvenient for political continuity.

DURING BREXIT: 'WE THOUGHT WE WERE FRIENDS!'[3]

The UK's vote to 'leave' the EU was as surprising to the majority of the French political class as it was to that of the UK, at least in the heat of the moment itself. As we will see, the decision forced France in many respects to henceforth take sides: to choose, in other words, between the bilateral relationship – the FBBR – and the EU which, as seen above, had provided the multilateral framework for that bilateral relationship. This was an uncomfortable position for France which it nevertheless assumed, causing expressions of consternation on the part of the UK – but 'we thought we were friends!' – that became all too familiar in the course of the Brexit negotiations as the UK chafed and baulked at its treatment by the EU as any other third country. By forcing the two countries onto opposing teams (literally, in the case of the negotiations), Brexit delivered a shock to the FBBR more comprehensive than previous significant differences, such as that over Iraq in 2003, because it tore more widely and deeply into the fabric of the relationship (Drake and Schnapper, 2021).

Learning the Ropes

French political rhetoric, as we have seen, underscored the overriding importance of maintaining the unity of the EU27, and the French approach from the very start of the Brexit clock was marked by what has been described as a strategic and unsentimental perspective on this new normal (Drake and Schnapper, 2021). Lequesne points to a tacit Franco-German agreement that France would play 'hardball' to Germany's 'softball' (2021). This came at some cost to the UK premiership of Theresa May (2016–19) who maintained cordial relations with French President Macron but was unable to convert these into any cushioning of the emerging realities – technical and administrative as much as political – of the Brexit negotiations. These talks began in 2017 and instantly imposed an altogether artificial separation of Franco-British bilateral business, on the one hand, and, on the other, the business of the EU-UK Brexit talks. The UK's invoking of Article 50 of the Lisbon Treaty was swiftly followed on the EU side by the statement of its negotiating positions and by the granting of the EU negotiating mandate to the European Commission, in the person of EU commissioner (and Frenchman) Michel Barnier and his Article 50 Task Force (European Council, 2017).

Henceforth, French officials were required to cease any other interactions with their UK counterparts that could either undermine the negotiating stance of the EU or, just as importantly, be seen to do so. Much routine contact dried up, and the FBBR in its old form withered, reduced to those areas which were exclusively bilateral affairs. These included negotiations over rail safety in the Channel Tunnel (where France was delegated the authority to negotiate on the part of the EU), the regulation of Channel crossings under the terms of the le Touquet Treaty and a number of additional bilateral deals in this matter. Also permitted was activity falling under the Lancaster House treaties; and those in the socio-cultural sphere broadly defined. The Sandhurst Summit agreement reached on 18 January 2018, for example, included a provision, amongst other things, for the loan to the UK of the famous Bayeux tapestry.

The ousting of UK PM Theresa May by Boris Johnson in 2019 was rapidly succeeded by the UK-EU deal reached in December 2019 that finally brought the first stage of the Brexit negotiations to their conclusion in the form of the Withdrawal Agreement and the Political Declaration on the Future EU-UK relationship (WA), which would be followed a year later by the Trade and Cooperation Agreement (TCA), as we see below. The relationship between the French and British leaders, Macron and Johnson, arguably reverted to the heteronormative familiarity between male leaders that so characterises contemporary diplomacy, with its illusionary promises of firm and decisive action (Alver and Stephenson, 2018). The French and UK administrative and diplomatic machines had by now learned the new ropes, easing the initial sense of dislocation and fracture experienced on both sides; a 'no-deal' had been averted, and the negotiations now turned to the future as the UK entered its 'transition' towards a full exit. At precisely this time, however, the Covid-19 global pandemic was about to hit, threatening to further derail a process hitherto hijacked by UK domestic politics.

The Bigger Picture

From the perspective of French leader Macron, the protracted negotiation of Brexit was an untimely distraction from what he saw as the EU's strategic priorities, a focus that only sharpened as Covid took its deathly toll on the EU and its member states. Macron's intentions for further European integration – for European 'sovereignties' – subsequently defined by him as European strategic autonomy stretching from technology to food and defence, had been explicit from the start of his presidential mandate in 2017; and he directed his energies to securing German support for the vision, with very modest success. In the course of 2019, Macron raised the stakes further still, notoriously pronouncing NATO 'brain dead', by which he meant falling short of the task of iteratively rethinking its role and its members' collective security to keep pace with fast-moving developments ('Emmanuel Macron warns Europe', 2019). He also pronounced the 'Washington consensus' for global governance similarly unfit for purpose. Into the void as he saw it should come a new 'Paris consensus' to which European strategic autonomy was central (le Grand Continent, 2020). From this broader perspective of global governance and Europe's place in the world, Brexit was an irritation but not a stumbling block: Macron's vision still included the UK as a vital player, Macron declaring in August 2019, in his annual speech to France's ambassadors, that 'whatever the outcome of Brexit, it is indispensable that we continue to think about our [European] sovereignty with Great Britain' ('Discours du Président de la République', 2019). In the course of 2020, as the pandemic raged, France and Germany did reach unexpected agreement on a 'NextGenerationEU' post-Covid recovery financial instrument (worth €750 billion at the time) but the Brexit talks, moved to the virtual realm for many months, continued to eat up time and attention, despite the deepening health crisis.

Towards the Trade and Cooperation Agreement (TCA) of 24 December 2020

Beyond the strategic interests discussed above and (thus) the firm French commitment to the unity of the EU27 in the Brexit negotiations, material French interests and stakes in Brexit were rather limited. While early political reactions to the Brexit vote were not in short supply, this faded over time. Public interest itself was muted, a reflection of 'indifference' (Lequesne, 2021). There was some sense of Brexit dividends and gains, unsurprising in the context of the habitual rivalry which characterises the Franco-British relationship just as much as an inclination to cooperate and collaborate. Thus, early noises were made regarding the prospect of London's lucrative financial services sector transferring to a Paris hub which did not turn out to be the case. Macron's first prime minister Edouard Philippe had already in 2017 enjoined his countrywomen and men based abroad, including the UK, to 'come home' (Drake, 2018), movement that was in fact subsequently accelerated by the conjoined facts of Brexit and Covid restrictions. With regards to French citizens in the UK, moreover, the 2019 WA had provided for the retention of pre-WA citizens' rights for all EU citizens residing in the UK (as well as UK citizens residing in EU countries). Where previously the exact number of French and UK citizens in each other's country had therefore been a matter of some guesswork, each individual was now to be numbered and counted, for good and bad.

In terms of trade flows, the UK arguably had more than France to lose in any 'no deal' scenario whereby trade would cease to be free (of tariffs and other barriers), given the trade balance between the two countries in France's favour. There were few vocal stakeholders making themselves heard above the voice of France's political executive; nor did the process of interest in aggregation in France or at EU level ahead of and during the negotiations structure in, to any significant extent, the inclusion of alternative voices and views.

In the event, the agreement reached between the EU and UK sides of the negotiating table on 24 December 2021 – the TCA – was minimalist and left much for further detailed talks over a drawn-out schedule, with an initial review due in 2026. These loose ends included numerous matters of significance to Franco-British cooperation, including the matter of the regulation of energy markets. Furthermore, key aspects on which France and the UK habitually or need to collaborate were excluded from the talks and therefore from the deal itself. This was the case notably for matters of security, defence and foreign policy coordination; and the life-and-death matter – for the migrants – of the handling of irregular Channel crossings from France to the UK by would-be asylum-seekers and refugees. These governance gaps meant that Brexit was far from 'done' by January 2021, despite the pronouncements of the UK Prime Minister Boris Johnson to the contrary. The TCA would now give way to multiple sets of new EU-UK negotiations (those over the Northern Irish Protocol would go particularly badly in the course of 2021; and the matter of fishing rights became very fraught) to be conducted not only in a tense period of crisis management of the Covid crisis, but after more than four long years of friction between the UK and the EU since the UK's 2016 Brexit referendum. This setting – this build-up of pressure – was not without dangers for the Franco-British relationship.

AFTER BREXIT: AFTERSHOCKS, BILATERALS AND TAKING SIDES

Indeed, relations in the final weeks of the 'transition' period to full exit (December 2020) and the first months of this exit, in 2021, got off to a difficult start, one that was significantly exacerbated by the cross-Channel politics of Covid. France, for example, reacted to the spread of a new variant of Covid-19 (initially dubbed the 'Kent' or 'English' variant, subsequently renamed the Delta variant) by hastily closing its borders with the UK on 19 December 2020, causing much disruption to cross-Channel crossings of trade and tourists alike, and presaging what would be a series of uncoordinated actions taken on one or other side of the Channel in the course of 2021 as France and the UK battled separately to contain the virus. With regards to the matter of vaccine procurement, early post-Brexit Franco-British relations were soured on a number of different levels. The EU negotiated its policy as a bloc, automatically placing France and the UK on different sides of what became a politically fraught situation. France itself, in the person of President Macron, made scientifically unsubstantiated criticisms of the safety and efficacy of the UK-developed Oxford-Astra Zeneca vaccine. In the UK, the false notion that the successful national vaccine rollout was one of the Brexit spoils – only possible thanks to the UK's departure from the EU – was never quashed by UK Prime Minister Johnson or his team; on the contrary, such jingoistic messaging served their broader purpose of rationalising Brexit.

Diplomacy – Business as Usual?

In other respects, diplomatic relations continued more or less as normal. France had not reacted negatively to the UK's wish to remove security and defence from the TCA negotiations on the grounds that France and the UK have the bilateral structures of the 2010 Lancaster House agreements as a basis for ongoing cooperation (Lequesne, 2021). The 10th anniversary of these agreements that fell in November 2020 was not, however, celebrated as might have been expected, a development largely ascribed to Covid restrictions but undoubtedly also complicated by the disruption of Brexit to Franco-British diplomatic channels. In a similar vein, according to Lequesne (2021), France had in practice become accustomed to conducting its foreign, defence and security policy via 'coalitions of the willing' rather than via formal institutions. In particular, according to Lequesne, and despite appearances to the contrary, France was never truly committed to the idea of a European Security Council, preferring instead to operate in multilateral formats such as the E3, and open to ongoing UK participation in such activity. The 'Paris Consensus' espoused by Macron as part of his big picture, strategic thinking, as seen above, indeed incorporated such perspectives.

Despite the potential of such post-Brexit common diplomatic ground between France and the UK, relations at the start of the after-Brexit era were nonetheless marked by tensions at the very top. These were apparent at the G7 summit held in the UK in June 2021 which was reported as having been 'wrecked' by Brexit (Helm and Steward, 2021), and in particular by undiplomatic exchanges between President Macron (as self-appointed EU spokesperson) on the one side, and UK PM Johnson on the other on the sensitive question of the Northern Ireland Protocol to the TCA (or more specifically, the UK government's explicit attempts to renege on or at least challenge a key component of the final Brexit deal). Accounts differ, and tiffs between leaders do not automatically spell diplomatic trouble, but their inevitable mediatisation do indicate strained relations.

It was also the case that Brexit had inflicted some damage on the reputation and image of the UK in France which further complicated the challenge of restoring diplomacy as usual between the two countries. Furthermore, and alongside the episodic political skirmishes outlined above, was the fact that the UK, by choosing Brexit, would now be far less open for business to French individuals, entrepreneurs and cultural artists for whom the UK, as an enthusiastic adopter of the EU's provisions for the freedom of movement of people, had hitherto opened its arms. For centuries, in matter of fact, the UK had been a lure for French individuals fleeing circumstances not of their choosing in their home country.

But as the UK's post-Brexit immigration legislation took shape, going to the House of Commons in July 2021 in the shape of the Nationality and Borders Bill, it became clear that for those French citizens not covered by the residency rights of the WA, entry to the UK's casual labour market, particularly in the service industry which had welcomed so many French workers since 1994, would henceforth be restricted. Furthermore, students of French nationality for whom the UK had typically been a sought-after destination under the Erasmus+ student mobility would now find that route cut off, despite early hopes to the contrary. In the context of the UK's notorious 'hostile environment' for immigrants, such developments could be expected to generate rather more than 'teething problems' as Brexit began to bite, for regular and irregular migrants alike. In the latter case, the UK government ramped up shows of its determination to 'take back control' of its borders. In the case of the Channel, these moves were marked by yet more funds sent in July 2021 to France to bolster French authorities' will if not capacity to stem the rising numbers of people using 'small boats' to cross the perilous waters. The Nationality and Borders Bill itself contained provisions to criminalise the fact itself of arriving by irregular means in the UK, ostensibly in order to stem the organised crime of people-trafficking.

Franco-British collaboration was thus essential to the UK's achievement of core Brexit promises on immigration; yet no amount of pressure from the UK could thus far induce the French into a bilateral agreement governing, in particular, the 'return' (readmission) of irregular migrants to French shores. Such matters come under the EU's 'Dublin' mechanisms to which France as EU member state is signatory (no matter how flawed those mechanisms may be). In July 2021 France did indicate support for a UK-EU agreement on such matters but will find itself balancing its operational commitments to Franco-British cooperation over Channel crossings, beneath and below the sea, regular and irregular (which have in any case failed in reducing the numbers of people seeking to cross the Channel in small boats) (Les traversées en 'small boats' en nette augmentation, 2021), with pressures from local (Calais) stakeholders, and the duties of EU membership. 2021 even featured an episode of so-called 'gunboat diplomacy' – a standoff between UK and French fishing fleets off the coast of Jersey, flanked by UK naval vessels, over the new TCA technicalities of fishing rights and licences, as the new economic realities of Brexit began to make themselves felt against a backdrop of political noise and distrust (Harrison, 2021).

Economic Interests and Other Voices

Lequesne (2021) identified certain 'French economic interests' lobbying the French government ahead of the many deals still to be struck within the terms of the TCA that will inevitably have an impact on French businesses trading with the UK (Kantor, 2021). Matters of French interest still to be agreed following the TCA ranged from the trading of energy and of financial services to the mutual recognition of qualifications. Of relevance is that at this early stage of the post-Brexit period, it was hard to disentangle the impacts of Covid and Brexit on trade flows and economic activity, meaning that the net impact of Brexit on these aspects of Franco-British interdependence remained to be seen. But both France and the UK had material interests in a strong partnership, given, by way of example, the UK's significant role in FDI in France (the third largest foreign investor in France in 2020); as well as in job creation (Business France, 2020); and in tourist revenue. The UK's Integrated Review explicitly refers to the 'economic relationship' between France and the UK that the UK intends to manage 'in a constructive and collaborative way, particularly in handling our shared border in relation to both trade and security' (UK Government, 2021).

CONCLUSIONS

We saw above that for France, Brexit posed a challenge on numerous levels. First, at the level of Franco-British bilateral relations, we saw that there was shock, disruption and aftershock: France and the UK were henceforth not only on different sides of the Channel, but also separated by the fact of their now membership and ex-membership of the EU, respectively. But there were also elements of continuity and cooperation, supported by the scaffolding of agreements institutionalised both by treaty and in material form. Bilateral diplomacy in the traditional areas of security, defence and military cooperation would for the foreseeable future have to do the heavy lifting of the bilateral relationship while other aspects of the diplomatic relationship, including public and commercial diplomacy, would take some time to navigate the realities of Brexit and the implementation of the TCA. Rebuilding trust between the two countries (and their citizens) was a work-in-progress, and opportunities for a growth in the Franco-British partnership were potential spoils of such a significant turning point.

In this context, it is of note that in August 2021 a new UK ambassador, Menna Rawlings, took up post in Paris. Not only the first ever female UK ambassador to Paris, Rawlings would also be the first to take up post in the after-Brexit era. We also note in passing that her academic and professional trajectory further distinguish her from the traditional image of the career diplomat, potentially opening up prospects for the more 'naked' diplomacy – open and exposed to new thinking and fresh ideas – espoused by some (Fletcher, 2016). The sustainability of bilateral relations typically comes from the depth and breadth of the relationship providing cover for temporary misalignments of or disagreements between political leaders, and there is much to play for here in the repairing of the fabric of Franco-British ties. The UK's 'Integrated Review' (see above) has little to say about either France or – especially – the EU, but we saw above that in Macron's thinking at least, the UK features as a key European diplomatic player despite Brexit; and for Whitman (2021), the UK has, in the Integrated Review, set its sights on a more sustainable diplomatic course than Macron's own 'fruitless unilateral diplomatic initiatives' (referring specifically to Russia). If the UK is indeed offering a 'vanguard role' and 'leadership on foreign policy issues', this could spell new opportunities for France to come on board.

Second, the FBBR had for almost 50 years before Brexit accommodated Franco-British differences over European integration. These differences ranged from the political economy of the EU to the role and reach of the EU in strategic global affairs. The UK's exit in combination with French president Macron's visions of European strategic autonomy could potentially construct a space for French leadership of the EU and a thus herald a return to a purported 'golden age' of French dominance in the EU. Some developments potentially point in this direction: in the first half of 2022, for example, France held the rotating presidency of the Council of the EU under the banner of keywords 'relaunch, power and belonging' (*relance, puissance, appartenance*; Vie publique, 2020). This provided France with a platform and some resources to push for strategic EU thinking on a range of issues. Yet the EU itself contains many fault lines, including the flouting of core democratic values by member states such as Poland and Hungary. On the occasion of numerous crises (the Eurozone; migrant flows from war zones including Syria; Covid-19) the EU has demonstrated just how hard it is to reach consensus and take collective action. The departure of German Chancellor Angela Merkel from the German and EU political scenes in 2022, furthermore, spells uncertainty for the Franco-German 'tandem' which, despite its difficulties, has been a bedrock of European integration for so many decades.

Finally, and with regards to domestic French politics, French president Macron sought and won a second term in the May 2022 presidential election. He beat his second-round opponent, Marine le Pen, by a decisive margin (58.55 per cent against 41.45 per cent of the votes cast). In so doing he somewhat bucked the trend of one-term presidents (Sarkozy, 2007–12; Hollande, 2012–17). But as in 2017, his victory in 2022 is likely to have owed as much to circumstances (including the war in Ukraine) and luck (the fragmentation of political opposition) as it did to more structural factors. The stiff resistance encountered by both his policies and persona during his first term, moreover, saw no sign of abating in the second (Bedock, 2021). Furthermore, and just as significant, Marine le Pen's score in these 2022 elections was an advance on her 2017 result, taking her support from over 10 million to more than 13 million votes five years on. Her party, the *Rassemblement national* (National Rally) then went on to win an unexpected 89 National Assembly seats in the June 2022 legislative elections (having broken through with eight seats in the previous 2017 elections). Macron's party, now renamed *Ensemble!* saw itself deprived of an absolute majority for this second term and guaranteed a politically turbulent second term.

During his first term, Macron opted to postpone a French overhaul of its EU membership in favour of a renewed French commitment to Europe as a global actor. This was a risky strategy, since not only is the 'bourgeois bloc' in France that supports further European integration in a minority, but the question of Europe hampers the political alignments across parties that are needed for electoral victory under the French electoral system (Amable and Palombarini, 2021). For some (Granville, 2021; Amable and Palombarini, 2021), moreover, France is experiencing a prolonged political crisis characterised by a marked lack of trust in politics and politicians; blocked institutions and processes; declining participation in the political process at all; and festering question marks over French national identity and the capacity of the current system to truly accommodate the diversity of its population and the challenges they face. If it is the case that France is 'complex and deeply troubled' (Smith, 2021), then the tangible significance of Brexit for France's next president is likely to be relatively minor in comparison with other challenges. In the longer term, however, Brexit may in retrospect appear as one of many external developments that will have nudged France into a reckoning with itself.

NOTES

1. Interview, Foreign, Commonwealth and Development Office (FCDO), London, UK official (8 October 2020).
2. As far as we know, this expression was first explicitly coined in 1953 when Georges Bidault, who had been French prime minister at the time of the Schuman Declaration, spoke in the French parliament in the heated debate in France around plans for a European Defence Community (ECD). The fear at this time was not just the undoing of mainland France, the hexagon, but of *l'Union française* – the French empire. In other words, France would be undone by a loss of its global influence, and the parliamentarians were not prepared to take the risk of such loss by transferring powers over foreign policy to a European-level body (so the EDC never saw the day). On 8 April 1992 the expression was next taken up as a political slogan, by then French prime minister, Pierre Bérégovoy. This was in the months leading up to the snap referendum called by then French President François Mitterrand on the Maastricht Treaty. That treaty provided for Economic and Monetary Union; for further integration on defence and foreign affairs, and it created the 'EU citizen'. Bérégovoy was

attempting to explain how Maastricht would make the EU more legitimate and democratic, by strengthening its institutions. Forty years after the Schuman Declaration, in other words, France was taking a further bold step down the path to remaking its identity around what French president François Mitterrand called its European future: France is our homeland (*patrie*), he had said in 1987, but Europe is our future.

3. British Embassy, Paris, two senior officials (interviewed 22 May 2019) cited in Drake and Schnapper (2021).

REFERENCES

Alver, J., and Stephenson, E. (2018, 5 December). Is diversity disrupting diplomacy – and are we doing enough to ensure it is? *King's College London News Centre*. https://www.kcl.ac.uk/news/is-diversity-disrupting-diplomacy-and-are-we-doing-enough-to-ensure-it-is. Accessed 21 September 2021.

Amable, B., and Palombarinil, S. (2021). *The Last Neoliberal. Macron and the Origins of France's Political Crisis*. Verso Books.

BBC. (n.d.). *On This Day (27 November)*. http://news.bbc.co.uk/onthisday/hi/dates/stories/november/27/newsid_4187000/4187714.stm. Accessed 21 September 2021.

BBC. (2018, 21 January). French President Emmanuel Macron on Brexit and Trump [TV series episode]. In A. Marr, *The Andrew Marr Show*. https://www.bbc.co.uk/programmes/p05vlv08. Accessed 21 September 2021.

Bedock, C. (2021). Understanding the unexpected: Emmanuel Macron's victory in the 2017 French Presidential Election'. In H. Drake, A. Cole, S. Meunier, and V. Tiberj (eds), *Developments in French Politics* (6th edn, pp. 37–55). Red Globe Press.

Bickerton, C.J. (2012). *European Integration. From Nation-States to Member States*. Oxford University Press.

Burgorgue-Larsen, L., Astresses, P-V., and Bruck, V. (2019). The Constitution of France in the context of EU and transnational law: An ongoing adjustment and dialogue to be improved. In A. Albi and S. Bardutzky (eds), *National Constitutions in European and Global Governance: Democracy, Rights, the Rule of Law*. T.M.C. Asser Press. https://doi.org/10.1007/978-94-6265-273-6_25.

Business France. (2020) *Annual Report: Foreign Investment in France*. https://investinfrance.fr/wp-content/uploads/2021/03/Annual-Report-FDI-in-France-in-2020-by-Business-France.pdf. Accessed 21 September 2021.

Collard, S. (2010). French municipal democracy: Cradle of European citizenship? *Journal of Contemporary European Studies*, *18*(1), 91–116. https://doi.org/10.1080/14782801003638760.

Discours du Président de la République à la conférence des ambassadeurs. (2019, 27 August). *Elysée*. https://www.elysee.fr/emmanuel-macron/2019/08/27/discours-du-president-de-la-republique-a-la-conference-des-ambassadeurs-1. Accessed 21 September 2021.

Drake, H. (2018). France, Britain and Brexit. In B. Martill and U. Staiger (eds), *Brexit and Beyond. Rethinking the Futures of Europe* (p. 104). UCL Press.

Drake, H., and Schnapper, P. (2021). We thought we were friends! Franco-British bilateral diplomacy and the shock of Brexit. *JCER*, *17*(4), 482–99. https://doi.org/10.30950/jcer.v17i4.1241.

Emmanuel Macron warns Europe: NATO is becoming brain-dead. (2019, 7 November). *The Economist*. https://www.economist.com/europe/2019/11/07/emmanuel-macron-warns-europe-nato-is-becoming-brain-dead. Accessed 21 September 2021.

EU. (2004). Directive 2004/38/EC of the European Parliament and of the Council of 29 April 2004. *Official Journal of the European Union*. https://eur-lex.europa.eu/LexUriServ/LexUriServ.do?uri=OJ:L:2004:158:0077:0123:en:PDF. Accessed 21 September 2021.

European Council. (2017, 29 April). European Council (Article 50) guidelines for Brexit negotiations. https://www.consilium.europa.eu/en/press/pressreleases/2017/04/29/euco-brexit-guidelines/. Accessed 21 September 2021.

European Council. (2020, 9 September). EU-UK relations: Coreper agrees mandate on Channel tunnel railway safety. https://www.consilium.europa.eu/en/press/press-releases/2020/09/09/eu-uk-relations-coreper-agrees-mandate-on-channel-tunnel-railway-safety/. Accessed 21 September 2021.

Européennes: comparez les programmes des principaux candidats. (2014, 22 May). *Le Monde*. https://www.lemonde.fr/les-decodeurs/article/2014/05/22/europeennes-comparez-les-programmes-des-candidats_4423193_4355770.html. Accessed 21 September 2021.
Financial Times. (2021). Trouble on the tracks. *FT.COM/Magazine*, *6*(7), 25–9.
Fletcher, T. (2016). *Naked Diplomacy: Power and Statecraft in the Digital Age*. William Collins.
Glencross, A. (2019). The UK-France diplomatic relationship. In A. Glencross, C. Gray, Y. Gürsoy, C. Rowe, and S.-I. Balazs (eds), *Renewing and Rethinking Bilateralism after Brexit* (pp. 22–7). Aston Centre for Europe, Aston University. https://publications.aston.ac.uk/id/eprint/39742/1/ace_report_bilateralism_after_brexit_july_2019.pdf. Accessed 21 September 2021.
Gordon, P.H., and Meunier-Aitsahalia, S. (2001). *The French Challenge: Adapting to Globalization*. Brookings Institution Press.
Granville, B. (2021). *What Ails France?* McGill-Queen's University Press.
Hanley, D. (2017). From 'la petite Europe vaticane' to the Club Med: The French Socialist Party and the challenges of European integration. *Modern & Contemporary France*, *25*(2), 135–51. https://doi.org/10.1080/09639489.2016.1256872.
Harrison, E. (2021, 6 May). Jersey officials hold talks with French fisherman over rights dispute. *BBC*. https://www.bbc.co.uk/news/uk-57003069. Accessed 21 September 2021.
Helm, T., and Stewart, H. (2021, 13 June). 'Mistrusted' Johnson feels full force of EU fury as Brexit wrecks G7 summit. *Guardian*. https://www.theguardian.com/world/2021/jun/13/mistrusted-johnson-feels-full-force-of-eu-fury-as-brexit-wrecks-g7-summit. Accessed 21 September 2021.
Hill, C. (2017). UK-France relations after Brexit. *E-International Relations*. https://www.e-ir.info/2017/01/22/uk-france-relations-after-brexit/. Accessed 21 September 2021.
House of Commons. (2004). Treaty between the Government of the United Kingdom of Great Britain and Northern Ireland and the Government of the French Republic. Implementation of Frontier Controls at the Sea Ports of both Countries on the Channel and North Sea, Le Touquet, 4 February 2004. *Parliamentary Papers online Treaty Series*, *18*.
Kantor, A. (2021, 13 April). How French companies are also being hit hard by Brexit. *Financial Times*. https://www.ft.com/content/0801cd6d-22c9-4e71-ae29-f6c857b69fe5. Accessed 21 September 2021.
L'INA. (n.d.). Conférence de presse du 27 novembre 1967. https://fresques.ina.fr/de-gaulle/fiche-media/Gaulle00139/conference-de-presse-du-27-novembre-1967.html. Accessed 21 September 2021.
Lastennet, J. (2019, 17 May). Européennes: le programme des Républicains en 2 minutes. *Toute l'europe*. https://www.touteleurope.eu/actualite/europeennes-le-programme-des-republicains-lr-en-2-minutes.html. Accessed 21 September 2021.
Le Grand Continent. (2020, 16 November). La doctrine Macron: une conversation avec le Président français. https://legrandcontinent.eu/fr/2020/11/16/macron/. Accessed 21 September 2021.
Lequesne, C. (2020). La Diaspora française de Londres à l'heure du Brexit. *Les Etudes du CERI*, 250. https://www.sciencespo.fr/ceri/fr/content/la-diaspora-francaise-de-londres-l-heure-du-brexit-0.html. Accessed 21 September 2021.
Lequesne, C. (2021). France. In *EU-UK 2030: UK in a Changing Europe*. https://ukandeu.ac.uk/wp-content/uploads/2021/06/EU-UK-2030-Report.pdf. Accessed 21 September 2021.
Les traversées en 'small boats' en nette augmentation. (2021, 27 July). *Le Monde*.
Lewis-Beck, M.S., and Morey, D.S. (2007). The French 'petit oui': The Maastricht Treaty and the French voting agenda. *The Journal of Interdisciplinary History*, *38*(1), 65–87. http://www.jstor.org/stable/4139670. Accessed 21 September 2021.
Pannier, A. (2018). La relation bilatérale. In T. Balzacq, F. Charillon, and F. Ramel (eds), *Manuel de Diplomatie* (pp. 28–41). Presses de Sciences Po.
Parsons, C. (2017). France and the evolution of European Integration. In R. Elgie, E. Grossman, and A. Mazur (eds), *The Oxford Handbook of French Politics* (pp. 585–605). Oxford University Press.
Parti socialiste. (2019). *Changeons d'Europe, Parti Socialiste*. European Parliament election manifesto. https://parti-socialiste.fr/wp-content/uploads/2018/10/Changeons-dEurope-1.pdf. Accessed 21 September 2021.
Reynolds, C. (2017). Presidential elections and Europe: The 2012 game-changer. *Modern and Contemporary France*, *25*(2), 117–34. https://doi.org/10.1080/09639489.2016.1248910.

Rozenberg, O. (2011). Debating about Europe at the French National Assembly: The failure of the rhetoric of unanimity. In K. Palonen, T. Turkka, and C. Wiesner (eds), *Parliament and Europe. Rhetorical and Conceptual Studies on Their Contemporary Connections* (pp. 145–64). Nomos Edizioni.

Rozenberg, O. (2020). France is back in a French Europe. In S. Bulmer and C. Lequesne (eds), *The Member States of the European Union* (3rd edn, pp. 73–100). Oxford University Press.

Shonfield, A. (1973). *Europe: Journey to an Unknown Destination (Reith lectures).* Allen Lane.

Smith, J. (2016). David Cameron's EU renegotiation and referendum pledge: A case of déjà vu? *British Politics, 11*, 324–46. https://doi.org/10.1057/bp.2016.11.

Smith, A. (2021). *Made in France. Societal Structures and Political Work.* Manchester University Press.

Tombs, R., and Tombs, I. (2007). *That Sweet Enemy: Britain and France: The History of a Love-Hate Relationship*. Pimlico

Tyerman, T., and Van Isacker, T. (2020, 9 October). Border securitisation in the Channel. *Border Criminologies blog*. https://www.law.ox.ac.uk/research-subject-groups/centre-criminology/centre border-criminologies/blog/2020/10/border. Accessed 21 September 2021.

UK Government. (2010, 2 November). UK-France Defence Co-operation Treaty announced. https://www.gov.uk/government/news/uk-france-defence-co-operation-treaty-announced--2. Accessed 21 September 2021.

UK Government. (2018). *UK-France Summit 2018 Documents*. https://www.gov.uk/government/publications/uk-france-summit-2018-documents. Accessed 21 September 2021.

UK Government. (2021). *Global Britain in a Competitive Age: The Integrated Review of Security, Defence, Development and Foreign Policy*. https://www.gov.uk/government/publications/global-britain-in-a-competitive-age-the-integrated-review-of-security-defence-development-and-foreign-policy. Accessed 21 September 2021.

United Nations. (n.d.). France and United Kingdom of Great Britain and Northern Ireland: Treaty concerning the construction and operation by private concessionaires of a channel fixed link. Signed at Canterbury on 12 February 1986. https://treaties.un.org/doc/Publication/UNTS/Volume%201497/volume-1497-I-25792-English.pdf. Accessed 21 September 2021.

van Kessel, S., Chelotti, N., Drake, H., Gonzalez, J-R., and Rodi, P. (2020). Eager to leave? Populist radical right parties' responses to the UK's Brexit vote. *The British Journal of Politics and International Relations, 22*(1), 65–84, https://doi.org/10.1177/1369148119886213.

Vie publique. (2020). Conseil des ministres du 4 novembre 2020. https://www.vie-publique.fr/discours/277068-conseil-des-ministres-4112020-presidence-francaise-du-conseil-de-lue. Accessed 21 September 2021.

Whitman, R. (2021). The United Kingdom: Europe's 'diplomatic vanguard'. *Council on Geostrategy*. https://www.geostrategy.org.uk/britains-world/the-united-kingdom-europes-diplomatic-vanguard/. Accessed 21 September 2021.

17. De-Europeanization of Eastern peripheries or testing the limits of differentiation: Poland in the post-Brexit European Union

Rafał Riedel

INTRODUCTION[1]

> For decades, Europe was about integration. Following the British referendum, the main issue is now disintegration. (Charles Wypłosz, 2016, p. 11)

As indicated by Charles Wypłosz's stark quote above, Brexit – both as an event as well as a process – changed the rules of the game in the European integration project and interpretations of it. The famous 'bicycle metaphor' suggested the need to move forward in order to avoid falling off. Arguably, previous attempts by the UK to cycle backwards had been so difficult (Wypłosz, 2016) that a Brexit was something that was 'waiting to happen'. The United Kingdom (UK) has always been a special case in the European integration project. British exceptionalism manifested itself in various forms and ways over the history of UK membership. The Brexit referendum on 23 June 2016 – and the victory for those who supported the UK leaving the EU – was the end of a long story of difficult relations with the UK's continental partners. It has never been an easy marriage and was threated many times by divorce. Instead of becoming ever closer, the UK's relationship with the European Union (EU) becomes ever looser with opt-outs. Brexit is not only vitally important for the British, it is potentially destructive for the EU and its core. Brexit may change the UK's status from an integration-tolerant country (if not a very ambitious one) to an integration unfriendly country, which endangers the very fundaments of the integration process. Brexit also produces externalities for other member states and non-members.

The UK's decision to leave the EU raises important analytical questions about consequences and implications for various EU member states, as well as the Union as a whole. This chapter examines perceptions and ramifications of the Brexit process from the perspective of the largest member state of the EU's Eastern periphery, namely, Poland. With the UK's withdrawal from the EU, Poland has gained the status of one of the Union's most problematic partners. This is both because of the openly Eurosceptic attitude of the ruling (after 2015) party – PiS (Prawo i Sprawiedliwość/Law and Justice) – and because of some structural incompatibilities that characterize the Polish economy. Therefore, the Polish case is interesting in the post-Brexit context, especially in post-pandemic times, when the system of European differentiated integration is dynamically changing.

It is important to start by asking what the consequences of Brexit are for a differentiated Europe. First, Brexit potentially strengthens Germany as the core of integration. Given France's weakened status after the previous economic crisis, the UK's withdrawal leaves even less of a balance to Germany. Second, the EU without Britain also means an EU without *free marketeers*. It was the UK (no matter if ruled by the Labour or the Conservatives) which brought the liberal component to the European integration project. Less Britain in Europe means also less liberal ideas. Third, we have learnt the limits of internal differentiation. Simply speaking, David Cameron overpaid in demanding more internal differentiation. The British political elites got lost in the attempts to play domestic politics in their relations with Brussels. Playing with egoistic interests, nationalisms and xenophobia got out of control – and, as a result, the UK found itself outside of the united Europe. Fourth, the British exit potentially also widens the circles of differentiated integration. It goes beyond the known schemes of inner and outer core as well as inner and outer peripheries. To the already existing categories of members and non-members, it adds the category of the former member, unknown so far to the EU or studies of it. This is an important lesson to be learnt by other EU member states, especially the ones that are on a trajectory of conflict with Brussels and with the European integration mainstream.

On the other hand, it is necessary to acknowledge that it was not the demand for differentiation that drove the Brexit referendum. It was the desire to leave the EU among large parts of the British public and political elites. Historically speaking, London was one of the major driving forces behind increased differentiation. Differentiation was treated as a kind of a compromise between the strong independence needs of the British and the consistency of the European project. However, it soon appeared that differentiation was a short-term tactic that did not offer a solid foundation on which the UK's presence in the EU could be grounded.

In this context, a key question is whether the British experience of leaving the EU can act as a ('good' or 'bad') example for other member states, in this particular case – Poland. The chapter asks if and how Brexit influenced Poland's European policies and politics, whether it served as a warning or as a stimulus to a more *sovereignistic* approach by the Polish government. The chapter will use considerations of policy, polity and politics to illustrate and explain de-Europeanization trends in Warsaw and how they, in turn, interacted with the Brexit process.

After providing an overview of the implications of Brexit as seen from the Polish perspective, this analysis will focus on the past years during which the ruling party in Warsaw converted from soft into hard Euroscepticism – in a way similar to the British Conservatives. The chapter argues that Brexit may lead the nationalist-populist government in Warsaw towards even more sovereignist attitudes against Brussels. Any perception of British success outside of the EU could support the Eurosceptic voices in Poland, feeding an illusion of Poland becoming the 'second Britain'. Just as the UK was one of the main advocates of EU's Eastern enlargement, its leaving the EU may serve as one of the main arguments for the Eurosceptics that 'there is life outside of the EU'.

BREXIT AND ITS IMPLICATIONS – POLISH PERSPECTIVE

Following the UK leaving the EU, the question arises whether other member states might follow. Although such a perspective seems unlikely and far away, it must be noted that before 2016 many had felt the same about Brexit. In one of the most globalized economies and one of the most internationalized societies, isolationist tendencies took over. Despite the fact that in today's world, national economies can hardly function as autarkic entities, still the depth and pace of internationalization processes can vary according to their readiness and willingness to integrate. From the time of the 2008 economic crises, through the migration and refugee crisis in Europe, up to the *Trumpism* era in America, we may observe increased protectionist and separatist practices across the globe. The coronavirus pandemic and associated restrictions accelerated this trend. Brexit has become the symbol of disintegration and isolationism. Whether others will follow this path, remains an open question, but certainly the path is getting wider.

This is especially so with Poland, which has joined the club of the most severe EU critics, together with Hungary. Despite the generally (exceeding 80 per cent in the public opinion polls) broad acceptance for Polish membership in the EU, many symptoms need to be seriously taken into account. More and more Polish youngsters (aged 18–29) claim that Poland would cope better with the challenges of the world if left to do so on its own. The flagship EU policies, like the green transition, or monetary integration, meet strong opposition in Poland. The public discourse is saturated with Euroscepticism, negative attitudes towards the main EU institutions as well as the largest and leading EU members (predominantly Germany). Poland is on a conflicting trajectory with the EU on most fundamental issues, like the rule of law (Matysek-Jędrych and Mroczek-Dąbrowska, 2021). Nevertheless, it is important to state that Poland remained loyal to the common EU negotiating position during the bargaining of the Withdrawal and Trade and Cooperation Agreements. The Polish government chose cooperation over trouble-making predominantly due to Poland's high exposition to the negative consequences of Brexit, especially under the conditions lobbied by London.

The UK had been perceived in Poland – especially by the nationalist-populist ruling PiS party – as a natural ally in the EU. In times of growing marginalization of Poland, losing such an important partner inside the Union is significantly disadvantageous. In the European Parliament, the PiS party lost their main ally – that is, *the Conservative* Euro-deputies. In the Council, UK had a reputation of a troublemaker, especially in times when Euroscepticism became British policy. That role of troublemaker is now seen as occupied by the illiberal democracies of Central and Eastern Europe, predominantly Poland (after Jarosław Kaczyński's party took power) and Hungary (after Victor Orban gained the constitutional majority in the Hungarian parliament).

The departure of one of the largest EU member states – the UK – has affected the voting power of the others in the EU institutional system. Comparative analysis of the allocation of votes, coalition-building potential and voting power in general before and after the Brexit show that the Visegrad Group will gain in voting power, with Poland experiencing the biggest increase statistically. How far it benefits from this power shift will, however, depend on how well the Polish authorities coordinate their voting behaviour (Goellner, 2017).

Seen from the economic point of view, one should not forget that Poland is not Britain as regards economic strength and potential. Additionally, Poland is far more dependent on trading with other EU countries (more than 70 per cent of all exports and 80 per cent of all imports are traded with EU economies). Trade flows are substantially different in the case of the two countries. Not only has the UK traditionally been a key player in the global economy, but the geographical allocation of trade flows also differ considerably. The share of UK's trade with its EU partners was remarkably lower than in the Polish case. For the UK, the first four trading partners are the USA, Germany, Switzerland and China – three out of four of the UK's leading trade partners are non-EU states. In contrast, 75 per cent of Polish trade is with EU economies. That said, despite the fact that Germany is Poland's most important partner, the UK remains an important market for Polish exports.

Bilaterally, we may observe a kind of asymmetry in terms of the importance of the mutual foreign trade between Poland and the UK. Great Britain is an important market for the Polish export (second largest, after Germany), whereas the Polish market does not seem to be significant for the UK (11th place). The relatively large trade surplus makes Poland more dependent on exports to the UK than on imports from the UK, which results in Poland being more vulnerable to all sorts of post-Brexit restrictions on access to the British market. It is the access to the UK market, much more than the resources coming from it, which make Poland dependent in economic relations with Great Britain (Matysek-Jędrych and Mroczek-Dąbrowska, 2021).

Another dimension that is of crucial importance is the large Polish diaspora living in Great Britain. Directly after the *big bang* enlargement, the UK (together with Sweden and Ireland) decided to open the labour market without taking advantage of the seven years transition period (which was the case of the other continental EU member states). This was mutually beneficial due to Poland's large unemployment rates at that time, as well as UK's economy needing labour in times of economic growth. As a consequence, the UK – as the large and dynamic economy – has remained the first recipient of Polish economic migrants for more than a decade after 2004. At the time of Brexit, it was still the second (after Germany) destination of Polish migrants, however on a seriously smaller scale compared to the levels immediately after enlargement. Nevertheless, for hundreds of thousands of Polish migrants, Great Britain leaving the EU translates into limiting labour mobility opportunities. This applies both to new waves of migration and to migrants who have already settled in the UK and did not meet the criteria of residency established by London as a consequence of the Brexit process. In times when the number of outgoing Polish migrants has decreased significantly, as well as in the context of 30 other labour markets remaining open for the potential migrants (beyond EU, also the European Economic Area and Switzerland), closing the British labour markets does not play that important a role, economically speaking. However, in terms of social aspects – it does. The established migration networks in Britain had been functioning effectively. Brexit closes off their further development. Linguistically, the British labour market was also more accessible for Polish migrants due to the relatively widely spread English language competences. Last, but not least, the liberal British economic model was also preferential for the easy flow of migrants, compared to other European labour markets.

It should also be remembered that the Brexit campaign was to a large extent fuelled by the anti-migration rhetoric. This is quite surprising in the face of the colonial British history and UK's traditional openness for migrants from across the globe. Nevertheless, the uncontrolled inflow of migrants from Central and Eastern Europe (and among them, proportionally the most from Poland) met strong criticism and opposition in Great Britain. It was reflected in the pre-Brexit referendum campaign, and it found its consequences in the post-Brexit settlement with the EU.

Limiting the free flow of EU citizens has many further consequences, spillovers and externalities, going beyond labour migration flows. For example, access to the British universities has been limited for continental Europeans, since they are treated as third country nationals. This translates into higher fees, limitations and other discriminatory practices, unknown in the EU. It may be expected that the Brexit process will have far wider implications for the free flow of people than limiting the movement of economic migrants. On all levels and dimensions, social interactions are likely to be limited with all sorts of effects on exchanges – from labour mobility, through students' exchange, up to scientific collaborations. All in all, limitations on free movement have serious implications not only for the Polish economic migrants. Wider social interactions will meet serious barriers and less privileged circumstances.

Summarizing this section, Poland has the most EU citizens living in the UK. After the UK's withdrawal, Poland is now the largest EU economy outside the Eurozone. Trade relations of the two countries are also going to be strongly affected by the Brexit process. Both the Polish and the British ruling parties (respectively PiS and the Conservative Party) were members of the same group in the European Parliament (*European Conservatives and Reformist*), sharing similar views on many aspects of European integration (Brusenbauch Meislova, 2019). Last but not least, Poland used to be (and still is) the largest recipient of EU funds, whereas the UK – despite the (in)famous British rebate – was a net contributor to the EU budget. For many, the simplistic view of the balance of EU budgetary transfers remains the key parameter of cost–benefit analysis of EU membership. This is why it was one of the main arguments in the Brexit campaign to leave. In the Polish case, it remains – and will remain for many years – a reason to be part of the EU project.

EUROSCEPTICISM OF EURO-ENTHUSIASTS

An important dimension that cannot be omitted in the context of Brexit and its ramifications is the phenomenon of Euroscepticism, which is present in very different ways in Poland and the UK. Undoubtedly, Brexit has been a manifestation of hard Eurosceptic views of large parts of the British citizenry. In contrast, Polish society represents exceptionally high levels of pro-EU attitudes, as demonstrated by public opinion polls. There are, though, similarities in attitudes towards the European Monetary Union. Both economies have notoriously remained outside of the Eurozone, partly as a result of highly Eurosceptic attitudes against the Eurozone in both societies. In this section, the focus is on the paradox of the highly pro-European support of the Polish citizens, accompanied with the (British-like) opposition to potential membership in the Eurozone. Analysing some specificities of Polish Euroscepticism is important in the light of Brexit, which is itself important to the Eurosceptic narrative.

Euroscepticism can be generally understood as a negative attitude towards the EU, the European integration process in general, some of its aspects or just the idea of uniting the continent in any respect (Taggart and Szczerbiak, 2004). In the case of the new member states (NMS), relatively few academic analyses have been conducted on Euroscepticism (Zuba and Riedel, 2015). In the first decade of full membership, the EU newcomers focused on proving that they are 'good Europeans'. Fairly successful rotating Presidencies of the Council of Ministers, a Presidency of the EU Parliament (Jerzy Buzek) and, not least, a Presidency of the European Council (Donald Tusk) were all signs that the NMS and their political elites felt more and more comfortable in the corridors of the EU institutions. However, this does not mean that all the new societies in the EU were and are unconditional Euro-enthusiasts. The Poles, Czechs, Hungarians and many others have shown their EU dissatisfaction on many different occasions. Yet the largest NMS, Poland, has remained a stable Euro-optimist. Even when governed by a moderate Eurosceptic coalition (2005–07), Polish society proved to be among the most Euro-enthusiastic in the Union. This was even more surprising after 2015, when the governing party in Warsaw took a more and more hard-Eurosceptic turn. The majority of society kept to highly pro-European positions.

What is similar in the case of Polish and British societies is the lack of appeal of monetary integration on the supranational level. Now, after Brexit, it is important to ask why Poles have an undisputed Euro-positive attitude whilst belonging firmly to the Eurosceptic camp when it comes to joining the Eurozone club. There is an important gap in Polish society between support for the European integration as such and opposition to supranational monetary integration in particular (Riedel, 2018a). And this cannot be understood just as an illustration of diversified public opinion typical of all democratic societies. In this case, the same people demonstrate a great deal of sympathy and support for the EU whilst at the same time being strongly Eurosceptic. In developing these attitudes, they refer to totally different, very often conflicting, sets of ideas, norms and values. Hence, there is a fundamental misunderstanding inside the Polish public opinion rather than a logical Euro-optimism combined with an equally rational Euroscepticism.

In Poland, directly after the transformation, there was very strong support for European integration and Polish participation in it. This was a result of a strategic turn narrated in public discourse as a 'Return to Europe'. The EU impressed the Poles as an area of economic prosperity, political stability and a promised land in general. So high expectations could only be disappointed. Once EU accession negotiations started and the EU became much more a set of figures, transition periods, opt-outs, etc., the fairy-tale picture disappeared. The first disappointments can be observed in the period 1998–2002. At that time, however, the government launched its information/promotional campaign before the accession referendum (2003). This stimulated an upward trend in support, which also continued after the momentous year of enlargement (2004). The enlargement enabled access to the Single Market and a 'rain' of cohesion money. Support for the EU thus reached its peak in 2008. Then the economic crises came to Europe (to Poland, however, to a lesser extent). As in many other EU member states, society started to become more Eurosceptic (Riedel, 2017). This downwards trend was broken again in 2014, following developments in Eastern and South-Eastern Ukraine. Poles saw with their own eyes the alternative to their Western orientation. Directly after the implosion of the Soviet Union in 1991, Polish and Ukrainian GDP were very similar. Two and a half decades later, Polish GDP is three times higher than Ukrainian, as a result of Leszek Balcerowicz's shock therapy and the strategic choices undertaken by the post-1989 governments. Poland is also the only EU member state that has a border with both Russia and Ukraine, which makes it more exposed to any effects of the Ukrainian-Russian conflict. This problematic situation spoke to the imagination of the Polish people to such an extent that their support for the EU skyrocketed and surpassed previous levels. In 2015, both the presidential and parliamentary elections were won by the PiS, which appeared as a self-proclaimed Euro-realist, but in practice a strongly Eurosceptic (by rhetoric and action) political actor. Jarosław Kaczyński, PiS's leader, read the Polish society's sentiments accurately and there are no surprises in the behaviour of his party (and government) towards Brussels. Perhaps it is even more representative than the public opinion polls that very often express a politically correct, rather than real, attitude of the Polish society.

One of the possible explanations for this phenomenon is the economic utility theory, which suggests that the more a society gains from the European integration project, the more positive it is about it. In economic terms, there are two strong arguments that persuade the Poles to be satisfied with their EU membership. One is participation in the Single Market which stimulated export growth (as an emerging market, the Polish economy is very much export dependent) and the second is the access to EU funds (cohesion and structural funds) which boosts public investments on an unprecedented scale. Here it is important to note that these two factors may disappear when Poland loses its competitive advantage (based on low labour costs) and when the voivodships (regions) stop qualifying for EU funds. All that suggests Poland's euro-enthusiastic attitude will decrease too. Additionally, other problems are seemingly cumulating inside and outside the EU project. These are, among others, the implications of the refugee/migration crisis, related collective decision problems in the allocation of the refugees, the recently overcome economic crisis, the unresolved Russian-Ukrainian conflict, pandemic-related restrictions, closed borders, etc. All in all, the EU is no longer seen as a promised land, a panacea for the inefficiencies of Polish politics and economy, or as a prize for transformation fatigue. Instead of being a solution, the EU has turned into a problem in the eyes of many Poles. The Euroscepticism of Poland's closest neighbours (like the Czech Republic) and partners (like Hungary or the UK) is also an important contextual factor.

The Brexit context is of highest importance for Eurosceptic actors. They can point to an example of a country that has left the EU and remained successful in many spheres of socio-economic life. Especially in the case of Poland, whose relations with the UK (trade flows, large diaspora, etc.) are quite special, Brexit is an exceptionally convincing example. Both in Poland and the UK, Eurosceptic parties remain in power. Britain ended up outside of the EU. Yet, even in the case of Poland, we are witnessing a process of worsening Brussels-Warsaw relations. This may have serious implications in the long term, since the ruling PiS party has all sorts of propaganda tools at its disposal and conducts an openly anti-EU narrative in Polish public discourse. The expression 'Pol-Exit' became *de-taboo-ized* and has entered the very centre of the political debate.

After Donald Tusk's return to Polish politics (2021), the pro/anti EU cleavage was promoted as one of the most crucial importance in the Polish public debate. This has not been the case since the accession referendum campaign in 2003. The old personal 'Tusk-Kaczyński' conflict was reactivated in new post-Brexit circumstances and it manifested in new ways and forms. Bearing in mind the pro-European attitude of the vast majority of the Polish society, Tusk and his party (Platforma Obywatelska/Civic Platform) have attempted to set the agenda of problematic (for PiS) topics, like the arguments between Warsaw and Brussels on the issues of green transition, judiciary reforms, rule of law standards, Article 7 procedure or the Recovery Fund. The PiS narrative, in return, became even more sovereignistic, and – as a consequence – openly anti-EU. Such a strong polarization in the debate among the political elites may bring about a similar effect among the Polish citizens. Pro-EU and pro-Western orientation has been an element of broad political consensus in the post-1989 Poland. Contesting and challenging it would mean a *Copernicus* turn in the Polish politics' paradigms.

TESTING THE LIMITS OF DIFFERENTIATION – DE-EUROPEANIZATION LESSONS

After the fall of the Berlin Wall, a group of the formerly East-bloc countries launched their journey towards the West under the 'Return to Europe' slogan. This Europeanization project resulted in accepting them in the 2004, 2007 and 2013 waves of enlargement as full EU members. Since that moment, their pro-EU commitment has been questioned many times, and the strongest trend observable in Poland and Hungary is an ostentatious U-turn that they took in the past years. It is characterized not only by democratic backsliding and illiberal tendencies, but also by accompanying de-Europeanization. It manifests itself in open anti-EU attitudes of the authorities as well as in various other spheres and dimensions from functional to normative ones.

Unsurprisingly for many Eurosceptic political actors (like for the PiS party in Poland), the UK (ruled by the Conservative Party) was an important ally. They watched the British case as an illustration of a de-Europeanization process. The Brexit process may be perceived as testing the limits of differentiation in Europe. Indeed it tests where differentiation may turn into disintegration and de-Europeanization. Before Brexit, the exemptions from the Eurozone and Schengen area had already been quite prominent examples of differentiation. But, undermining one of the four freedoms (free movement of people) – that became one of the bones of contestation in the Brexit process – attacked one of the fundamentals of the integration project and questioned the very idea of European integration. The British case showed that openly opposing the very core of the Single Market turned the direction of the integration trajectory. Economic theories of international integration tell us that it is not only the free movement of products and services that constitutes a single market; the creation and functioning of a single market is also conditional on liberalization and free movement of the factors of production: capital and labour. This is why the four freedoms have so far been treated as inseparable elements of one concept. At least, until 2020, when the UK succeeded in negotiating a status in which it has access to the Single Market, and the continental Europeans do not have open access to the British labour market.

For Poland and other Central and Eastern Europe (CEE) EU member states, the Brexit case is also instructive in terms of the dynamic process of European integration differentiation and fragmentation. Two decades ago, in the pre-accession phase, the 'Return to Europe' paradigm anticipated full and deep membership in the Western structures. In contemporary Central and Eastern Europe, the picture is much more mixed. Alongside the fully integrated states belonging to the core of the EU (e.g. the Baltic states or Slovakia), there are reluctant EU members who question the fundamentals of the European integration project (e.g. Poland and Hungary). In this context, it is worth reflecting on the lessons of Brexit for the better understanding of the system of European differentiation, specifically from the CEE perspective.

Both in academic debate and in real-life politics concepts of differentiated integration offer an alternative to dichotomous thinking about full membership and full non-membership. However, that possibility is itself closed down by extreme forms of opposition in the UK to Europe that cannot easily be comprehended in existing categorizations of differentiated integration (Leruth, 2015). The UK's decision to leave the EU has opened up a new chapter in discussions about future forms of differentiated integration in Europe (and, interestingly, inside the UK as well). Britain may itself end up differently integrated with the EU. Some parts of the UK may even end up reintegrating inside the EU. Some may end up in a grey zone that will only be defined in coming years as Brexit is concluded (Riedel, 2018b).

Differentiated integration as a scholarly concept grew together with the real-life increase in differentiation (opt-outs, exemptions, enhanced cooperation, constructive abstention, special clauses, additional protocols, etc.). London was an unquestioned leader in this exercise. In the last two decades, differentiation has been a dominant feature of European integration (Boerzel, 2005). It is argued that approximately half of the EU policies are implemented in different ways (Leruth and Lord, 2015). Undoubtedly, studying differentiated integration contributes to a better and more refined theoretical and empirical understanding of the European integration process (Genschel and Jachtenfuchs, 2014). Differentiated integration can be best understood as the institutional response to the increasing heterogeneity of member states' preferences and capacities resulting from the widening and deepening of the EU (Leuffen et al., 2013; Schimmelfennig, 2014). In the case of the UK, it was not capacities but preferences that kept London outside of the European core. It simply belongs to the category of the less willing countries, together with outsiders like the quasi-member (e.g. Switzerland). Some member states opt out (internal differentiation), whereas some non-member states opt in (external differentiation). That both contributes to – and creates further need for – reconciling heterogeneity inside and outside of the Union. Vertical differentiation is where policy areas are integrated at different speeds or with different degrees of centralization. Horizontal differentiation is where integrated policies are neither uniformly nor exclusively valid in all EU member states (Schimmelfenning et al., 2015). The UK did not participate in all EU policies (horizontal differentiation) and in some others it participated at its own speed and extent (vertical differentiation). This is undoubtedly also the wish of many Eurosceptic actors in the CEE, predominantly Poland and Hungary.

The Brexit issue tests differentiated integration in new ways. The story of European integration can be told as a story of its deepening and widening – these two dynamics form the mechanics of differentiation. Consequently, progress in integration has also meant an increase in differentiation over time (Schimmelfenning and Winzen, 2013). The UK supported the widening of the European Communities (later the European Union) as a constraint on deepening. The interplay between the two dimensions of integration seemed to effectively answer the British allergy to 'ever closer Union'. However the advance in integration in the 1990s, followed by the big bang enlargement (as well as subsequent waves in 2007 and 2013), meant that the idea that the EU had gone far enough became dominant in British public discourse. That dissatisfaction with membership was reinforced by the economic crisis (Schweiger and Magone, 2014), which hit the British economy severely. The party system reacted to it on the supply side, providing choices that would eventually make Brexit possible. In the case of Poland, the demand side (citizens' preferences) remain predominantly pro-European, whereas it is the supply side (the ruling party and its apparatus) that shapes the anti-EU discourse.

In the Brexit context, the European integration project is no longer just a game of deepening and widening. Brexit may also lead to a new generation of differentiation. The Brexit referendum – in its supranational dimension – was not only about Britain's position on the map of the EU (and its peripheries). It was also about the future of the integration project as such. The UK switched from an integration-tolerant country, to an integration unfriendly country whose behaviour and attitude endangers the very fundaments of the integration process. It produces externalities for other member states and non-members no matter if they are pro- or anti-integrationist. Given ways in which integration has evolved from one crisis to another, it is possible to interpret the Brexit decision as an opportunity for EU reform. The reformist impulse of Brexit may enhance European integration in two possible ways. First, it may help to reform the EU into a more differentiated system, which will allow countries to integrate at various speeds and extents. Second, 'getting rid' of Britain may even accelerate 'ever closer union' (Riedel, 2018b).

Another important lesson from Brexit is that the UK's European question was more than a question of whether to be or not to be in Europe. It was a question about party politics, identity, political economy, globalization and, last but not least, a changing Europe. The problem is that it can never be entirely answered (Oliver, 2015). It will come back in a reframed form with every new generation, every new treaty, every new enlargement. It is debatable though whether it is the referendum that is the most optimal method of dealing with it. At the same time, Brexit is not a one-day event that simply means walking out of Europe. Instead, it rather means a lengthy and complex process (Bernstein, 2016), which by no means ended in 2020.

Concluding this section, differentiation in Europe has plainly reached a scale and depth at which it can be described as a systematic characteristic of the European integration project in the 21st century. Frank Schimmelfennig, Dirk Leuffen and Berthold Rittberger wrote even about the system of differentiated integration, in which differentiation is an essential and enduring characteristic of the EU (Schimmelfennig et al., 2015). Directly after the Brexit referendum, the initial six founding states (Germany, France, Italy, Belgium, Luxemburg and the Netherlands) met in Berlin in order to discuss the new circumstances generated by the Brexit earthquake as well as to identify the options ahead. Symptomatically, the rest of the EU was called to a meeting in Warsaw a day later for the same purpose. The new divisions in Europe became even more clear in the sharp picture after the British decided to leave. Brexit gave the differentiated integration new impetus and dynamics. Whether it was not a turning point, reversing the trend towards disintegration remains an open question. Undoubtedly, the CEE peripheries could observe, whilst watching the Brexit process, where the lines are as regards the various circles of differentiated integration, as well as where the red line is beyond which the disintegration and de-Europeanization process starts.

CONCLUSIONS

The core period of the Brexit process (2016–20) coincided with the unprecedented de-Europeanization turn on the EU's Eastern flank. More than ten years after the EU's big bang enlargement, many of the new member states lost their initial pro-integration impetus and began flirting with Britain (and its EU-contesting attitude) both on the supranational level and in bilateral relations. Poland's nationalist-conservative government (2015–) chose the UK as the number one strategic partner in their foreign and EU policies. In the European Parliament, the British Conservatives allied with the Czech ODS (Občanská demokratická strana/Civic Democratic Party) as well as the Polish PiS (Prawo i Sprawiedliwośćb/Law and Justice) in the European Conservatives and Reformist group. Due to its economic and political weight, Poland is a critical case of general tendencies in the CEE region. However, the Polish case does more than exemplify some developments common to the CEE (semi-)periphery. Additionally, Poland is also one of the most Brexit-impacted states, given the geographical structure of its trade migration flows and its other socio-economic characteristics.

The Brexit process therefore offers a unique opportunity to draw important lessons for those states that deviate from the pro-European trajectory. De-Europeanization tendencies observed in many countries of the CEE region, here illustrated with the most significant example of Poland, should be seen in the context of differentiated integration discourse. The UK's experience with testing the limits of differentiation shows that DI's flexibility has its limits, even in the case of one of the strongest member states. Moreover, Brexit, with its profound implications, is set to be one of the most challenging phenomena facing the EU. It brings about serious consequences for the whole Union as well as the specific member states.

At the same time, the 23 June 2016 Brexit referendum brought some new stimulus to the reflection on the various forms of differentiation in Europe. Never before has an existing member state decided to leave the EU. At the same time, never before has a member state been so internally divided about its attitudes towards Brussels. With its imperial past and a long-lasting tradition of the 'splendid isolation' in its international relations, London has never been an easy partner for the other continental Europeans. It is true that the UK, historically speaking, had a specific attitude to the European integration project. However, the Brexit referendum brought about some new quality in the debate on differentiated integration in Europe. The UK was one of the most important of the older member states (though not a founding member), with one of the most powerful economies and high status in international relations. All that gave the UK bargaining power that it used to demand forms of differentiation in the EU (Schimmelfennig, 2014) that exempted it from commitments it did not want.

Even though the UK has always been on the positive side as regards the balance of discriminatory and exemptive differentiations, it appeared not enough for quite a portion of the British citizens and political elites. The UK, before the referendum, enjoyed a status of a preferential membership – the opposition of discriminatory membership (Schimmelfennig, 2014) – a case in which a member state is exempted from many rights and benefits of integration (which was the case of Poland and other new member states after the 2004, 2007 and 2013 rounds of enlargement). The UK was released from many undesired obligations that most of the other member states took. The rest of the EU was not determined enough to demand the full adoption of the EU law. The UK was strong by its Euroscepticism, economic as well as political power and, as a result, enjoyed a positive discrimination in the Community.

London's divorcing Brussels may provide a strong, disintegrative impulse for the whole project. And, as such, it has a destructive potential for the post-World War II economic and political order in Europe. The tsunami effect of Britain going out of the EU may be felt not only by the entrepreneurs operating across the Channel, but on the whole Single Market, including the barriers in migration traffic, capital flows, deficits in EU funds and policies. Brexit is a structural problem for the EU and its future (Riedel, 2018b).

Irrespective of the obvious prediction about Europe's future that the EU will continue to exist in one form or another, it is legitimate to assume that Brexit was one of the most salient symptoms of a brewing conflict between competing concepts of European integration. The UK as a member was presumed to be a crucial part of the fragile equilibrium in Europe standing behind market orientation, free trade, economic liberalism and balanced integration, and in contrast to dirigisme, protectionism, deeper integration and growing EU budgets (Goellner, 2017). The UK's leaving the EU bloc might possibly shift the focus away from liberal towards more regulatory concepts, gravitating in the direction of state-interventionism. The EU's matrix of interest will also evolve generating some new losers and winners of the new situation. Together with the Brexit process coming to its conclusion, the V4 countries – with Poland as the leading one – lost one of the closest allies in the EU. At the same time, their relative power grew proportionally in the supranational decision-making system.

In this way, Brexit opens up some potential for the CEE region to punch above its weight and play a crucial role in redefining the post-Brexit EU, or at least shape the debate on the future direction of the EU. At the same time, the V4 grouping (especially Poland and Hungary) voiced their concerns that Brexit could potentially serve to marginalize them further, in so far as Germany and EU institutions would use it to speed up the European integration (Brusenbauch Meislova, 2019).

Moreover, Poland has a chance to become the least compatible EU member state in the post-Brexit era. Its Eurosceptic political elite proved to be a troublemaker in Brussels on many occasions – from neglecting the migrants' allocation mechanism in 2017 to blocking the budgetary negotiations in 2020. Poland stands out in many policy areas as structurally incompatible with the EU's mainstream. Remaining outside of the Eurozone is a significant example. It is most clearly visible in the climate–energy domain, where Poland lags behind and is doing very little to catch up. And, since the Green New Deal for Europe remains one of the most important elements in the EU's political agenda, this incompatibility is critically important. Hence, there are several reasons to expect Poland to inherit the UK's status as the main troublemaker in EU politics.

NOTE

1. This research was supported by the NCN (Narodowe Centrum Nauki/National Center of Science) grant entitled 'Determinants and Dynamics of Differentiated Integration in (Post)Brexit Europe' (2020/37/B/HS5/00230).

REFERENCES

Bernstein, A. (2016, April). To Brexit or to Brexit? *News Extra*.

Boerzel, T. (2005). Mind the Gap! European Integration between Level and Scope. *Journal of European Public Policy*, *12*(2), 217–36. https://doi.org/10.1080/13501760500043860.

Brusenbauch Meislova, M. (2019). Great Expectations or Misplaced Hopes? The Role of the Visegrád Group in the Brexit Process. *Europe-Asia Studies*, *71*(8), 1261–84. https://doi.org/10.1080/09668136.2019.1643825.

Genschel, P., and Jachtenfuchs, M. (2014). Introduction: Beyond Market Regulation. Analysing the European Integration of Core State Powers. In P. Genschel and M. Jachtenfuchs (eds), *Beyond the Regulatory Polity? The European Integration of Core State Powers* (pp. 279–84). Oxford University Press.

Goellner, R.A. (2017). The Visegrád Group – a Rising Star Post-Brexit? Changing Distribution of Power in the European Council. *Open Political Science*, *1*, 1–6. https://doi.org/10.1515/openps-2017-0001.

Leruth, B. (2015). Operationalizing National Preferences on Europe and Differentiated Integration. *Journal of European Public Policy*, *22*(6), 816–35. https://doi.org/10.1080/13501763.2015.1020840.

Leruth, B., and Lord, C. (2015). Differentiated Integration in the European Union: A Concept, a Process, a System or a Theory? *Journal of European Public Policy*, *22*(6), 754–64. https://doi.org/10.1080/13501763.2015.1021196.

Leuffen, D., Rittberger, B., and Schimmelfennig, F. (2013). *Differentiated Integration. Explaining Variation in the European Union*. Palgrave.

Matysek-Jędrych, A., and Mroczek-Dąbrowska, K. (2021). Brexit and its Potential Consequences for Poland – the Perspective of Single Market Principles. In A. Visvizi, A. Matysek-Jędrych, and K. Mroczek-Dąbrowska (eds), *Poland in the Single Market: Politics, Economics, the Euro* (Series: Europa – Perspectives on the EU Single Market, pp. 299–313). Routledge.

Oliver, T. (2015). To Be or Not to Be in Europe: Is That the Question? Britains' European Question and an In/Out Referendum. *International Affairs*, *91*(1), 77–91. https://doi.org/10.1111/1468-2346.12187.

Riedel, R. (2017). The Evolution of the Polish Central Bank's Perspectives on the Eurozone Entry. *Post-Communist Economies*, *29*(1), 106–16.

Riedel, R. (2018a). EUROscepticism and Monetary Security in Europe. In P. Frankowski and A. Gruszczak (eds), *Cross-Disciplinary Perspectives on Regional and Global Security* (pp. 1–21). Palgrave McMillan. Doi.org/10.1007/978-3-319-75280-8_1.

Riedel, R. (2018b). Great Britain and Differentiated Integration in Europe. In T.D. Ramiro, K. Tanel, and C. Archil (eds), *Brexit – History, Reasoning and Perspectives* (pp. 99–112). Springer (Professional) International Publishing.

Schimmelfennig, F. (2014). EU Enlargement and Differentiated Integration: Discrimination or Equal Treatment? *Journal of European Public Policy*, *21*(5), 681–98. https://doi.org/10.1080/13501763.2014.897744.

Schimmelfennig, F., and Winzen, T. (2013). Instrumental and Constitutional Differentiation in the European Union. *Journal of Common Market Studies*, *52*(2), 354–70. https://doi.org/10.1111/jcms.12103.

Schimmelfennig, F., Leufen, D., and Rittberger, B. (2015). The European Union as a System of Differentiated Integration: Interdependence, Politicization and Differentiation. *Journal of European Public Policy*, *22*(6), 764–82. https://doi.org/10.1080/13501763.2015.1020835.

Schweiger, C., and Magone, J.M. (2014). Differentiated Integration and Cleavage in the EU under Crisis Conditions. *Perspectives on European Politics and Society*, *15*(3), 259–65. https://doi.org/10.1080/15705854.2014.912394.

Taggart, P., and Szczerbiak, A. (2004). Contemporary Euroscepticism in the Party Systems of the European Union Candidate States of Central and Eastern Europe. *European Journal of Political Research*, *43*(1), 1–27. https://doi.org/10.1111/j.1475-6765.2004.00143.x.

Wypłosz, C. (2016). Introduction: Cycling backwards. In C. Wypłosz (ed.), *What to Do with the UK? EU perspectives on Brexit* (pp. 1–17). CEPR Press.

Zuba, K., and Riedel, R. (2015). EUROsceptycyzm – próba konceptualizacji. *Europejski*, *3*(37), 26–48. http://dx.doi.org/https%3A//doi.org/10.31338/1641-2478pe.3.15.2.

18. Regional cooperation in the EU in the shadow of Brexit

Ian Cooper and Federico Fabbrini

INTRODUCTION

Within the European Union (EU), there are numerous regional groups of member states that engage in formalized cooperation that is separate from their cooperation within EU institutions. By our reckoning, there are 13 such groups that are currently active. They are found in every part of Europe – North, South, East and West – and every current EU-27 member state participates in at least one. These groups vary in numerous ways. Some of these groups are long-standing (e.g. Benelux, est. 1944) whereas others are quite recent creations (e.g. New Hanseatic League, est. 2018). They range in size from two members (Franco-German Cooperation, Iberian Summit) to 12 (Three Seas Initiative). Some are deeply institutionalized (e.g. Baltic Assembly) whereas others are only minimally so (e.g. Weimar Triangle, Slavkov Triangle). Some involve extensive cooperation across a range of policy areas (e.g. Visegrád Group) whereas others are focused on one policy area only (e.g. Salzburg Forum). Some are focused mainly on internal cooperation (e.g. Central European Defense Cooperation) whereas others are also concerned with policy coordination at the EU level (e.g. EuroMed7, the Nordic-Baltic Six). Despite these variations, all these groups represent forms of bottom-up cooperation that reside at an intermediate level between the individual member state and the EU as a whole.

The purpose of this chapter is to examine the phenomenon of regional caucusing in the EU, with the aim of mapping this unexplored political dynamic, and considering its consequences for the process of European integration. As such, this chapter pursues three objectives. First, the chapter endeavours to identify the bottom-up regional groups (BURGs) of cooperation existing in the EU, compare their function and assess their organization. Second, the chapter analyzes the impact that these regional groups have on EU integration, distinguishing between groups that pursue a purely administrative framework of cooperation and groups that instead are created to serve as agenda-setting arenas, multiplying the capacity of participating member states to shape EU policies within the EU governance architecture. Finally, the chapter also discusses BURGs in light of Brexit – the decision of the United Kingdom (UK) to withdraw from the EU – arguing that BURGs could provide a link between EU member states and the post-Brexit UK, even as the latter's departure has had the effect of strengthening BURGs within the EU.

This chapter fills a gap in the scholarly literature on European integration. While many regional experts may have studied one or another of these groups on an individual basis, there has been very little research conducted with the aim of analyzing and comparing them as a general phenomenon. Indeed, this is reflected in the fact that there is not even a commonly accepted name for these groups – variously called 'partnerships, alignments, blocs, alliances or groupings' (Rūse, 2014, p. 230) – let alone a commonly accepted definition of what they are.

Only a few works have sought to give a comprehensive survey of the BURGs within the EU. Those that have done so (Dangerfield, 2008; Inotai, 1998; Klemenčič, 2011; Rūse, 2013) are not up to date with recent developments in this rapidly evolving field, which has seen the creation of three new BURGs since 2015 (the Slavkov Triangle, the Three Seas Initiative, the New Hanseatic League) and the significant upgrade of an older one (Franco-German Cooperation, strengthened by the Aachen Treaty of 2019). More recent work in this field has been less comprehensive, tending towards shorter pieces analyzing the bottom-up cooperation among member states in the light of the policy challenges of Eurozone governance reform (Lewicki, 2019), Brexit (Brattberg et al., 2020) and Covid-19 (Lang and von Ondarza, 2020). Many of the works in the wider literature focus on one single BURG as their object of study (Górka, 2018; Kleinberga, 2019; Wouters and Vidal, 2017) rather than comparing them or studying them as a general pan-EU phenomenon. Some works have more broadly focused on BURGs in one particular region, that is, Central and Eastern Europe (Cabada, 2018; Jančošekovà, 2017), which has seen a proliferation of multiple adjacent, overlapping and nested BURGs. Some scholars have mainly focused their attention on one BURG but are also alert to broader questions such as how to typologize BURGs (Dangerfield, 2008) or how to study inter-BURG cooperation, as seen for example in the relations of the Baltic Assembly with Benelux and the Visegrád Group (Cutler and Von Lingen, 2019). Another scholarly angle is to look at how a single member state can stake out its diplomatic position through its engagement with multiple BURGs, for example, Poland (Kirpsza, 2019) or Austria (Müller, 2016). But, overall, it is evident that there is a gap in the literature, exposing a pressing need for an up-to-date and comprehensive survey of regional groupings within the EU.

This chapter therefore goes beyond this ad hoc scholarship by assessing the phenomenon of regional grouping from a broader theoretical perspective and reflecting on its implications for EU integration studies, and especially theories of differentiated governance. In particular, we argue that this kind of bottom-up political cooperation represents a particular form of differentiation within the EU, albeit one that is not always recognized as such. This is because much of the analysis of differentiated integration is focused on the extent to which common EU rules are not applied uniformly across the EU due to the various derogations and opt-outs that apply to different member states (Schimmelfenning and Winzen, 2020). This rule-based conceptualization however is effectively a top-down measure of differentiation in that it takes full application across the whole EU as the baseline and then measures deviations away from that. This is of course a valid and very useful kind of analysis, but it cannot capture the complete picture because it tends to leave out forms of bottom-up cooperation, such as those analyzed here.

The chapter is structured as follows. The second section provides a definition of regional groups, clarifying what properties we regard as necessary for a specific regional form of cooperation to fall within our definition of the concept and offers a list of existing EU regional groups. The third section compares the existing regional groups, classifying them with regard to their longevity (pre- versus post-accession), institutional structure (thick versus thin), policy scope (sectoral versus general) and the degree to which they are active/inactive. The fourth section examines the different purposes which the BURGs may serve – integration vanguard, functional cooperation, policy coordination or resistance. The fifth section discusses the interplay between BURGs and Brexit. The sixth section, finally, concludes, and reflects on the potential for further research on regional groups as a tool to enrich understanding of EU integration and differentiated integration.

DEFINING BURGS

Europe is a geographical region of complex interdependence in which there are multiple forms of international cooperation among states both within and outside the EU. In this chapter, we are only concerned with a particular form of cooperation, one that takes place inside the EU but is not part of the EU institutional structure. For this reason, we have five criteria by which we define an intra-EU bottom-up regional group (BURG). A BURG is a form of international cooperation that meets the following five criteria: (1) it is institutionalized cooperation; (2) it is currently active; (3) its participants are all current EU member states; (4) it is institutionally separate from the EU; and (5) the participating states are geographically proximate, by belonging to the same regional area of the EU. Further elaboration of these five criteria is provided below, along with examples of other forms of cooperation that they exclude, in order to clarify the nature of the BURGs that are the subject of this chapter.

Institutionalized Cooperation

We define an intra-EU BURG as a group that is institutionalized, that is, it has permanence that is regularly reproduced in practice. For example, a BURG could be classified as institutionalized if regular meetings, among ministers or parliamentarians, were held under its auspices – although, as we explain in the next section, the depth of organizational structuring of BURGs can vary significantly from one regional group to another. What this criterion excludes is temporary tactical alliances among member states such as are manifest, for example, when they cast their votes together in the Council of the EU (Hosli, 1999). It also excludes groups of EU member states that are sometimes described as having a collective identity but which lack any institutional form. For example, the 'Founding Six' – the original six member states of the European Coal and Steel Community (ECSC) and European Economic Community (EEC) – are sometimes described as a distinctive group, but we cannot find any extant institutional manifestation of this particular group identity – except, perhaps, a one-off meeting by the Foreign Affairs Ministers of the Six prior to the UK's Brexit referendum (Zalan, 2016) – and so we do not classify this group as a BURG.

Currently Active

Closely related to the previous criterion, we define an intra-EU BURG as one in which cooperation is currently active. The rationale for this criterion is that our purpose here is not to provide an historical account of all BURGs that have existed within the EU but only to survey those that currently exist. This excludes forms of cooperation among EU member states that existed previously but have been dissolved or fallen into disuse. One example of a BURG that no longer exists is the Western European Union (WEU), a military cooperation organization that was active in the late 1980s and 1990s, made up of EU member states that were also members of the North Atlantic Treaty Organization (NATO): over time the tasks of the WEU were transferred to the EU and it was dissolved in 2011. In this chapter, we have applied this criterion liberally so as to include those BURGs that are currently active even if there have been some gaps in their recent past activity – for example, they have not always held an annual meeting. For this reason, we include both the Slavkov Triangle (aka the Austerlitz Triangle/Trilateral) of Austria, the Czech Republic and Slovakia, founded in 2015 (Matovic, 2020), and the Weimar Triangle (France, Germany and Poland) founded in 1991, because both of them held meetings in 2020.

Only Current EU Member States

We define an Intra-EU BURG as one in which only current EU member states are full members. The rationale behind this criterion is that our purpose is to analyze BURGs as a phenomenon that is internal to the EU, and European integration. This criterion does have the effect of excluding important regional cooperation forums that include countries both inside and outside the EU, such as the long-standing Nordic Council (founded in 1952), which includes three EU member states (Denmark, Finland and Sweden) and two non-EU countries (Norway and Iceland), along with the semi-autonomous regions of Åland, the Faroe Islands and Greenland. This criterion also excludes regional cooperation that involves the UK (now an ex-member state as of 31 January 2020), although the interplay between Brexit and BURGs is discussed more at length in the fifth section below.

Institutional Separation from the EU

A BURG is a group of EU member states pursuing a form of cooperation that is separate from the common policies that are pursued at the EU level. By this definition, the Eurozone, in which currently 19 of the 27 EU member states share a common currency, is not a BURG because those states are pursuing a common EU policy, the third stage of Economic and Monetary Union (EMU). It is an instance of differentiated governance, but it is top-down rather than bottom-up in that the non-Eurozone states are opting out or derogating from the common policy. This is also true of many other common EU policies wherein certain member states exercise an opt-out. Even a group of member states pursuing 'enhanced cooperation' is not a BURG, because this is deeper integration authorized by the EU treaties. It should be noted however that sometimes a BURG will forge a common policy that is eventually adopted at EU level. The Schengen Agreement of 1985 is a good example: it was a pact made by five of the then ten EU member states to work to abolish internal border controls. As the Schengen area expanded, the EU eventually endorsed the policy of a Europe-wide passport-free travel zone. Thus, while the original Schengen Five were arguably a BURG, that is, distinct from the EU, this is no longer true because the Schengen acquis has been incorporated into the EU treaties (save for member states which have an opt-out or do not yet meet the criteria to join). Otherwise, the EU treaties are silent as regards the existence and status of the BURGs, with one exception – Benelux. As the oldest existing BURG, created in 1944, the Benelux is also the only regional caucus which is explicitly recognized in the EU treaties, as Article 350 TFEU (still) states that 'The provisions of the Treaties shall not preclude the existence or completion of regional unions between Belgium and Luxembourg, or between Belgium, Luxembourg and the Netherlands, to the extent that the objectives of these regional unions are not attained by the application of the Treaties.'[1] This provision, which was written into the EU treaties by the 1957 Treaty of Rome establishing the EEC, simply acknowledged the existence of the Benelux as a pre-EU BURG. There are no other provisions of the EU treaties which recognize the existence of individual BURGs or which permit or enable their creation; this absence underscores their institutional separation from the EU.

Geographical Proximity

The final criterion that determines whether states comprise a BURG is geographical proximity. This is admittedly the least precise criterion to define a BURG. In our view, this is met when states participating in a regional group belong to the same geographical area of Europe: as such, the relevant states do not need to be adjacent (with contiguous land or sea borders) but they should be situated in the same general region within Europe. This criterion arises from our observation that, with one exception (the Arraiolos Group), each group is concentrated in a particular region of Europe, even if the cooperating member states are relatively dispersed geographically. For example, the members of New Hanseatic League are all located in Northern Europe, even though they are spread over considerable distance (from Ireland to Estonia). Equally, the Weimar Triangle, comprising France, Germany and Poland, includes three bordering member states at the heart of the EU, which, due to their landmass, span from the Atlantic Ocean to the border with Russia and Belarus. Identifying a criterion of regional proximity excludes from our definition of BURGs forms of cooperation based on factors that are completely unrelated to region or geography. For this reason, our study excludes the Arraiolos Group – the one exception noted above – which is an informal summit, begun in 2003, of the presidents of EU member states that are parliamentary or semi-presidential republics.

With these criteria in hand, we can identify 13 groups of member states within the EU today that meet our definition of a BURG (Table 18.1).

COMPARING BURGS: KEY VARIABLES

Having identified the list of existing intra-EU BURGs, based on the definition provided in the prior section, we now offer a classification of these forms of regional caucusing. The phenomenon of BURGs, in fact, is quite heterogeneous, and the types of regional caucuses currently operational within the EU range across multiple dimensions. In particular, for analytical purposes we suggest it is helpful to differentiate BURGs according to these four variables: (i) their time of establishment – with old regional groups pre-dating EU membership and new regional groups post-dating EU membership; (ii) their level of institutionalization, which ranges from very light to very sophisticated machineries; (iii) their policy scope – with some regional groups dealing with sectoral-specific issues, and others dealing with a broader, general ambit; and finally (iv) their degree of activity, which ranges from very active, with BURGs that are regularly summoned, to fairly inactive, with BURGs that are only episodically revived by the participating member states for specific purposes. Understanding the features of these regional groups is helpful to assess their impact on EU integration (which we do in the next section); hence a further elaboration of these four criteria is offered below.

Longevity, Pre- or Post-Accession

BURGs can be classified depending on whether participating member states have created these frameworks of cooperation before joining the EU, or after joining the EU, or when some were in the EU and others were not at the time of creation. Of the 13 existing groups we have identified based on the definition given in the previous section, four were created prior

Table 18.1 Bottom-up regional groups in the European Union

Grouping	Countries Involved	Est.	Purpose	Institutional Features
Benelux	Belgium, Luxembourg, Netherlands	1944	Politico-economic union	Customs Union (1944); Parliamentary Assembly (1955); Economic Union (1958); Benelux Court of Justice (1965); Benelux Union (2008)
Franco-German Cooperation	France, Germany	1963	Political cooperation	Élysée Treaty (1963); Aachen Treaty (2019); Franco-German Parliamentary Assembly
Iberian Summit	Portugal, Spain	1983	Political dialogue	Bilateral summit of prime ministers
Visegrád Group	Czechia, Hungary, Poland, Slovakia	1991	Political cooperation	Ministerial meetings and summits of leaders; Visegrád Fund (2000); Interparliamentary cooperation (2003)
Baltic Assembly	Estonia, Latvia, Lithuania	1991	Political cooperation	Baltic Assembly (1991); Baltic Council of Ministers (1994)
Weimar Triangle	France, Germany, Poland	1991	Political dialogue	Meetings of foreign ministers; occasional summits of leaders
Salzburg Forum	Austria, Bulgaria, Croatia, Czechia, Hungary, Poland, Romania, Slovakia, Slovenia	2000	Home affairs cooperation	Meetings of interior ministers (2 times/yr); meetings of police chiefs; meetings on margins of EU
Nordic-Baltic Six	Denmark, Estonia, Finland, Latvia, Lithuania, Sweden	2004	Policy coordination	Ministerial meetings in proximity to EU meetings
Central European Defence Cooperation	Austria, Croatia, Czechia, Slovakia, Hungary, Slovenia (Poland: observer)	2010	Military collaboration, migration control	Meetings of defence ministers
EuroMed 7, now EuroMed 9	Cyprus, France, Greece, Italy, Malta, Portugal, Spain, now including also Croatia, Slovenia	2013	Political cooperation	Ministerial meetings; South EU Summit of national leaders (2016)
Slavkov/Austerlitz Triangle	Austria, Czechia, Slovakia	2015	Political cooperation	Summits of leaders
Three Seas Initiative	Austria, Bulgaria, Croatia, Czechia, Estonia, Hungary, Latvia, Lithuania, Poland, Romania, Slovakia, Slovenia	2016	Cooperation on North-South infrastructure, economics, energy, transport, business	Annual summits of national presidents; business forums
New Hanseatic League	Denmark, Estonia, Finland, Ireland, Latvia, Lithuania, Netherlands, Sweden	2018	Economic policy coordination	Meetings of finance ministers

to their members joining the EU (the Benelux, the Iberian Summit, and the Visegrád and the Baltic groups). However, Benelux may be described as a 'pioneer', that is, established before the EU, whereas the other three are 'followers' in that their members acceded together to the already-existing EU (Inotai, 2008, p. 80). The Benelux Customs Union (1944) foreshadowed and served as a working model for the EEC (1957), which it helped to found. As for the other three, a large part of their *raison d'être* was to help their members with preparation for EU accession in the intervening years after the BURGs' creation – 1983–86 for Portugal and Spain, 1991–2004 for the states of the Baltic Assembly and the Visegrád Group. However, the cooperation among participating states within these BURGs has persisted and continued to evolve in the decades since they became member states of the EU.

Just three of our 13 BURGs are hybrids, in that they were created by a mix of EU and non-EU states (the Weimar Triangle, Salzburg Forum, Central European Defence Cooperation). All three of these are in a way 'bridges' between East and West. The Weimar Triangle (est. 1991) enabled a high-level dialogue between East (Poland) and West (France and Germany) just as the Cold War was ending, the Salzburg Forum (2000) enabled home affairs cooperation between Austria and numerous acceding Central and Eastern Europe (CEE) states, and the Central European Defence Cooperation enabled military collaboration among five CEE states and Croatia prior to its accession. Here too, the cooperation persisted after all participating states acceded to the EU.

Finally, six BURGs were formed when all participating states were in the EU: the Franco-German cooperation, the Nordic-Baltic Six, EuroMed, the Three Seas Initiative, the Slavkov Triangle and the New Hanseatic League were created by states that were already members of the EU. With one exception (Franco-German cooperation), all of these are relatively recent creations, a fact which serves to highlight the extent of the tendency towards factionalism in the increasingly heterogeneous EU.

Institutional Structure

The BURGs also vary in the extent to which they are institutionalized. At the extremes, they range from Benelux, a complex organization with its own intergovernmental council, committee of ministers, parliamentary assembly, court of justice and secretariat (Wouters and Vidal, 2017) to the Nordic-Baltic Six, a group that has 'no leader and no formal structures', but rather is 'merely a loose, informal club whose members have a habit of consulting and coordinating with each other' (Kuusik and Raik, 2018, p. 2). A BURG may be more or less institutionalized based on a number of factors: (a) the number and complexity of its institutional structures; (b) the formal legal status of its founding document – treaty, declaration, joint statement, etc. – if it has one; and (c) whether it has a secretariat, that is, a dedicated civil service. Using these factors, we find that the 13 BURGs may be classified into three groups according to their level of insitutionalization. Four of them are *highly institutionalized* (Baltic Assembly, Benelux, Franco-German duo, Visegrád Group), in that they have (quasi-) permanent institutional structures that go beyond intergovernmental meetings to also include, for example, interparliamentary cooperation. We find that five BURGs are *moderately institutionalized* (CEDC, EuroMed, Iberian Summit, Salzburg Forum, Three Seas Initiative) in that while their cooperation is mostly confined to intergovernmental meetings, on this level their cooperation is relatively durable and robust. Finally, four BURGs are *minimally institutionalized* (New

Hanseatic League, Nordic-Baltic 6, Slavkov Triangle, Weimar Triangle) in that their cooperation is relatively tenuous and somewhat ad hoc, with little or no institutional footprint.

Within the four highly institutionalized BURGs the architecture of regional cooperation goes beyond simple summitry, as it is grounded on more permanent institutional structures of cooperation, which involve also other domestic institutions beyond national governments. In particular, the Benelux has since 1955 a Parliamentary Assembly – technically the Benelux Interparliamentary Consultative Council, which is composed of 21 Dutch MPs (elected from the 2 houses of Parliament), 7 Luxembourgish MPs (drawn from the unicameral Parliament) and 21 Belgian MPs (elected pro-quota by both the national/federal Parliament and the assemblies of the federated regions and communities).[2] The Parliamentary Assembly's seat rotates between the participating states every two years, but the body meets annually, with the task to advise the governments of the participating member states – which are also meeting at intergovernmental level in the Benelux Council of Ministers. Moreover, the Benelux also has a permanent secretariat, based in Brussels, as well as a Benelux court – established in 1965 and operational since 1974, which rules on requests for preliminary rulings from the Dutch, Belgian and Luxembourgish supreme courts regarding regulations which are common to the three countries and serves as a civil service tribunal for personnel of the Benelux Economic Union. Similarly, also the Baltic group has since 1991 its own Assembly, composed of 60 delegates elected, 20 each by the Parliaments of Estonia, Lithuania and Latvia, as well as a Baltic Council of Ministers, together with a secretariat, based in Riga, which supports the organization. The Visegrád Group does not feature a Parliamentary Assembly but there is interparliamentary cooperation in the form of regular meetings of parliamentary speakers and committees among its four members (Borońska-Hryniewiecka and Grinc, 2021).[3] In addition, there is a Visegrád Fund (est. 2000) which supports regional cooperation, with its own separate institutional structure, including a secretariat.

Similarly, Franco-German cooperation relies on an ever deeper system of bilateral governance, described by some as 'the most institutionalized form of member state cooperation within a regional political organization' (Krotz and Schramm, 2021). While the Elysée Treaty of 1963 established the foundations for bilateral relations between these two founding EU member states, with regular summits at level of heads of state and government, since 2003 a Franco-German Ministerial Council has been convening regularly twice a year – with the full cabinets of the two governments meeting jointly to discuss issues of common concern. Moreover, following the efforts by French President Macron to relaunch Franco-German cooperation, the Treaty of Aachen of 2019 has now established a Franco-German Parliamentary Assembly, which, as indicated in a follow-up interparliamentary agreement, is designed to 'draft proposition on all questions of interest for Franco-German relations with the aim to go towards convergence of French and German law' (Accord Parlamentaire Franco-Allemand, 25 March 2019, Article 6) (Assemblée nationale, 2019). The Parliamentary Assembly, which is composed of 100 members – 50 chosen among their MPs by the German Bundestag and 50 by the French Assemblée Nationale – has now adopted its standing orders and started operating. In sum, as the overview above outlines, BURGs can sometimes be largely unstructured forms of interstate cooperation, or they can become real unions within the EU, with proper executive, legislative and sometimes even judicial structures of their own.

Policy Scope

BURGs vary significantly in the extent of their policy concern, with some of them pursuing a rather specific task, focusing on pre-defined sectoral policies, and others instead covering multiple areas of cooperation between the participating member states. In particular, of the 13 existing BURGs we identified in the prior section, four – the Salzburg Forum, the Central European Defence Cooperation, the Three Seas Initiative and the Hanseatic League – pursue a limited remit, which focuses on the specific policy areas – namely, in the order of the four above-mentioned groups: home affairs cooperation, military coordination, cooperation on energy, transport, infrastructure and business, as well as economy policy coordination in the context of EMU reform. On the contrary, the other six BURGs have a much broader remit. This is clearly true for the highly institutionalized BURGs – Franco-German Cooperation, the Visegrád Group, the Benelux and the Baltics – which focus on cooperation both on economic and political issues. Yet, this is also true for the other five BURGs that are not highly institutionalized. The Nordic-Baltic Six is a configuration that permits coordination across a wide range of policy areas, as it enables participating ministers or officials from these states to meet prior to or on the margins of important EU meetings (Council, COREPER). As for the others, meeting in a format of national leaders or foreign ministers (as in the EuroMed, Iberian Summit, Slavkov Triangle, Weimar Triangle) does permit a wide-ranging policy discussion on any topic of mutual interest that can encompass high politics (diplomatic dialogue) and low (e.g. regional or local cross-border issues). For example, the Weimar Triangle, while mostly episodic in its operation (see below), focuses on security issues but within a broader scope of political dialogue. The EuroMed, while originally emerging as a Southern EU member state response to the euro crisis, from the start focused on issues beyond EMU reform, to address essentially any topic on the EU agenda (from migration, to respect for the rule of law and Brexit). This variation among BURGs and their different policy scope clearly influences their relevance, with groups having a broader remit generally playing a larger role in the EU (see the sixth section below).

Frequency of Meetings

As we explained in the introduction to this chapter, we are exclusively focusing on BURGs that are currently active, meaning in existence within the EU. Nevertheless, active BURGs still can differ significantly in the intensity of their activity, so a final criterion to classify BURGs is the frequency with which BURGs are actually convened and operational. By this metric, clearly four of the 13 BURGs identified in the prior section (the Weimar Triangle, the Salzburg Forum, the Central European Defence Cooperation and the Three Seas Initiative) are not very active. For instance, the Weimar Triangle, officially established in 1991, has met only erratically: the summit of foreign ministers, in October 2020, was the first meeting to take place since 2016, and there has not been a trilateral summit of national leaders since 2011. This confirms the uncertain strategic weight that the participating member states, particularly France, give to this BURG. Similarly, the Three Seas Initiative has so far produced limited output, even though the Initiative has organized an annual summit of national presidents (many of whom have limited constitutional powers) and on one occasion saw the participation of a US President (Donald Trump in 2017). In general, the 12 participating member states appear to grant limited institutional relevance to the initiative, whose value seems therefore mostly to operate at a lower institutional level, as a business forum.

The other BURGs appear to be much more active. In particular, the four BURGs which are endowed with a thick organizational structure (see above) – with both intergovernmental and interparliamentary cooperation, such as the Benelux, the Baltics, the Franco-German couple and the Visegrád Group – continue to actively engage with each other through the institutionalized forms foreseen by their partnership agreements. Nevertheless, also other BURGs which still rely on a much thinner institutional organization appear to be much more relevant. This is the case of the EuroMed, which despite being exclusively a leaders' summit, has allowed the heads of state and government of France, Spain, Italy, Portugal, Malta, Greece and Cyprus to develop common positions on issues of common concerns. In fact, the group has recently expanded also to Croatia and Slovenia. In all cases, it should be kept in mind that in addition to meetings in public, there may be many more behind the scenes meetings; ministers and officials from the BURGs are frequently in the habit of coordinating their position on the margins of meetings at the EU level.

EXPLAINING BURGS

What is the purpose of BURGs? Why are they created? This section seeks to answer this question by distinguishing between BURGs that serve exclusively a function to facilitate cooperation between participating states (e.g. Benelux, Baltics, Salzburg Forum) and BURGs that instead are designed as forums to develop common positions among the participating states, setting the agenda at EU level (Hansa, EuroMed, Franco-German, Visegrád). More specifically, regarding the purpose of the BURGs, we can identify a rough typology according to the different purposes that each of them serves. The list is non-exclusive, meaning that a BURG might fulfil multiple purposes at once, and the purposes it serves might change over time. We can identify four ideal-types of BURGs – what we will call, *integration vanguard*, *functional cooperator*, *policy coordinator* and *resistance cell*. These kinds of BURGs emerged – broadly in this order – through the history of the European integration process.

Integration Vanguard

An *integration vanguard* is a group of states that pursues further integration among themselves with a view to promoting integration in the whole of the EU. The best examples of this are Benelux and Franco-German cooperation, although in different ways. Benelux, begun in 1944 before postwar European integration began, is a *model*, in that it established forms of institutional cooperation among the three countries, for example, the common external tariff, that would later be adopted by the EU as a whole (Inotai, 2008, p. 80). Franco-German cooperation is a *motor*, in that the two countries jointly initiate further integration with a view that it should be adopted by the EU as a whole, exercising a style of joint leadership that has been termed 'embedded bilateralism' (Krotz and Schild, 2013). This bilateral relationship was formalized in the Elysée Treaty (1963), but it was prefigured in the 1950 Schuman plan, which in its original form involved only France and Germany but was joined by Italy and the Benelux countries to form the six-nation ECSC. Benelux and the Franco-German couple persist as separate entities within the EU to this day. Moreover, both of them continue to renew and strengthen their cooperation, as seen in the 2008 treaty instituting a Benelux Union (Wouters and Vidal, 2017) and the Franco-German Aachen Treaty of 2019 (Krotz and Schramm, 2021).

Functional Cooperation

A second purpose of a BURG may be as a *functional cooperator*. In this case, the focus is on internal cooperation among the participating member states rather than coordinating positions vis-à-vis common policies at the EU level. The focus of cooperation may be on matters not just of 'high politics' (e.g. diplomatic exchange, defence) but areas of 'low politics' tied to practical cross-border and regional issues (e.g. energy, transport, tourism). Many of the BURGs that enabled cooperation of this kind were founded by states that at the time were not yet EU members but aspired to join – the Iberian Summit, the Visegrád Group, the Baltic Assembly, the Salzburg Forum (which also included Austria, by then a member state). Functional cooperation also seems to be the main purpose of some of the other BURGs created more recently, including the Central European Defence Cooperation and the Three Seas Initiative. Of course, functional cooperation can co-exist with engagement at the EU level. The Salzburg Forum, which began as a forum mainly for internal cooperation in Justice and Home Affairs (JHA) and to prepare its members for EU accession, is now also engaged in policy coordination at EU level, where its seven members (one-quarter of EU member states) have the formal right of legislative initiative in certain JHA matters (Article 76 TFEU) (Müller, 2016, p. 28).

Policy Coordination

The third purpose of a BURG is as a *policy coordinator* that is focused externally on the EU level, as opposed to internal cooperation among the participating states. Perhaps the best example of this kind of BURG is the Nordic-Baltic Six (NB6), which is made up of the three Baltic states and the three Nordic EU member states (Denmark, Finland, Sweden). This group is a subset of a larger group, the Nordic-Baltic Eight (NB8) which also includes two non-EU states, Norway and Iceland (Kleinberga, 2019; Rūse, 2014). While the NB8 is a complex institution involving extensive internal cooperation among these eight countries, the NB6 exists mainly to allow the six members of the NB8 that are in the EU to coordinate their policy positions in the Council/European Council, typically through ministerial meetings prior to Council meetings. Other examples of BURGs whose purpose is policy coordination is the EuroMed, made up of the southernmost EU member states (Cyprus, France, Greece, Italy, Malta, Portugal, Spain, and now also Slovenia and Croatia) and the New Hanseatic League (made up of the NB6 countries plus Ireland and the Netherlands).

Unlike an integration vanguard, a BURG acting as policy coordinator is not necessarily advancing the cause of EU integration in general, but rather the particular interests of a sub-group of member states. Indeed, different BURGs with competing policy agendas may clash with one another when negotiating EU policy outcomes in the Council/European Council. This kind of political dynamic emerged in the late 2010s in the years following the Brexit referendum (2016), when the EU was grappling with proposals for the reform of the EU's economic governance regime, such as the idea of a fiscal capacity for the Eurozone (Fabbrini, 2019). Such reforms were supported by the EuroMed, which included countries that had been most affected by the euro crisis, who advocated greater solidarity in the form of shared debt. Northern member states – who no longer had the UK as their ally in this debate –

formed themselves in the New Hanseatic League to oppose these moves. The Franco-German duo tried to find a middle ground between the northern and southern positions, most notably with the 'Meseberg declaration' of June 2018 (Eichengreen, 2019), but this too failed to gain a consensus. The standoff between these different BURGs – each of which represented a different set of policy preferences for the EU – was eventually resolved in 2020 when the EU was hit hard by Covid-19, which necessitated the creation of a new Recovery Fund to address the economic consequences of the pandemic (Fabbrini, 2020). The New Hanseatic League was divided on the issue and opposition was reduced to four member states – the so-called frugal four of Austria, Denmark, the Netherlands and Sweden (which are not, by our definition, a BURG) – and so the Recovery Fund was eventually adopted. Even so, this dispute is a strong signal of the growing importance of the BURGs in EU politics.

Resistance

Fourth and finally, there is the possibility that a BURG could act as a *resistance cell*. In this case, a group of member states would actively work together against the fundamental values of the EU. Admittedly, this type of BURG is a sub-category of the previous group – namely, regional caucuses that pursue the functioning of coordinating policy priorities at EU level among the participating member states. Nevertheless, in this specific context, policy coordination is specifically directed towards frustrating the achievements of EU policy objectives, effectively evading or subverting EU norms (Dawson, 2020). As such, given its finality, we treat this as a distinctive function of a BURG. The most prominent example of a BURG taking action of this kind – although one that is highly contested – is the Visegrád Group acting to thwart the implementation of the Common European Asylum System (CEAS), and by extension the very foundations of the Rule of Law in the EU. As is well known, in response to the migration crisis of 2015, the EU adopted a number of emergency measures which, in a spirit of solidarity between the member states, established among others a temporary relocation mechanism of asylum seekers. However, even if these measures were legally binding, the Visegrád countries – acting in unison – refused to abide by the relocation mechanism, de facto sabotaging it (De Witte and Tsourdi, 2018). While action by Poland, Hungary and the Czech Republic was ultimately found in 2019 to be a breach of EU law by the European Court of Justice, the resistance coordinated by the Visegrád Group profoundly shaped EU responses to the migration crisis and plans to reform the CEAS.

BURGS AND BREXIT

The shock of Brexit has had profound ripple effects throughout Europe, with a disparate impact on the various EU institutions, policies and member states. In thinking about how to assess the relationship between Brexit and BURGs, it is useful to separate the period before the Brexit referendum, and the notification of withdrawal, and the period after the formal withdrawal from the EU.

Pre-Brexit, the UK was the champion of differentiated integration – in terms of pushing for derogations from common EU policies – but at the same time it was a reluctant participant in BURGs. On the one hand, the UK opted out of many common EU policies, including the single currency, the euro, and many elements of the Area of Freedom, Security and Justice, including the Schengen area. On the other hand, however, the UK had only a limited involvement in BURGs. While the above analysis only listed existing BURGs that are made up of current EU member states – and thus by definition excluded those with UK participation – the fact is that the UK participated little even when it was a member state.

The most clear-cut example of a pre-Brexit BURG involving the UK is its bilateral relationship with Ireland, which is extensively institutionalized. The closeness of this relationship is driven in part by circumstances of history and geography. In particular, since the 1920s, the UK and Ireland have had a Common Travel Area, an arrangement in which citizens of each country enjoy reciprocal rights to live, work, study, vote in elections and access social services in the other (Harvey, 2020). This existed for decades before EU accession in 1973 and persists after Brexit. Furthermore, the political relationship was further developed during the Northern Ireland peace process in the 1980s and 1990s culminating in the 1998 Good Friday Agreement, which formalized bilateral ties between the two governments in the form of the British-Irish Intergovernmental Conference (part of Strand 3, the East-West dimension of the agreement) (Murphy, 2019; Tannam, 2020).

Aside from its wide-ranging bilateral relationship with Ireland, the UK was largely disinclined to form BURGs with other EU member states – with the key exception of cooperation on foreign and defence policy. Pre-Brexit, the UK did engage with other EU member states on a multilateral, bilateral and trilateral basis in forms of security and diplomatic cooperation that were institutionally separate from the EU. In part this reflected the UK's long-held policy preference that the EU should not take on a significant role in the field of defence, because that could undermine the role of NATO as the primary international guarantor of European security. On a multilateral basis, the UK participated for many years in the WEU, an association of NATO members within the EU (which was abolished in 2011, as mentioned above).

Bilaterally, the UK developed significant security cooperation with France, the only other member state of the EU which is a permanent member of the UN Security Council and has a nuclear deterrent. In particular, in the Lancaster House treaties of 2010 on defence and security and nuclear cooperation, the two countries agreed to create a Combined Joint Expeditionary Force (CJEF) within ten years, a milestone reached in late 2020. This bilateral cooperation also builds on a diplomatic relationship that includes a periodic summit between the French President and the UK Prime Minister, who have met together 35 times since 1976, most recently in the Sandhurst summit between Emmanuel Macron and Theresa May in January 2018.

Finally, one other pre-Brexit group is the so-called E3, an informal forum for foreign policy coordination among the UK, France and Germany (Sepos, 2005, p.14). The E3 emerged in 2003 as a forum for the three largest EU member states to work out their differences after a major falling-out over the Iraq War; after that the group has released joint statements on matters of common concern in foreign policy, such as the conflicts in Syria and Libya and the Iran nuclear deal (Brattberg, 2020).

Turning to the post-Brexit era, is it possible that BURGs – forms of cooperation outside the formal EU structures – could serve as an ongoing connection between the UK and EU member states? One possibility may arise in the field of foreign and security policy (Tonra, 2021). In 2017, just one year after the Brexit referendum, 25 EU member states – all except Denmark, Malta and the withdrawing UK – moved to initiate Permanent Structured Cooperation (PESCO) as a form of enhanced cooperation within the EU's common security and defence policy (CSDP). Yet even though the Council of the EU in 2020 authorized selective third country involvement in PESCO, thus far the UK has expressed no interest in participating. In this circumstance, perhaps the most promising way forward would be for the UK to develop forms of collaboration with EU member states that are outside the institutional framework of the EU.

Since the referendum, while the UK has resisted engaging in security cooperation with the EU as a whole, it has sought to bolster bilateral relations with certain EU member states. As noted above, the UK has a well-established bilateral defence relationship with France. However, this has frayed somewhat in recent years, given that by mid-2021 there had not been a bilateral summit for over three and a half years, since Sandhurst in January 2018 (Momtaz, 2021). Regarding other EU member states, the UK signed two bilateral 'joint vision statements' on defence cooperation – one with the Netherlands in 2017, and one with Germany in 2018 (Brader, 2021).

There have been more wide-ranging proposals for initiatives that would restore the link between the UK and EU member states, if not with the EU itself. Two such ideas were aired by Emmanuel Macron in his Sorbonne speech in 2017, addressing the EU's post-Brexit future. One proposal was the European Intervention Initiative (EII/EI2), a forum for defence cooperation aimed at developing a 'shared strategic culture' that is separate from, but could be used to support either EU, NATO or ad hoc military actions. This was launched by nine EU member states (including the UK), which signed a 'letter of intent' in June 2018; the number of participating countries has since risen to 13, including two non-EU member states (Norway and the UK) (Directorate General for International Relations and Strategy, 2021). Another idea from Macron was to create a 'European Security Council' with the UK as a member, which could be smaller and less cumbersome than decision-making through the EU's Common Foreign and Security Policy. However, this idea has yet to be realized, and it is still unclear what the composition of a European Security Council would be, beyond the participation of the UK, France and Germany (Whineray, 2020).

Separately, a notable effect that Brexit has had on BURGs is the acceleration of new arrangements of regional cooperation within the EU-27. In particular, the New Hanseatic League emerged in 2017 as a response to Brexit by liberal, free trade-oriented member states from Northern and Western Europe. At the behest of the Netherlands, this group of like-minded member states, which on many issues shared the same policy preferences of the UK, came together to increase its voice on EU affairs and fill the void left by the UK withdrawal. From this point of view, therefore, Brexit triggered the emergence of a new, influential BURG, whose purpose was precisely to counter-balance other BURGs (e.g. the Franco-German duo and the EuroMed) in the new EU-27 without the UK (Puetter, 2017). In conclusion, while the UK's past participation in BURGs was limited, and its future involvement remains to be seen, Brexit has already had an impact on BURGs, causing the emergence of new initiatives of regional differentiated integration in the EU.

BURGS AND DIFFERENTIATED INTEGRATION

What do BURGs tell us about EU integration and differentiated governance? This chapter has examined regional caucusing as an unexplored side of differentiated governance in Europe. In their recent book, *Ever Looser Union?*, Schimmelfenning and Winzen (2020) examine in detail mechanisms of differentiated European integration, distinguishing between typologies of differentiation, explaining their drivers, and assessing their normative effects on EU integration. Nevertheless, by embracing a narrow definition of differentiation as a situation arising 'when the legally valid rules of the EU, codified in EU treaties and EU legislation, exempt or exclude individual member states explicitly from specific rights or obligations of membership' (pp. 3–4), Schimmelfenning and Winzen have left the phenomenon of BURGs out of their comprehensive analysis. Indeed, by their own admission 'there are other forms of flexibility such as ... informal cooperation among group of states' (p. 176), which must be researched further to obtain a clearer picture of all forms of differentiated integration in the EU. This chapter has attempted to do just that, focusing on the phenomenon that arises when 'groups of members [states ...] cooperate informally besides and beyond the institutional formats and legal rules of the EU' (p. 4).

To this end, the chapter has first defined BURGs, conceptualizing the phenomenon of bottom-up regional groups as a case of institutionalized cooperation among caucuses of EU member states belonging to the same geographical region. Moreover, the chapter has limited the scope of its analysis to currently active BURGs, leaving aside historical cases that were dissolved or absorbed into the EU structures. Based on this definition, the chapter has identified 13 BURGs, and classified them on the basis of several criteria – including their longevity (whether they were established before or after EU membership), their institutional complexity (whether they have a thin organizational structure, based purely on executive intergovernmental cooperation, or rather a thick and sophisticated one, including also interparliamentary cooperation and judicial settlement of disputes), their policy scope (whether they have a narrow focus on specific tasks or a broader mandate), and the frequency of their meetings and operations (whether regular or infrequent).

The chapter has then assessed BURGs, reflecting on their purposes. As such, we have distinguished BURGs that serve purely as frameworks for functional cooperation, increasing the ability of participating states to solve cross-border issues or promote projects of common interest from BURGs which instead fulfil a policy coordination function, hence increasing the abilities of their members to raise their voice in EU policy-making. A particular type of BURG we identified is that of vanguard of EU integration, with the Benelux and the Franco-German cooperation as examples of regional groups that provide, respectively, a model of integration on a small scale and a motor to develop further interstate cooperation among all countries that are willing to participate. Nevertheless, our analysis has also pointed out the case of BURGs that serve as cells of resistance towards further European integration. In this case, member states caucusing among themselves promote their shared preferences at EU level but do so evading or subverting EU laws that they dislike – a process dramatically visible in the Visegrád Group's refusal to abide by EU emergency laws on the relocation of asylum seekers in the aftermath of the migration crisis.

The assessment of BURGs allows us also to shed light on a topic that has attracted much attention in scholarly debate, namely, whether differentiated governance should be evaluated positively or negatively from the normative stance of European integration (Lord, 2015). While the political science literature tends to be cautiously supportive of differentiated integration – with Schimmelfennig and Winzen claiming that 'DI has enabled the EU to move to a level and scope of European integration ... that would have been impossible under the constraints of uniform integration' (2020, p. 179), our analysis has shown both the pros and the cons of BURGs for the process of integration. On occasion, BURGs can be positive for integration – as when they serve as vanguards, which other states may subsequently join – or in fact they can be neutral for integration – as when they serve as functional cooperation formats (not unlike the interstate compacts in the US federal system), or when they enable member states to coordinate their positions when engaging in policy debates at EU level. However, clearly BURGs can also be an obstacle to integration and indeed promote disintegration (intended here as the erosion of EU norms) when they become cells of resistance, promoting defiance of EU laws.

Be that as it may, BURGs remain a factor to be reckoned with in EU law and governance, and as such we hope this chapter may have opened a further avenue for research on differentiation. In fact, much work still remains to be done on BURGs, including by discussing their potential impact on the dynamics of domination at play in the EU (Fossum, 2019). Nevertheless, it is clear that regional grouping in the EU will continue to remain a facet of regional cooperation, also post-Brexit, and thus deserves additional scholarly analysis.

NOTES

1. In addition to Benelux, Article 350 also recognizes the even older Belgium-Luxembourg Economic Union (BLEU), which dates back to 1921 (Wouters and Vidal, 2017, p. 286). For our purposes, we consider the BLEU is not a separate BURG as it has effectively been subsumed by Benelux.
2. See https://www.beneluxparl.eu/fr/., last accessed 01 September 2021.
3. See 'Interparliamentary Cooperation of the Visegrad Group Countries' (n.d.).

REFERENCES

Assemblée nationale. (2019). *RÉSOLUTION relative à la coopération parlementaire franco-allemande*. https://www.assemblee-nationale.fr/dyn/15/textes/l15t0241_texte-adopte-seance.pdf, accessed 1 September 2021.

Borońska-Hryniewiecka, K., and Grinc, J. (2021). Actions Speak Louder Than Words? The Untapped Potential of V4 Parliaments in EU Affairs. *East European Politics and Societies and Cultures*. https://doi.org/10.1177/08883254211012770.

Brader, C. (2021, 9 March). UK Bilateral Defence Cooperation. *UK Parliament*. https://lordslibrary.parliament.uk/uk-bilateral-defence-cooperation/, accessed 1 September 2021.

Brattberg, E. (2020, 18 June). The E3, the EU, and the Post-Brexit Diplomatic Landscape. *Carnegie Endowment for International Peace*. https://carnegieendowment.org/2020/06/18/e3-eu-and-post-brexit-diplomatic-landscape-pub-82095, accessed 1 September 2021.

Brattberg, E., Brudzińska K., and Pires de Lima, B. (2020, 25 March). Contending European Views on a New Post-Brexit Balance. *Carnegie Endowment for International Peace*. https://carnegieendowment.org/2020/03/25/contending-european-views-on-new-post-brexit-balance-pub-81354, accessed 1 September 2021.

Cabada, L. (2018). The Visegrad Cooperation in the Context of Other Central European Cooperation Formats. *Politics in Central Europe*, *14*(2), 165–79. https://doi.org/10.2478/pce-2018-0014.

Cutler, R., and von Lingen, A. (2019). Emerging Interregional Parliamentarism: The Case of the Baltic Assembly. In M. Müftüler-Baç, K. Raube and J. Wouters (eds), *Parliamentary Cooperation and Diplomacy in EU External Relations* (pp. 120–38). Edward Elgar Publishing.

Dangerfield, M. (2008). The Visegrád Group in the Expanded European Union: From Preaccession to Postaccession Cooperation. *East European Politics and Societies*, *22*(3), 630–67. https://doi.org/10.1177/0888325408315840.

Dawson, M. (2020). Coping with Exit, Evasion, and Subversion in EU Law. *German Law Journal*, *21*(1), 51–6. https://doi.org/10.1017/glj.2019.95.

De Witte, B., and Tsourdi, E. (2018). Confrontation on Relocation: The Court of Justice Endorses the Emergency Scheme for Compulsory Relocation of Asylum Seekers within the European Union: Slovak Republic and Hungary v. Council. *Common Market Law Review*, *55*(5), 1457–94.

Directorate General for International Relations and Strategy. (2021). *European Intervention Initiative*. https://www.defense.gouv.fr/english/dgris/international-action/l-iei/l-initiative-europeenne-d-intervention, accessed 1 September 2021.

Eichengreen, B. (2019). The Euro after Meseberg. *Review of World Economics*, *155*(1), 15–22. https://doi.org/10.1007/s10290-018-0329-1.

Fabbrini, F. (2019). *Fiscal Capacity in the Eurozone: Study Commissioned by the European Parliament Constitutional Affairs Committee*. https://www.europarl.europa.eu/RegData/etudes/IDAN/2019/608862/IPOL_IDA(2019)608862_EN.pdf, accessed 1 September 2021.

Fabbrini, F. (2020). *Brexit & the Future of the European Union: The Case for Constitutional Reforms*. Oxford University Press.

Fossum, J.E. (2019). Europe's Triangular Challenge: Differentiation, Dominance and Democracy. *EU3D Research Paper* No. 1.

Górka, M. (2018). The Three Seas Initiative as a Political Challenge for the Countries of Central and Eastern Europe. *Politics in Central Europe*, *14*(3), 55–73. https://doi.org/10.2478/pce-2018-0018.

Harvey, C. (2020). The Irish Border. In F. Fabbrini (ed.), *The Law & Politics of Brexit* (Vol. 2, pp. 148–70). Oxford University Press.

Hosli, M.O. (1999). Power, Connected Coalitions, and Efficiency: Challenges to the Council of the European Union. *International Political Science Review*, *20*(4), 371–91. https://doi.org/10.1177/0192512199204004.

Inotai, A. (1998). Correlations between European Integration and Sub-Region Cooperation: Theoretical Background, Experience and Policy Impact. *Russian & East European Finance and Trade*, *34*(6), 3–91.

Interparliamentary Cooperation of the Visegrád Group Countries. (n.d.). *Sejm*. http://oide.sejm.gov.pl/oide/en/index.php?option=com_content&view=chapter&id=14731&Itemid=754, accessed 1 September 2021.

Jančošekovà, V. (2017). Regional Cooperation in Central and Eastern Europe and Its Implications for the EU. *European View*, *16*, 231–8. https://doi.org/10.1007%2Fs12290-017-0460-8.

Kirpsza, A. (2019). With Whom to Cooperate in Brussels? The Effect of Coalition-building with the Three Seas Initiative, Visegrad Group and Germany on Poland's Success in EU Lawmaking. In A. Mania, M. Grabowski, and T. Pugacewicz (eds), *Global Politics in the 21st Century: Between Regional Cooperation and Conflict* (pp. 205–33). Peter Lang Verlag.

Kleinberga, V. (2019). Bowling Together: Nordic Baltic Six in the European Union. In Ž. Ozoliņa (ed.), *Latvijas intereses Eiropas Savienībā* (pp. 17–31). Latvijas Politologu biedrība.

Klemenčič, M. (2011, 3–5 March). Formal Intergovernmental Alliances in the European Union: Disappearing or Still Alive? 8 [Paper presentation]. EUSA Twelfth Biennial International Conference, Boston, Massachusetts.

Krotz, U., and Schild, J. (2013). *Shaping Europe: France, Germany, and Embedded Bilateralism from the Elysée Treaty to Twenty-first Century Politics*. Oxford University Press.

Krotz, U., and Schramm, L. (2021). An Old Couple in a New Setting: Franco-German Leadership in the Post-Brexit EU. *Politics and Governance*, *9*(1), 48–58. https://doi.org/10.17645/PAG.V9I1.3645.

Kuusik, P., and Raik, K. (2018). The Nordic-Baltic Region in the EU: A Loose Club of Friends. *European Policy Analysis*, *18*(1–12).

Lang K.-O., and von Ondarza, N. (2020). Friends in Need: The Corona Pandemic Changes the Landscape of Groups and Coalitions in the EU. *SWP*, Comment 26. https://doi.org/10.18449/2020C26.

Lewicki, G. (2019). Hansa 2.0. A Return to the Golden Age of Trade? *Polish Economic Institute*.

Lord, C. (2015). Utopia or Dystopia? Towards a Normative Analysis of Differentiated Integration. *Journal of European Public Policy*, *22*(6), 783–98. https://doi.org/10.1080/13501763.2015.1020839.

Matovic: Borders between Slovakia, Czech Republic and Austria Remain Open. (2020, 9 September). *NewsNow*. https://newsnow.tasr.sk/foreign/matovic-borders-between-slovakia-czech-republic-and-austria-remain-open/, accessed 1 September 2021.

Momtaz, R. (2021, 2 August). Not Much entente, Barely cordiale: Franco-British Ties in the Doldrums. *Politico*. https://www.politico.eu/article/france-uk-relationship-entente-cordiale-emmanuel-macron-boris-johnson/, accessed 1 September 2021.
Müller, P. (2016). Europeanization and Regional Cooperation Initiatives: Austria's Participation in the Salzburg Forum and in Central European Defence Cooperation. *Osterreichische Zeitschrift fur Politikwissenschaft*, *45*(2), 24–34. https://doi.org/10.15203/ozp.1102.vol45iss2.
Murphy, M. (2019). The Brexit Crisis, Ireland and British–Irish Relations: Europeanisation and/or De-Europeanisation? *Irish Political Studies*, *34*(4), 530–50. https://doi.org/10.1080/07907184.2019.1669564.
Puetter, U. (2017). Brexit and EU Institutional Balance. In F. Fabbrini (ed.), *The Law & Politics of Brexit* (pp. 247–67). Oxford University Press.
Rūse, I. (2013). *(Why) Do Neighbours Cooperate? Institutionalised Coalitions and Bargaining Power in EU Council Negotiations*. Budrich UniPress.
Rūse, I. (2014). Nordic-Baltic Interaction in European Union Negotiations: Taking Advantage of Institutionalized Cooperation. *Journal of Baltic Studies*, *45*(2), 229–46. https://doi.org/10.1080/01629778.2013.846928.
Schimmelfennig, F., and Winzen, T. (2020). *Ever Looser Union? Differentiated European Integration*. Oxford University Press.
Sepos, A. (2005). Differentiated Integration in the EU: The Position of Small Member States. *EUI Working Paper*, RSCAS No. 17.
Tannam, E. (2020). The Future of British-Irish Relations after Brexit. In F. Fabbrini (ed.), *The Law & Politics of Brexit. Volume II. The Withdrawal Agreement* (pp. 254–73). Oxford University Press.
Tonra, B. (2021). Defense and Foreign Affairs. In F. Fabbrini (ed.), *The Law & Politics of Brexit. Volume III. The Framework of New EU-UK Relations* (pp. 179–97). Oxford University Press.
Whineray, D. (2020). The Pros and Cons of a European Security Council. *Carnegie Europe*. https://carnegieeurope.eu/strategiceurope/80869, accessed 1 September 2021.
Wouters, J., and Vidal, M. (2017). The Trials and Tribulations of Benelux. In T. Giegerich, D.C. Schmitt, and S. Zeitzmann (eds), *Flexibility in the EU and Beyond* (pp. 285–95). Hart Publishing.
Zalan, E. (2016, 10 February). EU Founding States Pledge Deeper Integration. *EuObserver*. https://euobserver.com/political/132204, accessed 1 September 2021.

PART IV

BREXIT AND AFFILIATED NON-MEMBERS IN EUROPE

19. The pattern of affiliations between the EU and its neighbours: Normative, Market and Governance Power Europe

Sieglinde Gstöhl

INTRODUCTION: EXPORT OF EU NORMS TO THE NEIGHBOURHOOD

Since the completion of the internal market in the early 1990s the European Union (EU) has significantly developed its neighbourhood relations. Starting with the creation of the multilateral European Economic Area (EEA) with the countries of the European Free Trade Association (EFTA), the EU negotiated a number of bilateral sectoral agreements with Switzerland after the latter's rejection of the EEA Agreement. The end of the Cold War opened an accession perspective not only for the neutral countries but also for the former Communist states in Central and Eastern Europe. As a result, EU membership almost doubled in the 2000s and, in turn, triggered the European Neighbourhood Policy (ENP) for the Union's new neighbours in the East but also those in the Southern Mediterranean. In 1999, in response to the violent conflicts in the Western Balkans after the breakup of Yugoslavia, the Stabilization and Association Process was launched to support those countries' gradual rapprochement with the EU. They soon obtained the status of (potential) candidates, and Croatia joined the EU in 2013, while bilateral Stabilization and Association Agreements are in force with all other countries of the region. Turkey has already been associated with the EU since 1963, entered in 1995 its customs union and obtained candidate status in 1999. The only other non-members in the EU's customs territory are Andorra, Monaco and San Marino, and they have since 2015 been negotiating association agreement(s) with the EU. Finally, the departure of the United Kingdom (UK) from the EU at the end of January 2020 has resulted in a Withdrawal Agreement that includes a special Protocol for Northern Ireland, aimed at avoiding a 'hard' border on the island of Ireland, and the conclusion of the EU-UK Trade and Cooperation Agreement (TCA).

In light of these developments, this chapter explores what kind of pattern of affiliations has emerged between the EU and its neighbouring countries, and how this pattern can be explained. This question is of relevance for the nature of the EU, the EU's current and future relations with European non-member states and the (emerging) regional order in Europe.

The argument unfolds in two steps. First, during the last three decades, the EU's development of its neighbourhood relations has resulted in a rather fragmented pattern of external differentiation. External differentiated integration occurs where non-member states adopt EU rules (Leuffen et al., 2013, pp. 17–18). The EU has not followed a 'one-size-fits-all' approach despite often dealing with groups of countries. However, since the 2010s the EU tries to consolidate the affiliations by insisting on certain core principles and precedents.

Second, the pattern of affiliation can largely be explained by conceptualizing the EU in three different ways which reflect different aspects of its nature: normative, market and governance power. The EU is a community of values, a large market with considerable regulatory capacity, and a legal-institutional order. It externalizes political and socio-economic norms, and the creation of partnerships (or associations) also allows it to export institutional norms. In a nutshell, the EU externalizes both substance and governance to its neighbours.

The next section sets out the conceptual framework before the various modes of affiliation of neighbouring countries with the EU are discussed. The chapter concludes with a brief comparative assessment.

CONCEPTUAL FRAMEWORK

The framework of analysis draws on a distinction between the substance and the governance of third countries' relations with the EU as well as, closely linked to that, on three conceptualizations of the EU as a power: normative, market and governance power.

The substance refers to how broad and deep the scope of a third country's access to the EU's internal market and other policy areas is, that is, its participation in the freedoms of the internal market (free movement of goods, services, capital and persons), horizontal and flanking policies (e.g. social policy, consumer protection, environment, research, education), the Schengen area or even the single currency.

Regarding the governance structure, most neighbourhood agreements now take the form of association agreements, including the two peculiar cases of the EU-UK TCA (although concluded as an EU-only agreement) and Switzerland's 1999 package of bilateral agreements (Van Elsuwege and Chamon, 2019, pp. 22–32). According to Article 217 TFEU, the common features of association agreements are 'reciprocal rights and obligations, common action and special procedure'. In the 1987 Demirel judgment, the Court of Justice of the EU (CJEU) stated that an association agreement creates 'special, privileged links with a non-member country which must, at least to a certain extent, take part in the Community system' (CJEU, 1987, para 9).

In the same year, the Commission had made clear that future EU-EFTA relations should be governed by three basic principles (the so-called Interlaken principles named after the meeting place): the priority of the Community's internal integration, the preservation of its decision-making autonomy and the maintenance of a balance of benefits and obligations (De Clercq, 1987). The latter includes preserving the integrity of the internal market by avoiding 'cherry-picking', ensuring homogeneity and a level playing field.

As pointed out in the literature on 'EU external governance', the EU's extension of regulatory boundaries does not necessarily go hand-in-hand with a parallel expansion of its 'institutional boundary' in terms of inclusion in EU policy-making processes (Lavenex, 2004, p. 683). When it comes to deep economic integration in its neighbourhood, the EU has increasingly attempted to ensure market homogeneity by concluding agreements which allow for a dynamic adaptation to the evolving *acquis* and its uniform interpretation, for independent surveillance and judicial enforcement as well as for dispute settlement between the contracting parties, with the EEA serving as the major source of inspiration (Gstöhl, 2016, p. 26). The Council of the European Union (2012, para 28) underlined 'that the principles of homogeneity and legal certainty guarantee the efficiency, sustainability and ultimately the credibility of the single market'. Moreover, it emphasized 'that the EU should have a consistent approach towards non-EU partners that participate in the extended Single Market' (Council of the European Union, 2014, para 4).

In general, it can be argued that the broader and deeper the scope of substance, and thus the export of socio-economic and political norms, the stronger the EU's quest to export institutional norms tends to be. Exceptions are only granted for very special cases that do not risk setting a precedent. Since the EU is usually the bigger power and the third countries demand access to its market, it matters what kind of 'norm-projecting' power the EU is. Three different conceptualizations can usefully be distinguished:

First, Manners's (2002, p. 236) seminal concept of 'Normative Power Europe' (NPE) – or 'the ability to define what passes for "normal" in world politics' – presents the EU primarily as a diffuser of political values and norms abroad. Hence, the most important factor shaping the EU's international role 'is not what it does or what it says, but what it is', with the core norms of the EU's identity being peace, liberty, democracy, rule of law and human rights, supplemented by the 'minor norms' of social solidarity, anti-discrimination, sustainable development and good governance (ibid., pp. 252–3). EU norm diffusion mainly takes place through procedural diffusion in an institutionalized relationship, contagion (unintentional diffusion), informational diffusion (e.g. strategic and declaratory communications), transference (e.g. through trade and aid) and overt diffusion (through physical EU presence), and it can be shaped by a cultural filter affecting the impact of norms in third countries (ibid., pp. 244–5). Conditionality facilitates procedural and transference diffusion.

Second, Damro (2012, p. 682) conceptualizes the EU as 'Market Power Europe' (MPE) which 'exercises its power through the externalization of economic and social market-related policies and regulatory measures'.

> [Such] externalization occurs when the institutions and actors of the EU attempt to get other actors to adhere to a level of regulation similar to that in effect in the European single market or to behave in a way that generally satisfies or conforms to the EU's market-related policies and regulatory measures. (Ibid., p. 690)

Three characteristics contribute to intentional or unintentional externalization: the presence of a large internal market, the EU's considerable regulatory capacity, and its function as an arena of interest contestation, including pressure from pro-externalization coalitions, help to determine the likelihood of the EU projecting its market power. The EU may use both persuasive and coercive tools to intentionally exercise its power, often linked to positive or negative conditionality, but also other tools such as international legal instruments or pushing EU standards in multilateral settings (ibid., pp. 691–2).

Third, Gstöhl and Phinnemore (2019b, p. 198) argue that by exporting its institutional norms and principles to the neighbourhood, the EU acts as 'Governance Power Europe' (GPE). The Union largely defines the macro-structures of 'privileged partnerships' with neighbours within the constraints of its own institutional DNA and existing precedents. Privileged partnerships are based on legally binding agreements which provide for both substance and governance (Gstöhl and Phinnemore, 2019a, p. 5): on the one hand, extensive reciprocal rights and obligations, selective *acquis* adoption, policy cooperation and integration, and on the other hand, extensive institutional arrangements for governing the relationship (e.g. joint council and committees, dispute settlement mechanism, access to EU bodies). Institutional norms are understood as forms of governance that encompass core principles such as the EU's quest to preserve the autonomy of its decision-making and legal order and a balance of rights and obligations or level playing field. The main diffusion mechanism is the reproduction of institutional norms. As expected by historical institutionalism, path dependence and the setting of precedents play a role for the replication of institutionalized relationships (Gstöhl and Phinnemore, 2021). At a critical juncture, the EEA was created with the EU's own institutional set-up as the template. The EEA in turn has served as a benchmark for later negotiations. Lavenex et al. (2009) find that beyond the macro-structures of neighbourhood relations, the modes of external governance in specific policy fields follow sectoral dynamics which are quite stable across countries and reflect the EU's internal modes of governance. Hence, reproduction also works on sectoral levels, and it matters for an institutional arrangement which areas of cooperation are included in an agreement with the EU.

The EU's market power attracts third countries seeking access to its large market, which allows it to export socio-economic norms; the EU's normative power promotes primarily political values vis-à-vis the neighbouring countries related to the EU's own nature as a peaceful community upholding democratic values and human rights; and the EU's governance power sets the parameters for the countries' institutional relations with the Union. The relative importance of the three concepts may vary with the neighbouring countries in question, reflecting their different preferences and relative bargaining power, including the fact that over time, precedents and path dependence can play a role in the EU's approach to privileged partnerships. Hence, the size and state of economic or political development of partners may play a role.

For MPE the internal market provides the material existence of the EU as a power that can externalize its socio-economic norms via persuasion, coercion or other tools. Damro (2021, p. 56) argues that 'the framework is open to the interplay of material/interest-based and/or social/ideational factors that contribute to the EU's identity and exercise of power across policy areas'. NPE focuses on ideational rather than material power and emphasizes the ability to use normative justification rather than material incentives or force for norm diffusion. Finally, GPE takes the EU's legal-institutional order as a starting point and is interested in explaining the institutional choices made regarding the affiliation of third countries. While NPE and MPE primarily focus on the effects that the EU's exercise of power has inside the third countries, they neglect the institutional form the relationship between the two is likely to take. GPE contributes to addressing this gap by focusing on the export of institutional norms through a 'reproduction' of the EU's own forms of governance and a replication of precedents of institutional arrangements with other third countries. GPE can thus be viewed as being complementary to the established concepts of NPE and MPE. Table 19.1 provides a simplified comparison.

Table 19.1 *The EU's power to externally project norms*

	Normative Power Europe	Market Power Europe	Governance Power Europe
Nature of EU	Community of values	Large internal market	Legal-institutional order
Main type of norms	Political	Socio-economic	Institutional
Main mechanisms of diffusion	Procedural diffusion and transference, including conditionality	Externalization through persuasion or coercion, including conditionality	Reproduction

PATTERN OF AFFILIATIONS: VARIATION IN SUBSTANCE AND GOVERNANCE

In the Brexit debate the following neighbourhood relations have often been referred to: the Norwegian, Swiss, Turkish and Ukrainian 'models' (see HM Government, 2016). These models concern countries of different size, level of economic development and democratization. They vary with regard to the substance covered and the governance arrangements. The pre-accession model for the Western Balkan countries is not considered here since its goal is not external differentiation as an alternative to but as a preparation for EU membership. Certain 'special cases' will be addressed as well. Finally, the 'British model' will briefly be presented.

The 'Norwegian Model'

This section introduces the integration arrangement of those EFTA countries which participate in the EEA, including the special case of Liechtenstein.

The European Economic Area

The EEA Agreement between the European Community (EC) and its then 12 member states, on the one hand, and the seven EFTA countries, on the other, was negotiated in 1989–92 against the backdrop of the end of the Cold War and the completion of the Community's internal market. Commission President Delors had proposed to switch from a sectoral to a global approach of cooperation, institutionalizing the relationship. By offering the EFTA countries an alternative to membership, the Community hoped to settle the 'deepening versus widening' debate in favour of deepening, as the Maastricht Treaty was taking shape. The EFTA countries, whose integration policy faced neutrality and domestic constraints, hoped to be able to avoid economic discrimination and marginalization by taking part in the internal market.

However, Austria, Sweden, Switzerland, Norway and Finland applied for EC membership in 1991–92 when it became clear that the EEA would not grant them joint decision-making (Gstöhl, 1994). In 1992 Switzerland failed to ratify the EEA Agreement due to a negative referendum outcome (see below). This withdrawal put its small neighbour Liechtenstein in a difficult position due to their customs and regional union (see below). In 1994 the Norwegian voters had – for the second time after 1972 – rejected EU membership in a referendum. In 1995, one year after the entry into force of the EEA Agreement, Austria, Finland and Sweden acceded to the EU, while Liechtenstein joined the EEA after positive referendums in 1992 and 1994. Since these developments only left Norway, Iceland and Liechtenstein on the EFTA side, the EEA is often referred to as the 'Norwegian model'.

In terms of substance, the European Economic Area covers the free movement of goods, services, capital and persons, competition rules as well as horizontal and flanking policies. Excluded are the EU's external relations, the common agricultural, fisheries and transport policies, regional policy, taxation as well as economic and monetary policy. The EFTA countries have in addition concluded a few bilateral sectoral agreements with the EU such as a Schengen association. Although they do not pay into the EU's budget, all EFTA countries are making substantial financial contributions to reduce economic and social disparities in certain EU member states. These grants are largely seen as being part of the price to pay for their participation in the internal market.

The governance of the EEA is based on an elaborate two-pillar system with 'quasi-supranational' features, aimed at matching the institutions on the EU side. The highest political body is the EEA Council where the EFTA Ministers for Foreign or European Affairs meet with representatives from the Presidency of the Council of the EU, the European Commission and the European External Action Service (EEAS). The EEA explicitly aims to create a homogeneous economic area. The homogeneity principle implies that the incorporation of new law into the EEA Agreement needs to happen as closely as possible to the adoption by the EU and that its interpretation should be as uniform as possible.

The European Commission retains the exclusive right to initiative. It transmits EEA-relevant proposals to the Council of the EU and the European Parliament as well as to the EEA EFTA states. The main consultations take place within the EEA Joint Committee in the so-called 'decision-shaping' phase. The EEA Joint Committee, usually composed of the EFTA ambassadors and representatives of the EEAS, decides by consensus. In case of an opt-out, the EFTA countries, which need to 'speak with one voice', face the threat of a suspension of related parts of the Agreement.

On the EFTA side, enforcement is carried out by the EFTA Surveillance Authority and the EFTA Court. It includes infringement procedures and advisory opinions delivered upon the request of national courts in EEA EFTA countries. The CJEU had in its famous *Opinion 1/91* objected to the proposed joint EEA Court of Justice, composed of EFTA and EU judges, on the ground that its legally binding interpretations could adversely affect the autonomy and exclusive jurisdiction of the CJEU. This ruling was later confirmed on several occasions. The CJEU and the EFTA Court maintain a close judicial dialogue.

While the EU has since the 1990s gone through several treaty revisions, the EEA Agreement itself has, despite the continuous incorporation of hundreds of new EU acts every year, remained largely unchanged. The relevant internal market legislation is often blurred with other policies that are not within the scope of the EEA Agreement, and EU agencies have gained importance. The creeping extension of the reach of the EEA Agreement did not go together with an enhanced participation of the EEA EFTA states in the relevant decision-shaping processes although some new institutional arrangements have been added in practice to counter the delays in the incorporation of new EU acts which often require adaptations by the EEA Joint Committee (Frommelt, 2020).

In sum, the EEA's broad and deep internal market association comes with a strong governance dimension which clearly reflects the power asymmetry in favour of the EU. This case therefore confirms the general argument: the broader and deeper the scope of substance, the stronger the governance. The EU has vis-à-vis the EFTA countries mainly been projecting market and governance power. It is not surprising that an exercise of its normative power has been limited given that EFTA consists of like-minded countries eligible for EU membership.

Although the UK was in 1960 a founding member of EFTA, the 'Norwegian model' was not an option for its post-Brexit relations with the EU (see Webb et al., 2018, pp. 32–42). Not only would it have to join EFTA again, but as an EEA EFTA member, the UK would have to 'speak with one voice' to the EU together with three small states. Moreover, the jurisdiction of the CJEU would have been replaced by the jurisdiction of the EFTA Court and the surveillance of the Commission by that of the EFTA Surveillance Authority, thus failing to 'take back control'.

Special case: Liechtenstein

Despite the Swiss 'no' to the EEA Agreement, Liechtenstein – located between Switzerland and Austria – had voted 'yes'. This outcome put their long-standing, close regional union and open border into question. Innovative adaptations of several bilateral treaties and the EEA Agreement were necessary to allow the principality to join the EEA. This 'squaring of the circle' was facilitated by the political will on all sides and the tiny territory of the principality (see Gstöhl, 1997). Part of the solution was the new principle of 'parallel marketability' of goods that enables Liechtenstein to apply on its very small domestic market Swiss rules in parallel with the EU rules incorporated into the EEA Agreement. Liechtenstein created a national market surveillance and control system in order to prevent Swiss products that differ from EEA standards being exported into EEA countries and products following different EEA standards being marketed in Switzerland. The convergence of Swiss rules to EU rules through the bilateral agreements and a policy of autonomous adaptation further facilitated this unconventional solution. The politically most sensitive innovation was a 'special solution' that allows Liechtenstein to use quantitative restrictions on the number of new EEA residents in light of its small territory and unusually high share of foreigners (Frommelt and Gstöhl, 2011).

These tailor-made arrangements for Liechtenstein show that flexibility is possible for very special, and small, cases that do not risk setting a precedent for other neighbours of the EU. They cannot be considered a model for much bigger countries like the UK, which in addition also had complied with full EU membership beforehand.

The 'Swiss Model'

Switzerland's opt-out of the EEA in 1992 also led to a 'freezing' of the EU membership bid it had launched in the same year and which was formally withdrawn in 2016. Instead, the country pursued a pragmatic bilateral approach, building on its 1972 free trade agreement (FTA) with the EC. The Swiss government and the EU concluded 16 new sectoral agreements in two packages in 1999 (free movement of persons, technical barriers to trade, public procurement, civil aviation, overland transport, agriculture, research) and 2004 (Schengen and Dublin association, taxation of savings, fight against fraud, processed agricultural products, environment, statistics, media, education, pensions) (see Schwok, 2021). Most of these 'bilaterals' are static, based on the equivalence of laws between the two parties, and some of them 'dock on' to EU law, for instance air transport and the free movement of persons. The Schengen and Dublin association agreements foresee a dynamic incorporation of new law, where new *acquis* requires approval from the Swiss legislature (but in case of a refusal, the agreement could be terminated) and Swiss representatives participate without a vote in the relevant committees and working groups. Unlike the second package, the 'bilaterals I' are linked through a so-called guillotine clause which implies that giving up one agreement would call into question all the others. Many referendums were since then held on various of these agreements. The package deals reflected the principle of 'appropriate parallelism' – the negotiation in parallel of separate agreements reflecting both sides' interests, or a balance of rights and obligations. Like the EEA EFTA states, Switzerland has also been contributing financially to a reduction of economic and social disparities in the EU.

Since the 'bilaterals II' entered into force a few additional agreements were concluded, in particular on Switzerland's participation in certain EU agencies (such as Europol, Eurojust or Frontex) and on cooperation between competition authorities. Besides, negotiations are still pending on electricity, agriculture, food and product security, public health, navigation by satellite and emissions trading. In fact, the EU had made the conclusion of further agreements allowing Swiss participation in the internal market conditional on the conclusion of an institutional framework agreement.

While the bilateral approach has expanded sector by sector, it lacks an overarching structure to deal with the around 20 main agreements, most of which are on a technical level run by a consensus-based Joint Committee (in addition to around 100 secondary agreements). For more than ten years, the EU and Switzerland sought to consolidate their relations, discussing various forms of governance. The Council of the European Union insisted on the limits of the static, sectoral approach, for instance the weak legal certainty:

> Due to a lack of efficient arrangements for the take-over of new EU acquis including CJEU case-law, and for ensuring the supervision and enforcement of the existing agreements, this approach does not ensure the necessary homogeneity in the parts of the internal market and of the EU policies in which Switzerland participates. (Council of the European Union, 2010, para 42)

The negotiations on an institutional framework agreement were concluded in late 2018. However, the Swiss government did not endorse the outcome and in May 2021 declared the end of the agreement (Swiss Federal Council, 2021). The institutional framework agreement would have entailed a dynamic adoption of relevant developments in EU law in some of the 'bilaterals' (those allowing participation in the internal market), granted Switzerland, in turn, more 'decision-shaping' access and introduced a dispute settlement with an arbitration panel (Oesch, 2020). The jurisdiction of the CJEU would have been limited to interpreting EU law adopted by Switzerland. Potential rebalancing measures in case of non-compliance could have included the suspension of agreements. Among the issues that led to the rejection were state aid, concerns with regard to safeguarding Swiss wage levels and social security costs. The EU side made it clear that without an institutional framework agreement, the bilateral agreements with Switzerland may not be updated and no new agreements will be concluded. Hence, the relationship risks eroding over time. Both sides still need to find a solution to this stand-off.

Although EU-Swiss relations are not as broad and deep as the EEA, they still cover a medium-level substance accumulated across sectoral agreements, yet with weak governance arrangements. The argument put forward in this chapter thus holds only partly, especially since the attempt to remedy this tilted situation with the institutional framework agreement has so far failed. The EU has been acting as MPE vis-à-vis Switzerland but its attempt to catch up as GPE has not been successful. Clearly, the 'Swiss model', which has emerged incrementally and rather haphazardly over the years, was not on offer to the UK from the EU side which was eager to preserve the integrity of the internal market (Tobler, 2021, p. 109).

The 'Turkish Model'

The Ankara Agreement of 1963, which established an association between Turkey and the EC, already foresaw the implementation of a customs union and the prospect of future membership. In 1987 the Turkish government applied for membership and in 2005 accession negotiations were finally opened but have seen many ups and downs since then. Whereas for Turkey the customs union was meant as a preparation for EU membership, for the small-sized countries surrounded by EU member states – Andorra, Monaco, San Marino – it has rather served as an alternative thereto.

Turkey between association and accession

The Ankara Agreement features not just provisions for the free movement of goods and a future customs union, it also foresaw the freedom of movement for workers, of establishment and to provide services as well as a common transport policy. None of these more far-reaching goals have, however, been achieved.

The *acquis* to be adopted by Turkey is laid out in decisions of the Association Council. Turkey's customs union with the EU, established in 1996, allows all industrial goods and processed agricultural products that comply with EU norms to circulate freely. Turkey adopted the common external tariff and the *acquis* in the areas of technical barriers to trade, and it aligns its legislation in other essential internal market areas, notably competition policy and protection of intellectual property rights. Legal convergence with relevant EU rules should take place as far as possible. This process was subsequently supported by the accession negotiations that also introduced political conditionality. The customs union binds Turkey to the EU's common commercial policy without offering it proper means of influencing that policy, and the EU's FTAs have opened up third markets for EU exports but not for Turkish exports (despite granting FTA partners access to the Turkish market). Turkey also remains outside the EU's single market and its regulatory and institutional framework. While such an arrangement might initially have been accepted by Turkish policymakers as a transitional measure on the way to EU accession, it has increasingly been put in question.

In recent years Turkey's accession negotiations effectively came to a standstill as a result of a major backsliding on domestic reforms and various foreign policy actions contrary to EU interests. In late 2016 the European Commission proposed to modernize the customs union by liberalizing trade in agriculture and services, public procurement and stronger commitments on competition, intellectual property rights and sustainable development. However, these efforts have two years later been suspended as well. Instead of further aligning with the EU, 'Turkey has been diverging in an increasingly systemic fashion from these rules over the past years', for instance levying additional customs duties on imports or concluding trade agreements not in line with those of the EU, despite its obligation to do so (European Commission and High Representative, 2021, p. 11).

The dialogue between the EU and Turkey on the customs union takes place in the Association Council and the Customs Union Joint Committee which the Council had set up. This governance structure suffers from a lack of effective consultation and dispute settlement mechanisms (Terzi, 2019). Both sides, the European Commission and Turkey, should exchange new proposed legislation of relevance to the customs union. However, the Association Council and its committees do not meet frequently. Moreover, in order to ensure the proper functioning of the customs union, Turkey should interpret provisions which are identical in substance to the corresponding provisions of the EU Treaty in conformity with the relevant EU case law. The Association Council tries to find a solution to any conflict and may unanimously decide to submit a dispute to the CJEU, another court or an arbitration tribunal. The latter options have not occurred in practice.

The partial customs union covers a narrow substance which a modernization would enhance, combined with a medium-degree governance that has not been fully applied. This generally confirms the argument that the broader and deeper the scope of substance, the stronger the governance. Whereas the EU acted as MPE and GPE vis-à-vis Turkey, its role as NPE remained restricted to the accession process, although a modernization of the customs union has also increasingly been linked to *ex ante* political conditions. For the UK a customs union was not an attractive option given its desire for an own trade policy.

Special cases: Andorra, Monaco and San Marino

While Turkey first entered an association and then a customs union with the EU, the reverse process applies to the European small-sized countries. The three states maintain historically very close relations with their neighbours: France and Spain for Andorra, France for Monaco, and Italy for San Marino. These special ties have involved deep bilateral integration in the form of customs unions, freedom of establishment for natural persons or the absence of border controls, but also to some extent an indirect integration with the EU. In 1990–91 Andorra and San Marino concluded own customs and cooperation agreements with the EU. They foresee the adoption of relevant EU customs legislation, to be determined by a Joint Committee, and an endeavour to take relevant case law into account in the interpretation of EU law-derived provisions. Only Monaco still relies on an indirect inclusion in the EU's customs territory via its agreements with France. When the Euro was introduced, the three states replaced the previously adopted currency of their neighbours by the single currency and concluded monetary agreements with the EU.

All three countries have in recent years expressed the wish to enhance their relations with the EU since they still face obstacles to internal market access (Maiani, 2019). They have since 2015 been negotiating association agreement(s) with the EU which will further integrate them into the EU internal market, for instance concerning the free movement of services and persons. In a declaration on Article 8 TEU Lisbon Treaty the EU commits to 'take into account the particular situation of small-sized countries which maintain specific relations of proximity with it'.

Unlike Turkey, the three very small countries have no participatory rights in the EU's decision-making process, but still have to implement the relevant *acquis*. Their monetary agreements with the EU grant exclusive competence to the CJEU. The European Commission (2012) had suggested a framework association agreement with the three states that will most likely consist of common institutional provisions and three bilateral parts. Unlike the EEA, such an association would not constitute a two-pillar system. It would entail consultation of the small-sized states ('decision-shaping') and the monitoring and enforcement of the relevant *acquis* would rather be carried out by the EU institutions, clearly reflecting the power asymmetry in favour of the EU (ibid., p. 17).

As argued by Maiani (2019), the small-sized countries are – similar to Liechtenstein – a special case insofar as they may, due to their peculiar geographic and demographic circumstances, get away with concessions that are unthinkable for other, more important partners of the EU. It is also noteworthy that there have been linkages – or 'cross-pollination' (ibid., p. 96) – between the EU's different partnerships and negotiations such as those with the UK, Switzerland and the three small states, but also Ukraine's Deep and Comprehensive Free Trade Area (DCFTA) with regard to the dispute settlement arrangement (Gstöhl and Phinnemore, 2021, p. 108).

The 'Ukrainian Model'

The ENP was first based on the bilateral Euro-Mediterranean Association Agreements, respectively, the Partnership and Cooperation Agreements with the transition countries to the

East, that were concluded throughout the 1990s. The latter have then for Ukraine, Georgia and Moldova been replaced by association agreements that were signed in 2014. Armenia had negotiated yet not signed such an agreement with the EU and instead joined the Eurasian Economic Union which was in 2015 launched by Russia, Belarus, Kazakhstan and Kyrgyzstan. Two years later Armenia signed a less ambitious Comprehensive and Enhanced Partnership Agreement with the EU. Azerbaijan and the EU are still negotiating a new framework agreement while Belarus has for many years already been facing EU sanctions. Additionally, the EU's approach to less developed neighbours willing to engage in closer ties builds on sectoral communities (see below).

The Eastern Partnership

The ENP's new bilateral association agreements comprise Deep and Comprehensive Free Trade Areas. The DCFTAs cover substantially all trade in goods and services as well as 'behind-the-border' issues, such as technical, sanitary and phytosanitary standards, competition policy, industrial policy, research cooperation, intellectual property rights, trade facilitation measures, company law, public procurement and financial services. In particular, the countries commit to incorporate the relevant *acquis* regarding technical barriers to trade and certain services. With its 'more-for-more' approach the ENP relies heavily on political conditionality and thus the EU's normative power (Manners, 2010).

The DCFTAs with Ukraine, Moldova and Georgia do not per se aim at the creation of a homogeneous and dynamic legal space. They contain several different legislative approximation mechanisms with varying degrees of obligation and various procedures to amend the incorporated rules. The decision to update the annexes to keep up with the relevant EU law is taken by mutual agreement in the Association Council or, if delegated, in the Association Committee. This process of (unilateral) legislative alignment has been rather slow and cumbersome. The piecemeal approach reflects the level of development. Furthermore, a few chapters include a unique form of market access conditionality, a mechanism which implies that the EU will only grant an associated country additional access to the internal market if its monitoring process shows that the country made sufficient progress in terms of legislative approximation, including aspects of implementation and enforcement (Van der Loo, 2016, pp. 247–76). The dispute settlement equally varies across sectors from consultation, arbitration or mediation to rulings by the CJEU (ibid., pp. 292–303). Overall, the governance arrangement is 'strongly tilted in the EU's favour' (Oppenheim, 2018, p. 4).

In terms of both substance and governance the DCFTAs can be assessed as of a medium degree. The association with its legal approximation, political and market access conditionality confirms the expectation of broader and deeper substance involving stronger governance arrangements. The EU has been projecting its market, normative and governance power. As an ex-EU member state wishing not to continue converging with EU rules, the 'Ukrainian model' was not an attractive option for the UK, as it follows a very different logic of rapprochement, with the degree of differentiation largely owed to the country's lack of capacity in certain sectors and the EU's interest in excluding areas such as the free movement of persons.

Sectoral communities

In addition to the bilateral neighbourhood relations, the EU has established sectoral cooperation in a few areas of internal policies with an important external dimension: energy, aviation and transport. These sectoral multilateral agreements extend the internal market *acquis* to the participating countries and also encourage closer cooperation between those countries (Öberg, 2020). They are complementary to the EU's enlargement policy and the ENP.

First, the Energy Community is the most advanced example for multilateral sectoral cooperation between the EU and some of its neighbours. The Energy Community Treaty – initially designed as an accession instrument – entered into force in 2006 and extends the EU's internal market for electricity and gas to South-Eastern Europe (Albania, Bosnia and Herzegovina, Kosovo, North Macedonia, Montenegro, Serbia), Moldova, Ukraine and Georgia. In addition, Armenia, Norway and Turkey take part as observers.

Second, the European Common Aviation Area with the Western Balkans, Iceland and Norway was signed in 2006 and entered into force in 2017. It liberalizes access to the aviation sector and exports relevant *acquis* in areas such as aviation safety, air traffic management, environment and consumer protection. Common Aviation Area agreements have also been opened up to the Eastern Partnership countries.

Third, the Transport Community Treaty with the six Western Balkans partners was signed in 2017 and entered into force in 2019. It focuses on integrating networks in the field of road, rail, inland waterway and maritime transport, and it covers areas such as technical standards, interoperability, safety, public procurement and environment.

Despite certain similarities, the governance structures of these three sectoral communities are not the same (Buschle and Karova, 2019). For example, in the European Common Aviation Area and the Transport Community the European Commission assesses the compliance of the non-EU contracting parties, while in the Energy Community that function is vested with the Secretariat. They also differ on the dispute settlement and on whether the case law of the CJEU after the signature of the respective agreement is binding. Unlike the EEA, they all lack a 'decision-shaping' access to EU institutions. The sectoral communities may take measures to implement amendments in line with the evolution of relevant *acquis*, but they are not obliged to do so. The *acquis* can be adapted to their institutional framework and to the specific situations of the non-EU contracting parties. The communities thus clearly have lower ambitions concerning homogeneity as compared to the EEA.

The substance is narrow but rather deep and combined with medium-strong governance mechanisms. Although this does not seem to correspond well to the overall argument, it can easily be explained by the communities' pre-accession rationale for South-Eastern Europe although other neighbours have later joined as well.

The 'British Model'

On 23 June 2016 a slim majority of the British people voted Leave in the Brexit referendum. The UK left the EU on 1 February 2020, the day when the Withdrawal Agreement entered into force. The UK government's red lines in the negotiations on a future partnership with the EU comprised the desire to conduct an independent trade policy, contain immigration from Europe, and take back control of laws (and the interpretation thereof). Given these red lines and the EU's principles, the outcome of the difficult negotiations was, not very surprisingly, an FTA. The Trade and Cooperation Agreement was signed at the end of the transition period in December 2020 and entered into force in May 2021. In order to avoid a physical border between Northern Ireland and the Republic of Ireland and to preserve the 1998 Good Friday (or Belfast) Agreement that had brought peace to a long-standing conflict, a protocol to the Withdrawal Agreement grants this British province a special status.

The United Kingdom's New Partnership with the EU

The TCA maintains the 'no-tariff, no-quotas' trade of goods with the EU and foresees cooperation on economic, social, environmental and fisheries issues, a close partnership on citizens' security, and an overarching governance framework. However, the non-tariff barriers to trade increased significantly for exporters and importers of both parties, and the provisions for services are rather weak, comparable to the EU's trade agreements with Canada or Japan. The level playing field chapters require the parties to maintain at least the same level of social, labour and environmental standards as prevailed at the beginning of 2021.

The guidelines of the European Council (2018, para 7) for the negotiations with the UK show that the 30-years-old 'Interlaken principles' still hold: they repeatedly stressed that any agreement would have to be based on a balance of rights and obligations, ensure a level playing field, as well as preserve the integrity of the internal market and the EU's autonomy. Legal as well as political constraints necessarily limit what the EU can offer without unravelling the Union.

With the governance framework the TCA provides the core of a legal structure defining the future bilateral relations between the EU and the UK. Hence, the EU seems to have drawn a lesson from the 'Swiss model' which consists of a dense network of sectoral bilateral agreements but lacks a common institutional framework. The main body is the Partnership Council which oversees the implementation and application of the TCA, with the assistance of 19 specialized committees. The agreement also provides various dispute settlement mechanisms, involving consultations and decisions by arbitration tribunals or panels of experts. The Partnership Council can amend parts of the TCA by mutual agreement. Yet, unlike in the other models discussed above, the UK does not have to take over any *acquis* and there is no role for the CJEU (except in Northern Ireland, see below).

The TCA is only a starting point for the new EU-UK relationship. Its substance is relatively narrow, more inspired by FTAs with countries further afar than those with EU neighbours. Consequently, the governance remains weak. Like in the Swiss case, despite being de facto highly integrated with the EU, the UK remains reluctant towards formal integration and frictions between the two sides are likely. The EU's market power is considerable, but its governance power is constrained by British sovereignty concerns. Although the UK might have liked to include more substance, it was not ready to pay the price required in terms of stronger governance arrangements.

Special case: Northern Ireland

Northern Ireland, although officially part of the UK's customs territory, remains under the EU's customs code and certain rules regarding goods, agri-products, state aid and wholesale electricity markets. Similar to the situation of Liechtenstein, which is both in the EEA and in a bilateral customs union with Switzerland (see above), Northern Ireland operates in two different integration regimes – the UK and the EU – simultaneously. In practice, the 'border' is therefore down the Irish Sea, managed by the UK authorities. Goods travelling from Northern Ireland to Great Britain have access to the UK internal market. By contrast, all commercial goods moving from Great Britain into Northern Ireland require customs declarations, and must respect product regulations, sanitary and phytosanitary standards. For those goods deemed to be at risk of subsequently entering the EU's internal market, tariffs have to be paid. Northern Ireland also applies the EU's value added tax rules on goods for sales across the Irish Sea.

The Protocol demands regulatory alignment of Northern Ireland to selective aspects of the EU's internal market legislation, managed through amendments to the annexes, which are decided by the Joint Committee. There is no 'decision-shaping', but the Legislative Assembly of Northern Ireland will have a vote every four (or possibly eight) years on the Protocol's continued application (Hayward, 2021). The CJEU retains jurisdiction in Northern Ireland as regards the provisions of EU law covered by the Protocol. Hence, the EU has shown some flexibility in accommodating the region's special circumstances by separating the four freedoms, by allowing a dynamic arrangement and by trusting the enforcement of a non-member state. Again, Northern Ireland is a unique case also because the EU needs to safeguard the interests of its continuing member state, Ireland.

CONCLUSION: FRAGMENTED YET CONSOLIDATING EXTERNAL DIFFERENTIATION

This chapter explored what kind of pattern of affiliations between the EU and its neighbours has emerged during the last three decades, and how this pattern can be explained. It argued that a certain consolidation has been taking place and that the governance arrangements tend to be stronger, the broader and deeper the scope of substance covered in a partnership. The EU acts not only as a normative power and a market power projecting its political and socio-economic norms abroad, but equally as a governance power exporting its institutional norms to the neighbourhood via partnership agreements. This latter aspect has so far largely been neglected in the literature.

The findings summarized in Table 19.2 show a clear correlation from the top left to the bottom right, except for the Swiss case and the sectoral communities. However, the institutional framework agreement would have moved Switzerland a cell further to the right, and the location of the sectoral communities can be explained by their pre-accession angle. A modernization of the customs union with Turkey and an association of the three small-sized countries would shift them downwards as well (and the latter possibly further to the right).

As shown by Gstöhl and Phinnemore (2019b, p. 195), there has been limited institutional innovation and significant path dependence since the creation of the EEA. Most neighbourhood relations take the form of association agreements. Regarding their substance, different additions to the free movement of goods are possible, but the EU insists on a balance of rights and obligations. Yet, the higher the degree of *acquis*-based integration, the more likely is an inclusion of third countries into the EU's decision-making processes via decision-shaping (and other governance mechanisms). Such an inclusion partially compensates the countries'

Table 19.2 Comparison of models

		Governance		
		Weak	*Medium*	*Strong*
Substance	*Narrow*	British model	Turkish model small-sized countries	Sectoral communities
	Medium	Swiss model	Ukrainian model	
	Broad and deep			Norwegian model

relative loss of autonomy and helps ensure the homogeneity of the shared legal space. Only in very special cases, such as those of the small-sized countries and Northern Ireland, have exceptional tailor-made arrangements been agreed. Öberg (2020, p. 153) rightly argues that over time:

> [t]he function of the internal market acquis has evolved from merely providing a legal framework for the functioning of the internal market among the EU Member States to also integrating third countries into the Union's sphere of influence beyond the accession process.

In this context the EU might offer different models of cooperation, yet in essence, it applies the same legal building blocks to extend EU rules on third countries in its proximity (Ott, 2021). Furthermore, the EU thereby insists on similar institutional arrangements in order to safeguard the functioning of the different agreements (Baur, 2019).

As a result, third countries generally face a trade-off between (market) access to the EU and convergence with EU rules which involves important dichotomies such as 'hegemony versus partnership' and 'differentiation versus homogeneity' (Bechev and Nicolaïdis, 2010). Other authors frame this built-in tension in terms of access and participation (Baur, 2019; Fossum et al., 2020). Baur makes a clear distinction between 'access to' the internal market (e.g. based on the conditions of the World Trade Organization or a free trade agreement) and 'participation in' the internal market. In the latter case the third countries are treated similar to EU member states based on an 'integration agreement' which contains the obligation for them to apply, implement or incorporate in their domestic legal order a predetermined selection of EU *acquis* (Van der Loo, 2016, p. 28). The power asymmetry generally works in favour of the bigger EU. The EU takes the level of economic development and the related administrative capacity of its partners into account, for instance in the form of political or market access conditionality.

If hegemony is understood as a polity using its superior capabilities to create an international order involving 'rules and norms of conduct, the topography of formal international institutions, [and] the (related) allocation of status and prestige' (Musgrave and Nexon, 2018, p. 595), then the EU can be viewed as a regional hegemon, and the pattern of affiliations it has been creating provides Europe with a certain order – an order that the UK wishes to escape. The challenge that all neighbours interested in a closer relationship with the EU face is to find an acceptable balance in the trade-off between substance and governance, or the benefits resulting from participation in the European project and the lack of real access to the related EU decision-making. This balance varies according to domestic preferences.

REFERENCES

Baur, G. (2019). Privileged Partnerships: The Partner Countries' (Institutional) Perspectives. In S. Gstöhl and D. Phinnemore (eds), *The Proliferation of Privileged Partnerships between the European Union and its Neighbours* (pp. 23–45). Routledge.

Bechev, D. and Nicolaïdis, K. (2010). From Policy to Polity: Can the EU's Special Relations with its 'Neighbourhood' be Decentred? *Journal of Common Market Studies*, *48*(3), 475–500.

Buschle, D. and Karova, R. (2019). The EU's Sectoral Communities with Neighbours: The Case of the Energy Community. In S. Gstöhl and D. Phinnemore (eds), *The Proliferation of Privileged Partnerships between the European Union and its Neighbours* (pp. 139–56). Routledge.

CJEU. (1987). Case 12/86, *Demirel v Stadt Schwäbisch Gmünd*, ECLI:EU:C:1987:400.

Council of the European Union. (2010). Council Conclusions on EU Relations with EFTA Countries, 3060th General Affairs Council meeting, Brussels, 14 December 2010. https://www.consilium.europa.eu/uedocs/cms_data/docs/pressdata/EN/foraff/118458.pdf (accessed 19 October 2021).

Council of the European Union. (2012). Council Conclusions on EU relations with EFTA countries, 3213th Transport, Telecommunications and Energy Council meeting, Brussels, 20 December 2012. https://eeas.europa.eu/archives/docs/norway/docs/2012_final_conclusions_en.pdf (accessed 19 October 2021).

Council of the European Union. (2014). Council Conclusions on a Homogeneous Extended Single Market and EU Relations with Non-EU Western European Countries, 3362nd General Affairs Council meeting, Brussels, 16 December 2014. https://www.consilium.europa.eu/uedocs/cms_data/docs/pressdata/en/er/146315.pdf (accessed 20 October 2021).

Damro, C. (2012). Market Power Europe. *Journal of European Public Policy*, *19*(5), 682–99.

Damro, C. (2021). The European Union as 'Market Power Europe'. In S. Gstöhl and S. Schunz (eds), *The External Action of the European Union: Concepts, Approaches, Theories* (pp. 54–68). Red Globe Press.

De Clercq, W. (1987). Speech at the EC-EFTA Ministerial Meeting. Interlaken, 20 May 1987. http://europa.eu/rapid/press-release_SPEECH-87-32_en.htm (accessed 19 October 2021).

European Commission. (2012). Communication 'EU Relations with the Principality of Andorra, the Principality of Monaco and the Republic of San Marino – Options for Closer Integration with the EU', COM(2012) 680 final, Brussels, 20 November 2012. https://eur-lex.europa.eu/LexUriServ/LexUriServ.do?uri=COM:2012:0680:FIN:en:PDF (accessed 20 October 2021).

European Commission and High Representative. (2021). Joint Communication to the European Council, State of play of EU-Turkey political, economic and trade relations, JOIN(2021) 8 final/2, Brussels, 22 March 2021. https://op.europa.eu/en/publication-detail/-/publication/2133b382-8b21-11eb-b85c-01aa75ed71a1/language-en (accessed 19 October 2021).

European Council. (2018). European Council (Article 50) (23 March 2018) – Guidelines, EUCO XT 20001/18, Brussels, 23 March 2018. https://www.consilium.europa.eu/media/33458/23-euco-art50-guidelines.pdf (accessed 19 October 2019).

Fossum, J.E., Quesada, M.G., and Zgaga, T. (2020). The EU's Non-Members: Key Principles, Underlying Logics and Types of Affiliation, EU3D Report, no. 1. *ARENA*. https://www.eu3d.uio.no/publications/eu3d-reports/report-1-20-fossum-et-al.pdf (accessed 19 October 2021).

Frommelt, C. (2020). Institutional Challenges for External Differentiated Integration: The Case of the EEA. EUI Working Papers, RSCAS 2020/65. *Robert Schuman Centre for Advanced Studies*. https://hdl.handle.net/1814/68538 (accessed 19 October 2021).

Frommelt, C. and Gstöhl, S. (2011). Liechtenstein and the EEA: The Europeanization of a (Very) Small State, Report, no. 18. *Utvalget for utredning av Norges avtaler med EU*.

Gstöhl, S. (1994). EFTA and the European Economic Area or the Politics of Frustration. *Cooperation and Conflict*, *29*(4), 333–66.

Gstöhl, S. (1997). Successfully Squaring the Circle: Liechtenstein's Membership of the Swiss and European Economic Area. In M. Hösli and A. Saether (eds), *Free Trade Agreements and Customs Unions: Experiences, Challenges and Constraints* (pp. 163–76). TACIS European Commission and European Institute of Public Administration.

Gstöhl, S. (2016). Mapping the European Union's Neighbourhood Relations: The European Economic Area as a 'Prototype' for the Integration of EU Neighbours? In S. Gstöhl (ed.), *The European Neighbourhood Policy in a Comparative Perspective: Models, Challenges, Lessons* (pp. 15–30). Routledge.

Gstöhl, S. and Phinnemore, D. (2019a). Introduction: Privileged Partnerships between the European Union and Third States. In S. Gstöhl and D. Phinnemore (eds), *The Proliferation of Privileged Partnerships between the European Union and its Neighbours* (pp. 1–22). Routledge.

Gstöhl, S. and Phinnemore, D. (2019b). Conclusion: The EU and its Privileged Partnerships – Governance Power Europe? In S. Gstöhl and D. Phinnemore (eds), *The Proliferation of Privileged Partnerships between the European Union and its Neighbours* (pp. 175–202). Routledge.

Gstöhl, S. and Phinnemore, D. (2021). The Future EU–UK Partnership: A Historical Institutionalist Perspective. *Journal of European Integration*, *43*(1), 99–115.

Hayward, K. (2021). 'Flexible and Imaginative': The EU's Accommodation of Northern Ireland in the UK–EU Withdrawal Agreement. *International Studies*, *58*(2) 201–18.

HM Government. (2016). Alternatives to Membership: Possible Models for the United Kingdom outside the European Union. *Cabinet Office*. https://www.gov.uk/government/publications/alternatives-to-membership-possible-models-for-the-united-kingdom-outside-the-european-union (accessed 19 October 2021).

Lavenex, S. (2004). EU External Governance in 'Wider Europe'. *Journal of European Public Policy*, *11*(4), 680–700.

Lavenex, S., Lehmkuhl, D., and Wichmann, N. (2009). Modes of External Governance: A Cross-national and Cross-sectoral Comparison. *Journal of European Public Policy*, *16*(6), 813–33.

Leuffen, D., Rittberger, B., and Schimmelfennig, F. (2013). *Differentiated Integration: Explaining Variation in the European Union*. Palgrave Macmillan.

Maiani, F. (2019). Unique, Yet Archetypal: Relations between the European Union and Andorra, Monaco and San Marino. In S. Gstöhl and D. Phinnemore (eds), *The Proliferation of Privileged Partnerships between the European Union and its Neighbours* (pp. 84–101). Routledge.

Manners, I. (2002). Normative Power Europe: A Contradiction in Terms? *Journal of Common Market Studies*, *40*(2), 235–58.

Manners, I. (2010). As You Like It: European Union Normative Power in the European Neighbourhood Policy. In R. Whitman and S. Wolff (eds), *The European Neighbourhood Policy in Perspective: Context, Implementation and Impact* (pp. 29–50). Palgrave.

Musgrave, P. and Nexon, D.H. (2018). Defending Hierarchy from the Moon to the Indian Ocean: Symbolic Capital and Political Dominance in Early Modern China and the Cold War. *International Organization*, *72*(3), 591–626.

Öberg, M.-L. (2020). Internal Market *Acquis* as a Tool in EU External Relations: From Integration to Disintegration. *Legal Issues of Economic Integration*, *47*(2), 151–78.

Oesch, M. (2020). Switzerland-EU Bilateral Agreements, the Incorporation of EU Law and the Continuous Erosion of Democratic Rights. *Yearbook of European Law*, *39*(1), 602–39.

Oppenheim, B. (2018, 27 February). The Ukraine Model for Brexit: Is Dissociation Just Like Association? *Centre for European Reform*. https://www.cer.eu/insights/ukraine-model-brexit-dissociation-just-association (accessed 19 October 2021).

Ott, A. (2021). The Building Blocks and Stumbling Stones of Constructing the European Legal Space. In W. Th. Douma, C. Eckes, P. Van Elsuwege, E. Kassoti, A. Ott, and R.A. Wessel (eds), *The Evolving Nature of EU External Relations Law* (pp. 205–29). T.M.C. Asser Press.

Schwok, R. (2021). The Bilateral Approach: Achievements and Limitations. In P. Dardanelli and O. Mazzoleni (eds), *Switzerland–EU Relations: Lessons for the UK after Brexit?* (pp. 38–55). Routledge.

Swiss Federal Council. (2021). Rapport relatif aux négociations sur un accord-cadre institutionnel entre la Suisse et l'UE, Berne, 26 May 2021. https://www.newsd.admin.ch/newsd/message/attachments/66827.pdf (accessed 19 October 2021).

Terzi, Ö. (2019). The EU-Turkey Customs Union: Shortcomings and Prospects for Modernization. In S. Gstöhl and D. Phinnemore (eds), *The Proliferation of Privileged Partnerships between the European Union and its Neighbours* (pp. 121–38). Routledge.

Tobler, C. (2021). The EU-Swiss Sectoral Approach under Pressure: Not Least Because of Brexit. In S. Lorenzmaier, R. Petrov, and C. Vedder (eds), *EU External Relations Law* (pp. 107–26). Springer.

Van der Loo, G. (2016). *The EU-Ukraine Association Agreement and Deep and Comprehensive Free Trade Area: A New Legal Instrument for EU Integration without Membership*. Brill Nijhoff.

Van Elsuwege, P. and Chamon, M. (2019). The Meaning of 'Association' under EU Law: A Study on the Law and Practice of EU Association Agreements. *European Parliament*. https://www.europarl.europa.eu/RegData/etudes/STUD/2019/608861/IPOL_STU(2019)608861_EN.pdf (accessed 19 October 2021).

Webb, D., Lang, A., Keep, M., Miller, V., Jozepa, I., Harari, D., and Gower, M. (2018). The European Economic Area. Briefing Paper, no. 8129, 21 December 2018. *House of Commons Library*. https://researchbriefings.files.parliament.uk/documents/CBP-8129/CBP-8129.pdf (accessed 19 October 2021).

20. The Swiss model in the context of Brexit: from 'side-street' to 'dead-end'?

Sandra Lavenex and Alexandre Veuthey

INTRODUCTION

Switzerland's special status as a quasi-member state enjoying many privileges of European integration without bearing the political costs of membership has certainly inspired Brexit debates. Yet, by the time of Brexit, Switzerland's unique model of association had increasingly come under strain – and what started as a 'side-street' to European integration had turned into a 'dead-end'.

Adamant of their national sovereignty and preferring trade liberalisation over political unification, Switzerland and the United Kingdom (UK) share many parallels in their relations to the European Union (EU). This also includes their ambivalent attitude towards freedom of movement which, at different points, has proved a stumbling block. Whereas the UK has opted for joining the EU, Switzerland has remained in the European Free Trade Area (EFTA) and has negotiated a unique set of bilateral agreements granting considerable access to the single market. It did not come as a surprise when in the context of Brexit, 'leave' proponents put forward the Swiss model as a way to reap the economic benefits while avoiding sovereignty losses of integration. What this debate failed to recognise, however, is that de facto Switzerland is subject to considerable sections of EU law – without participating in its development. Furthermore, the references to Switzerland failed to realise that the Swiss model of bilateral agreements increasingly stood under pressure both from within and from without.

This chapter examines the connections between the Swiss model of European integration and Brexit in two steps We start by retracing the trajectory of the Swiss model before turning to its relevance in the Brexit debates, on the one hand, and the reverberation of Brexit on Swiss-EU relations, on the other hand.

TRAJECTORY OF THE SWISS MODEL

A Side-Street Opening up: The Bilateral Agreements

The current model of EU-Switzerland relations finds its origins in the negative popular vote regarding accession to the European Economic Area (EEA) in 1992. Among the most decisive motives against EEA accession were opposition to freedom of movement for EU/EEA citizens and parallel endeavours of the Swiss Federal Government to move towards full EU membership. Indeed, in 1992, just a few months before the referendum, the Swiss government had sent a letter to Brussels asking for the opening of EU membership talks. This confounded the questions of EEA and EU membership in the eyes of the voters and increased opposition to the EEA (Dupont and Sciarini, 2001). The Swiss government's pro-European inclination coupled with popular opposition resulted in a unique 'side-road' of bilateral sectoral agreements. The bilateral agreements were negotiated in two rounds in 1999 and 2004, and came to supplement an existing set of agreements including the 1972 EU-Switzerland free trade agreement. One can say that despite recurrent politicisation of the bilateral arrangements (see below), this solution suited the Swiss interest in deep market access without supranational transfers relatively well. In any case, the letter expressing the willingness to accede to the Union was formally withdrawn in 2016.

Today, Swiss-EU relations are regulated by more than 120 mainly market access-related agreements (Dupont and Sciarini, 2007; Lavenex and Lehmkuhl, 2009; Oesch, 2018; Schwok, 2015).[1] The first bilateral agreements signed in 1999 came into force in 2002 and cover technical barriers to trade, public procurement markets, some agricultural products, overland transport, civil aviation, research and the free movement of persons. These agreements are legally bound by a 'guillotine clause': in case one of the agreements is unilaterally revoked, the other six agreements would also cease to have effect. The second round of bilateral agreements was signed in 2004. These cover a range of relatively minor issues (participation in EU education programmes and the MEDIA programme for the audio-visual industry; accession to Eurostat and the European Environmental Agency; reduced customs duties on processed agricultural products; and income tax exemptions for retired EU officials living in Switzerland) and more contentious points such as accession to the Schengen/Dublin agreements, the fight against fraud and taxation of savings. Of these, the agreement on Schengen/Dublin was subject to a referendum in June 2005. It was accepted by 54.5 per cent of the Swiss electorate (Schwok, 2009, pp. 53–66).

The evolving EU *acquis* and deepening interdependence motivated the Federal Council in 2008 to ask for a third round of bilateral agreements covering free trade in agricultural goods, public health, electricity, and participation in several EU institutions including the European Defence Agency, Galileo, the EU's emission trading system and ESDP Missions. After initial discussions, this eventual third round of sectoral negotiations has been stalled, mainly due to the EU's determination to reform the overarching institutional relations with Switzerland (see below).

A Unique Institutional Setting

The bilateral agreements between the EU and Switzerland differ from other forms of deep association and the EEA in various respects (Church, 2007; Gstöhl, 2002; Lavenex, 2011; Lavenex and Schwok, 2015). First, bilateral agreements have only been concluded in areas in which both parties share an interest in cooperation. Second, and contrary to the EEA, commitments under the bilateral agreements are, with the exception of the air transport and Schengen/Dublin agreement, static as they lay down the scope of necessary regulatory adaptation at the time of their conclusion (Lazowski, 2006, pp. 168, 172).

Most bilateral agreements are based on the mutual recognition of the 'equivalence of legislation'. This means that the 'equivalent' Swiss laws are explicitly listed in the annexes to the sectoral agreements. In case of legislative revisions equivalence must be reassessed. In practice, however, Switzerland has been assessing the 'euro-compatibility' of each legislative act prior to adoption since 1992; which constitutes a kind of voluntary adaptation to the *acquis* (dubbed 'autonomer Nachvollzug') (Church, 2000; Gava and Varone, 2012, 2014; Gava et al., 2014; Honegger, 2004, pp. 43–4; Jenni, 2014; Maiani, 2013).

Under the bilateral agreements the contracting parties are responsible for ensuring implementation on their respective territories, with the exception of the air transport case which recognises the jurisprudence of the Court of Justice of the EU (CJEU) and provides for dynamic legislative alignment with the EU *acquis*. In essence, the implementation of the bilateral agreements is based on the international law principle of 'good faith'. In order to deal with potential challenges arising in implementation, joint committees have been set up under each agreement. These committees are composed of experts from the responsible Commission Directorates General (DG) and the Swiss administration. These deal with potential disputes and can incorporate new EU legislation into the bilateral agreements, subject to the prior consent of the Swiss Federal Council. The agreements on air transport and free movement of persons also include a reference to relevant CJEU Case Law and the respective joint committees can decide on the inclusion of subsequent case law (Lazowski, 2006, p. 168). Meanwhile, Swiss Courts still diverge on whether they are under an obligation to take over further developments of the EU *acquis* or not (Tobler, 2021).

At least formally, the political monitoring procedure respects Switzerland's sovereignty as it avoids subjugation under a supranational jurisdiction. The only exception is the agreement on air transport, which is a partial integration agreement. It is, as noted above, dynamic because it provides for the steady incorporation of new EU legislative acts and it is subject to the monitoring and control functions of the European Commission and the CJEU.

In sum, EU-Switzerland relations have evolved along a functionalist, expert-based interaction 'from below' in a fragmented set of sectoral agreements. This fragmentation comes along with a particular degree of complexity and a lack of political leadership, which has posed challenges to overall strategic action – prompting the European Commission to seek a more centralised institutional relationship (see below).

The bilateral agreements also foresee Switzerland's participation in the decision-shaping process, but in a more restricted manner than for the EEA EFTA states. The formal rules are contained in a declaration on participation in the committees annexed to the bilateral agreements which stipulates that Switzerland has the right to participate as an 'active observer' with a right to speak, but not to vote, in the areas of research, air transport, social security and the recognition of diplomas (Grolimund and Vahl, 2006, p. 47; Honegger, 2004, p. 45). As in the Norwegian case, association with the Schengen and Dublin agreements involves the most far-reaching participation rights as Swiss officials have direct access to all relevant Council working parties, yet without the right to vote (Lavenex, 2015). In all other areas, the Commission has to consult with Switzerland on legislative proposals that further develop the *acquis* in areas in which legislation is equivalent. Once legislation has passed the pre-pipeline stage, the possibilities to influence it decrease markedly, in contrast to the arrangement found under the EEA (Grolimund and Vahl, 2006). This holds in particular for the elaboration of the implementing legislation in the comitology committees. As under the EEA, the Commission has to consult Swiss experts when drafting legislation in the areas relevant to the bilateral agreements and it mentions the Swiss positions in the pursuant Committee discussions. In contrast to the EEA EFTA states, however, the informal practice allowing EEA EFTA experts to assist comitology meetings as observers has not been extended in a general manner to Switzerland. Whereas the sectoral DGs have often been in favour of this informal practice, and have repeatedly allowed Swiss participation on an ad hoc and informal basis, the Legal Service of the Commission and DG Relex/European External Action Service (EEAS) have been increasingly disinclined to accept these special solutions for non-members (Honegger,

2004, p. 88). As we argue further below, tensions resulting from negotiations on an overarching Institutional Agreement and the Brexit process have reinforced these tendencies.

Swiss presence in EU agencies is also significantly more limited than Norway's. Switzerland participates in the Agency for Air Transport Security and the European Environmental Agency. Association with the Schengen and Dublin Agreements in justice and home affairs (JHA) has also implied the conclusion of cooperation agreements with Europol, the European Police College CEPOL, the prosecution agency Eurojust and the borders agency Frontex. With progressive implementation of the bilateral agreements Switzerland has expressed interest in joining more EU agencies, for instance, in the fields of medicines or energy regulation (Schweizerische Eidgenossenschaft, 2010). However, in the absence of agreement on a central institutional treaty (see below), the European Commission has refused formalising Swiss access to other decentralised agencies.

From the Swiss perspective, this bilateral model has provided the Swiss economy with satisfactory access to the single market. In addition, the negotiated issue-specificity of the bilateral agreements, their mainly static nature, as well as the lack of supranational enforcement mechanisms promised a stronger preservation of Swiss sovereignty vis-à-vis the EU than existing alternatives such as the EEA. Yet in reality, sovereignty has been compromised by the practice of autonomous adaptation to the *acquis*. Over the last decade, this delicate compromise has increasingly come under pressure from both domestic politicisation, symbolised most strongly in the 2014 Swiss popular vote against 'mass immigration' and from the EU's demands for the conclusion of an overarching institutional framework agreement.

First Potholes and a Dead-End

The first signs that the Swiss model of bilateral agreements would not hold for long can be traced back to 2008, four years after the conclusion of the second round of agreements. In its biennial conclusions on the EU's relations with Switzerland, the Council stated that 'taking part in the internal market requires a homogenous and simultaneous application and interpretation of the constantly evolving *acquis*' (Council of the European Union, 2008, para. 31). In 2010, the Council went one step further and explicitly declared its dissatisfaction with the bilateral agreements: while the 'system of bilateral agreements has worked well in the past, the key challenge for the coming years will be to go beyond that system, which has become complex and unwieldy to manage and has clearly reached its limits' (Council of the European Union, 2010, para. 48). The Council insisted that dynamic adaptation to the evolving *acquis*, homogeneous interpretation, surveillance and judicial enforcement mechanisms as well as a dispute settlement mechanism should be incorporated into the EU-Switzerland agreements (ibid.). The Council reaffirmed its previous conclusions in 2012. It concluded that 'the approach taken by Switzerland to participate in EU policies and programmes through sectoral agreements in more and more areas in the absence of any horizontal institutional framework, has reached its limits' (Council of the European Union, 2012, para. 31).

When domestic political actors in Switzerland started to question commitments made under the bilateral agreements, the European partners were thus already challenging the sustainability of the Swiss model. As noted above, the first important domestic challenge came in 2014 when the national conservative Swiss People's Party filed an initiative on 'mass immigration' that opposed the principles of freedom of movement. The initiative provided that all immigration to Switzerland should be limited by quotas and annual caps, and that employers should respect the principle of national preference in the hiring process – thereby annulling the privilege enjoyed by EU/EFTA nationals under freedom of movement. In a prospective manner, the text of the initiative also prohibited the conclusion of any international treaty contrary to its provisions.[2]

The initiative's approval by a narrow margin of 50.3 per cent came as a surprise. Not only was its call for quotas incompatible with the free movement agreement, such a unilateral breach also had the potential to annul all bilateral agreements due to the aforementioned 'guillotine clause'. Moreover, the reference to future international treaties had a straightforward implication as Switzerland was, at the time, expected to sign the Protocol extending the EU-Swiss agreement on free movement of persons to Croatia.

The success of the 'mass immigration' initiative led to a series of tensions that gradually undermined Swiss-EU relations. Because of the 'guillotine clause', the Swiss government was not able to sign the Protocol. In response, the EU decided to exclude Switzerland from European scientific research programmes such as Erasmus+ and the EU's framework programme for research and innovation, Horizon 2020. The situation was resolved when, in December 2016, the Swiss Federal Council adopted an implementation law[3] that is compatible with the free movement agreement. The law stipulates that in sectors where the unemployment rate of the Swiss population exceeds a certain threshold, employers are obliged to communicate vacancies first to Swiss residents, but it does not contain an obligation to favour Swiss applicants, nor does it impose quotas on EU/EFTA workers. This allowed the Swiss government to sign the Protocol and to return to full association status in Horizon 2020.

EU pressure for the negotiation of an overarching institutional framework agreement unfolded in parallel to these political tensions. As indicated above, under the bilateral agreements, Switzerland does not have to adopt the new EU *acquis* nor to follow the CJEU jurisprudence, and there is no supervisory authority nor a judicial dispute settlement mechanism. In the eyes of the EU, this legal framework threatens to undermine the homogeneity of the single market. The negotiations towards such an institutional framework agreement started in 2014, and lasted until the end of 2018[4] with the publication of a draft agreement. The draft agreement applied to five current market access agreements: the free movement of persons, land transport, air transport, technical trade barriers and agriculture – as well as all future market access agreements.[5] The proposal reflected a delicate balance between the EU's request for stronger enforcement mechanisms and Switzerland's opposition to 'foreign judges'. It proposed a 'two-pillar model' whereby Switzerland remained responsible for the proper implementation of the agreements on its territory without supranational supervision authority but provided for a dispute settlement mechanism, which could be triggered by the Commission. The dispute settlement mechanism would come into play when the joint committees were unable to find a compromise and would be conducted by an arbitration tribunal. This tribunal would be composed of one judge appointed by Switzerland, one appointed by the EU, and a third one appointed by the two aforementioned judges. Only when the interpretation or application of EU law was in doubt would the tribunal refer cases to the CJEU whose judgment would then be binding. The draft agreement also took a dynamic approach ensuring that relevant developments in EU law would be continuously incorporated.

In a surprising move, once the draft agreement was published, the Federal Council did not formally endorse it but decided to conduct consultations with the relevant stakeholders such as cantonal governments, political parties and interest groups (Federal Council, 2018) – arguably to address widespread discontent with specific provisions, notably concerning state subsidies, flanking measures for posted workers and the EU citizens' rights directive (Schwok, 2020). These concerns put socio-economic issues at the centre of the debate, notably the protection of wage levels and concerns about possible negative consequences for the Swiss social security system.

Following these consultations, the Swiss government requested clarifications and eventual amendments to ensure sufficient support among the Swiss population who would eventually have to endorse the agreement in a popular referendum (Federal Council, 2019). Then President of the EU Commission Jean-Claude Juncker stated that clarifications could be undertaken but that the agreement would not be renegotiated (Juncker, 2019). Despite several rounds of discussions between EU and Swiss negotiators, no compromise could be found on the Swiss concerns. In a sudden and widely unexpected move, the Swiss Federal Council in May 2021 announced one-sidedly – apparently without consultation with the EU counterparts – that it had decided not to sign the agreement and withdrew from the negotiations (European Commission, 2021a; Parmelin, 2021).[6]

In the run-up to this unilateral move, the EU had taken an unusually strong stance linking unrelated issues to the negotiations in order to put pressure on the Swiss government (Veuthey, 2020).[7] For instance, the Swiss stock exchange equivalence, which previously gave EU investment firms the right to trade shares on Swiss trading venues, was not extended after June 2019. Moreover, the EU froze the negotiations that had been on the table for several years, for example, the update of the Mutual Recognition Agreement on medical devices and an agreement in the field of electricity (European Commission, 2021b). As in 2014, the EU threatened to exclude Switzerland from research and innovation cooperation. Whereas under the Horizon 2020 regulation, Switzerland was entitled to be associated to the programme as an EFTA state (Official Journal of the European Union, 2013, Article 7), the 2021 Horizon Europe regulation opens association to EFTA states 'which are members of the EEA' (Official Journal of the European Union, 2021, Article 16) – de facto relegating Switzerland to a third country. This means Swiss research institutions can only participate in a consortium of at least three institutions from three different member states or associated countries (ibid., Article 22), and have to participate at their own costs (European Commission, 2021c, p. 14). Switzerland's change of status in Horizon Europe was confirmed by the Programme Guide published by the Commission in June 2021, after Switzerland's unilateral withdrawal from the negotiations on the Institutional Agreement. The Programme Guide does not include Switzerland in the list of countries to which the transitional provisions apply until the entry into force of the association agreements under negotiation and stipulates that 'legal entities established in Switzerland are currently not covered by these transitional arrangements' (ibid., pp. 12–13).

In conclusion, the 'Swiss Way' of EU association provides a unique pattern of decentralised sectoral agreements in fields of mutual interest. While effectively binding Switzerland to a very large share of the EU *acquis*, the existing arrangements formally preserve Swiss sovereignty as they omit the dynamic adoption of evolving EU law (except for the Schengen and air transport agreements) and the monitoring and/or sanctioning of compliance by EU institutions. This unique model has its origins in a phase when the Swiss government had signalled willingness to join the EEA and eventually also the EU – with the first years of implementation, however, the EU soon became dissatisfied and demanded reforms that would bring the Swiss model closer to the one of the EEA. By the time that the parties started the negotiation of the new Institutional Agreement, existing commitments, in particular regarding freedom of movement, had become increasingly contested in Swiss domestic politics – showing the potential vulnerability of an association based on the principle of 'good faith'. The draft Institutional Agreement paraphrased in 2018 proposed introducing, for five current and all future agreements, dynamic legal approximation and a 'two-pillar' supervisory mechanism involving a judicial dispute settlement system. Avoiding a direct implication for the CJEU, this system only acknowledged an indirect role for the court – thus minimising one of the key arguments of Eurosceptic parties in Switzerland. Nevertheless, socio-economic concerns regarding wage protection and social security systems came to dominate the debate. This mobilised political groups who had traditionally taken a rather pro-European stance, in particular the Socialist Party and trade unions. Whereas a solution to the EU's demands for a new institutional arrangement guaranteeing the continuation of the Swiss model seemed to be within reach, domestic politicisation in Switzerland and the limited flexibility of the EU have effectively turned the bilateral agreements from a 'side-street' to a 'dead-end'.

BREXIT AND SWISS-EU RELATIONS

Economic Ties and Political Barriers

Historically, Switzerland's and the UK's concerns with European integration have often converged, and can be summarised in the trade-off between maximising economic integration gains and minimising sovereignty losses (Dardanelli and Mazzoleni, 2021). Both countries were founding members of the 1960 European Free Trade Association (EFTA), which provided an economic alternative to supranational integration. Nevertheless, the European Economic Community (EEC) countries' rapid economic growth motivated the UK to seek EEC membership early on – despite vivid domestic opposition (HC Deb, 1972). The UK's accession to the EEC along with Denmark and Ireland in 1973 had an immediate impact on the remaining EFTA members as custom duties would have had to be reintroduced in relation to the UK and Denmark (Schwok, 2015, p. 15). As a result, Switzerland and the EEC concluded a free trade agreement in 1972 which, providing for the abolition of customs duties on industrial goods and certain processed agricultural products, laid the ground for Switzerland's gradual integration in the single market.

As an export-driven economy surrounded by EU member states, Switzerland has always been highly dependent on trade with its neighbours. In 2021, 51 per cent of Switzerland's exports went to the Union, and 69 per cent of its imports originated from the EU. On the side of the EU, Switzerland is the EU's fourth biggest export and import market for goods, after the US, China and the UK (accounting for 8 per cent of EU foreign trade). The EU is also the most important partner when it comes to direct investment. About 78 per cent of foreign direct investment in Switzerland originates in the EU. Conversely, approximately 51 per cent of Swiss direct investment abroad flows into the EU. Key Swiss export industries are machinery and electronics, precision tools, chemical and pharmaceutical products, and the financial business. In other sectors, interdependence with the EU stems from Switzerland's geographic position at the heart of Europe, for example, for land transport or electricity markets. Switzerland also has close ties with the EU when it comes to employment. At the end of 2018, more than 457,898 Swiss nationals were living and working in the EU, while 1.4 million EU 28/EFTA citizens were living in Switzerland – amounting to roughly 16.5 per cent of the overall Swiss population. In addition, more than 315,000 people from EU/EFTA countries commute across the border on a daily basis.[8]

In contrast to the UK, where economic interests led to a 'reluctant' membership,[9] Switzerland's political system with its direct democracy and its emphasis on popular sovereignty is seen as widely incompatible with this option (Linder and Müller, 2021). In fact, Switzerland's ambiguous status as non-member state progressively integrating the rules of the single market has provided fertile ground for the rise of Eurosceptic political forces. Classically, this role has been filled by the national conservative Swiss People's Party (SPP) which, combining an anti-European with an anti-immigration position, has grown to the largest party in Parliament (accounting for roughly 30 per cent of the seats) (Hutter et al., 2016). Swiss European policy has become even more complicated in recent years with parts of the second biggest political party in Switzerland, the Socialist Party (SP), joining the Eurosceptic camp (Schwok, 2020). Formally a loyal supporter of the government's European policy, the SP has played a key role in the contestation of the Institutional Agreement. As mentioned above, the key issues that brought the agreement to fail were not the compromise solution found regarding monitoring and enforcement. The main issues were a combination of leftist concerns for the protection of wages and work conditions, on the one hand, and more (but not exclusively) right-wing apprehension against the possible abuse of the social security system following adoption of the citizens' rights directive, on the other.

The Swiss Model in the Brexit Debates

Given the similarity of interests, it is not surprising that the Swiss bilateral model inspired Brexit debates. In the run-up to the Brexit referendum, the Swiss model was put forward as an example to follow for the UK. Concerning trade, it was argued that 'Switzerland has all the advantages of commercial access without the costs of full membership' (Hannan, 2012). Daniel Hannan, then Conservative MEP, emphasised that since the common external tariff does not bind Switzerland, it is free to define its own trade policy. For instance, Switzerland can freely sign trade agreements with third countries and does not have to consider the national interests of other EU member states when defining its trade position. Hannan also pointed out that Switzerland had an advantage over the UK in terms of per capita exports to the EU. Switzerland's economic success was, therefore, a strong argument for the Leave campaign. Nigel Farage even argued that Switzerland 'was an inspiration for the UK leaving the EU' (Swissinfo, 2020).

Yet, not all commentators understood the Swiss bilateral agreements correctly. This was for instance the case regarding freedom of movement. Regretting that the UK has 'been forced to surrender control of its own borders and is powerless to halt a new wave of immigration', David Campbell Bannerman (2013), then Conservative MEP, argued that the safeguard clause included in the bilateral agreement between Switzerland and the EU on the free movement of persons allowed Switzerland to refuse issuing residence permits to EU citizens. Yet this safeguard clause only applies to the accession of new member states and for a transitional period. It is therefore comparable with the transitional period that some EU member states had themselves imposed on citizens from the newly acceded Central and Eastern European countries. Whether by ignorance or in a deliberate move, Brexiteers thus misrepresented Switzerland's EU commitments.

The debates following the Brexit referendum also include various references to the Swiss model.[10] Some commentators suggested that this model granted advantageous access to the single market on a 'pick-and-choose' basis without an obligation to comply with EU rules and directives, or the CJEU.[11] As highlighted in the first part of this chapter, however, Switzerland has to follow the EU *acquis* to ensure continued access to the single market in the sectors covered by the bilateral agreements. Whether through updates to the bilateral agreements or through autonomous legal adaptation, Switzerland must maintain its standards and production norms at the same level as those of the EU and therefore must comply with EU rules over which it has no say. Another point that found insufficient reflection in the Brexit debates is that Switzerland was able to negotiate its access to the single market only because it accepted the free movement of people. Last but not least, those supportive of a Swiss-style UK withdrawal agreement failed to take into account that the EU was no longer satisfied with the system of bilateral agreements and had been pushing for a new setup already since 2008.

British hopes for a sector-by-sector withdrawal agreement were quickly dashed by the EU with the argument that this would undermine the integrity of the single market (Tobler, 2021, p. 124). In 2017, the European Commission clearly stated that 'preserving the integrity of the Single Market excludes participation based on a sector-by-sector approach' (European Commission, 2017, para. 9). This position was reaffirmed in February 2018 by the Commission's Brexit chief negotiator Michel Barnier who stated that the EU 'can't possibly imagine a situation in which it would accept cherry-picking' as the EU is 'responsible for guaranteeing the integrity of the single market' (Barnier, 2018). Michel Barnier's remarks followed press reports about what might be in the UK's post-Brexit trade proposal. That proposal, Theresa May's Chequers plan, was unveiled in 2018. The plan proposed leaving the single market, the customs union, the common agricultural policy, the common fisheries policy, and ending the free movement of persons as well as the jurisdiction of the CJEU (HM Government, 2018). At the same time, it would ensure frictionless trade in goods through a free trade area and that the UK maintains a common rulebook for goods, including agri-food (ibid.). The UK would also participate in some EU agencies and continue to cooperate with the EU in certain areas, including security and science (ibid.). The EU strongly rejected Theresa May's plan. Michel Barnier criticised the British customs plan and restated that the four freedoms of the single market were indivisible (Stone, 2018). During the State of the Union annual speech, Jean-Claude Juncker recalled that the EU was against cherry-picking and stated that the UK would not be part of the single market anymore 'and certainly not only in the parts of it they choose' (Juncker, 2018, p. 9). The EU finally rejected the Chequers plan in September 2018.

Brexit's Impact on Swiss-EU Relations

The Brexit referendum and the subsequent negotiations on a withdrawal agreement have generated much interest in Switzerland. The initial expectation was that by leaving the EU, the UK would be a strong ally for Switzerland in its negotiations with Brussels. Before the referendum, former Swiss president and foreign minister Micheline Calmy-Rey said it would be in Switzerland's interest for the UK to leave the EU (RTS, 2016a). She argued that the UK would have to renegotiate its partnership with the EU via bilateral agreements or by joining the EFTA and then the EEA. The latter solution would lead to a renewal of the EEA in a way that could be beneficial for Switzerland. Furthermore, joining forces with the UK would put Switzerland in a less asymmetric position in its negotiations with the EU (ibid.). These remarks were criticised by members of the Swiss Parliament who argued instead that a Brexit would cause an earthquake within the EU that would relegate the Swiss file to the bottom of the EU priority list (RTS, 2016b). At the time, Switzerland was in a defensive position seeking a solution with the EU regarding the 2014 initiative against 'mass immigration'. Therefore, a Brexit that would take all of Brussels' attention would not be in Switzerland's interest (ibid.).

After the referendum, Micheline Calmy-Rey reiterated her statement saying to the BBC that the UK and Switzerland should collaborate together to find a way to balance freedom of movement with single market access (Ahmed, 2016). In an interview with a Swiss newspaper, she also stated that Switzerland should let the UK negotiate first and play the role of 'snow plough' (Calmy-Rey, 2016). As a larger and more powerful country, she expected the UK to get more concessions from Brussels. Switzerland could then ask for the same.

However, the reality turned out to be the opposite. Brexit became Brussels' main concern, and Switzerland lost priority, as some members of the Swiss Parliament had predicted. Moreover, the fact that the EU found itself negotiating the UK withdrawal agreement and the Institutional Agreement with Switzerland in parallel did not serve Switzerland's interests. Indeed, having two countries seeking privileged access to the single market while insisting on their sovereignty made the EU tougher in both negotiations. The EU made it clear from the outset to Bern and London that its main objective was to preserve the homogeneity of the single market. In its negotiating mandate for the Institutional Agreement, the Council of the European Union declared that an overarching institutional framework was needed to 'protect the homogeneity of the internal market and ensure legal certainty' (Council of the European Union, 2014). In its guidelines for Brexit negotiations, the European Council also underlined that any agreement with the UK should be based on a balance of rights and obligations, the indivisibility of the single market's four freedoms, and the need to ensure a level playing field (European Council, 2017). As a result, it became clear that the Swiss model did not offer a potential alternative path of integration for other countries like the UK. The EU established a link between the two negotiations and ensured that no concessions that would undermine the homogeneity of the single market would be accepted. The link between the two negotiations is illustrated by an internal letter sent by Commissioner Johannes Hahn to Commission President Jean-Claude Juncker after the Swiss Federal Council decided in 2018 not to sign the draft Institutional Agreement and to hold domestic consultations instead. Commissioner Johannes Hahn stated that:

> We simply cannot accept further attempts of foot-dragging and watering down internal market rules, especially in what is probably the decisive phase regarding Brexit. I believe we have no choice but to pass this crystal-clear message that the Institutional Framework Agreement as it stands is as good as it gets. (Hahn, 2019)

In parallel to the negotiations, the EU has also hardened its position towards Switzerland in some areas of technocratic cooperation. Thanks to years of good cooperation, Swiss experts were invited to some EU technical meetings even when the bilateral agreements did not provide for it.[12] UK diplomats were well aware of that, and it has been reported to us that they were in weekly contact with their Swiss' counterparts to compare their access to EU instances.[13] As a result, the EU has excluded Swiss technocrats from all meetings where there was no legal framework that would provide for their presence in order to prevent the UK from exploiting this informal practice and demanding similar access.[14]

In sum, Swiss hopes to find a strong ally in the UK in their negotiations with the EU did not materialise. The EU has been intransigent in its negotiations with both countries insisting that privileged commercial access necessitates strong institutions guaranteeing the homogeneity of the single market. The EU's position can be illustrated with these words from a member of the EEAS in 2019: 'to protect the internal market it is necessary to enable everybody to interact according to the same rules and Switzerland should follow the Brexit negotiations to better understand the behaving of the EU'.[15] One can only speculate whether the EU would have been more compromising towards Switzerland had Brexit not happened. In any case, the EU's determination to review the legal framework of its relations with Switzerland predates Brexit. It can however be said that Brexit certainly did not help Switzerland in its negotiations with Brussels, as the EU took a tough stance towards both countries to preserve the integrity of its single market.

The Brexit Deal and its Perception in Switzerland

The UK's negotiated agreement with the EU has spurred some discussion in other closely associated non-member states such as Norway (Fossum and Vigrestad, 2021) and Switzerland in the potential advantages of aligning their EU affiliation more closely with that of the EU-UK agreement. When the EU and the UK announced on Christmas Eve 2020 that they had finally reached an agreement to govern their future post-Brexit relationship – the EU-UK Trade and Cooperation Agreement (TCA) – reactions in Switzerland were divided. The Swiss sovereigntist right welcomed the agreement negotiated by Prime Minister Boris Johnson.[16] Comparing the draft Institutional Agreement and the TCA, they stressed the absence of the CJEU in the dispute settlement mechanism, the fact that the agreement does not provide for dynamic adoption of EU law by the UK and that there is no guillotine clause to pressure the contracting partner. They also pointed out that since the free movement of persons is not part of the agreement, the EU Citizenship Directive does not apply. These four points were exactly what the Swiss sovereigntist right opposed in the Institutional Agreement's draft text – which led some to call the EU-UK agreement a 'heavy humiliation for Switzerland' (Schaller, 2020). The TCA raised attention also beyond the national conservative camp. Autonomiesuisse, an association of entrepreneurs, stated that the TCA gave 'Switzerland the opportunity to conclude a better framework agreement' (Autonomiesuisse, 2020). They felt that this agreement resolved the political issues of sovereignty and that Switzerland should follow suit. Some members of the Swiss Liberal Party also indicated that the Federal Council should seek a solution similar to what Johnson had negotiated with respect to the role of the CJEU (Tages Anzeiger, 30 December 2020). Herewith these members of the Liberal Party made a U-turn from their earlier support for the Institutional Agreement, thereby joining the widening camp of opponents.

On the other side of the spectrum, it has been argued that the two agreements are not comparable and that 'talking about Swiss failure and British success was like comparing apples and pears' (Schwok and Najy, 2020). These voices underline that the agreement negotiated by London is essentially a free trade agreement and is thus closer to the Swiss-EU free trade agreement signed in 1972 than to the system of bilateral agreements that goes much further in terms of market access (ibid.). Similarly, the CJEU plays no role in the 1972 free trade agreement, and that agreement anyway falls outside the scope of the Institutional Agreement (Cottier, 2020). The absence of the CJEU from the TCA – like the 1972 Switzerland-EU free trade agreement – is explained by the fact that these do not contain EU law (Tages Anzeiger, 28 December 2020). This is fundamentally different from the market access approach under the bilateral agreements, which, as discussed above, contain EU law. This is why the CJEU figures in the dispute settlement mechanism negotiated in the Institutional Agreement.

Also in substance, the TCA falls short of the EU-Switzerland bilateral agreements. The former is limited to avoiding the reintroduction of customs duties on trade in goods. Swiss-EU agreements remove a large number of non-tariff barriers thanks to the mutual recognition agreement and the equivalence of standards (phytosanitary, veterinary etc.). It should be noted here that following the Swiss Federal Council's decision not to sign the Institutional Agreement in May 2021, the EU decided not to update any market access agreements with Switzerland or to sign new ones (European Commission, 2021a). Therefore, the non-updating of the Swiss-EU mutual recognition agreement will inevitably create new non-tariff barriers over time. Nevertheless, Switzerland still has privileged access to the single market.

Post-Brexit discussions in Switzerland have also shown that the exclusion of freedom of movement from the TCA also comes at a price: it ends the mutual recognition of professional qualifications and the possibilities for British companies to send their staff for limited or extended assignments in the EU, and creates difficulties for some British companies to recruit qualified workers in the EU (Tages Anzeiger, 27 December 2020). London has also lost access to the Schengen Information System, the EU's police database containing information on individuals and entities that pose potential security threats.

In sum, the TCA clearly falls short of Swiss-EU bilateralism in terms of market access. Yet, the fact that this agreement excludes CJEU jurisprudence, the dynamic adoption of EU law and freedom of movement has been seen as attractive by the more Eurosceptic parts of the Swiss constituency. In any case, the TCA has not helped build support for the Institutional Agreement in Switzerland and may have contributed to the Federal Council's unilateral withdrawal.

CONCLUSION

Switzerland and the UK have historically shared an interest in the economic benefits of European integration with a concern over sovereignty losses. While the UK decided to join the EC/EU in 1973, Switzerland has sought a privileged partnership. The extent of market access and the lightness of sovereignty transfers found under the bilateral agreements benefited from a political climate in which the Swiss government had originally supported EEA membership and even eventual EU accession.

The Swiss 'side-street' has inspired Brexit supporters, and has recurrently been invoked as a possible model for the UK. However, these arguments have often misrepresented the actual functioning of the bilateral agreements – and failed to acknowledge that already starting in 2008 the Commission demanded substantive revisions of the Swiss model. The call for an Institutional Agreement providing for dynamic legal commitments and some form of judicial monitoring was justified by the need to protect the homogeneity of the single market. In parallel with the partial politicisation of bilateral agreements in Switzerland, the EU developed an increasingly tough stance on these institutional reforms. On the one hand, the EU decided not to sign or update any market access agreements with Switzerland as long as the institutional questions were not solved. On the other hand, the EU introduced issue-linkages making cooperation under existing agreements in research or financial markets conditional on the advancement of the Institutional Agreement.

The parallel EU-UK negotiations following Brexit did not alleviate the pressure on Switzerland, nor did they corroborate Brexiteers' interest in the Swiss model. The EU made it very clear that a partnership relying on sectoral agreements was no option. Instead of widening the scope of negotiations, Brexit therefore reinforced EU pressure on the Swiss model. The Swiss Federal Council's unilateral decision in May 2021 to end the negotiations on an Institutional Agreement is unlikely to reduce this pressure. Whereas the actual status quo with the bilateral agreements is not invalidated, without regular updates, their substance and hence market access will gradually erode.

Beyond the specific case of Switzerland and Brexit, the developments examined in this chapter highlight a new approach in the EU's relations with third countries, in which the homogeneity of the single market and the balance of benefits and obligations predominate over economic or other functional interests in promoting integration below the threshold of membership. Part of this package is the obligation to sign on to the dynamic adaptation of the evolution of the *acquis* and a dispute settlement mechanism, similar to the model of the EEA. In sum, the Swiss 'side-street' of bilateral sectoral agreements may well have turned into a 'dead-end'.

NOTES

1. For an inter-institutional analysis of the EU's position throughout these negotiations, see Najy (2019).
2. Initiative populaire fédérale 'Contre l'immigration de masse', https://www.bk.admin.ch/ch/f/pore/vi/vis413t.html (accessed 27 July 2021).
3. See Implementation of Article 121a Cst. Federal Council adopts ordinance amendments at https://www.sem.admin.ch/ejpd/fr/home/actualite/news/2017/2017-12-081.html (accessed 2 July 2021).
4. See Timeline of Swiss-EU relations since 2013 (aspects related to the Institutional Agreement) at https://www.eda.admin.ch/dam/europa/en/documents/abkommen/20210526-mm-europapolitik_beilage-8-2_chronologie_EN.pdf (accessed 28 July 2021).
5. Agreement facilitating bilateral relations between the European Union and the Swiss Confederation in the parts of the internal market in which Switzerland participates (final version), https://www.eda.admin.ch/dam/europa/fr/documents/abkommen/Acccord-inst-Projet-de-texte_fr.pdf (accessed 5 July 2021).
6. See Federal Department of Foreign Affairs, 'No signing of Swiss-EU institutional agreement', Press release, 26 June 2021, https://www.fdfa.admin.ch/eda/en/fdfa/fdfa/aktuell/news.html/content/eda/de/meta/news/2021/5/26/83705 (accessed 28 July 2021).
7. See Hahn (2019).
8. See the official information portal of the Swiss federal administration at https://www.eda.admin.ch/europa/en/home/europapolitik/ueberblick/wirtschaftliche-bedeutung.html.
9. See for example Margaret Thatcher, Speech to the College of Europe ('The Bruges Speech'), 20 September 1988, https://www.margaretthatcher.org/document/107332 (accessed 10 August 2021).
10. See for example Business Insider, 'May's government reportedly now wants a Swiss-style Brexit deal', 16 October 2017, https://www.businessinsider.com/mays-government-reportedly-now-want-a-swiss-style-brexit-deal-2017-10?r=US&IR=T (accessed 9 December 2021); Tony Connelly, 'Brexit talks: Goodbye Canada, hello Switzerland?', *RTE*, 12 January 2020, https://www.rte.ie/news/brexit/2020/0110/1105666-brexit-talks/ (accessed 9 December 2021).
11. See for example Senior European Experts, 'Switzerland and the European Union', *The expert's briefing*, 2020.
12. Interview with a Member of the Swiss Mission to the EU, Brussels, 10 September 2019.

13. Interview with a Member of the Swiss Federal Administration, online, July 2020.
14. Interview with a Member of the Swiss Mission to the EU, Brussels, 10 September 2019 and interview with a Member of the Swiss Federal Administration, online, July 2020.
15. Interview with a Member of the EEAS, Brussels, 12 September 2019.
16. Roger Köppel [@KoeppelRoger], Boris Johnson hat es richtig gemacht. Hart verhandelt, keine Unterwürfigkeit, Deal erreicht – ohne fremde Gesetzgeber und fremde Richter. Und ohne Personenfreizügigkeit. SEHR WICHTIG. [Tweet], Twitter, 24 December 2020, https://twitter.com/KoeppelRoger/status/1342174398783094785 (accessed 9 December 2021).

REFERENCES

Ahmed, K. (2016). Swiss offer EU solution for Britain. *BBC News*. 8 September. https://www.bbc.co.uk/news/business-37312807 (accessed 9 December 2021).

Autonomiesuisse. (2020). Autonomiesuisse salue l'accord du Brexit entre l'UE et le Royaume-Uni. Press release. 24 December. https://www.autonomiesuisse.ch/assets/Medien/Medienmitteilungen/20201224/fr/communique_de_presse_accord_du_brexit_autonomiesuisse_tableofvictories_fr_20201224.pdf (accessed 9 December 2021).

Barnier, M. (2018). General Affairs Council (Article 50). Press conference. 27 February. https://newsroom.consilium.europa.eu/events/20180227-general-affairs-council-art-50-february-2018 (accessed 6 December 2021).

Calmy-Rey, M. (2016). Wir sollten jetzt nicht nach Brüssel rennen. Interview. *Neue Zürcher Zeitung*. 26 July. https://www.nzz.ch/schweiz/alt-bundesraetin-micheline-calmy-rey-wir-sollten-jetzt-nicht-nach-bruessel-rennen-ld.107531?reduced=true (accessed 9 December 2021).

Campbell Bannerman, D. (2013). The only way is Swiss: How we can regain control of our borders. *The Telegraph*. 23 December. https://www.telegraph.co.uk/news/worldnews/europe/switzerland/10535146/The-only-way-is-Swiss-how-we-can-regain-control-of-our-borders.html (accessed 9 December 2021).

Church, C. (2000). Switzerland: An overlooked case of Europeanization? *Queen's Papers on Europeanization*. No. 3/2000. https://ideas.repec.org/p/erp/queens/p0003.html (accessed 4 December 2021).

Church, C. (ed.) (2007). *Switzerland and the European Union*. Routledge.

Cottier, D. (2020). UE-Royaume-Uni: attention aux faux-semblants, la Suisse ne peut que difficilement s'inspirer de l'accord britannique. *Le Temps*. 29 December. https://www.letemps.ch/opinions/ueroyaumeuni-attention-aux-fauxsemblants-suisse-ne-difficilement-sinspirer-laccord (accessed 9 December 2021).

Council of the European Union. (2008). Draft Council conclusions on EU relations with EFTA countries. Brussels, 5 December. https://data.consilium.europa.eu/doc/document/ST-16651-2008-REV-1/en/pdf (accessed 4 December 2021).

Council of the European Union. (2010). Council conclusions on EU relations with EFTA countries. Brussels, 14 December. https://eeas.europa.eu/sites/default/files/council_iceland.pdf (accessed 4 December 2021).

Council of the European Union. (2012). Council conclusions on EU relations with EFTA countries. Brussels, 20 December. https://eeas.europa.eu/archives/docs/norway/docs/2012_final_conclusions_en.pdf (accessed 4 December 2021).

Council of the European Union. (2014). Negotiating mandate for an EU-Switzerland institutional framework agreement. Brussels, 6 May. https://www.consilium.europa.eu/uedocs/cms_data/docs/pressdata/en/er/142503.pdf (accessed 4 December 2021).

Dardanelli, P. and Mazzoleni, O. (2021). Conclusions: Insights from Switzerland's experience. In P. Dardanelli and O. Mazzoleni (eds), *Switzerland-EU Relations: Lessons for the UK after Brexit?* (pp. 173–83). Routledge.

Dupont, C. and Sciarini, P. (2001). Switzerland and the European integration process: Engagement without marriage. *West European Politics*, *24*(2), 211–32.

Dupont, C. and Sciarini, P. (2007). Back to the future: The first round of bilateral negotiations with Europe. In C. Church (ed.), *Switzerland and the European Union* (pp. 202–14). Routledge.
European Commission. (2017). Annex to the recommendation for a Council decision supplementing the Council decision of 22 May 2017 authorising the opening of negotiations with the United Kingdom of Great Britain and Northern Ireland for an agreement setting out the arrangements for its withdrawal from the European Union, COM(2017) 830. Brussels, 20 December. https://www.europarl.europa.eu/RegData/docs_autres_institutions/commission_europeenne/com/2017/0830/COM_COM(2017)0830_EN.pdf (accessed 4 December 2021).
European Commission. (2021a). Commission statement on the decision by the Swiss Federal Council to terminate the negotiations of the EU-Swiss Institutional Framework Agreement, 21/2683. Brussels, 26 May. https://ec.europa.eu/commission/presscorner/detail/en/statement_21_2683 (accessed 4 December 2021).
European Commission. (2021b). Notice to stakeholders: Status of the EU-Switzerland mutual recognition agreement (MRA) for medical devices. Brussels, 26 May. https://ec.europa.eu/health/sites/default/files/md_dialogue/docs/mdcg_eu-switzerland_mra_en.pdf (accessed 4 December 2021).
European Commission. (2021c). Horizon Europe: Programme Guide. Version 1.0. Brussels, 17 June.
European Council. (2017). European Council (Article 50) guidelines for Brexit negotiations. Brussels, 29 April. https://www.consilium.europa.eu/media/21763/29-euco-art50-guidelinesen.pdf (accessed 4 December 2021).
Federal Council. (2018). European policy – Federal Council decides to launch consultations on the draft institutional agreement. Bern, 7 December. https://www.admin.ch/gov/en/start/documentation/media-releases/media-releases-federal-council.msg-id-73292.html (accessed 4 December 2021).
Federal Council. (2019). Institutional Agreement between Switzerland and the European Union. Letter to Jean-Claude Juncker. Bern, 7 June. https://www.eda.admin.ch/dam/europa/en/documents/bericht_konsultationen_insta/20190607_Lettre-CF-President-Commission-europeenne_en.pdf (accessed 4 December 2021).
Fossum, J.E. and Vigrestad, J. (2021). Is the grass greener on the other side? Norwegians' assessments of Brexit. *Politics and Governance*, *9*(1), 79–89.
Gava, R. and Varone, F. (2012). So close, yet so far? The EU's footprint in Swiss legislative production. In S. Brouard, O. Costa and T. König (eds), *The Europeanization of Domestic Legislatures: The Empirical Implications of the Delors' Myth in Nine Countries* (pp. 197–221). Springer.
Gava, R. and Varone, F. (2014). The EU's footprint in Swiss policy change: A quantitative assessment of primary and secondary legislation (1999–2012). *Swiss Political Science Review*, *20*(2), 216–22.
Gava, R., Sciarini, P. and Varone, F. (2014). Twenty years after the EEA vote: The Europeanization of Swiss policy-making. *Swiss Political Science Review*, *20*(2), 197–207.
Grolimund, N. and Vahl, M. (2006). Integration without membership – Switzerland's bilateral agreements with the European Union. Centre for European Policy Studies, Brussels. https://www.ceps.eu/wp-content/uploads/2013/02/1304.pdf (accessed 4 December 2021).
Gstöhl, S. (2002). *Reluctant Europeans: Norway, Sweden, and Switzerland in the Process of Integration*. Lynne Rienner Publishers.
Hahn, J. (2019). Letter to the President of European Commission. 17 June. https://asin.ch/content/uploads/2019/06/EU_Kommissar-Johannes-Hahn_Originalbrief-4.pdf (accessed 5 July 2021).
Hannan, D. (2012). Switzerland and Norway prove we can leave the EU. Interview. *London Loves Business*. 14 September. https://londonlovesbusiness.com/dan-hannan-switzerland-and-norway-prove-we-can-leave-the-eu/ (accessed 9 December 2021).
HC Deb. (1972). European Economic Community (Treaty of accession). Vol 829 cc677-809. 20 January. https://api.parliament.uk/historic-hansard/commons/1972/jan/20/european-economic-community-treaty-of (accessed 9 December 2021).
HM Government. (2018). The future relationship between the United Kingdom and the European Union. https://assets.publishing.service.gov.uk/government/uploads/system/uploads/attachment_data/file/786626/The_Future_Relationship_between_the_United_Kingdom_and_the_European_Union_120319.pdf (accessed 9 December 2021).
Honegger, E. (2004). Die Gemischten Ausschüsse in den Sektoriellen Abkommen zwischen der Schweiz und der EG. IDHEAP Report 216/2004. Lausanne: IDHEAP. https://serval.unil.ch/resource/serval:BIB_86859D95814F.P001/REF.pdf (accessed 4 December 2021).

Hutter, S., Grande, E. and Kriesi, H. (eds) (2016). *Politicising Europe: Integration and Mass Politics*. Cambridge University Press.
Jenni, S. (2014). Europeanization of Swiss law-making: Empirics and rhetorics are drifting apart. *Swiss Political Science Review*, *20*(2), 208–15.
Juncker, J.-C. (2018). State of the Union 2018. Speech. Strasbourg, 12 September. https://ec.europa.eu/info/sites/default/files/soteu2018-speech_en_0.pdf (accessed 4 December 2021).
Juncker, J.-C. (2019). Letter from the President of the European Commission to the Federal Council. Brussels, 11 June.
Lavenex, S. (2011). Concentric circles of 'EUropean' integration: A typology of EU external governance relations. *Comparative European Politics*, *9*(3), 372–93.
Lavenex, S. (2015). The external face of differentiated integration: Third country participation in EU sectoral bodies. *Journal of European Public Policy*, *22*(6), 836–53.
Lavenex, S. and Lehmkuhl, D. (eds) (2009). Switzerland's flexible integration in the European Union. *Swiss Political Science Review*, *15*(4). Special issue.
Lavenex, S. and Schwok, R. (2015). The Swiss way: The nature of Switzerland's relation with the EU. In E.O. Eriksen and J.E. Fossum (eds), *The European Union's Non-members: Independence under Hegemony* (pp. 36–51). Routledge.
Lazowski, A. (2006). Switzerland. In S. Blockmans and A. Lazowski (eds), *The European Union and Its Neighbours: A Legal Appraisal of the EU's Policies of Stabilisation, Partnership and Integration* (pp. 147–84). TMC Asser Press.
Linder, W. and Müller, S. (2021). *Swiss Democracy Possible Solutions to Conflict in Multicultural Societies*. Springer.
Maiani, F. (2013). Lost in translation: Euro-compatibility, legal security and the autonomous implementation of EU law in Switzerland. *European Law Reporter*, *1*, 29–35.
Najy, C. (2019). The EU in the negotiations of the bilateral agreements I with Switzerland (1992–99): Assessing the role of the European Commission and the Council. Doctoral Thesis. Université de Genève.
Oesch, M. (2018). *Switzerland and the European Union: General Framework, Bilateral Agreements, Autonomous Adaptation*. Dike.
Official Journal of the European Union. (2013). Regulation (EU) No. 1291/2013 of the European Parliament and of the Council of 11 December 2013 establishing Horizon 2020 – the Framework Programme for Research and Innovation (2014–2020) and repealing Decision No. 1982/2006/EC. L 347/104. https://eur-lex.europa.eu/legal-content/EN/TXT/?uri=celex%3A32013R1291 (accessed 9 December 2021).
Official Journal of the European Union. (2021). Regulation (EU) 2021/695 of the European Parliament and of the Council of 28 April 2021 establishing Horizon Europe – the Framework Programme for Research and Innovation, laying down its rules for participation and dissemination, and repealing Regulations (EU) No. 1290/2013 and (EU) No. 1291/2013. L 170/1. https://eur-lex.europa.eu/eli/reg/2021/695/oj (accessed 9 December 2021).
Parmelin, G. (2021). Accord institutionnel entre la Suisse et l'Union européenne. Bern, 26 May. https://www.eda.admin.ch/dam/europa/fr/documents/abkommen/20210526-brief-BR-vdL-InstA_FR.pdf (accessed 6 December 2021).
RTS. (2016a). La Suisse pourrait-elle tirer des avantages du Brexit? *Forum*. 6 June. https://www.rts.ch/info/suisse/7785590-critiques-sous-la-coupole-apres-les-propos-de-calmyrey-sur-le-brexit.html (accessed 9 December 2021).
RTS. (2016b). Critiques sous la Coupole après les propos de Calmy-Rey sur le Brexit. *Forum*. 7 June. https://www.rts.ch/info/suisse/7785590-critiques-sous-la-coupole-apres-les-propos-de-calmyrey-sur-le-brexit.html (accessed 9 December 2021).
Schaller, F. (2020). Brexit deal: lourde humiliation pour la Suisse. *Le Temps*. 28 December. https://blogs.letemps.ch/francois-schaller/2020/12/28/brexit-deal-lourde-humiliation-pour-les-suisses/ (accessed 9 December 2021).
Schweizerische Eidgenossenschaft. (2010). Bericht des Bundesrates zum Verhältnis der Schweiz zu den europäischen Agenturen. Bern. http://www.news.admin.ch/NSBSubscriber/message/attachments/20546.pdf (accessed 4 December 2021).
Schwok, R. (2009). *Switzerland-European Union. An Impossible Membership?* PIE Peter Lang.

Schwok, R. (2015). *Suisse-Union européenne: L'adhésion impossible?* Presses polytechniques et universitaires romandes.

Schwok, R. (2020). Switzerland-EU relations: The bilateral way in a fragilized position. *European Foreign Affairs Review*, *25*(2), 159–76.

Schwok, R. and Najy, C. (2020). Accord avec l'Union européennep: parler d'échec suisse et de succès britannique revient à 'comparer des pommes et des poires'. *Le Temps*. 28 December. https://www.letemps.ch/suisse/accords-lunion-europeenne-parler-dechec-suisse-succes-britannique-revient-comparer-pommes (accessed 9 December 2021).

Stone, J. (2018). Brexit: Michel Barnier rules out Theresa May's Chequers customs plan. *Independent*. 26 July.

Swissinfo (2020). Switzerland was 'inspiration' for Brexit, says Farage. *SWI swissinfo.ch*. 17 January. https://www.swissinfo.ch/eng/eu-relations-_switzerland-was--inspiration--for-brexit--says-farage-/45499628 (accessed 9 December 2021).

Tages Anzeiger. (27 December 2020). Das Brexit-Menü hat seinen Preis. https://www.tagesanzeiger.ch/das-brexit-menue-hat-seinen-preis-640898100302 (accessed 9 December 2021).

Tages Anzeiger. (28 December 2020). Christa Tobler: Grossbritannien hat eine andere Ausgangslage als die Schweiz. https://www.tagesanzeiger.ch/grossbritannien-hat-eine-andere-ausgangslage-als-die-schweiz-488667192367 (accessed 9 December 2021).

Tages Anzeiger. (30 December 2020). Verwirrspiel um die EU-Richter im Rahmenabkommen. https://www.tagesanzeiger.ch/verwirrspiel-um-die-eu-richter-im-rahmenabkommen-256904745851 (accessed 9 December 2021).

Tobler R.C. (2021). The EU-Swiss sectoral approach under pressure: Not least because of Brexit. In S. Lorenzmeier, R. Petrov and C. Vedder (eds), *EU External Relations Law. Shared Competences and Shared Values in Agreements between the EU and its Eastern Neighbourhood* (pp. 107–26). Springer.

Veuthey, A. (2020). Negotiating privileged partnerships: EU-Switzerland relations and the joined-up approach in practice. *College of Europe Policy Brief* (CEPOB) 10.20. http://aei.pitt.edu/103386/1/veuthey_cepob_10-2020_final.pdf (accessed 4 December 2021).

21. The Norway Model and the UK post-Brexit[1]

John Erik Fossum

INTRODUCTION[2]

The purpose of this chapter is to shed light on the nature of the so-called Norway Model and to reflect on how relevant (or not) it is for the United Kingdom (UK) post-Brexit. We obviously need to be clear on what we mean by the Norway Model, to establish whether it is relevant for the UK. From what we can discern from the UK debate, the Norway Model is a shorthand for the specific affiliation that Norway has developed with the European Union (EU). An important reason for paying explicit attention to this model is its role as an EU standard-setter or benchmark for the EU's affiliations with non-members: 'the EEA ... created a privileged partnership which soon became a stable point of reference for later relationships. Once in place, it structured the subsequent logic of EU neighbourhood relations' (Gstöhl and Phinnemore 2019, p. 187).

Nevertheless, the European Economic Area (EEA) agreement is not all there is to be said about the Norway Model. There are at least three different readings or interpretations of the Norway Model of relevance for the UK debate. The second section of the chapter provides an overview of these three different readings of the Norway Model. The third section provides an original contribution to the debate in the sense that it picks up on the third reading and outlines the ideas and institutional arrangements that we associate with the Nordic Model, which represents a distinct model for organising society in socio-economic and political terms. That yields important new information on horizontal Europeanisation pressures, so that the more Europeanised the Nordic EU member states, the stronger the Europeanisation pressure on Norway – to cohere with its closest Nordic neighbours. And the more Europeanised Norway is the less of a distinct affiliation model it constitutes. That has obvious implications for the UK's assessment of the Norway Model's relevance.

The fourth section of the chapter focuses on the two legal affiliation readings of the Norway Model and the domestic socio-political and economic conditions that embed these. As such, this section complements the assessment of the horizontal Europeanisation pressures on Norway from its Nordic neighbours with the vertical pressures that emanate from the legal framework that ties Norway to the EU, and how Norway domestically relates to this framework. Both assessments – third and fourth sections – will, when taken together, clarify the distinguishing features of Norway's EU affiliation and how it corresponds with or diverges from EU membership. That is important because formal arrangements are only the tip of the iceberg in terms of understanding affiliation arrangements.

The fifth section provides a brief overview of how the Norway Model has been discussed in the UK. The last section concludes.

WHAT IS THE NORWAY MODEL? THREE DIFFERENT READINGS

The first reading of the Norway Model basically equates it with the EEA Agreement, which pertains mainly to the EU's internal market and flanking areas. Many in the UK appear to associate the Norway Model foremostly with that agreement. That is, however, not a bilateral agreement between Norway and the EU, but a multilateral agreement that Norway, Liechtenstein, and Iceland (the EEA-European Free Trade Association (EFTA) states) have signed with the EU (it thus consists of these three countries and the EU's 27 member states). EU rule incorporation requires cooperation and joint consent among the three EEA-EFTA parties.[3]

A second reading of the Norway Model would refer to the entire body of well over 70 legal agreements that Norway has signed with the EU (NOU 2012, p. 2), agreements that complement the EEA Agreement and that cover almost the entire range of the EU's realm of action, that is, justice and home affairs and foreign and security policy in addition to the agreements governing access to the EU's internal market that are regulated by the EEA Agreement. As will be further explained below, the institutional arrangements that support this wide range of Norway-EU agreements differ, with the main difference between the EEA Agreement and the rest.

These two readings focus on the legal agreements that tie Norway to the EU. A third reading directs the attention to the political, economic, social, and cultural conditions that embed the legal arrangements and give shape and direction to Norway's EU affiliation (Fossum 2019a, 2019b). This third reading underlines that it matters to legal agreements how they are perceived, received, accepted, and/or challenged and whether states have arrangements (fiscal, administrative, etc.) that can compensate for negative effects of a given mode of affiliation. Such conditions are not simply Norway-internal. External conditions and Norway's external bonds and affiliations with other states also matter. Who Norway has the strongest bonds with and who Norway looks to for learning and inspiration matter to Norway's role as a possible model for the UK post-Brexit. Knowing that will shed added light on the values and worldviews that resonate most with Norway's. After all, who your friends are and whose company you keep says a lot about you.

There is no doubt that for Norway the Nordic region is at the top of the list on all these counts. Norway is then also a key carrier of the Nordic Model, which holds that the Nordic region shares a set of values that are closely associated with social democracy and that are sustained by historically entrenched political and socio-economic factors. In effect, Nordic Model proponents assert that the Nordic region is the bearer of a distinct socio-economic model upheld by a distinct set of political-democratic conditions. Thus, the third reading of the Norway Model underlines both the importance of ideology and distinctly institutionalised values. It shows that we need to complement the untangling of the legal specifics of a given country's EU affiliation with attention to the prevailing ideas, ideologies, values, and institutional arrangements that mark the affiliated state (and the EU). Legal affiliations are not value neutral. Free trade agreements are often associated with right-wing economic liberalism. In a similar manner, the countries that enter into such agreements have their own ideological dispositions. These countries' dispositions may correspond with the agreements or the two may clash.

Each of the three readings of the Norway Model points to a distinct set of factors that shapes Norway's EU affiliation. These are interpreted and understood differently, and they vary from one academic discipline to the next (such as law versus political science, versus political economy versus public administration, etc.). For instance, while the legal affiliation will tell us what issues are regulated and how, it will not tell us much about society's reception of these and how and the extent to which the legal provisions will transform Norwegian society over time. At the same time, Norway's socio-political and economic ideas, ideologies, values, and arrangements will be shaped by the legal arrangements in place, and both sets of factors will have bearings on Norway's relations with its closest Nordic neighbours.

Of particular relevance for this chapter is that the different readings of the Norway Model or Norway's EU affiliation vary in terms of the lessons that we can discern for the UK post-Brexit. We can for instance discern one set of lessons from the legal affiliation, others from socio-political, cultural, and economic conditions. If we look more closely at the least familiar and researched third reading, several questions emerge. One is how incongruent the Nordic Model and today's UK are. The answer does not only depend on how similar or different the Nordic Model is from the UK, but it also matters how Europeanised the Nordic region is, so that the more Europeanised, the less there is left of the distinctive traits of the Nordic Model. For the UK this matters since the UK has been pushing the EU in a neo-liberal direction (for the distinctive reading of neo-liberalism pursued by Thatcher, see Parsons, Chapter 6 in this volume). Its efforts were proven quite successful especially through the Single European Act (1987) (Lord 2020). Since then, Europeanisation has in overall terms been at odds with core tenets of the Nordic Model.

Presumably, then, given that Norway is not an EU member, it will be less Europeanised than the other Nordic EU member states. If so, might Norway then be more of a bearer of the Nordic Model than the Nordic states that are EU members? Or might Norway's EU affiliation be so close that Norway is better understood as an integral part of an increasingly Europeanised Nordic region? In the latter case, we should expect a mutually reinforcing Europeanisation impetus on Norway: from the EU (vertical) and from the closest neighbouring Nordic states (horizontal). The implication would be that the Norway Model is a matter of Europeanisation by other (non-membership) means. If so, there would be few distinct practical lessons for the UK to draw from Norway's EU affiliation. Conversely, if Norway is a stauncher supporter of the Nordic Model than the other Nordic EU member states, then Norway will be further to the left and not very compatible with the UK Conservatives' view of the UK's role post-Brexit. Norway would be closer to Labour's and much of Scotland's views.

STANDING OUT FROM THE REST? NORWAY, THE NORDIC MODEL, AND EUROPEANISATION[4]

The Norwegian Foreign Minister Anniken Huitfeld (2021), in her orientation to Parliament on important EU- and EEA-related questions in November 2021, noted that

> Nordic cooperation is an important part of the government's policy towards Europe. Nordic cooperation increases the likelihood for gains on the European arena. We have strong common interests with our Nordic friends. We have the same political vantage-point on key areas that are covered by the EEA agreement: industrial relations, welfare state and tripartite cooperation are keywords here. (Huitfeld 2021; author's translation)

The three issue-areas that Huitfeld highlights of the EEA are central ingredients in the Nordic Model. In effect, the Nordic Model's proponents claim that there are certain identifiable Nordic values that are institutionalised within and across the five states that make up the Nordic region (Denmark, Finland, Iceland, Norway, and Sweden). The literature on the Nordic Model – in line with the statement by Minister Huitfeld – holds up the core components of the Nordic Model in the socio-economic realm as macroeconomic governance; organised working life; public welfare services; and gender equality.

The countries in the Nordic region are among the countries that Hall and Soskice (2001) define as coordinated market economies (Germany, Japan, Switzerland, the Netherlands, Belgium, Sweden, Norway, Denmark, Finland, Austria), in contrast to liberal market economies (the USA, Britain, Australia, Canada, New Zealand, Ireland). The latter are '(n)ations with liberal market economies that tend to rely on markets to coordinate endeavors in both the financial and industrial relations systems, while those with coordinated market economies have institutions in both spheres that reflect higher levels of non-market coordination' (Hall and Soskice 2001, p. 19).[5]

Nordic Model proponents do not claim that the conditions that mark the Nordic Model are unique to the Nordic region. They argue that these traits are particularly pronounced, including how the socio-economic structure is embedded in and upheld by political parties and state institutions. Traditionally speaking, stable party constellations sustained the welfare schemes and were committed to 'fair, equitable distribution of benefits and burdens' (Dølvik et al. 2015, p. 20). The system whereby interest organisations – notably employers and employees – were closely linked to a state that was responsive to their concerns was based on a tightly coupled interaction between socio-economic concertation and political engagement and participation. It relied on democratic institutions configured to deal with large-scale political participation and a high level of transparency in political and economic matters.

A further delimiting feature of the Nordic Model is that it is based in the Nordic area as a distinct entity, sustained by a range of common (intergovernmental) institutions whose self-conception is that of a Nordic region. The Nordic region became institutionalised in formal terms through the Nordic Council, which instituted an open labour market and free movement in several steps from 1952 when the Nordic Passport Union was first established. Nordic regionalism over time became more firmly institutionalised with the Nordic Council of Ministers established in 1971.[6]

The institutional consolidation of the Nordic region in the post-war period coincided with the process of Europeanisation, that is, the forging of a set of governing institutions at the European level and how these institutions penetrate and reconfigure/transform the member (and affiliated) states (Olsen 2002). The Nordic states were gradually incorporated in this process, albeit at different times and in different manners: Denmark became an EU member in 1973 but is not in the Eurozone, Sweden (not in the Eurozone) and Finland (in the Eurozone) became EU members in 1995, whereas Iceland and Norway joined the EEA Agreement in 1992 and have rejected EU membership. All the Nordic states are in the Schengen area; hence have retained the system of open borders but now within the entire Schengen area. An open market in goods, services, persons, and capital requires low-threshold access and passage. That is one of the reasons why the EEA-EFTA states have signed the Schengen association agreements, which in effect locates them within the EU's external borders and systems of border controls. Norway (and Iceland) needed an association agreement with the EU to sustain the institutionalised system of Nordic cooperation. For Norway this issue was particularly pressing given that it has a 1630-kilometre-long border with Sweden that has been open for over 200 years.[7] When Sweden entered the EU in 1995, Norway could only keep this border open through affiliating with Schengen, which in turn would mean that Norway would be inside the EU's external border, with responsibility for border controls. Had Norway opted to stay outside of Schengen, it would have undermined the Nordic Passport Union and the provisions for free movement within the Nordic region (Fossum and Graver 2018).

An important aspect of Europeanisation is to pry open the Nordic region to the rest of the EU. In socio-economic terms, the Nordic region has been incorporated into a European setting that since the 1980s has become increasingly affected by a neo-liberal approach to politics and increasingly deregulated markets:

> By the beginning of the 1990s, a certain ideational uniformity prevailed among European political elites regarding the primacy of price stability, the limits of government intervention and the superiority of markets over planning as the pillars of societal organization. (Bickerton et al. 2015, p. 708)

But in contrast to what we see in the EU post-crises, the EU was less intrusive and left more scope for states and only parts of this programme were picked up by the Nordic countries:

> A special feature in the Nordic countries is that the economic liberalisation of the 1980s and 1990s was not accompanied by a corresponding deregulation of labour markets or dismantling of the welfare states as advocated by influential forces on the employer side and some right-leaning parties. (Dølvik et al. 2015, p. 32)

This does not mean that Europeanisation has been without effects, in particular in the last decades. A recent report on *The Nordics and Future Europe* (SAMAK 2019, p. 10) points to how

> (t)he 'Laval Quartet' (438/05, Laval C-341/05, Rüffert C-346/06, Finland C-319/06), and in Norway the Holship case, shows that there in some areas may exist a friction between EU/EEA rules and the ECHR and ILO core conventions. A social protocol in the EU, where the EU/EEA explicitly states that the ECHR/ILO core conventions is given prejudice if the conventions on any point collide with the four freedoms, can solve these issues satisfactorily on a permanent basis.

A similar argument is made with reference to the EU's provisions for state aid, which can give impetus to privatisation (Reegård 2020). These observations show that EU/EEA provisions on worker mobility and state aid can challenge aspects of the Nordic Model, with regard to its distinct labour market model, commitment to gender equality, and public welfare schemes.

These brief observations show that some of the institutional presuppositions for the Nordic Model have been affected by Europeanisation, both in terms of who has access to the Nordic region, and how the Nordic states regulate their economies and welfare systems. Having said that, it is important to underline that the literature on the Nordic Model has paid scant attention to Europeanisation,[8] and the literature on Europeanisation has not addressed the implications for the Nordic Model.[9] We therefore need more detailed and systematic knowledge of how (much) Europeanisation has transformed the social, economic, and institutional conditions that have been critical in sustaining the Nordic Model.

The Nordic Dimension and Norwegians' EU Voting

It is important to underline that it is not only the Nordic Model that figures when we discuss the Nordic influence on Norway's EU affiliation. There are also important historical and political factors that need to be taken into consideration.

One set of factors pertains to the different historical experiences that the Nordic states have of ruling and being ruled by each other. These historical experiences have had effects on Norway's EU affiliation. Norway's historical experience stands out from its two closest Nordic neighbours and associates, Sweden and Denmark, in that Norway was variously a junior partner and a semi-colony (a so-called lydrike) to Denmark (1389–1814), and thereafter in a monarchical union with Sweden (1814–1905). Finland (for a long time under Swedish rule and during 1809–1917 under Russian rule) and Iceland (1380–1918 under Danish rule) shared this experience of subservience with Norway.

Norway's historical experience of being ruled figured among the reasons that are presented for why Norway ended up rejecting EU membership in the two popular referendums in 1972 and 1994.[10] In the debate that led up to the 1994 EU membership referendum, Anne Enger Lahnstein, leader of the Centre Party and widely recognised as Norway's most prominent EU membership opponent, brought up Norway's subservient relation to Denmark and Sweden, and argued that joining the EU would subject Norway to a similar, if not worse, situation than what it had experienced during Danish and Swedish rule.[11] When the no side brought up the spectacle of union, it evoked the image of a regressive and undemocratic arrangement – in contrast to national independence that would ensure constitutional democracy. With that, the argumentative structure was set: any arrangement that could weaken the role and salience of the Norwegian Parliament, the Storting (due to its central role in the dissolution of the union with Sweden), could automatically be construed as an affront on the Norwegian nation and its constitution. As Iver Neumann succinctly states: 'Norwegian discourse on European integration played itself out in, and therefore on, the naysayers' own terms' (Neumann 2002, p. 90). This example shows that Norway's experience with its Nordic closest neighbouring countries was used as a means to bolster Norwegian national sovereignty.

Another historical example refers to the role of the Norwegian cleavage structure and the pattern of support – opposition to EU membership. This pattern is to a large extent reflected in the historical experience of foreign (read Danish and Swedish) rule. The major cities and the area around Oslo had the strongest foreign imprint through foreign officials and foreign languages, and the highest level of support for EU membership, whereas the relatively inaccessible countryside and the North were far less influenced by foreign rule and were strongly opposed to EU membership. Thus, deeply entrenched foreign exposure did not as is often assumed spur nationalism.

The EU membership issue contributed to activate structural cleavage lines that were important to the early stages in the development of Norwegian political parties (Valen 1999, p. 106). Both the 1972 and the 1994 results showed a strong split between centre and periphery, with the Oslo region being the only political centre unambiguously in favour of EU membership, and the Northern periphery the strongest opponent (but also with a majority in the West against). This centre-periphery division is common to Norway, Sweden, and Finland, but in Norway the contrast is more pronounced. Peripheral areas and what Rokkan (1999) referred to as 'counter-cultures' furnished no-voters during both referenda campaigns (Bjørklund 2005). It is interesting in this connection that the latter referendum was, as Tor Bjørklund (2005,

p. 183) notes, a 'carbon copy' of the former in terms of both the general results and the results in the various constituencies.

Nevertheless, there was a significant changeover of persons and other changes suggesting distinct dynamics. Bjørklund (2001) then also argues that the rejuvenation of the original cleavage model is overstated; new and more salient dimensions for the EU referenda results were gender (more women than men voted no) and the rise of public sector employees (more of them voted no). The underlying factor is defence of the welfare state and state regulation of the economy, both of which figure centrally in the Nordic Model.

A third example is that the Norwegian government decided that the 1994 popular referendum on whether to join the EU should come last among the Finnish, Swedish, and Norwegian EU referendums, to benefit from the so-called 'Sweden-suction'. The assumption was that Norwegian voters would be more compelled to vote yes once they knew the results from the Finnish and Swedish referendums in 1994. Close Nordic neighbours' decisions on their EU affiliations were assumed to affect Norwegians' EU voting choices.

These three examples show that aspects of Norway's Nordic experience thus figured both as a deterrent against EU membership and as a strategic device to induce Norwegians to vote yes. The deterrent worked along two quite different lines: the notion of the EU replacing the Danish-Norwegian and/or Swedish-Norwegian Union as a source of external domination, on the one hand, and voting no to preserve the values associated with the Nordic Model, on the other. The latter value-based defence was cast along national not Nordic lines, although it is quite clear that many Swedes were thinking the same and the margin of yes voters was very small in Sweden.

This brief overview shows that the Nordic dimension has played an important albeit still understudied role in shaping Norway's relationship to the EU. When considering the relevance of the Norway Model for the UK post-Brexit we cannot ignore this dimension which has bearings on values, socio-economic model, gender equality, and the governing system. The next section will relate this directly to Brexit.

The Nordic Dimension, Brexit, and the Norway Model

From the above we may draw out four sets of relevant observations of relevance for the Norway Model as a possible template for the UK post-Brexit. First, and as will be further detailed below, Norway is heavily Europeanised despite not being an EU member state. The implication for the discussion of the Norway Model as a possible template for the UK post-Brexit is that we need to take both the high degree of Europeanisation and the close links and value affinities that exist among the Nordic states into account. A critical issue is whether Europeanisation undermines the values and institutional arrangements associated with the Nordic Model; whether Europeanisation has limited impact on these; or whether Europeanisation is conducive to the preservation of these values and institutional arrangements. As was noted, in the 1980s and 1990s, Europeanisation did not represent a serious challenge. Developments since then appear more challenging, for instance, with regard to labour mobility-induced social dumping, and state aid rules giving impetus to privatisation (and perhaps particularly so in Norway, see Reegård 2020). The coronavirus pandemic has brought in new uncertainty, both with regard to the strength of Europeanisation pressures and with regard to the EU's future socio-economic direction, including the effects of the Green Transition.

Second, in terms of Brexit it looks like the Nordic region has voted with its feet: during the negotiations it remained bound to the EU rather than approximate to the UK. The Nordic EU member states did not break ranks with the other EU member states and instead helped to retain a common front in the EU-UK Brexit negotiations. In a similar vein, Norway did not use Brexit as an opportunity to try to renegotiate its relationship with the EU. On Norway's stance, former Foreign Minister Ine M. Eriksen Søreide, at a meeting in the Parliament's European Affairs Committee on 7 February 2018, noted that many people appear to think that Norway's relationship to the EU will change with Brexit. She rejected that assessment and instead noted that: 'It does not. Our relationship to the EU is there through the EEA Agreement and other agreements, but it is our relationship to Great Britain where we will form other agreements and build other frameworks' (Søreide 2018, author's translation).

Third, at least some of Norway's Europeanisation is driven by its close links to its Nordic neighbours (horizontal Europeanisation). The case of Norway's and Iceland's affiliation to Schengen shows that Europeanisation can put them in a quandary where they must choose more Europeanisation in order to retain core elements of Nordic cooperation. The direction of the EU's development thus matters to the future of the Nordic Model and the Nordic region. In this context, the EU's assessment of the membership-non-membership distinction matters: the more the EU is willing to consider the EEA countries as 'EU-insiders', the more uniform the Europeanisation pressures on the Nordic region. Conversely, the more the EU prioritises the distinction between members and non-members, the greater the wedge between Nordic EU members and Nordic EFTA-EEA members. The EU's experience with Brexit appears to have made it less tolerant of non-members' pleas for special arrangements, as is apparent in the Swiss case (see Lavenex and Veuthey, Chapter 20 in this volume). The Norwegian government appears cognisant of this (Fossum and Vigrestad 2021).

Fourth, the UK's exit from the EU positions Norway and Iceland in a potentially difficult squeeze between the EU and the UK. This is a matter of the more complex legal tapestry now that the EU-UK Trade and Cooperation Agreement TCA regulates EU-UK relations and the EEA (and other agreements) regulate Norway-EU relations, and the UK-EEA EFTA Free Trade Agreement regulates UK-Iceland, Liechtenstein, Norway (EEA-EFTA) relations (EFTA 2021). One issue is therefore how compatible these different legal arrangements are. The other issue is what form of spill-over there will be across relations when there is politicisation along one or more sets of relations. The former centre-right Norwegian government prioritised the EU dimension over the UK one, as was clear from Foreign Minister Søreide's remark as cited above. The present centre-left government even with the deeply Eurosceptic Centre Party does not seem to veer off this course. For the whole Nordic region composed as it is of small, internationally exposed, and adaptive countries, stable and predictable operating conditions matter greatly. The EU appears the stable anchor, the UK the politically volatile actor.

WHAT ARE THE DISTINCTIVE FEATURES OF NORWAY'S EU AFFILIATION?

The following provides a brief overview of Norway's affiliation with the EU. In line with what was said above about the Norway Model, there are at least three different readings of it. The presentation will shed light on all three: the EEA Agreement, the other agreements, and the political and social context that these agreements are embedded within. The need to pay particular attention to the political dimension stems from the fact that the issue of membership in the EU has figured as one of, if not the, most politically divisive issues in Norway in the post-war period. The membership issue remains controversial, and so the issue has long been kept away from the political agenda.

Given the high level of controversy, it is interesting to note that the EEA Agreement is the most comprehensive association agreement that Norway has entered in modern times, and it enjoys considerable popular support (see figures in Fossum and Vigrestad 2021). Norway's distinct EU affiliation is often presented as a domestic de-politicising compromise: it has enabled EU membership opponents to keep Norway out of the EU, and at the same time has provided EU membership proponents with guaranteed access to the EU's internal market (and almost all EU programmes). Norway entered the EEA Agreement with the EU before the 1994 EU membership referendum, where a small majority of the Norwegian population voted against EU membership. The membership rejection therefore had no bearing on the status of the EEA Agreement.

Overview of the Agreements: The EEA

Norway is associated with the EU through well over 70 agreements. Substantively, these range from the internal market, Schengen association agreements, agreements on asylum and police cooperation (Dublin I, II, and III), agreements on foreign and security policy (Norway participates in the EU's battle groups), agreements on internal security and justice, fisheries, agriculture, to name a few. Through these agreements, Norway has incorporated roughly three-quarters of EU legislation compared to those EU member states that have incorporated everything (NOU 2012, pp. 2, 3). Key areas that fall outside the scope of the cooperation are the euro, the customs union and foreign trade policy, the Common Agricultural Policy and taxation. Even some of these areas are affected by the rules of the single market. Free movement of capital affects taxation rules, and a substantial number of veterinary and food safety rules are included in the agreement.

The by far most important single agreement here is the EEA Agreement which came into effect in 1994 (Liechtenstein's took effect on 1 May 1995) and was intended to include the remainder of the EFTA[12] states in the EU's internal market. When the EEA Agreement took effect, the EEA-EFTA countries had to incorporate all relevant EU legislation that was in effect at the time of signing the agreement. The EEA Agreement is intended to ensure legal homogeneity within the entire 30-member EEA (the 27 EU members and Iceland, Liechtenstein, and Norway). The 'reward' for the EEA-EFTA states would be assured participation in the EU internal market basically on a par with an EU member state.

The main objective of the EEA Agreement was:

> to establish a dynamic and homogeneous European Economic Area, based on common rules and equal conditions of competition and providing for the adequate means of enforcement including at the judicial level, and achieved on the basis of equality and reciprocity and of an overall balance of benefits, rights and obligations for the Contracting Parties. (Official Journal of the European Communities 1994b)[13]

With homogeneity is meant:

> an economic area based on common rules and equal conditions of competition, and providing for the equivalent means of enforcement, including at the judicial level. Because it is dynamic, the homogeneity is also maintained when rules and interpretation of rules change in the EU. (Fossum and Graver 2018, p. xvii)[14]

The EEA-EFTA countries participate in most aspects of the EU's internal market (the agriculture and fisheries sectors are formally speaking exempted, but even here there is a lot of Europeanisation) even if they are not part of the EU's customs union (that is also the case with Switzerland). In contrast to Switzerland's (broad range of) sectoral bilateral agreements, the EEA Agreement is a broad and dynamic multilateral agreement between the post-Brexit 27 EU member states and the three EFTA states, Iceland, Liechtenstein, and Norway.[15]

The fact that the EEA Agreement is dynamic is intended to ensure effective market participation. Each EEA-EFTA state's compliance with the evolving EEA rules is closely monitored by the EFTA Surveillance Authority (ESA). The Single Market Scoreboard reveals that the transposition deficit in the three EEA-EFTA countries is not higher than the EU member state average; for Norway's case at 0.1, it is considerably lower (European Commission 2020).

With regard to the EEA Agreement, there has been considerable expansion into related flanking areas, such as for example environmental and social affairs. In addition, the dynamic nature of the EEA Agreement makes it difficult for a state to prevent areas that have been explicitly excluded from the agreement subsequently being pulled into its orbit. For Norway, a telling example is agriculture. It is politically very sensitive and was *explicitly excluded* from the initial EEA Agreement. At present, 40 per cent of the rules and regulations that Norway incorporates are in the field of agriculture. Important reasons for inclusion were the need for market access for fish and the sheer dynamics of horizontal expansion. These provisions are not confined to border crossing activities but cover internal affairs:

> In practice today, this body of regulations makes up the main portion of all public regulation pertaining to production, sale, labelling, hygiene and so forth with regard to fish and agriculture in Norway and to a large extent sets the standards in both these sectors. (NOU 2012, pp. 2, 646–7, author's translation)

The Norwegian government maintains a system of subsidies that it has considered necessary to sustain thriving rural communities in a country where the conditions for large-scale farming are challenging.

The situation of agriculture for Norway shows how the affiliated non-member loses control over an issue-area that it explicitly sought to *remove* from the trade-off equation and testifies to the manner in which a dynamic EU integration process undermines the prospects for states' self-rule.

EEA Article 105 states that the EEA Committee 'shall keep under constant review the development of the case law of the Court of Justice of the European Communities and the EFTA Court', and take measures 'to preserve the homogeneous interpretation of the Agreement' (Official Journal of the European Communities 1994a). Article 106 states that

> In order to ensure as uniform an interpretation as possible of this Agreement, in full deference to the independence of courts, a system of exchange of information concerning judgments by the EFTA Court, the Court of Justice of the European Communities and the Court of First Instance of the European Communities and the Courts of last instance of the EFTA States shall be set up by the EEA Joint Committee. (Official Journal of the European Communities 1994a)

In the event of differences or disputes over the interpretation of the agreement, EEA Article 111 empowers the EEA Joint Committee to settle the dispute according to principles laid down in that article. Thus, we see that, in the final instance the settlement of disputes over interpretation is political and not judicial (Fossum and Graver 2018, pp. 36–7).

The presentation shows that the EEA Agreement places the EEA-EFTA states in a quandary: they want and seek assured single market access while at the same time retaining national sovereignty. With assured market access comes a system of legal oversight and sanction that is clearly directed and operated by the EU. Even that does not ensure full homogeneity: when the EU undergoes a treaty change, there is no mechanism in the EEA Agreement to update its rules as a follow-up to such changes in the EU. A similar point applies to the fact that EU law develops through a dynamic interpretation by the Court of Justice of the European Union (CJEU), based on a teleological approach to the rules. The EFTA Court is anxious to ensure legal homogeneity, and therefore relates to the new EU legislation (Fredriksen and Franklin 2015, p. 649). The implication is that insofar as EEA rules are subsequently changed through legal interpretation, 'this means that legislation is changed without any collaboration from the EFTA countries' (Graver 2016, p. 818).

The EEA Agreement's institutional structure is designed as a two-pillar structure with bridging institutions, as well as a court and a surveillance body.[16] This arrangement (with the exception of EU agencification, see Egeberg and Trondal 2015) ensures formal sovereignty for the EEA-EFTA states. It does not, however, ensure autonomy, since the rule import is a one-way street, from the EU to the EEA-EFTA states. There is no mechanism for reciprocal rule export from the EEA-EFTA states to the EU. The institutional structure to some extent cloaks this, it does not, however, alter the facts on the ground.

Overview of the Agreements: Schengen and the Rest

The Schengen rules cover several areas, namely rules on checks on persons at the outer borders, harmonisation of the conditions of entry and of the rules on visas for short stays (up to three months), enhanced police cooperation (including rights of cross-border surveillance and hot pursuit), and stronger judicial cooperation on criminal cases through a faster extradition system and transfer of enforcement of criminal judgments on police cooperation. In addition, the agreement includes the establishment and development of the Schengen Information System (SIS). The SIS is a large-scale information system that supports external border control and law enforcement cooperation in the Schengen states. Schengen has its own institutional arrangements that differ from those of the EEA. The main institution is the Mixed Committee, which is made up of the EU member states, the European Commission and the four associated countries: Norway, Iceland, Switzerland, and Liechtenstein. All Schengen relevant issues that arise in the ongoing cooperation are discussed in this committee. There is no common decision-making body as within the EEA. The agreement has a guillotine clause: should either Iceland or Norway decide not to adopt new Schengen legislation that has been enacted in the EU, the agreement shall be considered terminated with respect to Iceland or Norway, unless the Mixed Committee, after a careful examination of ways to continue the agreement, decides otherwise within 90 days (Official Journal of the European Communities 1999, Article 8 (4)). The Schengen acquis is dynamic and develops by changes in the EU legislation that is included in the association agreement. There is no Schengen Court, and the EFTA Court is not empowered to deal with issues that arise under the Schengen agreements. Nevertheless, the

Mixed Committee keeps a watchful eye on the development of the case law of the CJEU and the competent courts of Norway and Iceland relating to such provisions.

Norway has signed a number of additional parallel agreements with the EU, including agreements on asylum and police cooperation (Dublin I and II) and on foreign and security policy – Norwegian troops are at the disposal of the EU's battle groups. The Norwegian Official Report that produced the largest-ever assessment of the EEA Agreement estimated that around 75 per cent of all of the EU's laws and regulations apply to Norway (NOU 2012, p. 2).[17]

The dense form of affiliation that makes up the sum-total of the Norway Model generates its own pressures for contiguity in norms, rules, and interpretations, which show up in how domestic institutions operate. Two telling examples pertain to how the Norwegian Supreme Court, in the rulings Nye Kystlink and Bottolvs, voluntarily adapted to EU law, and did so in issue-areas that were *not* regulated by the EEA Agreement (Fredriksen 2015). In a situation of tight regulation coupled with 'regulatory gaps', rule contiguity becomes important. The institutions within a closely associated non-member will feel strong domestic pressures for filling in whatever 'gaps' there are between the different agreements that the country has signed with the EU (Fredriksen 2018).

The onus on uniformity is not only to be found on the side of the EEA-EFTA countries. The recent CJEU Case C-897/19 I.N.:

> strengthens the impression of the EEA/EFTA States as 'insiders' rather than 'outsiders' also in matters where the application of EEA law is affected by parts of EU law that fall outside the scope of the EEA Agreement, but which are covered by other agreements between the EEA/EFTA States and the EU. (Fredriksen 2020)

Decision-Shaping and Scope for Political Participation

The presentation thus far has shown that the EEA-EFTA states have extensive rights and obligations in relation to the EU, and their participation in the EU's internal market is so extensive that it is almost on a par with member states. This form of market participation, similar to de facto economic membership, does not of course extend to the political realm, because the EEA-EFTA states have only limited access to EU decision-making forums; they are barred from participation with co-decision rights in the European Council, the Council, COREPER, and the European Parliament (EP).

Within the framework of the EEA Agreement, Norway has a number of experts in EU bodies and committees, especially under the Commission (NOU 2012, pp. 2, 824, 829–30). In issues regulated by the Schengen agreement, Norway has the right to participate in meetings (without voting rights) in the Council and has representatives in the committees under the Council.

The Norwegian Parliament has six representatives in the EEA Parliamentary Committee, gets access (through invitation) to the EU's system of interparliamentary coordination (COSAC), and has the right to be present in the interparliamentary committee on foreign and security policy. There are also explicit measures taken by Norway to get better access to the EU system. For instance, the Norwegian Parliament has an office in Brussels that is located in the EU Parliament. The Norwegian EU Delegation in Brussels understands itself as a spokesperson for Norwegian interests, and Norwegian regions and local government bodies have representatives present in Brussels.[18] The same applies to various business and trade union interests.

The fact that the EEA-EFTA states have comprehensive rights and obligations without participation in EU decision-making suggests that the relationship is a matter of taxation without representation given that EEA-EFTA member states and Switzerland contribute to the EU budget and take part in EU programmes such as Horizon 2020 and Erasmus+ as a crucial part of their integration in the internal market. The EEA Agreement makes explicit this commitment: the EU and the EEA-EFTA states:

> [S]hall take the necessary steps to develop, strengthen or broaden cooperation on matters falling outside of the four freedoms, where such cooperation is considered likely to contribute to the attainment of the objectives of [the] Agreement, or is otherwise deemed by the Contracting Parties to be of mutual interest. (Official Journal of the European Communities 1994a, Article 78)

Under the EEA Agreement the financial contribution is calculated by applying a proportionality factor. Since 2011 the overall level of net contributions expressed in terms of commitments has increased. Under this scheme, Norway's contribution to the EU budget during the 2014–19 period was 2,181,762,249 euros, whereas Switzerland's contribution for the same period was 2,196,864,781 euros (European Court of Auditors 2021).

The Domestic Norwegian Context: Adaptation, De-Politicisation, and Buffering/ Compensation

Norway's comprehensive incorporation in the EU through the EEA Agreement has sparked surprisingly little controversy, despite the fact that it has profound constitutional democratic implications. Since the EEA Agreement's inception, countless Norwegian governments have administered the agreement and complied with Norway's European commitments, as documented above. Norway's internal divisions over EU membership have therefore not affected the process of EU adaptation.

What then has sustained this close EU affiliation over time? Relevant factors are: legal certainty and a whole list of social, economic, and, not least, political reasons that explain the paucity of conflict. Economically speaking, Norway is highly internationally exposed and has a long history of adaptation to changing international circumstances and has a strong economy with a large sovereign wealth fund that forms a significant economic buffer. Politically speaking, Norway has a very competent public administration and an extensive welfare state, both of which help to alleviate social disruptions from international exposures. A further remarkable feature of Norway is that the public's trust in government is very high and has apparently not declined through EU adaptation.

In addition, political factors are important, especially given that most political parties have been divided on the EU membership issue (the largest party, the Social Democrats (AP) has for most of the time been split with a rough 60–40 divide in favour of EU membership), and some parties – notably the Centre Party which is now part of the ruling minority coalition – have been against not only EU but also EEA membership. Norway has, since the 1960s, had exceptionally strong anti-EU membership organisations, with the one from 1994 still very active. One important explanatory factor is that the Norwegian political system is hardwired as a consensus-seeking system. As was noted above, it operates in a complex cleavage structure, with divisions along value and functional lines, and where the EU membership issue twice has triggered deep-seated cleavages. Consensus-seeking behaviour is induced by the proportional electoral system that favours medium-sized parties, and works as a constraint on the largest parties. In addition, the political parties have instituted gag rules to keep the EU membership issue off the political agenda (Fossum 2010, 2019a, 2019b). All governments in Norway are coalition governments, and all coalitions have to consist of parties favouring Norwegian EU membership (even if internally divided) as well as parties opposing EU membership. As part of the coalition agreement – whether explicitly stated or tacitly agreed – the parties commit to retain the present EU affiliation. The two largest parties, the Conservatives (Høyre) and the Social Democrats (AP) are the ones most favourable towards EU membership. However, they form coalitions with small Eurosceptic parties that threaten to disband the coalition should the large party seek to apply for EU membership. These factors have enabled the political parties to separate the EU membership issue from the issue of EU adaptation.[19]

This has made it possible for coalitions which are deeply divided on EU membership to stay together and operate in a society that has become increasingly Europeanised. One important aspect of this bifurcating of EU membership and EU adaptation is to defuse the constitutional implications of the dynamic EU adaptation. That is probably a necessary concession to sustain the arrangement. It has proven possible to do so because the higher threshold procedures that we associate with constitutional change have only been triggered twice: in 1992 in connection with the EEA Agreement, and in 2016 in connection with Norway's accession to the EU's system of financial supervision. Legal scholars have argued that the government's very limited use of constitutional provisions is out of step with the magnitude of EU interference, and that the government's justification for this is anything but well grounded (Holmøyvik 2015).

The effect is to sideline the constitution's role as a vehicle for staking out the society's future role and direction. The membership–adaptation division serves as a rather peculiar type of funnel for handling political conflicts surrounding Norway's EU adaptation. It de facto directs the attention to single issues or single pieces of EU legislation, because there is no principled debate on the broader ramifications of how Europeanisation transforms Norway, and what the political cost of this mode of affiliation is in relation to EU membership.

The de-politicisation of this affiliation has been considered necessary in order to sustain the consensual element of Norwegian politics. It is also in a sense a functional necessity resulting from the nature of Norway's EU affiliation, because the affiliation leaves Norway with no real codetermination and a narrow channel for voicing its concerns.

These observations underline the distinct political logic and dynamics that underpin the so-called Norway Model. With regard to the question of the model's transferability to the UK such political realities must figure centrally in the UK's assessments. Have they?

HOW HAS THE NORWAY MODEL BEEN DISCUSSED IN THE UK?

If we look at UK parties' positions on the Norway Model, we find divides on the merits of the Norway option both between and within parties. What also matters given that there are three different readings of the Norway Model is which of these has been the main focus of the UK debate. The answer will tell us a lot about whether what was discussed was about the legal affiliation or how the affiliation is embedded in socio-economic and political conditions. The argument that is presented in this chapter is that the Norway Model should be construed as the latter, as the sum total of the three readings presented here.

The following statement is quite typical of how the Norway option was debated in the UK:

> Staying in the EU Single Market and leaving the Customs Union would mean full access to the Single Market for both goods and services, but the UK would have to continue to abide by the EU's four freedoms, including freedom of movement. It would have to accept the EU acquis and regulations, without having a say on what those rules might look like in the future. The UK would be subject to the European Free Trade Association Court (EFTA) rather than the ECJ (though that court follows ECJ judgements). The UK would be free to pursue its own independent trade policy, though in practice Norway, along with other countries in the EFTA, often negotiate as a bloc. (Institute for Government 2022)

It is quite apparent that this rendition focuses on the first reading, the EEA, only. We get the same general impression when we look at the key political figures in the debate. There is no reference to the Nordic Model in the UK debate; neither was there much concern with how Norway managed its affiliation, such as how it depoliticised the EU membership issue to enable ongoing EU adaptation.

Thus, when most interlocutors in the UK debate referred to the Norway Model the focus narrowed to the legally binding and dynamic affiliation with the EU, a mode of affiliation that would ensure the UK full incorporation in the EU's single market. The addition of a 'plus' – 'Norway plus' – referred to UK inclusion in the EU's customs union, which the EEA countries are not part of.

A further notable aspect of the UK debate is that many of the key figures in the debate changed positions on the desirability of the Norway Model (read the EEA plus a customs union) for the UK. For instance, prior to the Brexit referendum in 2016, many of the Brexiteers spoke favourably about the Swiss and Norway options, including then UKIP leader Nigel Farage (Express 2020). Farage as is well known adopted a far harder position after the 2016 referendum.

If we look more closely at the Conservative Party, it was internally divided. Tory ex-minister Nick Boles said: 'Norway-plus is a compromise that has broad appeal to the pragmatic middle. It delivers a softish Brexit with a deal that preserves membership of the single market and keeps the union of the UK intact' (Belfast Telegraph 2018). Conversely,

> (PM) May repeated her rejection of the 'Norway plus' model and suggested she would not be prepared to offer it as a compromise arrangement because it would mean the continuation of freedom of movement. That is regarded in Downing Street as the hardest of the prime minister's red lines ... 'What you see in the political declaration is what would be a deal for the United Kingdom that is not Norway, it is not Canada, it is a more ambitious free trade agreement than Canada, and it ends free movement – which Norway doesn't do.' (The Guardian 2018)

A survey by the ESRC of Conservative Party Members Project (2019) revealed members' reaction to the UK leaving with the kind of 'Norway-plus' deal some Tory MPs, such as Nick Boles, have touted. That arrangement would leave 38 per cent of grassroots Tories feeling betrayed, 11 per cent feeling angry, and 23 per cent disappointed.

Labour was also somewhat divided but with a larger contingent in support of the Norway Model than was the case in the Conservative Party. Labour MP Stephen Kinnock noted in the 6 November 2017 House of Commons debate on the EEA:

> Given that an off-the-shelf transition deal is inevitable, it is clear to me that EEA-EFTA is the only option. The EEA and EFTA are well-established and well understood arrangements that offer the

> clarity, stability and predictability that the British economy so desperately needs in these turbulent times. Transferring from the EU to the EEA and EFTA would allow us to balance sovereignty and market access. Crucially, such a transition deal would buy us time [to] negotiate the final comprehensive trade and strategic partnership deal that will shape the terms of the UK's relationship with the EU for decades to come, while also allowing us to enter into independent trade negotiations with third countries because we would be outside the customs union. (UK Parliament 2017)

Both Labour and Tory opponents of the Norway Model expressed strong doubts about the merits of replacing EU membership with the Norway Model.

In a joint foreword, Labour former foreign secretary David Miliband and Tory ex-minister Jo Johnson – who quit his Government role in November 2019 over Brexit – said: 'Norway-plus would represent a long-term commitment to pay to benefit from the European Union's regulatory structures while choosing to be outside it.' They added that while rejoining EFTA may limit the economic damage it would represent a 'significant loss of power' and influence. 'Both sides would be entitled to ask, if the past two and a half years of upheaval and tortuous negotiation culminated in a Norway-plus deal, what was the point of all that?' (Belfast Telegraph 2018).

When surveyed on the merits of the Norway Model, 24 per cent of Labour members said such a second-best outcome would make them feel disappointed, angry, or betrayed, compared to 52 per cent who said they'd feel relatively positive. That said, only 3 per cent chose 'delighted' as opposed to 12 per cent saying 'pleased' and 37 per cent 'relieved' (Bale 2019).

This brief overview shows that opinions were strongly divided and that the main focus was on the legal aspects of the affiliation. The main focus of the debate was on how binding or committing an affiliation the UK should retain with the EU and the Norway Model formed the most binding end-point of such a range of options. We also need to keep in mind that most MPs did not mention the Norway Model.

CONCLUSION

The main purpose of this chapter has been to increase our understanding of the Norway Model in order to shed light on how relevant it is for the UK post-Brexit. The chapter's point of departure is that in order to understand the Norway Model we need to complement the predominant legal narratives with an account that exposes how these legal arrangements are embedded in socio-economic and political conditions that give shape and direction to the affiliation. In effect, the key claim of this chapter is that we cannot tell how well such legal arrangements will work unless we take such socio-economic and political factors properly into account. The UK debate was surprisingly inattentive to such factors, which suggests that there would be some rude awakenings should it have embarked on such a route.

This chapter's distinct contribution is to show that we cannot confine the assessment of the relevant socio-economic and political conditions to Norway-domestic ones only. For Norway, the close links it has with its Nordic neighbours figure centrally in Norway's self-conception and in the values that Norway embraces. These institutionalised values are what make up the Nordic Model, which is referred to as a distinct subgroup of coordinated market economies. A critical issue in this context is how extensively this region has been Europeanised. It was pointed out in the above that the more Europeanised the Nordic region, the less scope for the distinctive traits of the Nordic Model. And whereas the countries in the Nordic region have developed different affiliations with the EU, three are EU members and two are in the EEA, it is readily apparent that they have all been extensively Europeanised. We still, however, lack adequate knowledge of how this extensive Europeanisation bears on the Nordic Model.

Since Norway is exposed to both vertical and horizontal Europeanisation pressures, there are few grounds for asserting that Norway's EU affiliation makes it a more devout carrier of the Nordic Model. In that sense, in order to establish how distinctive the Norway Model is as a mode of EU affiliation, it may be more important to clarify how extensively the Nordic region has been Europeanised than to look at the distinctive traits of Norway's legal affiliation with the EU.

A key point of this chapter has been to show that how we interpret the Norway Model matters for the UK's assessment of its situation and its range of choices post-Brexit. Focusing on the legal affiliation – whether the EEA or the whole gamut of legal affiliations – provides a one-dimensional debate that is only really concerned with the scope and legal certainty of the affiliation. Adding the Norway-internal and Nordic socio-economic and political reading yields a two-dimensional debate which must consider legal affiliation in relation to the underlying socio-economic model and the political conditions that rests upon. In order to expose how this left-right or ideological dimension intersects with the mode of affiliation we need more knowledge of how Europeanised the Nordic Model has become.

The obvious question for the UK is how separable the three aspects of the Norway Model are. Can the UK opt for one (EEA) without the other two? This question requires more scrutiny of the UK's situation along legal, political, and socio-economic lines. It would appear to be difficult for the UK simply to go for the EEA Agreement without any affiliation with Schengen, since that helps to ensure the integrity of the EU's single market which the EEA was intended to ensure. As a non-member the EU may be less willing to allow the UK to pick-and-choose elements of the justice and home affairs segment, which it could when it was an EU member. There would not seem to be any formal requirement for the UK to pay any explicit attention to the Nordic Model component. Having said that, there are actors in the UK, notably the Labour Party and Scotland, that would want to embrace all three aspects of the Norway Model.

NOTES

1. The research that went into this chapter has received support from the EU's Horizon 2020 programme (Societal Challenges 6: 'Europe in a Changing World – Inclusive, Innovative and Reflective Societies') under Grant Agreement No. 822419).
2. The author is grateful for comments and suggestions from Chris Lord and Jarle Trondal, excellent research assistance by Janna van Diepen and very proficient editing by Silva Malin Hoffmann.
3. Article 90.2 notes that 'Decisions by the EEA Council shall be taken by agreement between the Community, on the one hand, and the EFTA States, on the other.' Article 93.2 notes that 'The EEA Joint Committee shall take decisions by agreement between the Community, on the one hand, and the EFTA States speaking with one voice, on the other' (Official Journal of the European Communities, 1994a).
4. The author is grateful to Espen D.H. Olsen for a very fruitful collaboration on mapping the Europeanisation of the Nordic Model. See for instance Fossum and Olsen (2017).
5. A different and more culturally based distinction is Tony Judt's (2005) between the 'Nordic', the 'Rhineland', the 'Catholic' and variations within each of these.
6. In addition to the system of structured political cooperation there is a very dynamic administrative cooperation. See Stie and Trondal (2020). Jarle Trondal has in correspondence referred to that as a kind of 'Nordic administrative space'.

7. Pre-COVID this was very extensive, with almost all shopping traffic going from Norway to Sweden. It involved thousands of jobs on the Swedish side, see Statistics Norway (2021).
8. With some exceptions, notably Ingebritsen (1998), little attention has been paid to how, and in what sense, the preconditions for the Nordic Model have fundamentally changed, or not, after Europeanisation.
9. There is a large body of literature on Europeanisation, see e.g. Cowles et al. (2001); Featherstone and Radaelli (2003); Graziano and Vink (2007); Olsen (2002); Schimmelfennig and Sedelmeier (2005). Research on Europeanisation of the Nordic countries is often precisely that: single-case (see e.g. Claes 2003; Martinsen and Vrangbæk 2008; Spång 2007), comparative studies of Nordic states (see e.g. Jacobsson et al. 2004; Rieker 2006), or of Nordic cooperation (see e.g. Olsen and Sverdrup 1998). The book that most explicitly engages with Europeanisation is Grøn et al. (2015) with the telling subtitle highlighting exceptionalism: *Still the other European community?* 'Nordic exceptionalism' *within* European integration is detected with regard to issues such as compliance with EU norms and policies (Sverdrup 2004), or Euroscepticism (Raunio 2007). None of these studies, however, systematically assesses what Europeanisation entails for the core tenets of the Nordic Model.
10. Four times, in the 1960s, 1970s, and 1990s, Norway applied for membership of the EU. The two first instances, in 1962 and 1967 were aborted due to de Gaulle's veto against the UK's application (Bjørklund 1997, pp. 143–4). In connection with the two next applications, in 1972 and 1994, the EU membership question was voted over in popular referendums that were arranged after the negotiations had been completed. In both instances, a small majority of the population turned down EU membership. In 1972, 53.5 per cent voted against membership and 46.5 per cent voted for, and in 1994, 52.2 per cent voted against, whereas 47.8 per cent voted in favour. Voter turnout in the 1994 referendum was a whopping 89 per cent (Official Statistics of Norway 1995)!
11. Lahnstein argued in a newspaper interview that the EU post-Maastricht was more encompassing than the Norway-Sweden union, and in addition, that EU membership would subject Norway to a worse union than the one it had with Sweden during the period 1814–1905 (Dagbladet 28.03.92, cited in Køber 2001). This statement sparked a debate among historians, most of whom agreed that the EU was more encompassing. Historians were somewhat divided on whether the EU was worse than Norway's union with Sweden. Most historians were against Norwegian EU membership. Not long before the 1994 referendum, 84 Norwegian historians signed a petition against Norwegian EU membership (Køber 2001).
12. EFTA was established in 1960, and has now four members: Iceland, Liechtenstein, Norway, and Switzerland. Three of these countries are members of the EEA but not Switzerland.
13. For a comprehensive overview of the specific provisions of the EEA Agreement, see Arnesen et al. (2018).
14. On the principle of dynamic homogeneity in EEA law, see Hreinsson (2015).
15. For overviews of Norway's relationship with the EU, see Claes and Tranøy (1999); Eriksen and Fossum (2014, 2015); Fossum (2018, 2019b); Fossum and Graver (2018); NOU (2012); Sverdrup (1997). For Iceland's relationship, see Jonsdottir (2012); Thorhallsson (2004, 2019). For overviews of Liechtenstein's relations with the EU, see Frommelt (2016, 2017, 2018).
16. The first pillar is constituted by the EU institutions; the second one by the EEA-EFTA institutions. There are also joint bodies to implement the EEA Agreement. 'The two-pillar structure is necessary because the EEA-EFTA States have not transferred any legislative competences to the EU or to the joint EEA bodies. In addition, the EEA-EFTA States are also, … constitutionally unable to accept binding decisions made by the EU institutions directly' (Frommelt 2019).
17. For Iceland's agreements with the EU, see European Commission (2021).
18. See Oslo Region (2021).
19. The two-pillar structure of the EEA Agreement likely facilitates such dynamics because it retains formal sovereignty. At the same time, it also helps to cloak the extent of actual loss of autonomy involved. If we transfer this to the UK context, we see that the structural and partisan-political conditions are very different; hence, were the UK to join the EEA it is very unlikely that the UK would be able to bifurcate issue-specific adaptation from mode of affiliation.

REFERENCES

Arnesen, F.H., Haukeland Fredriksen, H., Graver, H.P., Mæstad, O. and Vedder, C. (2018) *Agreement on the European Economic Area A Commentary*, Baden-Baden: Nomos.

Bale, T. (16 January 2019) 'Would a Norway option break the Brexit stalemate? Here's what the polling says' [online], *The New Statesman*, available at https://www.newstatesman.com/politics/2019/01/would-norway-option-break-brexit-stalemate-here-s-what-polling-says (accessed 7 February 2022).

Belfast Telegraph (7 December 2018) 'At least 10 Cabinet ministers back Norway-style Brexit' [online], *Belfast Telegraph*, available at https://www.belfasttelegraph.co.uk/news/northern-ireland/at-least-10-cabinet-ministers-back-norway-style-brexit-37604287.html (accessed 17 January 2022).

Bickerton, C.J., Hodson, D. and Puetter, U. (2015) 'The new intergovernmentalism: European integration in the post-Maastricht era', *Journal of Common Market Studies*, 53(4): 703–22.

Bjørklund, T. (1997) 'Old and new patterns: The "no" majority in the 1972 and 1994 EC/EU referendums in Norway', *Acta Sociologica*, 40(2): 143–59.

Bjørklund, T. (2001) 'How appropriate is the cleavage model in explaining Norwegian voting behaviour from 1945 to 1997?', *Tidsskrift for Samfunnsforskning*, 42(1): 31–63.

Bjørklund, T. (2005) *Hundre år med folkeavstemninger – Norge og Norden 1905–2005* [*Hundred Years of Popular Referendums – Norway and the Nordics 1905–2005*], Oslo: Universitetsforlaget.

Claes, D.H. (2003) 'EØS-avtalen – mellom diplomati og demokrati', *Internasjonal Politikk*, 61(3): 275–302.

Claes, D.H. and Tranøy, B.S. (eds) (1999), *Utenfor, annerledes og suveren? Norge under EØS-avtalen*, Bergen: Fagbokforlaget.

Cowles, M.G., Caporaso, J. and Risse, T. (eds) (2001) *Transforming Europe: Europeanization and Domestic Change*, Ithaca: Cornell University Press.

Dølvik, J.E., Fløtten, T., Hippe, J.M. and Leirfald, B. (2015) 'The Nordic model towards 2030. A new chapter?', Oslo: Fafo report 2015(07).

EFTA (2021) *United Kingdom* [online], available at https://www.efta.int/free-trade/free-trade-agreements/uk (accessed 17 January 2022).

Egeberg, M. and Trondal, J. (2015) 'National administrative sovereignty – under pressure', in E.O. Eriksen and J.E. Fossum (eds), *The European Union's Non-Members: Independence under Hegemony?*, London: Routledge, pp.173–88.

Eriksen, E.O. and Fossum, J.E. (2014) (eds) *Det norske paradoks – Om Norges forhold til Den europeiske union*, Oslo: Universitetsforlaget.

Eriksen, E.O. and Fossum, J.E. (eds) (2015) *The European Union's Non-Members: Independence under Hegemony?*, London: Routledge.

ESRC Party Members Project (2019) 'No deal is better than May's deal' [online], available at https://esrcpartymembersproject.org/2019/01/04/no-deal-is-better-than-mays-deal/ (accessed 17 January 2022).

European Commission (2020) *Single Market Scoreboard* [online], available at https://ec.europa.eu/internal_market/scoreboard/performance_by_governance_tool/transposition/index_en.htm#changes-transposition-deficit (accessed 8 February 2022).

European Commission (2021) *Iceland* [online], available at https://ec.europa.eu/trade/policy/countries-and-regions/countries/iceland/ (accessed 17 January 2022).

European Court of Auditors (2021) *Financial contributions from non-EU countries to the EU and Member States* [online], available at https://www.eca.europa.eu/Lists/ECADocuments/RW21_03/RW_third_countries_contributions_EN.pdf (accessed 7 February 2022).

Express (3 December 2020) 'Brexit U-turn: Nigel Farage cited Norwegian model as "attractive option for Britain"' [online], *Express*, available at https://www.express.co.uk/news/uk/1367978/brexit-news-nigel-farage-eu-uk-trade-talks-no-deal-norway-eea-spt (accessed 17 January 2022).

Featherstone, K. and Radaelli, C. (eds) (2003) *The Politics of Europeanization*, Oxford: Oxford University Press.

Fossum, J.E. (2010) 'Norway's European "Gag Rules"', *European Review*, 18(1): 73–92.

Fossum, J.E. (2018) 'Brexit and the EU's affiliated non-members', in P. Diamond, P. Nedergaard and B. Rosamond (eds), *Handbook on Brexit*, London: Routledge, pp. 278–89.

Fossum, J.E. (2019a) 'What is the Norway Model? Mode of affiliation or political compromise?', Political Quarterly, 90(2): 266–73.

Fossum, J.E. (2019b) 'Norway and the European Union', in *Oxford Research Encyclopedia, Politics*, Oxford: Oxford University Press, pp. 1–30.

Fossum, J.E. and Graver, H.P. (2018) *Squaring the Circle on Brexit – Could the Norway Model Work?*, Bristol: Bristol University Press.

Fossum, J.E. and Olsen, E.D.H. (2017) 'The Nordic Model in a Europeanized Context', Unpublished paper.

Fossum, J.E and Vigrestad, J. (2021) 'Is the grass greener on the other side? Norwegians' assessments of Brexit', *Politics and Governance*, 9(1): 79–89.

Fredriksen, H.H. (2015) 'The EEA and the Case Law of the EU of the CJEU: Incorporation without participation', in E.O. Eriksen and J.E. Fossum (eds), *The European Union's Non-Members: Independence under Hegemony?*, Abingdon: Routledge, pp. 102–17.

Fredriksen, H.H. (2018) 'Article 107 [Preliminary rulings from the ECJ]', in F. Arnesen, H.H. Fredriksen, H.P. Graver, O. Mestad and C. Vedder (eds), *Agreement on the European Economic Area*, Beck-Hart: Nomos, pp. 837–40.

Fredriksen, H.H. (2020) 'A "special relationship" built on a patchwork: How the CJEU sees the EEA EFTA states' [online], *EFTA-Studies.org Blog*, 20 April, available at https://www.efta-studies.org/a-special-relationship (accessed 5 November 2020).

Fredriksen, H.H. and Franklin, C.N.K. (2015) 'Of pragmatism and principles: The EEA Agreement 20 years on', *Common Market Law Review*, 52(3): 629–84.

Frommelt, C. (2016) 'Liechtenstein's tailor-made arrangements in the EEA: A small state's creative solutions in European integration', in S. Wolf (ed.), *State Size Matters*, Wiesbaden: VS Springer, pp. 131–62.

Frommelt, C. (2017) In search of effective differentiated integration: Lessons from the European Economic Area (EEA), Unpublished doctoral dissertation, University of Zurich.

Frommelt, C. (2018) 'Liechtenstein and the EEA', in F. Arnesen, H.H. Fredriksen, H.P. Graver, O. Mæstad and C. Vedder (eds), *Agreement on the European Economic Area A Commentary*, Baden-Baden: Nomos, pp. 35–58.

Frommelt, C. (2019) 'The two-pillar structure of the EEA' [online], *EFTA-studies.org Blog*, 27 March, available at https://www.efta-studies.org/the-two-pillar-structure (accessed 17 January 2022).

Graver, H.P. (2016) 'Possibilities and challenges of the EEA as an option for the UK after Brexit', *European Papers*, 1(3): 803–21.

Graziano, P. and Vink, M. (2007) *Europeanization. New Research Agendas*, Houndmills: Palgrave Macmillan.

Grøn, C.H., Nedergaard, P. and Wivel, A. (eds) (2015) *The Nordic Countries and the European Union. Still the Other European Community?*, London: Routledge.

Gstöhl, S. and Phinnemore, D. (eds) (2019) *The Proliferation of Privileged Partnerships between the European Union and its Neighbours*, Abingdon, Oxon: Routledge.

Hall, P.A. and Soskice, D. (eds) (2001) *Varieties of Capitalism: The Institutional Foundations of Comparative Advantage*, Oxford: Oxford University Press.

Holmøyvik, E. (2015) 'Norway's constitutional acrobatics under the EEA Agreement', in E.O. Eriksen and J.E. Fossum (eds) (2015) *The European Union's Non-Members: Independence under Hegemony?*, London: Routledge, pp. 137–52.

Hreisson, P. (2015) 'General principles', in C. Baudenbacher (ed.) *The Handbook of EEA Law*, Berlin: Springer International Publishing, pp. 349–89.

Huitfeld, A. (2021) *Redegjørelse om viktige EU- og EØS-spørsmål* [online], Stortinget, 23 November, available at https://www.regjeringen,no/no/aktuelt/eu_utgreiing211123/id2888949/?utm_source=www.regjeringen.no&utm_medium=rss&utm_campaign=RSS-2581966-ownerid833-document Typeaktuelt (accessed 17 January 2022).

Ingebritsen, C. (1998) *The Nordic States and European Unity*, Ithaca: Cornell University Press.

Institute for Government (2022) 'The options for the UK's trading relationship with the EU' [online], available at https://www.instituteforgovernment.org.uk/explainers/options-uk-trading-relationship-eu (accessed 17 January 2022).

Jacobsson, B., Lægreid, P. and Pedersen, O.K. (2004) *Europeanization and Transnational States. Comparing Nordic Central Governments*, London: Routledge.

Jonsdottir, J. (2012) *Europeanization and the European Economic Area: Iceland's Participation in the EU's Policy Process*, London: Routledge.

Judt, T. (2005) *Postwar: A History of Europe since 1945*, New York: The Penguin Press.

Køber, L.K. (2001) 'Verre enn unionen med Sverige' – om bruken av unionsbegrepet og historiske sammenligninger med unionen med Sverige i EEC/EF/EU-debattene 1961–1994, Hovedoppgave i historie, Universitetet i Oslo.

Lord, C. (2020) 'Integration through differentiation and segmentation: The case of one member state from 1950 to Brexit (and beyond)', in J. Batora and J.E. Fossum (eds), *The EU Post-Crises: The Rise of a Segmented Political Order*, London: Routledge, pp. 243–64.

Martinsen, D.D. and Vrangbæk, K. (2008) 'The Europeanization of health care governance: Implementing the market imperatives of Europe', *Public Administration*, 86(1): 169–84.

Neumann, I.B. (2002) 'This little piggy stayed at home: Why Norway is not a member of the EU', in L. Hansen and O. Wæver (eds), *European Integration and National Identity – the Challenge of the Nordic States*, London: Routledge, pp. 88–129.

NOU 2012:2 (2012) 'Utenfor og innefor – Norges avtaler med EU' ['Outside and Inside: Norway's Agreements with the European Union'] [online], *Norwegian Ministry of Foreign Affairs*, available at https://www.regjeringen.no/no/dokumenter/nou-2012-2/id669368/ (accessed 17 January 2022).

Official Journal of the European Communities (1994a) Agreement on the European Economic Area. OJ L 1, 3 January.

Official Journal of the European Communities (1994b) Agreement between the EFTA States on the Establishment of a Surveillance Authority and a Court of Justice. L 344/1, 31 December.

Official Journal of the European Communities (1999) Council Decision of 17 May 1999 on Certain Arrangements for the Application of the Agreement Concluded by the Council of the European Union and the Republic of Iceland and the Kingdom of Norway Concerning the Association of Those Two States with the Implementation, Application and Development of the Schengen Acquis. L 176/31, 10 July.

Official Statistics of Norway (1995) *The 1994 Referendum on Norwegian Membership of the EU* [online], available at https://www.ssb.no/a/histstat/nos/nos_c235.pdf (accessed 17 January 2022).

Olsen, J.P. (2002) 'The many faces of Europeanization', *Journal of Common Market Studies*, 40(5): 921–52.

Olsen, J.P. and Sverdrup, B.O. (1998) *Europa i Norden. Europeisering av nordisk samarbeid*, Oslo: Tano Aschehoug.

Oslo Region (2021) *Oslo Region European Office* [online], available at https://osloregion.org/en/ (accessed 17 January 2022).

Raunio, T. (2007) 'Softening but persistent: Euroscepticism in the Nordic EU countries', *Acta Politica*, 42(2–3): 191–210.

Reegård, Stein (2020) 'Stort og smått; rødt og blått – Eksempler på hvordan en regjering tilpasser seg internasjonaliseringens utfordringer', in N. Veggeland (ed.), *Den Solbergske staten*, Trondheim: Sandnes Forlag, pp. 27–82.

Rieker, P. (2006) *Europeanization of National Security Identity. The EU and the Changing Security Identities of the Nordic States*, London: Routledge.

Rokkan, S. (1999) 'Cleavage structures and party systems', in P. Flora, S. Kuhnle and D. Urwin (eds), *State Formation, Nation-Building, and Mass Politics in Europe: The Theory of Stein Rokkan*, Oxford: Oxford University Press, pp. 1–191.

SAMAK (2019) *The Nordics and Future Europe* [online], available at https://samak.info/wp-content/uploads/2019/01/Norden-og-fremtidens-Europa-SAMAK-ENG.pdf (accessed 17 January 2022).

Schimmelfennig, F. and Sedelmeier, U. (eds) (2005) *The Politics of European Union Enlargement. Theoretical Approaches*, London: Routledge.

Søreide, I.M.E (7 February 2018) Møte i Europautvalget den 7. februar 2018 [Meeting in the European Affairs Committee 7 February 2018], available at https://www.stortinget.no/no/Saker-og-publikasjoner/Publikasjoner/Referater/Europautvalget/2017-2018/refe-201718-02-07/?all=true (accessed 30 September 2020).

Spång, M. (2007) 'Sweden: Europeanization of policy, but not of politics?' in T. Faist and A. Ette (eds), *The Europeanization of National Policies and Politics of Immigration. Between Autonomy and the European Union*, Berlin: Springer, pp. 116–35.

Statistics Norway (2021) 'Cross border trade' [online], available at https://www.ssb.no/en/varehandel-og-tjenesteyting/varehandel/statistikk/grensehandel (accessed 17 January 2022).

Stie, A.E. and Trondal, J. (2020) 'Introducing the study of Nordic cooperation', *Politics and Governance*, 8(4): 1–10.

Sverdrup, U. (1997) 'Norway: An adaptive non-member', in K. Hanf and B. Soetendorp (eds), *Adapting to European Integration – Small States and the European Union*, London: Longman, pp. 149–66.

Sverdrup, U. (2004) 'Compliance and conflict management in the European Union: Nordic exceptionalism', *Scandinavian Political Studies*, 27(1): 23–43.

The Guardian (30 November 2018) 'Theresa May rules out Norway-style Brexit compromise with Labour' [online], *The Guardian*, available at https://www.theguardian.com/politics/2018/nov/30/theresa-may-rules-out-norway-style-brexit-compromise-with-labour (accessed 17 January 2022).

Thorhallsson, B. (ed.) (2004) *Iceland and European Integration: On the Edge*, New York: Routledge.

Thorhallsson, B. (ed.) (2019) *Small States and Shelter Theory: Iceland's External Affairs*, London: Routledge.

UK Parliament (2017) 'European Economic Area: UK membership' [online], *House of Commons Hansard*, 6 November, Vol. 630, available at https://hansard.parliament.uk/Commons/2017-11-06/debates/FEEE4AD5-7465-47A4-97CA-A9B41B9DCAD9/EuropeanEconomicAreaUKMembership (accessed 17 January 2022).

Valen, H. (1999) 'EU-saken post festum', in B. Aardal, H.M. Narud and F. Berglund (eds), *Velgere i 90-årene*, Oslo: NKS Forlaget, pp. 106–19.

22. Liechtenstein and its relations with the EU[1]

Christian Frommelt

INTRODUCTION

With approximately 38,000 inhabitants, the Principality of Liechtenstein is Europe's fourth smallest country. Liechtenstein's sovereignty (in today's sense of the term) goes back to 1806 when the Holy Roman Empire was dissolved. Napoleon subsequently established the Confederation of the Rhine of which Liechtenstein was a member state. Due to its smallness, however, Liechtenstein has always closely leaned on neighbouring countries. From 1852 to 1919, Liechtenstein was in a customs and currency union with the Austrian monarchy. After this customs and currency union ended after World War I, Liechtenstein built up an even closer regional union with Switzerland. It is based on the Customs Treaty of 1923, but includes also many other agreements (inter alia the treatment of foreigners, the enforcement of civil judgments, the control of medicines, air traffic, patent protection and the currency). In addition to the close regional cooperation, Liechtenstein is also deeply Europeanised. On 2 May 1992, after long negotiations, representatives of the European Union (EU) and its member states and of the countries of the European Free Trade Association (EFTA) signed the Agreement on the European Economic Area (EEA). Today, as a member of the EEA, Liechtenstein finds itself half-way between Austria, a member of the EU, and Switzerland, which has stayed out of both the EEA and the EU.

The EEA membership marks an important step for Liechtenstein in its 'quest for independence and recognition as a sovereign state' (Pelkmans and Böhler, 2013, p. 12). At the same time, by focusing on economic integration EEA membership provided for a pragmatic approach to European integration. Liechtenstein may be a very small state with limited human resources, which begs the question whether that country is capable of managing its membership in the EEA. However, due to an efficient bureaucracy, a favourable legal culture and some flexibility on the part of the EU, its EEA EFTA partners and Switzerland it is able to comply with the obligations set out in the EEA Agreement. Indeed, Liechtenstein has even been able to turn its EEA membership into a boost to the economy.

This contribution analyses the specific features of Liechtenstein's relations with the EU. It will also address Liechtenstein's relations with the United Kingdom and how these have changed since Brexit took place. After this brief introduction the chapter describes Liechtenstein's cumbersome path to the EEA. The third section provides an overview of Liechtenstein's legal relations with the EU. The fourth section describes the domestic challenges associated with EEA membership. Likewise, the fifth section analyses Liechtenstein's tailor-made arrangements which exempt Liechtenstein from the implementation of certain EU legal acts. The sixth and seventh sections discuss, respectively, the public opinion on European integration and the effects of Brexit for Liechtenstein.

LIECHTENSTEIN'S PATH TO THE EEA: FLEXIBILITY FOR A MICROSTATE

Liechtenstein's accession to the EEA was the result of a lengthy and intense domestic debate, facing serious opposition by the local manufacturing sector as well as numerous trustees and other actors within the finance sector (Frommelt and Gstöhl, 2011, p. 14). The opponents of EEA membership argued in terms of Liechtenstein's smallness, in particular, the lack of bargaining power and the lack of administrative resources. But they also brought up the fear of uncontrolled immigration, high financial costs, the loss of democratic influence, and increased political pressure on Liechtenstein's financial centre. By contrast, the proponents of EEA membership argued primarily with reference to the negative externalities of being 'left behind' in an increasingly integrated Europe, but also with reference to the great economic potential that comes with a legally secured access to the EU's internal market. In addition, they pointed out that an EEA accession will strengthen Liechtenstein's reputation among the other European states and thus its recognition as a sovereign state.

In September 1992, the Liechtenstein parliament (Landtag) approved the EEA Agreement but decided to hold a national referendum. While the Swiss electorate and cantons rejected EEA membership, 55.8 per cent of Liechtenstein's population approved the EEA Agreement in the referendum. Of the possible 'yes/no' combinations between the two countries, this scenario was the most unexpected as the two economies seemed too tightly interwoven to permit a different choice of policy.

As a result, the Liechtenstein government first had to renegotiate relations with Switzerland, then have the solution approved by the EEA partners and finally overcome the domestic ratification hurdle again. In March 1995, the Landtag approved several changes to the Customs Treaty and other agreements between Liechtenstein and Switzerland. The Customs Treaty now allowed Liechtenstein to join international organisations and agreements without Switzerland as an intermediary. However, the parallel membership of Liechtenstein in two important economic and legal areas also required adaptations to the EEA Agreement. The solution of this 'Gordian knot' was found in the innovative principle of 'parallel marketability', which allows products meeting either EEA or Swiss requirements to circulate in Liechtenstein (Gstöhl and Frommelt, 2017, p. 4).

Due to the changes to the Customs Treaty and the EEA Agreement the members of the Landtag agreed to hold a second referendum. It took place in April 1995 after the approval by the Landtag and vivid campaigns in favour of and against EEA membership. With 55.9 per cent 'yes' votes the support was about the same as in 1992. On 1 May 1995 the principality became a full EEA member and thus achieved its first own treaty-based relationship with the EU.

Several factors contributed to 'squaring the circle' of participating in the extended internal market while maintaining the bilateral customs union with a non-member. The small size of Liechtenstein made it quite easy to observe the trade flows. The need to adapt the bilateral relations was mainly restricted to the free movement of goods and the differences between EU and Swiss rules that could potentially lead to conflict. The political will on all sides to honour the wish of the people of Liechtenstein to join the EEA despite Switzerland's rejection was strong: the Swiss had no interest in complicating their future bilateral negotiations with the EU while the EU was keen to demonstrate its understanding for the concerns of small states after the Danish 'no' to the Maastricht Treaty. Finally, Article 121(b) of the EEA Agreement

(1994) already recognised the regional union between Liechtenstein and Switzerland as being in conformity with the EEA Agreement to the extent that it did not impair its functioning. It would indeed have been paradoxical to force these two countries to reintroduce border controls after 70 years. Moreover, an additional EEA EFTA state was most welcome in view of the EU accession negotiations with Austria, Finland, Norway and Sweden.

Although EEA membership was hotly contested, the European question was no longer politicised after accession. That enabled the government to optimise the domestic framework conditions for EEA membership without much political resistance. In particular, the public administration was expanded. But parliamentary and direct democratic procedures were also adapted to enable efficient administration of the EEA Agreement despite the limited resources.

OTHER AGREEMENTS WITH THE EU

Liechtenstein, like the other EFTA states, has concluded bilateral agreements with the EU beyond the EEA Agreement. In 2004, Liechtenstein negotiated an agreement with the EU on the taxation of savings income. In 2015, the EU and Liechtenstein agreed on an amending protocol thereto, which entered into force on 1 January 2016. The revised agreement shall implement the OECD (Organisation for Economic Co-operation and Development) standard for automatic exchange of financial account information. It was widely seen as an important step for Liechtenstein to reaffirm its commitment to international cooperation on tax matters.

Liechtenstein has also concluded an agreement with the EU on security procedures for exchanging classified information as well as cooperation agreements with Europol and Eurojust. Another important integration step for Liechtenstein – like for Iceland, Norway and Switzerland – is the association with the Schengen area and Dublin convention. It requires Liechtenstein to adopt the relevant acquis and includes it in the European information and consultation mechanisms in the fields of border controls, international justice and police cooperation, visa and asylum policy. Similar to the EEA, the EFTA countries have the right to participate in decision-shaping, but they do not have a formal right to participate in decision-making in the further development of Schengen/Dublin law.

Liechtenstein's association to the Schengen area and the Dublin convention is not based on separate agreements with the EU, but it is linked to the respective Swiss bilateral agreements via protocols. Because these qualify as independent agreements in case the main agreement between the EU and Switzerland ceases to apply, Liechtenstein is formally a Schengen member in its own right since December 2011. It enjoys the same rights and obligations as Switzerland. Specific provisions are laid down for Liechtenstein concerning the time period required to implement new acquis, in case there is a domestic referendum (18 months).

In 2007, Liechtenstein concluded an additional agreement with the EU and Switzerland, extending the sectoral agreement between Switzerland and the EU on trade in agricultural products to Liechtenstein. The model of a trilateral supplementary agreement was already chosen in 1972 to extend the free trade agreement between Switzerland and the EU to Liechtenstein. Finally, Liechtenstein is included in the EU-Swiss agreements on processed agricultural products (2004) and the carriage of goods (2009). Those agreements apply to Liechtenstein although it is not an official contracting party because they are linked to the customs union between Switzerland and Liechtenstein. Hence, Liechtenstein representatives sit in the meetings of the respective mixed committees.

However, this close relationship with Switzerland, on the one hand, and with the EU, on the other, also carries the risk of getting out of control. Especially the fact that certain obligations stemming from the EEA Agreement are discharged by Liechtenstein joining respective agreements between the EU and Switzerland may not always prove to be a safe bet. If relations between Switzerland and the EU 'turn sour', as currently after the Swiss government's decision not to continue negotiations on an institutional framework agreement, existing (bilateral) agreements between the EU and Switzerland are likely to erode. That again will put pressure on Liechtenstein to revert to implementing EEA law if the eroded law between Switzerland and the EU is not in conformity with obligations stemming from the EEA Agreement anymore. Smallness could then become a curse.

To sum up, similar to Iceland and Norway, the EEA Agreement was not sufficient and Liechtenstein has concluded several other agreements with the EU. The overall level of integration is high. Nevertheless, Liechtenstein sometimes lacks the state capacity for full integration and therefore depends on tailor-made arrangements. Outside the scope of the EEA Agreement, Liechtenstein often depends on Switzerland in order to shape its relations with the EU. Finally, the legal and political cooperation with the EU in the area of taxation has improved the reputation of Liechtenstein's financial centre.

DOMESTIC INSTITUTIONAL CHALLENGES

In recent years, there have been several new institutional arrangements that have affected the functioning of the EEA's two-pillar structure and its nature as an agreement under public international law (Frommelt, 2020a). Whereas there were regular concerns about the compatibility of these institutional arrangements with the national constitutions of Norway and Iceland (Bekkedal, 2019), Liechtenstein's constitution like the entire legal order of Liechtenstein has proven to be very open to EEA law. This 'friendly' approach (Thürer, 1998) is mainly the result of Liechtenstein's monistic approach to international law. However, it must also be viewed in the context of Liechtenstein's specific legal culture of high jurisprudential reception of Swiss and Austrian law.

Article 8, paragraph 2 of the Liechtenstein constitution (1921) enables the Landtag to transfer sovereign rights to other states or international organisations as long as it does not restrict the fundamental rights laid down in the Liechtenstein constitution. Article 8 also forms the basis for the involvement of the Liechtenstein parliament in the EEA decision-making process. Each EEA EFTA state can indicate constitutional requirements to a decision of the EEA Joint Committee (JCD). This means that in certain cases the incorporation of new EU law into the EEA Agreement requires the formal ratification by the national parliament of the respective EEA EFTA state. Members of parliament of an EEA EFTA state, however, can only approve a JCD. They cannot make any changes or adaptations; neither to the JCD nor the EU act itself.

Each EEA EFTA state has its own criteria to follow before launching such a procedure. In Liechtenstein, the EEA/Schengen Committee of the Liechtenstein parliament meets a few days prior to the meeting of the EEA Joint Committee in order to decide whether a procedure that is in accordance with Article 103 of the EEA Agreement is necessary for a specific EU act. The parliamentary EEA/Schengen Committee makes its decision based on a recommendation from the EEA Coordination Unit of the Liechtenstein government. The recommendation itself is based on an expert opinion of Liechtenstein's Constitutional Court (Staatsgerichtshof).

Parliament's approval of a JCD is only necessary if the corresponding JCD changes domestic law or has financial consequences. By contrast, delegated and implementing EU acts, EU acts with a specific addressee, non-binding EU acts and EU acts that simply amend or consolidate other EU acts do not require approval by the Liechtenstein parliament.

The Constitutional Court also stated that the Committee's decision has to ensure the efficiency and proper working of the EEA Agreement. Finally, it highlighted the necessity of close cooperation between government and parliament to ensure the democratic legitimacy of the EEA policy-making process. These specifications give all players certain room for interpretation as to whether the stipulation of constitutional requirements is necessary or not. If Liechtenstein has pointed out the need to fulfil its own constitutional requirements to a JCD, parliament has to approve the respective JCD in a plenary meeting. While the number of reservations indicated is roughly the same for all three EEA EFTA states, the time needed for ratification is lower for Liechtenstein than for its EEA EFTA partners (Frommelt, 2020a, p. 24).

Legally speaking, every JCD represents an international treaty. It follows that a decision of the Liechtenstein parliament to ratify a JCD can be subject to a popular referendum within 30 days. In order for such a referendum to take place, 1,000 signatures of Liechtenstein citizens are required (out of a total of about 20,000 Liechtenstein citizens entitled to vote). If enough signatures are collected, a vote is held, with a simple majority of Liechtenstein citizens being sufficient to reject a JCD and thus the incorporation of new EU law into the EEA Agreement. Although the Landtag ratified more than 240 JCDs since 1995, a referendum against a JCD has never been held; nor has a referendum ever been held against a law implementing an EU act incorporated into the EEA Agreement.

Another element of direct democracy are popular initiatives. An initiative aims to enact a new law. Before parliament and ultimately the people can decide on a popular initiative, a sufficient number of signatures must be collected. However, before these signatures can be collected, the initiative is formally and materially examined by the government on whether it is compatible with the constitution, international law and EEA law. The government reports its examination to the parliament, which then decides whether the popular initiative is admissible or not. In case the parliament does not agree with the government, the government can ask the Constitutional Court to examine the initiative. Likewise, the initiator of an initiative can appeal to the Constitutional Court if he disagrees with the decision of parliament. It is therefore not possible for Liechtenstein's population to vote on an initiative that would initiate a new law that is not compatible with EEA law or that would change an existing law in a way that it would no longer be compatible with EEA law. The Liechtenstein examination procedure of popular initiatives differs greatly from that in Switzerland as in the Swiss case, a reported incompatibility with EU law does not stop the direct democratic procedure.

In summary, it can be said that Liechtenstein has built up a very favourable institutional and legal framework for its legal and political relations with the EU. First, the monistic legal tradition does not impede the delegation of national decision-making competence to an international organisation and enables the direct applicability of EU law incorporated in the EEA Agreement. Second, the participation of the Liechtenstein parliament in the EEA decision-making process is limited to the subsequent ratification of a JCD. The information and consultation rights of the Liechtenstein parliament are also less developed than in Norway and Iceland. Finally, in the course of EEA accession the system of direct democracy was adapted by allowing the examination of popular initiatives on the compatibility with EEA law in addition to the already provided examination of initiatives for their constitutionality. These examples show that the domestic implementation of the EEA Agreement in Liechtenstein is very pragmatic by design. In view of the limited human resources of the microstate, this is probably the only way for Liechtenstein to correctly implement the large amount of EEA law.

PUBLIC ATTITUDE TOWARDS EUROPEAN INTEGRATION

Liechtenstein's membership of the European Economic Area enjoys great support among Liechtenstein's citizens (Frommelt, 2020b). According to a recent survey (February 2020), the EEA evokes a positive image among 76 per cent of the people surveyed. In contrast, only 5 per cent of the Liechtenstein population have a negative image of the EEA. In addition, 84 per cent of Liechtenstein's citizens consider the EEA Agreement to be a good agreement for Liechtenstein and only 4 per cent consider it to be a bad agreement. The high level of support for the EEA among the Liechtenstein population is also reflected in the question of a possible withdrawal from the EEA. Accordingly, only 5 per cent of the people surveyed agree with the statement 'Liechtenstein should leave the EEA'.

A prerequisite for the high level of support for the EEA appears to be the preservation of the special rule regarding the free movement of persons. This allows Liechtenstein, despite its membership of the EEA, to restrict the right of residence in Liechtenstein also for EEA nationals. The retention of the special rule is supported by 67 per cent of the people surveyed. Only 6 per cent reject it. Another crucial factor is the compatibility of EEA membership with the Swiss-Liechtenstein customs union. Thereby, the perception of Liechtenstein's customs and monetary union with Switzerland is even more positive.

If the EEA Agreement were to be dissolved, the majority of respondents (51 per cent) would prefer an agreement equivalent in substance to the EEA Agreement. In such a case, EU membership would only be an option for 7 per cent. A less comprehensive agreement or even no contractual relations at all would be preferred by 17 per cent and 11 per cent of the respondents, respectively. The low level of support for EU membership is also confirmed by the question of the possible effects of EU membership on Liechtenstein. Accordingly, in the event of EU membership, a large majority of Liechtenstein citizens would expect an expansion in bureaucracy, increased financial transfers to other states and a restriction of their rights. In contrast, positively formulated arguments – such as more influence in Europe, an increase in competitiveness or an improvement in image – are rejected by the majority of those surveyed. Although the EU's image as a whole may not be particularly bad in Liechtenstein, the people of Liechtenstein have great reservations about EU membership.

Table 22.1 compares the respondents' attitude towards the possible effects of EU membership with the perceived effects of the EEA. The comparison shows the strongly contrasting perceptions of the EU and the EEA among the people of Liechtenstein. For example, 61 per cent of the people surveyed state that in Liechtenstein, the rights of the people would be restricted in the event of EU membership. In contrast, only 20 per cent agree with the statement that EEA membership would restrict people's rights. The perception of the EU and the EEA also differs greatly with regard to money payments to other European states. While in connection with EEA membership only 24 per cent of those surveyed agree with the statement that Liechtenstein has to pay too much money to other European states, 72 per cent believe that in the case of EU membership too much money would be transferred to other states. Furthermore, Liechtenstein citizens do not expect Liechtenstein's influence in Europe

Table 22.1 Comparison of the perception of the EU and EEA (percentage)

	Totally agree	Tend to agree	Neutral	Tend to disagree	Totally disagree	Don't know
The EEA has restricted popular rights	6	14	22	24	18	16
EU membership would restrict popular rights	36	25	15	7	5	11
The EEA has strengthened sovereignty	23	34	23	7	4	9
EU membership would bring more influence in Europe	5	12	17	27	32	7
The EEA means too much money to other European countries	7	17	29	14	7	25
EU membership would bring too much financial transfer to other countries	43	29	12	4	1	10
The EEA improved Liechtenstein's image abroad	22	35	25	6	2	10
EU membership would improve Liechtenstein's image abroad	6	14	26	26	19	8

Note: CAWI survey, February 2020, N = 869.
Source: Frommelt (2020b, p. 25).

to increase in the event of EU membership, while the majority considers EEA membership to be a gain in sovereignty.

The different perception of the effects of Liechtenstein's possible EU membership, on the one hand, and its EEA membership, on the other hand, cannot be objectively explained. Whether Liechtenstein is a member of the EU or the EEA does not change the above-mentioned direct democratic procedures much. Hence, the rights of Liechtenstein citizens would not be different in case of an EU membership. In the case of the image of Liechtenstein abroad or Liechtenstein's influence in Europe it is even likely that an EU membership would have a positive effect. In 1992 and 1995 when Liechtenstein decided on its EEA membership, some of those critical arguments about EU membership were used as arguments against EEA membership. Since opposition against the EEA was quite strong at that time, it is likely that many people now project their initial reservations about EEA membership onto an EU membership of Liechtenstein.

Public opinion in Liechtenstein shows an ambivalent relationship among Liechtenstein's citizens to European integration. The majority feels a sense of connection with Europe and attach great importance to the political and economic development of the EU. Positive terms such as peace, economic prosperity, freedom of travel and cultural diversity are also associated with the European integration process but not specifically with the EU. Indeed, the EU is increasingly rarely evoking a positive image in Liechtenstein. If Liechtenstein were to become a member of the EU, Liechtenstein's citizens themselves see hardly any advantages with respect to their country's competitiveness as a business location, its influence in Europe or its image abroad.

Low support for EU membership goes along with high support for EEA membership. Due to the high support for EEA membership, it is no surprise that there is very little controversy over EEA membership in Liechtenstein. The lack of debate may in turn explain why the actual level of knowledge among Liechtenstein's citizens on the institutional framework of the EEA as well as its scope and purpose is low (Frommelt, 2020b, p. 11). One can therefore argue that support for the EEA Agreement might be more related to vague sympathies, rather than stable attitudes. In this case, the high level of support for the EEA will only last as long as there are no alternatives to the EEA.

Although the different outcomes of the EEA referenda in Switzerland and Liechtenstein in 1992 showed that the Liechtenstein population has an independent opinion on European integration, the developments in Switzerland entail certain risks for Liechtenstein. As mentioned above, an increasing erosion of existing sectoral agreements could lead to more administrative burdens for Liechtenstein. Conversely, a clarification of institutional issues in the Swiss-EU relations could weaken the attractiveness of EEA membership.

SMALLNESS AND OTHER SPECIAL FEATURES

Theoretical approaches suggest that small states with market-oriented economic policies and high regulatory capabilities such as the EFTA states are more likely to join a common market than larger and less advanced states (Gstöhl, 2002, p. 532; Schimmelfennig and Winzen, 2020, p. 26). The incentives for integration increase when geographically close countries already participate in a larger market. But also the EFTA states' reluctance towards European integration can be explained by economic arguments such as wealth and economic prosperity (Mattli, 1999). Other explanations are: the specific characteristics of economic sectors, especially fishing in Norway and Iceland (Ingebritsen, 1998); the peculiarities of the political systems of the EFTA states, such as the long-standing rigidity of the Icelandic party system (Thórhallsson, 2015); the strong contrast between centre and periphery as well as the strength of the no movement; defence of the welfare state and gender equality in Norway (Fossum, 2019; Skinner Sundlisæter, 2012); the tradition of direct democracy, neutrality and federalism as the core of Switzerland's civic identity (Theiler, 2004); and the small size of Liechtenstein (Frommelt, 2016). Finally, strong national identities are likely to explain why sovereignty concerns are more salient in the EFTA states (Gstöhl, 2002).

Research on the causes of differentiated integration has so far been concentrated almost exclusively on the question of why the EFTA states have not yet joined the EU while there has been very little academic interest in the causes of specific opt-outs within the EEA acquis.

The demand for such opt-outs by Liechtenstein can be explained by five different dimensions (Frommelt, 2017, pp. 207–12). The first dimension relates to geographical factors such as the very small inhabitable area or the absence of specific geographical conditions such as waters which are used for navigation. In its decision of 10 March 1995, the EEA Council recognises 'that Liechtenstein has a very small inhabitable area of rural character' (EEA Council Decision 1/95, 1995, p. 80). The limited settlement area can be seen as a crucial factor to explain Liechtenstein's special solution in the field of free movement of persons (Frommelt, 2016). It is also likely to explain the fact that Liechtenstein could retain its legal provisions for foreign investments in the real estate market. Due to the absence of specific geographical conditions such as inland water or access to the sea, Liechtenstein is exempted from implementing the relevant acquis. Most of these opt-outs are not mentioned in the Annexes to the EEA Agreement but are notified by Liechtenstein to the EFTA Surveillance Authority (ESA). To give an example, Council Directive 96/50/EC of 23 July 1996 on the harmonisation of the conditions for obtaining national boatmasters' certificates for the carriage of goods and passengers by inland waterway is incorporated into the EEA Agreement but Liechtenstein has not transposed this directive into national law and ESA is very unlikely to ever require such a transposition.

Economic factors such as the limited market size or the lack of specific infrastructure can also explain Liechtenstein's numerous opt-outs. For example, an adaptation in Annex XI of the EEA Agreement refers to the small size of the Liechtenstein telecommunications market and thus the risk of market failure. Liechtenstein is not excluded from the implementation of the corresponding legal acts but the adaptation text states that the specific market conditions of Liechtenstein must be taken into account when examining its implementation, which gives the Liechtenstein legislator some kind of flexibility.

Administrative factors such as the number of administrative resources or a limited number of cases subject to a specific rule play a central role in explaining Liechtenstein's opt-outs from EU acts incorporated into the EEA Agreement. Due to its microstate structure, Liechtenstein's administration has only limited human resources. Accordingly, various adaptations to EU legal acts incorporated into the EEA Agreement provide for the delegation of certain implementation and surveillance tasks to neighbouring states – especially Switzerland, but also Austria and Germany. Examples of this can be found in air traffic or in the veterinary sector. Due to the small number of companies in Liechtenstein, certain statistical data cannot be collected or made publicly available, as it would be possible to draw conclusions about the companies concerned and thus data protection could no longer be guaranteed.

Liechtenstein is not only a member of the EEA, but is also in a customs union with Switzerland. Due to this 'parallel membership', Liechtenstein may require opt-outs from certain EU legal acts incorporated into the EEA Agreement. For example, Liechtenstein's accession to the EEA was only possible by a horizontal adaptation that allowed Liechtenstein to apply Swiss technical regulations and standards deriving from its regional union with Switzerland in parallel with EEA legislation on the Liechtenstein market (EEA Council No. 1/95, 1995). However, Liechtenstein was also granted specific exceptions in areas such as emissions trading, waste management, financial services or intellectual property in order not to jeopardise its regional union with Switzerland.

Finally, some of Liechtenstein's exceptions can be explained by its specific political and regulatory preferences. One example of this is Liechtenstein's non-membership in numerous EU programmes, which are in principle part of the EEA Agreement. Another example of a politically motivated opt-out is Liechtenstein's special solution in the field of transport, which allows Liechtenstein to levy a toll for heavy goods vehicles. Table 22.2 summarises the different explanations for Liechtenstein's country-specific opt-outs.

Various explanations of Liechtenstein's opt-outs are somehow related to the small size of Liechtenstein. However, it would be too simple to systematise all these opt-outs under the heading of limited state capacity. Indeed, it is not only a lack of capacity that explains the demand for opt-outs but the lack of political support to invest in capacity building and therefore to mobilise the respective capabilities. Given the large number of opt-outs, Liechtenstein is undoubtedly a special case. However, the explanatory patterns mentioned above can also be found in Iceland and Norway – albeit much less frequently. It can therefore be argued that

Table 22.2 Explanatory factors for Liechtenstein's differentiated integration in the EEA

Dimension	Cause	Example
Geographical factors	Small country size	Free movement of capital
	Geographical conditions	Inland waterways
Economic factors	Little market size	Telecommunication
	Lack of infrastructure	Combustion plants
Administrative factors	Limited administrative resources	Market authorisation
	Limited number of cases	Business statistics
Regional policy factors	Customs union with Switzerland	Parallel marketability
Political factors	Political preferences	Non-participation in EU programme Horizon 2020

Source: Own compilation; examples and legal references can be found in Frommelt (2017, p. 211).

within the scope of the EEA, the offer of exemptions for the EEA EFTA states is greater than for the EU states. This can be explained by the low negative externalities that the exceptions for the EEA EFTA states have on the EEA as a whole, but also by the complex institutional structure of the EEA.

WITHDRAWAL AGREEMENT BETWEEN THE EEA EFTA STATES AND THE UK

Following the referendum in the United Kingdom (UK) on leaving the EU (Brexit) in June 2016, the UK government formally notified the EU of its decision to leave on 29 March 2017. This marked the start of a two-year period of negotiations with the EU on the terms of an orderly withdrawal according to Article 50 TFEU. That proved, however, very difficult as the UK Parliament refused to give its consent to several draft agreements as none of these agreements could find a ready majority. Only in October 2019, the UK and the EU finally agreed on a withdrawal agreement. The agreement regulates in particular the acquired rights of citizens and the financial obligations of the UK. Until the end of 2020, the UK was to remain in the internal market (aka single market), but without co-decision rights. During this time, an agreement on future relations was to be negotiated.

For its future relations with the EU, the UK has opted for a free trade agreement (FTA) and against a closer integration model with the EU. The Trade and Cooperation Agreement (TCA) was concluded on 24 December 2020 and provisionally applied on 1 January 2021. Since 1 January 2021, the UK therefore is a third country. The character of the TCA, which – on insistence of the UK government – has no legal links to the EU's internal market, is only slightly more advanced than the standard FTAs the EU concluded with several EFTA states in 1972 and 1973. On that basis, a continuation of the previous level of integration and continued participation in the EU's internal market was not possible. In consequence, this also implied that the UK leaves the EU customs union and had to establish a customs border with the EU. That again caused problems on the island of Ireland where a visible border between Ireland and Northern Ireland had to be avoided to prevent civil unrest sparking again. Hence, the territory of Northern Ireland remained attached to the EU's internal market as far as the free movement of goods is concerned, 'along with all the guarantees it offers in terms of consumer protection, public and animal health protection, and combatting fraud and trafficking' (European Commission, 2020).

With Brexit accomplished, the UK has not only left the EU, but also the EEA. For almost 25 years, that agreement was the basis for economic relations between Liechtenstein and the UK. Based on the EEA Agreement, Liechtenstein citizens have numerous rights that they can invoke equally in all EU states and which they risked to lose once Brexit happened. Conversely, citizens from the UK had acquired numerous rights in Liechtenstein when the UK was still part of the EEA. These acquired rights had to be secured so that Brexit would not have a negative impact on life decisions that have already been made.

The withdrawal agreement between the EEA EFTA states and the UK (also known as 'Separation Agreement') (2020) ensures that EEA EFTA nationals already living in the UK or British nationals living in Iceland, Liechtenstein or Norway have largely the same rights as before. In addition to the right of residence, this also includes social security entitlements and the recognition of professional qualifications. Liechtenstein's right to restrict taking up residence under free movement rules remains untouched. As Norway, Iceland and Liechtenstein are part of the internal market, the separation agreement in addition to citizens' rights also deals with other issues arising from the UK's exit from the EU, such as data protection, intellectual property, goods already placed on the market and public procurement. For all of these issues, it is essentially foreseen that rights acquired before the end of the transition period will continue to be protected or that proceedings still ongoing at the end of the transition period will be terminated under the same provisions under which they were commenced. The Separation Agreement only applies to situations that existed before or on 31 December 2020. It does not regulate future relations with the UK.

The agreement was to be applied provisionally from 1 February 2020. This was guaranteed by Liechtenstein's Brexit Transition Act. This act also served as a legal basis for the national implementation of the transition period agreed between the EU and the UK. It states that the UK will continue to be considered an EEA or EU member state under Liechtenstein law during the transition period. This transition period, like that agreed under the respective Withdrawal Agreement between the EU and the UK, expired on 31 December 2020.

FUTURE ARRANGEMENTS

The general aim was to essentially replicate the legal relationship between the EFTA states and the UK when it still was an EU member state. Because Switzerland had rejected the ratification of its membership in the EEA in 1992, the basis for its trade with the UK was primarily the EU-Switzerland Free Trade Agreement from 1972 (FTA 1972). Subsequently, the bilateral agreements between the EU and Switzerland of which the first batch was signed in 1999 and the second in 2004 as well as several minor agreements were added. Iceland, Liechtenstein and Norway, however, joined the EEA and therefore had a more comprehensive legal basis to base their trade relations with the EU upon. Hence, the replication of these agreements under the new situation with the UK not being an EU member state anymore could not be the same at the outset. Furthermore, there was the special case of Liechtenstein: in 1923 Liechtenstein and Switzerland concluded the Customs Treaty (CT) by which Liechtenstein became a part of the Swiss customs territory. When Switzerland and the EU concluded the FTA 1972, that agreement was extended to Liechtenstein. It creates a free trade area for industrial products.

Later this was supplemented by the agricultural agreement between Switzerland and the EU which, again, was extended to Liechtenstein. Due to these different agreements and models of integration there was no solution that fits the relationship between the UK and all EFTA states.

For the last 25 years or more, trade in industrial and agricultural goods between Liechtenstein and the EU, and thus between Liechtenstein and the UK, have been governed by the FTA 1972 and the agricultural agreement between Switzerland and the EU. In addition to that, the EEA rules on the free movement of goods applied to the economic relations between Liechtenstein and the UK. On 31 December 2020, these two agreements, as well as the EEA Agreement, lost their applicability to the UK. Switzerland has concluded a trade agreement with the UK that more or less replicates six of the bilateral agreements between Switzerland and the EU in relation to the UK. Two of these agreements – the Free Trade Agreement and the Agreement on Agriculture – are extended to Liechtenstein via an additional agreement analogous to the two Switzerland-EU agreements (Trade Agreement between the UK and Switzerland, 2019). The supplementary agreement ensures the continuation of duty-free trade in industrial products and processed agricultural products between Liechtenstein and the UK. It entered into force on 1 January 2021.

The other parts of the EEA Agreement, like services, capital, movement of workers, intellectual property, competition, public procurement etc., that had ceased to apply between Liechtenstein and the UK had to be regulated through a new instrument. Therefore, the three EEA EFTA states and the UK concluded a free trade agreement (EEA EFTA-UK FTA), which was signed in London on 8 July 2021. From Liechtenstein's point of view this – for the moment – completes the reorganisation of economic relations with the UK. It covers cross-border trade in services, including financial services, as well as areas such as investment, intellectual property protection, digital trade, capital movements and public procurement. In particular, the agreement prevents discrimination against companies from the EU and offers Liechtenstein economic actors preferential market access compared to countries that do not have an agreement with the UK. The EEA EFTA-UK FTA essentially – as mentioned before – is a conventional FTA, albeit a very comprehensive one. In terms of content and structure, it is modelled on the Trade and Cooperation Agreement between the EU and the UK, but it also resembles many FTAs concluded by the EFTA states with third countries. The agreement entered into force at the beginning of September 2022.

INITIAL ASSESSMENT OF THE NEW ECONOMIC RELATIONS BETWEEN LIECHTENSTEIN AND THE UK

The new trade and economic relations between Liechtenstein and the UK are based on two (sets of) agreements: (1) the Additional Agreement of 11 February 2019 between the United Kingdom of Great Britain and Northern Ireland, the Swiss Confederation and the Principality of Liechtenstein and (2) the Free Trade Agreement between Iceland, the Principality of Liechtenstein and the Kingdom of Norway and the United Kingdom of Great Britain and Northern Ireland (2021). Generally speaking, the former covers the movement of goods while the latter covers all other areas, such as services, capital movements, sustainable development etc. Of course, a precise delimitation may at times be difficult. Therefore, the Agreement(s) by which Liechtenstein participates in the economic relation between Switzerland and the UK shall prevail 'in case of any inconsistencies' (Article 1.4 (2) EEA EFTA-UK FTA).

The aim of the EEA EFTA-UK FTA was to essentially replace the provisions of the EEA Agreement that applied between the parties before Brexit. The question may therefore be asked whether Liechtenstein being subject to the Additional Agreement UK-CH-LI (2019) – substantially inspired from the FTA 1972 – leads to another quality of the relation than if the part on goods from the EEA EFTA FTA were applicable to Liechtenstein as well. This is not the place to elaborate on a detailed comparison. The major feature of both agreements, however, is that they both are FTAs. In the EEA EFTA-UK FTA there is nothing left of an 'internal market logic' either (Baur, 2020). Hence, it can, again, be said that both agreements are rather conventional FTAs, albeit that the EEA EFTA-UK FTA is more modern and comprehensive.

It is, however, rather important to see where the new economic relation falls short of the legal framework as it exists in the EEA in an area that is very important to Liechtenstein, namely, financial services. These are covered in Articles 3.44 to 3.54 of the EEA EFTA-UK FTA. Contrary to the harmonised rules in the EEA, these are rather standard rules as can be found in many FTAs. For example, financial intermediaries do not have general access through 'passports' anymore but they depend on equivalence decisions for their market access in either market. Hence, respective EU equivalence decisions are applied in Liechtenstein via the EEA Agreement. The UK, for its part, has already issued several unilateral equivalence decisions which also apply to Liechtenstein. By comparison, the financial services policy of Switzerland and the UK – which is not yet supported by a respective agreement – in their mutual relation aims at a more ambitious agenda. In that vein, the UK and Switzerland are indeed negotiating a financial services agreement (Triebe, 2020). All this is, however, only early days of a new development altogether.

To sum up, with Brexit, economic and political relations with the UK had to be put on a new footing. After five years of negotiations, several agreements resulted that are quite significant for Liechtenstein's integration in Europe. The Liechtenstein government (2021, p. 10) describes the new FTA as the most comprehensive FTA Liechtenstein has ever concluded. However, the government does not hide the fact that the agreement is significantly less far-reaching than the previous relations with the UK based on the EEA Agreement. The room for manoeuvre in the negotiations on future relations with the UK was always limited by the fact that the functioning of the EEA should not be jeopardised. It is therefore not surprising that EEA EFTA-UK FTA is closely modelled on the EU-UK-FTA. Finally, the Brexit process showed how dependent Liechtenstein is on both Switzerland and its EEA EFTA partners, Norway and Iceland. The parallel membership in the EEA and the customs union with Switzerland is crucial for Liechtenstein but as long as the Swiss-EU relations do not match the scope of the EEA Agreement it is an ongoing institutional and administrative challenge.

CONCLUSIONS

We have shown that Liechtenstein, albeit a very small state that is compelled to lean on bigger neighbours for support, managed to join the EEA Agreement. It did so, despite Switzerland's abstention and against all odds, like limited human resources and administrative capacity etc. In the context of smallness, Liechtenstein's various exceptions need to be pointed out. These exceptions have different reasons, partly smallness as such, partly because Liechtenstein may be allowed to join Switzerland to regulate a question as a consequence of the Swiss-Liechtenstein customs union or other reasons. Also a factor of smallness, the narrative of the EEA as a gain in sovereignty has been addressed. It is this very context that explains why this contradicts the narratives in the other EEA EFTA states.

Another interesting point was the special ways in which Liechtenstein combines European integration and direct democracy. Mainly in comparison with the Swiss way of applying direct democratic principles and procedures to issues of European integration, Liechtenstein is, legally and in reality, much less exposed to the political instrumentalisation of direct democratic instruments such as referenda and popular initiatives to challenge national European policies. Legally, inasmuch as there is a clear procedure that aims at eliminating conflicts with international and European law and that is based on the principle of the rule of law. In reality, a consequence thereof is that no referenda have taken place since Liechtenstein joined the EEA.

Finally, we mentioned the example of how the EFTA states, but Liechtenstein in particular, solved their predicament of being left without agreement after Brexit. Again, a result at least partly due to its smallness, Liechtenstein could not join Iceland and Norway entirely in the agreement between the EEA/EFTA states and the UK. With regard to the free movement of goods, it had to join the framework agreement between the UK and Switzerland that essentially serves the same purpose, in an additional agreement. That agreement substantially refers to the Free Trade and the Agriculture Agreements between the EU and Switzerland, which apply to Liechtenstein due to the customs union. Their provisions apply between the parties *mutatis mutandis*. With regard to substance, however, there is little difference between either Liechtenstein being part of the EEA/EFTA-UK FTA and Liechtenstein being a party to the UK-Switzerland Trade Agreement.

Liechtenstein may be a very small state, but a certain pragmatism on all sides and Liechtenstein's openness towards international and European law helps finding solutions where, at first sight, none may seem available. And the fact that there was no 'ideological', EU-related antagonism between the UK and the EFTA states certainly helped as well.

NOTE

1. I would like to thank Dr Georges Baur for his support in the preparation of this chapter.

REFERENCES

Agreement on arrangements between Iceland, the Principality of Liechtenstein, the Kingdom of Norway and the United Kingdom of Great Britain and Northern Ireland following the withdrawal of the United Kingdom from the European Union, the EEA Agreement and other agreements applicable between the United Kingdom and the EEA EFTA States by virtue of the United Kingdom's membership of the European Union (EEA EFTA Seperation Agreement) (2020).

Agreement on the European Economic Area (EEA Agreement) (1994). *Official Journal of the European Union*, L 1/3.

Agreement on the withdrawal of the United Kingdom of Great Britain and Northern Ireland from the European Union and the European Atomic Energy Community (Withdrawal Agreement) (2019). *Official Journal of the European Union*, C 384 I/1.

Baur, G. (2020). *The European Free Trade Association*. Intersentia.

Bekkedal, T. (2019). Third state participation in EU Agencies: Exploring the EEA precedent. *Common Market Law Review*, *56*(2), 381–416.

Constitution of the Principality of Liechtenstein (1921). No 15. https://www.llv.li/files/rdr/Verfassung-E-01-02-2014.pdf.

Decision of the EEA Council No. 1/95 of 10 March 1995 in the entry into force of the Agreement on the European Economic Area for the Principality of Liechenstein (1995). *Official Journal of the European Union*, L 86/54.

European Commission (2020). Protocol on Ireland and Northern Ireland. *European Commission*. https://ec.europa.eu/info/strategy/relations-non-eu-countries/relations-united-kingdom/eu-uk-withdrawal-agreement/protocol-ireland-and-northern-ireland_en.

Fossum, J.E. (2019). Norway and the European Union. *Oxford Research Encyclopedia of Politics*. https://doi.org/10.1093/acrefore/9780190228637.013.1043.

Free Trade Agreement between the United Kingdom of Great Britain and Northern Ireland and Iceland, the Principality of Liechtenstein and the Kingdom of Norway (2021).

Frommelt, C. (2016). Liechtenstein's tailor-made arrangements in the EEA: A small state's creative solutions in European integration. In S. Wolf (ed.), *State size matters. Politik und Recht im Kontext von Kleinstaatlichkeit und Monarchie, Wiesbaden* (pp. 131–62). Springer.

Frommelt, C. (2017). *In Search of Effective Differentiated Integration: Lessons from the European Economic Area (EEA)*. Doctoral dissertation, ETH Zürich. https://www.liechtenstein-institut.li/application/files/7615/7435/5550/Thesis_Frommelt_final.pdf.

Frommelt, C. (2020a). *Institutional Challenges for External Differentiated Integration: The Case of the EEA*. Robert Schuman Centre for Advanced Studies, Research Paper No. RSCAS, 65. https://papers.ssrn.com/sol3/papers.cfm?abstract_id=3712440.

Frommelt, C. (2020b). *25 Years of Liechtenstein's EEA Membership – Survey Findings*. Study on behalf of the Ministry of General Government Affairs and Finance. Liechtenstein Institute. https://www.liechtenstein-institut.li/application/files/6016/0155/2129/Frommelt_2020.03.26_EEA_Membership_Final.pdf.

Frommelt, C., and Gstöhl, S. (2011). *Liechtenstein and the EEA: The Europeanization of a (very) small state*. Europautredningen. https://www.liechtenstein-institut.li/application/files/9515/7435/1176/Liechtenstein-and-the-EEA.pdf.

Gstöhl, S. (2002). *Reluctant Europeans: Norway, Sweden and Switzerland in the Process of Integration*. Lynne Rienner.

Gstöhl, S., and Fommelt, C. (2017). Back to the future? Lessons of differentiated integration from the EFTA countries for the UK's future relations with the EU. *Social Sciences*, *6*(4), 1–17.

Ingebritsen, C. (1998). *The Nordic States and European Unity*. Cornell University Press.

Liechtenstein Government (2021). Bericht und Antrag der Regierung an den Landtag des Fürstentums Liechtenstein betreffend das Freihandelsabkommen zwischen Island, dem Fürstentum Liechtenstein, dem Königreich Norwegen und dem Vereinigten Königreich von Grossbritannien und Nordirland, Nr. 77/2021.

Mattli, W. (1999). *The Logic of Regional Integration: Europe and Beyond*. Cambridge University Press.

Pelkmans, J., and Böhler, P. (2013). *The EEA Review and Liechtenstein's Integration Strategy*. Centre for European Policy Studies. https://www.ceps.eu/ceps-publications/eea-review-and-liechtensteins-integration-strategy/.

Schimmelfennig, F., and Winzen, T. (2020). *Ever Looser Union? Differentiated European Integration*. Oxford University Press.

Skinner Sundlisæter, M. (2012). Norwegian Euroscepticism: Values, identity or interest. *Journal of Common Market Studies*, *50*(3), 422–40.

Theiler, T. (2004). The origins of Euroscepticism in German-speaking Switzerland. *European Journal of Political Research*, *43*(4), 635–56.

Thórhallsson, B. (2015). Iceland: A reluctant European? In E.O. Eriksen and J.E. Fossum (eds), *The European Union's Non-Members. Independence under Hegemony?* (pp. 181–36). Routledge.

Thürer, D. (1998). Liechtenstein und die Völkerrechtsordnung. Ein Kleinstaat im völkerrechtlichen Spannungsfeld zwischen Singularität und Modell rechtlicher Integration. *Archiv des Völkerrechts*, *36*(2), 98–127.

Trade Agreement between the United Kingdom of Great Britain and Northern Ireland and the Swiss Confederation (2019).

Trade and Cooperation Agreement between the European Union and the European Atomic Energy Community, of the one part, and the United Kingdom of Great Britain and Northern Ireland, of the other part (EU-UK Trade and Cooperation Agreement) (2021). *Official Journal of the European Union*, L 149/10.

Triebe, B. (2020, 2 July). Die EU darf von der Schweiz lernen darf. *Neue Zürcher Zeitung*, p. 26.

PART V

BREXIT BEYOND EUROPE

23. The 2020 EU-UK Trade and Cooperation Agreement as a Canada style agreement

Nanette Neuwahl

INTRODUCTION[1]

On 31 January 2020 the United Kingdom (UK) became the first European Union (EU) Member State ever to leave the Union, following a popular referendum held three and a half years earlier, on 26 June 2016. Needless to say, the (economic and other) impact of Brexit depends much on the post-Brexit relationship between the EU and the UK, and it has often been suggested that the best form that that relationship could take would be a so-called 'Canada-plus' relationship (Neuwahl, 2017). However, the EU had made it quite clear when outlining its starting position in the negotiations that a 'Canada' style agreement would be available to the UK only under certain additional conditions, prompting British Prime Minister Boris Johnson to exclaim to a domestic audience that the EU was 'discriminating' against the UK. The EU on the other hand insisted that, due to the geographical closeness of the UK to the trading bloc, and in order to avoid unfair competition, it was necessary that it align with the EU in a number of policy fields, a requirement not asked of Canada. Thus, the idea that Canada could be a good model for the future relations between the UK and the EU has been disputed from the beginning of the negotiations on the future relations. Has the EU given in?

This chapter attempts to locate the 2020 EU–UK Trade and Cooperation Agreement (TCA) among other agreements that the EU has previously negotiated with third countries (European Commission, 2020a). It does so in the context of the EU3D research project coordinated by ARENA Centre for European Studies at the University of Oslo in Norway. EU3D looks into differentiation as a form of governance and its impact on society and democracy (Fossum, 2019a). As such, this chapter looks into the question of the EU's external differentiation, or differentiation in foreign policy. We are seeking more clarity on the following questions: Does the TCA fall within a familiar differentiation track? In particular, is it a 'Canada style' agreement rather than 'Norway style' agreement? In practical terms, to what extent is the TCA an attempt to nudge the UK towards conformity to the EU over time, which is the characteristic of a Norway style agreement? Is the TCA in any way a concession to the UK's pleas for a bespoke agreement? How, if at all, does the agreement show that 'geography matters' for the EU and the UK? Might the agreement be in a category all of its own?

Although EU Chief negotiator Michel Barnier at one point denied the UK a Canada style agreement, it will not have been lost on regular observers that, in parts, the agreement looks very much like one of those so-called mega-regional treaties that the EU has been negotiating and concluding across the globe – including the Comprehensive Economic and Trade Agreement with Canada (CETA). The TCA definitely shares objective characteristics with these agreements, which Velut et al. (2018) suggests in his introduction to an edited volume on these 'new generation' agreements, namely, the importance of the agreement in terms of GDP, its wide-ranging regulatory scope, and the fact of it being a 'living' instrument – meaning that such agreements are dynamic in character.

These are modern treaties, capable of dealing with the challenges of trading in an evolving regulatory environment, and in a context where the World Trade Organization (WTO), the global institution that governs trade, is paralysed by disagreements and polarisation. Historically, there have been several different waves of trade agreements. Classical bilateral agreements were followed, especially after the Second World War, by regional and global agreements such as the North Atlantic Free Trade Agreement (NAFTA) and the General Agreement on Tariffs and Trade (GATT). The recently negotiated mega free trade agreements are cross-regional agreements that seek to overcome the boundaries between existing trade blocs by building bridges between different regions (Velut et al., 2018). There is a strategic connotation to them, in the sense that they are about seeking trade alliances across the world between like-minded partners in order to overcome an impasse in global trade regulation. To draw a parallel between parts of the TCA and existing cross-regional trade agreements is not far-fetched in any way, and it even seems particularly appropriate in this case as there are socio-cultural aspects of Brexit that such mega-regional agreements are meant to address.

The TCA does not correspond in all respects to what mega-regional agreements seek to do. The 'strategic' aspects of the TCA have, so far, remained underdeveloped, and the discourse surrounding the TCA was not the same as that around CETA or Transatlantic Trade and Investment Partnership (TTIP). The dynamics of the negotiations between the EU and the UK during Brexit and the rhetoric surrounding it looked more like damage control than strategic partnership building. Yet, a partnership between the EU and the UK certainly can be conceived in a similar way to those other instances. Incidentally, CETA has been called a 'modest version of a mega-regional', a 'learning exercise' in experimentalist government or a WTO-plus agreement (Fahey, 2017), and also from this viewpoint it is an interesting comparison for the TCA.

Nevertheless, the question ought to be raised whether, in some respects, trade agreements between regional integration organisations and former Member States ought to be in a category all of their own. This may well be the case as regards the WTO's most favoured nation (MFN) principle (GATT Article I and GATS[2] Article II), an exception to which is laid down for customs unions and free trade areas in Article XXIV GATT, c.q. for integration agreements in Article V GATS. The exit of a Member State from a customs union puts a question mark over the continued availability of the exception to the MFN principle which the Member States of that union used to enjoy. The EU, like the WTO, is navigating in uncharted waters here. Arguably in the case of CETA, a new, deep trade agreement was being established, triggering the (cross-) regional integration exception to the MFN clauses. Such an argument seems compatible with the WTO's spirit. And indeed, Article 11.4 CETA states that the agreement is 'in conformity' with Article XXIV GATT and Article V GATS. The TCA does likewise (Article OTH.3: Establishment of a free trade area). However, the UK leaving the EU leads to the resurgence of previously eliminated trade barriers between WTO members. As a result, additional conditions might have to apply under WTO law before one might be able to invoke an exception to the MFN principle. One might have to show that, substantially, Brexit does not change much from a trade point of view as compared to the previously existing situation, especially since there is no change in tariff treatment. In particular, it might be required that there be little or no adverse effects on third countries and that there be a comprehensive approach to trade liberalisation. In order to rule out regression, perhaps a level playing field has to be agreed to, such as that which existed before the split. Since WTO members do not take a legalistic approach to these questions (CBC News, 1999), a definitive answer may not emerge anytime soon. However, it gives scope for thinking that the TCA still needs to find its place in the midst of a growing body of international economic law.

It is worth stressing also that the TCA, like CETA, seeks to address non-trade issues, which today may be considered just as important as the elimination of tariffs and quantitative restrictions to trade. In the latter, the character of the TCA as a 'living instrument' may be relevant. If the parties would be concluding a static trade agreement of a technical character, then everything would be relatively simple, but as soon as the agreement becomes a commitment to an evolving cooperation, with decision-makers being able to make a difference to the social and environmental circumstances of ordinary citizens, then democratic accountability becomes important (see, however, the peculiar situation of Norway as explained in: Fossum, 2019b). The TCA certainly shares distinct democratic challenges with the mega-regional trade agreements, including the intentional flexibility of the agreement with regard to future developments. This is in part concomitant with the new, digital age, affecting the growing service industry in particular. To enable the development of a legitimate, modern international regulatory framework, the process of regulatory change must be transparent and accessible to stakeholders and/or parliaments. What we will see in these agreements, therefore, is a tendency to involve stakeholders. Stakeholder empowerment leads to direct involvement in the life of the agreement and, to some extent, a reproduction of political life, externalising it to the international level. This is definitely uncharted territory in terms of WTO law.

In line with these developments we will also see, in such agreements, tendencies (1) to exclude rights of private parties and domestic justiciability ('direct effect'); (2) to avoid institutionalised international courts; and (3) to allow intergovernmental solutions, including through the suspension of rights by parties as a retortion for violations of the agreement by the other party. The TCA excludes all direct effect in domestic law as of principle (Article COMPROV.16: Private rights). In this respect, it is different from classical bilateral agreements concluded by the EU. The Court of Justice of the European Union (CJEU) has not yet clearly expressed itself on the constitutionality of restricting the effect of 'partnership provisions' in EU courts. While recognising that the TCA may eventually have to be considered in a category of its own for WTO purposes, the following section considers how this new agreement compares to a 'Canada style' agreement as regards its scope, its institutional features and its dynamic character.

The next section deals with the similarities and differences in the substantive remit of a 'Canada style agreement' and the TCA. The third section compares the institutional set-up of the CETA and the TCA, including adjudicatory dispute settlement and governmental control on it. The fourth section then deals with the dynamic aspects of a Canada style agreement and the requirement of a level playing field as opposed to a mere regulatory cooperation. In the fifth section we will by way of conclusions summarise and evaluate our findings. It will appear that the TCA is a variant of a Canada-type agreement and that both the UK and Canada could constitute valuable partners of the EU on the international scene.

SUBSTANTIVE REMIT

Since both the UK and the EU have referred to a Canada style relationship during the negotiations of the TCA, Canada-EU relations are a good point to start looking for comparisons. EU-Canada relations are governed by a whole set of international agreements (Neuwahl, 2018a), but predominantly by the Comprehensive Economic and Trade Agreement (CETA) and the Strategic Partnership Agreement (SPA) that complements it (Neuwahl, 2018a; Prince, 2017; Van Overmeire and Nichay, 2016). CETA is a document of almost 1,600 pages and annexes (Council of the EU, 2016). Its main objective is to eliminate, as far as possible, all obstacles to trade and investment between the parties. The official negotiations started on 6 May 2009, after an important scoping exercise of several years, and they were concluded on 26 September 2014. After a period of 'legal scrubbing', the agreements were eventually signed on 30 October 2016 and approved by the European Parliament on 15 February 2017. Just like the SPA, CETA has been applied provisionally since September 2017[3] and consequently binds Canada and EU and its Member States, while the latter are ratifying the agreement for matters in their competence – essentially, portfolio investment and (aspects of) Investor-State Dispute Settlement (ISDS). Ninety per cent of the subjects covered come under the external trade powers of the EU, while the Member States internally still share powers for implementation. Whereas CETA is the economic and trade pillar of the partnership, the SPA provides a framework for security, justice and foreign policy coordination that was conceived specifically for EU-Canada relations. Although this chapter deals mainly with CETA, politically, the SPA is closely related to it. Together, they form the two main pillars of the relationship between the EU and Canada, with a number of sectoral agreements 'floating around' that mainly existed before the conclusion of CETA (Neuwahl, 2018a).

Could CETA and the SPA have inspired EU-UK relations? Most definitely, although there was never any attempt to cut and paste their provisions directly into EU-UK relations, since such agreements are negotiated chapter by chapter, line by line and tariff schedule by tariff schedule. Nevertheless, an EU-Canada style relationship has undeniably been considered relevant for post-Brexit EU-UK relations, because its appeal is at least fourfold:

1. CETA eliminates all tariffs and quotas on goods originating in the territory of its members, with the exception of just a few sensitive areas (cars, dairy products). Customs controls, VAT checks and sanitary checks are not affected by it. The TCA is based on similar principles, and for good reason. Under the TCA the UK and the EU profit from the continuation of tariff-free access to each other's markets. Since tariffs make imports more expensive, their elimination helps to maintain an attractive level of consumer prices and competitive costs of production inputs. Under the WTO's MFN rules this is permitted when a regional agreement liberalises trade for substantially all goods.
2. CETA reaffirms the principle of national treatment (non-discrimination) between the parties as regards goods and services and recalls the commercial defence mechanisms and other rules that apply in the WTO context.
3. The deep trading relationship between the EU and Canada is furthermore inspired by a wish to expand and modernise WTO regimes, mimicking to a certain extent the EU common market (regulatory cooperation) without exactly copying it, and tending to both commerce and security objectives. It is an attempt at policy alignment between Canada and the EU, although each party retains the right to legislate. Due to its comprehensive

character, the EU and Canada aspire to creating a special regime relative to global rules while contributing to a rules-based international order.

4. CETA and SPA put into place a coordination of Canada's and the EU's policies that is transposable to the UK-EU partnership. Clearly, it has never been the intention of either party to simply 'copy-paste' CETA or the SPA to UK-EU relations as the commercial and other relationships are different from the start. But those agreements contain rules and concepts that are of considerable interest when considering EU-UK relations. This is not only because the agreements establish privileged relationships. It is because they regulate matters in an orderly fashion. There is much value in making agreements between the EU and the UK, but perhaps even more in ensuring that they are compatible with other agreements, so as to minimise disputes.

What has been lacking from the relations between the UK and the EU is a joint 'scoping exercise' spanning several years, involving civil society and stakeholders, which could have served to help decide on the orientation of the negotiations. The Political Declaration on the future relations between the UK and the EU (European Commission, 2019), although important, does not fulfil the same objectives, nor does it give insight into the consequences for different sectors of the economy. This did not really help decide which areas to include or to exclude. On both sides there was hope that cooperation between the EU and the UK could be more ambitious than any previous agreement, but there emerged no clear strategy as to how to achieve that. In the end, a number of issues had to be deferred to sometime in the future. Given the time pressure, the parties could not be overly ambitious due to at least three aspects: (1) the sensitivity of certain topics; (2) the severability of less urgent topics; and (3) a desire to avoid a mixed agreement – an agreement that covers areas of both Union and Member State competence and is signed by both the former and the latter.

Judging from its substantive provisions alone, the TCA resembles a Canada style agreement. Like CETA, it goes beyond classic bilateral free trade agreements, covering a great range of subjects such as trade in goods and in services, trade-related matters, investments, digital trade, intellectual property, public procurement, aviation and road transport, energy, fisheries, social security coordination, law enforcement and judicial cooperation in criminal matters. A full overview of the TCA is given in a European Parliament Research Report (EPRS, 2021) together with the negotiating positions of both the EU and the UK. The core, however, consists of trade and (non-trade but) trade-related issues. In the following we will compare the commitments under CETA with the TCA as regards the most salient issues in UK-EU relations.

Trade

Two-way zero-tariff access of goods is an important part of the TCA, but not the one promising most economic growth. Commentators have pointed to the fact that the 'Canada model' hardly covers services that are key to UK industry – particularly financial services – and many considered this one of the most prominent 'disadvantages' of the Canadian model for EU-UK relations. To be sure, CETA does cover services. In this context as well as in relation to goods, it includes provisions that both reiterate and reinforce the WTO principle of national treatment, combined with an obligation of non-regression or stand-still: 'once liberalised, always liberalised'. Even so, CETA allows the parties to exempt certain sensitive aspects from the scope of the agreement, and the EU has used this option regarding financial services; local licensing requirements, a formidable obstacle to the provision of financial services for third states, are essentially not in conflict with CETA and there is no provision made for passporting (automatic recognition) the way the UK was accustomed to in the EU Single Market (Norton Rose Fulbright, 2017). None of this breaches WTO law, which leaves a discretion to the contracting parties in this respect.

There are good reasons why this 'plus' bit of the 'Canada-plus' model was not going to be achieved. Oppenheim and Grant (2017) have argued that if Britain would propose the inclusion of its cherished service industries ('Canada-plus'), the EU would make it 'costly' by requiring the UK to pay into the EU's budget. However, referring just to cost is missing an important aspect. The free movement of services has long been a challenge for the EU legislator in many sectors. The EU Services Directive 2006/123/EC (2006) excluded many sensitive sectors from its remit. One of the great harmonisation achievements was the Financial Services Regulations (BBA, 2016) which provided for the automatic admission of financial services provided by subsidiaries from banks in other Member States, given certain sector-specific conditions under the (regularly supervised) responsibility of the country of origin. If the EU would continue to give such 'passporting rights' to the UK after Brexit and without guarantees, it would be surrendering control to a foreign country. This would be just as much a red line for the EU as it would be for the UK. Rather than to outsource consumer protection in this area entirely to an entity it could not supervise at all, the EU would exclude the issue from the negotiations. What was offered instead for goods and services was tariff-free access to each other's markets, principles of national treatment, and non-regression clauses and cooperation. The UK needed to accept that it would lose the privileged position it had in financial services when it was still a member of the Single Market. In this context, it may not have helped the UK that under the provisions of CETA, if the EU would be giving the UK unrestricted access to the financial service market of the EU, it would have to offer the same right to Canada.

The services part of the TCA therefore is comparable to CETA's. Like CETA, the TCA has substantial sectoral coverage, including professional and business services (e.g. legal, auditing, architectural services), delivery and telecommunication services, computer-related and digital services, financial services, research and development services, most transport services and environmental services. The actual level of market access depends on the way the service is supplied: whether it is supplied on a cross-border basis from the home country of the supplier, for example, over the internet ('mode 1'); supplied to the consumer in the country of the supplier, for example, tourism ('mode 2'); supplied via a locally established enterprise owned by the foreign service supplier ('mode 3') or through the temporary physical presence in the territory of another country ('mode 4').

Like under CETA there are non-discrimination obligations ensuring that service suppliers or investors from the UK will be treated no less favourably in any Member State than it treats its own operators. This entitles them to receive more favourable treatment than that granted to service providers or investors of third countries without similar provisions in place. However, UK service suppliers have lost automatic rights to offer services across the EU. Like Canadian service suppliers they will have to comply with a patchwork of host-country rules in each Member State, and may need to establish themselves in the EU to continue operating. Many have already done so. The TCA does not provide for the recognition of mutual qualifications but, like CETA, it allows the parties to agree, on a case-by-case basis, additional arrangements for the mutual recognition of certain professional qualifications.

As regards legal services, the TCA (Part Two, Title II, Articles SERVIN.5.47-50) gives UK solicitors, barristers and advocates the right to advise clients across the EU on UK and public international (not EU) law while using their home professional titles, except where EU Member States have placed specific limits on this activity as specified in the Annex to the agreement. There is no automatic right to advise cross-border, over the internet ('mode 1') or through a temporary presence ('mode 4'). This is because individual states retain their own rules for how third country lawyers may practise in their jurisdiction. In the past, UK solicitors have been able to establish under 'home' title in any EU Member State, and to offer advice on UK law or the law of the host state, including EU law. They were also able to provide temporary cross-border legal services, without the need to register with the host Member State's authorities. By contrast, the TCA contains an innovating title on digital trade and data protection (TCA, Part Two, Title III, Articles DIGIT.1-DIGIT.7).

Non-Trade Issues

One of the most innovative areas of cooperation of CETA was sustainable development. This is dealt with in CETA Chapters 22–24, including more specific chapters on trade and labour (CETA, Chapter 23) and on trade and the environment (CETA, Chapter 24). Arguably, those provisions are of special importance. In CETA, one finds no hard commitments as regards chemicals, biotechnology, the transition towards renewable energy and the decarbonisation of industry. CETA does not foresee a 'duty to regulate' of the kind which appears in human rights discourse relating to the environment. This is no doubt due to the fact that, whereas the right to a healthy environment is being recognised in European law, in practice, Canada and the EU do not share precisely the same values (Misonne, 2016) and they have not signed up to the same multilateral agreements. In comparison, the UK starts off from a position of close alignment to the EU on environmental standards. However, in future it may be tempted, in light of the promise of new trade deals with Canada and the US, to relax its rules on the admissibility of products such as hormone treated beef, chlorinated chicken and produce obtained through genetical engineering or the use of dangerous pesticides, in particular by abandoning the precautionary principle that applies in the EU context. For this reason, the TCA contains provisions seeking to prevent this from happening, to which we shall return later (third and fourth sections). In CETA, commitments to uphold sustainable development standards are 'soft' or 'cooperative' – there is no recourse to standing dispute settlement mechanisms for their enforcement. If a party claims that CETA is being violated, an expert panel may be established to find a 'mutually satisfactory plan' (CETA, Articles 23.10.12 and 24.15.11). This is in marked contrast to a 'Norway type agreement' that asks for alignment with the EU under the supervision of an EFTA court and involving interpretation of EU law by the European Court of Justice (Tatham, 2014).

During the negotiations between the EU and the UK, the EU at first insisted on full and dynamic alignment of the UK, also because of its suspicion that the UK would roll over CETA in its relations with Canada, and perhaps the US, which would leave the UK exposed to transatlantic pressure: if the UK would conclude deep trade agreements with Canada and the US, it might adopt environmental laws of a lower standard than hitherto, in order to accommodate the export interests of those countries. The TCA, while not obliging Britain to align with the EU, contains non-regression clauses forbidding it to regress from the level attained by the end of the transition period (TCA, Part Two, Title XI, Chapter Six, Article 6.2: Environmental levels of protection). As regards the chapter on trade and labour, the issues are not fundamentally different, be it that the subject is of course workers' protection (TCA, Part Two, Title XI, Chapter Seven, Article 7.2: Labour and social standards). CETA is a trade agreement and therefore not principally concerned with labour and social standards. Nevertheless, such standards have an impact on the competitiveness of exports in goods and services, as well as a relevance to the EU's post-Lisbon external non-trade (social) objectives. Whereas CETA uses soft commitments and diplomacy in this area, the EU's stance towards the UK was to ask for alignment. The EU has since dropped the requirement of dynamic alignment, as well as introduced unique dispute settlement provisions. We shall get back to this later (see the fourth section below 'Freedom to legislate and dynamics of alignment' and the subsection 'Dispute settlement' in the third section). The TCA furthermore forbids to drop taxation standards (Title XI, Chapter Five, Article 5.2: Taxation standards).

Other

In theory, the partnership between the EU and the UK could well have been more ambitious than the relation with Canada, in the sense that it could include continued advanced security and defence cooperation, financial services and civil aviation. But most of these matters have been postponed to be agreed upon later, separately or under the umbrella of the TCA partnership. Given the short time-span until the end of the transition-period (which the UK did not intend to prolong), and given the differences between the positions of the parties, not everything that was on the table was agreeable this time round. Even on fisheries there was little common ground. However, the TCA explicitly provides for the possibility of a growing body of agreements to be concluded in the framework of one 'Partnership' (TCA, COMPROV.2). Meanwhile, especially in the context of the – unprecedented – COVID-19 crisis of 2020, it had become important to focus particularly on trade (certainly in connection with non-trade matters) and on setting up an evolving cooperation driven by innovative institutional provisions like those under other deep trade agreements.

The content of the TCA may also have been affected by the intention to avoid a mixed agreement. The disadvantage of a mixed agreement is that until the agreement is ratified by all the 27 Member States, the EU can only apply it provisionally, leaving both parties the possibility to put a stop to the application under public international law. Several commentators have suggested that the EU might want to avoid a mixed agreement by concluding and bringing into effect an agreement that covers only matters that come under the exclusive competences of the EU as defined by the CJEU in its Opinion 2/15 on the EU-Singapore Free Trade Agreement (CJEU, 2017). In the case of the TCA a mixed agreement could be avoided by providing for a gradually growing body of agreements (TCA, COMPROV.2), making the TCA flexible enough to avoid the inclusion of matters coming under exclusive (or even shared) Member State external competences. This way, the partnership could be brought into force immediately (subject to European Parliament approval) as regards matters coming within EU competence, while referring any issues that did not have to be tackled immediately to a later stage, including Investor State Dispute Settlement (ISDS) and portfolio investments. As we shall see later, ISDS is currently excluded from the TCA, and so are portfolio investments.

INSTITUTIONAL FEATURES

A Canada style relationship has certain institutional arrangements that it shares with several other deep trade agreements and which are different from those applying in the EU Single Market, the European Economic Area (EEA) and other models that may be used for comparison. Whereas the EU and the EEA basically have one set of institutions for the entire range of issues covered, CETA allows for much more differentiation, and so does the TCA. The most important institutions and their field of application are considered in this section. The first subsection will deal with dispute settlement provisions and the second with the committee structure and governmental control.

Dispute Settlement

CETA provides two main types of dispute resolution mechanisms: intergovernmental (through diplomatic or adjudicatory channels) and ISDS. The latter constitutes an innovative system of international arbitration between private parties and public authorities. Both CETA and the TCA explicitly exclude national courts. One of the reasons for doing so could be that domestic court adjudication might lead to a more fragmented interpretation of international legal provisions. Article 30.6 of CETA, a provision echoed by the TCA (Article COMPROV.16: Private rights), excludes any 'direct effect', which means that their provisions cannot be invoked before a national court. This domestic non-justiciability knows only small exceptions. CETA Article 19.17 evokes the possibility of domestic judicial review procedures in the specific field of government procurement. This leaves at least a possibility to use CETA in domestic law for the interpretation of executive decisions taken in this field. (Similarly, TCA, Article PPROC.11: Domestic review procedures, paragraph 6.)

Exclusion of direct effect

In EU legal practice, the general exclusion of direct effect is quite remarkable for a bilateral agreement. The explicit exclusion of direct effect is at odds with the general principle of EU law that any provisions of EU measures ('acts') that lend themselves to judicial application can be invoked in national EU courts. Bilateral agreements to which the EU is a party are assimilated, for the purpose of domestic law, to acts of EU institutions. Therefore, self-executing provisions contained in them will normally have direct effect in EU law. Unless the matter is specifically provided for in the agreement itself, the CJEU will hold that a bilateral agreement will have direct effect as long as the CJEU does not find a persistent non-application by the other party (Hauptzollamt Mainz v C.A. Kupferberg, 1982). As long as the latter has not happened, the national courts in the EU would have to apply such provisions and so would the CJEU itself. In the case of the EEA, this agreement and its implementing acts have direct effect in EU law for as long as the EFTA countries faithfully implement the agreement. The fact that many of CETA's provisions are closely related to multilateral WTO provisions may have played a role in the parties excluding direct effect of CETA. These have persistently been denied direct effect (Neuwahl and Hammamoun, 2015; Petersmann, 2016), arguably so as to avoid unduly upsetting the equilibrium between parties, but also to prevent fragmentation of jurisprudence in a global context. In the jurisprudence of the CJEU, regional deep trade agreements like CETA will likely be considered exceptions among bilateral agreements. And this applies in the same way to the TCA.

Meanwhile, the Court of Justice of the European Communities, as it was then called (CJEC) has provided well-known exceptions to the absence of direct effect, even in the context of the multilateral GATT in the cases of 'Nakajima' and 'Fediol' (Fédération de l'industrie de l'huilerie de la CEE (Fediol) v Commission of the European Communities, 1989; Nakajima All Precision Co. Ltd v Council of the European Communities, 1991). The judgment of the CJEC in the Fediol case concerned a regulation authorising producers to complain to the Commission about the unlawful commercial practices of a third country. One affected producer argued that the failure to prosecute in the case of an Argentinian producer was incorrect, particularly in view of the fact that Argentina had violated several GATT provisions. Although the CJEC found that GATT law has no direct effect, it also declared that action would be authorised on the basis of this violation because the regulation itself made explicit reference to the GATT (Fediol v Commission of the European Communities, 1989). In Nakajima, a litigant argued that a Council anti-dumping regulation had failed to comply with the anti-dumping measures set out in the GATT. The CJEC found that the regulation had specifically been adopted to comply with the Union's obligations under the WTO and that, therefore, the regulation could be interpreted as to its legality, taking into account the obligations established on this basis in the context of the WTO (Nakajima All Precision Co. Ltd v Council of the European Communities, 1991). The application of CETA provisions in internal law is therefore possible, as an exception to an exception, which could increase the effectiveness of some of its provisions as well as (very important for EU law) their harmonious interpretation in the EU. One field where this could be relevant could be government procurement (CETA, Article 19.17). The TCA equally contains such a possibility in the area of public procurement (Article PPROC.11: Domestic review procedures, paragraph 6).

Investment tribunal

The most publicised and controversial institution of CETA has undoubtedly been the Investment tribunal, with jurisdiction over ISDS. Whereas the European Commission is in favour of including provisions of this type in deep trade agreements, doing so will make the conclusion of such an agreement more complicated, especially since the provisions concerned may touch upon competences of the Member States as defined by the CJEU in its Opinion 2/15 on the EU-Singapore Free Trade Agreement. Although ISDS clauses arguably benefit Central European states the most, the West European members are less concerned by them. They do allow the EU itself to better defend common interests, but experience has shown that their inclusion can lead to strong resistance both from citizens and from governments. For this reason, the future of these clauses is uncertain, and many scholars have suggested that ISDS should be included in a separate agreement rather than in the trade agreement itself. Indeed, the TCA does not include ISDS, at least for the moment. This need not really surprise. Ever since the Brexit process was triggered, the UK, even though it had ratified CETA for its part, has shown a strong aversion to supranational courts and tribunals. The negative image of ISDS may also have played a role.

Inter-state dispute settlement

Given the limited role for private party litigation, as described above, inter-state litigation acquires greater interest. The TCA adopts and further develops a dispute settlement mechanism of a type that can also be found in CETA and other regional free trade agreements. It consists essentially of government-to-government dispute settlement procedures that do not exclude unilateral measures by the parties, such as tariffs or restrictive measures, but that seek to avoid this from happening by having recourse to consultation, negotiation and/or adjudication by institutions other than standing courts. In this respect, CETA follows a trend that likely has inspired the TCA and is present in other deep trade agreements, for example, the Trans-Pacific Partnership. The inclusion of intergovernmental dispute settlement mechanisms in CETA and other deep trade agreements should be seen in light of the intention to enhance the overall effectiveness of the commitments while, at the same time, preserving a great extent of control for the parties. The power of adjudicatory institutions can be restricted also due to a shared resolve to avoid interfering with the workings – where there is an overlap – of the WTO's dispute settlement system (Schill, 2017; Schill and Vidigal, 2018).

One of the characteristics of a CETA-type dispute settlement system is the general preference for ad hoc arbitration and mediation over more institutionalised forms of dispute settlement. This sets the 'Canada-type' agreement apart from other model-type agreements such as 'Norway' (EEA), and the trend is picked up also in the TCA. In CETA, ad hoc arbitration is the go-to solution, as it is an effective way of getting to a decision which settles a dispute, without establishing a full-fledged court system. It is preferred to mediation, where nothing happens without both parties' acceptance – which can be both an advantage and a disadvantage. In an arbitration context the parties retain a great extent of control, for instance, by regulating who the arbiters would be or what qualities they should have (as regards CETA's financial services chapter, see CETA Article 13.20(4)), and also by reserving the power to agree with the other contracting partner on binding interpretations of the agreement. Meanwhile, in sensitive cases a more direct government control is required, and mediation can be resorted to if appropriate, supplemented by inter-party consultations. Ad hoc arbitration can then be excluded altogether for certain areas, or directions can be given as to the modalities or standards of review (e.g. CETA, Article 28.6(b)).

CETA excludes both Chapter 23 on Trade and Labour and Chapter 24 on Trade and the Environment from ad hoc arbitration. The way to go here is either intergovernmental cooperation mechanisms (CETA Article 23.9 resp., 24.14), non-binding decisions of expert panels or mediation (CETA Articles 23.11(2) and 24.16(2). According to CETA Article 17.4, competition policy is also excluded from inter-state adjudication. Other instances are CETA Article 3.7 (anti-dumping), Article 7.9 (subsidies) and Article 8.45 (Investment Canada Act). CETA thus shows where the sensitivities of the parties can be, and that there are different ways to deal with them.

The TCA uses a horizontal as well as field-specific dispute settlement mechanisms (EPRS, 2021), including arbitration tribunals and panels of experts (e.g. in the field of energy), for which the rules of procedure and a code of conduct are provided in an annex. In addition to the above, however, the TCA has been endowed with a bespoke dispute settlement regime in the context of the chapter Level Playing Field and Sustainability (LPFS). It is this aspect of dispute settlement (applying only in respect to LPFS and, in another variant, state aids) which makes the TCA into a 'treaty for divergence'. This expression, coined by Collins (2020), means that the TCA is not necessarily coaxing parties into convergence. Rather the opposite. The treaty is quite permissive towards divergence. First of all, the bar for protective measures against 'social dumping' is quite high. It allows countermeasures only in case of 'significant divergence' accompanied by 'material damage', proven by 'facts' (TCA, Title IX, LPFS, Article 9.4: Rebalancing, paragraph 2). That is more demanding than the WTO system, to which CETA refers. Secondly, the party who finds a measure by its counterpart thus unacceptable will not be able to obtain the adaptation of the measure, it can just impose tariffs (TCA, Title IX, LPFS, Article 9.4: Rebalancing). Thirdly, the reaction (tariffs) must be proportional and time-limited and restricted to what is strictly necessary, and all this is subject to institutionalised arbitration. So too, in case subsidies affect trade between the parties, the party who is hit can take remedial action, under slightly revised conditions (TCA, Title IX, LPFS, Article 9.4: Rebalancing, paragraph 3 and Article INST.34B: Special procedures for remedial measures and rebalancing). This provides a basis for immediate counteraction, unless the other party starts a procedure of arbitration. In absence of a decision within 30 days, the affected party may take rebalancing measures, and in that case the other party may retaliate (Mariani and Sacerdoti, 2021).

The TCA does not foresee an obligation for a party to recover the amounts of money that were paid as a subsidy or attributed as a tax advantage, although this could flow from implementing legislation. Interestingly (EPRS, 2021), the LPFS provisions not only provide for a rebalancing mechanism due to a party 'lowering' standards, but they also allow a party to increase their own standards and adopt measures that rebalance the material impact and preserve fair competition. Last but not least, an 'overuse' of retaliation by tariffs may trigger a review of the level playing field provisions altogether (TCA, Title IX, LPFS, Article 9.4, paragraph 6).

All in all, this is a case of 'managed divergence': the TCA manages increasing regulatory divergence in an orderly way. In doing this, it does not regulate harmonisation but it manages the reaction to divergence. One may suspect that these arrangements are quite unique. At any rate, it is quite possible for the EU to argue that these arrangements are a one-off, acceptable only in case of outgoing Member States. They tie its hands. The EU will not want to extend the privilege to any other state who is (near) perfectly aligned, such as the EEA or Turkey. Such negotiations are not on the EU's priority list exactly because they already have agreements that do not include such provisions. This is not just the EU being unwilling. The exception to the WTO's MFN principles is available only to integration projects like customs unions and previously non-existing free trade areas. In order for it to continue to be available, it may be required that any new obstacles to trade accompanying an exit of a Member State are exceptional, and that they do not harm the interests of other WTO states. Although the TCA states that the agreement conforms with the WTO (Article OTH. 3), this has not been confirmed in the WTO. In view of this uncertainty, the negotiation of such diversification will not be a priority for the EU. One can therefore say that the TCA closely resembles a Canada relationship, but it can also be seen, in some respects, as a new model that may come in handy in case another Member State might decide to leave the EU, ensuring a level playing field in relation to both legislative differentiation and state aids while facilitating divergence by regulating disputes over those.

Comitology

A cross-regional agreement like the one with Canada has a particular institutional structure allowing for regular cooperation between the parties. As we shall see, there is a parallel between the Canada agreements and the TCA as regards the many political and expert committees set up or proposed by them. They are meant to contribute to the 'dynamic character' of the agreement (discussed in the next section), although their usefulness and legitimacy are sometimes disputed (Griller et al., 2017; Weiss, 2019; Wetzels, 2020). The democratic character or otherwise of their decisions (Weiss, 2019) is a question outside the scope of this chapter.

The most prominent treaty committee of CETA is the so-called Joint Committee, co-chaired by the Canadian Minister of Commerce and the EU Trade Commissioner or their representatives (CETA, Article 26.1 paragraph 1). It can amend CETA in certain aspects (CETA, Article 26.1.5(c) in conjunction with Article 4.1(f), Article 8.1, Article 8.10, 3, Article 20.22) as well as amend annexes and protocols to CETA (CETA, Article 30.2.2) and prescribe binding interpretations of CETA rules (CETA, Article 26.1(e)). It can set up and assign tasks to other specialised committees (CETA, Article 26.1. 5(g) and (h)), monitor their performance and, if appropriate, revoke their mandate. Among the CETA special committees that have been created, the most notable are the Committee on Trade in Goods, which can decide on measures to implement the exchange of product warnings (Article 21.7. 5) and the Committee on Services and Investment which, once the investor-state arbitral tribunal is in force, has the power to amend the code of conduct of the judges of the tribunal and the applicable procedural rules (CETA, Article 8.44. 2 and 3(b)). Other committees are the Joint Management Committee on Sanitary and Phytosanitary Measures, the (previously existing) Joint Customs Cooperation Committee, the Committee on Government Procurement, the Financial Services Committee and a Committee on the Recognition of Professional Qualifications, the Committee on Trade and Sustainable Development and the Regulatory Cooperation Forum and the Committee on Geographical Indications (CETA, Article 26.2.1). Working groups can also be set up (CETA, Article 5.14.4). It should be noted that there is no equivalent institution to the European Free Trade Association (EFTA) Surveillance Authority tasked with the surveillance of obligations in the field of the Internal Market, State Aids and Competition Policy.

In principle, all treaty committees are co-chaired by a representative of Canada and of the EU, and they are composed of representatives of Canada and the EU, but not of representatives of the EU Member States. Member State officials may, however, occasionally be included where considered appropriate. The Regulatory Cooperation Forum may include 'relevant officials of the Parties' as members (CETA Article 21.6.3). Other specialised committees can also include national delegates, such as: representatives with competence for SPS measures for regulatory and the trade matters (CETA, Article 5.14.1); representatives of customs, trade or other competent authorities (CETA Article 6.14.2); representatives of financial services authorities (CETA Article 13.18.1); and generally national representatives of any kind (CETA Article 19.19.1). According to CETA, Article 26.2.5, 'Each Party shall ensure that when a specialized committee meets, all the competent authorities for each issue on the agenda shall be represented …'. The institutional framework of the EU-Canada SPA is lesser known. Of particular interest in the SPA is that the parties affirm their commitment to fostering cooperation between law enforcement authorities, notably by pursuing cooperation between them and Europol of the type previously agreed in a Cooperation Agreement (Cooperation Agreement, 2005). The SPA created a Joint Ministerial Committee co-chaired by the Minister of Foreign Affairs of Canada and the European Union High Representative for Foreign Affairs and Security Policy, as well as a Joint Cooperation Committee made up of officials, which may be assisted by subcommittees, ensuring regularity, monitoring and exchange of information.

The SPA with Canada is founded on the premise that there exists a certain community of values between the parties. It creates an institutional framework aimed at deepening these common values and promoting them in relation with third countries. It establishes a partnership wider than commerce, allowing active cooperation on a whole series of issues – including security, development questions and judicial cooperation – both bilaterally and in the framework of bilateral, regional and multilateral international relations. As such, the SPA is an example of how to (jointly) take leadership in the international arena on such issues as weapons proliferation, counterterrorism and the International Criminal Court, but also climate change and a rules-based international order. According to Burnett (2019), sanctions, visa liberalisation for Georgian citizens as an incentive for political reform and future EU accessions can equally be discussed in this context, and so can the establishment of a multilateral ISDS tribunal within the WTO framework. As a European Parliament report sets out (EPRS, 2021), the core governance component of the TCA is the Partnership Council, co-chaired by a member of the European Commission and of the UK government and assisted by 19 specialised committees. It will oversee the attainment of the TCA objectives and supervise its implementation and application in addition to the dispute settlement mechanisms. The specialised committees that are established are the following (TCA, Article INST.2): the Trade Partnership Committee which supervises in turn the following ten trade specialised committees: Committee on Goods, Committee on Customs Cooperation and Rules of Origin, Committee on Sanitary and Phytosanitary Measures, Committee on Technical Barriers to Trade, Committee on Services, Investment and Digital Trade, Committee on Intellectual Property, Committee on Public Procurement, Committee on Regulatory Cooperation, Committee on a Level Playing Field, Commission on VAT and the Recovery of Taxes and Duties. There are also eight non-trade specialised committees: on Energy, on Air Transport, on Aviation Safety, on Road Transport, on Social Security Coordination, on Fisheries, on Law Enforcement and Judicial Cooperation, and on Participation in Union Programmes. Provision is made for four working groups (TCA, Article INST.3). The Partnership Council and the Committees adopt binding decisions by mutual consent (TCA, Article INST.4). The Trade Partnership Committee may dissolve trade specialised committees or establish new ones (TCA, Article INST.2, paragraph 2). It can thus be imagined that a Committee on the Recognition of Qualifications is established like the one under CETA.

Whereas the TCA essentially covers economic matters, it does provide for some continuity of the past in law enforcement and judicial cooperation in criminal matters (EPRS, 2021). Among others, it provides for the exchange of data between the parties, but without granting the UK access to the EU's databases and information systems, and it introduces a new surrender mechanism for persons accused or convicted of crimes – to replace the European Arrest Warrant. The UK will also continue to cooperate with the EU agencies in this field (Europol and Eurojust). Of course, the parties could have decided to be more ambitious in questions of security and justice cooperation. The UK initially wished to remain included in the Schengen Information System, Europol, the European Arrest Warrant and Eurojust. It also showed a willingness to continue to participate in joint defence programmes. However, the EU would only allow the UK to participate in such cooperation if it maintained an equivalent protection in matters of data protection and human rights. To verify this thoroughly without exceeding the period available for negotiation and ratification of the future partnership appeared impossible. In addition, it is unprecedented for a country to have full access to Europol without being subject to the jurisdiction of the CJEU. As Burnett (2019) reports, the US maintains a liaison office with Europol and posts liaison officers to the EU Intelligence and Situation Centre (INTCEN), and this arrangement could be copied to the UK in agreement with Europol. In addition, the EU's Political and Security Committee (PSC), consisting of ambassadors to the EU and dealing regularly with Common Foreign and Security Policy (CFSP) and Common

Security and Defence Policy (CSDP), invites future Member States and non-EU NATO countries like Canada and the EU to ad hoc meetings (PSC+7 and PSC+9). Although these meetings are currently infrequent, they could be held more regularly if the UK were involved (Burnett, 2019). Last but not least, one of the EU's concerns in security cooperation is the harmonisation of the definition of terrorism (Dumitriu, 2004; EU Directive, 2017/541). Evidently, when on 31 December 2020, Britain left not only the EU but also its place in CETA, it lost a great amount of influence, and it is hard to believe that it should want to be in a lesser position than Canada when it comes to intergovernmental cooperation on such matters in the interest not only of accessing valuable channels of information and cooperation with its largest trading bloc, but also as a way of exercising direct, sovereign control at an equivalent level to the EU.

The comitology of the TCA, while largely developing in parallel to that of CETA, is still in evolution and most of the committees still have to be set up. In this context it is worth noting that the setting of the agendas is a question of political priorities. For instance, the Financial Services Committee is among the committees that, right now, fail to take flight. In part this is due to the virtual exclusion of the sector from the TCA as a whole (EPRS, 2021, pp. 8–10; Foster, 2021). In addition, the downgrading of the EU representative in London from ambassadorial level to that of representative of an international economic organisation may not have helped to speed up the implementation process.

FREEDOM TO LEGISLATE AND DYNAMICS OF ALIGNMENT

In Brexit, one of the central questions, if not the central question, was 'control'. Consequently, a big issue concerned the extent of alignment that the UK had to accept as a condition for continued (two-way) market access for goods, services and investments. After being aligned with the rest of the EU in many areas for many years, the UK now wanted to be able to diverge. Freedom to legislate was a red line for the Johnson government, since, in their view, that was what Brexit was all about. And what could be wrong with that, given that the EU and its 27 Member States remain free to determine what commerce is admissible within their market and what is not? To the extent that the EU-27 are in command of access to their market, they do not depend on the UK adopting harmonised policies. Besides, Britain's departure will allow the EU to advance more easily in areas that have faced UK opposition in the past.

So, what is the issue? Alignment between the UK and the EU-27 is important for several reasons. First of all, it facilitates commercial relations with the other party's market for goods and services. Apart from opening new markets, alignment helps to prevent companies from having to follow two sets of regulatory provisions, which would cause them reduced profitability because of greater production costs, viz. reduced benefits of scale. This affects buying, selling, transport, research and development and more. The logistical implications may differ from sector to sector: for some products, alternative trade partners and markets may exist. On the side of both the UK and the EU there seems to prevail a certain reliance on the fact that if policy divergence occurs, businesses and labour will adapt. They will choose their preferred markets, sometimes taking losses. Regardless of whether there is regulatory alignment, businesses will continue to seek optimal profitability. Meanwhile, for the EU, alignment is not just about trade opportunities. It ensures that third countries do not frustrate certain social, health and environmental issues that the EU is set out to solve for and on behalf of its Member States. The EU's legal system helps prevent social dumping between Member States, that is, a race to the bottom for economic gain. But because the same may not be easy to obtain in relation to a country that is no longer a Member State, the EU is keen on making access to its market dependent on alignment. In this way, the EU hopes to prevent that countries in its proximity undercut EU standards in order to have an advantage on the EU market. In particular, the EU wishes to make access to the Single Market dependent on the UK:

1. Not using state aids to undercut the EU's competitiveness.
2. Not relaxing (current or future) environmental protection standards.
3. Not decreasing social and workers' protection standards.
4. Not having recourse to unfair fiscal competition.

In the following, we shall distinguish between voluntary cooperation and enforcement in these fields. Alignment can namely be attained in two ways: by obligation (such as in the 'Norway model' or in a 'backstop' situation, read: Northern Ireland) or by voluntary decision – notably if the two parties develop standards together but then allow each other to adopt them separately into their own law or not. Here too, the Canada style relationship provides a useful model.

Regulatory cooperation

In a CETA-type relationship the importance of regulatory alignment is clearly recognised and effectively addressed without there being an obligation of harmonisation. In CETA, alignment is first and foremost discretionary. Both parties remain free to regulate what can be sold in their markets, and it is this freedom to regulate social, health and environmental standards that may cause obstacles to trade to arise. To get around this, CETA provides a rather effective framework allowing coordination to happen so as to minimise disruption to trade and hence to encourage market integration. In practice, for both parties regulatory cooperation serves primarily to avoid unintentional obstacles to trade. CETA does not affect the sovereignty of the parties. It leaves untouched their right to make social, environmental and human rights choices and to close their market to products that originate there or abroad and that do not conform to those policies and laws. While western democracies generally have comparable ideas on what deserves public protection, and similar conceptions of threats, innovation, new merchandise, new ways of commerce and new scientific data bring along new regulative proposals. To prevent businesses from having to cope with different sets of market legislation, governments need to coordinate positions at an early stage. Regular information exchange and action taken upon it are of the essence.

Regulatory cooperation has been practised for decades in the framework of the WTO and bilateral agreements, even without a formal treaty. While the TTIP negotiations between the EU and the US have stalled, there has always been great interest, on both sides of the Atlantic, in regulatory cooperation on commercial and security matters (Bercero et al., 2018). The added value of the new generation free trade agreements is that they establish an institutionalised framework to conduct and improve communication, increase transparency and determine the regulatory priorities of the parties. This institutional framework can only be amended by all the parties concerned, including the parliaments.

Naturally, the emphasis here is again on the removal of barriers to trade caused unintentionally, or due to a mere lack of interest of a party in the impact of any measure on the other partner. The goal is not to remove barriers to trade caused by deliberate political choices that may be justified in the public interest. Issues that are politically sensitive to one of the partners (such as genetically modified organisms or glyphosate) are preferably left aside or treated in full knowledge of the facts by each of the parliaments concerned. This certainly results in a preference for technical and depoliticised cooperation when setting the agendas. Certainly, there is no automatic and unlimited mutual recognition. By virtue of the CETA protocol on the mutual recognition of the results of conformity assessment, national treatment will apply, and this only if the Canadian conformity assessment body (CAB) has been recognised by an accreditation body designated by a Member State or by the EU. The same goes for Canada and the European accreditation bodies (Hervé, 2017). Furthermore, there are no obligations directly on individuals, and there are no procedural rights for companies affected by discrepancies between legislations. As explained before, the agreement is not directly effective. This leaves the parties in charge. Regulatory cooperation is essentially an obligation of endeavour rather than an obligation of result; there are no sanctions for failure to arrive at any decision, and parties remain free to apply their national law, subject essentially to a principle of equal treatment. However, the regularity of meetings on all levels may well result in a coordination reflex, and, hopefully, better governance – similar to the 'open method of coordination' practised inside the EU (Nedergaard, 2007; Radaelli, 2003). Given the TCA's comitology provisions described in the previous section, it is fair to expect that similar cooperation will take place in the framework of the TCA, even if we saw that political priorities may vary and some subjects may be sensitive right now, including financial services and the recognition of qualifications or (business) migration.

Level playing field and sustainability

In addition to its provisions concerning voluntary regulatory cooperation, there is, in the TCA, a requirement of a Level Playing Field and Sustainability (LPFS), to which a specific chapter is devoted. CETA lacks a chapter on a level playing field, although it contains legal instruments that have a bearing on it. CETA contains chapters on state aid, competition policy and public undertakings as well as two chapters on sustainable development that have similar objectives as LPFS, complementing the WTO in this field. The TCA's Title on LPSF for its part contains the following chapters: State aid control, Agreements between undertakings, State-owned enterprises, Taxation standards, Labour and Social Protection, Environment and Health, Climate Change, and Other instruments. In respect of those fields there is a subsection on inter-state adjudication that contains a sanctioning mechanism with unique features whose purpose is to allow policy divergence. As explained before, it provides for 'managed divergence', making space for increasing regulatory divergence in a peaceful way by limiting the freedom of parties to take unilateral countermeasures. This 'rebalancing system' is the one feature where the TCA's institutional features are clearly distinct from CETA's.

The draft agreement proposed by the negotiating team of EU negotiator Michel Barnier (European Commission, 2020b) contained particular ratchet clauses for some areas – Labour and Social Protection, Environment and Health, Climate Change and Taxation standards, respectively (Draft Article LPFS.2.28: Future levels of protection, Draft Article LPFS.2.31: Future levels of protection Article LPFS.2.3.3(b): Future levels of protection and Draft Article LPFS.2.26: Taxation standards). They would have required that if a party admitted higher standards after the coming into force of the agreement, it could not individually diminish the level of protection any longer. While they did not entail an immediate obligation for the UK to align with the EU, in the end, they would have limited its freedom to legislate since, once the measure would be adopted, the country could no longer undo it on its own, or only at the risk of sanctions from the EU. These proposals did not survive as such in the final agreement. The

TCA does not contain those clauses, although parties agree to maintain the level of protection which existed at the time of the entry into force of the agreement. In case of breach the other party is entitled to take countermeasures in accordance with the procedures provided for.

In conclusion to this section, it is fair to say that, on the matter of freedom to legislate, the TCA indeed resembles CETA, while displaying certain features that are unique and which are justified by the possibility of increasing divergence between the UK and the EU in certain areas.

CONCLUSIONS

This chapter has aimed at locating the TCA among existing affiliations of agreements negotiated between the EU and third countries. In particular, the question was asked, is it a 'Canada style' agreement (rather than, say a 'Norway style' agreement)? We have seen that in many fields the TCA resembles a new generation deep trade agreement like CETA. We looked at the comparison with a Canada-type agreement from the following perspectives: substantive remit, institutional layout, freedom to legislate and dynamics of alignment.

As regards the substantive remit, the cooperation between the UK and the EU is, at least potentially, very broad, in accordance with the 2019 Political Declaration which presented ambitious plans, laying the foundation for a cooperation in a wide range of fields surpassing even a Canada style partnership. Because the relations between the UK and the EU had become rather acrimonious in 2020 the full potential of an ambitious partnership could not be realised in any way. Nevertheless, in addition to the principle of 'zero tariffs', a governance structure could be agreed allowing the agreement to evolve over time in function of the common interests of the UK and the EU. The TCA clearly profited from the experience made with regional deep trade agreements in relation to institutional provisions, and this bodes well for the future 'life' of the partnership and the realisation of its potential.

As regards dispute settlement, there is, like in CETA, the exclusion of 'direct effect', which stands out as an exception for bilateral agreements concluded by the EU (we have suggested why this might have been done, and we have noted that it may not exclude all domestic application). Instead, there is – again like in CETA – a variety of inter-state dispute settlement mechanisms, including arbitration and mediation, together with basic procedural rules of a binding nature. In addition, the TCA foresees a flurry of committees intended to give life to the agreement over time. While under CETA these have been meeting progressively ever since the provisional application of the agreement, those of the TCA still have to become functional for the most part. The Northern Ireland committee (set up not under the TCA but under the Northern Ireland Protocol of the 2019 Withdrawal Agreement) is unique to UK-EU relations. Given the at times acrimonious relations between the UK and the EU, it may take time for some of the comitology provisions to be put into effect. Like under CETA, committees can also be abolished if they are not seen to fulfil a useful function. While it is too early to compare their performance today, at some point further research may have to be undertaken to evaluate developments.

As regards the freedom to legislate, we enquired to what extent the TCA is an attempt to nudge the UK towards conformity to the EU over time. The UK withdrew from the EU and thereby rid itself from its obligation to pool sovereignty in restricted fields. It is a now an equal partner to the EU, a situation that is more comfortable than in an EEA context. There are indeed limits, including the requirement of a level playing field, the alignment of Northern Ireland laid down earlier in the Withdrawal Agreement, and human rights commitments. But the way in which such obligations can be enforced is, like in CETA, through unilateral action in the form of the denial of rights and the suspension of parts of the agreement in certain circumstances. In both agreements this can be avoided through consultation, and mediation or arbitration is available. One aspect (which is thought by some to be little used in practice) is the unique procedure of 'managed divergence' of the TCA. As we saw, this consists in the strict regulation of the conditions in which parties can take countermeasures against legislative divergence, and it is found in the chapter on LPFS. It represents a concession from the EU, which agreed to limit its power to take countermeasures against the UK in case of legal divergence by raising the bar for such measure and by imposing unique procedural prescriptions. These modalities can be seen as a 'British variant' of the Canada model. They constitute a novelty in a free trade agreement, and it is not certain whether the EU would want to consider introducing this feature in other bilateral agreements.

These findings concern the perspective looking from the inside out. It is not established here that looking from the outside, that is, from the viewpoint of WTO law, CETA and the TCA, are in all respects in the same category. As pointed out, it may yet take some thinking about this question from the viewpoint of international trade law. However, both CETA and the TCA are clearly free trade agreements aspiring to build upon WTO rules by establishing and developing substantive and procedural rules that complement those rules in a harmonious way. And both aspire to establishing exceptions to the MFN obligations under GATT and GATS. Finally, there is no doubt that both CETA and the TCA are important building blocks of the EU's legal politics on the international plane and give rise to partnerships which, potentially, can have a sizeable impact on the development of regional international custom and law.

NOTES

1. An earlier version of this chapter was published in June 2020. The author would like to thank Professors Dia Anagnostou, John Erik Fossum, Christopher Lord and Sabine Saurugger for their helpful comments on the earlier version of this work. The usual disclaimer applies.
2. General Agreement on Trade in Services (GATS).
3. On the side of the EU, CETA and the SPA are mixed agreements. The Member States are parties next to the EU because certain matters are agreed for which they have retained power. As not all Member States have ratified the agreement for matters in their competence yet, the agreement is being applied provisionally by the EU and Canada for matters within its exclusive competence. Provisional application is to be understood as (mutually agreed) unilateral application, which basically implies each party is free to withdraw its consent to such application should there be reason to do so (Neuwahl, 2013b). Arguably, Brexit might constitute such a reason.

REFERENCES

BBA. (2016). What is 'passporting' and why does it matter? *Brexit Quick Brief No. 3.* British Bankers Association.

Bercero García, I., Emberger, G. and Vandenberghe, J. (2018). EU-US engagement on regulatory issues: Lessons learnt notably in the context of the TTIP negotiations. *European Foreign Affairs Review, 23*(2), 149–66.

Burnett, A. (2019, 23 April). EU strategic partnerships: A model for future EU-UK relations? *Atlantic Community*. https://atlantic-community.org/eu-strategic-partnerships-a-model-for-future-eu-uk-relations/. Accessed 1 October 2022.

CBC News. (1999, 14 October). WTO tells Feds to dismantle auto pact. https://www.cbc.ca/news/business/wtotells-feds-to-dismantle-auto-pact-1.195639. Accessed 1 October 2022.

CJEU. (2017). Opinion 2/15 of the Court (Full Court) of 16 May 2017. https://eur-lex.europa.eu/legal-content/EN/TXT/?uri=CELEX%3A62015CV0002%2801%29. Accessed 1 October 2022.

Collins, D. (2020, 28 December). A treaty for divergence, a treaty for a sovereign state. *Politeia*. https://www.politeia.co.uk/a-treaty-for-divergence-a-treaty-for-a-sovereign-state/. Accessed 1 October 2022.

Cooperation Agreement. (2005). Agreement between the Government of Canada and the European Police Office, signed and entered into force on 21 November 2005.

Council of the EU. (2016, 14 September). Comprehensive Economic and Trade Agreement between Canada, of the One Part, and the European Union and Its Member States, of the Other Part. http://data.consilium.europa.eu/doc/document/ST-10973-2016-INIT/en/pdf. Accessed 1 October 2022.

Directive 2006/123/EC of the European Parliament and of the Council on services in the internal market. *Official Journal of the European Union, L376*, 36–68.

Directive 2017/541 of the European Parliament and of the Council on combating terrorism, replacing Council Framework Decision 2002/475/JHA and amending Council Decision 2005/671/JHA. *Official Journal of the European Union, L88*, 6–21.

Dumitriu, E. (2004). The EU's definition of terrorism: The Council Framework Decision on combating terrorism. *German Law Journal*, *5*(5), 585–602.

EPRS. (2021). EU–UK Trade and Cooperation Agreement. An analytical overview. In-Depth Analysis, European Parliament Research Service. https://www.europarl.europa.eu/RegData/etudes/IDAN/2021/679071/EPRS_IDA(2021)679071_EN.pdf. Accessed 1 October 2022.

European Commission. (2019). Political Declaration setting out the Framework for the Future Relationship between the European Union and The United Kingdom. https://ec.europa.eu/info/publications/revised-political-declaration_en. Accessed 1 October 2022.

European Commission. (2020a, 31 December). EU-UK Trade and Cooperation Agreement. https://ec.europa.eu/info/relations-united-kingdom/eu-uk-trade-and-cooperation-agreement_en. Accessed 1 October 2022.

European Commission. (2020b, 18 March). Draft Text of the Agreement on the New Partnership with the United Kingdom. https://ec.europa.eu/info/publications/draft-text-agreement-new-partnership-united-kingdom_en. Accessed 1 October 2022.

Fahey, E. (2017). CETA and global governance law: What kind of agreement is it really in law? *European Papers*, *2*(1), 293–302.

Fédération de l'industrie de l'huilerie de la CEE (Fediol) v Commission of the European Communities [1989] 70/87 (CJEC); 1781.

Fossum, J.E. (2019a). Europe's triangular challenge: Differentiation, dominance and democracy. *EU3D Research Papers No. 1*. https://ssrn.com/abstract=3505864.

Fossum, J.E. (2019b). What is the Norway model? Mode of affiliation or political compromise? *The Political Quarterly*, *90*(2), 266–73.

Foster, P. (2021, 1 April). Future of financial services agreement remains unclear. *Financial Times*.

Griller, S., Obwexer, W. and Vranes, E. (eds) (2017). *Mega-regional Trade Agreements: CETA, TTIP, and TiSA: New Orientations for EU External Economic Relations*. Oxford University Press.

Hauptzollamt Mainz v C.A. Kupferberg & Cie KG a.A. [1982] 104/81 (CJEC); 3641.

Hervé, A. (2017). La loi du marché: Réflexions sur la coopération réglementaire instaurée par l'AECG. *Revue des Affaires Européennes*, *2*, 235–42.

Mariani, P. and Sacerdoti, G. (2021). Trade in goods and level playing field. *Brexit Institute Working Paper Series No. 7*. https://ssrn.com/abstract=3797021.

Misonne, D. (2016). Exploring CETA's relation to environmental law. *Environmental Law Network International*, *2*, 46–53.

Nakajima All Precision Co. Ltd v Council of the European Communities [1991] 69/89 (CJEC); I-2069.

Nedergaard, P. (2007). Maximizing policy learning in international committees: An analysis of the European Open Method of Coordination (OMC) committees. *Scandinavian Political Studies*, *30*(4), 521–46.

Neuwahl, N. (2017). CETA as a potential model for (post-Brexit) UK-EU relations. *European Foreign Affairs Review*, *22*(3). 279–301.

Neuwahl, N. (2018a). Canada et Union Européenne: Un partenariat innovateur et hors du commun. *Encyclopédie du Jurisclasseur: Europe (Traité).* LexisNexis.

Neuwahl, N. (2018b). Ratification risks in mixed agreements: The case of CETA. *European Foreign Affairs Review*, *23*(3). 145–8.

Neuwahl, N. and Hammamoun, S. (2015). Les effets des accords internationaux en droit de l'Union. In S. Adams, S. Hammamoun, E. Lannon, J-V. Louis, N. Neuwahl and E. White (eds), *Commentaire Mégret sur le droit de l'Union européenne, Relations extérieures* (3rd edn, pp. 185–222). Editions de l'Université de Bruxelles.

Norton Rose Fulbright. (2017). Examining regulatory equivalence. *A FSN Forum and Norton Rose Fulbright Paper.* https://www.nortonrosefulbright.com/en/news/bbc5ed2b/examining-regulatory-equivalence---a-fsn-forum-and-norton-rose-fulbrightpaper. Accessed 1 October 2022.

Oppenheim, B. and Grant, C. (2017, 1 December). UK + EU = Canada+? *Centre for European Reform, Insight.* https://euagenda.eu/publications/uk-eu-canada. Accessed 1 October 2022.

Petersmann, E-U. (2016). The European Union's 'cosmopolitan foreign policy constitution' and its disregard in transatlantic free trade agreements. *European Foreign Affairs Review*, *21*(4), 449–68.

Prince, H.A. (ed.). (2017). *Accord économique et commercial global entre le Canada et l'Union Européenne: Esprit et dynamique d'un bilatéralisme nouveau.* Éditions Yvon Blais.

Radaelli, C. (2003). The Open Method of Coordination: A new governance architecture for the European Union? *SIEPS Report No. 1*. Swedish Institute for European Policy Studies.

Schill, S. (2017). Authority, legitimacy, and fragmentation in the (envisaged) dispute settlement disciplines in mega-regionals. In S. Griller, W. Obwexer and E. Vranes (eds), *Mega-regional Trade Agreements: CETA, TTIP, and TiSA: New Orientations for EU External Economic Relations* (pp. 111–50). Oxford University Press.

Schill, S., and Vidigal, G. (2018). Reforming dispute settlement in trade: The contribution of Mega Regionals. *International Centre for Trade and Sustainable Development (ICTSD) and the Inter-American Development Bank (IDB).*

Tatham, A.F. (2014). Diffusing EU law beyond the borders of the Union: The judicialisation of the European trading area. *Colombia Internacional*, *81*, 27–66.

TCA. (2020). Trade and Cooperation Agreement between the European Union and the European Atomic Energy Community, of the one part, and the United Kingdom of Great Britain and Northern Ireland, of the other part. *Official Journal of the European Union, L 444.*

Van Overmeire, X. and Nichay, N. (2016). *The Comprehensive Economic and Trade Agreement between Canada and the EU: An Overview*. Lexis-Nexis.

Velut, J-B., Dalingwater, L., Boullet, V. and Peyronel, V. (eds) (2018). *Understanding Mega Free Trade Agreements: The Political and Economic Governance of New Cross-regionalism.* Routledge.

Weiss, W. (2019, 4 November). The role of treaty committees in CETA and other recent EU free trade agreements. *Foodwatch.*

Wetzels, H. (2020, 9 January). CETA puts pressure on precautionary principle: Glyphosate implicated. *Bilaterals.* https://www.bilaterals.org/?ceta-puts-pressure-on. Accessed 1 October 2022.

Withdrawal Agreement. (2019). Agreement on the withdrawal of the United Kingdom of Great Britain and Northern Ireland from the European Union and the European Atomic Energy Community. *Official Journal of the European Union, C 384 I/1.*

24. The impact of Brexit on EU-US political relations and NATO

Roy H. Ginsberg

THE STAKES

There is no paucity in the 2020s of challenges facing the security of the twin pillars of the transatlantic relationship: NATO (North Atlantic Treaty Organization) and the EU (European Union). Of the 30 members of NATO, 25 are either EU and European Economic Area (EEA) members, or formal or potential candidates for EU membership. Ninety per cent of EU citizens live in a NATO member state. If Brexit results in a less capable, less secure, and more divided Europe at home and abroad, NATO will be weakened. As the United States (US) and Canada are NATO members and thus the North American links to the security of Europe, they too have a stake in Brexit outcomes. This chapter evaluates the impact of Brexit on EU-US political relations and NATO but does so as a function of how Brexit changes the United Kingdom (UK), the EU, and their bilateral relationship.

The EU-US relationship has evolved from its beginning as a largely commercial partnership when the two established diplomatic relations in the 1950s. It pays to recall the role of the US through the Marshall Plan and its focused attention on post-war Franco-German political reconciliation through regional economic integration in mid-20th century Europe. Bilateral trade and foreign direct investment, taken together, make the EU-US commercial relationship the largest in the world. Over time, these relations began to extend to foreign policy cooperation/coordination in areas of common accord just as the EU was developing its Common Foreign and Security Policy (CFSP) and its Common Security and Defence Policy (CSDP). There is hardly a troubled or insecure region of the world where collaboration between the EU and its member states and the US is not already occurring.

There was a time when the US and some NATO countries in the EU did not want to see the EU develop a defence dimension, concerned that it would duplicate NATO and diminish American support. In recent years, the US and NATO have come to welcome and support EU efforts to contribute to transatlantic and international security in ways that strengthen NATO.

EU-US relations, severely tested and undermined during the Trump period, are still fundamentally sound given the alternative – a divided west welcomed by Moscow and Beijing. Any weakening of the scope of EU-US foreign policy and security cooperation would neither be in the interests of the EU nor of the US and NATO. Russia continues to menace and interfere with its neighbours, sowing distrust by means of disinformation and cyber intrusions to its advantage. China grows into a technological, economic, and military behemoth with a worldview at odds with many western interests and most values. Each attempts to divide the EU and NATO and discredit the western liberal democracies in favour of one-party authoritarian rule.

Brexit is not an advantageous development in EU-US and transatlantic relations, at least in the short term. It complicates and divides the European pillar of the western security alliance. Brexit alienated the UK's European partners who had expected a softer exit on foreign and security policy (FSP). Such an exit was the intent of Prime Minister Theresa May but not of her successor, Boris Johnson. However, there is reason to expect that the EU and the UK will come to terms with their divorce. They are likely to inch towards a new modus operandi in FSP cooperation to their mutual advantage and that of the US and NATO. The next section focuses on the near-term (three to four years) impact of Brexit on the divorcees as it affects EU-US political relations and NATO. The third section picks up with a forecast of EU-UK and EU-US relations in the medium term (five to seven years). The fourth section looks over the horizon to imagine how the Brexit drama may play out for the principal actors by the 2030s in an international system increasingly influenced by China.

THE PARTING

The post-Brexit condition of the EU and the EU-UK relationship directly affects core US interests on both sides of the Channel. After all, the EU and the UK are American partners of the first resort. Brexit is a game-changer for the EU and UK in the near term. Put bluntly, the EU has suffered an historic loss in international reputation, prestige, and scale – no member state has ever left until the UK. The loss to the EU of the UK's considerable diplomatic influence, expertise, and military capabilities is of concern given the EU's own developing and *sui generis* role in international politics and security. That role depends on the combined weight and capability of its member states for more effectiveness. When considering the hard and soft power assets that the UK lent to EU foreign policy one realises how much it brought into – then took out of – the EU.

There are, however, some compensatory benefits of Brexit for the EU. The EU has a long history of rallying in response to adverse external stimuli by deepening integration (e.g., aftermath of the oil embargo and price hikes in 1973). Even when the UK was an EU member, it was often an awkward and equivocating partner, never a good fit, and opting out of important pieces of the European project.

The jolt of the UK's exit may further the deepening of regional cooperation and integration. For example, Brexit has stimulated a renewed push within the EU to improve and expand needed capabilities for its CSDP civilian and military crisis management operations (for an analysis of the impact of crisis management deployments on host countries, see Ginsberg and Penksa, 2014). Indeed, with German and French impetus, the EU launched the European Defence Fund (EDF) in support of the CSDP without the UK. In the past two decades, the EU deployed 30 CSDP operations across Europe, Africa, and Asia; 5,000 military and civilian staff have been deployed. Inside the EU, the UK was chief among NATO-firsters to dampen enthusiasm for the EU to develop an autonomous defence capability. With the leading Atlanticist gone, the Europeanists have more scope to act in matters of defence if they are prepared to do so, but they will carry less weight without the UK, at least for now.

At the same time the EU adjusts to consequences of the post-Brexit era, it has a rational concern over the reliability and endurance of the US as an ally and partner given Trump's legacy and large domestic following. Europeans are wary that Congressional elections could bring back a GOP ('Grand Old Party') majority in the US House of Representatives by 2023 and thus more divided government and a return of Trump or Trumpism to the White House by 2025. Some states, particularly France and Germany, do not see Trumpism as a passing phenomenon but detect deeper nationalist, demographic, and generational shifts within the US body politic away from Europe. Others, including Poland and the Baltic Republics, embrace American security regardless of who sits in the White House.

Of course, European elections also affect the climate of EU-US relations. The EU's own direction has already been influenced by the departure of Chancellor Merkel and the outcome of the French presidential elections. Whether in North America or Europe, election results in a period of national populism and nativism are reminders of the importance of domestic politics in shaping transatlantic relations, windows of opportunity to seal efforts of EU-US collaboration, and the need to cultivate a new generation in support of those relations.

One of the challenges faced by the EU is the certainty that the UK will approach individual member states or sub-groups to gather information and to work with or against EU foreign policy activity. EU High Representative Borrell warned the member states to repel UK efforts to 'bilateralise' relations with them and 'cherry-pick' when, where, and how to collaborate at the EU's expense (Borrell, 2021). Dividing the EU could backfire. It could harm prospects for a revival of cross-Channel foreign policy and security cooperation, which both the US and NATO consider important.

The net advantages of Brexit for the UK's aspirant global foreign policy free of EU constraints remain to be seen. Clearly the UK has lost the platform, politics and economies of scale, cover, and force multiplier its EU membership offered. That platform offered an amplified voice for and support of UK influence and vital interests (Falklands War); politics and economies of scale reduced the costs to the UK of combined EU action and amplified its influence (EU sanctions on Russia for poisoning UK residents); cover allowed the UK to hide behind the EU when taking joint actions that the UK would not likely have taken on its own, particularly when the US opposed such actions (West Bank settlements); and force multiplier refers to benefits of EU action in international security that have add-on effects on other organisations (NATO).

At the same time, it would be unrealistic to underestimate the internal challenges facing the UK that will weigh heavily on the costs of its foreign policy aspirations outside the EU. First, Brexit has divided the country. Scottish and Northern Irish voters voted overwhelmingly to remain in the EU in the 2016 referendum. Scottish nationalists stand to gain support for calls for another referendum on independence. The future of Northern Ireland also remains in question. Second, the UK economy following Brexit and Covid-19 restrictions and related costs has been hit hard. Trade with the EU has significantly fallen, while public debt has grown larger than the size of the country's economy.

In general, Brexit does not mean the UK will substantially increase its hard power in all sectors of the military. Spending for the British Air Force and army will decrease (as well as the number of troops, a concern raised by the Pentagon). However, the number of nuclear warheads will increase. The Royal Navy will get an increase in funding. It retains a symbolic hold on public perception of the UK as a great power. While the UK's significant cache of soft power remains influential, spending is under pressure. The UK has reduced ODA spending from 0.7 to 0.5 per cent of GDP. In time, as aspirations encounter fiscal reality, it will likely be compelled to reconsider collaborating with the EU to achieve economies and politics of scale when interests converge. And they do.

Even with the UK's impressive measures of influence, it will be nearly impossible for an 'upper-tier middle power' (Hill, 2019) in a multipolar world of great power rivals to succeed in standing alone against the rapid advance of Chinese economic, technological, and military power and assertiveness. Outside the EU, the UK will not necessarily be safer nor more influential. Three ironies of its own making exasperate the Remainers and the country's friends in the EU and US. One, the EU member states retain sovereignty over foreign and defence policy, may and do opt out of common EU actions, and retain the veto over anything the EU proposes that adversely affects vital national interests. Therefore, the UK did not need to leave the EU to retain sovereignty over its FSP. Two, the UK left the CFSP that it once helped shape to its advantage and, three, leaving the EU weakens CFSP to its disadvantage. Now alone and outside the EU, the UK will need to demonstrate its relevance to friends (US), adversaries (Russia), and systemic rivals (China).

The UK risks losing influence with the US if it presumes the Special Relationship will provide the same kind of cover and collaboration the EU did. The US has developed special relationships with other countries in and outside the EU. The UK is negotiating free trade agreements (FTAs) with third countries (already concluded, for example, with Australia and Singapore), but the prize, an FTA with the US, is not an immediate priority of the Biden White House. That said, as announced in September 2021, the UK joined the US and Australia in an agreement to provide the technology for building a fleet of nuclear submarines for the Australians. The deal supplanted a Franco-Australian agreement for France to build conventional submarines for Australia, infuriating Paris. However, it does point to British relevance to western security interests in Asia in cooperation with the US and at the same time lends weight to France's call for its EU partners to take a more active role in matters of Indo-Pacific security.

EU and UK

The EU and UK are off to a rocky start even as both sides are anxious to move on. No sooner had the UK exited than a row broke out with the EU in the Irish Sea of concern to all parties, including strident supporters of Ireland in the US Congress and White House. Provisions were made in the Protocol on Ireland and Northern Ireland in the UK-EU Withdrawal (October 2019) to keep Brexit from disrupting the delicate peace codified in the 1998 Good Friday Agreement and creating division between the Irish Republic and Northern Ireland. The Protocol signatories agreed to eliminate border controls on trade between the Irish Republic and the North. However, the Protocol calls on the UK to establish custom checks and health and safety inspections at Northern Irish ports for certain goods (e.g., meat products) entering from Great Britain by the start of 2021. Once those goods enter Northern Ireland they flow freely across the border with the Irish Republic and into the EU Single Market, which is why the EU insists on customs regulations.

After a grace period to set up customs posts ended on 1 April 2021, the UK unilaterally announced postponing implementation until October ostensibly to give traders more time to adjust to the new requirements. Meanwhile, there have been shortages of imported food and other goods in the North. The Protocol allows grace periods for further adjustment, but extensions would have to be negotiated between the signatories. Concern by Unionists over any effort that appears to detach Northern Ireland from the UK has caused them to complain about the newly required customs formalities in no uncertain terms.

Ireland defends the interests of the peace process in the North and the EU, which protects the integrity of the Single Market, is in no mood to give London the benefit of the doubt. It has charged the UK with a breach of international law, though the row ought to be settled sooner than later. The UK is caught between a rock (Unionists) and a hard place (EU). No one wants peace in Northern Ireland to be a victim of Brexit. Friction across the Channel and the Irish Sea are plainly not in US interests. The US favours good EU-UK relations. More worrisome strains followed.

Britain's initial and general foreign policy aspirations in relation to the EU are found in the 'Political Declaration Setting Out the Framework for the Future Relationship Between the EU and the UK', which was agreed concomitantly with the Withdrawal Agreement covering the terms of Brexit (October 2019). The Declaration, which reflected then Prime Minister May's earlier expectation, affirmed continued EU-UK foreign policy and security cooperation including 'close cooperation in Union-led crisis management missions and operations, both civilian and military' (European Council, 2019, p. 189). The assumption was that the UK was on board to negotiate the modalities of a post-Brexit foreign policy cooperation mechanism with the EU. That was not to be the case.

The December 2020 UK-EU Trade and Cooperation Agreement (TCA) set out the framework for bilateral duty-free trade in goods and provisions for anti-crime cooperation, counter-terrorism, and cyber-security after Brexit. However, Prime Minister Johnson's government chose to exit the EU with no framework for future foreign policy and security cooperation, abruptly reversing the cooperation affirmed in the Political Declaration. The unilateral move stunned and 'dis-Mayed' Remainers in the UK and those in the EU (and the US) who favoured continued UK-EU cooperation. It gets worse.

As if that were not enough, the EU lambasted the UK decision not to grant normal diplomatic privileges to the EU's London Ambassador in early 2021 (since resolved). The EU's 143 other delegations around the world enjoy full diplomatic status. The decision was designed to send a message: the EU is not a sovereign equal, a point repeated in 2021 with the release in London of 'Global Britain in a Competitive Age: The Integrated Review of Security, Defence, Development and Foreign Policy', a sweeping display of foreign policy goals and aspirations. The EU is barely mentioned. Instead, priority is placed on cooperation with individual EU member states and NATO, bypassing the EU as if it did not matter. The act confirms Johnson's *volte face* after decades of UK collaboration with the EU in foreign policy and a blatant pandering to the Conservative right-wing. The UK Government has taken a hard exit from EU foreign and security policy, one of the main reasons it joined the European Commision 47 years earlier.

In sum, Brexit seems like a needless zero-sum game between London and Brussels, at least for now, which disadvantages US and NATO interests at particularly dangerous and turbulent times for western democracies at home and abroad.

EU, US, NATO

Notwithstanding Trump's bombastic support of Brexit, it is difficult to make the case that Brexit advantages the US, given its historic role in supporting post-war European integration, close ties with the UK, and support of the UK in the EU. No longer will the UK be a real or perceived bridge or voice between the US and the EU. Brexit badly divided the EU and the UK. It severed the UK from the regional body on which it depended for its own economic and political security. It risks exposing an 'aspiration-capabilities' gap that leaves the UK worse off outside the EU. The UK's go-it-alone global ambitions run up against its more modest resources as a top-tier middle rank power (Hill, 2021).

The EU has been given a needed boost by the timely election of President Biden whose Administration welcomes re-engagement with European partners, making renewed EU-US cooperation possible, and bringing multilateral cooperation back into the fold of American foreign policy. Already rhetoric and action from Washington and Brussels point to a new push to collaborate on solving global problems and issues.

The European Commission wasted no time in late 2020. It proposed a 'once-in-a-generation' opportunity to design a new transatlantic agenda for global cooperation with the Biden Administration (European Commission, 2020, p. 1). Such an agenda would according to the Commission leverage the combined global economic influence of the two centres of advanced democracies and transatlantic partners to jointly cooperate on the major global issues of the times. 'This comes at a time when there is a commonality of outlook and priorities on domestic and international agendas between the incoming US administration and the EU' (European Commission, 2020, p. 1). The Commission proposed to strengthen democracies in view of the spread of authoritarian powers; increase multilateral cooperation on climate change, global health, Covid-19 vaccines, post-pandemic prevention/preparedness and cyber-security; resolve bilateral trade disputes; strengthen the WTO, WHO, and other functional bodies; move on arms control/disarmament; and establish new bilateral dialogues in such arenas as security, defence, and science and technology.

In a series of statements leading up to the June 2021 EU-US Summit, the US embraced the call for a new Transatlantic Agenda.

- At a meeting of the EU Foreign Affairs Council, Secretary of State Blinken committed the US to repair, revitalise, and increase the ambition of the EU-US relationship based on common democratic values and multilateralism (US Department of State, 2021);
- At a meeting of the Munich Security Conference, President Biden vowed to rebuild trust with and engage the European partners, make the partnership a cornerstone of US foreign policy, and work closely with EU partners to meet the global problems of our time (Biden, 2021a);
- At the European Council Summit President Biden reaffirmed his commitment to revitalise EU-US relations and buttress the world's democracies against the authoritarian tide (The White House, 2021);
- In his Administration's Interim National Security Guidance, President Biden called for recommitment to the transatlantic partnership and forging a common agenda with the EU (Biden, 2021b); and
- At the EU-US Summit, the two partners agreed to a new Transatlantic Agenda to cooperate on bilateral and global issues including health, climate change, trade, technology, and security and defence. Various new councils, working groups, dialogues, and task forces were initiated or proposed. In FSP, the two affirmed an 'unwavering support for robust NATO-EU cooperation' (European Council, 2021, p. 7).

The UK's absence at the June 2021 EU-US Summit was a stark reminder of what has changed in Europe and how much the Summit partners have moved on, leaving the UK outside the expanding EU-US relationship. Cooperation with the former EU member was nary a thought as the Europeans and Americans laid out their new post-pandemic agenda for cooperation.

From an historical perspective, the EU and US have agreed on some international issues and agreed to disagree on others. In recent examples of policy coordination resulting in common action, the US joined the EU to help fund the COVAX facility to get vaccines to needy countries and agreed to temporarily suspend tariffs related to the World Trade Organization (WTO) aircraft disputes. They agreed to issue sanctions on Russian officials for the poisoning of Andrei Navalny and the occupation of Crimea, on Belarus officials for election fraud, on Myanmar for overturning democratic elections and shooting to kill civilian protestors, and on China over the treatment of the Uighurs of Xinjiang.

Conversely, examples of policy differences include: the Nord Stream 2 gas pipeline; the US decision not to join the International Criminal Court; Trump's decision to withdraw from the Joint Comprehensive Plan of Action (JCPOA) (reversed by Biden subject to negotiation talks coordinated by the EU); closing of Gitmo; tariffs on trade in steel and aluminium; public procurement practices; data privacy; digital technology; and Israeli settlements in the West Bank. Another policy difference is the US concern over the terms of the EU-China investment treaty (not ratified) and the rush by the EU and Germany to conclude negotiations for that treaty days before the Biden Administration took office; and Italy's decision to join China's belt and road initiative. The US has expressed concern over China's financial investments and growing strategic interest in Europe, including purchases of ports, other critical infrastructure, and energy companies in southern Europe; and China's use of mask and vaccine 'diplomacy' that divided EU members.

Such differences come as no surprise; 'the whole point of European FSP was to be able to disagree with the US without endangering NATO and the US'.[1]

As far as the US and NATO are concerned, they are not advantaged by the souring of EU-UK relations. This is a particularly critical time due to the rise of China as a systemic rival in the Asia-Pacific and beyond and unabated Russian interference in democratic elections, threats to the Baltic Republics, wrenching sovereign territory from the Ukraine and Georgia, and hybrid attacks and disinformation campaigns that originate in Russia. The melting ice in the Arctic region opens up new areas of concern for the security of the EU and NATO. Just when the EU and NATO are ramping up their security relationship, the UK has stepped back from the EU. However, as discussed below, new areas of EU-NATO security cooperation may provide a basis for the EU and the UK to work, at least indirectly, on security matters.

Since 2016 the EU and NATO consult and cooperate on procurement of needed and complementary defence capabilities to address shortfalls, avoid duplication, and achieve interoperability and force-multipliers. NATO has a stake in EU members' efforts to narrow its capabilities gap in such areas as air and sea lift, air-to-air refuelling, strategic lift, combat search and rescue, intelligence, surveillance, and reconnaissance, and military mobility. The North Atlantic Council and the EU Political and Security Committee hold regular meetings on these and other topics including efforts to counter disinformation activities, hybrid security threats, terrorism, terrorist financing, and improvised explosive devices. The EU-NATO consultative partnership in turn deepens EU-US political links in areas not previously covered in the bilateral relationship, especially if real 'deliverables' are the outcomes of the process of consultations and information-sharing.

NATO Secretary-General Stoltenberg has spoken widely on strengthening NATO-EU cooperation and partnership. He attends meetings of the European Council and now the European Commission just as EU High Representative Borrell participates in meetings of the NATO Foreign and Defence Ministers. He has suggested the two collaborate more closely on cyber- and maritime security and climate change: 'When we work together we are stronger and more capable of managing the difficulties we face' (Stoltenberg, 2020). Stoltenberg has welcomed EU members' efforts to raise defence spending on new military capabilities and streamline their defence industries, which remain fragmented. 'All of that will be good for European and transatlantic security, so long as they complement NATO' (Stoltenberg, 2020). 'The EU cannot defend Europe' (Stoltenberg, 2020).

At the June 2021 NATO Summit, the allies emphasised the essential importance of the NATO-EU strategic partnership for the security of the Euro-Atlantic area. They emphasised how NATO-EU cooperation has reached unprecedented levels, for example, in countering cyber threats (increasingly viewed not just as criminal acts but as national security threats), strategic communications, operational cooperation on maritime issues, military mobility, defence capabilities, counterterrorism, and defence and security capacity building. NATO underscored the importance of NATO-EU cooperation given current and evolving security challenges, for example, resilience issues, emerging and disruptive technologies, security implications of climate change, disinformation, and growing geostrategic competition.

The improvement in transatlantic relations during the early months of the Biden Administration suffered a set-back over the chaotic and frightful manner in which the US and allied forces withdrew from Afghanistan following the Taliban's sudden takeover in August 2021. However, the EU and its member states and the US still remain partners in foreign policy cooperation in areas of common concern and agreement. The Biden Administration and the EU are recommitting themselves to common causes when policy preferences converge. Of course, the proof of the pudding is in the eating, but at least a new page has turned, or a window of opportunity has opened – depending on the metaphor one chooses. Even as the western democracies compete for global influence and dominance in each other's and world markets, and even in the roughest times, complementary and enduring democratic values and often similar (not identical) interests point to the logic of partnership.

Brexit is history. The EU and UK are now apart. The UK, a partner of first resort in international security for the US, is no longer in the EU – its other partner of first resort. Their separation occurred just when EU-US and EU-NATO cooperation is expanding in historically unprecedented terms. Still, once the dust settles on EU-UK relations, is there reason to anticipate that a new modus operandi in FSP will develop across the English Channel? Can the two who seemed so apart in the wake of Brexit come 'together apart' as they find new modalities of FSP cooperation? After all, this was the thrust of the aborted 2019 Political Declaration that set out the framework for future EU-UK relations. Will the EU and US adjust to the UK outside the EU by finding ways to cooperate trilaterally?

TOGETHER APART

As with many divorces, grievance gives way to acceptance as both sides adjust and move on. So too will the EU and UK. Foreign policy was a primary reason the UK joined the European project in 1973, but not a primary reason it left in 2020. The UK and EU still share the same regional space and environs, start from the same base of values, and have similar interests. They face an assertive and meddlesome Russia and a systemic rival in China; they cannot afford to work at cross-ends and duplicate resources if they are to remain resilient against the tide of change and retain American support of and for European security. They will likely agree in the medium term to a modus operandi so 'together apart' they can cooperate/collaborate on FSP when interests converge. Such an arrangement would allow the UK and EU to compensate in part for what each lost over Brexit and bolster the European wing of NATO, now the institution that most closely connects the UK with majority of EU members. However, looking from the outside in is not the same as looking from the inside out. The UK may have less influence as a non-member state but likely have much more than most.

EU and UK

EU foreign policy will neither wither on the vine nor sprout the hardiest grape, but the jolt of Brexit will likely stimulate a renewed commitment to act with more effect abroad. The weight of France and Germany in EU foreign policy and EU-US relations will increase. Within the EU, Germany will (by necessity) grow more comfortable as a player in and provider of international security. The EU after Brexit will continue if not hasten efforts to increase and improve its strategic autonomy and structured cooperation for deployments of CSDP civilian and crisis management operations.

Strategic autonomy refers to an ongoing effort of EU members to own more of their security, particularly defence and cyber-security, the defence industry and industrial base, and supply chains. The Permanent European Structured Cooperation (PESCO) framework refers to binding agreements among member states to invest in, develop, and operate defence capabilities needed for CSDP and NATO missions. PESCO projects include maritime and air systems, military mobility, and cyber-security. Many PESCO projects relate to NATO priorities.

The EU will slowly make progress on needed reforms in defence procurement to standardise deployments of CSDP and NATO missions, aiming to reduce costly duplication of assets. Pressure will remain from the US (building on former President Trump's lead but doing so in diplomatic terms) and the NATO Secretariat on EU NATO members to bring agreed defence spending up to 2 per cent of GDP. Progress has been made but not uniformly, for example, Italian and German defence spending each account for under 1.6 per cent of GDP. Only 20 per cent of NATO's spending on defence comes from EU NATO members. Neither NATO nor the US have reservations about improved EU security capabilities. The EU will never replace NATO, but it can complement it.

A primary concern of UK allies is not the agency of its soft power but the limits to its hard power, even with its nuclear deterrent and deployments of the Royal Navy to fly the Union Jack and demonstrate its presence in Asia-Pacific. Although the UK exceeds NATO's 2 per cent defence spending threshold, it is not capable of deploying independent military force in a major conflict outside the US or NATO (Hill, 2019). Many analysts conclude that Global Britain's tilt to the Asia-Pacific to play a major role in the security of that region is mostly aspirational. The UK risks harming its own interests if it puts significant military resources into the Asia-Pacific at the expense of those needed in its own region, especially given continued Russian militarism (Harris, 2021).

The UK's aims to expand cooperation with other groups or networks of states are promising for specific tasks, for example, in monitoring China's territorial expansion in the South and East China Seas. Five Eyes – the UK, US, Canada, Australia, and New Zealand – share intelligence on China's growing assertiveness in the Asia-Pacific. Networks are useful as the UK seeks a 'tilt' to the region but do not compensate for the loss of its security from the break with the EU.

The UK needs the EU in its relations with China. Alone it is too small to influence China on human rights, the Uighurs, trade barriers, Hong Kong, and the militarisation of the South

China Sea islets, which could affect strategic shipping lanes. For some of these issues, the EU and the member states, including the US, will struggle to exert influence over the Chinese. Should the UK challenge China unilaterally, it is more vulnerable to Chinese retaliatory sanctions than it would be inside the EU, given its smaller weight in China's foreign trade and investment. As for the Commonwealth, it is not likely to be a partner of first or second resort in FSP for the UK outside the EU, chiefly because of its large heterogeneous composition and the long shadow cast by the legacy of British colonialism.

The UK's aspiration to remain a special partner of the US may also fall short. The US values its relationship with the UK and recognises its leadership in intelligence-gathering, counter-terrorism, and cyber-security. It values the UK nuclear deterrent and British overseas bases. Overall, however, outside the EU the UK may be somewhat less relevant to the US and subject to more dependence on it. Recent US pressure prompted it to phase out all fifth generation (5G) networks supplied by the Chinese company, Huawei, by 2023.

France, Germany, and other member states will be courted by the UK for access to information and influence, but as they continue to work on strategic autonomy and structured cooperation, they are not likely to soon open the door widely to the country that left. If by turning its back on the EU and playing second fiddle to the US, the UK risks being more alone and less influential than it was inside the EU, the outcome would hardly be acceptable to the body politic. As that body politic takes note of the gap between the promise of 'Global Britain' and its costs and limitations, there will be pressure on Johnson's successors to strike a more balanced relationship with the EU for the same reasons the UK originally joined the European Community. The time will come when the UK recognises that the most advantageous way to retain global influence will be in partnership with the EU (Harris, 2021). For its part, the EU will want to work on a path to cooperation with the UK to strengthen its own effectiveness abroad. Four passages in the EU-UK foreign policy and security relationship seem plausible:

1. *After the fait accompli*. As the bitterness over the hard Brexit concerning FSP cooperation with the EU begins to ebb, it will likely be followed by acceptance of a *fait accompli*; the two will muddle through as they begin to re-engage in selected areas of common interest on an ad hoc and trial-by-error basis (Whitman, 2016, 2020). As trust begins to rebuild, consultations between the UK Foreign and Development Office and the EU member foreign ministries and EU institutions will start to take shape. Some information will begin to be shared again. Consultations will lead to cooperation and some coordination, but not yet alignment, of policy.
2. *Variable geometry*. EU-UK cooperation/coordination will likely accelerate between the two and across different sub-groups of EU member states and the UK (and US) but linked to CFSP (e.g., G-7; E3 – France, Germany, UK; E3 plus the High Representative or the US; UK-France, UK-Germany). Such a variable approach, already at play, provides more flexible and speedier responses to world events.
3. *Negotiations*. Negotiations proceed for the terms and modalities of foreign policy cooperation and coordination as the benefits of re-engagement outweigh the costs, and with a wider comfort zone for not just more EU 27+1 joint statements but, increasingly, policy alignments; and
4. *New modus operandi*. Completion of negotiations for a new institutional *modus operandi* whereby the UK attends and participates, as a non-voting non-member, in EU foreign policy bodies. Here the two engage in policy coordination and alignment leading to selec-

tive joint actions. The UK could be invited to attend the Foreign Affairs Council (FAC), European External Action Service (EEAS), and other meetings as an observer, participate in and contribute to PESCO and EDF projects, and affiliate with the European Defence Agency (EDA). Its embassies would cooperate, even coordinate, with EU delegations on in-country matters of common interest. UK personnel would participate in planning, financing, and deploying CSDP civilian and military crisis management operations. Agreements on the exchange of classified material would be required. In other words, a quiet reconvergence will take place.

EU-US-NATO

If history is any judge, the logic of transatlantic cooperation has staying power. After all, relations have survived the French withdrawal from the NATO command structure in the 1960s; US war in Vietnam by the 1970s; controversial deployment of short- and medium-range missiles in Europe in the 1980s; end of the Cold War in the 1990s; unresolved trade disputes from aircraft to steel; and the Trump Administration's hostility to the European project. Competition for markets and foreign policy spats exist along a continuum of relations over time.

Brexit seemed to have no advantage for EU-US relations in the near term. However, in the medium term those relations stand to benefit once the Brexit dust settles and improvement in EU-UK relations occur, which will be encouraged by the US. It would then be plausible for the EU and US relationship in FSP to evolve into an EU-US-UK relationship, as discussed in the next section. Restoring trust in EU-US relations and resetting EU-UK relations will strengthen NATO.

In the immediate aftermath of Brexit, the EU-UK relationship was defined by a zero-sum game. As time passes, and the two recognise anew the value of collaboration, the relationship will be more likened to a positive-sum game. There is no certain linearity about the future course of EU-UK-US relations and where the EU-NATO relationship may go but given what we know of the world at present, the bet is that the west will come together to survive given the alternative. It is the future of these relations well into the next decade to which we now turn.

FULL CIRCLE?

It was suggested in the last section that the EU and UK are likely to develop a new foreign policy modus operandi in the 2020s. What would those relations look like alongside EU-UK-US relations and NATO in the international system of the 2030s? Would a modus operandi be the terminus of how far the EU and UK would go, or would relations develop further? This section offers two likely scenarios for the future of EU-UK-US political relations and NATO, keeping in mind how those relations are affected by China. China is the one power most likely to rival, divide, and test the resolve and resilience of the EU and the transatlantic relationship.

Scenarios

1. *The EU-UK association scenario.* The anticipated modus operandi of the 2020s could be a stepping-stone for negotiations leading to an EU-UK association agreement in the 2030s.

Such an accord would codify the arrangements developed in practice in the modus operandi. An association agreement is a ratified treaty between the EU and a non-EU state that establishes a framework of privileged links to foster flexible cooperation on and action in a wide variety of policy areas. A putative EU-UK association accord could include terms of freer trade, political and economic cooperation, and participation in CSDP operations, police and anti-crime cooperation, and counterterrorism. Association accords establish institutions, such as an Association Council at ministerial level, for implementation and monitoring. Morocco and Ukraine are among the 20 countries with whom the EU has association accords. Given its size and history with the EU, a putative association accord would be a five-star one rather than boilerplate.

Association makes sense since the UK is not likely to rejoin the EU in the foreseeable future. It would codify the first steps of cooperation and consultations in FSP and provide mechanisms for coordination and alignment of policy actions. The 2019 Political Declaration, which set out the scope for – but not the blueprint of – EU-UK cooperation in FSP, was ignored by the UK upon exiting the EU. Association would return to that unfinished work, putting the Political Declaration into practice. In that sense, the EU and UK in the 2030s may come 'full circle' to the intent of the Political Declaration.

Association would repair EU-UK political relations, pick up from a long pre-Brexit history of collaboration, strengthen the European pillar of NATO favoured by the US and NATO, amplify the UK's soft and hard power assets, particularly in cyber-security and intelligence, and reap economies and politics of scale for the EU and UK to carry more weight with more effect in the international system. The UK and EU have relative strengths, expertise, and resources in different regions and across different issue areas. Association would be the framework within which the UK and EU could cooperate on how best to position the partners in relation to managing China's growing influence.

In 2021 the UK became a non-member 'third country'. By the 2030s that designation will likely evolve with association into a more affirming EU 27+1 configuration. The US would advocate for and welcome resumed collaboration between its partners of first resort.

2. *The trilateral cooperation scenario.* As the EU-UK relationship evolves into a new compact, so too is the EU-US relationship likely to evolve in the 2030s to include consultation and cooperation among the EU, UK, and US on FSP, trade, and the range of international issues from climate change to global health and the internet of things. Trilateral cooperation would be driven by the economies of acting together, building on common values and similar interests, and responding to external pressures on the western liberal democratic order. The three will face an even more intense and immediate systemic Chinese rival at home and abroad than they did in the 2020s and continued Russian interference in and disruptions on the EU's doorsteps.

   In this scenario, the EU and US will have finally negotiated and concluded an FTA. This would put their bilateral commerce and trade dispute settlement mechanisms under an institutional framework for the first time. The EU and the UK will likely have extended their limited FTA of the 2020s into a fuller one, including services. Should that happen, a trilateral FTA would be within the realm of reason, building on earlier aborted attempts at negotiating transatlantic free trade.

   Trilateral cooperation would entail a framework of consultative meetings at the working group, political director, and ministerial levels. The principals share information, seek common ground, and act on issues of common concern in foreign policy and security, new technologies, and threats to common interests.

The EU's PESCO framework to jointly develop defence capabilities among its members will have grown into an important EU-NATO bridge and a deeper EU-US security and defence partnership. It will likely build on the first ever EU agreement with the US, Canada, and Norway to participate in the PESCO Military Mobility Project that began in 2021. That project facilitated rapid and seamless movement of military personnel and assets throughout the EU. The US will likely have cultivated its working relationship with the EDA, participated in EDA projects, and contributed to several CSDP deployments.

The trilateral approach would draw on combined strengths, talents, and resources to compete with China on trade and investment and set standards for future 6G wireless networks, artificial intelligence (AI), digital trade, and other emerging technologies before China does. The trio would harness their collective strength to address the new foreign-domestic security agenda of modern times – climate change, global public health, pandemic preparations, supply chains, cyber-security, and disinformation and electoral interference, among other items. The impact of solidifying the common economic, political, and security interests of the EU, UK, and US would in turn bolster NATO in a decade when China's weight in the international system will continue to rise.

The China Effect

This chapter began with concern over the impact of Brexit on EU-US relations and NATO in the 2020s. It ends with concern over the looming impact of China on EU-US-UK relations, the EU, and NATO in the 2030s. Will China be the external catalyst that compels a deeper EU-UK and EU-US foreign policy relationship and more unified response? Or will China divide and weaken Europe and the transatlantic alliance?

China's commercial-cum-political influence rivals the western countries and reaches the four corners of the world. The metrics of such influence include: vaccine and mask diplomacy, the belt and road initiative, loans at favourable terms for developing countries to finance massive infrastructure investments that trap them into a downward spiral of dependence and unpayable debt; 'Made in China 2025' strategy, and rapid increases in research and development spending in science and technology for tomorrow's technologies. China is now the world's second largest military spender.

To be blunt, Taiwan may be 'the most dangerous place on earth' (Metz, 2021). If China were to succeed in launching an invasion and repelling an American defence, it would fundamentally alter the balance of power in the Asia-Pacific; upend the international system, unleash a horrific humanitarian disaster; and give China control of the world's largest manufacturer of microchips (located in Taiwan) for semiconductor production. China's grab of contested islets in the East and South China Seas and construction of military installations on them could affect shipping routes vital to global trade. Its rapid and huge increases in defence spending and build-up of defensive and offensive military capabilities raise questions about purpose and intent. Repression in Tibet, Xinjiang, and Hong Kong raises questions across the world over what kind of state Xi's China has become at home and abroad.

China and the west are locked in a global contest over which system best leads others by example. However, neither wants a new cold or hot war, but that does mean turning a blind eye to actions that upend long-established international norms and laws on which the functioning of world order depends. The more the west is united on China policy, however this takes shape, the less likely it is to be divided. A unified China policy would require the EU and NATO member states to first agree among themselves on the desired path. This is the nub around which the partners either bridge their differences on how to relate to China from the position of unity and strength or remain divided and weakened.

The US sees China as a strategic threat and trade competitor and is engaged in both a costly arms race with China and a race to stay ahead in the next generation of wireless technology and AI. It has been less hesitant than the EU to infuse a values-based approach in its relations with China, yet Americans are hooked on purchases of goods made in China that are no longer made in America and China holds billions of dollars in US debt obligations. The EU in general, and Germany in particular, are more dependent on trade and investment flows (and the jobs that come with that commerce) with China than the US. They view China as a systemic rival and trade competitor and aim to maintain trade and investment flows concomitant with taking up concerns on human rights – employing sanctions as a last resort.

However, the EU and most member states are beginning to recognise the risks of efforts by China to divide them, are increasingly concerned over President Xi's authoritarian rule, and have begun to respond not just in words but with action (Small, 2020).

> Deliberations in Europe over long-term issues ranging from supply chain diversification to telecoms security will take place in an atmosphere of intensified distrust of the Chinese government, as well as greater clarity about the nature of the actor China is becoming ... (Small, 2020, p. 2)

For example, France, following the UK, will ban 5G equipment from Huawei by 2028. The EU, UK, and US imposed sanctions on China over its suppression of the democratic rights and autonomy of the people of Hong Kong 'guaranteed' for 50 years in the 1997 Anglo-Chinese agreement ending British rule. The EU, UK, and US imposed sanctions on China for its treatment of the Uighurs; China imposed counter sanctions. In this heated environment the EU is putting on hold ratification of the EU-China investment treaty.

A trilateral approach to China within the transatlantic framework is far better than a go-it-alone approach. The collective way offers the scale needed to respond to China. On human rights, there are signs of a more common approach among the EU, UK, and US. On the principle of the freedom of navigation on the high seas (*mare liberum*), the US, France, and the UK deploy naval missions to the South and East China Seas – and their vessels have sailed through the Taiwan Strait – to ensure shipping routes remain open under international law. Future joint naval and other military exercises require interoperability, a goal set by NATO and the EU.

To ensure trilateral cooperation on China into the 2030s, the principals would need to:

> [F]ind common ground in identifying together where China can be a potential partner, where it is a competitor, the ways in which it is a systemic rival, and what each partner can do, together or separately, to address opportunities and challenges that accompany China's rise. (Hamilton, 2021, p. 4)

Only if the political will can be mustered, as it was when the Atlantic Alliance of the 1950s stood firm during the Cold War, can the west best manage relations with China to minimise conflict without sacrificing values. Managing western relations with China to avoid domination of the international system will be tough in the 2020s and tougher in the 2030s. There is scope for common approaches among the western allies, including the EU and the UK … together.

NOTE

1. The author expresses appreciation for this comment by Professor Christopher Hill.

REFERENCES

Biden, J.R. (2021a, 19 February). Remarks by President Biden at Pfizer Manufacturing Site [Transcribed speech]. The White House. https://www.whitehouse.gov/briefing-room/speeches-remarks/2021/02/19/remarks-by-president-biden-at-pfizer-manufacturing-site/. Accessed 4 October 2022.

Biden, J.R. (2021b). Interim National Security Strategic Guidance. The White House. https://www.whitehouse.gov/wp-content/uploads/2021/03/NSC-1v2.pdf. Accessed 4 October 2022.

Borrell, J. (2021, 30 January). After Brexit, how can the EU and UK best cooperate on foreign policy? *HR/VP Blog*. https://eeas.europa.eu/headquarters/headquarters-homepage/92345/after-brexit-how-can-eu-and-uk-best-cooperate-foreign-policy_en. Accessed 4 October 2022.

European Commission. (2020, 2 December). *Joint Communication to the European Parliament, the European Council and the Council. A New EU-US Agenda for Global Change*. JOIN(2020)22 final. https://ec.europa.eu/info/files/joint-communication-new-eu-us-agenda-global-change_en. Accessed 4 October 2022.

European Council. (2019). *Political declaration setting out the framework for the future relationship between the European Union and the United Kingdom*. OJ C 384I/178. https://eur-lex.europa.eu/legal-content/EN/TXT/PDF/?uri=CELEX:12019W/DCL(01)&from=EN. Accessed 4 October 2022.

European Council. (2021, 15 June). EU-US summit statement: 'Towards a renewed Transatlantic partnership'. https://www.consilium.europa.eu/en/press/press-releases/2021/06/15/eu-us-summit-statement-towards-a-renewed-transatlantic-partnership/. Accessed 4 October 2022.

Ginsberg, R., and Penksa, S. (2014). *The European Union in Global Security: The Politics of Impact*. Palgrave Macmillan.

Hamilton, D. (2021). *First Resort: An Agenda for the United States and the European Union*. Woodrow Wilson Center.

Harris, M. (2021, 2 January). Britain needs a post-Brexit foreign policy. *The Economist*. https://www.economist.com/briefing/2021/01/02/britain-needs-a-post-brexit-foreign-policy. Accessed 4 October 2022.

Hill, C. (2019). *The Future of British Foreign Policy: Security and Diplomacy in a World after Brexit*. Polity Press.

Hill, C. (2021, 15 March). *UK Foreign Policy and the Special Relationship Post-Brexit* [Video]. Youtube. https://www.youtube.com/watch?v=tS838qgK06I&ab_channel=SMUTowerCenter. Accessed 4 October 2022.

Metz, J. (2021, 1 May). The most dangerous place on earth. *The Economist*. https://www.economist.com/leaders/2021/05/01/the-most-dangerous-place-on-earth. Accessed 4 October 2022.

Small, A. (2020, 13 May). The meaning of systemic rivalry: Europe and China beyond the pandemic. *European Council on Foreign Relations*. https://ecfr.eu/publication/the_meaning_of_systemic_rivalry_europe_and_china_beyond_the_pandemic/. Accessed 4 October 2022.

Stoltenberg, J. (2020, 15 December). Secretary General: NATO-EU cooperation has reached unprecedented levels. NATO. https://www.nato.int/cps/en/natohq/news_180092.htm. Accessed 4 October 2022.

The White House. (2021, 25 March). President Biden participates in EU Council Summit. https://www.whitehouse.gov/briefing-room/statements-releases/2021/03/25/president-biden-participates-in-european-council-summit/. Accessed 4 October 2022.

US Department of State. (2021, 22 February). Secretary Blinken's participation in the EU Foreign Affairs Council. https://www.state.gov/secretary-blinkens-participation-in-the-eu-foreign-affairs-council/. Accessed 4 October 2022.

Whitman, R. (2016). The UK and EU foreign, security, and defence policy after Brexit: Integrated, associated or detached? *National Institute Economic Review*, *238*(1), 43–50.

Whitman, R. (2020). Missing in action: The EU and UK foreign, security, and defense policy relationship after Brexit. *European View*, *19*(2), 222–9.

25. Post-Brexit opportunities: what exactly does Australia offer the EU and the UK?

Russell Solomon

INTRODUCTION

Brexit should, of course, be considered a global as well as a regional and local issue for the United Kingdom (UK) and European Union (EU). Despite this, it has not captured much attention from either the Australian government or the population at large. Where there has been any attention paid this has been largely directed at what possible trade or other economic opportunities might be available for Australian exporters in their dealings with either the UK, the EU or both. Once the EU and the UK completed their post-Brexit economic deal, the *Trade and Cooperation Agreement* (TCA), as meagre as it was, other countries including Australia began to consider more seriously the kinds of economic relationships they are likely to experience with each of these polities in a post-Brexit era.

Historically, Australia's relations with the EU have been the converse of those with the UK where antagonism and only episodic engagement with the EU was in contrast to a deep, ongoing and often close one with the UK. If the EU was seen as marginal in Australia's political considerations in the first 40 years of its existence, then Australia was seen as even more peripheral by the EU. The relationship with the EU has, over time, been influenced by the nature of Australia's relationship with the UK and thus Brexit may well be a liberating impulse for EU-Australia relations just as much as it might open up new opportunities for the UK-Australia relationship.

Australia's post-Brexit political relationship with the UK can be expected to remain important. Unfortunately, the close relationship between the two countries from Australia's colonial past, inherited political institutions and intelligence sharing has encouraged some, rather nostalgically, to seek to oversell the economic returns for both from engaging with a 'newly liberated' UK. The in-principle *UK-Australia Free Trade Agreement* (FTA) of June 2021 is a narrow one focused mainly on goods trade and with long lead times for the removal of some tariffs. On the other hand, the political and security relationship offers more promise if the rhetoric of Global Britain is to be believed though, again, there are doubts as to how these relations can be further advanced from where they currently stand.

Over the last 20 to 30 years EU-Australia relations have seen a softening of the rhetoric around the trade and economic relationship as well as a broadening of its scope. Importantly, Australia now sees the value of a closer relationship. Australia has moved on in terms of its trade and economic profile since the early 1970s when the UK was seen as having betrayed it by joining the then European Economic Community (EEC), a body considered obstructionist to the liberalisation of Australia's important agricultural trade. However, just as geography still matters in terms of goods trade, the importance of EU-Australia trade in services and the investment relationship means trade and economic relations will be an integral dimension of any future relationship.

In considering what Brexit might mean for Australia's relations with both the EU and the UK this chapter gives the strong proviso that any post-Brexit scenario is likely to reveal unanticipated outcomes for the EU and the UK that could, in turn, influence the nature of Australia's future relations with each. The prospect of bilateral FTAs will continue to loom large but the negotiating path ahead is unlikely to be a smooth one and whether Australia's relationships with each becomes more institutionalised will depend on a broad range of policy engagements. With a focus on their trade and economic as well as security relationships, the chapter will address Australia's post-Brexit relationship with the UK, followed by that with the EU and conclude with some reflections on the possible future implications of Brexit for these two sets of relationships.

POST-BREXIT UK AND ITS RELATIONS WITH AUSTRALIA

The UK government has presented Brexit as a particular break with the past and in doing so has reconstructed what it considers the past to have been. The perceived constraints of the EU upon the UK, both politically and economically, as seen by this Brexiteer-dominated government have been widely discussed. What has not been so widely considered is this government's interpretation of the post-Brexit world and its past relationships with countries outside Europe. With the view that the UK's new-found liberation from the EU will open up new opportunities has come the misperception, fed by certain prominent Australians such as former Prime Minister Abbott,[1] that a new Commonwealth economic space of the UK's ex-colonies will emerge (Cleverly and Hewish, 2016, p. 4). UK nostalgia for past affiliations, as constructive as these notions may be presented, runs the risk of appearing delusional.[2] Yet, as the UK seeks to 'leverage past greatness into future progress' the Commonwealth of nations offers poor prospects for economic advancement (Agnew, 2020, p 267) as was the case for some time even before the UK acceded to the EEC (Bailey and Budd, 2019, p. 163; Hearne et al., 2019, p. 342).[3] While such groupings undoubtedly reflect strong people-to-people connections, they hold much less relevance in terms of developing further trade and other economic links. In addition, there is no certainty that the UK's ex-colonies will agree to such an arrangement (Campanella and Dassu, 2019, p. 107) particularly if their people-to-people connections are undermined by a UK immigration policy that offers limited access into the UK for foreign citizens.

While Australia and the UK share an adherence to a rules-based international political order and trading environment as well as a shared language, legal system and dominant culture and heritage, to date this has not translated into material trade benefits despite the relative complementarity of their respective trade profiles. There was no evidence of nostalgia for their past relationship translating into a closer economic partnership either in the early days of Brexit (McDougall, 2016, p. 565) or more recently as the two countries finalised their FTA (Besser, 2021). Australia's application of a pragmatic diplomacy to its bilateral trade relations since the UK joined the EEC in the early 1970s is now firmly established. This has proved successful for Australia even if arguably forced upon it 50 years ago as it shifted its trade focus to countries with whom it had no historical or cultural affinity.

The Johnson government had sought to pivot the UK's approach to both political and economic relations post-Brexit as being about the development of a grand strategy that it calls 'Global Britain'[4] which also fits with the government's view of portraying Brexit as either a break with or a continuation of the past (Adler-Nissen et al., 2017, p. 576).[5] Now placing itself outside of the networks of the EU and, mindful of the problems of 'going it alone' in the world, the UK is naturally reaching out to other possible alternatives (Hill, 2018, p. 188). The UK's rhetoric about removing itself from the constraints of a neighbouring supranational entity and having the independence and flexibility to engage with other players around the world is an understandable extension of the Brexit campaign. However, it remains to be seen whether it makes economic sense, or even political sense, for the UK to downplay its 'regional destiny'.

What this pivot might mean for Australia's relations with the UK going forward still requires further examination and their FTA deal, once further details are available, may assist in giving the notion of Global Britain some content. Former Australian High Commissioner Downer is correct in saying that the bilateral relationship with the UK is strong and that both pursue the principles of trade liberalisation and anti-protectionism (Downer, 2016), and that they have shared, for some time, many trade and foreign policy positions (Barber, 2017). Yet, as hard-headed foreign and trade policy bureaucrats in Canberra will know, what Australia shares with the UK is also largely shared by many other countries, many of whom are more important to UK's global projections, be they economic or strategic.

UK-Australia Trade Relations

The UK's 2017 Department of International Trade White Paper outlined the UK's trade policy approach as including transparent and inclusive trade, a rules-based global trading environment including the World Trade Organization (WTO), plurilateral arrangements and free trade globally (HM Government, 2017). This general approach, not surprisingly, accords with Australia's trade policy approach as well as that of other liberal trading states. At the same time, Australia's Department of Foreign Affairs and Trade (DFAT) in a submission to a parliamentary inquiry indicated that the impact of Brexit on Australia's trade with the UK is expected to be limited given the country's strong orientation towards Asia and the relatively small share of each other's trade.[6] However, DFAT did see Brexit providing opportunities to 'strengthen further our close and effective partnership with the UK' (Department of Foreign Affairs and Trade et al., 2017, p. 10) while highlighting the continuing importance of the UK's economic relationship with the EU.

In February 2020, UK Prime Minister Johnson, in referring to the UK's choice as to what kind of Brexit deal to have with the EU, stated that 'the choice is emphatically not "deal or no-deal" ... The question is whether we agree a trading relationship with the EU comparable to Canada's – or more like Australia's' (HM Government, 2020a). However, it was to take a further six months after the TCA for the UK to have even an in-principle deal with Australia. The TCA, once finalised, was a somewhat thin document representing a relatively hard Brexit and thus providing a reasonably wide scope for Australia's FTA talks with the UK. They have relatively complementary trade flows given that while Australia is a large commodity exporter, the UK specialises in exporting high-value industrial goods and services. Yet, by the UK government's own estimate, the UK's benefit from such an FTA only amounts to a 0.02 per cent increase to Gross Domestic Product (GDP) over 15 years (David, 2021) though Australian exports (particularly in terms of beef and lamb) are expected to increase in value much more over time (Besser, 2021; Morris, 2021).

Despite Australia and the UK initiating a trade working group and conducting subsequent government-to-government talks around an FTA since September 2016,[7] the in-principle FTA of June 2021 is a narrow one focused almost entirely on the more easily monitored goods trade. There will be a transition period with tariffs on certain agricultural imports from Australia progressively removed but with quantities capped for 15 years.[8] UK farmers strongly lobbied that the lower cost and allegedly hormone and pesticide-affected Australian beef and lamb will put UK farmers out of business if allowed into the UK tariff free. It remains to be seen whether this lobbying will be effective (Gregory, 2021; Walker et al., 2021). This opposition may make it harder to gain parliamentary approval for the deal and, with Scottish and Welsh farmers amongst those facing considerable pressure from Australian agricultural imports, may also later hamper UK government efforts to address devolution concerns and discourage Scottish moves for independence (Inman, 2021). If services trade is to be included in the FTA, certainly to the advantage of the UK, more complex negotiations will be needed. Services make up a large proportion of each economy[9] and non-tariff barriers (NTBs) in this sector will need to be addressed for the UK to make inroads into the Australian market. Any difficulty for the UK in accessing the Australian services market is likely to be exacerbated by Australia's proximity to the highly developed Singapore and Hong Kong financial markets.

The finalisation of this UK-Australia FTA was not conducted in isolation or concluded purely for trade or other economic benefits to the parties. Australia has exhibited a long-standing and bipartisan drive for striking bilateral FTAs to complement regional trade and economic groupings, though these have been principally focused upon the Asia-Pacific region. An FTA with the UK not only represents market diversification for Australia,[10] but understandably feeds off the political affinity towards the UK felt by most of its political class. For the UK, the FTA is more important politically and symbolically than economically. Australia is seen as a like-minded country and the making of such a deal signals that the UK is both ready and able to do the same with other more important potential trading partners such as the US. The in-principle deal also represents the first such FTA for post-Brexit UK other than those already rolled over from previous EU FTAs. The nature of this first FTA by a post-Brexit UK may give us the first inkling of what Brexit actually means (Menon, 2021) and indicate, if the deal means anything, which sectors might be compromised, such as agriculture, in future and much larger trade deals (David, 2021).

The deal is seen by the UK as a 'stepping-stone' to more deals with the trans-Pacific group of the *Comprehensive and Progressive Agreement for Trans-Pacific Partnership* (CPTPP), a regional FTA of 11 countries. While this group accounts for 13 per cent of global GDP and an important part of UK efforts towards greater involvement in the Asia-Pacific region (Packham, 2021), their trade only amounted to 8 per cent of UK trade in 2019 (Wintour, 2021, p. 23). Negotiations are unlikely to be straightforward given the different regulatory disciplines of many of the group's members and the UK will need to sign up to accession agreements with all members before it can join the CPTPP (Darkin, 2020). Then UK Trade Minister Truss refers to the accession to the CPTPP as a 'huge opportunity … [and] will help shift our economic centre of gravity away from Europe towards faster-growing parts of the world and deepen our access to massive consumer markets in the Asia-Pacific' (Department for International Trade, 2021). Upon accession, the UK will then need to secure its own versions of the EU FTAs with a number of these countries while it negotiates FTAs with others. As well as possible trade and economic gains, the UK has also identified geopolitical advantages from joining this regional economic grouping (Kane, 2021).[11]

UK-Australia Migration and Worker Access Issues

Australia is amongst a number of Commonwealth countries, including New Zealand and India, that early on expressed in-principle interest in free trade deals with a post-Brexit UK while, at the same time, demanding easier migration into the UK (Onslow, 2016). Soon after the Brexit referendum, then UK Home Secretary Amber Rudd made it clear that Australians wanting visas to work and live in the UK should not expect any special treatment (Bourke, 2016). Immigration control was a key driver of the Leave campaign as that campaign tapped into the widespread sentiment that workers from the EU were taking the jobs of UK citizens. Prime Minister Johnson made no secret of his interest in adopting Australia's 'points-based system' that has been used to control immigration.[12]

In promoting this 'points-based' approach, Johnson no doubt saw this system as both strictly controlling those coming into the UK while also signalling to business that he was supporting them get the skilled and talented people from overseas that they sought. This double function served by the rhetorical adoption of the Australian approach at the time,[13] while symbolically useful, presented a problem for Johnson as he still needed to choose between a stricter approach or one more aligned with amending the existing employer-sponsored system (Morris, 2019). The Australian system was unlikely to be workable in the UK given it produced high levels of immigration while, if adopted and linked to the issue of asylum in Europe, would also have raised alerts around the much-criticised Australian approach to addressing refugee issues (Morgan, 2017, p. 122).

The UK's points-based system adopted and implemented in 2021 (HM Government, 2020b) differs from Australia's scheme in being an employer-led scheme similar to that which existed before Brexit and, apart from treating EU citizens the same as citizens from the rest of the world, is more open to skilled migration. For a Skilled Worker visa, applicants must have a specific job offer for which they are sponsored (Walsh, 2020). It remains uncertain how the UK's new immigration points system will impact its ability to make trade deals around the world. It may even hinder the making of a more developed one with Australia given that government's desire to gain enhanced access for both businesspeople and young people into the UK. Indeed, what a post-Brexit UK government can actually deliver in terms of trade outcomes may well only surface when negotiations with various countries reveal their various trade-offs between migration and market access (Menon and Wager, 2020, p. 282).

The recent in-principle Australia-UK FTA offered little in terms of mobility and people access. It addressed only one particular concern with the removal of the requirement for UK backpackers to work on farms or in construction in Australia in order to extend their working visas. The reciprocal deal provided three-year work visas for people under 35 years in each other's country without any occupational restrictions,[14] but greater access for Australians and British citizens to each other's country, be it for business or otherwise, is yet to be considered. Mutual recognition of qualifications is also provided in the FTA though more concerning for the Australian union movement is the possibility that the agreement removes labour market testing allowing Australian employers to fill vacancies without first determining whether Australian workers can do the job (Murphy, 2021).

UK-Australia Security and Defence Relations

Australia and the UK already have strong security and defence links through a range of bilateral and multilateral partnerships outside the Australia-EU relationship and this is manifested in the annual *Australia-UK Ministerial Dialogue* (AUKMIN). The important multilateral intelligence network known as the *Five Eyes Intelligence Alliance* (Australia, Canada, New Zealand, the UK and the US) will remain an important aspect of Australia's overall security relationship with the UK regardless of whatever other groupings the UK may join. Both countries are also members of the *Five Eyes Defence Arrangements* and in 2018 they established the *Australia-UK Leadership Forum*. The UK government's new Global Britain approach, currently expressed in the broadest of terms, has yet to reveal a noticeable change to the UK's security and defence posture so far as Australia is concerned.

The UK, in its 2015 *National Security Strategy and Strategic Defence and Security Review*, referred to the importance of the Asia-Pacific region and that it would work with like-minded states such as Australia to 'defend and protect our global shared interests' (HM Government, 2015, pp. 57–8). Certainly, the UK government's desire is apparent with the UK's First Sea Lord Tony Radakin recently stating that 'the Indo-Pacific is this incredible hub and so is somewhere the UK is looking to have a larger say in' (Wintour, 2021, p. 22). Whether this interest in the broader Indo-Pacific region is being driven by economic interests, looking perhaps for new fishing grounds, or purely strategic issues such as the need to address the rise of China, the UK will need to engage more seriously in Australia's part of the world if it is to be a global player. As yet, despite the desire for regional economic links, there is no certainty that the UK will feel the need to project itself militarily or in any other security sense into the Indo-Pacific any more than it currently does. Whether it can actually afford to extend its military forces into this region must be another consideration.

For its part, Australia emphasised in its 2017 *Foreign Policy White Paper* (Australian Government, 2017, p. 80) the importance of cooperation with the EU and the UK as 'like-minded partners who support strong rules and institutions' and referred in its 2016 *Defence White Paper* to the relationship being 'based on deep historical and cultural ties' (Department of Defence, 2016, p. 137). However, legitimate questions remain as to whether the parties share the same meanings of (or ascribe the same importance to) such exhortatory phrases and how these will be translated into meeting the various challenges that each face (Allison-Reuman, 2019, p. 571). Of course, any discussion of a changing security and defence relationship with the UK would also need to take account of Australia's historically important and enduring close relationship with the US under *the Australia, New Zealand and United States Security Treaty* (ANZUS Treaty). Any UK claims that it has special responsibilities for international order beyond its own particular national interests are thin (Hill, 2018, p. 190) and Australia would be less than prudent to expect, without evidence, that the UK would use its Global Britain posture in any military or security sense in regions far from home.

POST-BREXIT EU AND ITS RELATIONS WITH AUSTRALIA

EU-Australia Trade and Economic Relations

Despite Australia's feelings of being betrayed by the UK when it joined the then EEC in 1973, it had largely seen its relations with the EEC through a UK lens. This was a product of both the close affinity between Australia and the UK as well as Australia's perceived intransigence and even antipathy towards the EEC. This view was something encouraged by both the EEC's relative indifference to Australia's part of the world and Australia's failure to understand the EEC's powers and range of activity in the 1970s (Benvenuti, 2018, p. 203). Not surprisingly, Australia's view of the EU up until the late 1990s was coloured by both the UK's own awkward relationship with the EU as well as some stridently Eurosceptic UK media (Murray, 2018, p. 210). While agricultural trade tensions over market tariffs and subsidies shaped the early relationship, other disputes such as the Howard government's refusal to entertain a human rights clause in any trade agreement during the 1990s helped feed the Australian view that institutionalising relations with the EU was just too difficult. Together with Australia's concern at the asymmetry of the trade relationship and its trade deficit with the EU was the view, not without foundation, that the EU was reluctant to embrace trade liberalisation.

Australia's relationship with the EU had, historically, been shaped by trade even though the investment relationship has become far more important over time. The EU's Common Agricultural Policy (CAP), with its subsidisation of agricultural trade, was the chief focus and cause of Australia's antagonistic approach to dealing with the EEC and then the EU up into the 1990s.[15] This Australian focus coupled with the limitations on the role that the EEC could play in trade and foreign relations meant their relationship remained a 'residual' one until the late 1990s.[16] From this time there were gradual changes in policy, approach and importantly perceptions of Australia and the EU towards each other. The CAP ceased to be so significant in shaping the overall relationship and the McSharry CAP reforms of that time, together with reforms through the Uruguay Round of international trade talks, meant that the CAP ceased to be an obstacle to the further development of Australia-EU relations. Australia's access to new and closer markets for its agricultural products as well as the now shared Australian and EU support for multilateral trade liberalisation (as revealed from 2001 with the Doha round of trade talks)[17] have helped to move the relationship on to more solid and positive ground. The successful negotiation of the 2010 wine trade agreement gave Australia a confidence boost and would have also helped change Australian perceptions towards further institutionalising their economic relations.[18]

Brexit can be expected to influence the approach taken by each in finalising an FTA. The EU is now 15 per cent smaller without the UK in trade terms but remains a major global player with which Australia would want to have favourable market access.[19] Brexit will also have changed the EU's internal dynamics as it proceeds with trade agreements without having within its ranks the relatively strong liberalising force of the UK. The absence of the UK may thus result in the Australia-EU deal being a shallower one though Brexit itself may have served to hasten its finalisation (Winters, 2018, p. 62). With the largest share of Australia's investment and services trade with the EU being with the UK pre-Brexit,[20] and with serious doubts raised about how liberalising the EU will be on digital services trade (Drake-Brockman, 2018, p. 30), a post-Brexit FTA with the EU is more likely to focus on goods.

For Australia, the EU27 remains economically very important given its current trade with Australia is something in the order of three to one times greater than that with the UK.[21] Negotiating an FTA with the EU makes sense for Australia given the complementary nature of their trade profiles while it holds the potential to improve Australia's participation in global value chains given the current relatively low value added nature of its exports (Suder, 2018, p. 97). Australia remains mindful of the significance of the EU having already made or currently negotiating FTAs with many of Australia's major markets in Asia and with almost all of Australia's major trading partners within the Organisation for Economic Co-operation and Development (OECD). Australia recognised the importance of a deal before Brexit with the then Turnbull Coalition government seeing progress on an FTA with the EU as a higher priority than any deal with the UK (Yencken, 2018b, p. 27). More recently, Australia's Foreign Affairs and Trade department underlined the importance of an FTA as '[building] upon Australia and the EU's natural partnership, arising out of a shared commitment to the rule of law, global norms and free and open markets' and that such an FTA would 'set the benchmark for what can be achieved between like-minded partners' (Department of Foreign Affairs and Trade, 2021a).

Both Australia and the EU recognise that their bilateral economic relationship is no longer adequately regulated by the WTO (Villalta Puig, 2014, p. 300) and, with WTO reform remaining unresolved, they each have an additional incentive to conclude a bilateral trade agreement. An Australia-EU agreement will necessarily have a key focus upon what the EU terms 'new generation free trade agreements' (McKenzie, 2018, p. 259) that seek to liberalise non-tariff barriers and address regulations that impede trade.[22] Apart from agriculture, Australia and the EU have relatively low tariff rates and any gains will likely come from liberalising these 'behind the border' barriers (Elijah and O'Neill, 2018, p. 64). Both have well-developed regulatory standards and enjoy 'high equivalence of regulatory intent'. Thus, the mutual recognition of technically different but broadly equivalent standards impacting their trade should not be difficult to achieve across a wide range of products and services (Kenyon and van der Eng, 2017, p. 260).[23]

Beverages (wine) and meat are two particular export concerns for Australia, but financial and other services may be attractive sectors for both parties. As these negotiations proceed, a sector-by-sector agreement is more likely to emerge and, while still representing a step forward in their relationship, it will be nowhere near as ambitious as when the Framework was initiated. One other possible opportunity which may be included in the negotiations is that of enhanced mobility easing the entry of EU citizens into Australia and vice versa now the UK, with its aversion to granting visas, has left the EU.

While the focus has been upon the trade relationship, there have been attempts to broaden and institutionalise Australia's relationship with the EU since the 1990s. This began with the Howard government's relatively brief 1997 *Joint Declaration on Relations between Australia and the EU*, progressed with the 2003 *Agenda for Cooperation* agreement and then continued with the Rudd/Gillard government's support for the 2008 *Australia-European Union Partnership Framework* that opened the way to a treaty-level agreement. The Framework's ten separate dialogues covered a wide range of areas as well as trade and economic matters. They included science, technology, research and innovation, education and culture, migration, counterterrorism, the fight against organised crime and cybercrime as well as judicial cooperation and intellectual property. Climate change was included in the dialogues but the Abbott Coalition government abandoned Gillard's Emissions Trading Scheme in 2013 placing

Australia out of alignment with the EU on this important issue (Yencken, 2018b, p. 26) while otherwise continuing to move the relationship away from the antagonism of yesteryear.

Rights issues may also become the subject of negotiations and create some difficulties for Australia if the EU introduces conditions into its FTA negotiations around the implementation of certain rights standards.[24] Just as the Howard government rejected these in the 1990s, so negotiations on the Framework were stalled in 2014 by the Abbott government due to the EU's proposed human rights clause. This move by Australia occurred even though the EU was expected to examine possible breaches before invoking retaliatory measures (Stats, 2015, p. 293). It remains unclear whether the recently installed Australian Labor government will baulk at the inclusion of such conditions in a finalised FTA[25] revealing much about the hypocritical position on rights so prevalent amongst Australia's political class. Should the EU inject such conditions into future negotiations which are then seriously entertained by Australia, this will provide insights into both the nature of any asymmetrical interdependence and Australia's realisation that it needs a more formal arrangement with one of its major trading partners.

When an FTA arrives it will only be a step, albeit an important one, on the path to a broader and more robust relationship between the parties. Given the time taken to reach the treaty stage it will undoubtedly be a trade agreement that goes beyond a literal reading of trade provisions and have a political resonance for both parties (Capling and Ravenhill, 2011, p. 556; Mascitelli and Wilson, 2018, p. 347). That Australia and the EU can make a formal agreement and work together is revealed by their delegated aid agreement of 2014,[26] something which formed part of the EU's 2006 Pacific Strategy (European Commission, 2006b). The ability of Australia and the EU to work together to finalise an FTA has, however, been brought into question with the fallout from Australia's September 2021 nuclear submarine deal with the US and the UK (the AUKUS deal). This saw Australia cancel its AUD$90 billion submarine contract with France and, in solidarity with France's annoyance at how it was treated by Australia, the FTA talks were delayed a month despite being one of the final rounds. Questions of trust in dealing with Australia have been raised and Australian negotiators will be mindful that it only takes one EU member state to refuse to ratify an FTA for it to fail to be finalised.

As well as slowly developing the Australia-EU economic relationship since the turn of the century,[27] the changing regional context is important with geopolitical developments in the Asia-Pacific serving to promote their closer relations. The EU's more assertive posture has reflected its own institutional developments around increased integration and enhanced trade and economic competencies as revealed through the implementation of the Maastricht Treaty, the Single Market and the European Monetary Union. An example of EU signalling that it aimed to be a more globally engaged player came with its 2006 *Global Europe* strategy and with it a new trade policy direction posturing that trade agreements can go 'further and faster in promoting openness and integration' (European Commission, 2006a, pp. 5–8).

Despite this recent change in the EU's approach, it should be noted that the EU is not a recent arrival to the Asia-Pacific region and has been involved in the *Asia–Europe Meeting* (ASEM) and the *ASEAN Regional Forum* (ARF) for some years. Australia and the EU's shared involvement with these bodies has provided opportunities for them to become better acquainted around a shared interest in seeing a stable Asia-Pacific region (Matera and Murray, 2021, p. 327). The growing strength and assertiveness of the current regime in China coupled with Australia's recent problems in developing a dialogue with that regime have added to Australia's desire to see the EU becoming even further involved in the region.

Over recent decades, just as the EU has come to accept and promote its enhanced role,[28] so its involvement in the Asia-Pacific region has been taken more seriously by regional players, including Australia. In this regional context, there may be a valuable spinoff for Australia with the EU's potential to be an important interlocutor on issues of shared relevance (Yencken, 2018a, p. 585). Developing a regional focus was also seen as economically beneficial for the EU and Commissioner Malmström, in launching the Australia-EU FTA talks, referred to in trade agreements with Australia and New Zealand as providing 'EU businesses with a valuable entry point into the wider Asia-Pacific region' and placing 'European companies on an equal footing with those from the other countries in the area that have signed up to the *Comprehensive and Progressive Agreement for Trans-Pacific Partnership*' (European Commission, 2018).

EU-Australia Security Relations

The enhanced global role adopted by the EU, partly resulting from its internal institutional developments and perception of geostrategic and other global threats, has prompted a more serious tilt to the Asia-Pacific. In April 2021, the EU Council approved the *EU Strategy for Cooperation in the Indo-Pacific* seeking cooperation through partnerships with 'all partners in the region who share common objectives' including in security and defence and presaging a 'meaningful' European naval presence. This general strategic document saw the EU working through regional organisations to address a range of global issues, such as climate change, with this considered crucial to implementing its global agenda (EEAS, 2021; European Council, 2021).

Over the past 20 years the EU and Australia have applied their shared values and norms around a rules-based international order to a number of security related agreements including around law enforcement, data sharing, the promotion of peace and stability and crisis management (Matera and Murray, 2018, p. 185). The 2017 *EU-Australia Framework Agreement* sought to strengthen future security cooperation and referenced the promotion of international peace and stability; countering the proliferation of weapons of mass destruction (WMD) and illicit trade in small arms and light weapons; and working together to prevent and fight against terrorism, organised crime and cybercrime (Department of Foreign Affairs and Trade, 2017, Articles 6–11).

Australia and the EU have made other more specific agreements including an operational agreement to share information by the Australian Federal police and the EU's EUROPOL. They have also made an *Agreement on the Security of Classified Information* in 2010, a 2014 *EU-Australia Counter Terrorism Dialogue* and, from 2015, a *Framework Partnership Agreement on Crisis Management*. These agreements should be seen more as steps along the path towards an overall closer relationship and while representing specific areas of convergence, they do not lock either party into agreeing with the other or necessarily seeing particular security challenges through the same lens. That said, this progressive institutionalisation of Australia's relations with the EU has aided their mutual socialisation and helped to lower any perceptions of distance (Murray, 2018, p. 213). Just as their material interests around trade and economic issues will not necessarily converge, so the EU and Australia are unlikely to see threats in identical terms or that their political and strategic interests will necessarily align, as shown with climate change.[29] The institutionalisation of their relations based as it is on an ideational affinity and some shared material interests, expressed both bilaterally and within a regional context, is likely to mean that their relations can be expected to remain largely a matter of 'business as usual' both politically and strategically after Brexit.

Brexit, of course, is more of a political and economic schism than a security or defence one between the EU and the UK. The security-related arrangements with the EU, engaged in prior to the UK's departure will, if anything, be strengthened after Brexit and sit easily alongside Australia's well-developed intelligence and defence arrangements with the UK. The extent to which the EU will further develop its security relations with Australia will depend on how much of its soft or diplomatic power it is prepared to expend in the Indo-Pacific region. That will largely, but not entirely, be a product of the EU's economic and related support to countries of the region while the values and norms it shares with Australia will enable it to call upon Australia to be an important conduit and facilitator of that regional engagement.

CONCLUDING REFLECTIONS

Brexit has changed the political dimension of Australia's relationships with the EU and the UK but is expected to have only a marginal impact on the economic dimension despite some rhetoric claiming otherwise. While the historical and cultural links between Australia and the UK are often highlighted, Australia's multi-ethnic character reveals a strong people-to-people affinity with nations of the EU. More important, however, is Australia's ideational affinity with both the UK and the EU around governance and the liberal international order. This has provided a foundation for institutionalising aspects of their respective relationships through various arrangements. This convergence of ideas does not, of course, automatically translate into an agreed hierarchy of interests and the parties will need to accommodate any differences through various levels of negotiation.

For Australia, its economic priority list will be different from that which it applies to addressing defence and security issues. Australia sees itself as a global trading nation even as it has had to look much closer to home, and particularly to China, for the bulk of its exports by value and volume. Australia acknowledges a need to try and diversify the markets for its exports, particularly given its recent political and trade problems with China. Both the UK and the EU show potential for improved market access for Australia though negotiating for improved market access from each will inevitably be on a sector-by-sector basis. Australia has come to recognise, perhaps partly as a result of the UK's entry into the EEC, the value of its own pragmatic diplomacy. It understands that any incentives for an early and successful resolution of FTA talks will be balanced against the influence of the parties' respective domestic economic interests.

Despite being highly influenced by the Eurosceptic media of pre-Brexit UK, both Australian governments and businesses remained in no doubt about the potential economic benefits to be gained from further engagement with EU markets. The UK's departure from the EU has further emphasised the need for Australia to no longer see the EU through 'UK eyes' while also serving to remove any lingering EU perceptions that Australia sits within a UK-centred 'anglosphere'. This will be confirmed if Brexit proves a catalyst in hastening progress towards the finalisation of an Australia-EU FTA. It is a testament to the development of Australia-EU relations over the previous 20 years, and particularly since the Framework Agreement was signed, that Brexit can be seen as creating further incentives for institutionalising rather than undermining relations with the EU. While the EU is overall weaker economically with the departure of the UK, it remains a major player economically and politically on the global stage. Its presence in the region of greatest relevance to Australia, the Asia-Pacific, is becoming more important as it channels its influence through various forums and arrangements. A bilateral FTA with the EU would be a critical indicator of the maturing of their trade relationship, economically important for Australia and politically significant for both parties. Given Australia's ideational affinity with the EU, its strategic position geographically and experience of regional collaboration, Australia will be an important hub for the EU's projection of its 'soft power' into the Asia-Pacific region, something both see as being of mutual benefit.

The recent in-principle Australia-UK FTA is of greater significance politically and symbolically than economically, and probably more so for the UK, given it is the first post-Brexit FTA that is not rolled over from a previous EU-negotiated FTA. For Australia, with its ongoing concerns over multilateral trade liberalisation, the FTA offers the potential for further diversification of its trade by destination. Australia may have hoped for enhanced access for those Australians seeking to enter the UK as well as further economic gains with Boris Johnson, a supposed 'Australophile', as Prime Minister. However, these have not materialised and his replacements, initially Liz Truss and then Rishi Sunak, were both expected to temper such expectations. Moving beyond the in-principle agreement may prove difficult for both parties given FTAs include more than tariff arrangements, such as a number of legal areas covering services regulation, intellectual property and immigration while placing procedural as well as substantive requirements on the parties. Importantly, the finalisation of this FTA would involve, as all FTAs do, some sacrifice of a country's 'sovereign rule-making power' (Hestermeyer and Ortino, 2016, p. 455). Even a government that favours liberalised bilateral trade like the UK government will be keenly aware that each FTA potentially undermines making the Brexit mantra of 'taking back control' a reality.

Even though the UK's pivot to a more assertive global role has been presented as addressing defence and security issues as well as trade and economic ones, there is no certainty that its departure from the EU will enhance its strategic importance to Australia. For Australia, the security relationship with the US remains paramount and unlikely to be displaced in the near future. The North Atlantic Treaty Organization (NATO) and the EU have already been working more closely together on a range of global security matters such as counterterrorism, crime and migration. While the UK will still be working on these issues with European states it will be doing so more as an outsider and further attention and resources will need to be devoted to this more local engagement. The UK's post-Brexit Global Britain pitch appears so far to be little more than a trade and economic slogan and evidence is yet to appear that it will result in a serious and sustained projection of UK defence and security interests into the Asia-Pacific region. The budgetary difficulties currently experienced by the UK as a result of Brexit and COVID-19 would seem to indicate quite the reverse.

As the UK government moves beyond Brexit, it may find it difficult to shift its focus away from domestic issues. A volatile Northern Ireland situation has already resulted from the effects of the Northern Ireland Protocol while the Scottish National Party's recent electoral win has placed a possible Scottish independence poll firmly back on the agenda. For the EU, Brexit is unlikely to negatively impact its moves towards further engagement in the Asia-Pacific region unless post-Brexit ramifications amongst EU27 states draw the EU's attention back to Europe thereby making the region a lesser priority. In terms of its political engagement with Australia, the progressive institutionalisation of its relations through various trade as well as other frameworks and agreements will still serve to progress the bilateral partnership even if Australia's value to the EU as a regional hub is lessened by events back in Europe.

NOTES

1. Tony Abbott was appointed a trade envoy for the UK Board of Trade in 2020.
2. Allison-Reumann refers to the need to distinguish between reflective nostalgia and the more damaging restorative nostalgia which seeks to recreate the way things were in the past (2019, p. 570).
3. Even a doubling of Commonwealth trade would only offset a small fall in EU trade post-Brexit (Hearne et al., 2019, p. 357).
4. Global Britain is about the UK continuing to be 'open, inclusive and outward facing; free trading; assertive in standing up for British interests and values; and resolute in boosting our international standing and influence ... active in every region; global interests, working with our allies and partners to deliver the global security and prosperity that ensures our own ...' (UK Foreign and Commonwealth Office, 2018).
5. Global Britain has also been referred to as the 'Brexiteers' principal form of offensive nostalgia' (Campanella and Dassu, 2019, p. 108).
6. In 2019–20, in terms of merchandise trade, the UK with a 4.1 per cent share (AUD$15,803 million) was Australia's fifth most important in terms of exports while imports from the UK with a 2.2 per cent share (AUD$6,954 million) made it the tenth most important market for Australia. Overall, Australia is the 20th most important market for UK merchandise exports and the 17th most important for such UK imports. The investment relationship is more evenly balanced between the countries (Department of Foreign Affairs and Trade, 2021c).
7. In 2019, Australia and the UK negotiated two bilateral agreements, a wine agreement and a *Mutual Recognition Agreement* to secure the continued flow of trade and current arrangements once the UK left the EU.
8. Australian beef and lamb exports from Australia will enjoy immediate access to increased duty-free quotas. Tariffs on dairy products will cease in five years, eight years for sugar and ten years for beef and lamb from Australia (Minister for Trade, Tourism and Investment, 2021).
9. In 2020, the services sector in the UK accounted for 70.9 per cent of GDP while in Australia the services sector provided 66.04 per cent of that country's GDP (Statista, 2021a, 2021b).
10. Given Australia's high dependence on trade with China and its recent political difficulties with that country, it now has an additional political as well as an economic incentive to diversify its trade, particularly if that involves an agreement with a country with whom it has had long and close relations.
11. Australia has also been assisting the UK in joining the ASEAN Regional Forum as a dialogue partner.
12. This system is a way of ranking or prioritising applicants for jobs based on their characteristics, such as education, language skills and work experience. In Australia, those with the highest number of points based on these characteristics are invited to submit a visa application. Thus, they are selected for economic purposes rather than for being family migrants, refugees or international students (Sumption, 2019).
13. The UK government's own Migration Advisory Committee criticised the Australian system and concluded that if the government wanted a points-based system then it should only introduce it for skilled workers without a job offer. The Committee's recommendations were largely ignored by the government (Gentleman et al., 2020).
14. A proposed reciprocal agricultural worker visa is aimed at addressing the expected shortfall of workers on Australian farms.
15. The relationship from the early 1970s to the late 1990s has been characterised as 'intransience on the one side and blunt recrimination on the other' (Elijah and O'Neill, 2018, p. 62).
16. Australia and the EEC related to each other only after they had 'exhausted themselves engaging with their immediate region' (Kenyon and Kunkel, 2005, p. 63).
17. Both Australia and the EU have more recently signed up to a joint Ministerial Communique calling for reforms to the WTO.

18. This wine agreement followed a 1994 one and showed that the parties could successfully negotiate a trade deal while a 1998 *Mutual Recognition Agreement* proved an important trade facilitation measure between them at the time.
19. In 2019–20, Australia's exports of merchandise trade to the EU (AUD$11,723 million) accounted for only 0.4 per cent of EU imports while Australia's imports from the EU (AUD$58,681 million) accounted for 15.1 per cent of Australia's imports. Australia's services exports to the EU were valued at AUD$7,087 million while its services imports were valued at AUD$12,931 million (Department of Foreign Affairs and Trade, 2021b).
20. For example, the UK took nearly 40 per cent of Australia's total exports to the EU and 80 per cent of Australia's exports of financial services to the EU pre-Brexit.
21. Australia's two-way trade with the EU amounted to AUD$78.7 billion in 2019–20 making the EU a key trading partner.
22. For Australia, much of its focus will remain on agricultural trade and it would be seeking improved market access from an FTA for its beef, grains, sugar, dairy products and lamb.
23. Australia is seen as a reliable and 'easy' place to do business (World Bank, 2020) with a 'trade policy formulation and evaluation structure [that] continues to be very transparent' (World Trade Organization, 2020, p. 26).
24. The EU has trade and cooperation agreements with over 120 countries and they all include a human rights clause stipulating that human rights are central to relations with the EU. These clauses are not without consequences with sanctions having, on occasion, been imposed for breaches.
25. While the international rights standards that Australia has signed up to in international treaties do not become effective until implemented in domestic law, human rights breaches within bilateral agreements will be the subject of each agreement's arbitration provisions.
26. The EU gave aid to Pacific countries while Australia gave aid to countries in Africa, an example of cooperation in action as well as a manifestation of shared norms and values around aid (Yencken, 2015, p. 434).
27. Prior to Brexit, the EU had become Australia's foremost source of inward investment, the second most important source of imports and its fourth biggest export market.
28. The EU had launched its *New Asia Strategy* in 1994 but it was the more pragmatic approach outlined in *The EU and Asia: Strategic Framework for Enhanced Partnership* in 2001 that began to engage countries like Australia (Yencken, 2015, p. 430).
29. For a discussion of convergence and divergence in their security interests, see Matera and Murray (2021).

REFERENCES

Adler-Nissen, R., Galpin, C., and Rosamond, B. (2017). Performing Brexit: How a Post-Brexit World Is Imagined Outside the United Kingdom. *The British Journal of Politics and International Relations*, *19*(3), 573–91. https://doi.org/10.1177/1369148117711092.

Agnew, J. (2020). Taking Back Control? The Myth of Territorial Sovereignty and the Brexit Fiasco. *Territory, Politics, Governance*, *8*(2), 259–72. https://doi.org/10.1080/21622671.2019.1687327.

Allison-Reumann, L. (2019). After Brexit: Australia's Relations with the EU and the UK. *Global Affairs*, *5*(4–5), 567–73. https://doi.org/10.1080/23340460.2020.1714466.

Australian Government. (2017). *Foreign Policy White Paper*. Department of Foreign Affairs and Trade https://www.dfat.gov.au/publications/minisite/2017-foreign-policy-white-paper/fpwhitepaper/index.html. Accessed 29 June 2021.

Bailey, D., and Budd, L. (2019). Brexit and beyond: A Pandora's Box? *Contemporary Social Science*, *14*(2), 157–73. https://doi.org/10.1080/21582041.2019.1621365.

Barber, T. (2017, 7 February). Australia Offers Hope for Brexit Trade Deal. *Financial Times*. https://www.ft.com/content/604687ba-ea08-11e6-893c-082c54a7f539. Accessed 10 May 2021.

Benvenuti, A. (2018). Australia's Relations with the European Community in a Historical Perspective: An Elusive Partnership. *Australian Journal of International Affairs*, *7*(3), 194–207. https://doi.org/10.1080/10357718.2018.1453476.

Besser, L. (2021, 24 April). Trade Minister Dan Tehan Says Free Trade Deal with UK Ready by June. *ABC News online*. https://www.abc.net.au/news/2021-04-24/australia-uk-free-trade-agreement-close/100092630. Accessed 30 May 2021.

Bourke, L. (2016, 4 October). Amber Rudd Rules out Australians Having Easier Immigration to UK after Brexit. *The Sydney Morning Herald online*. https://www.smh.com.au/world/amber-rudd-rules-out-australians-having-easier-immigration-to-uk-after-brexit-20161004-gru3ev.html. Accessed 17 May 2021.

Campanella, E., and Dassu, M. (2019). Brexit and Nostalgia. *Survival: Global Politics and Strategy*, *61*(3), 103–11. https://doi.org/10.1080/00396338.2019.1614781.

Capling, A., and Ravenhill, J. (2011). Multilateralising Regionalism: What Role for the Trans-Pacific Partnership Agreement. *Pacific Review*, *24*(5), 553–75. https://doi.org/10.1080/09512748.2011.634078.

Cleverly, J., and Hewish, T. (2016). *Reconnecting with the Commonwealth: The UK's Free Trade Opportunities*. Free Enterprise Group. https://static1.squarespace.com/static/5f74ad4afd34df5b8a3b53a3/t/5fd8a1430cb5764bbd4bbfcf/1608032583267/FEG_Commonwealth-Trade_web.pdf. Accessed 1 June 2021.

Darkin, E. (2020, 30 September). An Unlikely Trans-Pacific Alliance? The UK's Case for CPTPP Membership. *Global Counsel blog*. https://www.global-counsel.com/insights/blog/unlikely-trans-pacific-alliance-uks-case-cptpp-membership. Accessed 15 May 2021.

David, D. (2021, 16 June). Australia Deal Will Not Hit UK Farmers, Says Liz Truss. *BBC News online*. https://www.bbc.com/news/business-57478412. Accessed 25 June 2021.

Department of Defence. (2016). *2016 Defence White Paper*. Commonwealth of Australia. https://www.defence.gov.au/WhitePaper/Docs/2016-Defence-White-Paper.pdf. Accessed 30 June 2021.

Department of Foreign Affairs and Trade. (2017). *Framework Agreement between the European Union and Australia*. https://www.dfat.gov.au/sites/default/files/european-union-australia-framework-agreement.pdf. Accessed 29 June 2021.

Department of Foreign Affairs and Trade. (2021a). *Australia-European Union Free Trade Agreement* [Fact sheet]. https://www.dfat.gov.au/trade/agreements/negotiations/aeufta/australia-european-union-fta-fact-sheet. Accessed 5 July 2021.

Department of Foreign Affairs and Trade. (2021b). *European Union Country* [Fact sheet]. Australian Government. https://www.dfat.gov.au/sites/default/files/eu-cef.pdf. Accessed 5 July 2021.

Department of Foreign Affairs and Trade. (2021c). *United Kingdom Country* [Fact sheet]. Australian Government. https://www.dfat.gov.au/sites/default/files/uk-cef.pdf. Accessed 5 July 2021.

Department of Foreign Affairs and Trade, Austrade, Efic and Tourism Australia. (2017). Submission to *Inquiry into Australia's trade and investment relationship with the United Kingdom*. Submission 29. Parliament of Australia. https://www.aph.gov.au/Parliamentary_Business/Committees/Joint/Foreign_Affairs_Defence_and_Trade/tradewithUK/Submissions. Accessed 30 June 2021.

Department for International Trade (2021, 2 June). UK Welcomes CPTPP Nations' Invitation to Begin Accession. Media Release of Rt Hon Elizabeth Truss MP. *Government of the United Kingdom*. https://www.gov.uk/government/news/uk-welcomes-cptpp-nations-invitation-to-begin-accession. Accessed 5 June 2021.

Downer, A. (2016, 17 December). Australia Was Wounded When Britain Joined the EU: Now We Can Make Things Right – as Partners. *Telegraph*. https://www.telegraph.co.uk/news/2016/12/17/australia-wounded-britain-joined-eu-now-can-make-things-right/. Accessed 30 May 2021.

Drake-Brockman, J. (2018). An Australian Perspective on the Australia-EU Free Trade Agreement. In J. Drake-Brockman and P. Messerlin (eds), *Potential Benefits of an Australia-EU Free Trade Agreement* (pp. 9–36). University of Adelaide Press.

EEAS (European Union External Affairs Service). (2021, April). *EU Strategy for Cooperation in the Indo-Pacific* [Fact sheet]. https://eeas.europa.eu/sites/default/files/eu-indo-pacific_factsheet_2021-04_v.5.pdf. Accessed 5 May 2021.

Elijah, A., and O'Neill, A. (2018). Australia and EU Trade: Potential and Pitfalls in a Changing Global Context. In B. Mascitelli and B. Wilson (eds), *'So Distant So Close': Australia and the European Union in the 21st Century* (pp. 58–76). Australian Scholarly Publishing.

European Commission. (2006a). Global Europe: Competing in the World – a Contribution to the EU's Growth and Jobs Strategy [Communication from the EC to the EC, EP and EESC]. COM(2006)

567 Final. https://eur-lex.europa.eu/LexUriServ/LexUriServ.do?uri=COM:2006:0567:FIN:EN:PDF. Accessed 30 April 2021.

European Commission. (2006b, 29 May). EU Relations with the Pacific Islands – a Strategy for a Strengthened Partnership [Communication from the EC to the EC, EP and EESC]. COM(2006) 248 final. https://eur-lex.europa.eu/legal-content/EN/TXT/PDF/?uri=CELEX:52006DC0248&from=EN. Accessed 30 April 2021.

European Commission. (2018, 22 May). Commission Welcomes Green Light to Start Trade Negotiations with Australia and New Zealand [Press Release]. *European Commission*. https://ec.europa.eu/commission/presscorner/detail/en/IP_18_3881. Accessed 30 April 2021.

European Council. (2021, 16 April). EU Strategy for Cooperation in the Indo-Pacific. Doc.7914/21. https://data.consilium.europa.eu/doc/document/ST-7914-2021-INIT/en/pdf. Accessed 30 April 2021.

Gentleman, A., Walker, P., and O'Carroll, L. (2020, 29 January). Migration Committee Rejects Full Points-based System for UK. *Guardian Online*. https://www.theguardian.com/uk-news/2020/jan/28/migration-committee-advises-against-full-points-based-system-for-uk. Accessed 29 April 2021.

Gregory, A. (2021, 23 May). Brexit: Opposition to 'Irresponsible' Australia Trade Deal Rages on as Minister Urged to 'Fight back' or Resign. *The Independent*. https://www.independent.co.uk/news/uk/politics/australia-trade-deal-farmers-snp-b1852370.html. Accessed 29 May 2021.

Hearne, D., De Ruyter, A., and Davies, H. (2019). The Commonwealth: A Panacea for the UK's Post-Brexit Trade Ills? *Contemporary Social Science*, *14*(2), 341–60. https://doi.org/10.1080/21582041.2018.1558277.

Hestermeyer, H., and Ortino, F. (2016). Towards a UK Trade Policy Post-Brexit: The Beginning of a Complex Journey. *King's Law Journal*, *27*(3), 452–62. https://doi.org/10.1080/09615768.2016.1254416.

Hill, C. (2018). Turning back the Clock: The Illusion of a Global Political Role for Britain. In B. Martill and U. Staiger (eds), *Brexit and beyond: Rethinking the Futures of Europe* (pp. 183–92). UCL Press.

HM Government. (2015, November). *National Security Strategy and Strategic Defence and Security Review 2015: A Secure and Prosperous United Kingdom*. https://assets.publishing.service.gov.uk/government/uploads/system/uploads/attachment_data/file/555607/2015_Strategic_Defence_and_Security_Review.pdf. Accessed 28 April 2021.

HM Government. (2017, 9 October). *Trade Policy White Paper: Our Future UK Trade Policy*. https://www.gov.uk/government/publications/preparing-for-our-future-uk-trade-policy. Accessed 28 April 2021.

HM Government. (2020a, 3 February). Prime Minister Boris Johnson's speech in Greenwich [Transcript of speech]. https://www.gov.uk/government/speeches/pm-speech-in-greenwich-3-february-2020. Accessed 3 May 2021.

HM Government. (2020b, July). *The UK's Points-based Immigration System. Further Details*. Home Office. https://assets.publishing.service.gov.uk/government/uploads/system/uploads/attachment_data/file/899755/UK_Points-Based_System_Further_Details_Web_Accessible.pdf. Accessed 7 May 2021.

Inman, P. (2021, 21 May). UK-Australia Trade Deal: What Are the Key Issues? *Guardian Online*. https://www.theguardian.com/politics/2021/may/20/uk-australia-trade-deal-what-are-the-key-issues. Accessed 30 May 2021.

Kane, J. (2021, 2 February). *Comprehensive and Progressive Agreement for Trans-Pacific Partnership (CPTPP)*. Institute for Government. https://www.instituteforgovernment.org.uk/explainers/trade-cptpp. Accessed 6 May 2021.

Kenyon, D., and Kunkel, J. (2005). Australia and the European Union in the World Trade Organization: Partners or adversaries? *Australian Journal of International Affairs*, *59*(1), 55–69. https://doi.org/10.1080/1035771042000332048.

Kenyon, D., and van der Eng, P. (2017). Australia and the EU: Partners in the New Trade Agenda. In A. Elijah, D. Kenyon, K. Hussey, and P. van der Eng (eds), *Australia, the European Union and the New Trade Agenda* (pp. 267–76). ANU Press.

Mascitelli, B., and Wilson, B. (2018). Against the Odds – a Free Trade Agreement between the European Union and Australia. *Asia Europe Journal*, *16*(4), 333–49. https://doi.org/10.1007/s10308-018-0500-2.

Matera, M., and Murray, P. (2018). Australia's Relationship with the European Union: From Conflict to Cooperation. *Australian Journal of International Affairs*, *72*(3), 179–93. https://doi.org/10.1080/10357718.2018.1453475.

Matera, M., and Murray, P. (2021). Security Relations between the EU and Australia. In T. Christiansen, E. Kirchner, and S.S. Tan (eds), *The European Union's Security Relations with Asian Partners* (pp. 323–45). Palgrave Macmillan.

McDougall, D. (2016). Australia and Brexit: Déjà vu All over Again? *The Round Table*, *105*(5), 557–72. https://doi.org/10.1080/00358533.2016.1233759.

McKenzie, L. (2018). Overcoming Legacies of Foreign Policy (Dis)interests in the Negotiation of the European Union-Australia Free Trade Agreement. *Australian Journal of International Affairs*, *72*(3), 255–71. https://doi.org/10.1080/10357718.2018.1453480.

Menon, A. (2021, 4 June). Brexit: Has Ambiguity Run Its Course? *UK in a Changing Europe*. https://ukandeu.ac.uk/brexit-has-ambiguity-run-its-course/?mc_cid=1b270f9c56&mc_eid=e90cb65751. Accessed 8 June 2021.

Menon, A., and Wager, A. (2020). Taking back Control: Sovereignty as Strategy in Brexit Politics. *Territory, Politics, Governance*, *8*(2), 279–84. https://doi.org/10.1080/21622671.2019.1702895.

Minister for Trade, Tourism and Investment. (2021, 15 June). New free trade agreement to deliver jobs and business opportunities in Australia and The United Kingdom. Joint Media Release with Prime Minister. *Australian Government*. https://www.trademinister.gov.au/minister/dan-tehan/media-release/new-free-trade-agreement-deliver-jobs-and-business-opportunities-australia-and-united-kingdom. Accessed 30 June 2021.

Morgan, J. (2017). Brexit: Be Careful What You Wish For? *Globalizations*, *14*(1), 118–26. https://doi.org/10.1080/14747731.2016.1228785.

Morris, C. (2021, 17 June). UK-Australia Trade Deal: What are the Arguments for and Against? *BBC News Online*. https://www.bbc.com/news/57173498. Accessed 2 July, 2021.

Morris, M. (2019, 26 July). Boris Johnson's 'Australian Points-based System' Announcement Is Symbolic and Open-ended. *LSE Politics and Policy blog*. https://blogs.lse.ac.uk/politicsandpolicy/johnson-australian-points-based-system/. Accessed 30 July 2021.

Murphy, K. (2021, 16 June). Unions Demand Detail of Australia's Free Trade Deal with UK Citing Concerns for Workers. *Guardian Online*. https://www.theguardian.com/australia-news/2021/jun/16/unions-demand-detail-of-australias-free-trade-deal-with-uk-citing-concerns-for-workers?utm_term=8c25d220f443c3c0d56c62825fa8f439&utm_campaign=AustralianPolitics&utm_source=esp&utm_medium=Email&CMP=aupolitics_email. Accessed 30 June 2021.

Murray, P. (2018). Australia's Engagement with the European Union: Partnership Choices and Critical Friends. *Australian Journal of International Affairs*, *72*(3), 208–23. https://doi.org/10.1080/10357718.2018.1453477.

Onslow, S. (2016, 7 July). What Brexit Means for the Commonwealth. *The Conversation*. https://theconversation.com/what-brexit-means-for-the-commonwealth-61941.

Packham, C. (2021, 3 June). UK and Australia Bid to Strike Trade Deal by Mid-June. *Reuters*. https://www.reuters.com/world/uk/uk-australia-hold-further-talks-bid-strike-trade-deal-within-weeks-2021-06-03/. Accessed 10 June 2021.

Statista. (2021a). *United Kingdom: Distribution of Gross Domestic Product (GDP) across Economic Sectors from 2010 to 2020*. https://www.statista.com/statistics/270372/distribution-of-gdp-across-economic-sectors-in-the-united-kingdom/. Accessed 30 July 2021.

Statista (2021b). *Australia: Distribution of Gross Domestic Product (GDP) across Economic Sectors from 2010 to 2020*. https://www.statista.com/statistics/375558/australia-gdp-distribution-across-economic-sectors/. Accessed 30 July 2021.

Stats, K. (2015). Antipodean Antipathy: Australia's Relations with the European Union. In N. Witzleb, A.M. Arranz, and P. Winand (eds), *The European Union and Global Engagement: Institutions, Policies and Challenges* (pp. 279–304). Edward Elgar Publishing.

Suder, G. (2018). Australia-European Union Trade and Investment Dynamics: Member State Considerations for the Free Trade Agreement. In B. Mascitelli and B. Wilson (eds), *'So Distant So Close': Australia and the European Union in the 21st Century* (pp. 77–100). Australian Scholarly Publishing.

Sumption, M. (2019, 2 August). *The Australian Points-based System: What Is It and What Would Its Impact be in the UK?* The Migration Observatory at the University of Oxford. https://migrationobservatory.ox.ac.uk/resources/reports/the-australian-points-based-system-what-is-it-and-what-would-its-impact-be-in-the-uk/. Accessed 10 August 2021.

UK Foreign and Commonwealth Office. (2018, March). The government's vision of Global Britain and the role of the Foreign and Commonwealth office in supporting and enabling government departments to deliver this vision [Memorandum]. *UK Parliament*. https://publications.parliament.uk/pa/cm201719/cmselect/cmfaff/780/78008.htm#_idTextAnchor035. Accessed 30 May 2021.

Villalta Puig, G. (2014). *Economic Relations between Australia and the European Union: Law and Policy*. Kluwer Law International.

Walker, P., Harvey, F., and O'Carroll, L. (2021, 16 June). Fears UK-Australia Trade Deal Could Cause Surge in Tariff-free Meat Imports. *Guardian Online*. https://www.theguardian.com/politics/2021/jun/15/uk-australia-trade-deal-to-include-15-year-cap-on-tariff-free-imports. Accessed 30 June 2021.

Walsh, P.W. (2020, 17 May). Policy Primer: The UK's 2021 Points-based Immigration System. *The Migration Observatory at the University of Oxford*. https://migrationobservatory.ox.ac.uk/resources/primers/policy-primer-the-uks-2021-points-based-immigration-system/. Accessed 30 May 2021.

Winters, L.A. (2018). What Difference Does Brexit Make? In J. Drake-Brockman and P. Messerlin (eds), *Potential Benefits of an Australia-EU Free Trade Agreement* (pp. 61–72). University of Adelaide Press.

Wintour, P. (2021, 26 March). A Great Trade-off. Why Britain Is Tilting towards the Indo-Pacific. *The Guardian Weekly*, *204*(14), 21–3. Accessed 30 April 2021.

World Bank. (2020). Ease of Doing Business in Australia. https://www.doingbusiness.org/en/data/exploreeconomies/australia. Accessed 3 May 2021.

World Trade Organization. (2020). Trade Policy Review. Report by the Secretariat: Australia. https://www.wto.org/english/tratop_e/tpr_e/s396_sum_e.pdf. Accessed 3 May 2021.

Yencken, E. (2015). Like-minded Partners in the Asia-Pacific Region? The EU's Expanding Relationship with Australia. *Asia Europe Journal*, *13*(4), 425–41. https://doi.org/10.1007/s10308-015-0414-1.

Yencken, E. (2018a). From the Common Agricultural Policy to the Eurozone Crisis: Bilateral Disputes in the Australia-EU Relationship. *The Round Table: The Commonwealth Journal of International Affairs*, *107*(5), 585–600. https://doi.org/10.1080/00358533.2018.1527519.

Yencken, E. (2018b). From the 'British Betrayal' to Brexit: The UK in European Union-Australia Relations. In B. Mascitelli and B. Wilson (eds), *'So Distant So Close': Australia and the European Union in the 21st Century* (pp. 10–34). Australian Scholarly Publishing.

26. China views Brexit: the impacts of the UK's withdrawal from the European Union in Chinese eyes

Biao Zhang and Shaohua Yan

INTRODUCTION[1]

Since the British decision to leave the European Union, scholars have been busy with assessing the impacts of Brexit. Existing assessments focus mainly on the impacts of Brexit on the United Kingdom (UK) (e.g. the British constitution, devolution, and party politics), and the European Union (EU) (e.g. integration, institutions, and governance). Few of them, however, assess how Brexit may affect an emerging global power like China. A handful of exceptions exist. Summers, Yang, and Yu assess how Brexit will affect China-EU relations. Whereas Yang (2020) argues that China holds 'an optimistic attitude' towards a post-Brexit EU and China-EU relations, Summers and Yu argue that the importance attached by China to the EU will decline, and the post-Brexit China-EU relations will continue to be hindered by the dispute over issues such as market economy status (Summers, 2017; Yu, 2017).

While these existing assessments provide insights into the impacts of Brexit on China-EU relations, they suffer from several limitations. First, these assessments focus exclusively on the implications of Brexit for China-EU relations. Brexit will significantly affect China's relations with the EU when the Union loses one of its key members. But so do China's bilateral relations with the UK, and China's 'strategic environment' in which the US, Japan, and Russia will change their policies because of Brexit. Second, within the existing assessment, the focus is mainly on the economic consequences.[2] Trade, investment, and finance have taken centre stage of the existing assessments. Other significant issues such as China's strategic aim of pushing for 'multilateralism' (i.e. understood by the Chinese government as equivalent to 'multipolarity'), however, are marginalized in the discussion. Third, the existing assessments say relatively little about what different segments of China make of Brexit. Except for Yang, these assessments make relatively little effort to present various Chinese perspectives on Brexit and its influences.

In this chapter, we seek to provide an assessment of Brexit's impact on China that distinguishes itself from existing ones in three respects. First, we seek to broaden the focus from China-EU relations to China's relations with the UK and China's broader foreign relations. As we will show below, Chinese assessments of Brexit are sophisticated because China is not only concerned with the 'direct' impact of Brexit on China-EU relations and China-UK relations, but also the 'indirect' impacts on the US-UK relations, UK-Japan relations, and UK/EU-Russia relations that will in turn shape China's 'strategic environment'. For China, Brexit's influences are felt through many channels and relationships.

Second, we seek to broaden the focus from the economy to other fields such as global order, great power politics, security and strategy. With the China-US strategic rivalry and many countries' turn to the 'Indo-Pacific', China becomes increasingly concerned with the broader consequences of Brexit.

Third, we seek to bring more Chinese assessments to light. Since June 2016, Chinese officials (incumbent or retired), state media, and analysts (government-affiliated or university-based) have repeatedly made their assessments. State media, such as *Xinhua News*, *Guangming Daily*, *People's Daily*, and *Global Times*, have published many commentaries, editorials and observations on Brexit and its impacts. Analysts from the Chinese Academy of the Social Sciences (CASS), the Ministry of Security's China Institutes of Contemporary International Relations (CICIR), Ministry of Foreign Affairs' China Institute of International Studies (CIIS), the Ministry of Finance's Chinese Academy of Fiscal Sciences (CAFS), the Ministry of Commerce's Economic Cooperation Research Institute (ECRI), the Chinese Communist Party's Central Party School (CPS), and many leading universities, all have made their assessments. This wide range of sources provides a bigger window into the Chinese thinking on Brexit.

Drawing on policy documents, news reports, speeches, and academic articles,[3] we show that Chinese assessments of the impacts of Brexit concentrate on four aspects. First is the impacts of Brexit on the UK itself. In China's view, Brexit is harmful to the UK's political thinking, economy, party politics, international influence, and global role. Second is the impacts of Brexit on China-UK relations. Chinese evaluations are mixed with both negative and positive views: while Brexit may pose a challenge to China-UK relations, it would also create more opportunities for China and the UK to 'cooperate' in strategic, trade and investment relationships. Third is the impacts of Brexit on China-EU relations. China views that Brexit will undermine China-EU relations in the strategic, political, and economic dimensions. Fourth is the impacts of Brexit on what China calls 'great power relations', including UK-US relations, UK-Japan relations, and UK/EU-Russia relations. China is concerned with these relationships because they constitute China's 'strategic environment'.

In the end, we conclude that the Chinese understanding of the impacts of Brexit is important in several senses. First, China's view of Brexit provides an international perspective on what an emerging global power located in the Indo-Pacific makes of Brexit (see e.g. Oliver, 2016). Second, China's view of Brexit will significantly affect China's foreign policy. Although many Chinese observers are not officials, they still play a key role in shaping China's foreign policy. Third, the Chinese reception of Brexit is important to the success of British and European foreign policy in the post-Brexit era.

Before moving further, it is important to make clear two points. One is that before *and* after the British decision to leave the EU, the Chinese government keeps articulating its position as a strong supporter of European integration. For instance, during his state visit to the UK in October 2015, the Chinese President Xi Jinping urged the UK to remain in the EU (Financial Times, 2015). The day before the referendum, *Global Times* (2016b) published an editorial to warn that if the Brexiteers won the vote, for the UK 'it would be like a person who was walking a tightrope at high altitude and falls off inadvertently without wearing a safety belt'. Furthermore, after Brexit, the Chinese government did not change its position towards European integration. For instance, about a month after the referendum, the Chinese Premier Li Keqiang expressed his support of European integration in the China-EU business summit (MFA, 2016b). Zhang Ming, Chinese ambassador to the EU, stated that China's policy has 'high consistency and constancy', because 'regardless of whether the EU is in adversity or prosperity, China will firmly support the European integration process, firmly support the unity and development of the EU, and firmly support Europe in playing a greater role in international affairs' (Chinese Embassy to the EU, 2020). China's policy paper on the EU in 2018 also articulated its support for European integration (Gov.CN, 2018).

The other is, paradoxically, that China declares that it accepts Brexit and respects the British choice and wants to develop relations with the UK in parallel with that of the EU, as if there is nothing contradictory in supporting *both* Brexit and European integration. For instance, in his speech delivered at the World Economic Forum on 27 June 2016, just three days after the referendum result was revealed, Li Keqiang declared that China wanted to 'work hard to maintain and develop China-EU and China-UK relations': 'We want to see a united and stable European Union, and we also want to see a stable and prosperous Britain' (Li Keqiang, 2016). In her comment on Brexit, Ministry of Foreign Affairs (MFA) spokeswoman Hua Chunying stated that China 'respects the choice of the British people' and 'supports the development path independently chosen by Europe' (MFA, 2016a). The Ministry of Commerce (Mofcom) spokesman Shen Danyang also commented that the Chinese government 'respects' the British people's choice; while the Chinese government will 'closely monitor the situation after the UK's referendum', they 'remain confident in the prospects of China-EU economic and trade relations, and are willing to work with the EU and the UK to deepen cooperation in various fields, realize the smooth transition and development of China-EU economic and trade cooperation mechanisms' (SCIO, 2016). As China's most recent policy paper on the EU put it, 'China hopes to see Brexit proceed in an orderly fashion and stands ready to advance China-EU and China-UK relations in parallel' (Gov.CN, 2018). Thus, for the Chinese government, there is no conflict between respecting the British choice of leaving the EU, on the one hand, and supporting European integration, on the other.

BREXIT FOR BRITAIN

China's assessments of the impacts of Brexit on the UK itself are important, because these assessments shape Chinese calculations of how China will deal with a post-Brexit UK. In contrast to the official position that China 'respects' the British choice of leaving the EU, Chinese assessments of how Brexit impacts the UK are quite nuanced.

In general, Brexit is widely viewed as harmful to the UK in every aspect. First, Brexit, which is attributed to the prevalence of 'populist' and 'irrational forces' in the UK,[4] will further unleash more powerfully 'irrational forces' that shape the UK's internal and external policies. For instance, state media and scholars express their concerns that the forces that make Brexit possible would change the UK's outlook and mind. *Global Times*'s Editorial criticizes Brexit as a demonstration that the UK is turning inwards and closing its doors to the outside world. While attacking Brexiters as extremely xenophobic and narrow-minded, who care only about 'the guarantee of pension, fewer immigrants appearing in their community, less places taken by foreigners' and marginalized 'topics such as national ambitions and global strategy', the Editorial condemns Brexit for demonstrating that 'the British have lost psychologically', and 'moving towards a small nation and narrow-mindedness [*Xiaoguo Guamin*] and kicking the can down the road [*Poguanzi Poshuai*]' (Global Times, 2016c). Another Editorial from *Global Times* says that Brexit reveals how 'populist sentiments have been integrated into the democracy of contemporary Western countries, and the rational elements of scientific decision-making have been continuously squeezed out'. Brexit is 'tantamount to Britain's self-isolation … [and] the UK after Brexit will lose some opportunities to participate in leading major international affairs' (Global Times, 2019).

This feeling is shared by the Chinese analysts. 'The current rise of populism in the UK', a researcher from CIIS writes, 'may lead to the rise of protectionism and isolationism in the country' (Jin, 2016, 36). Two other scholars warn that 'the mainstream political parties in the UK', in their responses to the challenge of populism, 'have continued to cater to their propositions, which has also increased the influence of populism on foreign policy decisions in British domestic politics' (Wang and Lv, 2020, 53). This attribution of Brexit to the irrational, populist forces rather than a calculated, hard-headed choice leads many to view that Brexit would unleash 'irrational forces' into the UK's internal and external policies.

Second, Brexit will considerably harm the UK economy. First, Brexit will slow down the UK's economic growth and reduce its national incomes. *Xinhua*'s (2019) official 'International Commentary' reports on the exodus of foreign companies from the UK, with the comment that 'Whether it is for the macro-economy or for the development of individual enterprises, uncertainty is harmful and without benefits.' 'The typical feature of Brexit', it continues, 'is precisely its uncertainty and unpredictability.' Chinese scholars also express their concern that Brexit will give a blow to the UK's economic growth (Liu and Feng, 2017, 51; Wang, Xu, and Zhang, 2016, 6). Second, Brexit will send shockwaves to the financial industry. Ma Zhengang, a former Chinese ambassador to the UK, warns that Brexit would undermine the UK economy and hit London's position as one of the leading international financial centres. Likewise, Cui Hongjian, a leading and influential analyst from CIIS, points out that 'The biggest problem [caused by Brexit] is that if the world position of the British financial industry cannot be preserved, the British economy will fall sharply', even to the extent that the UK 'will quickly withdraw from the world's major economies' (Global Times, 2016a). There are pervasive concerns with the UK's financial passporting right, and with the move of financial institutions to Frankfurt and Paris (e.g. Wang and He, 2020, 74). Third, Brexit will affect the UK's inward investment. State media and analysts alike suggest that once the UK leaves the EU, it will no longer serve as the most attractive European destination for foreign investment. Instead, countries on the European continent will become homes for foreign investment (Xinhua, 2017a).

Third, Brexit will continue to shape British party politics and the political system. First, most Chinese commentators notice the role played by UKIP in the Brexit campaign, and thus conclude that British politics is no longer dominated by the established parties such as the Conservatives and Labour. Instead, British politicians will respond more to 'the people' (e.g. Wang and Liu, 2020). Second, in many observers' view, Brexit changes the balance of power between the Parliament and the government. The Parliament has been reasserting its power against the government during the process of Brexit and will continue to do so (He and Shi, 2019; Liu, 2017; Wang and Lv, 2020). In short, as one commentary by *Xinhua* (2016) puts it, Brexit will not only 'trigger a major earthquake in the political realm' but also 'produce a "domino effect"' on the British political system in the future.

Fourth, Brexit threatens the very existence of the UK. Chinese analysts consider that Brexit will have serious consequences for Scotland and Northern Ireland. For instance, Qiao Liang, a leading Chinese military strategist who co-authored *Unlimited War*, argues that once the UK leaves the EU, Scotland and Northern Ireland will also leave the UK, making 'three British Isles become one isle'. The vice head of CICIR argues that 'the unity of the UK will be threatened' (Feng, 2016, 3), and the head of the European Institute of CICIR notes that Brexit will cast a 'huge question mark over the integrity of the UK' (J. Zhang, 2019, 44).

A CIIS researcher remarks that 'The issue of domestic regional separatism will once again be put on the political agenda, and national unity faces challenges' (Jin, 2016, 31). Wang and Zhang (2019, 18–24) suggest that Brexit will not only affect devolution, but 'give a blow to the Irish peace process' and 'trigger the debate over the referendum on Ireland's unification'. The concern with the very existence of the United Kingdom is widely shared (see also Wang and Liu, 2020, 151).

Fifth, Brexit will undercut the UK's 'international influence' for a variety of reasons. Some think that the UK's slowing economic growth will drain its resources for military and political action. For instance, a researcher from the Central Party School argues that an economic downturn will 'cause the UK's defense and foreign affairs resources to shrink, [and] thereby reducing its support for US international operations' (Cao, 2019, 50). Others think that managing Brexit negotiations will make the UK less visible in international events. The UK will lose its international influence because of its focus on Brexit negotiations and repairing the effects of Brexit: as Zhang Jian (2019, 44) writes, 'In the past three years, due to Britain's busy Brexit, its visibility in international affairs has declined significantly.' Still others suggest that it is the exit of the EU that would reduce the British influence. Many analysts think that Britain's 'international status' is weakened once it gets out of the EU (Feng, 2016, 4).

Sixth, Brexit forces the UK to redefine its role in the global political economy, starting the process of finding a new role after its departure from the EU. Here, state media and many analysts have noticed the UK government's rhetoric of building a 'Global Britain'. However, they express considerable doubt over this post-Brexit image. For instance, commentaries on the UK's attempt to send the Queen Elizabeth Strike Carrier to the South China Sea by *People's Daily* (Overseas Edition, 2019a) openly express 'scepticism' towards the idea of Global Britain. *Xinhua*'s commentary, under the title of 'Britain's global positioning in the "post-Brexit" era is questioned', is widely circulated within China by state media (Guangming Daily, 2021; Xinhua, 2021). *China Youth Daily* states that it is impossible for the UK to pursue a Global Britain, when it is dealing with the 'sequela of Brexit' (China Youth Daily, 2021).

This scepticism towards the post-Brexit role is also shared by Chinese scholars. One of the earliest assessments contends that Global Britain lacks 'coherency', because the objective of maximizing trade with China is contradictory with the promotion of human rights in China; it also lacks 'feasibility', since it fails to enlist support from other parties and societal actors (B. Zhang, 2018). Ruike Xu (2020) tests the rhetoric of 'Global Britain' against the facts such as the leadership visits to foreign countries, finding instead that the UK becomes less global. Researchers from CASS and CICIR argue that the UK's ability in expanding its influence across the world, from Africa to Asia, is limited (Li, 2017; Qu and Wang, 2021).

In short, in Chinese assessments, Brexit will considerably affect the UK's outlook, economy, politics, unity, international influence, and global role, and these impacts are negative.

BREXIT FOR CHINA-UK RELATIONS

Unlike China's assessments of Brexit's impacts on the UK that are largely negative, the Chinese assessments of the implications of Brexit for China are mixed with both negative and positive views.

On the one hand, there are the negative views that Brexit may hinder China-UK political and economic relations. First of all, Brexit may destabilize China-UK relations. Some attribute this to the rise of populism and irrationalism in the UK. Under the sway of populism, China-UK relations will be disrupted because the UK politicians will respond more to domestic demands than Chinese interest. 'The current rise of populism in the UK', which leads to the rise of protectionism and isolationism in the country, as Jin (2016, 36) observes, 'will affect the overall situation of the "Golden Era" of Sino-British relations'. Wang and Lv (2020, 53) caution that 'The influence of populism will become a new challenge facing the development of China-UK relations.' Others, however, attribute this to the UK's diminished international influence after Brexit. Since the UK will lose its international influence, it will tend to demonstrate its global presence and influence by challenging China's claims on the South China Sea and Hong Kong and Xinjiang. Hence Jian Zhang (2020, 57–8) speaks of the UK's 'contradictory' policy towards China, and Wang and Lv (2020, 52) of the UK's 'dualistic' policy towards China. These scholars share the view that despite the UK's attempt to develop its economic relations with China, it will challenge China on several fronts in order to show its presence and recompense for its diminished international influence (Zhang, 2019a).

Second, China-UK trade relations will be negatively affected. Brexit will decrease China's exports to the UK. This reduction in Chinese exports may be partly due to the slowing down of British economic growth and decreasing national incomes that will reduce the demand for Chinese products, and partly due to the choices of many Chinese companies to stop using the UK as their transit point for exporting their goods to the EU (Liu and Feng, 2017, 51–2). Either way, Brexit will cut Chinese exports to the UK. Also, Brexit will make it less easy to strike a free trade agreement (FTA) between China and the UK than is commonly expected. Jian Han (2020, 66) identifies four obstacles for China and the UK to reach an agreement: FTA requires the recognition of market economy status (MES), but the UK would face enormous third-party pressure from other Western countries in granting China this status; the US, which is in a trade war with China, will not let a China-UK FTA undermine the US objective of pressuring China; as one of the UK's key trade partners, the EU has extended influence on the UK's trade negotiation; finally, human rights concerns will step in the way towards the UK and China's FTA. Similarly, Xu, Garcia-Herrero, and Zhang (2017, 46–7) argue that the EU will wield significant influence over the UK's trade negotiations. Given that the UK will also need to renegotiate with other World Trade Organization (WTO) members, which is time-consuming and burdensome, it would be impossible for China and the UK to strike a quick FTA.

Third, Brexit will affect Chinese investment in negative ways. Chief among the many considerations is that, as state media and scholars point out, Chinese companies' interest in 'going out' to the UK would be reduced, because the UK would lose its 'gateway' function. As the UK loses its function of a 'bridge' to the EU, Chinese investors would reconsider their choice of destination and reallocate their investment (Feng, 2016, 4; Yu, 2017).[5] Chinese businessmen and scholars also express their concerns about the uncertainty of Brexit. For instance, Wang Jianlin, the owner of Dalian Wanda, one of the major Chinese real estate developers, openly warned that Brexit will deter Chinese investors from putting money into the UK. Xu Weiping, the chairman of the Advanced Business Park (ABP) that pledged to rebuild Royal Albert Dock into a new financial centre, said that uncertainty around Brexit had a significant effect on marketing and letting of the property (Clarence-Smith, n.d.). Like businessmen, Chinese scholars also express their worries about investing in the UK. For them, the UK government may not keep the door open to Chinese investment, and the newly established investment screening regime will prevent Chinese investment from entering into the UK (Yu, 2017; Zhang, 2019b).

In short, Brexit will create considerable challenges to China-UK relations on the political, trade, and investment fronts.

On the other hand, there are feelings that Brexit might give a boost to China-UK relations. Unlike the pessimists who focus on the negative effects on China-UK relations, the optimists argue that Brexit creates opportunities for China to develop relations with the UK precisely because Brexit does considerable damage to the UK, and thus creates a 'gap' for China to fill.

First, Brexit creates a strong incentive for the UK to develop its relations with China. Liu Xiaoming, former Chinese ambassador to the UK, writes that 'Brexit posed more opportunities than challenges to China-UK relations.' For him, Brexit creates triple opportunities: the 'strategic opportunity' for China and the UK to cooperate, when the UK's pursuit of the 'strategy of Global Britain' matches with China's 'New Era Socialism with Chinese Characteristics'; the 'development opportunity' for both sides to cooperate, including infrastructure, the One Belt and one Road (OBOR) Initiative, RMB internationalization, green finance and technology; and the 'cooperative opportunity', including global governance, climate change, anti-terrorism for both sides to solve (Xinhua, 2018a). Similarly, state media also reports how Brexit creates enormous opportunities for China and the UK to 'cooperate'. Zhongsheng from *People's Daily*[6] calls for building an 'enhanced version of the "Golden Era"', because in the post-Brexit era the two sides' positions on 'major international issues such as supporting economic globalization, opposing protectionism, reforming the global economic governance system, and tackling climate change have become more prominent, and their interests more aligned' (Zhongsheng, 2018). *China Daily* (2018) reports, under the title of 'Brexit can bring China-UK closer together', how Chinese diplomats speak of 'a [post-Brexit] time of new and historic opportunities'. *Guangming Daily* says that 'Brexit would be an opportunity for China's development', and 'China should seize the opportunity to strengthen cooperation with the UK in every field', 'especially the large number of cooperation opportunities brought by the Belt and Road Initiative (BRI) and Northern Powerhouse, and strengthen the economic, trade, and commercial partnership between the two sides' (Q. Li, 2016). Finally, this optimistic feeling is widely shared by Chinese scholars. Brexit will create a demand for both sides to have more 'intimate cooperation' (Feng, 2016, 5), or 'strategic coordination' (Wang and Lv, 2020).

Second, Brexit will significantly deepen the China-UK bilateral trade relationship for several reasons. First is that after Brexit, China and the UK would be freer to do their trade. Officials and analysts argue that Brexit makes it easier for China and the UK to strike an FTA. For instance, Li Ruogu, former Chief of China's Ex-import Bank, said in the Boao Forum for Asia (BFA), one of the key forum institutions created by China, that China and the UK have less restraints after Brexit than before to do their trade (China Daily, 2017). Similarly, Chinese analysts also express the view that Brexit might boost China-UK trade. A research team from Mofcom's ECRI suggests that both sides would attach more importance to their trade relationship; China should take this 'strategic opportunity' to strengthen cooperation with the UK on 'advanced manufacturing' such as aviation, auto industry bio-technology, and telecommunication (ECRI, 2017, 59–60). Feng (2016, 4) writes that after leaving the EU, the UK will be 'free from the constraints of the EU and accelerate the establishment of a closer economic cooperation system with China'. *China Daily* (2021) comments that 'The UK should seize the opportunity to strengthen multilateral cooperation with other countries in the world, and at the same time deepen trade cooperation with China, to welcome new breakthroughs.'

Third, Brexit creates opportunities for China and the UK to deepen their financial cooperation. Here, the voices from China's financial sector express their strong expectation of a post-Brexit development. For instance, *Xinhua* publishes an exclusive interview with the head of the London Branch of Bank of China, Sun Yu, suggesting that the UK would need RMB to maintain its leading position as an international financial centre, and China should seize the opportunity of Brexit to enhance its RMB internationalization (Xinhua, 2017b). *People's Daily* commentary is that there is enormous 'further space' for the Chinese offshore market to grow, and in the future, the UK's financial industry will significantly benefit from the offshore RMB business (People's Daily, 2017). The Financial Research Institute from one of China's biggest commercial banks estimates that Brexit will significantly promote the collaboration on RMB internationalization (Financial Research Institute ICBC, 2016).

Fourth, Brexit will bring more Chinese investment into the UK. First, the devaluation of the British pound will create the opportunity for China to acquire assets in the UK for a lower price (Wang and He, 2020, 78). Also, as the UK's economy was undermined by Brexit, Chinese money will be needed for development. Li Daokui, one of China's leading economists, argues that he is optimistic because most Chinese investment flows into the UK's real estate sector (People.Cn, 2016). In sharp contrast to the pessimistic evaluation, the optimists see that Chinese investment into the UK will continuously grow.

In short, Brexit will create both challenges and opportunities for China-UK relations, especially in the bilateral political, trade, financial and investment relationship. As the recent events between China and the UK show, the pessimistic assessment seems to win the debate.

BREXIT FOR CHINA-EU RELATIONS

Unlike the Chinese assessment of its relations with the UK which is characterized by domestic contestation over the good and bad effects of Brexit, China's evaluation of Brexit's impact on China-EU relations is dominated by the pessimistic view that Brexit will harm both sides (cf. Yang, 2020). Some Chinese scholars have argued that 'the economic and political relations between the two sides will not change much' (Feng, 2016, 4); that China-EU trade relations will be boosted because the EU will need to significantly develop its relations with China to avoid economic recession, making a China-EU trade deal easier (Wang, Xu, and Zhang, 2016, 7). But the overall feeling is that Brexit would cause significant disruptions to the bilateral strategic and economic relationship.

First, at the EU member state level, Brexit will result in Chinese loss of one of its key advocates within the EU. Here, Brexit will diminish the Chinese influence over the EU members in at least three ways. First, the UK is a strong advocate for granting China Market Economy Status (MES). There will be fewer supporting voices of granting China the MES within the EU. Second, Brexit will make it harder for China to gain support from the member states for striking an FTA. As one of the countries that has high trade complementarity with China, the UK has been a leading advocate of a China-EU FTA. However, Brexit would reduce the possibility of a China-EU free trade deal. Third, Brexit will make China lose a country that can exercise a leadership effect over others in dealing with China-led initiatives. In the last few years, the UK has been responding quickly and warmly to China's initiatives such as OBOR and the Asian Infrastructure Investment Bank (AIIB), even to the extent of displeasing the US and incurring warnings. The UK's action often leads other EU member states to act, exercising a kind of demonstrative effect on the EU member states. With Brexit, China will lose a country that can exercise such a demonstrative effect on other countries. Thus, the influence of China over the EU members will be diminished.

Second, at the Union level, Brexit will undermine China's strategic aim of pushing for multipolarity. Since the early 2000s, China has been trying to work with the EU on building a 'multilateral' world. The Chinese objective is to work with the EU on balancing against the US influence, constraining its use of force and unilateralism. The election of Donald Trump in 2016, the outbreak of a trade war with China, and the 'Indo-Pacific' strategy further make the Chinese believe that their need of the EU is growing unprecedentedly. Nevertheless, Brexit weakens the EU's material capability, reducing the EU's capability of undertaking actions in various fields. This reduced material capability will undermine China's strategic aim of building a multipolar world. 'As a pole in the multipolar international structure', Jin writes, 'the European Union advocates multilateralism and plays an important normative role in many fields.' But as the EU's material capability is weakened, China's strategic aim of balancing against the US would be less feasible (2016, 34). While Chinese assessments view Brexit as undermining China's strategic aim of 'multilateralism', there is also the apprehension in China that Brexit, which reduces the EU's material capability, will (further) shift the EU's 'perception' of China from a 'strategic partner' to a competitor. Cui (2018) writes, for instance, that Brexit constitutes one of the two 'turning points' in China-EU relations. With the withdrawal of a key member from the Union, the EU will perceive China from a position of weakness. China is more likely to be viewed as a competitor.

Third, Brexit would significantly affect China-EU trade relations in several ways. First, its immediate result is to reduce the scale of China-EU trade relations. Because the UK's trade with China is approximately 15 per cent of the overall EU trade with China, the UK's decision to leave the EU would decrease the total trade volume between China and the EU. Second, without the UK, the EU will be more likely to compete with China. The UK economy has more complementarity with China; without the UK, the EU would intensify its competition dimension with China.

In short, the Chinese assessment of the impact of Brexit on China-EU relations focuses on China's diminished influence over other member states, the undermined Chinese objective of multilateralism, and the downturn in China-EU trade relations. It seems that these assessments are more pessimistic than existing studies suggest.

INDIRECT INFLUENCES: BREXIT AND 'GREAT POWER RELATIONS'

Apart from Brexit's impacts on Britain, China-UK relations, and China-EU relations, China is also concerned with the broader implications of Brexit for China's 'strategic environment' or 'great power relations'. In Chinese eyes, Brexit will definitely affect UK-US relations, UK-Japan relations, and UK/EU-Russia relations. As the US, Japan, and Russia are China's 'neighbouring great powers', influences on them would change China's 'strategic environment'. Feng (2016, 4) speaks for many when he writes that 'Brexit has rewritten the geopolitical map of Europe, and new changes have taken place in the relations between great powers, and all this will inevitably affect China's international strategic environment.'

First, Brexit would reduce the importance of the UK to the US, which makes the UK's China policy vulnerable to US influences. There is a consensus within the Chinese scholarly circle and state media over the decreased importance of the UK to the US after Brexit. Some analysts attribute this decreased importance to the UK's withdrawal from the Union and thus the inability of influencing EU policies (Feng, 2016, 5; Lu, 2016a; Jin, 2016, 33; J. Zhang, 2019, 48; Zhao, 2020). Others, however, attribute it to the UK's inability to support the US across the world because Brexit has damaged the British economy and the UK's already shrinking size of military expenditure (Cao, 2018, 50; Zhao, 2020). State media echoes this feeling of increased American influence over the UK after Brexit. For instance, *People's Daily* reports how the UK is 'anxious to negotiate a trade deal with the US' (People's Daily (Overseas Edition), 2019b). *Xinhua* (2018b) reports that the US and the UK have 'unequal enthusiasm' for strengthening the special relationship. *Global Times* (2016b) published an Editorial to warn that Brexit would lead the UK to losing its influence over the US, and turn the UK into an 'Atlantic Orphan'.

Moreover, the consequence following this change is that the US would have greater influence over the UK's China policy. Once the importance of the UK to the US decreases, the asymmetry in the UK-US relationship would make the UK subordinate itself to the US when making policy towards China. Ding Yuanhong (2016), a former Chinese ambassador to the EU, writes that although the UK may 'give priority to safeguarding Britain's own interests and to reflect greater autonomy', its tendency to 'follow the United States on major international issues will not weaken, or even become more obvious'. Jian Zhang's (2020, 59) assessment is that 'the American factor will become more prominent, which will affect Britain's China policy to a greater extent'. *Global Times*'s opinion piece also suggests that post-Brexit UK 'will become even more subordinate to the US inevitably affecting Britain-China relations favouring provocative foreign policy such as sending the aircraft carrier Queen Elizabeth to the South China Sea'.

Second, Brexit would move the UK closer to Japan, increasing China's pressure when the two countries are unfolding their security cooperation. There is a consensus among Chinese scholars that Brexit would warm up the UK's relations with Japan, even to the extent of forging a 'quasi-alliance' (Zhao and Lv, 2020). Some scholars attribute this to the fact that 'the strategies of the two countries quickly converged and interacted' (Zhao and Lv, 2020, 50–52); others think that this is because both countries are US key allies and pursuing 'common interest' in the Indo-Pacific and 'common values' (Meng, 2020). Also, the warming relations between the two countries would put more pressure on China. A CICIR researcher's view is that their defence cooperation destabilizes security in the region, complicating the South China Sea issue, and furthering the 'soft balancing' against China (Meng, 2020, 20–21). Thus, Brexit eventually puts more pressure on China because of the British weight added to Japan.

Third, China is also concerned about Brexit's impacts on EU-Russia relations and UK-Russia relations. Primarily, the Chinese concern is with EU-Russia relations. Chinese analysts argue that after Brexit, EU-Russia relations will likely be improved. Given that the UK is the leading hardliner towards Russia, its departure from the EU will make it possible for other countries to pursue less confrontational relations with Russia (Feng, 2016, 5; Lu, 2016b; Jin, 2016, 33; Ren, 2016, 29; A. Xu, 2016, 30; J. Zhang, 2019, 49). This might take the form of an EU decision to lift sanctions on Russia under the pressure of some member states. Or it might also take the form of a Russian active push for the EU 27 to lift sanctions on Russia (Feng, 2016, 5), even using tactics such as 'intensifying EU's internal division' (A. Xu, 2016, 30). Thus, losing one of the firm hardliners on Russia, the EU would improve its relations with Russia.

Second, Brexit may also create an opportunity for the UK and Russia to have a rapprochement in their relationship and dealings with the EU. For instance, an influential researcher from CICIR argues that 'the attitudes and policies of the two sides [UK and Russia] towards each other will gradually be adjusted and changed', because the UK will find itself 'in a place similar to Russia', geographically located 'on the fringe of Europe', and facing similar pressures from the EU. As the EU would not want its ex-member to prosper, which would demonstrate that Brexit was the right choice, 'There will be more room for the integration of interests and cooperation on the EU issue, and it does not even rule out the possibility that the two sides will jointly deal with the EU on certain issues' (J. Zhang, 2019, 49).

In short, Chinese assessments are concerned with the broad influence of Brexit on 'great power relations' and China's 'strategic environment'.

CONCLUSION

In this chapter, we seek to show that Chinese assessments of the impacts of Brexit on China go beyond the narrow focus on China-EU relations and the economic dimension. In Chinese eyes, Brexit will not only affect the UK and China's relations with the UK and the EU, but also the great power relations such as between the US and UK, the UK and Japan, and the EU and UK-Russia that shape China's foreign relations. Furthermore, what Brexit means for China is not only about economics, but also about politics, strategy, and global order. Finally, Brexit's influences are assessed by a wide range of Chinese subjects. While the Chinese official rhetoric emphasizes 'consistency and constancy' towards the EU and 'respect' of the British choice to leave the EU, assessments by state media and government-affiliated or university-based analysts display much nuance towards Brexit.

Chinese assessments have focused on the implications of Brexit for four subjects. First, Chinese assessments focus on the impacts of Brexit on the UK itself. In China's view, Brexit may be harmful to the UK's outlook and thinking, economy, political system, the UK union, international influence and global role. Second, Chinese assessments focus on the impacts of Brexit on China-UK relations, with both negative and positive views expressed. While for the pessimists Brexit may destabilize China-UK relations, reduce Chinese exports to the UK, and decrease Chinese investment into the UK, for the optimists it would create more opportunities for China and the UK to cooperate in strategic and economic fields. Third, Chinese assessments analyze the impacts of Brexit on China-EU relations. What Brexit means for China-EU relations is basically negative, because the Chinese objective of pursuing 'multilateralism' and promoting trade with and investment in the EU would be undermined. Fourth, Chinese assessments focus on the broader impacts of Brexit on US-UK relations, UK-Japan relations, and EU/UK-Russia relations. These countries are important players in China's foreign relations, and will shape China's strategic environment.

In the end, understanding what China makes of Brexit is important in several senses. First, China's view of Brexit provides an international perspective on how an emerging global power located in the Indo-Pacific understands and appraises the British decision to leave the EU. Although much has been known about what the UK, the EU, and US make of Brexit, much less has been known about how China understands Brexit. Second, China's view of Brexit will significantly affect its foreign policy towards the UK and EU. Although many commentators are not officials, they play a key role in shaping China's foreign policy by offering policy advice. Third, the Chinese reception of Brexit is important to the success of British foreign policy in the post-Brexit era. As the UK seeks to build a 'Global Britain', and the UK's economic relations with China are deemed as crucial for its prosperity, Chinese assessment shows how Brexit is received in China, providing a test of the extent to which the UK's aim is likely to be achieved.

NOTES

1. We are grateful to John Erik Fossum for his detailed comments on earlier versions of the draft. Biao thanks Wuhan University's Center for Economic Diplomacy, where he is serving as a research fellow, for providing support and Guowei Wang for his research assistance.
2. That said, it is important to notice that the existing assessment sometimes touches on the effects of Brexit on several non-economic issues, such as China-EU educational and security relationships (e.g. Summers, 2017, 13–14).
3. We seek to provide a window into the Chinese thinking, rather than exhaust all the texts related to Brexit and conduct an analysis.
4. Chinese scholars often consider the decision as an emotional way of expressing frustration with the British or European economic, political, and social condition, instigated by the populist politicians. Brexit is 'the growing extremist and populist forces represented by the UK Independence Party that ultimately made Brexit successful in the referendum' (Feng, 2016, 2).
5. But according to the Heritage Foundation's China Global Investment Tracker (CGIT), China's investment has decreased continuously from $46.8 billion in 2016 to 5.7 billion in 2017, $3.8 billion in 2018, $2.2 billion in 2019, $9,530 million in 2020.
6. Zhongsheng means 'voice for China', which is widely regarded as quasi-editorial.

REFERENCES

Cao, X. (2019). '试论英国脱欧对英美特殊关系的影响'. *Contemporary International Relations*, *5*, 47–53.

China Daily. (2017, 11 April). 评论：积极看待英国脱欧对华影响. http://cn.chinadaily.com.cn/2017-04/11/content_28876224.htm. Accessed 31 October 2021.

China Daily. (2018, 20 June). Brexit can bring China-UK closer together. https://www.chinadaily.com.cn/a/201806/20/WS5b294210a3104bcf48c1562a.html. Accessed 8 November 2021.

China Daily. (2021, 25 February). 中国日报网评：中英贸易不断增长 抓住机遇深化合作方为正解. https://cn.chinadaily.com.cn/a/202102/25/WS60375df3a3101e7ce9741037.html. Accessed 21 October 2021.

China Youth Daily. (2021, 16 September). 受困于'脱欧'后遗症 '全球化英国'力不从心. http://zqb.cyol.com/html/2021-09/16/nw.D110000zgqnb_20210916_3-09.htm. Accessed 1 November 2021.

Chinese Embassy to the EU. (2020, 21 January). 驻欧盟使团团长张明大使就中欧关系接受《中国青年报》专访. http://www.chinamission.be/chn/stxw/t1731626.htm. Accessed 9 October 2021.

Clarence-Smith, L. (n.d.). Developer Advanced Business Park in threat to pull plug on Royal Albert Dock funds. Retrieved 4 February 2021, from https://www.thetimes.co.uk/article/developer-advanced-business-park-in-threat-to-pull-plug-on-royal-albert-dock-funds-295vnhhf7.

Cui, H. (2018). '中国欧盟关系的结构性变化及其前景'. *International Studies*, *1*, 41–59.

Ding, Y. (2016). 丁原洪：英国脱欧后的英美'特殊关系'. http://comment.cfisnet.com/2016/0725/1305411.html. Accessed 11 September 2021.

Economic Cooperation Research Institute (ECRI). (2017). '英国脱欧谈判与中英经贸合作战略契机'. *International Economic Cooperation*, *10*, 56–61.

Feng, Z. (2016). '英国脱欧及其对中国的影响'. *Contemporary International Relations*, *6*, 1–6.

Financial Research Institute ICBC. (2016). 英国脱欧中长期利好人民币国际化. https://www.icbcstandardbank.com/icbc. Accessed October 2022.

Financial Times. (2015, 23 October). China's Xi Jinping urges UK to stay in EU. *Financial Times*. https://www.ft.com/content/df78cae4-797e-11e5-933d-efcdc3c11c89. Accessed 18 December 2017.

Global Times. (2016a). 六大专家谈英国脱欧影响：世界格局将因此走向何方？. https://world.huanqiu.com/article/9CaKrnJWajb. Accessed 12 May 2021.

Global Times. (2016b, 23 June). 社评：英国脱欧公投 高空走钢丝表演. https://opinion.huanqiu.com/article/9CaKrnJW40E. Accessed 24 September 2021.

Global Times. (2016c, 24 June). 社评：英国回300年前原点，欧洲加速衰落. https://opinion.huanqiu.com/article/9CaKrnJW6dr. Accessed 26 August 2021.

Global Times. (2019, 16 January). 社评：英式民主将脱欧吊在了半空中. https://opinion.huanqiu.com/article/9CaKrnKh64B. Accessed 24 September 2021.

Gov.CN. (2018). 中国对欧盟政策文件 (China's Policy Paper on the EU). http://www.gov.cn/xinwen/2018-12/18/content_5349904.htm.

Guangming Daily. (2021, 18 March). '英国谋划'后脱欧'时代全球定位遭质疑'. https://m.gmw.cn/baijia/2021-03/18/34695360.html . Accessed 1 September 2021.

Han, J. (2020). '"全球英国"理念下的英国自贸协定谈判及中英FTA前景展望'. *International Trade*, *5*, 61–7.

He, Y. and Shi, Z. (2019). '脱欧背景下的英国政府、议会和政党关系的变化——以威斯敏斯特为视角'. *Journal of European Studies*, *4*, 49–66.

Jin, L. (2016). '英国脱欧：原因、影响及走向'. *International Studies*, *4*, 24–36.

Li, J. (2017). '英国与欧盟中东政策的未来走向: 以英国脱欧为视角'. Western Asia and Africa, *5*, 20–41.

Li, K. (2016). 夏季达沃斯论坛致辞实录 [Record of the 2016 Summer Davos Forum Speech]. http://www.gov.cn/zhuanti/2016-06/27/content_5085953.htm. Accessed 10 August 2021.

Li, Q. (2016, 4 August). 英国'脱欧'对中国经济的影响. *Guangming Daily*. https://opinion.huanqiu.com/article/9CaKrnJWSON. Accessed 16 May 2021.

Liu, Y. (2017). '英国'脱欧'公投中的民粹主义现象分析'. *Journal of Jiangsu Administration Institute*, *4*, 83–9.

Liu, J. and Feng, Q. (2017). '英国脱欧后中英贸易的影响及对策研究'. *International Trade*, *1*, 49–53.

Lu, Z. (2016a). 英美'特殊关系'会否一脱就变. *Xinhua*. http://www.xinhuanet.com/world/2016-07/02/c_129109557.htm. Accessed 12 May 2021.

Lu, Z. (2016b, 25 July). 英国脱欧对国际战略格局的影响. *Guangming Daily*. https://epaper.gmw.cn/gmrb/html/2016-07/25/nw.D110000gmrb_20160725_1-12.htm. Accessed 12 May 2021.

Meng, X. (2020). '"印太战略"与'全球英国'战略交汇下的日英安全合作. *Contemporary International Relations*, *3*, 11–21.

MFA. (2016a, 24 June). 2016年6月24日外交部发言人华春莹主持例行记者会. https://www.fmprc.gov.cn/web/fyrbt_673021/t1375085.shtml. Accessed 4 July 2021.

MFA. (2016b, 13 July). Li Keqiang and President Jean-Claude Juncker of the European Commission jointly attend 11th China-EU Business Summit and deliver speeches. https://www.fmprc.gov.cn/mfa_eng/zxxx_662805/t1381876.shtml. Accessed 12 May 2021.

Oliver, T. (2016). European and international views of Brexit. *Journal of European Public Policy*, *23*(9), 1321–8. https://doi.org/10.1080/13501763.2016.1174534.

People.Cn. (2016). '李稻葵：英国脱欧对中国投资不会有太大影响'. http://finance.people.com.cn/n1/2016/0626/c1004-28479134.html. Accessed 3 April 2021.

People's Daily. (2017, 30 March). 既然要'分手'，英国想快点（经济透视. http://world.people.com.cn/n1/2017/0330/c1002-29178188.html. Accessed 10 May 2021.

People's Daily (Overseas Edition). (2019a, 26 February). '全球英国'能重振英国吗. *People's Daily Overseas*. http://paper.people.com.cn/rmrbhwb/html/2019-02/26/content_1910776.htm. Accessed 1 December 2021.

People's Daily (Overseas Edition). (2019b, 13 August). 英国急着想谈拢对美自贸协定(环球热点. http://world.people.com.cn/n1/2019/0813/c1002-31291100.html. Accessed 1 December 2021.

Ren, L. (2016). '英国脱欧对全球治理及国际政治经济格局的影响'. *International Economic Review*, *6*, 21–30.

Qu, B. and Wang, S. (2021). '后脱欧时代'全球英国'外交战略及其前景. *Contemporary International Relations*, *1*, 21–8.

SCIO. (2016). 商务部举行7月初例行发布会. http://www.scio.gov.cn/ztk/xwfb/jjfyr/34996/wqfbh35004/Document/1488907/1488907.htm. Accessed 10 May 2021.

Summers, T. (2017). *Brexit: Implications for EU-China Relations*. Chatham House.

Wang, X. and Liu, J. (2020). '结束还是开始?——民粹主义视阈下的英国脱欧及其走向'. *Foreign Theoretical Trend*, *3*, 140–51.

Wang, Y. and He, Y. (2020). '"后脱欧时代"的英欧贸易谈判及其影响'. *Contemporary World*, *10*, 74–9.

Wang, Y., Xu, Z. and Zhang, X. (2016). '英国脱欧对中英和中欧贸易投资的影响'. *International Economic Cooperation*, *12*, 4–9.

Wang, Z. and Lv, D. (2020). '英国脱欧与中英关系的未来'. *Contemporary World*, 48–54.

Wang, Z, and Zhang, X. (2019). '脱欧背景下英国权力下放的演变及其影响'. *Journal of European Studies*, *4*, 1–25.

Xinhua. (2016, 24 June). 新华国际时评：英国'脱欧'，政治豪赌的失败. http://www.xinhuanet.com//world/2016-06/24/c_1119106584.htm. Accessed 10 May 2021.

Xinhua. (2017a, April). 英国'脱欧'使德国成为全球第二大最具吸引力投资地. http://www.xinhuanet.com/world/2017-04/20/c_129555585.htm. Accessed 11 May 2021.

Xinhua. (2017b, 13 April). 专访：在英国'脱欧'进程中抓住人民币国际化历史机遇. http://www.xinhuanet.com//fortune/2017-04/13/c_1120802903.htm. Accessed 11 May 2021.

Xinhua. (2018a, 26 January). 中国驻英大使：英国'脱欧'对中英关系发展机遇大于挑战. http://www.xinhuanet.com/2018-01/26/c_1122317551.htm. Accessed 9 September 2021.

Xinhua. (2018b, 14 July). 国际观察：'特殊关系'难加强 英美热情不对等. http://www.xinhuanet.com/2018-07/14/c_1123126270.htm. Accessed 9 September 2021.

Xinhua. (2019). 新华国际时评：企业'出走'凸显英国'脱欧'尴尬. http://www.xinhuanet.com/world/2019-02/21/c_1124146012.htm. Accessed 12 December 2021.

Xinhua. (2021). 英国谋划'后脱欧'时代全球定位遭质疑. http://www.xinhuanet.com/world/2021-03/17/c_1127222747.htm. Accessed 4 December 2021.

Xu, A. (2016_. '英国脱欧对全球经济的可能影响'. *People's Forum*, *7*, 28–30.

Xu, R. (2020). '英国外交形势', in Zhanpeng Wang and Ruike Xu (eds), *UK Development Report*. Beijing: Social Science Press, 99–120.

Xu, J, Garcia-Herroro, A., and Zhang, J. (2017). '英国脱欧会影响中欧贸易吗?'. *International Economic Review*, *3*, 45–57.

Yang, Y. (2020). After Brexit: the certainty and uncertainty of China-EU relations in academic discourse. *European Foreign Affairs Review*, *25*(1).

Yu, J. (2017). After Brexit: risks and opportunities to EU–China relations. *Global Policy*, *8*(S4), 109–14. https://doi.org/10.1111/1758-5899.12440.

Zhang, B. (2018). '全球英国: 脱欧后英国的外交选择'. *Contemporary International Relations*, *3*, 18–25.

Zhang, B. (2019a). '英国的南海政策：变化，动因与走向'. *Contemporary International Relations*, *7*, 29–44.

Zhang, B. (2019b). State transformation goes nuclear: Chinese National Nuclear Companies' expansion into Europe. *Third World Quarterly*, *40*(8), 1459–78. https://doi.org/10.1080/01436597.2019.1627189.

Zhang, J. (2019). 英国脱欧的战略影响. *Contemporary International Relations*, *11*, 43–50.

Zhang, J. (2020). 后脱欧时代英国对华政策前瞻. *International Economic Review*, *2*, 56–70.

Zhao, H. (2020). '英美防务关系的特性及其演变'. *Contemporary World and Socialism*, *4*, 148–55.

Zhao, Y and Lv, Y. (2020). '印太'视阈下日英'准同盟'关系的构建与局限. *Pacific Journal*, *8*, 43-55.

Zhongsheng. (2018). 打造中英黄金时代的增强版. *People's Daily*. http://www.gov.cn/xinwen/2018-02/02/content_5263045.htm. Accessed October 2022.

PART VI

BREXIT AND QUESTIONS OF LEGITIMACY

27. Brexit and political legitimacy

Albert Weale

INTRODUCTION

'Any Member State may decide to withdraw from the Union in accordance with its own constitutional requirements.' So runs Article 50 of the Consolidated Version of the Treaty on European Union (2012). To date only the United Kingdom (UK) has invoked the article, and it is likely to remain the only state to do so for some time, if ever. For that reason alone, Brexit is the focus of intense study, as it involves many issues about the role of democracies in an inter-dependent international order. Did Brexit reflect anything more than passing domestic political trends? How far was it a local expression of a more general wave of populist nationalism? What are the limits of supranational authority and how far can states make credible commitments to one another to join in an ever-closer union of their peoples?

These and similar questions typically involve controversies over political legitimacy – controversies that were at the heart of Brexit in a number of different ways. In requiring the withdrawal process to be in accordance with the constitutional requirements of the Member State, Article 50 itself requires the withdrawal process to be legitimate. How far were those constitutional requirements met and what problems of constitutional legitimacy did the Brexit process reveal? Moreover, the turning point of Brexit was the referendum of 23 June 2016, and there are profound questions in democratic theory concerning the role of referendums in political decision making and the obligations they imply for citizens at large, particularly with decisions as fundamental as matters of trade, migration, environmental protection and international security, which were all bound up with leaving the European Union (EU). Moreover, withdrawal from the EU was withdrawal from a form of political association involving supranational authority. So, central to Brexit is the question of how far respect for supranational authority is compatible with political legitimacy deriving from domestic democratic control, an issue that will continue in respect of the UK's conduct in future relations with the EU. Finally, Brexit threatens the political legitimacy of a unitary state that seeks to hold together a union of the nations that make up the UK.

POLITICAL LEGITIMACY

The idea of legitimacy is a complex one (Beetham, 2013). However, for the purposes of this analysis, it may be understood as conformity to the requirements of a normative order. In the case of Brexit this means both the legal-constitutional order – constitutional legitimacy – on the one hand and the normative order of democratic principles – democratic legitimacy – on the other.

The constitutional order defines the offices and powers of those entitled to act with political authority, and in the UK is determined through custom, statutory provision and judicial judgement. This is not to say that the determination of constitutional norms and principles is easy or uncontentious. However, what the law required and permitted in the case of Brexit could be determined by established practices that were independent of the Brexit issue itself. In other words, the legal-constitutional assessment of the issues prompted by Brexit did not depend on the specifics of the Brexit process itself but could be defined by more general constitutional principles.

It is often claimed that the UK does not have a constitution. Does this mean that it is not possible to talk about the constitutional legitimacy of the Brexit referendum? If 'constitution' means a single document, like the US Constitution or Germany's Basic Law, containing fundamental legal provisions both for the functioning of government and for the rights of citizens, then the UK does not have a constitution. However, if by 'constitution' we mean a set of rules and legal requirements for government together with certain agreed conventions, then the UK does have a constitution, though it is spread across many documents.[1]

The existence of the constitution should not be confused with its character. The standard characterization of the UK constitution is that it is flexible. What is meant by this is that it is easily changed. In legal terms, all that is required is parliamentary consent by a simple majority vote; royal assent can be assumed. By contrast with rigid constitutions, there are no entrenched powers held by different bodies and no counter-majoritarian procedures required for constitutional change. The House of Lords, as the second chamber, has relatively weak delaying powers, and by convention will not oppose legislation that fulfils a manifesto promise of a party with a majority in the Commons. Since the electoral system tends to bestow large parliamentary majorities on a governing party, even when that party has only secured a plurality of the popular vote (normally at just above 40 per cent), constitutional change can normally be secured without cross-party negotiation. It is a measure of the political turbulence created by Brexit that the normal ability of a governing party to control the Commons was lost between the election of June 2017 and that of December 2019, when the Conservative government lacked a majority in the House.

The flexibility of the UK constitution is best illustrated by reference to the scale of constitutional reforms of the last 40 years or so. These include the rise of judicial review, the reduction in the responsibilities of local government, devolution to Scotland and Wales, reform of the House of Lords and the use of referendums, most notably in relation to devolution and the Good Friday Agreement in Northern Ireland (see King, 2007). However, although the UK constitution is flexible and has experienced considerable change in a few decades, there is also a sense in which it is also remarkably stable. In particular, the principle of parliamentary sovereignty, which extends back to the seventeenth century, is still central to the exercise of governmental authority, a fact that was to become both decisive and highly charged in the Brexit process.

By contrast with constitutional legitimacy, the norms and principles that make up democratic legitimacy are harder to define. They lack a generally recognized process of authoritative determination, so that their meaning is contested. They are also cast at a high level of generality such that they can take different plausible interpretations. For example, it is a principle of democratic theory that a political system should facilitate opposition as well as government. Indeed, this is one principle that picks out democratic political systems from non-democratic ones. However, the precise interpretation of this principle will vary from one democratic political system to another. In some, it will require a sharing of power among the principal parties that make up the legislature, particularly in matters of constitutional change. In others, it will require only that the opposition is allowed to criticize and campaign against the government of the day, without expecting to have any say in the formal powers of decision. Similarly, there are important questions about the scope of majority rule. In a political system in which there are distinct territorial authorities associated with nationhood or strong provincial identity, it is possible to argue that legitimate decision making should rest on a super-majority principle of concurrent majorities among the affected parties, requiring consent from those territorial authorities regarded collectively, as well as a majority of the population taken as a whole. Given these disputes and the indeterminacy to which they give rise, the only approach to the democratic evaluation of legitimacy is to state explicitly the presumed principle of democratic theory that is being used to evaluate a political process in any particular context.

Even allowing for a generally recognized authoritative process of determination, there are likely to be disagreements within any political culture about what the constitution requires, alongside disagreements about the meaning of democracy. During Brexit conflicting and contradictory appeals were made to both the constitutional and the democratic normative order. Although the courts were able to settle some of the constitutional questions, others were resolved only through political contest. Only political processes could resolve, or at least determine, the interpretation of democratic principles that were to prevail in this contest. It was not simply that Brexit divided the population on the merits or otherwise of membership of the EU. It was that in doing so, it also opened up severe and possibly permanent disagreements about the democratic legitimacy of the UK as a sovereign political entity. Both the constitutional controversies and the controversies in democratic theory were so sharp because they involved competing visions (the religious overtones of the word 'visions' are not entirely coincidental in this context) of what living in a constitutional democracy in an inter-dependent world involves.

Because the referendum was the decisive turning point in Brexit, questions of legitimacy must initially focus upon that event. Those questions can be usefully divided into three, corresponding to the three stages of the process: the legitimacy of holding a referendum on the issue; the problems of legitimacy arising from the conduct of the referendum; and the authority of the result and its implications for the conduct of government and the obligations of citizens. At each stage, the political struggle became more intense. Over the holding of the referendum, there was virtually no controversy. With the coming of the campaign itself the debate became rancorous. The aftermath of the referendum and withdrawal involved, and continues to involve, deep and possibly permanent disputes about political authority in the UK and the manner in which it can continue to be exercised, as well as what standards of political legitimacy in the international order need to be respected.

CALLING THE REFERENDUM

The parliamentary decision to hold a referendum on Cameron's renegotiated terms was relatively uncontroversial. The Conservative Party had promised a referendum in their 2015 manifesto, and Labour also supported the principle. Various issues about the conduct of the referendum and about the implications of leaving the EU were raised in the second reading debate in the House of Commons, but there was little opposition to the principle of having such a referendum (see HC Deb, 2015).

In constitutional terms the referendum was a 'consultative' one. After the result some Remainer voices interpreted this to mean that Parliament was not obliged to implement the result. However, in UK constitutional terms, consultative status has a specific meaning, as (Uberoi, 2015) pointed out in its briefing paper on the subject. A consultative referendum is one in which a point of political principle is being decided rather than popular agreement being sought to a particular piece of legislation. The contrasting case was the 2011 UK referendum on changing the electoral system, in which a particular set of proposals were put to the popular vote. Although the proposal for a change in the electoral system was lost on that occasion, had the result gone the other way, the particular electoral system put to voters would have been the basis for legislation. Constitutionally, the UK Parliament, being legally sovereign, could have chosen to treat the referendum result as merely an opinion poll. However, there is a constitutional principle that Parliament does not legislate in vain. Legislating for a referendum implied acting on its result. In any case, what might have been constitutionally permissible was not politically feasible. Having handed the decision to the people in a referendum, Members of Parliament (MPs), when they passed the legislation, were politically committing themselves to implementing the result.

What are the relevant considerations in democratic theory? The principle of popular sovereignty does not of itself imply the use of referendums in matters of European integration. After all, Article 20(2) of the German Basic Law affirms that all state authority derives from the people, but despite its commitment to deep European integration, Germany has not held referendums on, say, the Maastricht or Lisbon treaties, as other countries have done and are sometime required to do by their constitutions. Some parliamentarians may have thought that they were either implicitly or explicitly acknowledging the sovereignty of the people in legislating for a referendum, but the principle of popular sovereignty alone does not require a referendum. Rather, it seems, the referendum was adopted by the Conservatives as a response to the rise of the UK Independence Party (UKIP) and, once the Conservatives unexpectedly won a majority in the Commons in 2015, it because politically impossible for other parties substantially to oppose the policy.

One way of interpreting the parliamentary support for the referendum was as an expression of the ideal of government by consent. Suppose that there had been a clear and ardent majority of voters in favour of leaving the EU, then it could be argued that keeping the UK in the EU was, in effect, constraining the majority of voters to stay in a political association against their will. Holding a referendum might then be a way of testing whether this proposition was true. For the majority of MPs, who voted Remain three to one, it might seem a relatively harmless way of demonstrating lack of popular support for leaving the EU. For Leave MPs it was an opportunity to achieve their long-sought goal. They then found it easier to mobilize discontent than Remainers found it to mobilize content. The referendum need not be seen as an expression of popular sovereignty, but rather as a case in which a sovereign parliament delegates to the body of citizens a particular decision of principle.

THE CONDUCT OF THE REFERENDUM

The conduct of the referendum raised three issues of importance to questions of legitimacy: the extent of the franchise, the counting rule used for the voting, and the conduct of the campaigners. These are primarily questions in democratic theory. Although there were legal problems with the funding of the Vote Leave campaign, the House of Commons Public Administration and Constitutional Affairs Committee (2017), taking evidence from a wide range of witnesses, concluded that in general the conduct of the referendum meant that it was a free and fair process.

The Extent of the Franchise

For national elections, UK law gives the vote to all citizens aged 18 or older, with certain restrictions, for example with respect to prisoners. Other categories of those eligible to vote include UK citizens living abroad for less than 15 years and Irish citizens resident in the UK. However, some two million EU resident citizens, other than Irish citizens, were only entitled to vote in local and EU elections, not national ones. Parliament decided not to extend the franchise to EU residents for the referendum, though it would have been legally possible to do so. The principle of parliamentary sovereignty made this a constitutionally valid decision.

However, the constitutional question is one thing, the issue of democratic principle another. Depriving EU nationals the right to vote in the referendum may have been constitutionally legitimate, but to what extent was it consistent with democratic principles? As Sandra Kröger (2019, pp. 287–9) notes, there are two principles that have been theoretically discussed in respect of the scope of the franchise: the all-affected principle and the all-subject principle. The first affirms that those who are affected by a political decision should have a say in the making of that decision. The second affirms that only those subject to the authority of the decision should have a say.

Olsen and Rostbøll (2017) have advanced a version of the all-affected principle, according to which the people of no state in the EU have the democratic right unilaterally to withdraw from the Union. Their argument is that the withdrawal of one state affects the political status of all citizens of the EU and so unilateral withdrawal would be a violation of the principles of political equality and non-domination. In reply, it might be said that this conclusion is an illustration of just how expansive, and therefore how implausible, any version of the all-affected principle is. In making the withdrawal of a Member State from the EU a matter to be decided by all citizens of the EU, the all-affected principle would render nugatory the right of any Member State to withdraw, since the exercise of the right would be conditional upon agreement from citizens in other states. The EU would cease to be a voluntary union of states as representatives of their peoples. Moreover, the argument depends less on a democratic principle of equality, but more on a claim about the extent to which the fact of interdependence calls for the creation of a common political authority (Olsen and Rostbøll, 2017, pp. 445–7, 454, 459). However, the extent to which interdependence calls for the creation of common political authority is a matter to be judged by those affected, not externally. The citizens of a Member State may well decide that they would prefer to limit the growth of interdependence in order to protect domestic democratic control.

Consequently, the all-subject principle seems a more plausible basis on which to argue that EU citizens residing in the UK should have had the right to vote in the referendum. As Kröger points out, such persons had a vital stake in the decision, since they had made the choice to settle in the UK under EU freedom of movement rules. Continued residency after a Leave vote would make them subject to whatever changes in their status was legally decided, including the possibility, for example, that they could not continue their residency without being naturalized as citizens. So, on the twin basis of the all-subject principle and a recognition of the stake that resident EU citizens had in the decision, it can be argued that their exclusion from the franchise was democratically illegitimate.

It would not follow that lack of legitimacy, in this particular respect, undermined the legitimacy of the conduct of the referendum as a whole, since a process may have defects but still be above a threshold to meet an overall test of legitimacy. Moreover, it is likely that had two million resident EU citizens been given the vote, the result would have been different, given that the winning margin was only 1,269,501. Had this happened, Leavers might then have argued that the result was illegitimate, since a reason for being opposed to EU membership was that it led to a situation in which non-citizens could be decisive in what was essentially a matter for the national body of citizens. There is obviously a danger of question-begging in respect of this argument, since the issue should turn on whether those who had, on perfectly bona fide grounds, an intense stake in the issue were entitled to the vote, rather than on the question of whether, if they were to receive the vote, the result would have been different. Nonetheless, had EU citizens been given the vote and the result turned on their participation, it might have been a perceived source of illegitimacy.

The exclusion of resident EU citizens might have been justified if the UK government had made a firm and clear commitment to retaining their rights of residence irrespective of the result. It would then have acknowledged their rightful claims in respect of continuity of status without conceding that this involved the right to vote in national elections, which after all had not been a feature of their status prior to Brexit. Contrary to this, it might be argued that the denial of the right to vote before Brexit was itself objectionable, given the stake that EU residents had, and this alone should be sufficient to have granted them the franchise. Conceptually, this means that the all-subject test for those residents in the country is only a necessary condition of the franchise, and the question at issue between those who wish to grant and those who wish to withhold the franchise from EU residents is how far the additional stakeholder test is sufficient. (For non-resident citizens with the franchise, the all-subject test is not even necessary.) In the event, the UK government chose to use the rights of EU residents as a bargaining counter in the negotiations over the Withdrawal Agreement. The issue of legitimacy was therefore overridden by considerations of pragmatic interest.

The Counting Rule

An issue that never seems to have been raised throughout the process is the question of what the counting rule for the vote should have been. It was taken for granted that the referendum would be decided by a simple majority of those voting. This was the rule used in the 1975 referendum on continued membership of the Common Market (as it then was), and it was also the rule used in all other referendums, both UK-wide and non-UK-wide, except the 1978 referendum held in Scotland on devolution. The 1978 devolution referendum required a simple majority of those voting and, in addition, at least 40 per cent of the eligible electorate to be in favour of devolution if it was to go forward, in effect imposing a super-majority requirement.

Would it have been democratically unfair, and therefore politically illegitimate, to have imposed a similar requirement on the EU referendum? It is possible to argue that such an approval quorum can lead to a sense by the majority that they have been unfairly deprived of victory. Indeed, had the same percentage of registered voters been used in the EU referendum as in Scotland in 1978, then the referendum result would have been Remain, since only some 37 per cent of registered voters favoured Leave. This in itself could have been a source of discontent on grounds of perceived unfairness. Moreover, by 2016, it could be argued that it would be unfair to treat the EU referendum differently to all the other referendums bar one. Precedent for a simple majority decision could have been invoked. To have required an approval quorum would suggest that the government was seeking to rig the process in order to obtain the outcome that it wanted. Indeed, Leavers did express concerns about the government seeking to bias voting, raising the question in the Commons second reading debate about the information the government would provide to voters and whether it would be impartial. The use of a super-majority principle would have fed into those concerns as a point of discontent with the legitimacy of the process.

On the other hand, it might be argued that leaving the EU was such a significant act, and one with serious long-term consequences, that to require a super-majority would be the best way of ensuring that there was a substantial and settled body of opinion in favour of leaving. The long-term consequences of leaving did figure in the debate about the referendum, but only indirectly with the suggestion that the voting age might be lowered to 16 to recognize that the young would have to live with the consequences. Moreover, there is another reason in favour of a super-majority stemming from the requirements of legitimacy in international agreements. In order to be effective, the parties to an international agreement have to be able to rely upon the credible commitment of other parties to the agreement. This is particularly so in the case of the EU where long-term cooperation is required as a condition of achieving the goals of the Union (see later discussion). In this context, the conservative bias of a super-majority rule might be justified by the fact that it makes departure from the EU less likely, and so increases commitment. Against this line of argument, it can be urged that Article 50 itself leaves it up to the constitutional requirements of the Member State as to how the article is to be triggered. Insofar as precedent is an important element of UK constitutional conventions, the vast majority of the precedents suggest that a simple majority of those actually voting ought to be sufficient. Moreover, a decision to leave the EU is not irreversible. Article 49 envisages the possibility that a state could reapply for membership. So, though the consequences of leaving are serious, the possibility of reapplying means that the effects may not stretch to the long term.

The Conduct of the Campaigners

The campaign itself did not resemble anything like a Habermasian ideal speech situation, in which all sides recognized that the force of the better argument should prevail. In general terms, Remainers exaggerated and Leavers both exaggerated and lied (see Clarke et al., 2017, chapter 3; Evans and Menon, 2017, pp. 51–68).

The Remain campaign seems to have been conducted as though those devising it had read and internalized the political science literature on the supposed success of negative campaigning. Apart from the general appeal to the risks of being outside one of the largest single markets in the world, claims were made that taxes would rise in the near future, public expenditure would be cut and house prices fall. (This last point was a rather curious argument, since there were swathes of the electorate for whom a fall in house prices would be an advantage.) Membership of the EU was presented as a reluctant necessity rather than a political ideal. Remainers did not campaign on the promise of an ever-closer union among the peoples of Europe.

The Leave message was premised on the principle that it would be possible, in the words of Boris Johnson, later PM but at that stage the leader of Vote Leave, for the UK to have its cake and eat it (Musolff, 2020). According to prominent Leavers, there were no downsides to Brexit, only upsides. However, optimistic exaggeration passed into lies with the Vote Leave campaign bus carrying a display on its side promising an extra £350 million per week for the National Health Service were the UK to leave the EU and so save on its contribution to the Union budget. The UK Statistics Authority felt obliged to write an open letter to Vote Leave complaining about its misuse of official statistics by presenting a gross figure – before the rebate and EU spending in the UK – as though it were a net figure (UK Statistics Authority, 2016).

Did this failure to reach high standards of political communication undermine the legitimacy of the referendum? It certainly means that the campaign was not a well-functioning one that presented the electorate with the trade-offs and compromises inevitably involved in whether the UK chose to leave or remain. Leave was never one option but several, depending on whether it meant staying inside the Customs Union, the Single Market, neither or both. The Leave side had an incentive to present matters as though these were minor choices, when in fact they were highly significant. On the other hand, Remain would involve continued loss of freedom in respect of migration policy and international trade negotiations as well as the prospect of being drawn closer to a political association that would become a transfer union. A mature democracy would wish to discuss and deliberate upon such trade-offs, but that did not happen.

However, if referendums ceased to be legitimate because those campaigning for one outcome rather than another make exaggerated or false claims about the result, then no referendum could never be legitimate. Decision making in a democracy must presuppose that citizens in general can exercise judgement on the truth of the claims that are being made by campaigners. Moreover, fact-checking was not a difficult or costly exercise. The BBC and others went to great lengths to verify or disconfirm claims that were made on both sides. The referendum was not a façade in which the result can be known before any votes are cast. There was a genuine popular choice, despite the fact that the conduct of the campaigning should have reached higher standards according to criteria of deliberative justification.

THE REFERENDUM AFTERMATH: THE AUTHORIZATION OF GOVERNMENT

Leading politicians in both the Conservative and the Labour Parties took the referendum result to be decisive, understanding that it authorized a policy of withdrawal from the EU. On becoming Prime Minister, Theresa May famously asserted that 'Brexit means Brexit', intending to silence any attempt to weaken the implications of the referendum result (Mardell, 2016). She also held the view that the result of the referendum was sufficient to authorize the government to trigger the Article 50 process, and that this was not a matter for Parliament. At the Conservative Party conference in October 2016, she said that those who argued that initiating the process for leaving the EU could only happen after agreement in both Houses of Parliament were not standing up for democracy but trying to subvert it. By this logic 'the people' had replaced Parliament as the sovereign body. The referendum of June 2016 had expressed the will of the people, and it was not the place of Parliament to undermine that will. Instead, it was a matter of exercising what in the UK constitution is known as the Royal Prerogative, a form of executive action.

The government's position was challenged by a judicial review brought by Mrs Gina Miller. On 3 November 2016, the High Court gave its judgment in the *Miller* case, a judgment later to be confirmed by the Supreme Court. At issue was the question of whether the UK government needed parliamentary approval to inaugurate the Article 50 process. The government argued it did not need such approval. The three judges, in a judgment that invoked the principle of parliamentary sovereignty going back to seventeenth-century cases, ruled it did. The following day the Brexit-supporting press attacked both the verdict and the judges who had made it. 'The judges versus the people' exclaimed the *Daily Telegraph* (Dominiczak, 2016). 'Enemies of the people' pronounced the *Daily Mail* in chorus (Slack, 2016). Moreover, no Cabinet Minister, including the Secretary of State for Justice and Lord Chancellor, was prepared publicly to explain and defend the role of the courts in judging constitutional controversies, even though the government admitted that the case was justiciable (Weale, 2018, pp. viii–x). This failure led to Lord Lexden, a Conservative peer, to inaugurate an urgent debate in the House of Lords on the question of what steps the government were taking to ensure that the Lord Chancellor, then Liz Truss, would fulfil her duty to uphold the independence of the judiciary (HL Deb, 2016; see also Ponsford, 2016).

The case settled the issue as a matter of constitutional law, making Parliament the ultimate source of legitimate decision making. However, of itself that does not settle the matter of democratic principle. If the courts decided that the people by means of a referendum vote could not as a matter of constitutional law transfer their authority to the government directly, might it not still be the case that this ought to be possible according to the principles of democratic theory? Might not the position of Theresa May and her government have been right in democratic theory, even if their position was not upheld as a matter of UK constitutional law? If sovereign authority resides in the people, why could the people not directly legitimize an act of government? Even if one took the view that Parliament had only delegated its sovereign authority to the people for the particular purpose of deciding on Brexit, that might still imply that, in virtue of the delegation having taken place, the people then determined a general will according to which the government should act.

However, there are major problems in democratic theory with this argument. A well-functioning democracy requires respect for the rule of law as a value. If the people are not sovereign according to the standards of constitutional law, then they cannot be treated as sovereign. Of course, while it would be possible to change the constitution, and declare that in place of parliamentary sovereignty, the UK was now based on a principle of popular sovereignty. If this were to happen, Parliament would have transferred its sovereignty as a whole rather than just delegating it for a particular question. However, this was not the constitutional position at the time of the referendum and, given that fact, it is not plausible to suppose that putative democratic principles can override established constitutional principles. A democracy the practice of which was not consistent with the rule of law could not preserve political freedoms at its core.

Moreover, there is a problem with supposing that popular sovereignty allows the people directly to mandate the government in the conduct of its affairs. The referendum had posed the question of Leave or Remain. When Theresa May asserted that 'Brexit means Brexit', the widely cited retort was 'But what does "leave" mean?' (Mardell, 2016), a question that could only be answered through the negotiations between the EU and the UK. Leaving the EU was in principle consistent with a wide variety of possible final outcomes, including staying in either the Customs Union or the Single Market, or both. In other words, though the referendum may, in some sense, have been authoritative, there was no one negotiating mandate that it authorized. The eventual outcome, by which Northern Ireland was in effect kept in the Single

Market and Customs Union was a possibility that no one ever raised during the referendum campaign. A popular sovereignty that stops short of choosing among options with substantive and important implications for the life-chances and economic well-being of citizens cannot amount to meaningful sovereignty at all.

More generally, it does not make sense to suppose that the people can mandate a government directly, short of there being clear and unambiguous choices involved or with there being a high degree of consensus about issues in the general population, with neither condition seldom met in politics. The idea that a UK Prime Minister can act as the agent of a Rousseau's general will fails to do justice to the complexity of issues and the reasonable pluralism that obtains among citizens. So, to the question, what possibly could the referendum have authorized, the only answer, both in legal constitutional terms and in terms of democratic theory, is deliberation and choice in Parliament about the triggering of Article 50. When it came to the crucial vote, the majority in favour of triggering Article 50 turned out to be overwhelming.

In determining the UK's options on withdrawal and any agreement on the future relationship with the EU, parliamentary deliberation and decision were profoundly affected by Theresa May's decision to call an election for 8 June 2017. The Article 50 notice had already been given in March of that year. However, the government only had an overall majority of 17 seats, and it was clear that it would be difficult for the government to secure a majority in the Commons for any agreement that it would be able to negotiate with the EU. The Fixed Term Parliament Act prevented the Prime Minister alone from calling an election, but the opposition Labour Party was willing to support the government to obtain the two-thirds majority needed by the Act to override its normal provisions and hold an early election. The result, however, went contrary to what many observers, and presumably the Prime Minister herself, expected. In place of the 17 seat overall majority, the Conservatives were returned as the largest party, but with only 318 seats in the Commons, eight short of what an overall majority would require. There then followed an unprecedented series of defeats of the government for the succession of potential EU agreements that were laid before Parliament, defeats that were only resolved by the resignation of Theresa May as Prime Minister, her replacement by Boris Johnson, his negotiation of a Withdrawal Agreement and another general election in December 2019, which returned an 80 seat majority for the Conservatives, sufficient for the eventual Withdrawal Agreement to be passed.

In terms of political legitimacy, the period between June 2017 and December 2019 highlighted the shortcomings of the principle of majority rule in the Commons when faced with more than two alternatives. While it is true that a majority vote in the Commons is normally sufficient warrant for a legitimate political decision, nothing follows when voting takes place when no alternative can command a majority. In normal situations, a failure to overcome a veto on change preserves the status quo. However, with the triggering of Article 50 in March 2017, there was an automatic default to third country status without any agreement on withdrawal or the future relationship. Moreover, a central difficulty in negotiating the Withdrawal Agreement was the situation in Northern Ireland, the only part of the UK to have a land border with an EU state. Keeping that border open had been a central element in the 1998 Good Friday Agreement between the Irish and UK governments, and it was feared that imposing a border to protect the Customs Union and the Single Market would reintroduce the most visible symbol of division associated with the Northern Irish 'troubles'. As we shall see, this issue, along with the status of Scotland, created one of the long-term problems of political legitimacy for the internal integrity of the United Kingdom.

THE REFERENDUM AFTERMATH: THE OBLIGATIONS OF CITIZENS

What duties did the referendum place on citizens, particularly those who were opposed to Brexit? The straightforward populist answer to this question was that a referendum had been held and the losers should simply accept the fact. This principle was sometimes accompanied by the claim that, had the result gone the other way, Remainers would have expected Leavers to abide by the result, so that it was only fair that Remainers should accept defeat.

Although there is some substance to these arguments, they do not carry the weight that Leavers assumed or required. It is perfectly possible to hold that the referendum was a crucial step in authorizing the triggering of Article 50 but deny that this implied that there was an obligation on Remainers to give up campaigning for a change of policy. There is no inconsistency in supposing that the referendum was a genuine act of authorization, on the basis of which the government could pursue a policy of leaving the EU and continuing to campaign for a reversal of that decision. There are plenty of examples in British politics in which controversial, but procedurally legitimate, legislation has been passed, only for it to lead to widespread protests and campaigns to repeal that legislation, of which the most obvious is the legislation creating the Community Charge (the Poll Tax as it was known) in 1989. Had the campaigns been more effective in stopping implementation and forcing repeal, public life would have done better all round.

It can be argued (Bellamy, 2019, p. 131) that there is in principle a clear distinction between decisions on policy questions, like the Poll Tax, and constitutional or constitutive questions, and that the latter, being concerned with the basic political framework within which citizens live and plan their lives, should only be reversed once in a generation. This argument might of course have permitted a second referendum very quickly after the first one, since a speedy reversal of the decision would not have created a situation in which citizens and EU nationals were making plans on the assumption that the UK would leave. Yet, this pragmatic argument seems not to do justice to the principle that major constitutional decisions should be relatively infrequent.

Both Leavers and Remainers during the campaign spoke of its being a 'once in a generation' decision. Leavers did so in the sense of urging voters to seize the moment, consistent with a more general narrative that political and economic elites had been responsible for driving forward European integration without the consent of the people. Remainers did so in order to underline the risks that might lead to irretrievable loss from a decision to leave. Either way, the phrase 'once in a generation' gave the sense that once the referendum result had been decided, campaigners on both sides should accept the result, at least for some time.

However, the concept of a generation has no clear meaning in public discourse, democratic theory or the UK constitution. Since the electorate is constantly being replenished each year with new voters while other voters die or emigrate, there is not a succession of future generations who take the place of existing ones. Moreover, there are different possible ways of interpreting the idea of a generation. For example, one might say that there should be no referendum until someone born in 2016 came of voting age, which would imply no repeat referendum until 2034, or 2032 were the voting age to be lowered to 16. On the other hand, one might pick the year at which the UK actually left the EU, 2020, and count the emerging generation from then. No doubt there could be many other tests, which is simply a way of saying that the 'once in a generation' test is highly indeterminate, and so cannot be a sound basis for obligations.

In any case, any application of the 'once in a generation' test that extended the required period beyond the life of a parliament would run into conflict with a fundamental UK constitutional principle, namely that no parliament can bind its successors. It is not difficult to imagine a majority party being elected on a promise of hold a referendum on rejoining the EU sometime in the 2020s. Even if the referendum were taken to be the key point of authorization for Brexit, that fact could not be interpreted to mean that a future parliament was precluded from seeking to reverse the decision. If so, there is an argument akin to one of backwards induction that a Remainer turned Rejoiner could use: since a future parliament could constitutionally decide to reverse the referendum decision or at least hold another referendum, it makes it more likely that it will do so if the campaign is effective and active as early as possible.

It is of course a reasonable principle to expect reciprocity of obligation among citizens. So, it is certainly true that those Remainers who held that Leavers would have had an obligation to stop campaigning should not deny that the same obligation applied to them. Equally, however, it is possible to have voted Remain and yet hold, on democratic principles, that there was no obligation on Leavers to stop their campaign had they lost the referendum vote, though they might have hoped that the campaign might fade from a sense of futility. It is one thing to hope, as a prediction, that the campaign to leave the EU would fail, without supposing that ceasing the campaign was an obligation of citizenship.

Does anything follow about citizen obligation from the conduct of the referendum? As already suggested, doubts have been raised about the democratic legitimacy of the referendum from the fact that there was systematic misinformation during the campaign, the most egregious example of which was the Vote Leave campaign bus promising an extra £350 million per week for the NHS as a result of leaving. Suppose that Leave was disproportionately responsible for the misinformation, does that make a difference to the sense of obligation that Remainers should feel? It only plausibly makes a difference if the balance of forces for and against in the referendum were decisively tipped by the misinformation. After all, if Leave would have won the referendum even without the misinformation, then the fact of misinformation itself cannot affect how Leavers should subsequently conduct themselves. In any case, the indeterminacy of the constitutional status of the referendum means that as a matter of obligation (the question of political prudence is different), Remainers had no reason to hold back from campaigning to reverse the result.

An ardent Remainer might argue a stronger case, however. Such a person might say that the systematic misinformation in the campaign, supposing it to have been decisive, gives the freedom to engage in civil disobedience and disruption. In other words, general democratic principles give citizens a right to campaign to overturn a policy decision, even one determined by a referendum, but, if there is misinformation that is material to the result, then that fact alone licenses a campaign of civil disobedience. As it happens, there were no major instances of civil disobedience by Remainers. No one invaded the Commons chamber or blocked traffic in Whitehall gluing themselves to the road. (The contrast with protest over failure to act over the climate emergency is instructive here.) However, it is not clear on what principle an ardent Remainer could mount a campaign of civil disobedience simply on the grounds that there had been asymmetric misinformation between the two sides of the campaign. Prudence would suggest keeping the protest campaign lawful.

LEGITIMACY AND INTER-STATE RELATIONS

So far, this analysis has been concerned with domestic political legitimacy, whether thought of in terms of constitutional doctrine or democratic principle. However, issues of legitimacy also arise in respect of the external conduct of the UK. We cannot of course apply domestic constitutional or democratic standards, but we can consider how far Brexit is consistent with the norms of the international order. Those norms may be regarded as basically Grotian in character (Sidgwick, 1891, p. 230; Weale, 2005, pp. 102–6). They include the equality of states in the international order and the duty of non-intervention. From this international state of nature, states can then negotiate with one another in agreements to mutual advantage, a crucial condition of which is that there must be reasonable expectation on both sides that the commitments embodied in any agreement will be kept, otherwise there would be no point to the agreement.

As far as withdrawal itself is concerned, these principles do not impugn the legitimacy of Brexit. It is true that an ongoing union of states, like that of the EU, does presuppose a willingness of the state parties to make continuing political and economic enforceable commitments as a condition of being able to secure any agreement at all. No state would freely enter into agreement with the other states unless those commitments were present. However, the EU treaties do not make reference to 'perpetual union' or anything similar. Article 50 explicitly allows for withdrawal and it has been argued that ensuring the freedom of state association within the EU requires a right of withdrawal akin to the right of secession in a federal association. Given the existence of prior open-ended commitments, most notably in respect of the EU budget and the continuing liabilities that have to be met from that budget, for example in respect of pensions for UK officials working in the Union, there is a legitimate obligation to settle such accounts. Yet, although settling outstanding liabilities is a condition of legitimate withdrawal, they concern how to withdraw. They do not invalidate the right to withdraw.

The future legitimacy challenge arises from the willingness of the UK government to abide by the terms of the Withdrawal Agreement particularly in respect of the Northern Ireland Protocol, where the UK is required to apply customs and standards checks for goods moving from Great Britain to Northern Ireland. Within the first three months of the UK leaving the EU, the Commission has already initiated legal proceedings against the UK for its delaying application of the agreed checks, although it should also be noted that the attempt by the Commission to close off the border between Ireland and Northern Ireland (if only for a short time) in order to protect supplies of Covid vaccines complicated the issue. Legitimacy is likely to turn on the good faith with which any future UK government abides by the terms of the Withdrawal Agreement, since the EU can use the terms of the Trade and Cooperation Agreement to impose sanctions if it senses a breach. Meanwhile, in terms of its own sphere of authority, the UK did not initially apply customs and standards checks on imports because it lacked the necessary administrative infrastructure to do so, a situation described by one EU diplomat as 'taking back control by not taking control'.

LEGITIMACY AND THE UK STATE

The Brexit referendum and the circumstances that surrounded it inaugurated a highly turbulent period of UK politics. However, this is not to say that the process was substantially illegitimate. The requisite legislation was passed according to due form, the principle of parliamentary sovereignty was reaffirmed in the UK, and the EU avoided a situation in which the UK left without an agreement on the terms of withdrawal or on the future relationship. In some respects, these are modest achievements. The legislation may have been passed with due form, but that is not to say that it was passed with sufficient scrutiny. The Trade and Cooperation Agreement, for example, was passed in one day in Parliament. Similarly, the principle of parliamentary sovereignty was reaffirmed in the High Court decision on *Miller*, but it only needed to be reaffirmed in that way because a UK government threatened it with an attempt at executive privilege. Finally, withdrawal and future cooperation agreements were reached, but they were modest in many ways, and pressure will accumulate from business and others to go beyond them in the future. The 2019 election campaign slogan from the Conservatives was 'Get Brexit done', but Brexit is an agenda for future action, not an event in the past.

The most substantive issue is the future integrity of the UK state itself, which Brexit threatens. The Scottish referendum results produced a large majority against Brexit, and this has reinforced the Scottish National Party's campaign for a second independence referendum in Scotland. How strong the pressure for independence will be is hard to say, and there are significant economic and practical arguments against independence. Yet, of course, there were significant economic and practical arguments against Brexit. Similarly, the future of Northern Ireland within the UK has been put into question by Brexit. Northern Ireland voted leave, but the Northern Ireland Protocol means that there are now administrative barriers to trade between Northern Ireland and the rest of the UK. Sentiment in Northern Ireland would have to move substantially to produce pressure for a re-unification referendum. However, there is no escaping the persistence of the issue.

There are many ways of interpreting the politics of Brexit. However, it is hard to avoid the interpretation that sees as one essential element a movement asserting a particular vision of nationalist democracy, associated with the view that 'a people' is entitled to govern itself. If so, then perhaps a major irony of Brexit is that a nationalist movement to withdraw from the EU has generated its own internal nationalities problem, threatening the political legitimacy on which any multi-national polity depends.

NOTE

1. For a valuable compilation, bringing the documents together in one place, see House of Commons Political and Constitutional Reform Committee (2014).

REFERENCES

Beetham, D. (2013). *The Legitimation of Power* (2nd edn). Basingstoke.

Bellamy, R. (2019). Was the Brexit Referendum Legitimate, and Would a Second One Be So? *European Political Science*, *18*, 126–33. https://doi.org/10.1057/s41304-018-0155-x. Accessed 4 October 2022.

Clarke, H.D., Goodwin, M., and Whiteley, P. (2017). *Brexit: Why Britain Voted to Leave the European Union*. Cambridge University Press.

Consolidated Version of the Treaty on European Union. (2012, 26 October). *Official Journal of the European Union*, C 326/13. https://eur-lex.europa.eu/resource.html?uri=cellar:2bf140bf-a3f8-4ab2-b506-fd71826e6da6.0023.02/DOC_1&format=PDF. Accessed 4 October 2022.

Dominiczak, P. (2016, 3 November). Judges vs the People: Government Ministers Resigned to Losing Appeal against High Court Ruling. *The Telegraph*. https://www.telegraph.co.uk/news/2016/11/03/the-plot-to-stop-brexit-the-judges-versus-the-people/. Accessed 4 October 2022.

Evans, G., and Menon, A. (2017). *Brexit and British Politics*. Polity Press.

HC Deb vol 596 (2015, 9 July). Hansard. https://hansard.parliament.uk/Commons/2015-06-09/debates/15060939000001/EuropeanUnionReferendumBill. Accessed 4 October 2022.

HL Deb vol 776 (2016, 15 November). Hansard. https://hansard.parliament.uk/lords/2016-11-15/debates/2B30457F-04CC-42AA-857B-5C7C691B1BDC/JudiciaryIndependence. Accessed 4 October 2022.

House of Commons Political and Constitutional Reform Committee. (2014). *A New Magna Carta?* https://publications.parliament.uk/pa/cm201415/cmselect/cmpolcon/463/46302.htm. Accessed 4 October 2022.

House of Commons Public Administration and Constitutional Affairs Committee. (2017). *Lessons Learned from the EU Referendum*. HC 494. https://publications.parliament.uk/pa/cm201617/cmselect/cmpubadm/496/496.pdf. Accessed 4 October 2022.

King, A. (2007). *The British Constitution*. Oxford University Press.

Kröger, S. (2019). The Democratic Legitimacy of the 2016 Referendum on EU Membership. *Journal of Contemporary European Research, 15*(3), 284–98. https://doi.org/10.30950/jcer.v15i3.1052.

Mardell, M. (2016). What Does 'Brexit Means Brexit' Mean? *BBC News*. https://www.bbc.com/news/uk-politics-36782922. Accessed 4 October 2022.

Musolff, A. (2020, 13 February). Having Cake and Eating It: How a Hyperbolic Metaphor Framed Brexit. *LSE Blog*. https://blogs.lse.ac.uk/brexit/2020/02/13/having-cake-and-eating-it-how-a-hyperbolic-metaphor-framed-brexit/. Accessed 4 October 2022.

Olsen, T.V., and Rostbøll, C.F. (2017). Why Withdrawal from the European Union Is Undemocratic. *International Theory, 9*(3), 436–65. https://doi.org/10.1017/S1752971917000094.

Ponsford, D. (2016, 7 November). IPSO Chair Sir Alan Moses: Lord Chancellor Should Do More to Protect Judges from 'Ignorant Criticism'. *Press Gazette*. https://www.pressgazette.co.uk/ipso-chair-sir-alan-moses-lord-chancellor-should-do-more-to-protect-judges-from-ignorant-criticism/. Accessed 4 October 2022.

Sidgwick, H. (1891). *The Elements of Politics*. Macmillan.

Slack, J. (2016, 4 November). Enemies of the People: Fury over 'Out of Touch' Judges Who Have 'Declared War on Democracy' by Defying 17.4m Brexit Voters and Who Could Trigger Constitutional Crisis. *The Daily Mail*. https://www.dailymail.co.uk/news/article-3903436/Enemies-people-Fury-touch-judges-defied-17-4m-Brexit-voters-trigger-constitutional-crisis.html. Accessed 4 October 2022.

Uberoi, E. (2015). *European Union Referendum Bill 2015–16*. House of Commons Library Briefing Paper no. 07212. https://commonslibrary.parliament.uk/research-briefings/cbp-7212/. Accessed 4 October 2022.

UK Statistics Authority. (2016, 27 May). UK Statistics Authority Statement on the Use of Official Statistics on Contributions to the European Union. https://uksa.statisticsauthority.gov.uk/news/uk-statistics-authority-statement-on-the-use-of-official-statistics-on-contributions-to-the-european-union/. Accessed 4 October 2022.

Weale, A. (2005). *Democratic Citizenship and the European Union*. Manchester University Press.

Weale, A. (2018). *The Will of the People: A Modern Myth*. Polity Press.

28. Political constitutionalism and referendums: the case of Brexit

Richard Bellamy

The British referendum on leaving the European Union (EU) has attracted much controversy regarding the legitimacy of both the process and the handling of the result. Predictably, those who agree with the result have tended to view it as a supreme democratic and constitutive act, while those who disagreed have questioned both its democratic and constitutional validity, seeing it as exemplifying the worst characteristics of populism. Here I discuss one version of this latter critique: namely, the compatibility of referendums generally – and this referendum in particular – with political constitutionalism.

A key feature of the United Kingdom's (UK) legal and political system is typically claimed to be that it possesses a political rather than a legal constitution (Griffith, 1979; Tomkins, 2005, pp. 1–6; Loughlin, 2013, pp. 11–12; Sumption, 2019, p. 76). A legal constitution is standardly associated with an entrenched legal document that codifies certain individual rights, the rules of the political process, and the role and relations of the main legal and political institutions. This legal constitution provides a 'higher' law that frames the operation of politics and allows politicians and public servants to be held accountable and obliged to abide by the terms of the constitution via the courts by citizens and other individuals who are subject to their authority. Instead, a political account of constitutionalism designates an approach that locates the constitution in the character and design of the political system and the modus operandi of its component political processes (Bellamy, 2007; Gee and Webber, 2010). According to this political conception, there can be no higher laws other than the laws that emerge from a duly constitutive and constitutional political process. Instead, citizens can hold governments and the administration accountable via democratic, political institutions. In the British case, such political accountability occurs indirectly through elections and directly by elected parliaments and the need for the government to abide by existing laws and to govern and legislate with the support of a plurality of the population and a majority of MPs (Griffith, 1979; Tomkins, 2005, pp. 1–10).

A central feature of the British political constitution, therefore, is the doctrine of the sovereignty of Parliament (Ewing, 2013, p. 2118; Gordon, 2019, pp. 133–7). On this account, it is the representative and parliamentary process that gives the democratic system its constitutional qualities. However, despite the UK having held 11 referendums since 1973 – mainly on devolution – this doctrine is often viewed as incompatible with referendums given their justification standardly rests on an appeal to popular sovereignty. Indeed, it has been viewed as 'paradoxical' (Bogdanor, 1994, p. 34) that A.V. Dicey, whose *Introduction to the Study of the Law of the Constitution* (1885 [1915]: Part II, chapter 13, pp. 402, 405) offers the *locus classicus* of the doctrine of parliamentary sovereignty, became the first to advocate the referendum in Britain (Dicey, 1890).

Unsurprisingly, perhaps, the Brexit referendum has given rise to two divergent and opposed criticisms of political constitutionalism and its relationship to referendums in general and that on Brexit in particular, each made in contrary ways by critics and supporters of that referendum. On the one hand, referendums – and especially the Brexit referendum – have been seen as at odds with the political constitution, which involves a form of democracy possessing constitutional qualities that is only found in representative systems based on free elections between competing parties (Bellamy, 2007). Critics of referendums view this incompatibility positively, regarding referendums as a disfigurement of democracy (Urbinati, 2019) that deny the pluralism and tolerance of true democratic decision-making through emphasising the existence of a mythical and singular people's will (Weale, 2018). By contrast, advocates of referendums have seen this potential incompatibility negatively, as an indication of political constitutionalism's elitism and failure to provide sufficient space for citizen participation through more truly democratic avenues (Tierney, 2013). On the other hand, political constitutionalism has been considered as encouraging populism. Critics of referendums allege that it prioritises democracy over constitutionalism, which necessarily takes a legal form. As a result, it offers no adequate check on exercises of 'executive dictatorship' that take a populist turn by asserting that any government possessing a stable majority can be 'judge in its own cause', effectively able to make and interpret the law as it wishes (Hailsham, 1978, p. 127; Pettit, 1999, p. 176). By contrast, advocates of referendums consider them as a truer form of political constitutionalism, offering an opportunity for the direct expression of popular political sovereignty on which the legitimacy of parliament's legislative sovereignty ultimately rests (Tierney, 2013).

This chapter puts to one side the strictly legal issue of the compatibility of the referendum with prevailing UK public law and explores instead the broader normative issue of the compatibility of referendums in general, and this one in particular, with the very notion of a political constitution. I shall argue that referendums can play a valid political constitutional role as part of a system of checks and balances on executive authority so long as they are appropriately embedded within a system of representative democracy. On this account, referendums do not displace parliamentary sovereignty with popular sovereignty. As a result, they can encourage popular participation without producing populism.

The argument proceeds as follows. First, I briefly outline both the constitutional qualities political constitutionalists associate with a parliamentary representative democracy and some of the limitations that critics attribute to it. Second, I explore how far referendums can be said to be compatible with the former while potentially addressing the latter. I shall argue this can be possible to the extent referendums can be nested within, and made a component of, the standard picture of the political constitution so as to form part of a system of political checks and balances with constitutional qualities. Third, I turn to the Brexit referendum and consider whether, while far from perfect, it was so nested and can be regarded as democratically and constitutionally legitimate in terms of the political constitution, performing an important supplementary function appropriate to such constitutive issues.

POLITICAL CONSTITUTIONALISM

Political constitutionalism proceeds from the argument that the laws determining the terms of social and political co-existence, including the basis and interpretation of fundamental rights, are matters of reasonable disagreement among those who are subject to them (Waldron, 1999, pp. 107–18; Bellamy, 2007, pp. 4–5). Political constitutionalists claim that the most appropriate way of recognising the contested nature of these terms and rights is to subject them to a collective decision-process as to their content and implementation that treats all concerned impartially and promotes reciprocity among them, so all are regarded with equal respect and concern, respectively (Waldron, 1999, chapter 11; Bellamy, 2007, chapter 4). Representative democracy linked to parliamentarism is held to satisfy these desiderata in a manner that deploys certain qualities standardly associated with constitutionalism (Griffith, 1979; Gordon, 2019, pp. 131–3; Tomkins, 2005, pp. 1–10; Bellamy, 2007, pp. 12, 259, 260).

These constitutional qualities are achieved not through legal mechanisms that hold politicians and the administration to the norms of a codified and entrenched constitution that acts as a higher law, but through the operation of a political system that renders them subject to authorisation by and accountable to citizens (Bellamy, 2007, chapter 6). However, these political mechanisms incorporate two key constitutional devices – those of checks and balances (Bellamy, 2007, chapter 5), reflecting respectively negative and positive aspects of constitutionalism (Barber, 2018, pp. 2–9). On the one hand, governments are checked through requiring authorisation by, and being held regularly accountable to, citizens through the electoral process. These mechanisms provide checks on arbitrary rule and the protection of individual rights. They can also be supplemented by weak form judicial review that highlights the adverse impact of general legislation on the rights of particular individuals (Bellamy, 2011; Waldron, 2016, chapter 9). On the other hand, governments, and indirectly those citizens supporting them, are balanced by having to compete against opposition parties – both in elections and in the legislature, and hence must 'hear the other side'. These balances promote the participation in decision-making by citizens so as to support the need for politicians to appeal to their commonly avowable reasoning and interests and enhance identification with the public good. Bicameralism, federalism and a proportional electoral system can all, where appropriate, provide further sources of balance that foster deliberation and the need to address all sections of the community (Waldron, 2016, chapters 3–5).

All these mechanisms can be seen as sharing a lineage with the ancient notion of the mixed constitution, which aimed at achieving a degree of mutual checks and balances between the different classes of a society (Bellamy, 1996). Although in their modern incarnation they involve democracy, their virtues lie not as means for collective self-rule or popular will formation, as in certain theories of deliberative and direct democracy. Rather, as per the neo-Roman republican tradition, their core concern is with the promotion of freedom as non-domination and relatedly of equality (Tomkins, 2005, chapter 2; Bellamy, 2007, chapter 4). From this perspective, what matters is that public authorities cannot act arbitrarily, that is, simply as they will, without consulting the views and interests of those subject to their rule.

The capacity for arbitrary rule arises when there is an inequality of power and a relationship of dependence of the ruled on the rulers (Lovett, 2001). Political constitutionalists regard a democratic system as a way of overcoming this possibility by placing rulers under the equal influence and control of the ruled, and rendering all equal before the laws (Bellamy, 2007, chapter 6). Indeed, given citizens are both rulers and ruled in turn, with politicians elected by appealing to a majority among them, citizens too can be considered as mutually influencing and controlling each other. In such a situation, no politician or citizen can reliably will what the collective rules should be without consulting others and appealing to their commonly avowable judgements, while personal dependence on a particular master or patron is replaced by the mutual dependence of equals for their considered and voluntary support.

By advocating an institutional framework for a non-dominating system of democratic government, political constitutionalism seeks to achieve a form of rule that treats all with equal respect and concern (Bellamy, 2007, chapter 4). The securing of equal respect can be regarded as an intrinsic feature of political constitutionalism. Elections based on one person, one vote and majority rule treat all citizens as possessing equal status, and provide a mechanism that gives equal weight to their views and interests and that is neutral and impartial with regard to their worth for any collective decision (Christiano, 2008). This proves instrumental to securing equal concern and the negative and positive constitutional purposes of protecting rights and fostering participation and the public interest, respectively (McGann, 2004, pp. 56, 71). The balancing features of the political constitution encourage reciprocity among citizens and a willingness to compromise to create viable party programmes with broad popular appeal. For example, competition between different parties incentivises politicians to fish for votes and construct programmes that build coalitions between different groups of citizens that appeal to the median voter – usually that set of preferences that represent the Condorcet winner across the electorate (Ordeshook, 1986, pp. 245–57). As R.A. Dahl famously observed, within pluralist societies majority rule tends to be the rule of an alliance of various minorities (Dahl, 1989, p. 218). Given many minorities could swap allegiance this motivates both a regard for minority rights and the need to frame policies in terms of their benefit to the public interest rather than particular sectional interests.

Meanwhile, the prospect of future elections constrains arbitrariness by governments, which will be held accountable for their failings when they next seek authorisation to rule. That parties may alternate in power also creates a reason to wish the rules of the game to remain fair and for the judiciary to be independent and ensure all are equal under the law. As noted above, bicameralism – especially where the second chamber is selected by different electoral rules to the first – may likewise provide a spur to inclusive deliberation and a regard for the public interest. The precise nature of these institutional arrangements will tend to reflect the social characteristics of the polity concerned (Dahl, 1989, pp. 251ff.).

Of course, there are numerous imperfections and flaws in any extant political constitution. Many of these problems are those associated with representative democracy more generally (Dunn, 2005, p. 19). Critics focus on the elite character of representative systems, the lack of responsiveness of parties and the ways collusion between them can keep key issues off the electoral agenda, and the resulting disempowered nature of citizen participation, limited as it is to a periodic vote on the, often overlapping, programmes offered by politicians (Tierney, 2012, pp. 3–4; 2013, pp. 2187–8). These failings are held to largely depoliticise democracy and limit both its checking and balancing capacity, thereby weakening its negative and positive constitutional qualities. If parties fail to adequately contest each other and offer clear alternatives, then it becomes harder to check governments and hold them to account. Likewise, if the main parties ignore the preferences of certain groups of citizens and take them off the electoral agenda, then these preferences will carry no weight in the balance of political priorities within any of the party programmes (Mair, 2013). The danger in such cases is less that of the tyranny of the majority as of a tyranny of a minority – a feature exacerbated in plurality electoral systems such as that of the UK, which reduce the number of viable parties in play, and result in parliamentary majorities that rarely represent a majority of voters. This possibility has seemed particularly perilous in the case of constitutional rules – especially those relating to the political process, where a government or politicians as a class can have an interest in enacting policies that entrench their own position and weaken competition, as with gerrymandering (Ginsburg and Aziz, 2018). Indeed, a number of authors sympathetic to the political constitutionalist position on matters of substance, such as abortion rights, have advocated judicial review on matters of democratic process on these grounds (Dahl, 1989, pp. 188–92).

Given that the normative case for political constitutionalism has been linked, as we saw, with republican notions of citizenship and the avoidance of the domination resulting from arbitrary rule, the participatory deficits of representative democracy have appeared to many critics as in conflict with the aspiration of its advocates to offer an alternative to liberal accounts of democracy (Tierney, 2013, p. 2187). After all, a key criticism of legal constitutionalism by political constitutionalists relates to its alleged elitist and anti-democratic character. Against this criticism, some legal constitutionalist critics have countered that contestation through legal challenges, such as class actions, offer an avenue for more citizen participation, and an important supplementary legal source of constitutional checks and balances (Lafont, 2019, chapter 8). I leave these arguments to one side (see Bellamy, 2013 for a discussion). However, other, more radical republican and democratic critics argue that referendums – especially on constitutional and constitutive issues, but also with regard to certain policies – provide a way of both giving such legal constitutionalism a political endorsement of a democratic kind (Ackerman, 1991), and providing a more directly democratic form of political constitutionalism (Tierney, 2012, 2013). As they typically note, referendums would seem, at least prima facie, to provide a stronger realisation of the intrinsic quality of democracy than voting in elections, in that it gives each citizen a direct say on a salient issue – one that may even have been occluded by parties (Tierney, 2012, p. 19, quoting approvingly Bogdanor, 1981, p. 93). However, even if this obtains, worries persist that referendums may lack many of the instrumental constitutional qualities associated with a representative democratic system (Lord, 2021). Nevertheless, as was suggested above, suitably designed, they could possibly provide a potential check and balance to the legislature on matters where incentives are lacking for politicians not to put their own interests in holding on to power above those of the public at large. It is to these issues that we now turn.

THE CONSTITUTIONAL QUALITIES OF REFERENDUMS

Referendums typically fall into three rough issue categories and take two broad forms, with two distinctive modalities. With regard to issues they can be categorised as related to constitutive, constitutional or policy matters (Tierney, 2012, pp. 11–15). The first involves decisions that redefine either the polity, as in referendums on secession – such as the recent Scottish referendum on independence, or the fundamental form of its regime, as in referendums on an entirely new constitution. The second relates to more limited amendments to an already existing written constitution or constitutional statute, which operate within the prevailing constitutional structures with regard to both the polity and the regime, such as the recent Irish referendum on abortion or the British referendum on changing the electoral system. Finally, the third concerns policies ranging from changes in local planning regulations, as is common in Swiss communal and some English Parish referendums, to major policy decisions, such as the California Proposition 218 that – while technically a constitutional amendment – was designed to give voters a direct say over levels of local government taxes. As this last example indicates, there can be some overlap between the issue types – a policy issue can have constitutional implications, as in this case, while most constitutive referendums will raise both constitutional and policy issues, as was the case with Brexit. It will also be a matter of degree as to how far a constitutional amendment can be regarded as altering the nature of the regime or polity, as might have been the case with electoral reform, or in referendums on establishing elected Mayors.

As to forms, referendums can be regarded as either top down, where the government calls and frames the referendum, or bottom up, where a process exists for citizens to request a referendum – for example, by gathering a prescribed number of signatures. Here too there are forms that combine elements of both, such as the Irish use of citizen juries to identify issues on which referendums might be called.

Finally, concerning modalities referendums may be negative, called to abrogate an existing law or arrangement, or positive, aimed at approving a proposal for a new measure or arrangement. Once again, this distinction may not be clear-cut. In some cases, a successful negative referendum may entail the need for new positive measures or arrangements, though the precise nature of these may not be clearly specified. Likewise, if a positive proposal has failed to get approval it has by implication been abrogated.

The degree to which referendums can be regarded as either possessing themselves constitutional qualities or complementing those of representative and parliamentary forms of democracy will depend on the particular ways the issue, forms and modalities interact with each other and, where relevant, with the system of representative democracy (Lord, 2021). Broadly speaking, the intrinsic securing of equal respect appears strongest in referendums that are bottom up and allow citizens to propose new policies, and weakest in those that are top down and merely seek approval of a government measure (Cheneval and el-Wakil, 2018). Referendums of the former type that belong to the policy issue category, take a bottom-up form and involve a positive modality approximate most closely to exercises of direct democracy that can be characterised as embodying popular sovereignty. As such, prima facie at least, they appear best placed to counter the criticism of representative democracy for its lack of participation and elitism. However, these types of referendum are also those where critics have most doubted their instrumental constitutional qualities. These worries involve the limitations of referendums with regard to collective policy making; citizen competence and elite manipulation; majority tyranny; and the lack of accountability or undermining of the role of representatives (Tierney, 2012, pp. 22–4; Lord, 2021, p. 35). I shall consider each of these worries in turn, although, as we shall see, they relate in various ways to each other.

The key problem for referendums with regard to collective policy making relates to the weighting of citizens' preferences across the whole domain of policy options (Bellamy, 2018, pp. 314–16). A referendum necessarily focuses on a single issue, whereas elections focus on party programmes that bundle together a range of policies and seek to weigh them against each other, including giving consideration for the knock-on effects of decisions in one policy area for decisions in others (Tierney, 2012, p. 37). A decision on a policy taken in isolation from others risks producing policy incoherence – as when voters vote for tax cuts that would undermine the government's ability to fund public services and infrastructure that they wish to see expanded (Haskell, 2001, p. 16). True, the Ostrogorski paradox suggests the possibility that bundling may involve putting together a number of policies, many of which taken on their own are not supported by a majority (Setälä, 2006; Lord, 2021, p. 34). In this scenario, a bottom-up, positive, policy referendum might be justified to challenge parties having taken off the agenda or ignored a majority view in a given area. However, that would depend on the policy being discrete, which in most cases is unlikely.

The policy implications of a popular vote may also be imprecise. This is especially true of negative, abrogative referendums, where what is to be put in place of the rescinded measure – if anything – may be unclear. Yet, positive referendums may also be imprecise unless the policy proposal is clearly specified. A related issue stems from the binary nature of many referendums, whereby the two options on offer may be arbitrary and suppress alternatives that would have been the most preferred (i.e. the Condorcet winner), particularly if voters could rank their preferences among multiple possibilities (Bellamy, 2018, pp. 317–18; Weale, 2018, pp. 62–6). Of course, voters could be given multiple options to choose from and allowed to rank them, as occurs in some Swiss referendums (Lord, 2021, p. 36). Yet, these are likely to still be options relating to a single policy.

Worries about citizen competence enter here. Some advocates of policy referendums claim they benefit from the 'wisdom of crowds' (e.g. Landemore, 2013). However, that depends on citizens possessing sufficient knowledge about the relevant policy area to be able to make a reasonable guess as to which of the available options might be best. Meanwhile, the aforementioned problems regarding policy connectedness and the representativeness of the options on offer still apply. Even referendums that emerge from a popular initiative can be subject to elite manipulation (Honohan, 2002, pp. 220–30), as they will generally arise as a result of a campaign led by a small group of activists, who will then seek to shape the referendum question so as to favour their preferred result. In the absence of personal expertise, most voters will also follow elite cues from media and other campaigns (Honohan, 2002, p. 218). In these respects, referendums may at best allow for a similar degree of misrepresentation and manipulation as elections, and at worst an even greater degree given party ideology tends to act as a relatively stable indicator of the overall direction of the policies advocated taken as a whole, whereas such guides may be lacking when it comes to a single issue. Of course, as advocates of these initiatives note, the issue concerned may be one that divides parties, with support and opposition cutting across standard party lines (Glencross, 2021, pp. 57–8). A referendum in such circumstances may help overcome such divisions. Yet, it could also be seen as an abnegation of responsibility by politicians to take a difficult decision. After all, free votes in legislatures can often be among the most deliberative precisely because politicians do not simply follow the party lead. By the same token, though, the fact that politicians have no clear mandate for how they would vote could be seen as legitimising a popular debate and decision.

Nevertheless, so far as policy issues are concerned, the disadvantages of referendums may outweigh the advantages. As was noted in the last section, the need to fish for votes from a diverse electorate and build a coalition for a party programme helps support minority interests. But when it comes to a vote on a single issue the need for coalition building is likely to be less. That increases the danger of majority tyranny, since the need for compromise and accommodation is greatly reduced, as is the capacity, within the procedure, to develop a compromise (Haider-Markel et al., 2007; Bellamy, 2018). Meanwhile, policies that are so decided tend to become entrenched – politicians will be wary of reversing a measure possessing a popular mandate, even if they regard the policy as deleterious. Moreover, they will bear no personal responsibility for it and so cannot be held to account for its failings. Once again, the worry is that referendums may not only lack adequate instrumental constitutional qualities themselves but also undermine those associated with representative democracy.

These concerns arise when referendums are seen as instances of direct democracy, involving the exercise of popular sovereignty. Some theorists have argued that while referendums with this quality may be inappropriate on policy issues, they are suitable for constitutive and constitutional issues (Tierney, 2012, 2013). As I noted above, referendums on these two issues concern, respectively, the definition of the polity and its demos, and the character of the regime – particularly the rules of the democratic game. Both these issues have been regarded as being suitably conceived as expressions of 'we the people' (Ackerman, 1991). In the first case, a referendum could be seen as providing a way for those concerned to contract to form a people who then subject themselves to a common authority under their mutual control. In the second case, a referendum allows the secondary rules that define the legal and political system to be authorised directly by the people to whom they will apply, encouraging them to identify with these rules as theirs.

Two additional claims are often made in regard to both issues (Tierney, 2012, pp. 12–15; 2013): first, that these are matters of collective and common interest that transcend the particular interests individuals may have with regard to specific policies; and second, that referendums spark a more participatory and deliberative debate of a kind that promotes public reasoning on a topic that defines both the public or demos and their public interactions. On this account, constitutive and constitutional referendums form part of a dual democracy (Ackerman, 1991): they provide a democratic mechanism for bringing into being a democratic system that can address policy issues. Yet, it is disputable whether they can escape the problems identified above with regard to policy referendums. To do so, it must be assumed that the referendum does indeed take the form of a contract whereby all citizens agree on fair terms of cooperation and consent to them, with constitutional and constitutive politics differing in deliberative and epistemological quality to normal politics, such that citizens are moved by the better argument and avoid the conflicts of interest and ontological disagreements typical of policy debates (Habermas, 1996, pp. 278–9). However, there is no compelling reason to believe this will be the case (Bellamy and Schönlau, 2004).

If, as political constitutionalists argue, rights and procedural rules can be matters of reasonable disagreement, then there is no more reason to expect a consensus will be reached on them through a public wide discussion and referendum than in a legislative debate. Nor are such discussions necessarily any more bottom up and free from elite manipulation, given that – as with policy proposals – they are likely to be prompted by political entrepreneurs and the debate heavily influenced by the media. Meanwhile, such a discussion may lack the incentives of checks and balances that lead to legislators 'hearing the other side'. Indeed, as the 2008 Swiss referendum on minarets, recurrent Swiss referendums on immigration and residence of foreign criminals, and California Proposition 8 illustrate (Frey and Goette, 1998; Moeckli, 2011; Hainmueller and Hangartner, 2019), such exercises of popular democracy may allow minority rights to be abrogated by tyrannous majorities. Some such checks might be incorporated into the referendum process – for example, it might be necessary to have a threshold for the turnout of over 50 per cent and/or to achieve a super majority if the measure is to carry. However, while these requirements may prevent certain unjust proposals carrying they can also inhibit reforms that remove injustices from the prevailing status quo (Schwartzberg, 2013). They can only be justified if it is reasonable to assume that most changes would be likely to be worse than the prevailing system – hardly an endorsement of popular sovereignty. Arguably, a comprehensive constitutional reform might allow for more compromise to arise of a balancing kind between the representatives of different groups, and – as with the Icelandic constitutive assembly – there could be a direct crowdsourcing of ideas by the public, with the whole package then put to a referendum. However, this proposal seems to suggest that constitutive and constitutional referendums become more acceptable the more they develop the characteristics of representative, competitive party politics.

Although there is some evidence that Dicey may have come to regard referendums in this light (Weill, 2003), the development of his argument seems to have been driven by the desire to stop Irish Home Rule at any price (Cosgrove, 1980, pp. 105–10, 247). However, that need not mean that referendums could not be incorporated into a Diceyan version of political constitutionalism where political sovereignty lies with the people but legal sovereignty rests with Parliament, which retains both constitutional and legislative authority (Weill, 2003, pp. 474–5). Dicey's point – at least until 1911 – seems to have been that an executive required a significant level of popular political authorisation for major constitutional change. However, as with the Great Reform Act of 1832, he considered – at least initially – an election victory in which the change figured prominently in the campaign as sufficient (Weill, 2003, pp. 478–9). He only turned to advocating a referendum as Home Rule appeared unlikely to be opposed. The logic of his argument was not to consider the people as possessing legislative sovereignty, though, as some have argued. Rather, he saw referendums as a means for exercising a popular political constraint on the legislature in the case of significant constitutive or constitutional laws that paralleled – and could even be exercised by – the withdrawal of their authorisation of a government at an election (Weill, 2003, pp. 480–88).

In a similar manner, Eoin Daly (2015) has argued, referendums may be considered as forming a part of the mixed constitution, adding another political channel for checks and balances in areas that legislatures may be ill-suited to provide for themselves (Daly, 2015, p. 32). Rather than being bottom-up and positive exercises of popular legislative sovereignty, and as such rivals to parliamentary sovereignty, he contends that referendums are better seen as negative and top down, serving a contestatory function aimed at guarding against arbitrary rule and promoting public justification (Daly, 2015, p. 37). As such, they can contribute to the negative and positive instrumental constitutional functions identified above, usefully supplementing representative democracy in the process.

Daly considers referendums of this kind as particularly relevant for constitutive and constitutional issues. Both these issues could be regarded as relating to areas where politicians might have an interest at variance with those they represent. For example, a government might wish to introduce electoral reforms or constitutional amendments that make it more likely they remain in power or the policies they favour are entrenched. He contends that forcing governments to put proposals on these two sorts of issues to a referendum can promote a wider public discussion and promote civic participation. As he notes, in Europe Ireland, Switzerland and Denmark, all have mandatory constitutional amendment referendums for issues of this kind (Daly, 2015, p. 38), as does Australia (Daly, 2015, p. 41). Even in Germany, which had been thought averse to referendums given their use by the Nazis, the Basic Law has been amended to allow for a referendum on changes to the Basic Law itself (A146) (Lord, 2021, p. 31). Their aim is to reinforce the likelihood such measures treat all with equal respect and concern by giving all citizens an equal vote on them while having the proposal itself and its implementation the product of coalition building and compromise by parties in the legislature, whose actions remain electorally authorised and accountable. He distinguishes referendums that still retain parliamentary legislative sovereignty from those, such as De Gaulle's 1962 referendum amending the rules on Presidential elections, that involve a direct populist appeal by a political leader to the 'people's will' in order to bypass parliamentary amendment procedures (Daly, 2015, pp. 36–7). Daly likens referendums of the former type to the role of a second chamber that adopts a different form of representation to the first and primary legislative chamber. As a form of multicameralism (Daly, 2015, p. 43), referendums both support the representation of all relevant interests on such important questions, and promote their balancing through enhancing the scrutiny to which they are subjected.

Daly's argument presents an account of referendums that can be reconciled with political constitutionalism in so far as it distinguishes political and legal sovereignty, leaving the latter with Parliament. So conceived, referendums introduce a check and balance that possess the intrinsic and instrumental constitutional qualities of democracy that political constitutionalists seek to deploy, at least when they are embedded within a system of representative democracy and act as a supplement to it. However, his account gives referendums a largely negative, contestatory role. They operate not to propose change so much as to approve or reject changes proposed by the legislature. As such, they only partly address the alleged failings of representative democracy. They operate against elites when they are acting against the public interest, but not when they are failing to act in the public interest. Yet though any given individual act of omission may pose less of a danger than any single act of commission, taken cumulatively over time they may do as much, if not more, to undermine popular support for democracy.

Even in pluralist systems such as the UK, though, electoral competition may work against parties successfully colluding to take certain constitutional issues completely off the agenda. For example, although the two main parties have generally opposed any move towards proportional representation for national elections, the hung parliament of 2010 gave the Liberal Democrats the opportunity to push for electoral reform. Given the type of issue and the fact that no parliamentary majority probably existed for this measure, putting a proposal to a referendum could be regarded as a legitimate alternative to canvas the support of the broader public for such a fundamental reform. Likewise, the Northern Ireland referendums on remaining part of the UK (1973) and the Good Friday Agreement (1998), and the Scottish (1979, 1997) and Welsh (1979, 1997, 2011) referendums on devolution, and in the case of Scotland independence (2014), all deal with constitutional issues where it is conceivable no majority would exist at Westminster for the change, and those voters with a strong interest in the issue lacked sufficient representation. Even though not all of these detailed the precise form the proposal would take, they can be seen as a means for checking against potential inaction by politicians on a core constitutive or constitutional issue through canvassing the wider and more diverse chamber of the relevant public as a whole. It would be misleading to regard them as operating as expressions of popular sovereignty or consent. It remains to be seen whether the Brexit referendum can be understood in similar terms.

THE BREXIT REFERENDUM AND POLITICAL CONSTITUTIONALISM

The Brexit referendum has been subjected to a high degree of criticism, especially, but not solely, by those favouring remaining in the EU. These criticisms have ranged from concerns about the misleading character of the Leave campaign, including financial irregularities, misinformation and the use of algorithms for media advertising that derived from dubiously obtained personal information (Hansson and Kröger, 2021), to dissatisfaction with the franchise, especially for its failure to include resident EU nationals or to reduce the voting age to 16 (Grayling, 2017, pp. 189–97). The evaluation developed here focuses on the second set of criticisms relating to the referendum's institutional design and constitutional credentials rather than the first set relating to its conduct. However, neither the referendum's conduct nor design need to be perfect for it to be legitimate. Though both were flawed in various ways, it was arguably no worse in these respects than current general elections in the UK or most other advanced democracies, such as the United States (USA). These too rightly attract criticism for their many shortcomings. For example, similar campaign techniques to those of the Brexit referendum feature in normal elections in these countries, while a case exists in both the UK and USA for allowing permanent residents to vote, lowering the age of the franchise, and changing the electoral system to some form of proportional representation (PR). Yet, though undoubtedly improvable, both systems are regarded as possessing sufficient democratic qualities to be legitimate processes. The Brexit referendum arguably meets a similar threshold of legitimacy, despite its manifold faults (Electoral Commission, 2016; Bellamy, 2019a). Granting this to be the case, my concern is whether it could be regarded as compatible with political constitutionalism along the lines given in the last section.

Note, if it can, that would offer a different ground for the referendum's legitimacy than was given by not only many Leave supporters but also others, such as the former Prime Minister Theresa May, who supported Remain but felt obliged to honour the referendum's result: namely, that it was an expression of the people's will, with popular sovereignty trumping parliamentary sovereignty (Weale, 2018, pp. ix–x). It also provides a response to those who considered the referendum as unconstitutional – either in principle, or due to the absence of its procedures forming part of a legal constitution (Grayling, 2017, pp. 189–97). Instead, it could be seen not as a form of direct democracy requiring constitutional regulation but rather as a constitutional form of democratic politics as part of a mixed political constitutional system.

To fit this role, a referendum needs to be both embedded within and regulated via the system of representative democracy, and as such subject to the legal authority of parliamentary sovereignty, while offering a justified check and balance upon it issuing from the political authority of the people taken as a whole. The argument of the previous section suggested this is most likely to be the case in referendums on constitutive and constitutional issues, which are top down and related to affirming or contesting a proposal from the executive, and that can only take place when legislated for by a duly elected legislature, which retains the responsibility for acting on the result as its members think fit. How far was this true of the Brexit referendum?

The decision to call the referendum resulted from a manifesto pledge of the Conservative Party in the 2015 election. That origin has been viewed as somehow tainted – a hypocritical move to blunt the electoral threat posed by the UK Independence Party (UKIP) to the Conservatives. Yet, it could equally be seen as a mechanism for giving voice to an issue that the major parties had largely kept off the electoral agenda. True, the Conservatives had tried to make the EU an electoral issue in the 2001 and 2005 elections without success, a point to which I return below. However, to the extent that EU membership forms a constitutive issue as to the very nature of the polity, then it can be regarded as rightly a matter on which the people as a whole should be consulted. Indeed, across the EU that has steadily become the norm, including in Germany where the Constitutional Court (2009, paras 179 and 263) has recently argued that the development of a 'federal state' at the European level could reach a point that would require 'a decision of the German people beyond the present application of the Basic Law' (German Federal Constitutional Court, 2009). If a referendum is increasingly seen as necessary for not only joining the EU but also for any significant deepening of European integration, then the same should hold for a decision to leave the EU altogether. Making that possibility a manifesto pledge within an election can be regarded as providing a democratic test of its significance for the electorate. Meanwhile, doing so to fend off a challenge from a small party with significant but diffuse support (UKIP has only won one parliamentary seat in an election, which was held by a popular MP, who had defected from the Conservative Party) can be regarded as providing a form of balance within a plurality system for views that might otherwise go unheard.

I also noted how referendums are likely to most fit with political constitutionalism to the extent they are regulated by parliamentary legislation. Here too that was the case. Legislation governing referendums in general had been passed under the Political Parties, Elections and Referendums Act 2000, and this was specifically applied to the Brexit referendum in the European Referendum Act 2015. This Act was passed with an overwhelming majority in the Commons of 544 to 53 in favour, with only the Scottish National Party voting against.

As I remarked above, the main complaints with this legislation related to the franchise, the lack of supermajority rules, the length and rules for the conduct of the campaign and the alleged vagueness of the question posed. The relevant question to ask here is whether the proposed changes could be justified as necessary for the referendum to perform its checking and balancing role. My claim will be that at best they were unnecessary for the constitutional legitimacy of the referendum and at worst they would have been illegitimate.

With regard to the franchise, the referendum adopted that used for national elections under the provisions of the Representation of the People Act 1983 and 2000. Although those provisions are contestable, they are largely consistent with those found in other established democracies. A related but distinct issue is whether a reasonable case can be made for keeping to those provisions, or whether not to depart from them in this case involved an unequivocal injustice. Here it is useful to distinguish between who can be legitimately included in making a decision and the side constraints that might arise with regard to those affected by a decision. In the case of a constitutive referendum, which concerns the very shape of the demos, a reasonable case can be made for restricting the decision to citizens. On the stakeholder account of political rights and obligations (Bauböck, 2015), the claim to being a citizen of a given sovereign political community belongs to those whose freedom and rights are inherently linked to the collective self-government and flourishing of this polity over time. This argument links citizenship rights to the performance of civic and social duties and a commitment to the political community and its members, including to future generations. On this view, rightful inclusion in the demos depends on assuming the obligations entailed by long-term membership of a community, not least by naturalising as a citizen of the host country – something that was relatively easy for long-term resident EU citizens to do. This view also seems the most consistent with political constitutionalism, which concerns the ability for citizens to decide the rules governing their social co-existence on an equitable basis. It would be inapposite to include in such a process those who are not committed to living under those rules over time. That said, EU citizens are certainly affected by the decision, and for any Brexit deal to be legitimate it should also be constrained in ways that acknowledge their legitimate expectations regarding their rights to remain – as the EU negotiators justifiably insisted.

What about the argument that the franchise ought to have included 16 year olds? Critics of this decision argue that it excluded those most directly affected by the proposal. They note that while those aged over 65, many of whom may never have to live with the consequences of their vote, divided 66–34 pro-Leave, the excluded younger generation, whose future will be profoundly shaped by Brexit, were 72–27 pro-Remain (Clarke et al., 2017, p. 155). Again, these are important objections. Cohort injustices are possible, and some have even suggested disenfranchising the elderly from voting on certain issues (Van Parijs, 1998). Still, the elderly tend to have children and grandchildren, so are not entirely without any concern for securing the interests of future generations, while any economic downturn as a result of Brexit would also have short-term and direct effects on their pensions and access to health care.

Supermajority thresholds are often required for constitutional and constitutive referenda. For example, the 1979 referenda on devolution in Scotland and Wales required the approval of at least 40 per cent of the eligible electorate rather than just a majority of those who voted, a threshold they failed to meet. Neither did the Brexit referendum, where the majority of 51.89 per cent on a participation rate of 72.21 per cent represented just 37.4 per cent of the electorate – although it was achieved by the 1975 referendum, which had a lower turnout (64.62 per cent) but a higher majority in favour (67.23 per cent). The argument favouring such criteria is that the (constitutional or quasi-constitutional) infrastructure of a polity should be relatively stable, particularly in those respects where it matters greatly for some members (perhaps a minority) in the society: for example, they have built their lives around the assumption that it will remain in place. Putting part of that infrastructure up for a 50–50 vote is like playing dice. This may be because there will always be some who vote against the status quo on the basis of frustration with the government on any front or because those affected will not realise, until it is too late, how badly they will be affected. For any such reason there will always be noise in the system, so to speak. This is an important consideration. However, a supermajority is an illegitimate way to address this point. For a supermajority violates a basic democratic and liberal norm that decision-making processes should be impartial and neutral between views in order to be fair (May, 1952). Supermajorities entrench the status quo and may consequently lock in inefficient or unequal measures that generate injustices (Schwartzberg, 2013). Instead, the issue was addressed in part by the referendum being advisory to Parliament, which subsequently had to debate and implement relevant legislation. In that sense, there was an opportunity for Parliament to deliberate the implications of the decision, and for it to be reconsidered by the electorate – a point I return to below.

A slightly different version of the supermajority argument is whether the vote should have obtained a majority among – or even in all – of the different 'nations' of the UK. The devolved regions argued that the UK included at least four demoi: those of Scotland, Wales and Northern Ireland, as well as England. Indeed, a case could even be made for suggesting that London, with a population almost as large as that of Scotland and Wales combined and devolved powers of its own, represented a fifth demos. Of these five, only two: Wales and England (minus London) voted to leave the EU. This requirement could be conceived as an additional political check and balance necessary in multinational political systems. However, it is not at present one that exists within the UK for non-devolved matters. Rather, power is devolved downwards from Westminster to these authorities for the purpose of managing domestic issues. The UK at present is not formally a federation and even if it has federal-like features, federative powers with regard to the sovereignty of the British state, such as the ability to contract obligations under international law, remain at Westminster, for which purpose the UK operates as a single nation – much as the EU represents all the member states in those areas where competences have been conferred upon it, notably the negotiation of trade issues within the World Trade Organization (WTO). Nor is this an unusual arrangement – it is true of federations such as the USA and Germany, for example. It reflects the fact that the federal parts ultimately form a unitary state, which in the area of external affairs has to be able to act as a single unit, for example on issues such as defence. The two parts of the UK most likely to leave – Scotland and Northern Ireland – had had, respectively, referendums on independence (2014) and joining the Republic of Ireland (1973), with the referendum on the Good Friday Agreement (1998) also, in part, a referendum on the conditions under which Northern Ireland might leave the UK and join the Republic – and although Brexit may prompt them to be repeated sooner rather than later, at the time of the EU referendum a reasonable case existed for saying that for these purposes the UK formed a single demos.

With regard to the question posed, unlike the referendum on electoral reform of 2011 the electorate were not asked to accept or reject a specific constitutional proposal, which would then automatically become legislation. Formally speaking, as with the other UK referendums hitherto, it was a consultative referendum and the EU Referendum Act did not include any requirement that the government implement the decision. As such, it was consistent with parliamentary legislative sovereignty. Instead, the question was 'Should the United Kingdom remain a member of the European Union or leave the European Union?' However, this could be seen as a referendum on whether to accept or reject David Cameron's, the then Prime Minister, renegotiation of the terms of Britain's EU membership. In other words, it offered a check on the prevailing view of the government and in the legislature more generally – and, indeed, was the first – and so far the only time – that view has been rejected in a referendum. The issue then turned to what terms of leaving the EU should follow from that decision, and should the electorate have been consulted via a second referendum on them?

The argument against a repeat referendum tended to take the form that these should be a once in a generation exercise. Adapting a parallel argument to Thomas Jefferson's for a periodical ratification of the terms of the US Constitution to ensure they still reflected 'we the people' (Jefferson, 1984), the argument goes that repeat referendums should only occur once the generation that decided the original referendum no longer form a majority. The reasoning is that with constitutive and constitutional referenda, which concern the basic political and legal framework, there is a need for continuity of a kind associated with the rule of law, whereby individuals can plan ahead. That criterion was met in 2016 with regard to the first EU referendum of 1975, but would require at least a decade for a repeat of the 2016 referendum to be legitimate. However, that objection does not really address two different arguments for a second referendum: one addressing the case for a supermajority in a way more consistent with democratic norms, and that fits with the checks and balances rationale given for them here, the other raised by the need for a ratification of the terms of the withdrawal from the EU.

With regard to the first argument, the case for a second referendum might proceed as follows. In his novel *The Life and Opinions of Tristram Shandy Gentleman* (1762, Vol. VI, chapter XVII), Laurence Sterne has Shandy, the novel's narrator, report, misremembering Herodotus on Persian customs, that the ancient Goths of Germany took major decisions twice: first drunk and second sober, with only those drunken resolutions that met with sober approval being acted on. Shandy remarks that his father was much taken with this argument but being teetotal adapted it to involve discussing important domestic matters with his wife on the first Saturday night of the month and then on the following Sunday morning, referring to these two deliberative occasions as his 'beds of justice' (Waldron, 2016, pp. 76, 327, n. 29). Adapting this argument, it can be maintained that, for the reasons given earlier, decisions involving changing the very rules of the political game deserve to be considered especially carefully. At the same time, such consideration ought to respect democratic norms and allow all views to be fairly weighed and expressed. Balancing passionate frustration with the possible inadequacies of the status quo against reflective consideration of the consequences of changing it, potentially for an even worse arrangement, reflects a well-established deliberative norm of 'hearing the other side' that informs adversarial debate in Parliament and the Courts as well as normal elections. Indeed, Sterne's 'two bed' argument has been employed to justify bicameralism, in which the second chamber acts as a scrutiny chamber, and could be equally employed to allow for judicial review (Waldron, 2016, p. 77). This argument responds to the common criticisms of the first referendum while reflecting general considerations that derive from the reasoning underlying political constitutionalism rather than being ad hoc arguments that reflect one's view of the issue the referendum sought to decide. Unfortunately, the early triggering of Article 50 rendered it impossible to hold a second referendum before time ran out. However, arguably doing so for this reason would have been appropriate from a political constitutionalist perspective, and not to do so was a missed opportunity.

The second argument, that a vote should have been held on the specific terms of withdrawal, rather than the general issue of whether to withdraw at all, is more problematic. This moves the decision from a strictly constitutive and constitutional issue to something more like a policy issue, where as we saw referendums prove more problematic. Parliament – arguably like the public as a whole – was divided between (a) remaining in the EU, (b) leaving and staying in the single market (roughly Norway/ European Economic Area) or customs union, (c) leaving and not staying in the single market and customs union (a version of which would have been Theresa May's amended Chequers deal or the withdrawal agreement ultimately negotiated by Boris Johnson), and (d) leaving without a deal (WTO rules). One solution, proposed by Justine Greening, would have been to offer voters these choices and accepted either the plurality winner or, using a Borda or Condorcet count, the most preferred of these options. However, that would still not have necessarily weighed the impact of these options against the full range of other policies of importance to voters. For this purpose, a general election in which voters have an opportunity to see how these options fit into a programme of government offers a better solution. As it happens, voters were given such a choice, with elections in both 2017 and 2019. The latter election gave Boris Johnson's Conservative Party a landslide victory, with the party winning 43.6 per cent of the vote – the highest percentage obtained by a party since 1979, and a parliamentary majority of 80 seats. Arguably, therefore, the second argument was met and there can be no doubting that 'getting Brexit done' was the settled preference of the British electorate.

Of course, criticisms continue about the conduct of both the election and referendum campaigns and especially the misinformation and failure to discuss certain key issues, notably Northern Ireland. Yet, these failings are arguably down as much to the failure of the opposition parties as the process itself. After all, the referendum and election were overseen by an independent regulator, the Electoral Commission, which in its report argued that no procedural failures were serious enough to invalidate the result. In other words, while flawed and improvable, the process cannot be regarded as so defective as to justify being annulled. Indeed, recent opinion polls suggest that even with the many problems attendant on leaving the EU already having become apparent, a re-run of the referendum at the time of writing would be unlikely to produce a different result.

CONCLUSION

Disillusionment with the result of the Brexit referendum has led many critics to dispute the democratic or constitutional validity of referendums in general. They are seen as populist instances of popular sovereignty that are at odds with a properly constituted form of democracy (Weale, 2018). Indeed, this was often assumed to be the position in any case of political constitutionalists – and was in fact a view I personally held (Bellamy, 2007, pp. 135, 263). However, despite regarding the decision to leave the EU as both economically and morally mistaken (Bellamy, 2019b, pp. xii–xv), I consider we should accept that decision and the legitimacy of the referendum for making it. Liberals consider that individuals have the right to make mistakes, hoping they – or at least the rest of us – may learn from their errors. The best one can seek to achieve is that a mistake is made in a considered way. Indeed, one must allow that maybe Brexit is not the mistake many of us consider it to be.

Political constitutionalism offers a system of checks and balances for resolving disagreements, such as those relating to membership of the EU, in a fair manner, and which forces citizens and politicians to hear the other side. This chapter has argued that referendums can form a justifiable part of such a system, and that this was the case with the 2016 referendum. However, that does not mean that we should accept Brexit as reflecting the will of the British people. Rather, we should accept that the plurality of citizens who voted for this result made their case in a fair way that was suitably checked and balanced. The disagreement remains, making it justified to argue that those opposed to leaving the EU can continue to campaign for better terms with the EU (Weale, 2017), and ultimately – ten years or more, as per the Jeffersonian principle discussed earlier – for a further referendum on rejoining.

REFERENCES

Ackerman, B. (1991). *We the People: Foundations*. Harvard University Press.

Barber, N.W. (2018). *The Principles of Constitutionalism*. Oxford University Press.

Bauböck, R. (2015). Morphing the Demos into the Right Shape. Normative Principles for Enfranchising Resident Aliens and Expatriate Citizens. *Democratization*, *22*(5), 820–39. https://doi.org/10.1080/13510347.2014.988146.

Bellamy, R. (1996). The Political Form of the Constitution: The Separation of Powers, Rights and Representative. *Political Studies*, *14*(3), 436–56. https://doi.org/10.1111%2Fj.1467-9248.1996.tb00593.x.

Bellamy, R. (2007). *Political Constitutionalism: A Republican Defence of the Constitutionality of Democracy*. Cambridge University Press.

Bellamy, R. (2011). Political Constitutionalism and the Human Rights Act. *International Journal of Constitutional Law (I-Con)*, *9*(1), 86–111. https://doi.org/10.1093/icon/mor024.

Bellamy, R. (2013). The Democratic Qualities of Courts: A Critical Analysis of Three Arguments. *Representation*, *49*(3), 333–46. https://doi.org/10.1080/00344893.2013.830485.

Bellamy, R. (2018). Majority Rule, Compromise and the Democratic Legitimacy of Referendums. *Swiss Political Science Review*, *24*(3), 312–19. https://doi.org/10.1111/spsr.12315.

Bellamy, R. (2019a). Was the Brexit Referendum Legitimate, and Would a Second One Be So? *European Political Science*, *18*(1), 126–33. https://doi.org/10.1057/s41304-018-0155-x.

Bellamy, R. (2019b). *A Republican Europe of States: Cosmopolitanism, Intergovernmentalism and Democracy in the EU*. Cambridge University Press.

Bellamy, R., and Schönlau, J. (2004). The Normality of Constitutional Politics: An Analysis of the Drafting of the EU Charter of Fundamental Rights. *Constellations: An International Journal of Critical and Democratic Theory*, *11*(3), 412–33. https://doi.org/10.1111/j.1351-0487.2004.00385.x.

Bogdanor, V. (1981). *The People and the Party System*. Cambridge University Press.
Bogdanor, V. (1994). Western Europe. In D. Butler and A. Ranney (eds), *Referendums Around the World: The Growing Use of Direct Democracy* (pp. 24–97). Palgrave.
Cheneval, F., and el-Wakil, A. (2018). The Institutional Design of Referendums: Bottom-up and Binding. *Swiss Political Science Review*, *24*(3), 294–304. https://doi.org/10.1111/spsr.12319.
Christiano, T. (2008). *The Constitution of Equality*. Oxford University Press.
Clarke, H.D., Goodwin, M., and Whitely, P. (2017). *Brexit: Why Britain Voted to Leave the European Union*. Cambridge University Press.
Cosgrove, R.A. (1980). *The Rule of Law: Albert Venn Dicey, Victorian Jurist*. University of North Carolina Press.
Dahl, R.A. (1989). *Democracy and Its Critics*. Yale University Press.
Daly, E. (2015). A Republican Defence of the Constitutional Referendum. *Legal Studies*, *35*(1), 30–54. https://doi.org/10.1111/lest.12038.
Dicey, A.V. (1885). *Introduction to the Study of the Law of the Constitution* (8th edn). Reprinted in 1915, MacMillan.
Dicey A.V. (1890). Ought the Referendum to be Introduced into England? *Contemporary Review*, *57*, 489.
Dunn, J. (2005). *Setting the People Free. The Story of Democracy*. Atlantic Books.
Electoral Commission. (2016). *The EU Referendum: Report on the 23 June 2016 Referendum on the UK's Membership of the European Union*. Retrieved 2 February 2018 from https://www.electoralcommission.org.uk/who-we-are-and-what-we-do/elections-and-referendums/past-elections-and-referendums/eu-referendum/report-23-june-2016-referendum-uks-membership-european-union.
Ewing, K.D. (2013). The Resilience of the Political Constitution. *German Law Journal*, *14*(12), 2111–36. https://doi.org/10.1017/S2071832200002698.
Frey, B.S., and Goette, L. (1998). Does the Popular Vote Destroy Civil Rights? *American Journal of Political Science*, *42*(4), 1343–8. https://doi.org/10.2307/2991861.
Gee, G., and Webber, G. (2010). What Is a Political Constitution? *Oxford Journal of Legal Studies*, *30*(2), 273–99. https://doi.org/10.1093/ojls/gqq013.
German Federal Constitutional Court. (2009). Judgement of the Second Senate of 30 June 2009, 2 BE 2/08 (Lisbon Treaty). Retrieved 30 September 2022 from http://www.bundesverfassungsgericht.de/SharedDocs/Entscheidungen/EN/2009/06.
Ginsburg, T., and Aziz, H.Z. (2018). *How to Save a Constitutional Democracy*. University of Chicago Press.
Glencross, A. (2021). History. In J. Smith (ed.), *The Palgrave Handbook of European Referendums* (pp. 49–66). Palgrave Macmillan.
Gordon, M. (2019). Parliamentary Sovereignty and the Political Constitution(s): From Griffith to Brexit. *King's Law Journal*, *30*(1), 125–47. https://doi.org/10.1080/09615768.2019.1594614.
Grayling, A.C. (2017). *Democracy and Its Crisis*. Oneworld.
Griffith, J.A.G. (1979). The Political Constitution. *Modern Law Review*, *42*(1), 1–21. https://doi.org/10.1111/j.1468-2230.1979.tb01506.x.
Habermas, J. (1996). *Between Facts and Norms: Contributions to a Discourse Theory of Law and Democracy*. Polity.
Haider-Markel, D.P., Querze, A., and Lindaman, K. (2007). Lose, Win, or Draw? A Reexamination of Direct Democracy and Minority Rights. *Political Research Quarterly*, *60*(2), 304–14. https://doi.org/10.1177/1065912907301984.
Hailsham, L. (1978). *The Dilemma of Democracy: Diagnosis and Prescription*. Collins.
Hainmueller, J., and Hangartner, D. (2019). Does Direct Democracy Hurt Immigrant Minorities? Evidence from Naturalization Decisions in Switzerland. *American Journal of Political Science*, *63*(3), 530–47. https://doi.org/10.1111/ajps.12433.
Hansson, S., and Kröger, S. (2021). How a Lack of Truthfulness Can Undermine Democratic Representation: The Case of Post-Referendum Brexit Discourses. *The British Journal of Politics and International Relations*, *23*(4), 609–26. https://doi.org/10.1177/1369148120974009.
Haskell, J. (2001). *Direct Democracy or Representative Government? Dispelling the Populist Myth*. Westview.
Honohan, I. (2002). *Civic Republicanism*. Routledge.

Jefferson, T. (1984). Letter to Madison of September 6, 1789. In M.D. Petterson (ed.), *Thomas Jefferson: Writings* (pp. 959–64). Library of America.
Lafont, C. (2019). *Democracy without Shortcuts: A Participatory Conception of Deliberative Democracy*. Oxford University Press.
Landemore, H. (2013). *Democratic Reason: Politics, Collective Intelligence, and the Rule of the Many*. Princeton University Press.
Lord, C. (2021). Referendums and Democratic Theory. In J. Smith (ed.), *The Palgrave Handbook of European Referendums* (pp. 29–48). Palgrave Macmillan.
Loughlin, M. (2013). *The British Constitution: A Very Short Introduction*. Oxford University Press.
Lovett, F. (2001). Domination: A Preliminary Analysis. *The Monist*, *84*(1), 98–112. https://doi.org/10.5840/monist20018414.
Mair, P. (2013). *Ruling the Void: The Hollowing out of Western Democracy*. Verso.
May, K. (1952). A Set of Independent, Necessary and Sufficient Conditions for Simple Majority Decision. *Econometrica*, *20*(4), 680–84. https://doi.org/10.2307/1907651.
McGann, A.J. (2004). The Tyranny of the Supermajority: How Majority Rule Protects Minorities. *Journal of Theoretical Politics*, *16*(1), 53–77. https://doi.org/10.1177%2F0951629804038902.
Moeckli, D. (2011). Of Minarets and Foreign Criminals: Swiss Direct Democracy and Human Rights. *Human Rights Law Review*, *11*(4), 774–94. https://doi.org/10.1093/hrlr/ngr026.
Ordeshook, P.C. (1986). *Game Theory and Political Theory*. Cambridge University Press.
Pettit, P. (1999). Republican Freedom and Contestatory Democratization. In I. Shapiro and C. Hacker-Cordón (eds), *Democracy's Value* (pp. 163–90). Cambridge University Press.
Schwartzberg, M. (2013). *Counting the Many: The Origins and Limits of Supermajority Rule*. Cambridge University Press.
Setälä, M. (2006). On the Problems of Responsibility and Accountability in Referendums. *European Journal of Political Research*, *45*(4), 699–721. https://doi.org/10.1111/j.1475-6765.2006.00630.x.
Sterne, L. (1762). *The Life and Opinions of Tristram Shandy Gentleman* (Vols V and VI). T. Becket and P.A. Dehondt.
Sumption, J. (2019). *Trials of the State: Law and the Decline of Politics*. Profile Books.
Tierney, S. (2012). *Constitutional Referendums. The Theory and Practice of Republican Deliberation*. Oxford University Press.
Tierney, S. (2013). Whose Political Constitution? Citizens and Referendums. *German Law Journal*, *14*(12), 2185–96. https://doi.org/10.1017/S2071832200002728.
Tomkins, A. (2005). *Our Republican Constitution*. Hart.
Urbinati, N. (2019). *Me the People: How Populism Transforms Democracy*. Harvard University Press.
Van Parijs, P. (1998). The Disenfranchisement of the Elderly, and Other Attempts to Secure Intergenerational Justice. *Philosophy & Public Affairs*, *27*(4), 292–333. https://doi.org/10.1111/j.1088-4963.1998.tb00072.x.
Waldron, J. (1999). *Law and Disagreement*. Clarendon Press.
Waldron, J. (2016). *Political Political Theory: Essays in Institutions*. Harvard University Press.
Weale, A. (2017). The Democratic Duty to Oppose Brexit. *Political Quarterly*, *88*(2), 170–81. https://doi.org/10.1111/1467-923X.12338.
Weale, A. (2018). *The Will of the People. A Modern Myth*. Polity.
Weill, R. (2003). Dicey Was Not Diceyan. *Cambridge Law Journal*, *62*(2), 474–94. https://doi.org/10.1017/S000819730300638X.

29. Exceptionally exceptional? A postscript on Brexit in the guise of a conclusion

Kalypso Nicolaïdis, with comments by Albert Weale, Christopher Lord and John Erik Fossum

By God, I do love the Ingles. God dammee, if I don't love them better than the French![1]

Will Brexit finally free the French from Voltaire's infatuation? Or will it vindicate his fascination – if that is what his love was – for an exceptionally exceptional nation and people?

For its protagonists, Brexit is nothing if not a story of triumphant exceptionalism. The story of a people enslaved by the shackles of Brussels, now embarking on a journey of escape, served by daring prophets bargaining over terms of departure with a stubborn Pharaoh-Brussels, complete with the parting of the seas. Egyptians, EUians: let the people go!

Admittedly, you've got to be quite special, or high, to 'see the sounds' at Mount Sinai ('All the people saw the sounds … they saw and trembled', says the Torah). But who in this day and age still believes in 'Chosen People', except as some sort of collective narcissistic disorder?

And yet, British exceptionalism feels like a conspiracy these days. The British identity complex and separation gene scrutinised under the microscope by historians, sociologists, anthropologists, geopoliticians alike, with the old Victorian story of the commonalities between the Israelites and the British people no longer needed as a prop, but nevertheless always there as decoys.

This is comfortable play for social scientists where rational calculations, interests and plans win the day. Leavers warned us from the early days, Brexit would not be primarily about doing but about being, be-leaving, a leap of faith at the edge of the Sea, leaving the army of EU bureaucrats in pursuit to drown in their own red tape. Leavers may have disagreed among themselves on the ethics of unleashing some kind of modern plague on the wretched Europeans (a Kent variant maybe?), or whether 40 years of wandering in the wilderness before reaching the Promised Land ought to be part of the package, but they agreed on one thing: the Sea shall part.

Brexit would be *our* catharsis, a voyage from self-doubt to self-rediscovery, the old Anglosphere our new Jerusalem, connecting Great Britain's future with its glorious past, and the English heartland with its British parts. For in order to rekindle the old imperial flame in a new key, the English nationalist spark would now need to define some sort of identity for itself as the offshore 'other' of the European continent, a continent where 'multinational' means something very different. The more European tongues echoed inside its cities' double-deckers, the greater the appeal of Churchill's 'community of English-speaking peoples'. The great escape from the European Union (EU) was to allow for a politically correct Englishness which loves 'our' Pakis and paints Euro-centredness (read favouring white European over brown Commonwealthians) as parochial. Ah, the particular mix of triumph and drudgery that is a Great Escape!

In *this* Exodus story, it is not Britain that is narrowing its horizons but its European neighbours who have failed to enlarge theirs. The whole thing wasn't about curbing the freedom of nomads but about conquering 'ours' as settlers. The leave vote was truly exceptional wasn't it, a vote *against* the status quo, an exception to the golden rule of voting behaviour, driven by anti-establishment anger. Or could it be seen as an even deeper measure of British exceptionalism, a vote for a reconstructed status quo, reflecting a widespread belief that we never truly were part of the EU to begin with: not the euro, Merkel, Brussels or power structures on the other side of the Channel, this ever-remoter Union. To leave was to revert to the *status quo ante*, back to the place where we used to be before the exile into Egypt/Brussels actually took place. Back to our world.

To be sure, Leavers have had radically different ways of 'not being European enough' à la de Gaulle. Some wanted to leave because they found Europe too big, others because they found it too small. For a promised land, the parochials dreamt of the shires, the globalists of the Antipodes. The former want more protection and to pull up the drawbridge, the latter less protectionism and to build bridges. While the former exude resentment about the EU's place in the United Kingdom (UK), the latter exude confidence about the UK's place in the world. It is not clear what version other Europeans dislike more, both alienating in their own way. If the Brits have left us because they find Europe too big, we can confine Brexit to all that is pathetic about Little Britain. If they have left because they find Europe too small, there might be some *panache*, however delusional, in their story of Cool Britannia goes global.

But who truly believes in this exceptional synthesis of retreat and conquest?

If in the Bible story, despite the promise to go free, many Israelites do not want to leave at all ('Why hast thou done this to us, that thou hast led us out of Egypt?'), the 13 tribes do eventually come together in the desert. Not so of course in our version of the Exodus story, where doubt, division and resistance are likely to prevail for years to come. Like all revolutions, this cannot be a unanimous moment. As an English revolution, it has meant England without London, Oxford or Bristol. As a British revolution, it has meant the UK without Scotland or Northern Ireland. For these parts, Brexit means leaving an imagined colonial rule from Brussels only better to be subjected to our home-made internal colonialism. Never forget Drogheda (1649) say the Irish …

What if our real exceptional destiny is not your version of milk and honey but what we already had, ask the tribes who had elected to stay? How do you expect us willingly to get lost in a legal and political no man's land, to leave a Euroland governed in our language, literally as well as ideologically, whose achievements like the single market, enlargement and free trade deals with the rest of the world stand as blinding markers of British influence? When, even on the global scene, 'British' had become the voice of European diplomacy and Britain's waning power has been magnified for decades by its EU back-office? In that land we are masters, masters of the treaties and masters of the agenda, not slaves!

Perhaps then the exceptional in this story is its intensity, its binary character over an object, the EU, which elsewhere and in other times, could be painted in shades of grey. Dreyfus@GB. In this tale of two Britains, the voting map eerily reflecting our ancestral political geography, the camps of the Civil War, conservative North and West supporting King and Court against the merchants and the liberal South, bolstered by the Scottish rebellion and Cromwellian Ireland. Or no! forget the old divides over region, class, church, party! This is a modern cultural war between the more or less young, schooled or urban, and between two sides who differ on everything from the death penalty to gay rights – even sexual fantasies!

These are not passing opinions. Five years later, each side has absorbed its new identity with a passion: I leaver, I remainer. *They* are unpatriotic, traitors, coward, unimaginative, rootless, *we* are patriotic, courageous, honest, irreverent. *They* are uneducated, irrational, insular, bigot, xenophobes, racist, dupes, *we* are open-minded, open-hearted, open-*tout court*. My virtue is bigger than yours. At its height, the story exudes with emotional clarity, feelings oddly physical, involving dead torn skin, one side shackled to an EU corpse, the other amputated from Europe's body politics. Never the wounds shall heal.

* * *

The Brits can argue among themselves as to whether British exceptionalism is about the election of a people or childish delusions. But for most on the continent it could only be indulged if it meant one thing: Britain has been and will remain the exception.

We get it, say Britain's continental neighbours. We know: you withstood Spanish, French and German kings, emperors, dictators and armadas. We admire your unique blend of healthy democratic disrespect for authority and necessary deference to government. We understand: your leaving is the price we pay for those nasty continental traits you thankfully do not share with us – memories of occupation, a need for a supranational antibody against nationalism, a yearning for stability after centuries of border swaps. Lucky you! Good luck, Lords of the Churchillian Rings!

No sour grapes, they add disingenuously. We won't even comment on the parochialism of your globalism, your deluded imperial revisionism and custodianship of great powerlessness. While we admit that the colonial gene remains part of Europe's DNA – at least in all its former imperial nations – you alone let it define your future.

And so, the Exodus story of exceptionalism has not only been a heroic tale sung by Brexiters. Eurofederalists on the continent have also admitted that letting *this* people go would be quite a relief. What could we do anyway with these islanders cut off from the continent by any hint of 'fog in the Channel'; a continent whose aspiration to harmony they never quite bought. De Gaulle was right, they say, even if for the wrong reasons (we are all schizophrenic about Americans these days): the Brits are simply 'not European enough' to remain in the club. Let them delude themselves in their fantasyland. 'Tired of the fog? Try the frogs!' teased French recruiters with glee in the early days.

* * *

Hasn't it been taboo for other Europeans to admit to the Brits' 'can-do' exceptionalism? To admit that only they do not mind acting as political eccentrics who question received wisdom? To note that with Orwell, the Brits tend to believe that if liberty means anything at all, it means the right to tell people what they do not want to hear. Sadly, they are often misunderstood by others when they do so in their own cryptic way, 'with the greatest respect' and all. And sadly, they do not deserve to be when healthy disrespect turns into contempt.

Be that as it may, can EU-central admit that the Brits have been the only ones with not only the mindset but the muscle power to be capable of doing the deed (even if those with the mindset and those with the muscle are not the same people)? That no other EU country could have achieved such an amazing, deluded act of stubborn self-confidence, invoking memories of past noble defeats, Dunkirk spirit and all, along the way. The drafters of the EU Treaties' exit clause knew it: only the British civil service would be capable of revisiting the following in two years: 12,000 European regulations, 7,900 legal implementation instruments and

80,000 pages of so called *acquis communautaires*, the laws passed by the EU in the last seven decades.

'Could the queen stop Brexit?' a student asked me in a Moroccan university adorned with the portrait of King Mohammed VI. 'Hum', I replied, 'couldn't, wouldn't …' For many around the world, the commitment shown by the British elites to go through with a popular mandate most of them profoundly disagreed with has been a political phenomenon truly worthy of admiration. Will the Moroccan people ever be allowed to force their own top brass to do their bidding in this way?

But then again, will the Moroccans, or anyone else for that matter, ever experience such a parliamentary melee, with its mindboggling mash of procedures and passions, rippling down through the centuries from its original font, another (glorious) revolution. The drawn-out Brexit political saga may have seemed like democratic chaos, vacuous slogans, inveterate lies, violations of electoral funding laws, and some say, the worst media in the world, alongside the best. In the fray, an MP was murdered for playing the game in a different way.

But we could also agree that far from making a fool of itself, the UK has demonstrated to the world what an epic political struggle can look like, where both publics and politicians mobilise mostly peacefully against the other side while mingling in Westminster square and in Westminster lobbies. Seldom in Europe have we been graced with such genuinely heartfelt debates about Europe. Granted, the timing is a bit odd. Most of it took place *after* the vote. But better late than never. And is it really better to repeat the referendum until the people vote the right way, or until we can re-elect the people as Brecht would say?! Ah, the Ingles!

* * *

And yet …

How exceptional can British exceptionalism really be? After all, nothing is less exceptional than exceptionalism, that sense of specialness at the heart of every national identity, starting in Europe. Think of the Portuguese and their oceanic melancholy, the Poles and their own messianic story, the Estonians and their avant-gardism, the French and their grandeur, the Greeks and their worship of resistance, the Spaniards and their buccaneering past, the Italians and their world-class taste, the Belgians and their dark chocolate wrapped in ever darker humour …

In truth, the claim to exceptionalism may be the most widely shared feeling among EU members, each with its own 'proud tradition' and 'finest hour', each with the unique palimpsest of its language, as Elena Ferrante would say, each with its own fierce debate about the fit between the national and EU projects. We may prefer one exceptionalism over another, of, say, the self-deprecating Belgians over that of more self-satisfied nationals, or of smaller nations over bigger ones, and you may deplore any sense of uniqueness based on self-abasing contempt for others, but we can't deny the ubiquity of exceptionalism.

Perhaps the British are only more exceptional in being most oblivious to the uniqueness of others? Who knows. The British mystery, to take Karl Popper's formulation, may have captured the imagination of many in Europe for a long time, but fascination wears off.

Perhaps the British have always been the most ambivalent of all Europeans about the EU, half in, half out for the last four decades, sometimes in, sometimes out in the last four centuries. But which national public is not ambivalent about the EU these days? And which country has given the project such extremes, from Winston Churchill's original vision and Harold Wilson's entry combat to Clement Attlee's bailing out and Thatcher's turnaround.

Perhaps the Brits simply take problematic trends to their ultimate logic. Take the British brand of neoliberalism, probably the ultimate condition of possibility for Brexit. Or the country's unwillingness to submit to the post-war notion of democracy constrained (Müller, 2011), allowing for the almost untrammeled power of the executive to dictate the terms of Brexit. But the ills of neoliberalism have touched many other shores. And these days, parliaments and courts have been subdued around Europe. Is anyone taking back control these days, from bullying markets or bullying governments? Will there be future disrespect for authority?

Or perhaps the British thrive better than others on inconsistency. How can you be both insecure enough so radically to underestimate your influence in Brussels, and secure enough so blindly to trust that you can go it alone?

Is the separation gene not a matter of degree, a lower capacity for dual allegiances between island and continental European peoples, a greater British unwillingness to admit to its dependence on neighbours? But then again, the UK gave birth to the world's largest and most resilient federation of nations. Ironically, by exacerbating internal tension around the division of powers repatriated from Brussels, Brexit has brought the UK closer to EU member states like Spain, Italy and Belgium, which have long had to battle centrifugal forces. There are few exceptions when it comes to separatist demons.

Has the never-extinguished imperial urge present among some pathetic oldies not turned into dying embers among younger Brits? Just like, more or less, in Portugal or France? If you ask them, most millennials on both sides of the Channel would prefer to take part in a European peace-corps than be asked to rule a far-flung land. Alongside mobile phone roaming, the interrail pass, Erasmus romance and euros-across-borders, British kids embrace 'Banal Europeanness' (Cram, 2009) like the next Europeans.

Or is the whole specialness business a collective prank, a very English one at that, best expressed after the war by Flanders and Swann, that most notable of British comedy duos. 'The English, the English, the English are best/I wouldn't give tuppence for all of the rest' echoes to this day their 'Song of Patriotic Prejudice'. And piling it on to the audience in their introductory wit: 'Thanks to the English you are not … Spanish.' For every Englishman who rages about Battles for Britain knows in his heart that invaders make a habit of becoming ancestors, right?

In the end, British citizens understand as well as their continental neighbours the power of cooperation. They just want to do it on their own terms. Annoying! Asked before the vote whether there should be more decision-making at the European level, the result was close to the European average (above 50 per cent) regarding health care and social security, stimulating investments and jobs, securing the energy supply, protecting the environment, promoting the equality of men and women and even dealing with immigration issues. They do get it: no country is an island, or two.

* * *

Some of us may have preferred a British conversion to a nearby like-minded exceptionalism, replete with similar talk of unacceptable outside interference and national identity: that of the Danes. And yet, Brexit only encouraged the Danes' EU-ness, at least in its immediate aftermath. Perhaps when your exceptionalism lies with the delights of hygge, which elects a cuddly present by the fireplace over a glorious past or future, stepping out alone into the cold is a step too far (although of course such a courtesy does not extend to asylum-seekers who have had to experience a very un-hyggeish Denmark). Mindfulness versus Exodus.

In fact, other Europeans may be more like the UK than they will admit. Which country in the EU does not have a transactional view, asking 'What's in it for me?' Are there examples of a member state willing to override its own interest for the sake of something called EU interest? This is the beauty of an EU game honed over decades to extract positive sums from individual national calculations: the European interest is not some transcendental truth known to the happy few in Brussels. The European interest is the final compromise, the never-ending quest for agreement, the seeming devotion of the many busy bees of European diplomacy to the overall balance of the hive. The Brits are only exceptional in telling it as it is – and in their belief that leaving the table altogether could strengthen their hand.

* * *

More prosaically, all this talk of exceptionalisms obscures the reality that there are only better or worse answers to the same sets of globally recurring dilemmas thrown up by our ubiquitous liberal capitalist modernity – control versus cooperation, local versuss global, order versus justice … The idea of an exceptional EU as some special *sui generis* project embarking on a reinvention of shared sovereignty may just cloak the banality of it all.

At the very least, isn't the EU's own claim to exceptionalism predicated on its capacity to accommodate the many variations of exceptionalism in its midst? To be sure, reconciling the different national attitudes to striking the balance while committing to mutually binding forms of cooperation is a harder calling than functionalists would have it. Britain may have just been leaning too far on the 'control' side of the equation. And yet, there were alternatives to Brexit in the kind of 'managed discretion' its government was asking in the run-up to the referendum. At its best, the EU must serve as a multifaceted mirror in which all exceptionalisms can be reflected and deflected in equal measure, a machinery designed to turn exceptions into rules, and exceptional countries into rule-bound ones. Some will say that British exceptionalism lay in part in its vulnerability to this logic, in its willingness to be law-abiding, its propensity to take the EU too literally when others (Italy?) know how to bow to the rule without enforcing it. Why has the UK not followed the lead of Germany's supreme court and asserted its own constitutional integrity? Could it be that the EU lost the British people because they took it too seriously?

Not so, say the 27 in unison. The Brits are addicted to the special status we have offered them in the last two decades and the conviction that we owe it to them. How else could the City have been for so long the master of euro-clearing in spite of the country's disdain for the euro? Exceptional treatment is a privilege for members, they say. Even if they had become out-almost-in, they cannot get the same treatment they got before Brexit, as in-almost-out. The more out they chose to be, the less exceptions they can claim! Brexit can only remain an exception, the first and last to leave, they say, if we no longer treat the UK exceptionally as we have over the last decades. It makes sense that the bar be set higher when you are outside the club. Respect by the EU for the constitutional integrity of its member states and by the member states for the EU's integrity is a daunting balancing act best practised from within.

But can some be more equal than others, even as all non-member states are lumped together under third country status? After all, doesn't the fate of a 'former member state' deserve the ultimate claim to exceptionalism?

Ironically, both sides may continue to argue that the UK does deserve special treatment when it comes to equivalence, qualifications or data exchange, but mean very different things: continued special access for London, protective special exclusion for Brussels.

Thankfully for the British psyche, Commonwealth citizens are expected to step right in, all 2.4 billion of them, and demonstrate life's bounty outside the euro-perimeter, still there for the picking. But in the rest of the world, including the Anglosphere, British exceptionalism is an old story that may be past its sell-by date. For all the hope that the empire will strike back, Commonwealth countries have moved on, worrying about their globalised youth and localised poor, not the UK's regional woes. And from China to Brazil, South Africa to Japan, those tuning in have asked the same question: if British exceptionalism cannot be soluble in a union which tamed its imperialist undertones, what makes the Brits think that we, the rest of the world, will step in as their new Promised Lands? In spite of the old ties, isn't it more likely that Sudan, Sierra Leone, Kenya, Lesotho, South Africa, India, Myanmar or Sri Lanka will get used to dealing directly with Brussels without a London gateway? When British Prime Minister May rightly invoked the extraordinary wealth and breadth of the relationships Britain already has, from Mauritius to Madras, from Newfoundland to Swaziland, did she explain what it was about the EU that prevented these relationships from flourishing before Brexit?

Or is it a mark of British exceptional attention deficit disorder that it could not do both at once when in the EU: continental and global politics. Has membership of the EU club prevented its members from going about their global business? … If they so chose of course. What is true, however, is that without the EU, Britain needs to creatively reinvent its bilateral relations around the world, a deflated global island, but global nevertheless.

Let's face it. Even if exceptionalism in Europe is no exception, the British brand has long predestined the country to hit the road first and probably alone. Always prone to out-Asterix the French, always the *empecheur de tourner en rond*, the spoilsport, no matter that this was precisely why others valued its hard-headed intuition that the EU was going around in circles. They were annoying but kept us on our feet, like …

… una *mosca cojonera* (literally a fly with balls), quipped a Spanish friend.

* * *

POSTSCRIPT

In the years following the Brexit referendum, many scholars, including the brilliant contributors to this volume, engaged earnestly and honestly with the why and the how, as well with the 'what next'. Whatever his or her prior beliefs as citizens, whether British or not, the political scientist's calling is to dissect and analyse this unfolding reality. But when the moment under scrutiny is so pregnant with historical resonance and yet so entwined with everyday life, and when witnessing the stubbornness and grandstanding of politicians on all sides, the scholar may become irritable, cannot help but note the value left on the table, and fall prey to her normative biases.

Some of us sought to imagine and promote an Exodus lite, to sketch out more enticing future entanglements and exit about peaceful coexistence rather than harsh separation. And so we ask, can the British tribes learn again to walk together? If so, remainers must recognise that there was no 'Brexit tide of hate', that their fear of otherlessness was broadly unfounded. And leavers that if democracy calls for losers' consent, that covenant is predicated on giving them a stake in the process.

Ultimately, should we not also, as both scholars and citizens, help shape a European politics which embraces the ambivalence that all have on fundamental questions of cooperation and control? Who truly is simply sovereigntist or cosmopolitan? Can the former acknowledge that the EU's job is to manage the inevitable loss of sovereignty in our modern world, and the latter that it may have gone too far in so doing? Brussels used to encourage everyday bonds, twinning cities, universities, festivals, schools. Did it need to tie the European dream to bond yields? Is it too late for Brexit to serve as a backdrop for the EU's democratic reckoning? It would help for the EU to at least acknowledge the great symbolic gift Brexit has bestowed unto it: to demonstrate to the world and to its own citizens that it is an association by choice.

Perhaps then Brexit boils down to the contrasting connotation of one word: bond. Bond as bondage or servitude for some, bond as the ties that bind for others. Shackles versus Sharing. And maybe this is where the exceptional synthesis may lie, with all those in the UK who can hear both words, who might contemplate retaining a bit of bondage in exchange for some ties. Non-believers who let go of their nostalgia, who chose to give the promise a go, refusing to be treated as ineffective rebels. And leavers who while contemplating our unfolding global power politics are drawn back to a familiar spot on the map, Europe.

* * *

COMMENTS ON KALYPSO NICOLAIDÏS' POSTSCRIPT

Albert Weale

The EU promises an ever-closer union of the peoples of Europe. To make such a union possible the 'stories of peoplehood' – to borrow the phrase of Rogers Smith (2003) – that help define the political culture of the member states must make logical room for the recognition of supranational authority in at least some important domains of social and economic life. In her insightful, not to say exuberant, comment, Kalypso Nicolaïdis examines the extent to which the British/English story of peoplehood (the conflation of Britishness and Englishness is obviously an important element of the significance of the story to which I shall return at the end) lies behind Brexit. She concludes that, though every member state can make a claim to exceptionality, the British brand was long predestined 'to hit the road first and probably alone'.

Whenever a political system seems to buck a trend, there is a tendency in political science to analyse the process in terms of long-standing distinctive features of its political culture. Thus, the lack of universal health care in the USA is sometimes said to be a reflection of its foundational liberal tradition. The German authoritarian experience is said to have its origins in Prussian militaristic culture and the apolitical orientation of the German middle classes. The differences in political and economic performance between the north and south of Italy have been ascribed to the civic culture of the north and the hierarchical culture of the south derived from the Normans. India remains exceptional as a low-income country that has been a long-lasting democracy due, so it is claimed, to its argumentative culture. In each case, the claim is that political choice and outcome have decisively shaped those traditions of thought that define a distinctive political identity.

It is this mode of analysis that Nicolaïdis invokes. On this account, Brexit has its origins in a particular story of British peoplehood, an island people that stood valiantly alone against the

Armada and the Luftwaffe but with global ties to Empire and Commonwealth, ties that were forged in large part through an English-speaking union. Its parliamentary tradition of government withstood test after test. As Ed Murrow, a member of the American press core in London, once said of the Second World War, '... British armies retreated from many places, but ... there was no retreat from the principles for which your ancestors fought' (cited in Hennessy, 1992, p. 19). No wonder, it might seem, that the UK was long predestined to hit the Article 50 road first and alone.

Yet, there is one obvious fault in this line of argument. If the UK was predestined to leave the EU by virtue of its long-standing political traditions and culture, why did it ever join in the first place, rather than remain, along with Switzerland and Norway, in close association with the EU rather than part of it? If a long-standing tradition and culture explain a 52 per cent Leave versus a 48 per cent Remain vote in 2016, how do we explain a 33 per cent Leave to a 66 per cent Remain vote in 1975?

One answer to these questions is the one that Brexiteers, for whom the island story is canonical, give, namely that it was a mistake to remain in 1975 or that, even if it was not a mistake to remain when the EU was primarily a free trade association as in 1975, it would be a mistake – and a big mistake, one that was contrary to UK identity – to remain once the EU had developed sufficient supranational authority to become a 'European super-state'. The merit of this account is that it maintains the idea that the distinctive political culture of the UK is incompatible with EU membership while allowing for the possibility of EU membership. Yet this one merit is outweighed by many demerits.

Firstly, it conflates free trade with a single market. By the time that the UK joined, the EU had in effect achieved free trade within the customs union. What remained was the problem of the non-tariff barriers to trade, things like the *Reinheitsgebot* by which the purity of beer sold in Germany was regulated and with the effect of reducing competition from foreign beers. (Although this example was often cited at the time of the creation of the single market, I have never been sure whether it was apocryphal or not. Policy makers are as prone to convenient mythical examples as anyone.) It is possible to have tariff-free trade with regulation by a relatively weak international organisation like the World Trade Organization, but it is not possible to have a single market without strong political and legal authority over the rules applicable to goods and services. A single market among a number of nation states entails some supranational authority.

Secondly, the global dilemma facing the UK in the latter half of the twentieth century was pithily summarised in Dean Acheson's remark at West Point, that Britain had lost an empire and not found a role. One role that UK governments have aspired to play was that of Athens to the USA's Rome. There is some substance in the special relationship, particularly in the field of defence and security cooperation. But a close trading relationship with the USA, perhaps the major prize of the Brexiteers, could never substitute for membership of the EU. Free trade with the USA, even if it could get through Congress, would never spill over into greater political cooperation in a US-UK Anglosphere (the kindly version of Orwell's Oceana). To suppose so is to ignore the one-sided dependence the UK would have on its larger partner, a dependence revealed in the failure through US pressure of the Suez venture, the cancellation of Blue Streak, the invasion of Grenada, the vital role of the USA in enabling the Falklands War, not to mention the hazards implicit in the vicissitudes of a Trump. Against this background, and in a frequently hostile world, the effective choice for the UK is either political cooperation with the EU or becoming an outsized New Zealand.

The choices and trade-offs implicit in international political and economic cooperation were never discussed during the referendum. Instead, discussion of relatively short-term circumstances prevailed. These included: a public expenditure squeeze over a number of years that make imagined savings on the UK contribution to the EU budget attractive to those ignorant of detail; the scandals associated with corruption and sleaze in Parliament that unfairly tarnished the whole political class; regional inequalities that highlighted the prosperity of London and the south east by contrast with northern industrial towns that had lost their civic pride; and migratory flows from Central and Eastern Europe after 2004 together with the scenes of Syrian migrants in mainland Europe that provided fodder for anti-immigrant populists. Against this background, the rhetorical appeal of 'Take back control', with its tacit invocation of a particular story of UK peoplehood, defeated a poorly conducted campaign by Remain that relied upon arguments of economic interest reluctantly advanced. The failure was not a failure of the people but of a political class that should have been more responsible.

A game I sometimes like to play is to ask people when the boundaries of the present UK state were established. The replies are instructive. Some, like Hugh Gaitskell in his opposition to the Common Market, invoke 'a thousand years of history'. Others refer to the Tudors and the union of England and Wales in 1536. Yet others, think of the 1707 Act of Union, which joined Britain with Scotland. Few say 1922, when that portion of Ireland that constituted the Irish Free State seceded from the UK. Behind that secession lay an Irish nationalism with its own distinctive story of peoplehood, a story that has evolved since 1973 to make room for its full participation in the EU. If the Irish border is the flash point of continuing negotiations between the UK and the EU, such that no one can say that Brexit is ever done, there is a certain irony in the thought that it arises because one story of peoplehood has met its match in another.

* * *

Christopher Lord

In this contribution and others, Kalypso Nicolaïdis identifies the critical importance of understanding Brexit through its own foundation myth(s): through the stories that are told to justify it, to give it coherence, to celebrate it, to inspire its followers and sometimes even to make its opponents feel better about it. Kalypso cunningly frames the problem as one of 'exceptional exceptionalism'. The difficulty, she notes, is that most peoples can claim to be exceptional in some way. So, claims to exceptionalism usually amount to claims to being 'exceptionally exceptional'. That, in turn, puts them at risk of collapsing into banality or absurdity: either the banality of not really being any more exceptional than others or the absurdity of having to exaggerate in order to claim to be exceptional at all.

But just why is it so important for Brexit to have a foundation myth that makes claims to being 'exceptionally exceptional?' There was a time when Brexit bumped along happily as an inconsistent coalition of neoliberals and those whose reasons for voting to leave implied a 'big-state', big-spend commitment to the regeneration of left-behind parts of the UK. However, with winning comes the embarrassment of winning. If history is written by winners, the first thing winners may need to do is write their own history. That threatened a struggle over the meaning of Brexit. Yet, storytelling, myth creation, selective remembering and forgetting even more can also help synthesise the contradictory. Many of its supporters whose hopes for Brexit conflicted could agree there was something exceptionally exceptional about the UK that justified its withdrawing from the EU: perhaps its global character, perhaps its strong sense of itself as a self-governing people constructed around some kind of sovereignty, parliamentary or popular?

An even larger embarrassment that comes from winning is having to do something about it. Brexit would now have to be turned into a definite programme of internal and international transformation. If a member state is a specific kind of state organised for membership of the European Union (Bickerton, 2012), Brexit now requires a form of state organised for withdrawal from the European Union. The key problem was that so much about the UK – its political economy, its international relationships beyond the Union, its law, its definition of rights, its constitution and its territorial settlement (Bogdanor, 2019) – had come by 2020 to assume a membership of the European Union that no longer existed.

So, the Brexit state will probably have to thoroughly change the UK or settle for the ultimate BRINO (Brexit in name only) by keeping much that originated from the EU or by unilaterally following many Union policies and laws from the outside. The latter would mean membership without membership rather than any exceptional exceptionalism. But even the former requires an exceptional exceptionalism that is defined against half a century of the UK's own past and not just in contrast to 'less happy lands'. Hence, the importance of the idea of 'captivity' in Kalypso's reconstruction of claims to exceptional exceptionalism. The captivity from which the exceptionally exceptional need to escape is not just that of the EU pharaoh but that of their own timidity in failing to understand how much more they could achieve outside the EU. Brexit, as Kalypso puts it, would need to present itself as a 'voyage from self-doubt to discovery'.

Maybe it all comes down to two contrasting understandings of politics. As Kalypso observes, much of Brexit is about being rather than doing. On the 'being' side of politics is the value of being a citizen of somewhere whose claims to being 'exceptionally exceptional' are easily misunderstood if they are thought just to be nostalgia for a shared past. Rather, they are at least as much a wish to make a future together: to decide together because of the intrinsic value of deciding together and not as part of some other unit. On the 'doing side' of politics are the systems needed to deal with collective action problems: the systems needed to trade, to ensure a stable financial system, to provide security, to cooperate over the handling of pandemics, to deal with climate change.

Here we can see the special acuity of Kalypso's contribution. For her, the exceptionally exceptional includes the asking of questions that do not occur to others. It can hardly be said of arguments for Brexit that they were all about the 'being side of politics'. To the contrary, they made their own assumptions about democratic political systems, economic systems, security systems and other international systems. So, let's assume that any European Union needs to be justified as a means by which Europe's highly interconnected democracies can manage their collective action problems in ways that, in turn, help them meet their own needs and their own obligations to their own publics. Let's also assume that better ways can be identified of doing that than the existing form of European Union. Wouldn't member democracies then be justified, or even required, to seek some new form of European Union or even to leave it? Hasn't Brexit been exceptionally exceptional in showing that arguments for a European Union might themselves imply the possibility of exiting it?

Perhaps that gets us to a distinction that is as simple as it is fundamental. Some claims to being exceptionally exceptional need only convince those making them. Some, however, need to be arguments capable of convincing others. How far will any justifications for leaving the

EU that assume some exceptional exceptionalism need also to be able to convince the 48 per cent in the UK, the 56 per cent in Northern Ireland and the 63 per cent in Scotland who voted to remain? Will they also need to convince younger generations who voted to remain, or even generations too young to vote at all on that single day that created the leave and remain tribes? Democratic politics brings no closure even to questions as exceptionally exceptional as Brexit.

How far, indeed, will convincing others also require convincing other democracies within and beyond the EU? Here Kalypso remarks that 'In the end, British citizens understand as well as their continental neighbours the power of cooperation. They just want to do it on their own terms.' An obvious difficulty is that 'you can't play cricket when others want to play football'. Ok, that was amongst the most irritating clichés of the Brexit story? But, it's true, you can't play cricket when others want to play football. When does the exceptional become the delusional? When does Brexit cease to be Exodus and when does it become Monty Python's Search for the Holy Grail?

* * *

John Erik Fossum

The Brexit process was given momentum by the rhetorical invocation of the notion of 'taking back control'. The reward at the end of the line, as Kalypso Nicolaïdis so nicely put it, would be for the UK to remove itself from the shackles of Brussels' controls. This stark UK choice of a clean break with the EU and with that the invention of a new status as the first ex-member state, stands out as the exception. In the EU sovereignty is not accumulated in a unified political centre but is pooled and shared in a set of common institutions that the representatives of the EU's peoples participate in and co-determine. British exceptionalism thus entails taking exception from a European exceptionalism bent on revising Bodinian sovereignty. In doing so, the Brexiters take exception from the EU exception. Viewed in that light, the UK's actions are entirely conventional. They pay homage to and affirm the normative hegemony of nationalism as the world's most widely shared and largely taken-for-granted conception of identity and community. But rather than the Holy Grail the Brexiters have thus far found it to be a rather hollow grail, with aggrieved UK nations actively punching holes in the national walls and wanting out. They are not seduced by the lure of a reinvigorated British (or better English) nationalism. Should we be surprised? Are they simply bad losers, or is there something else unfolding?

Nicolaïdis provides a set of very sophisticated and nuanced renditions of the complex notion of exceptionalism, both on the side of the UK and the EU. When we think of exceptionalism in relation to nationalism, I think there are some additional aspects of nationalism that bear mentioning. They pertain to interesting ambiguities in nationalism's nature and role in today's world. For one, nationalism serves as a kind of script and set of prescriptions for community and identity with near-global reach. This serves to unify the discourse on community and identity. At the same time, the unifying thrust is tempered by the highlighting of national specificity. Precisely what this specificity is nationalism appears to be quite flexible or elastic about, given that it can be attached to so many different phenomena or traits. We might then say that nationalism is also quite chameleonic, in the sense that it can be adapted to so many different contexts and circumstances and can be associated with so many aspects of human existence. We see that even in rather surprising places. Consider capitalism whose genetic make-up is global and unbounded. Nationalism can avail itself of it to help flag the nation by proudly announcing where a product is made, and ads can flood the airwaves with appeals to buy American. Nationalism's marriage with the state has given it a house that it controls. In every room of the large house nationalism is flagged, in the kitchen through flags on Norwegian cucumbers, in the living-room through sports events draped in national colours, and in the garden through the national flag waving proudly on the flagpole.

Nationalism's inherent flexibility and adaptiveness combined with its very ubiquity makes it probably the most perfect power-legitimating doctrine that has ever been invented. Nationalism's normative isomorphism ensures the ready acceptance that comes with deep and almost taken-for-granted familiarity (note Michael Billig's, 1995 notion of banal nationalism); nationalism's claim to ground the community in the past and in a sense of shared history (however brutally that 'sense of sharing' has come about) serves as a perfect recipe for creative historical (re)construction by leaders, political entrepreneurs and intellectuals of all stripes. All contribute to 'write the nation into existence'. Nationalism's close affiliation with democracy through a territorially demarcated popular sovereignty crowns this edifice and grants it the finest of all wrappings: popular sanction.

It is well known that the nationalist thrust can aid a politics of exclusion. It can also be used to legitimise a national self-contained discourse that does not feel a strong compunction to engage with 'the other'. Brexit is precisely about 'othering'. The national frame gave impetus to the Brexit process as made up of two solitudes. There was very little real discussion across the Channel of the world we share and of the world that we would lose as a consequence of cutting or weakening the bonds; both sides were preoccupied with recovering as much as possible of the world that they felt that they were about to lose.

It is in this context that there is a profound irony at the heart of the European political experiment. For all the talk there is about establishing Europe as a federation, the onus is on establishing the institutional-constitutional hardware of the federation. That is good as far as it goes, but in a context of institutionally entrenched nationalism there is the issue of how far federal-type institutions can ensure federal-type mentalities. There is a distinct spirit of federalism (Burgess, 2012). In my view, at the heart of federalism lies not nationalism's certainty of community but rather a fundamental ambiguity of community that stems from balancing or reconciling shared rule with self-rule. In the EU context, one hitch is that the process of coming together is depicted (and conducted) as one of integration, not federalisation. Federalisation refers to a process of coming together that is at the same time wholly attentive to the preservation of sub-unit self-rule. Intrinsic to such a process is a constant search for the appropriate balance of shared rule and self-rule. The UK for a long time served as a useful democratic critic of the EU's integrationist teleology but here the irony is that despite having bequeathed several of the world's largest (in popular: India and territorial: Canada) federations and having functioned as a world-encompassing empire it never sought to instil a spirit of federalism in the European enterprise. In that sense, the nationalist leanings of Brexit appear as an instance of taking exception from the UK's globalist part.

This is unfortunate since a critically important albeit missing link in the European enterprise is a viable federalism: a sense of attachment to multiple communities at different levels of governing that is at the same time both critical of centralisation and of fragmentation. This spirit has never been allowed to replace the stubborn vestiges of nationalism even if it would serve Europe much better. For such a spirit to emerge critical engagement with any agglomeration of power is a *sine qua non*, as is also the onus on developing the requisite capacity to solve common problems. Such a federalism must be properly subjected to democratic norms and rules. The UK has at several instances played that critical corrective role, especially with regard to democracy. With regard to federalism, however, the UK's critical approach has come with a rather twisted notion of federalism which sees it as akin to centralisation.

NOTE

1. This conclusion is adapted from my *Exodus, Reckoning, Sacrifice: Three Meanings of Brexit* (2019, London: Unbound), a book inspired in part by the work of many of this *Handbook*'s authors. I would like to thank the editors, John Erik Fossum and Chris Lord, for engaging with this out-of-the-box format. The conversation will no doubt continue in the spirit of the overall *Handbook*.

REFERENCES

Bickerton, C. (2012) *European Integration. From Nation States to Member States*, Oxford: Oxford University Press.

Billig, M. (1995) *Banal Nationalism*, London: Sage.

Bogdanor, V. (2019) *Beyond Brexit, Britain's Unprotected Constitution*, London: Tauris.

Burgess, M. (2012) *In Search of the Federal Spirit: New Theoretical and Empirical Perspectives in Comparative Federalism*, Oxford: Oxford University Press.

Cram, L. (2009) Introduction: Banal Europeanism: European Union Identity and National Identities in Synergy, *Nations and Nationalism*, *15*(1): 101–8.

Hennessy, Peter (1992) *Never Again: Britain 1945–51*, London: Jonathan Cape.

Müller, J.W. (2011) *Contesting Democracy: Political Ideas in Twentieth-Century Europe*, New Haven: Yale University Press.

Smith, Rogers M. (2003) *Stories of Peoplehood: The Politics and Morals of Political Membership*, Cambridge: Cambridge University Press.

Index